$42.95

# CANADIAN HUMAN RESOURCE MANAGEMENT
## THIRD EDITION

CANADIAN HUMAN RESOURCE MANAGEMENT, Third Edition. Copyright © McGraw-Hill Ryerson Limited, 1990. CANADIAN PERSONNEL MANAGEMENT AND HUMAN RESOURCES, Second Edition. Copyright © McGraw-Hill Ryerson Limited, 1985, 1982. PERSONNEL MANAGEMENT AND HUMAN RESOURCES, Third Edition. Copyright © McGraw-Hill Inc., 1989, 1985, 1981. All rights reserved. No part of this publication may be reproduced, stored in a retrieval system, or transmitted, in any form or by any means, electronic, mechanical, photocopying, recording, or otherwise, without prior written permission of McGraw-Hill Ryerson Limited.

ISBN: 0-07-549799-9

2  3  4  5  6  7  8  9  0    THB    9  8  7  6  5  4  3  2  1  0

Printed and bound in Canada

Care has been taken to trace ownership of copyright material contained in this text. The publishers will gladly take any information that will enable them to rectify any reference or credit in subsequent editions.

Text Design by Janet Riopelle
Cover Design by Patti Brown

**Canadian Cataloguing in Publication Data**
Main entry under title:

Canadian human resource management

3rd Canadian ed.
Earlier eds. published under title: Canadian personnel management and human resources.
ISBN 0-07-549799-9

1. Personnel management.  2. Personnel management—Canada.  I. Werther, William B.
   II. Title: Canadian personnel management and human resources.

HF5549.C35  1990     658.3     C90-093503-0

# CONTENTS

○ ○ ○ ○ ○ ○ ○ ○ ○ ○ ○ ○ ○ ○ ○ ○ ○ ○ ○ ○ ○ ○ ○ ○ ○ ○ ○ ○ ○ ○ ○ ○

## PART *1* ○ ○ ○ ○ ○ ○

## FOUNDATION AND CHALLENGES
### 3

## PART *2* ○ ○ ○ ○ ○ ○

## PREPARATION AND SELECTION
### 105

PART 4 ○ ○ ○ ○ ○ ○ ○

COMPENSATION AND PROTECTION
367

# P A R T 5 ○ ○ ○ ○ ○ ○

## *EMPLOYEE AND LABOUR RELATIONS*
### 471

PART *6* ○ ○ ○ ○ ○ ○

HUMAN RESOURCE MANAGEMENT IN PERSPECTIVE
601

# P R E F A C E

*We believe that human resource departments will play a critical role in determining the success of Canadian organizations, and of our society, in the future, especially in the 1990s.*

The Authors

*T*eachers and students ultimately determine the value of any university text book. *Canadian Human Resource Management* is no exception. Its second edition passed the test of the market place by earning adoptions and re-adoptions in more than seventy colleges and universities in Canada and becoming the best-selling human resource management text in this country. The book's thrust on presenting key concepts, issues, and practices of this exciting field without being encyclopedic, its practical focus, and its emphasis on readability have endeared it to hundreds of instructors and thousands of students in Canada. Equally gratifying, a large number of students retained this book for their professional libraries after course completion, suggesting that they found real value in the book.

## BALANCED COVERAGE

We attribute the book's popularity to its balanced coverage of both theory and practice, and of traditional materials and emerging concerns. Regardless of their orientation, readers will sense our belief that people are the ultimate resource for any employer. How well an organization obtains, maintains, and retains its human resources determines its success or failure. And the success or failure of our organizations shapes the well-being of every individual on this planet. If the events of late 1989 and early 1990 are any indication, the human race is entering a totally new phase in its evolution. The break-up of protectionist trade barriers and ideological walls that separate countries of the world may mean that the manager of the nineties has to operate in a more complex and dynamic global setting that is also much more interdependent. Training in human resource management (HRM) may become even more critical in the new setting.

The third edition of *Canadian Human Resource Management* builds on the strengths of the second edition and further expands several key human resource functions. The book is divided into six parts. Part 1, ''Foundations and Challenges'' makes clear the dynamic nature of human resource management, discussing in detail the organizational and environmental challenges facing a human resource manager. Part 2, ''Preparation and Selection,'' discusses in detail all the steps involved in planning and hiring people in an organization. Part 3, ''Development and Evaluation,'' discusses the importance of preparing employees for new challenges through training and development and providing timely performance feedback. Part 4, ''Compensation and Protection,'' reviews the many ways a human resource department can contribute to a more effective organization through effective and fair compensation and benefits administration and adhering to high safety standards. Part 5, ''Employee and Labour Relations,'' discusses in detail the union-management framework, union organizing, collective bargaining and collective agreement administration, and the management's role in improving the quality of life of employees. The final part, Part 6, ''Human Resource Management in Perspective,'' reveals how human resource departments should evaluate their own effectiveness and prepare themselves for future.

Within this format, both present and emerging concerns of a significant nature are highlighted. This edition has a very thorough coverage of Canadian Human Rights Legislation and an in-depth discussion of the Charter of Rights (in Chapter 3). This discussion of human rights and Canada's emphasis on providing employment equity is carried through later chapters on Job Analysis, Recruiting, Selection, Training and Development, Performance Appraisal, and Compensation. This integration of human rights legislation to all key human resource activities makes this third edition of *Canadian Human Resource Management* unique in its field.

The text in its third edition also introduces the concept of productivity and discusses how HRM departments and specialists may contribute to organizational productivity through their efforts. Chapter 2 has a new discourse on automation and its effects on HRM. Chapter 4 has a new section on human resource accounting and its relevance to salary administrators, trainers, and human resource planners who are interested in monitoring changes in employee productivity. The expanded chapter on selection, the new chapter on orientation, the additional material on profit sharing in the chapter on compensation—all these are just a few examples of our concern with productivity improvement in the Canadian setting.

The third edition also emphasizes evaluating the effectiveness and efficiency of the human resource department. Chapters on key human resource activities such as recruitment, selection, orientation, and training have new sections detailing evaluation criteria. There is a new section on utility analysis in the chapter on selection.

A number of recent trends and potentially promising HRM strategies have also been incorporated into appropriate chapters of the new edition. In recognition of Canada's role in emerging world markets and global competition, the authors have added a new section on cross-cultural management training; the promising field of computer-assisted training programs is given some attention in the chapter on training; the compensation chapter has a new discussion on the Pay Equity legislation that has been passed in Ontario and Manitoba and may soon be the reality in several other Canadian provinces; the occupational health and safety chapter has a discussion on the new Workplace Hazardous Materials Information System; the trend towards separate Canadian unions and away from international unions is noted in the chapter on management-union relations; finally, the emerging challenges of technological revolution, dual career families, and the shift in Canadian demographics and its effect on the work force and work environment are noted in all appropriate chapters and especially in the future challenges context.

## KEY FEATURES

Although balanced and thorough coverage is the most important feature of this book, we believe that readers and instructors want more than that. Comments from colleagues and students convince us that an introductory human resource management text should also be readable and teachable. To fine-tune the focus and style of this book, we surveyed more than thirty instructors in the HRM area from all over Canada using an extensive questionnaire. The changes that we have incorporated into this edition are partially based on the feedback we have received from these instructors. Considering all available information, we felt that a HRM text should:

. Capture the interest of readers through an easy reading style and tie each major concept with an example of an existing practice,
. Reflect all changes and important challenges facing the field,
. Provide instructors with a flexible teaching tool.

To enhance the book's appeal to both students and instructors, we have incorporated a variety of features that add relevance and interest to the material:

1.  *Real-life examples.* The third edition contains more than 200 anecdotes and examples drawn from the case histories of business and government organizations. These are integrated into the text material to illustrate and reinforce key concepts.

2.  *Two-colour figures.* These are more than 100 two-colour figures that illustrate concepts and their relationships while adding visual variety to the book.

3.  *Chapter objectives.* Each chapter begins with a list of learning objectives that prepare the reader for the major ideas ahead. Students will also find these objectives to be useful review tools.

4.  *Chapter opening quotation.* Each chapter is headed by at least one brief quotation from a leading scholar or practitioner in the field, to stimulate interest and provide a perspective on the chapter.

5.  *Opening issue.* The text of each chapter starts with an issue or a matter of practical concern. This helps the reader to focus attention on the different perspectives discussed in the following pages and integrate the various ideas in resolving the central issue or problem.

6.  *Chapter summary.* Each chapter concludes with a brief summary of its main thoughts.

7.  *Terms for review.* Following the summary is a list of the key terms introduced in the chapter. These terms are italicized in the chapter text for easy cross-reference.

8.  *Review and discussion questions.* Each end-of-chapter section includes several review and discussion questions. Some of these require a summarizing of ideas found in the chapter; others, an application of the chapter's concepts to specific problems.

9.  *Chapter incidents.* Each chapter presents real or invented case histories, called "incidents," that are suitable for classroom discussion or independent study. These classroom-tested exercises emphasize the application of the material in the chapter to realistic situations that readers may encounter.

10. *Case studies.* Most chapters in this third edition present a long case that requires the students to consider the many demands on a human resource manager and the many issues that the person has to consider before making any decision. This helps the students to prepare for his or her future job where decisions have to be made bearing in mind needs of the larger organization and its surrounding environments.

11. *Suggested readings.* At the end of each chapter, at least three readings to help the student conduct further research on the topic are listed.

12. *References.* Each chapter provides a mix of classic and current references that enable the reader to pursue study of text concepts in greater depth.

13. *Glossary.* Since this book is intended as an introduction to human resource management area, a thorough glossary is included. This material is useful as a reference and review tool.

## SUPPLEMENTARY MATERIALS

To augment the balanced coverage and interest-building features of the book, a comprehensive, one-volume combined instructor's manual and test bank is made available to all adopters of the text.

**Instructor's Manual.** The manual portions of the volume comprise: Section I with a sample course syllabus, alternative course designs, suggested term projects, a film and videotape bibliography, and other instructional resources; Section II, with chapter-by-chapter materials such as lecture notes keyed to chapter outlines, experiential in-class exercises, answers to review and discussion questions, comments on chapter incidents, and comments on chapter cases; and section IV, with a complete set of transparency masters selected from the figures in the text.

**Test Bank.** The test bank, Section III of the volume, presents approximately 1,000 questions drawn from the text material. Questions include true-false, multiple choice, essay, and other formats.

WILLIAM B. WERTHER, JR.
KEITH DAVIS
HERMANN F. SCHWIND
HARI DAS

January, 1990

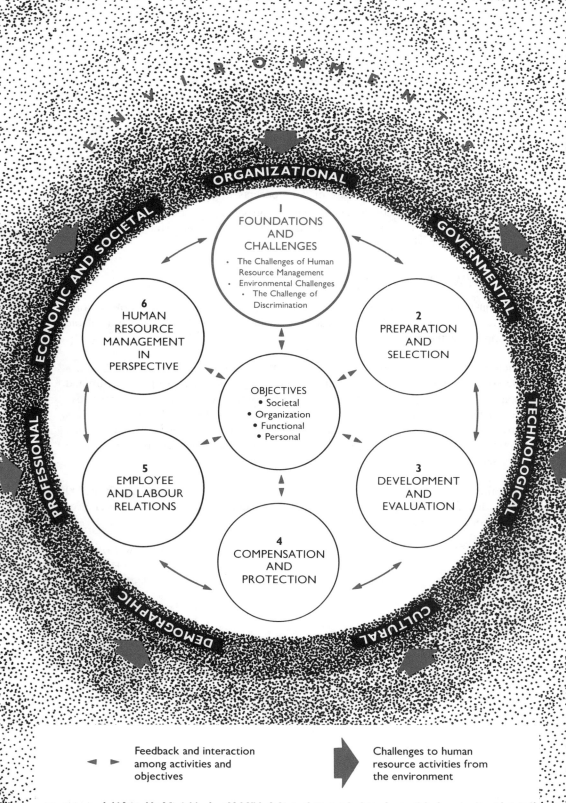

ENVIRONMENTS

ORGANIZATIONAL

GOVERNMENTAL

TECHNOLOGICAL

CULTURAL

DEMOGRAPHIC

PROFESSIONAL

ECONOMIC AND SOCIETAL

**1**
FOUNDATIONS AND CHALLENGES
• The Challenges of Human Resource Management
• Environmental Challenges
• The Challenge of Discrimination

**2**
PREPARATION AND SELECTION

**3**
DEVELOPMENT AND EVALUATION

**4**
COMPENSATION AND PROTECTION

**5**
EMPLOYEE AND LABOUR RELATIONS

**6**
HUMAN RESOURCE MANAGEMENT IN PERSPECTIVE

OBJECTIVES
• Societal
• Organization
• Functional
• Personal

Feedback and interaction among activities and objectives

Challenges to human resource activities from the environment

# PART 1 ○○○○○○

## *FOUNDATIONS AND CHALLENGES*

*A* human resource department helps people and organizations reach their goals. But it faces many challenges along the way. These challenges arise from the demands of people, the organization, and the environment. Other challenges result from laws, especially the need for equal employment opportunity.

The first three chapters explore these challenges and set a foundation upon which the rest of this book builds. Your success as a manager of people or a specialist in human resources depends on how you meet these challenges. Whether you are a manager, an employee, or any citizen, you are affected because organizations touch your life every day. How well our organizations succeed also determines your well-being and the well-being of our society.

# CHAPTER *1* ○○○○○○

# *THE CHALLENGES OF HUMAN RESOURCE MANAGEMENT*

*What differentiates companies today is the calibre and commitment of their staff—managers recognize that and look to their human resources people for strategy to manage people effectively.*

JIM KEYSER[1]

○ ○ ○ ○ ○ ○ ○ ○ ○ ○ ○ ○ ○ ○ ○ ○ ○ ○ ○ ○ ○ ○ ○ ○ ○ ○ ○ ○ ○ ○

## *CHAPTER OBJECTIVES*

After studying this chapter, you should be able to:
1. *Discuss* the central challenge facing our society.
2. *Explain* the purpose and objectives of human resource management and how they are linked to an organization's overall strategy.
3. *Summarize* the major activities associated with human resource management.
4. *Describe* the human resource responsibilities of all managers.
5. *Identify* the key jobs in a human resources department.

○ ○ ○ ○ ○ ○ ○ ○ ○ ○ ○ ○ ○ ○ ○ ○ ○ ○ ○ ○ ○ ○ ○ ○ ○ ○ ○ ○ ○ ○

*N*ame the greatest accomplishment of the twentieth century. Landing on the moon? Computers? Biogenic engineering? The most significant achievement may not even have happened yet. But every major advance of this century shares a common feature: organizations.

A large part of today's Canada (originally known as Rupert's Land) was opened up to settlers by the Hudson's Bay Company. Canada is the world's largest producer of newsprint, nickel, and asbestos, thanks to the efforts of several companies and small organizations in those industries. The Canadian Broadcasting Corporation, which owns and operates several radio and television stations and networks, brings you the news, music, and entertainment. In each case, it is organizations that have marshalled the resources needed to achieve these results.

Even on a more day-to-day basis, organizations play a central role in our lives. The water we drink, the food we eat, the clothes we wear, and the vehicles we drive are products of organizations. When future historians view our era, they may see twentieth-century organizations as our greatest accomplishment. Certainly, they will agree with this assessment:

> Organizations are the most inventive social arrangements of our age and of civilization. It is a marvel to know that tens of thousands of people with highly individualized backgrounds, skills, and interests are coordinated in various enterprises to pursue common institutionalized goals.[2]

People are the common element in all organizations. They create the objectives, the innovations, and the accomplishments for which organizations are praised. When looked at from the perspective of the organization, people are resources. They are not inanimate resources, such as land and capital; instead, they are human resources. Without them, organizations would not exist. The following incident shows how decisively important human resources can be.

> TransCanada Minerals was a small company that owned several nickel and zinc leases. In exchange for several million dollars, it sold all its mineral claims. Total balance sheet assets consisted of some office furniture, miscellaneous prospecting equipment of little value, and nearly $8 million on deposit with the Royal Bank of Canada. While the president of the company looked for investments in the brewing industry, one of the firm's few remaining geologists discovered a large deposit of zinc. Within a short period the company's stock doubled.

It can be seen that although TransCanada Minerals' balance sheet did not list the human "assets," these resources were at work. Before the zinc discovery, a casual observer would have considered the $8-million deposit as the company's most important asset; afterward, he would have considered the mineral claim the major asset. However, a keen observer would have noted that neither the bank account nor the mineral claim could be of great value without capable people to manage them.

More and more top managers are beginning to recognize that organizational success depends upon careful attention to human resources. Some of the best managed and most successful Canadian organizations are those that effectively make employees meet organizational challenges creatively.

> In a high-tech organization such as Northern Telecom, this often means getting the best out of engineers, who tend to be creative problem solvers by nature. In other organizations such as the MDS Health Group Ltd. of Toronto, the management fosters creativity by encouraging a free flow of ideas up and down the organizational hierarchy. As Ed Boyce, the senior vice president of Human Resources, points out, MDS people are made to think as a team. "It is sort of an unwritten rule," he

observes, "that although we have different titles and different roles in the hierarchy — for order and to make the team work — we're all equal as people."[3]

People and organizations depend upon each other.[4] Individual employees rely on organizations for jobs, and increasing resource constraints coupled with rising societal expectations mean that they have to use the available resources more effectively. The current national debate over the need for controlling ever-rising medicare costs is a good example of this.

How can organizations be improved? Organizations improve through the more effective and efficient use of their resources. *Effective* means producing the right goods or services that society deems appropriate.

For an airline, effective means providing safe, convenient, and reliable air transportation of people and freight. Efficient means that an organization must use the minimum amount of resources needed to produce its goods and services. If Air

FIGURE 1-1    The Central Challenge of Organizations

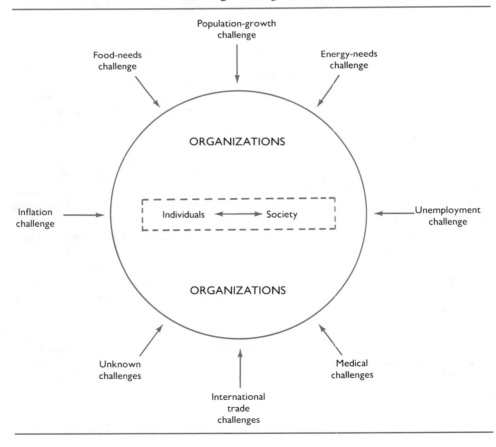

Canada, for example, can do a better job of scheduling its planes with the same amount of other resources, it can serve more customers with fewer planes, pilots, and fuel. Other airlines must then serve more customers with fewer planes to remain competitive. The result for society is an improvement in the industry's productivity.

*Productivity* refers to the ratio of an organization's outputs (goods and services) to its inputs (people, capital, materials, and energy).[5] (See Figure 1-2.) Productivity increases as an organization finds new ways to use fewer resources to produce its output. In a business environment, productivity improvement is essential for long-run success. Through gains in productivity, managers can reduce costs, save scarce resources, and enhance profits. In turn, improved profits allow an organization to provide better pay, benefits, and working conditions. The result can be a higher quality of work life for employees, who are more likely to be motivated toward further improvements in productivity. Human resource managers contribute to improved productivity directly by finding better, more efficient ways to meet their objectives and indirectly by improving the quality of work life for employees.[6]

How to measure productivity? The index that relates all inputs (e.g., capital, raw materials, labour, etc.) to outputs (shown in Figure 1-2), while theoretically meaningful, may not help decision makers to pin-point potential areas of improvement. For practical use, productivity measures of each of the major components of production may be more meaningful. For example, one can think of labour productivity, productivity of machinery, and so on. Employee productivity can be measured using output per worker or output per work-hour while productivity of equipment and machinery may be measured by sales or production per dollar of investment in equipment and so on.

The major challenge facing Canadian managers is productivity improvement while maintaining a high quality of work life for the employees. Work-place innovation and re-design of jobs to facilitate achievement of high productivity levels will be two of the means used to attain these objectives. As two authors[7] noted, innovation on two fronts, namely people and technology, will be the major challenge of the 1990s. Failure to innovate on these fronts will result in an erosion of competitiveness and a loss of jobs and prosperity in this decade.

Statistics Canada figures[8] indicate that during 1971-1981, more than half a million jobs were lost due to technological changes. However, this was more than compensated for by the more than 2.5 million jobs created by growth in demand due to new technologies. Updating technology to increase our productivity levels, quality of life, and competitiveness in international markets would seem to be a high priority task facing managers in this country.

Yet the innovation record of Canadian companies is far from reassuring. In a survey of more than 1000 private sector businesses by the Economic Council of Canada,[9] it

FIGURE 1-2   Productivity Defined as a Ratio

$$\text{Productivity} = \frac{\text{outputs (goods and services)}}{\text{inputs (people, capital, materials, energy)}}$$

was found that most Canadian companies continue to use traditional practices to facilitate innovation. The most popular internal processes were setting up joint committees and introducing profit-sharing plans. Fewer than 25% of respondents had programs for redesigning jobs; few firms had implemented other changes such as innovative compensation arrangements, participative decision making, and payments to workers for knowledge acquired.

In a time of rapid technological change, managing or facilitating organizational change is a vital part of human resource management. The human resource manager can significantly contribute to an organization's health, productivity, and capacity for innovation through activities such as job analysis, quality of work life programs, innovative compensation and communication systems, and organizational development efforts.

> The experience of Camco Inc., the country's largest appliance manufacturer, illustrates the importance of sound human resource management in raising employee productivity and organizational profits. After eight years of operation, Camco management decided to break its organizational chain of command and listen to the workers. The organization's structure became "flat" when every worker was encouraged to talk to everyone else. The results went beyond the most optimistic expectations. Employees made several recommendations that at first seemed not workable, but because of the commitment of employees, they became realities. For example, in the production of glass microwave shelves, the employees made a suggestion originally considered to be impractical, but when implemented it saved Camco $25,000 annually. Productivity improvement in just one year after the change was 25% and absenteeism was reduced by 30%.[10]

Canada has created more new jobs between 1985 and 1988 than the twelve nations of the European Community have in the past fifteen years.[11] Similar results emerge when Canada is compared to the U.S. For instance, in 1987, employment was up in Canada by 2.5%; the corresponding figure for the U.S. was only 2%, while all other major economies of Europe and Japan had only 1% or less. According to a forecast by the Organization for Economic Cooperation and Development, the net gain of jobs in West Germany, Italy, and Britain in 1989 would be nil, while France would lose jobs as it has done steadily since the early 1980s. This is, however, not true for Canada and the U.S., where the job markets will keep growing.

However, a discouraging fact is the productivity of Canadian workers. In Canada, the growth rate in worker productivity in the recent past has been slow. For example, in this country, the output per employed person in manufacturing went up by 1.4% between 1979 and 1985. The comparable figures for West Germany and Japan were 2.4% and 6.3%, respectively. What this means is that "we have more Canadians at work per widget. And ultimately, this is likely to make us less competitive. . . ."[12]

In another study of twenty-eight industrialized countries of the world, Canada ranked seventh in overall competitivenes, but was last in productivity growth and twenty-third in responsiveness to foreign market conditions.[13] Clearly, there are no simple solutions to these problems. However, a review of management practices in companies such as Cooperators General Insurance Company (Guelph, Ontario), Inco (Copper Cliff,

Ontario), IBM Canada, Xerox Canada (some of which won Awards of Excellence and Awards of Merit for productivity improvement) indicates that top-level commitment, employee involvement, a conscious strategy to encourage innovation, and entrepreneurship are critical for productivity improvement.[14] Needless to say, all these actions necessitate the presence of an enlightened and proactive human resource department. Herein lies the importance of the human resource management function in modern organizations.

## THE RESPONSE OF HUMAN RESOURCE MANAGEMENT

*improving the productive contribution of individuals in orgs. while also attaining other societal + indiv. interests.*

As society's challenges have become more complex, organizations have responded with increased sophistication. *Human resource management*—also called personnel management — *is an activity aimed at improving the productive contribution of individuals in organizations while simultaneously attempting to attain other societal and individual objectives.* The field of human resource management, thus, focuses on what managers — especially human resource specialists—do and what they should do. In practice, the above definition requires that the organizations engage in activities that enhance the contribution of individuals to the organizations' productivity and effectiveness and meet larger societal and individual goals.[15]

Improving the contribution of human resources is so ambitious and important that all but the smallest firms create specialized personnel or human resource departments to enhance the contributions of people. It is ambitious because human resource departments do not control many of the factors that shape the employee's contribution, such as the capital, materials, and procedures. The department decides neither strategy nor the supervisor's treatment of employees, although it strongly influences both.[16] Nevertheless, the purpose of human resource management is important. Without gains in employee productivity, organizations eventually stagnate and fail. However, to guide its many activities, a human resource department must have objectives.

## OBJECTIVES OF HUMAN RESOURCE MANAGEMENT

*The purpose of human resource management is to provide organizations with an effective work force. To achieve this purpose, the study of human resource management reveals how employers obtain, develop, utilize, evaluate, maintain, and retain the right numbers and types of workers.* The importance of these activities is illustrated by this example:

> The Atlantic Brewery always sought the best workers it could find. "Best" meant, among other things, brightest and most reliable. Usually, the company recruited students from surrounding schools and universities. With one job, however, this strategy created problems. The job required the worker to stand in the bottling plant eight hours a day inspecting beer bottles for damage. The work floor was damp, noisy, and full of fumes coming from the beer tanks. Employees usually quit within four months.

Bright, ambitious persons found this simple, repetitive job boring. Probably, a solution for this would be to give the job to individuals with lower ambitions and career expectations. Human resource management can succeed only when it provides a work force appropriate to the jobs to be done.

In practice, human resource management achieves its purpose by meeting objectives. *Objectives* are benchmarks against which actions are evaluated. Sometimes these objectives are carefully thought out and put in writing; more often, they are never formally stated. Either way, objectives guide the human resource function in practice. To do this, human resource objectives must recognize challenges from society, the organization, the human resource function, and the people who are affected. Failure to do so can harm the firm's performance, its profits and even its survival. These challenges spotlight four objectives that are common to human resource management.

- *Societal objective.* To be responsive to the needs and challenges of society while minimizing the negative impact of such demands upon the organization. The failure of organizations to use their resources for society's benefit may result in restrictions on the organizations.[17] For example, society may pass laws that limit human resource decisions.

- *Organizational objective.* To recognize that human resource management exists to contribute to organizational effectiveness. Human resource management is not an end in itself; it is only a means of helping the organization achieve its primary objectives. Simply stated, the department's role is to serve the rest of the organization.

- *Functional objective.* To keep the department's contribution on a level appropriate to the organization's needs. Resources are wasted when the human resource department is more or less sophisticated than the organization demands. The department's level of service must be appropriate for the organization it serves.

- *Personal objective.* To assist employees in achieving their personal goals, at least insofar as these goals enhance the individual's contributions to the organization. If the personal objectives of employees are ignored, employee performance may decline, or employees may even leave the organization.

These four objectives are beacons that guide the day-to-day activities of human resource management. However, not every human resource decision meets the above four objectives every time. Trade-offs do occur. But these objectives serve as a check on decisions. The more these objectives are met by the human resource department's actions, the better will be its contribution to the organization. Moreover, by keeping these objectives in mind, human resource specialists are able to see the reasons behind many of the department's activities.

## HUMAN RESOURCE MANAGEMENT ACTIVITIES

To fulfil these objectives, human resource specialists engage in activities that lead to an effective work force for the organization. These activities exist to obtain, develop, utilize, evaluate, maintain, and retain employees. Figure 1-3 shows how these activities contribute to the purpose of human resource management if all four objectives are met. When other nonhuman resources also contribute properly, the organization achieves its

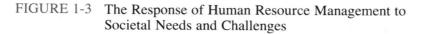

FIGURE 1-3    The Response of Human Resource Management to
Societal Needs and Challenges

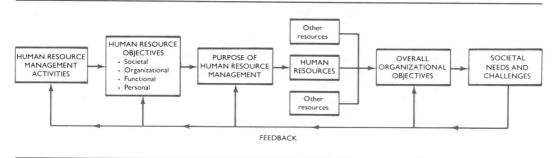

overall objectives, which are to meet societal needs and challenges. As the figure points
out, human resource activities are essential to organizational objectives and the needs
of society.

Senior managers in many successful Canadian organizations have come to realize
the importance of human resources in maintaining the competitiveness of an organization
and even in ensuring its survival.

> In the mid-1980s, the senior management at a major Ontario tire manufacturing
> company developed a mission statement with the cooperation, advice, and support
> of union representatives. This participative style helped to build a cohesive work
> team, which in turn resulted in a five-fold improvement in the company's return
> on assets in a two-year period. During the same period, at Garrett Canada of
> Rexdale, Ontario, an aerospace manufacturing firm, the company's management
> actively attempted to build a "family" atmosphere for its 900 employees. In a three-
> year period, Garrett's focus on its people paid off handsomely; it resulted in the
> identification of a profitable new product line and additional sales of an estimated
> $5 million.[18]

## MANAGING HUMAN RESOURCES STRATEGICALLY

Human resource management as a specialized function evolved from very small beginnings. In the beginning (as will be detailed in Chapter 2), the role of a personnel manager
(or "welfare secretary" as it was known then) was merely to help employees with their
personal problems such as housing and medical help. Over a period of time, the personnel
function grew beyond its clerical, liaison, and service role. Today it is an integral part
of the strategic position that an organization assumes—inseparable from key organizational goals, product-market plans, technology and innovation and, last but not least, an
organization's strategy to respond to governmental and other pressures.

A human resource management strategy, to be effective, should be formulated after
considering an organization's objectives, environmental threats and opportunities, and the

firm's internal strengths and weaknesses. Typically, the strategy formulation process consists of the following steps:

1. *Environmental analysis.* A careful analysis of environmental threats and opportunities should precede the identification of a strategy. By continuously monitoring trends in the economy, society, and labour market and noting changes in governmental policies, legislation, and public policy statements, a human resource manager will be able to identify new action guidelines.

A large electric utility, sensing society's increasing concern about air pollution, decided to reduce coal burning and shift to hydro power. This in turn necessitated replacement of its plant and equipment as well as making major changes in its human resource strategy. Not only were new skills required, but the changeover from existing procedures and systems (e.g., compensation, appraisal, training) had to be smooth and cause as little disruption to the work as possible. A strategy based on considerable in-house and external training was drawn up and implemented. By the time the utility switched to hydro power, it had the necessary supply of skilled technicians and other human resource support systems.

2. *Internal analysis.* An analysis of what the organization is capable of doing in view of its resource profile is a second integral aspect of identifying human resource strategies. To perform the internal analysis, the human resource manager should collect information on employee characteristics, technical skills, experience, existing organizational structure and systems, and standard operating procedures that are currently used within the organization. The objective is to match corporate objectives and strategies with the realities that surround the organization and its managers.

Calgary Electronics, which employs twelve sales people and seven service and repair personnel, was concerned about the growing competition in the electronics equipment market. Historically, the firm had sold and repaired all makes of electronic and electrical equipment (ranging from blenders to large screen TV and complex security alarm systems). To meet the competition, the firm initially decided to go on an aggressive advertising and personal selling strategy. However, a detailed investigation into the company's past performance indicated that the strength of the firm lay in its prompt and cheap repair service. A review of the employee skills and training also indicated that several of the sales people did not have any formal training in selling. Based on the results of the internal analysis, Calgary Electronics decided to focus on repairs and after-sales service in its advertising campaigns.

3. *Assess strategic options.* Given the objectives, the environmental threats and opportunities, and internal strengths, an organization has to assess each strategic option for its viability. It is also necessary to anticipate the likely competitive responses to each option. Can competitors match, offset, or go beyond any advantages conferred by a chosen option?

4. *Identify strategy and implement it.* Unsuitable strategic options have to be dropped

from consideration. The ones that appear viable have to be scrutinized in detail for their advantages and weaknesses before being accepted for implementation. Some of the questions to ask at this time include:

- Are our assumptions realistic?
- Do we really have the skills and resources to make this strategy viable?
- Is this strategy consistent internally? Do the various elements of the strategy "hang together"?
- What are the risks? Can we afford them?
- What new actions have to be taken to make the strategy viable?

> Before implementing a "service at your door step" policy, Calgary Electronics analyzed the potential competitive response. To reduce the likelihood of its competitors' matching its strategy, Calgary Electronics decided to extend its service to after-hours and in-house. The rates charged by the firm were to be advertised (along with going market rates). The service personnel were also to be given some sales training. When they visited a house, they were to supply the resident with discount coupons and a brochure giving details of products and services offered by the firm. In this way, the firm's service personnel could play a dual role.

Strategy implementation involves securing, organizing, and directing the use of resources both within and outside the organization. In the human resource management area, this translates into staffing, compensating, evaluating, counselling, training, and continuously developing the personnel. It will also involve an examination of the entire management philosophy, the formal and informal organizational structures, and the climate of the organization. The incentives needed to motivate organizational members, the appropriate leadership style needed when dealing with employees, and the planning and control systems that should be installed — all these, and several other related issues, are of prime concern at the implementation stage.

5. *Evaluate strategies.* Strategies, however effective they proved to be, have to be examined periodically. An organization's contextual factors such as technology, environments, government policies, etc., change continuously; so do several of its internal factors, such as membership characteristics, role definitions, internal procedures, etc. All these changes necessitate periodical examination of strategies to ensure their continued appropriateness.

To recognize the increased importance of human resources in the strategic success of a firm, the term "personnel" has been increasingly replaced by "human resource management" (or HRM for short). The objective of HRM, however, continues to be achieving effective utilization of human resources so as to accomplish the societal, organizational, *and* personal objectives of its employees. The term "personnel" is still used in several organizations to refer to the department that deals with employee selection, orientation, compensation, training, and record keeping; however, many successful organizations have realized the critical nature of the HRM activities and appointed senior managers to head the human resource department.

Human resource activities are, thus, actions taken to provide the organization with an effective work force. Some of the more important ones are described in the following paragraphs.

Once an organization grows beyond a few employees, attempts are made to estimate the organization's future human resource needs through an activity called *human resource planning*. With an idea of future needs, *recruitment* seeks to secure qualified job applicants to fill those needs. What results is a pool of applicants who are screened through a *selection process*. This process chooses those people who meet the needs that were uncovered through human resource planning.

Since new workers seldom fit the organization's needs exactly, they must be *trained* to perform effectively. Subsequent human resource plans reveal new demands upon the organization. These demands are met by recruitment of additional workers and by *development* of present employees. Development teaches employees new skills to ensure their continued usefulness to the organization and to meet their personal desires for advancement. Then as demands change, *placement* activities transfer, promote, demote, lay off, or even terminate workers.

To check on these various activities, individual performance is subject to *appraisal*. This activity not only evaluates how well people perform, but also indicates how well human resource activities have been carried out. Poor performance might mean that selection, training, or developmental activities should be reconsidered. Or there may be a problem with employee relations (e.g., poor motivation and lack of job satisfaction).

When employees perform acceptably, they must receive *compensation*. This form of reward includes wages, salaries, incentives, and a wide variety of fringe benefits such as insurance and vacations. Some rewards are *required services* dictated by *legal compliance*, such as the Canada Pension Plan, safe working conditions, and the like. *Communications* and *counselling* efforts are other techniques used to maintain good employee relations.

If human resource management activities do not meet employee needs successfully, workers may band together to take collective action. Then management is confronted with a new situation, *union-management relations*. To respond to collective demands by employees, human resource specialists may have to negotiate a *collective agreement* and administer it.

Even when human resource activities appear to be going smoothly, modern human resource departments apply *controls* to evaluate their effectiveness. Besides traditional budgetary limitations, the human resource department may elect to conduct an evaluation of each activity's effectiveness in meeting the HRM objectives.

Figure 1-4 matches these different activities against the four objectives previously discussed. The figure shows that each activity contributes to one or more objectives. For example, appraisal contributes to organizational, functional, and personal objectives.

If an activity does not contribute to one or more of the department's objectives, the resources devoted to that activity should be redirected.

## *Responsibility for Human Resource Management Activities*

The responsibility for HRM activities rests with each manager. If a manager does not

FIGURE 1-4    The Relation of Human Resource Management Activities to
Human Resource Management

| HUMAN RESOURCE OBJECTIVES | SUPPORTING ACTIVITIES |
| --- | --- |
| 1. Societal objective | a. Legal compliance<br>b. Required services<br>c. Union-management relations |
| 2. Organizational objective | a. Human resource planning<br>b. Recruitment<br>c. Selection<br>d. Training and development<br>e. Appraisal<br>f. Placement<br>g. Control activities |
| 3. Functional objective | a. Appraisal<br>b. Placement<br>c. Control activities |
| 4. Personal objective | a. Training and development<br>b. Appraisal<br>c. Placement<br>d. Compensation<br>e. Control activities |

accept this responsibility, then human resource activities may be done only partially or not at all.

When a manager finds that HRM work seriously disrupts other responsibilities, this work may be reassigned. The assignment might be to a worker or a specialized department that handles human resource matters. This process of getting others to share the work is called *delegation*. But delegation requires the manager to assign duties, grant authority, and create a sense of responsibility; if these three elements are not explained clearly to the delegate, delegation often fails. And even though others may have been asked to handle human resource activities, the manager still remains responsible. Delegation does not reduce a manager's responsibility; it only shares that responsibility with others. For example, many managers ask a senior worker to train new employees. However, if the senior worker errs and the new employee makes a costly mistake, the manager will properly be held responsible by superiors.

## THE ORGANIZATION OF HUMAN RESOURCE MANAGEMENT

A separate department usually emerges only when human resource activities would otherwise become a burden to other departments in the organization, i.e., when the expected benefits of a human resources department usually exceed its costs. Until then, managers handle human resource activities themselves or delegate them to subordinates.

When a human resources department emerges, it is typically small and reports to some middle-level manager. Figure 1-5 illustrates a common placement of a human

FIGURE 1-5   The Human Resource Department in a Small Organization

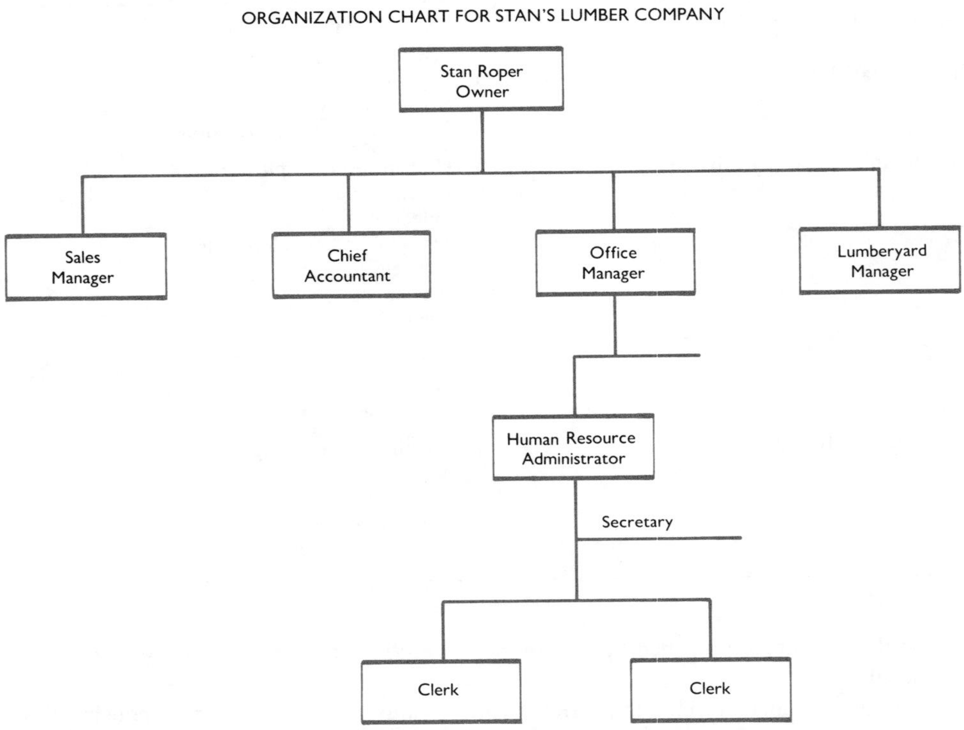

ORGANIZATION CHART FOR STAN'S LUMBER COMPANY

resources department at the time it is first formed. The activities of such a department are usually limited to maintaining employee records and helping managers find new recruits. Whether the department performs other activities depends upon the needs of other managers in the firm.

As demands on the department grow, it increases in importance and complexity.[19] Figure 1-6 demonstrates the increased importance by showing the head of human resources reporting directly to the chief operating officer, who is the company president in this figure. The greater importance of the head of human resources may be signified by a change in title to vice president. In practice, increased complexity also results as the organization grows and new demands are placed on the department; jobs in the department become more specialized. As the department expands and specializes, it may become organized into highly specialized subdepartments.

The size of the human resource department varies widely, depending largely on the size of the organization being supported. One study reported a high ratio of workers to human resource employees of 277 to 1. The low ratio in that study was 29 to 1.[20] Another study reported an average of 36 human resource professionals per 1000 employees for a ratio of 28 to 1.[21] By and large, a ratio of 1:100 (i.e., 100 employees to 1 human resource staff) may be adequate in most settings. The numbers may reflect the more strategic role played by human resource departments today.

FIGURE 1-6   The Hierarchy of Jobs Within a Large Human Resource
Department

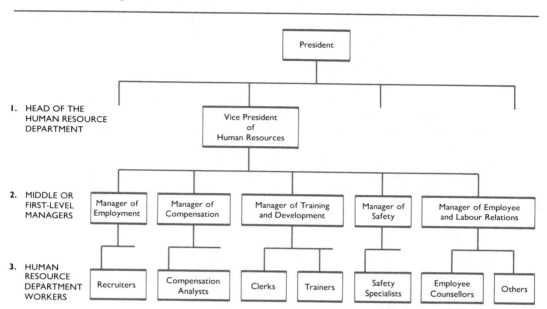

*Departmental Components*

The subdepartments of a large human resource department approximately correspond
with the activities already mentioned. For each major activity, a subdepartment may be
established to provide the specialized service, as shown in Figure 1-6. The employment
department, for example, handles recruitment and selection. Other divisions perform the
activities implied by their names in the figure. This specialization allows members of
the department to become extremely knowledgeable in a limited number of activities.

Activities not shown in Figure 1-6 are shared among the different sections. For
example, employment, training, and development managers may share in human
resource planning and placement. Performance appraisals are used to determine pay,
and so the compensation division may assist managers in appraising performance.
Required services fall to the benefits and safety sections. Control activities (communications and counselling) are divided among all subdepartments, with employee and labour
relations doing much of it. Employee and labour relations sections also provide the
official union-management coordination.

*Key Roles in the Human Resource Department*

The human resource department contains a hierarchy of jobs, also shown in Figure 1-
6. The top job varies in importance and title in different organizations.[22] When the

department is first formed, the head of it is often called a personnel manager, director, or administrator. The title of vice president of personnel or vice president of human resources is more likely when the department's contribution, sophistication, and responsibility have grown. If unions make a major demand on the personnel function, the title typically becomes director or even vice president of industrial relations.

Human resource departments in large organizations have a variety of positions whose holders report to the top person. The manager of employment assists other managers with recruiting and selection. The compensation manager establishes fair pay systems. The training and development manager provides guidance and programs for those managers who want to improve their human resources. Other activity managers contribute their expertise and usually report directly to the head of personnel.[23]

Activity managers may be supported by an assortment of specialists, secretaries, and clerks who carry out the department's activities. It is the specialists in large organizations who actually do the recruiting, training, and other necessary tasks. And it is these specialist positions that are sought by college graduates starting careers in this field.

### The Service Role of the Human Resource Department

Human resource departments are service departments. They exist to assist employees, managers, and the organization. Their managers do not have the authority to order other managers in other departments to accept their ideas. Instead, the department has only *staff authority*, which is the authority to advise, not direct, managers in other departments.

*Line authority*, possessed by managers of operating departments, allows these managers to make decisions about production, performance, and people. It is the operating managers who normally are responsible for promotions, job assignments, and other people-related decisions. Human resource specialists merely advise line managers, who alone are ultimately responsible for employee performance.

In highly technical or extremely routine situations, the human resource department may be given *functional authority*. Functional authority gives the department the right to make decisions usually made by line managers or top management. For example, decisions about fringe benefits are technically complex, so the top manager may give the human resource department the functional authority to decide the type of benefits offered employees. If each department manager made separate decisions about benefits, there might be excessive costs and inequities. To provide control, uniformity, and the use of expertise, functional authority allows human resource specialists to make crucial decisions effectively.

The size of the department affects the type of service provided to employees, managers, and the organization. In small departments, the human resource manager handles many of the day-to-day activities related to the organization's human resource needs. Other managers bring their problems directly to the head of human resources, and these meetings constantly remind the human resource manager of the contribution expected.

When the human resource function grows larger, more problems are handled by subordinates. Not only do human resource managers have less contact with lower-level managers, but others in the department grow increasingly specialized. At this point, human resource managers and their subordinates may lose sight of the overall contributions expected of them or the limits on their authority. Experts sometimes become more interested in perfecting their specialty than in asking how they may serve others. While improving their expertise, they may fail to uncover new ways of serving the organization and its employees. Or specialists may try to exercise authority they do not have. For example, consider what happened at a fast-growing maker of minicomputers.

> For the past five years, Harris Minicomputers Limited had grown at an average rate of 25% a year. To keep up with this growth, the personnel department manager, Earl Bates, used budget increases to hire new recruits. His strategy meant that the personnel department was well prepared to find new employees. But recruiting specialists paid little attention to other human resource problems. In one month, three of the company's best computer design engineers quit to go to work for a competitor. Before they left, they were interviewed. They complained that they saw desirable job openings being filled by people recruited from outside the organization. No design engineer had been promoted to supervisor in three years. So each of these engineers found jobs where the promotion possibilities looked better.
>
> When Earl reminded these engineers that they lacked experience or training as supervisors, one of them commented that the company should have provided such training. With the next personnel department increase, Earl hired a specialist in employee training and development.

The personnel manager and the recruiting specialists at Harris Minicomputers overlooked the variety of activities that the personnel department is supposed to perform. And they failed to identify the services that the organization needs from the personnel department. They also did not recognize the connection between different human resource management activities.

## THE HUMAN RESOURCE MANAGEMENT MODEL

Human resource management is a system of many interdependent activities. These activities do not occur in isolation. Virtually every one affects some other human resource activity.

> In preparing a bid for the construction contract, an estimator miscalculated the human resource requirements. Too many unskilled workers and too few skilled employees were hired. As the construction of the hockey arena fell behind schedule, supervisors tried to get the work done more quickly. This speedup led to complaints from the union. Finally, the project manager realized the problem. The manager fired one-third of the unskilled workers and replaced them with skilled cement masons and carpenters. This decision led to legal problems over unemployment compensation claims, and the higher-paid skilled workers caused the original payroll estimates to be wrong. The human resource manager had to intervene. The arena seats were in place by the first home game. But the contractor lost $385,000 on the job.

As this illustration shows, human resource activities are connected. A poor decision about human resource requirements led to problems in employment, placement, legal compliance, union-management relations, and compensation. When human resource activities are viewed as a whole, they form an organization's human resource management system.

## A Systems Model

When activities are related, a system exists. A system is two or more parts (or subsystems) working together as an organized whole with identifiable boundaries, inputs, and outputs.[24] Examples are everywhere. A car is a system composed of subsystems called the engine, the transmission, the radio, and so on. A human body is a system with respiratory, digestive, circulatory, and other subsystems. Moreover, cars, people, and human resource departments all have identifiable boundaries, inputs, and outputs.

Figure 1-7 shows how human resource management activities form an interconnected system with boundaries. It indicates that each activity (or subsystem) relates directly to every other activity. For example, the challenges faced by human resource departments affect their selection of employees. The selection subsystem influences the department's development and evaluation of human resources. In addition, each subsystem is affected by the department's objectives and the external environment in which human resource management takes place.

Thinking in terms of systems is useful. It causes one to recognize the relationships between parts. If one adopts a systems view of human resources, the relationships between human resource activities are less likely to be overlooked. In the example of the hockey arena, the manager, when firing one-third of the unskilled workers, failed to take into account the interdependence of the subparts of the human resource system.

Systems thinking also requires the recognition of the system's boundaries, which mark the beginning of its external environment. The environment is an important consideration because most systems are open. An *open system* is one affected by the environment. Organizations and people are an open system because they are affected by their environments. Human resource management is also an open system, influenced by the external environment. The arena contractor's organization was an open system because laws, unions, and other elements in the environment affected the manager's decision to replace unskilled workers.

The following brief discussion of this model's parts explains the role of major human resource subsystems and serves as a preview to the six parts of this book and its major topics. (Each part is identified below and in the foregoing model by a roman numeral.)

**I.** *Foundations and challenges.* Human resource management faces many challenges in dealing with human resources. These challenges arise from the environment in which organizations operate; economics, markets, pressure groups, professional ethics, and government are just a few environmental factors. Perhaps the most pervasive environmental force is government requirements for equal employment opportunity. Challenges also spring from within the organization. For example, other departments compete with the personnel department for larger budgets. Or human resource departments are sometimes expected to improve the quality of work life within the organization.

FIGURE 1-7   A Model of the Major Human Resource
Management Subsystems

These challenges and others usually demand that the human resource department find ways to make jobs more meaningful and more productive.[25] To perform effectively, personnel specialists need to consider a broad spectrum of challenges before undertaking traditional personnel activities.

   **II.** *Preparation and selection.* To meet their challenges, human resource departments commonly develop a human resource information base. Data are gathered about each job and the organization's future human resource needs.[26] With this data base, employment specialists are then able to recruit and select new workers.

**III.** *Development and evaluation.* Once hired, new employees are oriented to the organization's policies and procedures and placed in their new job positions. A sound human resource information system also indicates which employees need training and development. Training is often provided by human resource departments to enable workers to do their jobs better. On the other hand, development helps new and old employees prepare for future responsibilities. Truly effective developmental activities are preceded by career planning, wherein individuals attempt to identify their career objectives. Periodically, employees are evaluated through formal performance appraisals. Appraisals give workers feedback on their performance and can help the human resource department identify weaknesses.

**IV.** *Compensation and protection.* Human resource specialists help provide the organization with effective performers. One important element in maintaining employee satisfaction is compensation programs. These include wages, benefits, incentives, and other services the employer makes available. The human resource manager should also ensure that the organization complies with the various statutory requirements relating to minimum wages, pension plans, and unemployment insurance contributions.

**V.** *Employee and labour relations.* For a variety of reasons, employees may decide to join together and form self-help groups called unions. When this happens, the human resource department is usually responsible for handling the organization drive, negotiating a contract with the union, and administering the contract once signed. The human resource manager is also responsible for counselling and disciplining employees, communicating with them, and improving the overall quality of work life within the organization.

**VI.** *Human resource management in perspective.* As with any social system, departments need to uncover their successes and failures through self-evaluation. Increasingly, sophisticated human resource departments conduct audits of the various subsystems in order to implement solutions to emerging problems. At the same time, human resource specialists seek to remain aware of future challenges in order to anticipate their impact on the organization and its human resources.

## An Applied Systems View

Since human resource subsystems affect each other, human resource specialists must remain aware of this interdependency. Perhaps the most effective way to recognize possible implications is through systems thinking. Figure 1-8 provides a simplified visual model for applying systems thinking.

An applied systems view describes human resource activities as taking inputs and transforming them into outputs. Then the human resource specialist checks on the results to see if they are correct. This checking process produces feedback, which is information that helps evaluate success or failure. Consider the situation faced by Natalie Marchand, the human resource manager at Municipal General Hospital:

> A predicted shortage of medical technologists caused Natalie to start an in-house development program to prepare six lab assistants to become licensed medical tech-

FIGURE 1-8   The Input-Output Simplification of the Human Resource Management System

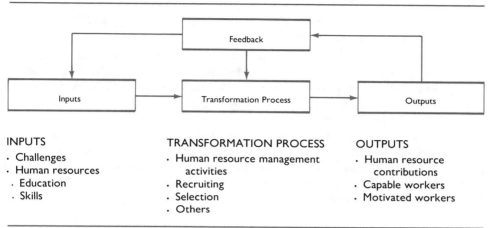

**INPUTS**
- Challenges
- Human resources
- Education
- Skills

**TRANSFORMATION PROCESS**
- Human resource management activities
- Recruiting
- Selection
- Others

**OUTPUTS**
- Human resource contributions
- Capable workers
- Motivated workers

nologists. After fifteen months, they finished the program and passed the provincial certification test. Since the program was a success and the shortage had grown worse, eight more lab assistants were recruited for the second program.

The prospect of a shortage was one input. Another input was the lab assistants who signed up for training. The program itself was the transformation process that created the desired output, a new supply of technologists. When all six technologists passed the provincial certification test, those results gave Natalie feedback that the program was a success.

In summary, the human resource management system transforms inputs into desired outputs. The inputs are challenges (usually in the form of information) and human resources. Through human resource activities, these inputs are transformed into the desired outputs, which become feedback to the human resource management system.

In practice, systems thinking helps identify the key variables. After viewing new information as an input, specialists decide what the desired output is. With inputs and outputs known, decision makers draw on their knowledge of human resource activities to transform the inputs into outputs in the most effective way. To verify their success, they acquire feedback about the outcome. Negative feedback means that other inputs (information or people) are needed or that the transformation process (a specific human resource activity) is malfunctioning. Negative feedback demands corrective action.

## Proactive Versus Reactive Human Resource Management

Human resource departments cannot always wait for feedback and then respond, however. Waiting may expose the organization to damage from the external environment.

For example, reconsider Natalie Marchand's situation when she learned of the impending shortage of technologists:

> NATALIE MARCHAND:   My department budget must be increased by $12,000 so we can train more technologists.
>
> ANNA NEWMAN:   Hold on! The municipality has put a freeze on the hospital budget for six months and as director of administrative services my hands are tied. Why not wait until we can show the Municipal Council of Supervisors complaints from the doctors? Then the shortage will be real and we can get the board to react to it.
>
> NATALIE MARCHAND:   But then we will probably have to spend $15,000 for training. We will probably have to pay another $30,000 for overtime to the technologists we now have while we train new ones. Besides, with all that overtime, error rates will jump and so will lawsuits for faulty lab work. All I need is $12,000, but I need it now.

Anna was suggesting that Natalie's department wait until an actual problem occurred and then react. Natalie wanted to take action in anticipation of the problem without waiting for the feedback of doctors' complaints or lawsuits. Anna's approach to this human resource challenge was reactive, while Natalie's was proactive.

Reactive human resource management occurs when decision makers respond to human resource problems. Proactive human resource management occurs when human resource problems are anticipated and corrective action begins before the problem exists.[27]

> A large electronics firm uses contract labour to staff its human resource needs during periods of peak business activity (contract labour consists of persons who are hired — and often trained — by an independent agency that supplies other companies with needed human resources for a fee). When this electronics firm finds that it needs electronic component assemblers to finish a project, for example, it recruits, hires, and trains most of these people through its own human resource department. But some of the workers it uses will be contracted from a temporary help agency. Not only can the agency provide extra staff more quickly, but these agency workers do not become the firm's employees; instead, they work for their agency and are assigned by it to meet the temporary need for more workers. When the project is completed or when the business cycle declines, the electronics firm informs the agency that it needs fewer of these temporary contract workers. The result is that the human resource department is able to meet the staffing needs of its divisions while providing high levels of employment security to its own employees.

This policy of using contract labour is another example of how proactive human resource departments seek ways to meet the needs of an organization and its employees while remaining sensitive to the firm's economic environment. In the electronics example, the firm did not wait for the economy to go up or down and then react. Rather, it developed policies that allowed the organization to adjust smoothly to changes caused by technology, the economy, and other factors.

## HUMAN RESOURCE MANAGEMENT APPROACHES

Throughout this chapter several approaches to personnel management stand out. They provide complementary themes that we will pursue throughout the book to keep personnel management and human resources in their proper perspective. They include:

- *Human resource approach.* Human resource management is the management of people. Thus human resource management should be done professionally — in fact, humanely![28] The importance and dignity of human beings should not be ignored for the sake of expediency. Only through careful attention to the needs of employees do organizations grow and prosper.
- *Management approach.* Human resource management is a responsibility of every manager. The personnel department only provides a service for other departments; in the final analysis the performance and well-being of each worker is the dual responsibility of that worker's immediate supervisor and the human resource department.
- *Systems approach.* Human resource management takes place within a larger system, the organization. Therefore it must be evaluated with respect to the contribution it makes to the whole. In practice, experts must recognize that the human resource management model is an open system of interrelated parts, each of which affects the others and is influenced by the external environment.

As for the question of precisely how human resource management is affected by the environment, the next chapter reviews the major environmental challenges.

## SUMMARY

The central challenge for organizations is maintaining their high productivity and their effectiveness. Human resource management exists to improve the contribution made by human resources to organizations as well as to achieve societal and individual objectives.

Human resource management fulfils its purpose by obtaining, developing, utilizing, evaluating, maintaining, and retaining an effective work force. To carry out its role, personnel management needs to satisfy several objectives generated by society and the organization. The objectives are achieved through a variety of activities. These activities are the responsibility of all managers, but many of them may be delegated to specialists in a human resource department. Human resource departments often begin as small offices that grow as the demands upon the organization increase.

The activities of a human resource department are best viewed as a system of actions, each of which affects others directly or indirectly. Human resource specialists take information and human resources as prime inputs and through different activities produce outputs that help the organization achieve its objectives. Ideally, human resource experts undertake this role proactively.

## TERMS FOR REVIEW

| | |
|---|---|
| Human resources | System |
| Productivity | Open system |
| Purpose of human resource management | Inputs and outputs |
| Effectiveness | Feedback |
| Delegation | Reactive |
| Labour-management relations | Proactive |
| Staff authority | |

## REVIEW AND DISCUSSION QUESTIONS

1.  What is productivity and why is it important to organizations?
2.  Give the purpose, definition, and objectives of human resource management.
3.  Explain the relationship between societal needs and the activities of a human resource department.
4.  Make a diagram of a large-scale human resource department and label the likely components of such a department.
5.  Of what use is a systems model of human resource management?
6.  Explain the difference between proactive and reactive approaches to human resource management.
7.  Suppose your employer is planning a chain of high-quality restaurants to sell food products it already produces. Outline what areas of human resource management will be affected.
8.  If a bank is going to open a new branch in a distant city, with what inputs will the human resource department be concerned? What activities will the department need to undertake in the transition to a fully staffed and operating branch? What type of feedback do you think the department should seek after the branch has been operating for six months?

## INCIDENT 1-1
### The Birth of a Human Resource Department

> In 1983, Karen and Alice Bloodsworth decided to form a business to advise women executives on financial planning. Their decision coincided with a rapid increase in women executives. By the end of 1988, Alice was still handling all personnel records, employment, and compensation for sixty employees in three cities in eastern Canada.
>
> Talking with Karen, Alice listed the following reasons why she thought a personnel department should be formed.

   **a.** "I don't like to do recruiting or interviewing."

   **b.** "The human resource paperwork interferes with my time to line up new accounts."

   **c.** "Certainly, someone else could do this human resource work better."

   **d.** "I've never had any training in human resource work, and I fear I might be unknowingly breaking laws."

   **e.** "Without a human resource department, there is no one to whom I can delegate these thankless tasks."

   **f.** "I've done this human resource work long enough."

   It was decided to hire a recent graduate of a reputable university for training as a human resource manager.

1.   Of the reasons Alice gave, which should properly be considered in deciding whether to start a human resource department? Which should be ignored?

2.   What is Alice's view of human resource management?

3.   If you were hired to fill the new opening of human resource director, what personnel responsibilities do you think Alice would delegate to you?

## INCIDENT 1-2
## Human Resource Decision Making at Calgary Importers Limited

Calgary Importers Limited is a very large importer of linens, china, and crystal. It has branch offices in six provinces and has long been plagued by problems in its human resource practices. These problems led to the following discussion between the vice president of human resources and the vice president of distribution:

**Rob Whittier:** You may not agree with me, but if we are going to have consistency in our human resource policies, then key decisions about those policies must be centralized in the human resource department. Otherwise, branch managers will continue to make their own decisions differently. Besides, the department has the experts. If you needed financial advice, you would not ask your doctor; you would go to a banker or other financial expert. When it comes to deciding compensation packages or hiring new employees, those decisions should be left to experts in salary administration or selection. To ask a branch manager or supervisor to make those decisions deprives our firm of all of the expertise we have in the department.

**Henri DeLahn:** I have never questioned your department's expertise. Sure, the people in human resources are more knowledgeable than the line managers. But if we want those managers to be responsible for the performance of their branches, then we must not deprive those managers of their authority to make human resources decisions. Those operating managers must be able to decide whom to hire and whom to reward with raises. If they cannot make those decisions, then their effectiveness as managers will suffer.

1. If you were the president of Calgary Importers Limited and were asked to resolve this dispute, whose argument would you agree with? Why?

2. Can you suggest a compromise that would allow line managers to make these decisions consistently?

## INCIDENT 1-3
## North Star Airlines

North Star Airlines is a small commuter airline based in Montreal. Its president, Jean Galipeau, was a major force in its creation. As its long-time president, he stamped his image on the company through his employee relations philosophy. He treated employees as if they were part of a large family. Policies and management actions were designed to take care of North Star's human resources. The company went beyond merely promoting from within and offering superior wages and benefits.

For example, when other airlines furloughed employees during fuel crises and during reduced activity due to changes in economic and environmental conditions, North Star put surplus pilots and flight attendants to work selling tickets, loading bags, and even washing airplanes. Through these turbulent times, not one full-time North Star employee was laid off. As North Star's senior vice president for administration observed, "All the employees in North Star saw what we did for our pilots and flight attendants. Everyone knows we went the extra mile for them. Today, our employees are willing to go the extra mile for us."

True enough. In 1989, it gave an 8% raise when other airlines barely gave a 5% raise. The majority of North Star's employees responded by chipping in to buy their employer a $40-million jet. Today, some of North Star's policies include:

- Reassignment of employees to avoid layoffs, even at the expense of short-term profits and productivity.
- Wages that are five to ten cents per hour above the rates paid to unionized workers in other airlines.
- Fringe benefits that are considered some of the most generous in the industry and that provide employees with sound economic security in the event of disability or retirement.
- Rewards for employees who do an exceptional job of helping passengers in need of assistance.
- Communications from top management with all employees in groups of twenty-five to thirty every year-and-a-half.

Although good planning, modern planes, lean staff, and effective equipment scheduling contribute to North Star's favourable record, the core of its success is those people who do the planning and scheduling, and who serve the customers. By creating and maintaining an effective work force, North Star has been able to grow and prosper in times when other airlines have declared bankruptcy.

1. Since North Star must pay approximately the same for its planes, equipment, fuel,

and facilities as other airlines, how can it pay higher wages and fringe benefits and still remain one of the industry's most profitable carriers?

2.   From this incident, give examples of how North Star management uses the human resource, management, systems, and proactive approaches discussed in the chapter.

## SUGGESTED READINGS

Andrews, Janet R., "Where Doubts about the Personnel Role Begin," *Personnel Journal*, Vol. 66, No. 6, June 1987, pp. 84-89.

Blake, R. W., "The Role of the Senior Human Resource Executive: Orientation and Influence," *ASAC Personnel and Human Resources Division Proceedings* (edited by T. H. Stone), Halifax, St. Mary's University: June 1988, pp. 62-71.

Bowen, D. E. and L. E. Greiner, "Moving from Production to Service in Human Resources Management," *Organizational Dynamics*, Summer 1986, pp. 35-53.

Dickson, Nancy E., "Personnel Policies Take Form," *Personnel Journal*, Vol. 66, No. 4, April 1987, pp. 52-61.

Hackett, Thomas J., "The Real Role of Personnel Managers," *Personnel Journal*, Vol. 67, No. 3, March 1988, pp. 70-75.

Halcrow, A., "Operation Phoenix: The Business of Human Resources," *Personnel Journal*, Vol. 66, No. 9, September 1987, pp. 92-101.

Magnus M., "Personnel Policies in Partnership with Profit," *Personnel Journal*, Vol. 66, No. 9, September 1987, pp. 102-109.

Niminger, James N., *Managing Human Resources: A Strategic Perspective*, Ottawa: The Conference Board of Canada, 1982.

Tsui, Anne S. and George T. Milkovich, "Personnel Department Activities: Constituency Perspectives and Preferences," *Personnel Psychology*, Vol. 40, 1987, pp. 519-537.

## REFERENCES

1.   Jim Keyser, manager in charge of human resources at Coopers & Lybrand Consulting Group, Toronto, quoted in the *Globe and Mail*, September 14, 1987, page B-11.

2.   Robert Granford Wright, "Managing Management Resources through Corporate Constitutionalism," *Human Resource Management*, Summer 1973, p. 15.

3.   David Gilburt, "Top Secrets of Management," *Canadian Business*, July 1987, p. 32.

4.   Karen E. Debats, "The Continuing Personnel Challenge," *Personnel Journal*, May 1982, pp. 332-336, 338, 340, 342, 344.

5.   William B. Werther, Jr., William A. Ruch, and Lynne McClure, *Productivity through People*, St. Paul: West Publishing Co., 1986, pp. 3-5.

6.   Harold C. White, "Personnel Administration and Organizational Productivity: An Employee View," *Personnel Administrator*, August 1981, pp. 37-42, 44, 46, 48, also see, Walter Kiechel III, "Living with Human Resources," *Fortune*, August 18, 1986, pp. 99-100; "Improved Productivity Ensures Survival," *Work Life*, 1986, Vol. 4, No. 6, pp. 6-8.

7.   K. Newton and G. Betcherman, "Innovating on Two Fronts: People and Technology in the 1990s," *Canadian Business Review*, Vol. 14, No. 3, Autumn 1987, pp. 18-21.

8.   Statistics Canada figures, ibid., pp. 18-21.

9.   Results of the survey, ibid.

10.   Andrew Campbell, "Turning Workers into Risk Takers," *Canadian Business*, February 1985, p. 109.

11.   P. Cook, "Is Canada's Economic Machine Making too Many Jobs?" *Globe and Mail*, February 15, 1988, p. B-2.

12.   Ibid.

13.   W. Nymark, "Leadership in Canadian Business: A Pressing Need," *Canada Commerce*, Summer 1986, pp. 14-16.

14.   *Work Life*, op. cit.

15.   Joyce D. Ross, "A Definition of Human Resources Management," *Personnel Journal*, October 1982, pp. 781-783.

16.   Dennis R. Briscoe, "Human Resources Management Has Come of Age," *Personnel Administrator*, November 1982, pp. 75-77, 80-83.

17. Harold A. Gram, Gunther Brink, and John Smola, *Business Policy in Canada*, Toronto: John Wiley & Sons (Canada) Ltd., 1980, pp. 453-457.

18. *Work Life*, ibid.

19. David E. Dimick, "Who Makes Personnel Decisions?", *The Canadian Personnel & Industrial Relations Journal*, January 1978, pp. 23-29.

20. "HRM Measurement Projects Issues First Report," *Resource*, December 1985, p. 2.

21. "Personnel People," The *New York Times*, May 11, 1986, p. 3-1.

22. Roger Kenny, "The Future Top Personnel Executive," *The Personnel Administrator*, December 1978, pp. 17-19. See also John Sussman, "Profile of the Successful Personnel Executive," *The Personnel Administrator*, February 1980, pp. 77-82.

23. Herbert E. Meyer, "Personnel Directors Are the New Corporate Heroes," *Fortune*, February 1976, pp. 84-88, 140. See also Wendell French and Dale Henning, "The Authority-Influence Role of the Functional Specialist in Management," *Academy of Management Journal*, September 1966, pp. 187-203.

24. Rabindra N. Kanungo and Harish C. Jain, "Why Behavioural Science in Management?" in H.C. Jain and R.N.

Kanungo (eds.), *Behavioural Issues in Management*, Toronto: McGraw-Hill Ryerson Ltd., 1977, pp. 4-5.

25. Rabindra N. Kanungo, Gerald J. Gorn, and Henry J. Dauderis, "Motivational Orientation of Canadian Anglophone and Francophone Managers," in Jain and Kanungo (eds.), op. cit., pp. 85-99. See also James G. Goodale, "Job and Personal Factors Affecting Worker Attitudes and Performance," in Jain and Kanungo (eds.), op. cit.

26. T.F. Hercus, "Management Inventory Systems," *The Canadian Personnel & Industrial Relations Journal*, January 1973, pp. 22-29.

27. Paul R. Westbrook, "A Practical Approach to Personnel," *Personnel Journal*, September 1977, p. 459. See also Alfred W. Hill, "How Organizational Philosophy Influences Management Development," *Personnel Journal*, February 1980, pp. 118-120, 148.

28. C.W. Memeth and J.I.A. Rowney, "Professionalize or Perish," *The Canadian Personnel & Industrial Relations Journal*, January 1981, pp. 27-31. See also Walter R. Nord and Douglas E. Durand, "What's Wrong with the Human Resource Approach to Management?" *Organizational Dynamics*, Winter 1978, pp. 13-25.

# CHAPTER 2 ○○○○ ⊗ ⊗

# *ENVIRONMENTAL CHALLENGES*

*Given increasingly fierce global competition, the corporate emphasis in Canada has shifted markedly to productivity and quality. . . . If you don't own the patents to the ultimate technology (no one anywhere really does any more) and you don't have exclusive access to a source of low cost money, the only factor that can give you a competitive edge is your people.*

EVA INNES, ROBERT L. PERRY, and JIM LYON[1]

○ ○ ○ ○ ○ ○ ○ ○ ○ ○ ○ ○ ○ ○ ○ ○ ○ ○ ○ ○ ○ ○ ○ ○ ○ ○ ○ ○

## *CHAPTER OBJECTIVES*

After studying this chapter, you should be able to:

1. *Explain* the historical challenges that have led to the emergence of the human resource management function.
2. *Identify* the external forces that affect today's human resource management practice.
3. *Isolate* the challenges to human resource management that come from within the organization served.
4. *Describe* the challenge of professionalism facing the human resource management field.

○ ○ ○ ○ ○ ○ ○ ○ ○ ○ ○ ○ ○ ○ ○ ○ ○ ○ ○ ○ ○ ○ ○ ○ ○ ○ ○ ○

*H*uman resource management occurs within an environment filled with challenges. These challenges make human resource management an appealing career choice for people who seek an opportunity to help others.

> "Why would you want to go into human resource management as a career? There are so few challenging things to do," commented Tom Corlini, the resident assistant in Mike Ferguson's dorm.
> "I like to work with people," Mike confidently responded.

> "Come on, name two jobs where you don't work with people," chuckled Tom. "Why not major in something more challenging?"
>
> "Like what? I think the human resource management field will be challenging. Not only do you work with people, but you help them — help them get jobs and promotions and reach other personal objectives. There are challenges of recruiting new workers, developing training programs, and coping with constantly changing demands. When changes take place in society, people in organizations are usually affected. And when people in organizations are affected, human resource management is involved. You name two interesting jobs with more challenge," Mike argued.

Not every human resource specialist is as enthusiastic about the work as Mike. But few practitioners ever complain that their careers lack challenge.

Challenges to human resource management practices may result from changes within the historical, external, organizational, or professional environments. Although some challenges are unique to a firm or an industry, many of them affect personnel professionals in all organizations. For example, most human resource management practices have historical origins earlier in this century and have led today's managers to use similar methods and procedures. However, today's practitioners must adapt these practices or create new ones to meet the challenges that result from the external, organizational, and professional environments in which they work. Their proactive responses assume an awareness of their organization's environment and how it may affect their efforts. An example of how the policies and practices of human resource departments are affected by technological changes is illustrated in the Ottawa-Carleton Transit case:

> Ottawa-Carleton Regional Transit Authority planned to introduce a computerized traffic scheduling system and informed the union about its plans shortly after the signing of a two-year collective agreement. The union foresaw a loss of several jobs and was very concerned about these proposals. It filed an application to the Canadian Labour Relations Board complaining that the employer had not given proper notice of the change and that the proposed changes went beyond simple changes in job descriptions.

Source: Ottawa-Carleton Regional Transit Commission and Amalgamated Transit Union Locals 1502 and 279, 1982, 1 Can. LRBR 172.

The changes in the external environment meant that the transit authority had to adapt its business and human resource strategies to the new realities. The sources of the major challenges facing the human resource management system are shown in Figure 2-1; the rest of this chapter explains these challenges. Throughout the book, we will return to these challenges to see how they affect the specific human resource activities.

## HISTORICAL CHALLENGES

The field of human resource management did not suddenly appear. It evolved into its present form. A review of this evolution shows how the efforts of early pioneers led to

FIGURE 2-1   A Model of the Human Resource Management System and
Its Major Environmental Challenges

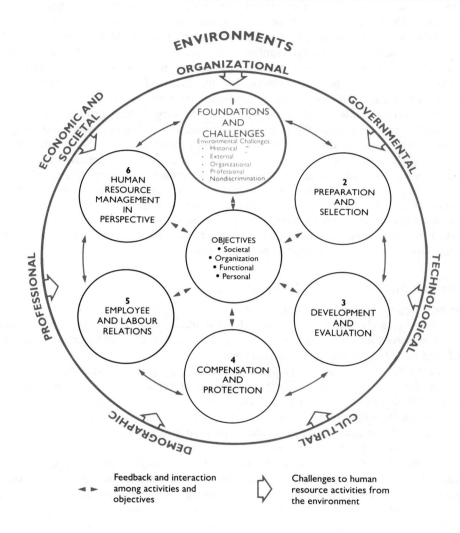

today's more proactive methods. By tracing this evolution, we also can sense the newness
and growing importance of human resource management.

### Early Causes and Origins

The origins of personnel management are unknown. Probably the first cave dwellers
struggled with problems of utilizing human resources. Even the Bible records selection
and training problems faced by Moses.[2]

During the thousands of years between Moses and the Industrial Revolution, there were few large organizations. Except for religious orders (the Roman Catholic Church, for example) or governments (particularly the military), small groups did most of the work. Whether on the farm, in small shops, or in the home, the primary work unit was the family. There was little need for a formal study of management of personnel.

The Industrial Revolution changed the nature of work. Mechanical power and economies of scale required large numbers of people to work together. Big textile mills, foundries, and mines sprung up in England and then in North America. Collectively, people were still an important resource, but the Industrial Revolution meant greater mechanization and unpleasant working conditions for many workers.

By the late 1800s, a few employers reacted to the human problems caused by industrialization and created the post of *welfare secretary*. Welfare secretaries existed to meet worker needs and to prevent workers from forming unions. Social secretaries, as they were sometimes called, helped employees with personal problems such as education, housing, and medical needs. These early forerunners of personnel specialists also sought to improve working conditions for workers. The emergence of welfare secretaries prior to 1900 demonstrates that the personnel activities in large organizations had already become more than some top operating managers wanted to handle. Thus social secretaries marked the birth of specialized human resource management, as distinct from the day-to-day supervision of personnel by operating managers.

## Scientific Management and Human Needs

The next noteworthy development was scientific management. The scientific management proponents showed the world that the systematic, scientific study of work could lead to improved efficiency. Their arguments for specialization and improved training furthered the need for personnel departments.

Stimulated by the developments of scientific management and early unions, the first decades of this century saw primitive personnel departments replace welfare secretaries. These new departments contributed to organizational effectiveness by maintaining wages at proper levels, screening job applicants, and handling grievances. They also assumed the welfare secretary's role of improving working conditions, dealing with unions, and meeting other employee needs.

By World War I, personnel departments were becoming common among very large industrial employers. But these early departments were not important parts of the organizations they served. They were record depositories with advisory authority only. At that time, production, finance, and marketing problems overshadowed the role of personnel management. The importance of personnel departments grew slowly as their contribution and responsibilities increased.

From the end of World War I until the Great Depression in the 1930s, personnel departments assumed growing roles in handling compensation, testing, unions, and employee needs. More and more attention was paid to employee needs. The importance of individual needs became even more pronounced as a result of the research studies in the United States at Western Electric's Hawthorne plant during this period. These studies showed that the efficiency goals of scientific management had to be balanced by considerations of human needs. These observations eventually had a profound impact on personnel management. But the Depression and World War II diverted attention to more urgent matters of organizational and national survival.

## Modern Influences

The Depression of the 1930s led citizens to lose faith in the ability of business to meet society's needs. They turned to government. Government intervened to give workers minimum wages and the right to join labour unions. In 1940 Canada started an unemployment insurance program to help alleviate financial problems during the transition from one job to another. In general, the government's emphasis was on improving employee security and working conditions.

This outpouring of legislation during the 1930s helped to shape the present role of personnel departments by adding legal obligations. Organizations now had to consider societal objectives and the need for legal compliance, which elevated the importance of personnel departments. In practice, personnel departments were made responsible for discouraging unionization among employees. But with new-found legal protection, unions grew dramatically. These organizing successes startled many organizations into rethinking their use of *paternalism*, their ''management knows best'' approach to employee welfare. Personnel departments began replacing paternalism with more proactive approaches that considered employee desires. When workers did organize, responsibility for dealing with unions also fell to the personnel department, sometimes renamed the industrial relations department to reflect these new duties.

Personnel departments continued to increase in importance during the 1940s and 1950s. The recruiting and training demands of World War II added to the credibility of the personnel departments that successfully met these challenges. After the war, personnel departments grew in importance as they contended with unions and an expanding need for professionals such as engineers and accountants. The increasing attention given to behavioural findings led to concern for improved human relations. These findings helped underscore the importance of sound personnel management practices.

In the 1960s and 1970s the central influence on personnel was again legislation. Several laws were passed that affected the working conditions, wage levels, safety, and health and other benefits of employees. These acts began to provide personnel department managers with a still larger voice — a voice that began to equal those of production, finance, and marketing executives in major corporations.

Human resource management—as the personnel function is known today—did not emerge until recently. It is only very recently that human resource specialists have started to exert great influence on organization strategy or have begun to be chosen as chief executives.

> The late Ross Hennigar of Suncor Inc. was one of the few who reached the level of chief executive of an organization. Larry Bowk of Constellation Assurance Company is yet another human resource specialist who became the company's CEO. In recent years the number of senior-level jobs in the human resources management field has increased. Whereas ten years ago a firm would have advertised for a Personnel Manager, today it typically asks for a ''Senior Executive — Human Resources'' or a ''Vice President of Human Resources.''[3]

## EXTERNAL CHALLENGES

Organizations are surrounded by an external environment filled with variables — variables over which the organization has little influence. This leaves personnel departments with two choices: to wait for the variables to change and then react, or to anticipate what changes will take place and plan accordingly.

> The Depression of the 1930s caused the birth rate to decline. The Prairies were severely hit by the Depression and the population actually declined in Saskatchewan during the 1930s and 1940s. This meant there were fewer people in the thirty-five to forty-four age range during the late 1960s and throughout the 1970s. This age group is the primary source of middle-level managers. Reactive personnel departments did little until the shortage became acute. Proactive personnel departments implemented training programs in the early 1960s to groom lower-level managers to fill the foreseeable shortages.

Human resource departments could do nothing about the lower birth rates, but proactive firms treated this change as an input and developed programs to transform their employees into capable workers before the shortage of human resources harmed operations.

The specific external challenges that face human resource management vary. The most common ones include technology, economics, changes in the labour force, cultural values, and government. The steps that human resource specialists follow to keep up with these diverse changes are outlined in Figure 2-2. As it explains, human resource experts must constantly watch the environment for changes and evaluate their implications for the organization. Once conceived, proactive plans are developed and implemented. Their success is determined through feedback about the changes. Although numerous challenges face the field, the major ones are discussed in the following sections.[4]

FIGURE 2-2   Steps in Dealing with Environmental Challenges

1. **Monitor the environment.** Human resource specialists must stay informed about likely changes in the environment by belonging to professional associations, attending seminars, furthering their formal education, and reading widely.
2. **Evaluate the impact.** As new information is acquired, human resource experts ask: "What impact will this information have on the organization today? Tomorrow?" Specialists must diagnose the future meaning of today's events.
3. **Take proactive measures.** Once changes and their impact are evaluated, human resource specialists implement approaches that help the organization reach its goal.
4. **Obtain and analyze feedback.** The results of proactive personnel activities are then evaluated to see if the desired outcomes were brought about.

## Technological Challenges

Technology influences human resource management in two general ways. One way is for technology to change entire industries.

The technology of cars and airplanes modified the transportation industry. Automobile and aviation companies grew. Growth created demand for more employees and training. For those already employed within this industry, growth provided promotional opportunities. Railways were also affected by the same technology, but the personnel management challenges differed. Revenue was lost to cars, trucks, and airplanes, limiting growth in that sector of the transportation industry. Advancement opportunities — even employment opportunities — shrank. Personnel departments in these companies had to reduce the work force and create early retirement systems.

Automation is the other main way technology affects human resource management.

The introduction of computers into banks changed employment needs. Before computers, personnel specialists recruited large numbers of unskilled and semiskilled clerks. Computers, however, required highly skilled programmers and systems analysts. Also needed were semiskilled employees to process information into computer-usable form. To outsiders, banks changed little, but their personnel departments had to change recruiting and training programs significantly.

Since the early 1980s, Canada has witnessed the rapid growth of computerization, affecting almost all walks of life. An unprecedented degree of computerization and automation has changed the way we work, play, study, and even entertain ourselves. Indeed, robots are increasingly playing such a key role in Canadian industry today that the field of *robotics* is gaining attention from practitioners and researchers alike.[5]

Why do organizations automate various activities? There are several reasons for automating. The first is the push for speed. Competition from other countries has made it imperative that we improve our manufacturing practices if we want to stay competitive. For instance, capital equipment items that on average take six to twelve months to make in Canada take six to twelve weeks to make in Japan. A survey of 206 Canadian chief executives by Andrew Templer found that the major reasons for introducing robots into the workplace were the increasing cost of labour, concern over product quality, concern over the loss of market share, declining productivity of employees, and the general trend toward robotization in Canadian industry.[6] The same study also found that lack of skilled workers, employee unwillingness to perform certain types of jobs, and top management values also contributed to the prevailing trend. Only 16% of Templer's respondents had actually introduced robots in their workplace at the time of the survey; however, another 15% were preparing for their use in the near future and 38% were actively considering their use in the long term.

A second reason for automation is to provide a better service to the customer, to increase predictability in operations, and to achieve higher standards of quality in production. Machines do not go on strike, nor do they ask for raises.

Automation also allows flexibility in operations. In the future, "the range of manufacturing systems and all hardware and software must be greatly extended in order to accommodate the variations that will become accepted as normal."[7] Thus, the production facility should be versatile enough to produce many different products; the time, cost, and effort involved in changing set-ups should be reduced to a point where they are not a factor in costs. Even very small batches can then be economic.

Automation also permits us to rely on machine intelligence. Machines can process enormous quantities of data in seconds and microseconds and take corrective actions. When logical or rational decision making is important, machines can be employed, thus saving valuable human resources and time. They are, however, unlikely to be very helpful when creative or intuitive decisions are to be made.

Automation, to be beneficial, should permit the integration of technologies. Thus, the technologies should also mesh with each other in an elegant manner. It should be noted that automation is not the answer to all of Canada's economic problems.

The lack of availability of capital for buying expensive robots puts such purchases beyond the reach of most small- and medium-sized organizations. Negative union attitudes towards mechanization is another barrier to the introduction of robots in the workplace. Automation is also no substitute for entrepreneurial decision making. The human resource manager's functional expertise and judgement will continue to be critical. However, it is a reasonable prediction that in the future, most hazardous and boring jobs will be taken over by robots. Dangerous jobs — such as working with toxic chemicals and paints — will be changed by substituting robots for people. Likewise, highly repetitive assembly tasks will continue to be taken over by robots during the early 1990s. General Motors, for example, planned to use more than 1,500 robot painters by 1990, when it would have more than 13,000 robots doing welding, assembly, and other work.[8] New jobs will appear for engineers, technicians, and assemblers of robotic equipment. The result will be more challenges for human resource departments to recruit and train these specialists. Those jobs that remain are likely to be upgraded in importance and pay because those who control and maintain the robots will require higher level skills than the less skilled workers who will be replaced.

The bad news is that human resource professionals may have to contend with increased worker alienation, since job opportunities may shrink along with opportunities for socialization on the job. To effectively utilize expensive robots, more and more factories may find it necessary to work two or three shifts a day. If these changes do occur on a wide scale, human resource departments will face even more challenges in recruiting and retaining qualified workers. And it is likely that these departments will become more involved with helping line managers introduce robots into the workplace in ways that minimize employee fears of displacement and unemployment.[9] It is also possible that automation will adversely affect the overall quality of work life.[10]

Yet another factor that has very great significance for the human resource manager is the increasing computerization of major organizational functions. The computer has already become (and will increasingly become) an essential part of most organizations. Some of the possible consequences of computerization on organizations are shown in Figure 2-3.

The *exact* effects of computerization on decision making will vary from one organization to another (depending on size, management practices, technology, culture, etc.). Figure 2-3 is intended to show some broad patterns in this context. The significance of these trends for personnel selection, training, and evaluation practices cannot be overemphasized.

## Economic Challenges

The business cycle challenges the skills of human resource specialists. A recession cre-

FIGURE 2-3  Possible Consequences of Computerization on Organizations

---

- Increased delegation of decision making to lower levels (with clearly established constraints), with implications for the training function, performance evaluation, and reward systems.
- More unit-level data analysis with implications for performance evaluation procedures.
- Changes in work procedures, increasing the importance of frequent job analysis, greater focus on job design, more flexible procedures, etc.
- Increased separation between managers and computer specialists, necessitating new reporting procedures, leadership training, and performance evaluation measures.
- Task specialization and fragmentation, with implications for all human resource activities.
- Changed work hours and procedures affecting several of the human resource functions.

---

Source: From a talk given by F.C. Miner, ''Impact of Computers on Management Training,'' Saint Mary's University, Halifax, March 16, 1984.

ates a need to maintain a competent work force and reduce labour cost. Decisions to reduce hours, lay off workers, or accept lower profit levels intimately involve human resource departments. The more carefully human resource departments monitor the economy, the better they can anticipate the organization's changing needs. This means control strategies can be less drastic because they are begun sooner.

> Gemini Contractors supplied roofing and siding materials to the construction industry. When in 1987 the human resources manager of the company, monitoring the monthly earning figures of that industry, noticed the earnings beginning to drop, he recommended an employment ''freeze'' and no new workers were hired. Sure enough, Gemini's sales to the construction industry in 1988 were about half those of a few years back; yet no one was put on layoff because normal employee departures had reduced labour costs sufficiently.

On the other hand, as the economy expands, the demand for new employees and training programs grows. Voluntary departures by employees also increase. These developments bring pressure for higher wages, better benefits, and improved working conditions. Human resource departments must act cautiously, however. Overstaffing, bloated benefit programs, and high wages aggravate the problems of a declining business cycle.

A major economic challenge now facing Canadian organizations is dealing with free trade with the U.S. The Canada–U.S. Free Trade Agreement, which was finally ratified in December 1988, calls for tariff reductions on commodities in stages over ten years, beginning January 1, 1989. The stages are set at one, five, and ten years, so the first group of commodities began to cross the border tariff-free in January 1989.

Although the effects of free trade on the country, its manufacturing companies, labour force, and standard of living are hard to predict, almost all commercial and many other business organizations are likely to feel its impact.[11] The U.S. buys almost 75% of our exports, and free trade between the countries can have significant repercussions for both trading partners. It is clear that Canadian companies will be challenged to increase productivity and efficiency, thereby increasing their competitiveness. This means that human resource departments in Canadian organizations will have to pay particular attention to training their workers and re-designing the jobs to increase the overall productivity levels.

## Demographic Challenges

The demographics of the labour force describe the composition of the work force: the education levels, the age levels, the percentage of the population participating in the work force, and other population characteristics.[12] Demographic changes occur slowly, are usually known in advance, and are well measured. Decisions to have smaller families in the 1930s, 1960s, or 1970s, for example, take decades to influence the work force. Increases in the educational levels of the population are another slow-moving trend.

A close look at the labour market, however, indicates several trends:

*Trend 1: the increasing number of women in the work force.* Figure 2-4 shows the labour force participation rates for males and females in Canada for the last several years and estimates for the year 1995. The figure indicates increasing participation by women. One projection estimates that by 1995, 57% of Canadian women (above fifteen years of age) will enter the labour force[13]; another study reported in the *Financial Times* expects 85% of Canadian women aged 25-54 years to enter the labour force by the year 2005.[14] It is interesting to note that compared to several other industrialized nations, the participation rate of Canadian women is high.

More women have also been entering unconventional jobs. Today many women prefer to leave their traditional, non-professional occupations (such as clerical and sales) and work in management, law, engineering, and medical fields. The fact that women accounted for 70% of the total employment growth in Canada between 1976 and 1985[15] has raised new issues of child care, counselling for two-career families, employment equity and equity in compensation systems.

*Trend 2: Shift from primary and extractive to service jobs.* Currently, there is a shift from employment in primary and extractive industries to service and professional jobs.

FIGURE 2-4   Labour Force Participation Rate in Canada

|  | MALE | FEMALE | COMBINED |
|---|---|---|---|
|  |  | (all in % of total population) |  |
| 1951 | 83.8 | 24.1 | 54.2 |
| 1961 | 77.7 | 29.5 | 53.7 |
| 1966 | 79.8 | 35.4 | 57.3 |
| 1971 | 77.3 | 39.4 | 58.1 |
| 1976 | 77.6 | 45.2 | 61.1 |
| 1980 | 78.4 | 50.4 | 64.1 |
| 1985 | 76.7 | 54.3 | 65.2 |
| 1995 | 77.1 | 58.4 | 67.9 |

Source: Statistics Canada, *The Labour Force*, Bulletin No. 71-001, 1966-1981; Pradeep Kumar, Mary Lou Coates, and David Arrowsmith, *The Current Industrial Relations Scene in Canada: 1986*, Kingston, Ont.: Industrial Relations Centre, Queens University, 1986; Woods Gordon and Clarkson Gordon, *Tomorrow's Customers* 20th Edition, Toronto, 1986; David K. Foot, *A challenge of the 1980s: Unemployment and Labour Force Growth in Canada and the Provinces*, Toronto: Institute for Policy Analysis, University of Toronto, 1981; 1995 projections by the authors.

Figure 2-5 indicates the shift in proportions of the labour force employed in different industries over the last two decades. Apparently, occupations employing white-collar workers (e.g., clerical, professional, sales) are increasing in number, while those employing blue-collar workers (e.g., skilled and semiskilled technicians) are decreasing.

*Trend 3: Educational attainment of workers.* A look at the educational attainment of Canadian workers presents an intriguing picture. On the one hand, the educational attainment of Canadians has been increasing dramatically over the past several years (see Figure 2-6) and is expected to maintain its upward trend. More and more Canadian adults seem to like the idea of going back to school, as the following quote points out:

### FIGURE 2-5   Distribution of Employment by Major Occupational Groups

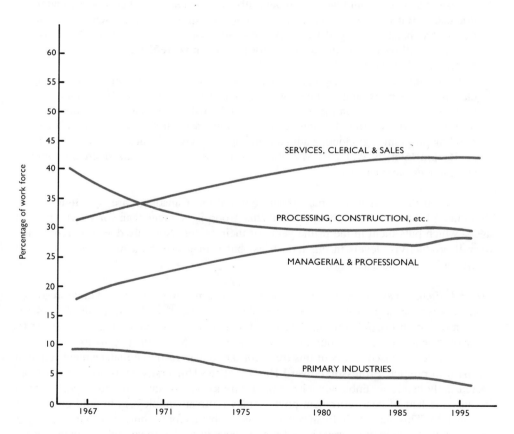

Source: Statistics Canada, *The Labour Force*, Bulletin No. 71-001, 1967–1981 and Bulletin No. 94-736, 1975–1981. Peter Dungan, *PRISM Projection Through 1995*, Toronto: Policy and Economic Analysis Program, Institute for Policy Analysis, University of Toronto, July 21, 1986; Projections for 1995 shown here are by the authors based on *Statistics Canada* and other available data.

FIGURE 2-6   Educational Attainment of Canadian Workers

| EDUCATIONAL LEVEL ATTAINED | YEARS | | | (PROJECTED) | |
|---|---|---|---|---|---|
| | 1961 | 1971 | 1981 | 1989 | 2000 |
| Elementary School | 45.3 | 25.8 | 15.2 | 9.2 | 6.8 |
| Secondary School | 46.2 | 52.7 | 53.0 | 49.5 | 48.5 |
| Post-Secondary Level | 8.5 | 21.4 | 31.8 | 41.3 | 44.6 |

Source: W.D. Wood and P. Kumar (ed.), *The Current Industrial Relations Scene in Canada 1981*, The Industrial Relations Centre, Queen's University, Kingston, 1981; *The Labour Force*, Dec. 1981; Statistics Canada, *The Changing Educational Profile of Canadians*, Ottawa, 1980; adapted from *The Labour Force*, Statistics Canada, Catalogue 71001, 1989.

Across the country thousands of Canadian adults are now hitting the books. Twenty years ago an adult would have been painfully conspicuous in a classroom of undergraduates. But the notion that education ends abruptly after high school or university has been challenged by a new generation of life-long learners. No fewer than two million Canadians over twenty-five are now refusing to bury learning along with their year books. . . .

At the University of Guelph urban teachers mingle with airline pilots for evening classes on sheep farming—all hoping to become part-time farmers. Union members spend weekends at Simon Fraser University in British Columbia studying the art of negotiating. At the tiny Université Sainte Anne in Church Point, N.S., a boat-building program is graduating adults who hope to revive a local ship-building yard. At Rankin Inlet, N.W.T., RCMP officers while away hours with degree-earning correspondence courses . . . [16]

The disturbing news is that about four million Canadians are still functionally illiterate.[17] What is worse, about 40% of this group is younger than forty-five years of age — which puts them in the prime years of their career. Not only does this reduce the overall productivity levels in our industries, but it may also be a major contributor to safety violations and accidents.[18]

*Trend 4: Employment of older workers.* One of the impending issues for human resource managers is what *Maclean's* termed "our old age crisis."[19] In 1996, about 28% of the population (or almost 7.6 million Canadians) will be more than fifty years old. By 2000, the sixty-five and over age group may reach close to 13.5% of the population.[20]

The exact consequences of this trend for the human resource management function are hard to predict. Professor Edward Harvey of the University of Toronto predicts an increasingly hectic scramble for jobs in the future as one possible consequence.[21] This is because the fear of post-retirement poverty may motivate employees to hold on to their current jobs. This may create fresh concerns and problems for the human resource manager who may be faced with unprecedented bottle-necks in professional and unionized industries. Many factors influence an individual's decision to retire (including health status, adequacy of pensions, demands of the job, etc.). Understanding and preparing well ahead for the challenge may be the only recourse to meet the demands of the future retirees; in any case, pressures for expanded retirement benefits, variable work schedules, coordination of government benefits (e.g., Canada Pension Plan benefits) with company benefits, and retraining programs are just a few of the challenges that await human resource specialists of the future.

Further, if fertility rates in Canada remain at modest rates, the average age of our population is likely to increase steadily (see Figure 2-7). The consequences of population aging could include a deluge of pensioners expected in the early to mid-2000s. It is also pointed out that a shifting age structure will bring less consumerism, demand for different types of products and alterations in labour productivity levels.[22] Whatever the precise consequences, an aging population has major implications for the human resources function, especially in the areas of recruitment and selection, job design, training, appraisal, and compensation and benefits administration.

FIGURE 2-7  Population Projections for Canada

| | (UNDER ASSUMPTION OF FERTILITY RATE OF 1.5) % DISTRIBUTION OF POPULATION BY AGE GROUP | | | |
| | 0-14 | 15-64 | 65+ | MEAN AGE |
| --- | --- | --- | --- | --- |
| 1991 | 20.5 | 68.1 | 11.4 | 35.5 |
| 1996 | 19.0 | 68.9 | 12.1 | 36.8 |
| 2001 | 17.2 | 70.2 | 12.6 | 38.2 |
| 2011 | 15.2 | 70.5 | 14.3 | 40.8 |
| 2021 | 14.3 | 66.7 | 19.0 | 43.2 |
| 2051 | 13.0 | 61.2 | 25.8 | 46.2 |

*Source: Statistics Canada, *Current Demographic Analysis: Fertility in Canada—From Baby Boom to Baby Bust*, November 1984, Catalogue #91-524E, Ottawa.

*Trend 5: More part-time workers*. The structure of employment in Canada has also been changing slowly over the years. There are more part-time workers now than ever before. More than 15% of all employment now is represented by part-time workers (numbering about 1.8 million).[23] Eighty per cent of part-time workers are women who typically work at low-paying sales and service jobs.[24] Several of the full-time jobs were converted into part-time jobs during the recession in the early 1980s to reduce labour costs. The increasing proportion of part-time workers has raised new concerns about pay inequity in this country and has provided momentum to the equal-pay-for-work-of-equal-value concept.

*Trend 6: Youth unemployment*. Yet another crisis facing the Canadian economy is youth unemployment. Although in general the Canadian economy has been robust since the mid-1980s, the youth unemployment rate in this country continues to be relatively high. In 1986, the unemployment rate for young persons who were in the fifteen to twenty-four age group was 15.2%; the corresponding figure for the twenty-five years and up group was only 8%.[25] Also, earnings of younger workers in Canada (less than twenty years old) have been traditionally lower than that of older workers. One study showed that this has been changing for the worse in recent years. The decline in youths' earnings relative to mean earnings of the population continued and accelerated in the early 1980s.[26]

Unemployment rates in some of the provinces were significantly higher than the national average and the rates in economically prosperous provinces. Newfoundland continues to have the highest degree of unemployment in the country (at about 20%), while Ontario with a 7% unemployment rate had the lowest unemployment rate in the country. Overall, Canada had an unemployment rate of 9.1% in July 1987.[27]

Some available research has shown a link between unemployment and poor physical and mental health. Leandre Desjardins, chairman of the Canadian Mental Health Association (CMHA), suggests that unemployment may lead to poor health because of poor diet, stress, and inactivity.[28] The unemployed also periodically go through emotional highs and lows (called a "roller-coaster effect" by CMHA). The longer a young person remains unemployed, the less the person will be able to adjust to the discipline required in steady jobs and to maintain good work habits. As Elizabeth Beale, chief economist with the Atlantic Provinces' Economic Council, pointed out, "If someone is unemployed for the first five or six years of his adult life, then their ability to hold a job suffers drastically."[29] Alienation, a sense of hopelessness, and an increasing crime rate may be some of the many social costs associated with youth unemployment. Clearly, the challenges facing the human resource managers are complex indeed.

Yet this picture may change drastically in the future years. Because of the low birth rates of the 1960s and 1970s, the population of young workers in Canada may actually decline in the 1990s and into 2000. One estimate shows that by 1996, there will be 600,000 fewer adults in the age group of twenty to thirty-four years (and about 50,000 fewer teens);[30] this may mean a shortage of teenage workers beginning in the 1990s. This could affect many of the service industries seriously; it also may mean a shortage of middle-management talent near the end of the next decade.

## Cultural Challenges

As cultural values change, human resource departments discover new challenges. The increased participation of women in the labour force is an example of a cultural change that has demographic implications.

> Between 1970 and 1980 the labour force in Canada grew by roughly three million workers. The participation of women (as a percentage of the total labour force) grew from 37% to 44% during that decade.[31] The old cultural value judgement that "men work and women stay home" underwent radical modification during that period. This shift carries implications for personnel management. For example, child-care facilities provided by the employer will become a more common demand confronting human resource departments. Sick days—paid days off for illness—may become "personal leave days," so that working parents can care for the needs of children.

Changing attitudes towards work and leisure have confronted human resource departments with requests for longer vacations, more holidays, and varied workweeks.[32] Supervisors increasingly turn to human resource managers for help with employee motivation. Even attitudes towards honesty are reflected in the growing rates of employee theft with which many human resource departments must contend.

Over the last several decades, Canadian society has developed through advanced industrialization towards what has been called the post-industrial stage.[33] As mentioned

FIGURE 2-8   Forming a Cultural Mosaic

Immigrants are vital to the growth of the Canadian labour force. Government projections of our country's population and labour force usually include assumptions incorporating varying immigration rates. When the economy is expanding and the demand for labour increases, typically we have to meet this by increasing the immigration levels. Given Canada's low birth rate, our overall population may start declining in the next fifty to one hundred years unless immigration levels are increased. The "business immigrants" (who can enter under the Investor category with a net worth of at least $500,000) and the "entrepreneurs" (who are expected to set up and manage a new business) have often acted as catalysts of economic growth in this country, while immigrants from nontraditional sources such as Hong Kong, Vietnam, India, Sri Lanka, and the Philippines have added to the cultural diversity and richness of this country. Unlike the American notion of the "melting pot," Canada has encouraged each ethnic minority to maintain its unique cultural heritage to form part of the Canadian cultural mosaic. For the practising manager, this cultural diversity brings simultaneously additional opportunities and challenges.

Although there is no statistical proof that racism is increasing, the arrival of many immigrants from Asia, Africa, and other countries in South America has sparked new social tensions in major cities in Canada. In recent years, there have been charges of racism against police in Toronto and Montreal and in Nova Scotia. In the years to come, the human resource manager's job of maintaining a just and equal-opportunity work setting will become even more important.

earlier, this has led to a shift in the labour force from primary, extractive occupations to secondary (manufacturing and processing) and service industries. In the past fifteen years, women's employment has increased by approximately 80%. More and more young persons have also been entering the work force. This increase in the number of women and young persons working has led to some changes in the expectations and demands of the labour force.

There has also been a change in Canadian values in recent years. The Canadian national character has been described succinctly in the past as a "conservative syndrome"[34] made up of a tendency to be guided by tradition, to accept the decision-making functions of elites, and to put a strong emphasis on the maintenance of order and predictability. Canadians are typically viewed as a hybrid product of several nationalities and ethnic groups "not quite as American as the Americans, not quite as British as the British . . . and not quite as French as the French."[35] However, in recent years Canada's national self-image has changed somewhat (witness the new Constitution, with its Charter of Rights and Freedoms). The coexistence of Anglophones and Francophones along with dozens of other national, racial, and ethnic groups, each with its unique cultural and social background, makes Canadian society a "vertical mosaic."[36] (See Figure 2-8.) This has led to a few unique issues and problems for the human resource administrator. Sociologists who have compared Canadian patterns with those of the U.S. have suggested that in Canada the "sorting" of people proceeds in terms of ascriptive criteria (e.g., sex, ethnic origin).[37] For example, in Canada gender is a clearer indicator of where men or women will be located in the labour force than it is in the U.S. Another study on occupational distribution by ethnic origin found that the cultural pluralism ideal in Canada (in contrast to the so-called "melting pot" ideal in the U.S.) results in unequal job placement of different ethnic groups.[38] Greater governmental intervention has at times been necessary to eliminate such imbalances (the Canadian Bill of Rights of 1960 is an example).

It is, of course, impossible to identify every changing value in any society. However, organizations represent only a small sample of society, so as cultural values change, human resource departments can anticipate the impact of some of the changes and act accordingly. Failure to make the attempt can lead to lower effectiveness or government involvement.

A *Maclean's* survey of a cross-section of Canadians in 1987 indicated that Canada was on the threshold of profound social changes.[39] Historically, Canadians have always been far more positive than Americans to government participation in economic activities (e.g., in the early days of Canadian history itself, private and public capital was combined to create the Canadian Pacific Railway). However, in recent years, government is slowly falling out of favour with many Canadians. As the *Maclean's* survey concluded, "With parts of the country in the grip of economic stagnation, many Canadians are growing pessimistic about the nation's economic future while scrambling to support themselves. As a result, individuality, a kind of do-it-yourself citizenship, appears to be supplanting faith in government in the minds of many."[40] Canadians are also "turning inward to families and careers in search of personal rewards."[41] Forty per cent of the respondents stated that religion is becoming more important in their life. However, the same survey also indicated that "a majority [of Canadians] are shedding idealism in favour of pragmatism. Many acknowledge a willingness to sacrifice principles to get what they want out of life."[42] Canadians surveyed in this poll had also moved, though fractionally at 3%, to the political right.

## Government Challenges

Few challenges encountered by human resource departments are as overwhelming as those presented by government. Government—through the enforcement of laws—has a direct and immediate impact on the human resource function. The federal and provincial laws that regulate the employee-employer relationship challenge the methods human resource departments use. Some laws, such as the Canada Labour Safety Code of 1968, make major demands on human resource departments. The impact of these laws has helped elevate the importance of human resource decisions.

Government involvement in the employment relationship seeks to achieve societal objectives—usually the elimination of practices considered contrary to public policy. To human resource specialists, government involvement requires compliance and proactive efforts to minimize the organizational consequences. At appropriate points throughout this book, employee-related laws are explained, to illustrate the challenges modern human resource departments encounter and the actions they must take.

In 1983 the British Columbia government sought to rewrite the rules of bargaining, especially in the public sector. Bill 3, the Public Sector Restraint Act, attempted to remove job security from civil servants, while Bill 2, the Public Service Labour Relations Amendment Act, if passed, would have had the effect of stripping unions of the right to negotiate a variety of items, including work scheduling. The proposals would have also limited wage increases and reduced the importance of the Human

Rights Commission within the province. The proposed legislation immediately sparked off a series of strike threats, including those from the 40,000-member British Columbia Government Employees Union (BCGEU). The Solidarity Coalition, a 950,000 member protest movement, threatened a general strike all over the province.

An important piece of government legislation that has profound implications for the human resource management profession is the Constitution Act of 1982, which contains a Canadian Charter of Rights and Freedoms. The Charter provides some fundamental rights to every Canadian. These are:

1. Freedom of conscience and religion;
2. Freedom of thought, belief, opinion, and expression, including freedom of the press and other media of communication;
3. Freedom of peaceful assembly; and
4. Freedom of association.

The Charter provides protection to every Canadian in the following specific areas:[43]

1. Fundamental freedoms;
2. Democratic rights;
3. The right to live and seek employment anywhere in Canada;
4. Legal rights;
5. Equality rights for all individuals;
6. Officially recognized languages of Canada;
7. Minority language education rights;
8. Canada's multicultural heritage; and
9. Native people's rights.

The Meech Lake Accord, by which the province of Quebec officially signed the Constitution, is yet to be ratified by New Brunswick and Manitoba. At the time this book goes to press, there is also some uncertainty about Newfoundland's support for the accord. If and when the accord becomes a reality, it could have major implications for human resource management practices in Canada. The Charter's section on equality rights provides protection to individuals against discrimination in hiring or in the work place on non-job-relevant criteria. Affirmative action plans, however, continue to be legal. Under section 15(2) of the Charter, the legality of special programs or affirmative action cannot be questioned. This section explicitly states that none of the other provisions of the Charter ''preclude any law, program or activity that has as its object the amelioration of conditions of disadvantaged individuals or groups including those that are disadvantaged because of race, national or ethnic origin, colour, religion, sex, age or mental or physical disability.''[44] It is, however, too early to delineate the precise implications of the accord for human rights' legislation in Canada and its provinces.

The Abella Commission on Equality in Employment was appointed in 1983 to inquire into the most effective, efficient, and equitable methods of promoting employment opportunities for four designated groups: women, disabled persons, native people, and visible minorities. The commission recommended that all organizations set mandatory equality programs. The commission also urged the provincial and federal governments to pass equity legislation—a recommendation that has since been implemented by some Canadian provinces.[45]

The significance of the Charter of Rights on the human resource function can not be overemphasized. It affects practically every aspect of a human resource manager's job —especially recruitment, selection, training, compensation, appraisal, and collective bargaining. The Canadian Human Rights Legislation and its impact on human resource management practices in this country will be discussed further in Chapter 3.

## ORGANIZATIONAL CHALLENGES

Besides external demands, human resource departments find current challenges within the organizations they serve. Internal challenges arise because employers pursue many objectives. These objectives require trade-offs between financial, sales, service, production, employee, and other goals. Since human resource objectives are just one set among many in the eyes of top management, human resource managers must confront internal challenges with a balanced concern for other needs. The employer does not exist solely, or even largely, to meet human resource objectives. Rather, human resource departments exist to assist the organization in meeting its other objectives successfully. Human resource departments find several internal challenges in helping the organization achieve its objectives. Included are challenges from unions, informational needs, and organizational character.

### Unions

Unions represent an actual challenge in unionized companies and a *potential* challenge in those that are not. In companies with unions, the employer and the union sign a labour agreement that specifies compensation (wages and benefits), hours, and working conditions. The agreement limits the human resource activities of supervisors and human resource specialists. For both, the challenge is to achieve objectives without violating the agreement.

> Karl McPheters wanted to promote Jill Wang to chief switchboard operator because Jill was an excellent employee. The labour contract called for promotions to go to the most experienced worker, which meant Pam Hale. To promote Jill, Karl found Pam a production job at more money. She took it. This now made Jill the senior switchboard operator and next in line for the promotion. The contract was honoured, and management achieved its objective of promoting the best person, Jill.

The formation of unions necessitates major changes in management procedures and systems especially during a strike or lockout.

> The Mount Saint Vincent University Faculty Union in Nova Scotia, which was formed in 1988, attempted to negotiate its first contract with the university management in June 1988. For the next several months, both the management and union were

engaged in a long negotiation. When the negotiations broke off in April 1989, the faculty went on strike. This meant that alternative arrangements had to be made for administering and grading exams, preparing student convocation lists, etc. Since several other labour unions refused to cross the picket lines set up by the faculty union, alternative arrangements had to be made for receiving supplies.

Employees *without* unions are affected too. To retain the flexibility of nonunion status, human resource departments implement compensation policies, hours of work, and working conditions similar to those found in unionized operations. Here the human resource challenge is usually determined by top management: try to operate so that unionization is discouraged. For example, in November 1980, Michelin Tires actively lobbied with the provincial government in Nova Scotia to discourage unionization within its plants and was successful in its attempt.[46]

The emerging challenges confronting western industrial countries, according to one author, would seem to be to identify new policies and programs that are consistent with the economic realities of the future.[47] Unions are increasingly drawing closer to Social Democratic and Labour parties; in other cases they are realizing how important it is to maintain their close ties with each other and to coordinate their efforts if they are to maintain their power in the wake of Conservative administrations in several countries. Employers caught between increasing labour costs and declining profit margins in several of the traditional industries may turn to human resource managers for their "expert" handling of the situation. What are the causes of industrial disputes? Are they identifiable or are they too diffuse? Are there other alternatives to work stoppages? Which of the available alternatives are consistent with present-day values and social aspirations? These are some of the questions for which human resource managers will be required to find adequate answers in the future.[48]

## Information Systems

Human resource departments require large amounts of detailed information. Increasingly, the quality of the department's contribution depends on the quality of its information. Such questions as the following hint at just a very few of these information requirements:

- What are the duties and responsibilities of every type of job in the organization?
- What are the skills possessed by every employee?
- What are the organization's future human resource needs?
- How are external constraints affecting the organization?
- What are the current trends in compensation of employees?

And this list could be continued for pages!

A good Human Resource Information System (HRIS) is important for a variety of reasons: first, it helps the human resource manager to carry out routine activities without having to guess about past activities and occurrences. A good HRIS would provide the decision maker with all relevant past data so that current decisions and policies are consistent with past decisions. Second, a good HRIS enables the manager to make human resource decisions more effectively and efficiently. Decisions on hiring, transfer, promotion, training, compensation, and development of employees can be made in time, more efficiently, and considering all constraints facing the organization. HRIS is, thus, an integral aspect of a strategic human resource management system discussed in Chapter 1. Third, a good HRIS helps the organization to comply with all legal and human rights provisions. By keeping track of the employee profile, compensation figures, and career growth patterns, an organization will be able to avoid discrimination charges. Finally, an HRIS enables the human resource manager to monitor various activities and to take timely control action. This is particularly useful for monitoring the cost effectiveness of various HR activities (e.g., selection, training) and appropriateness of various organizational procedures (e.g., safety).

Clearly, the acquisition, storage, and retrieval of information present a significant challenge. To meet this challenge, human resource departments increasingly rely on computer-based information systems — systems that store detailed information about employees, jobs, laws, unions, economic trends, and other internal and external factors. But massive information systems challenge the human resource department's ability to safeguard the privacy of employee records. And failure to provide such safeguards may well lead to increased government intervention in the form of privacy legislation.[49] HRIS will be discussed in further detail in Chapter 22.

## Organization Character

Every employer is unique. Similarities between organizations can be found among their parts, but each whole organization has a unique character.[50] *Organization character* is the product of all the organization's features: its employees, its objectives, its technology, its size, its age, its unions, its policies, its successes, and its failures. Organization character reflects the past and shapes the future.

The challenge for human resource specialists is to adjust proactively to the character of the organization. For example, it is sometimes overlooked that objectives can be achieved in several acceptable ways. This idea, called *equifinality*, means there are usually many paths to any given objective. The key to success is picking the path that best fits the organization's character.

> Human resource manager Aaron Chu feared that a request that he be permitted to hire a training assistant would be turned down. So instead of asking for funds to hire someone, Aaron expressed concern that poor supervisory skills were contributing to employee complaints and some resignations. He observed at the weekly management meeting that unskilled replacements could lead to rising labour costs.
>
> Knowing that top management was concerned that the company remain a low-cost producer, Aaron was not surprised when the plant manager suggested hiring ''someone to do training around here.'' Aaron got a budget increase for training. By adjusting to the organization's character, he achieved his objective.

Indeed, well-managed companies seem to be able to create a culture that encourages risk taking, innovation, and entrepreneurship. Much of this ''culture'' may not be measurable in the traditional way. Often, the culture of an organization is conveyed through stories, myths, ceremonies and symbols.

At a large Canadian telecommunications company, there is a story about prospective employees being asked to come for a job interview at 9 A.M. on a Sunday morning. The intent is to weed out undedicated applicants who do not want long hours and who are not prepared to make sacrifices. As the company chairman puts it, "We are in business to be a success, to win."[51]

In Mary Kay Cosmetics Inc. of Canada, there is a slogan "Do unto others what you would have them do unto you." In operational terms this means not only some personal touches such as birthday cards, wedding gifts, flowers at funerals, picnics, and Yuletide gatherings but also helping one's colleagues when the work load gets heavy. The employees are aware that their colleagues will, in return, show concern for their lives outside the office.[52]

## PROFESSIONAL CHALLENGES

*Professionalism* provides yet another challenge to human resource managers. In the last decade or so, there has been an enormous growth in the number of human resource managers. Between 1971 and 1981, the number of human resource managers in Canada grew from 4,055 to 25,110 (or over six times). By 1991, this number is expected to reach 28,659.[53] Other executives and staff involved in human resource activity are also expected to go up to 44,018 by 1991 (the corresponding figure in 1981 was 38,332). Despite this enormous growth, human resource management as a profession has been slow to evolve into a full-fledged profession. Until recently in many Canadian provinces, there were no minimum qualifications for practising as a human resource professional. Since the actual capabilities of practising human resource experts vary widely, it became increasingly evident during the 1970s that professionalism of the human resource management field was needed. Kumar, in his study of personnel managers, personnel and industrial relations officers, and personnel clerks, concluded that:

> Against the background of growing professionalism and complexity in personnel and industrial relations, the P&IR staff in Canada appears to be under-educated and under-trained. A majority of managers and personnel officers have only a high school education with little vocational training. Only two-fifths have had any university education and only one in four has a university degree.[54]

Several formal programs are currently available for educational training in human resources and its related areas.[55] However, as pointed out by Memeth and Rowney, several of the available college and certificate programs in human resource management may only enhance the technical and job-related skills of the persons involved.[56] This has led many a top executive to lose faith in the human resource staff's ability to think in terms of the entire organization rather than in terms of a few departments or individuals involved.[57] In the words of Burack and Miller:

> To meet the changing needs and circumstances of organizations, substantive changes in the orientation of personnel specialists, let alone curriculum, faculty preparation and pedagogical techniques will be demanded. For example, the descriptive and recipe approaches to personnel or human resources management should be replaced

by a more comprehensive approach, which incorporates policy, environment and people and particularizes these to specific organizational or situational conditions.[58]

The education programs should thus focus not merely on human resource management but on developing flexible and broad decision makers in an organizational context.[59] Further, to build the profession of human resource management, accreditation and/or certification would seem to be called for.

## The Issue of Accreditation/Certification

The American Society for Personnel Administration (ASPA) established, in late 1975, standards and credentials for accreditation in the field of human resource management. The credentials are now earned through successful completion of various tests by a candidate. This ensures a minimum level of competence among those who receive a professional designation from ASPA.

ASPA created four professional designations to distinguish between different levels of specialists and generalists in the human resource field. Specialists have to pass a test in one area of human resource management. Generalists must pass tests in three areas for the designation of accredited personnel manager (APM) or four areas to receive the accredited executive in personnel (AEP) designation. Tests are given by ASPA in the following areas:

1. Employment, placement, and personnel planning
2. Training and development
3. Compensation and benefits
4. Health and safety
5. Employee and labour relations
6. Personnel research

Canada has been somewhat slow in the move toward certification of human resource managers. Although it is generally agreed that the establishment of a uniform standard of education and minimum professional qualifications would further the interests of practitioners and would also provide a better framework for the administration of upgrading courses, the efforts toward certification have been only recent.[60] In the past, the Council of Canadian Personnel Associations (CCPA) had been a national voice for personnel and industrial relations practitioners in Canada.[61] At a provincial level, Alberta, Manitoba, Ontario, and Quebec have made significant progress towards certification. The efforts taken by the Human Resource Institute of Alberta are particularly noteworthy in this context.

If more education and training are needed to improve the skill levels and status of human resource managers, what should such a training program contain? In one survey involving 154 human resource practitioners in Canada, a majority of the respondents recommended five or more years of work experience as a requirement for effective performance in the field. On formal education and training, approximately two-thirds of the respondents felt that a university degree was an essential requirement for such jobs. Also, those respondents who considered personnel and industrial relations as a professional vocation stated that in addition to a good general education, candidates should have received a prescribed course of academic training.[62]

Figure 2-9 shows a list of courses required by the Personnel Association of Ontario (PAO). The results of a survey done by Kumar at Queen's University are also shown in the same figure.[63] As may be seen, there is considerable similarity across the lists.[64]

FIGURE 2-9  Subject Areas for Certification

---

### (PERSONNEL ASSOCIATION OF ONTARIO AND KUMAR SURVEY FINDINGS)

---

**PAO**

| Tier I (all) | Tier II (any 3) |
|---|---|
| 1. Labour Economics | 1. Industrial Relations |
| 2. Organizational Behaviour | 2. Manpower Planning |
| 3. Finance/Accounting | 3. Training and Development |
| 4. Personnel Research | 4. Compensation |
| 5. Personnel Administration | 5. Health and Safety |

**Kumar Survey**
**(In order of importance)**

| | |
|---|---|
| 1. Human Resource Management | 7. Communication Skills |
| 2. Sociology/Psychology | 8. Labour Relations |
| 3. Management Skills | 9. Collective Bargaining |
| 4. Industrial Relations | 10. Statistics/Computers |
| 5. Economics/Labour Economics | 11. Organizational Theory/Behaviour |
| 6. Labour Law | 12. Labour History |

---

Source: D.A. Ondrack, ''P/IR Professional Certification in Ontario: The PAO Model,'' paper presented at a symposium on professional education in P/IR, Canadian Industrial Relations Association (CIRA), Dalhousie University, Halifax, N.S., May 26, 1981.

Certification alone does not make human resource management a profession or improve its status in the eyes of organizations. Indeed, some argue that the field will never become a profession because there is no common body of knowledge.[65] Human resource management is not a clearly separate discipline like law, medicine, or economics. It draws on a variety of disciplines.

One approach to improving the human resource manager's status within the organization may be to strengthen the position's contribution to the enhancement of organizational performance and effectiveness. This is already beginning to take place. The higher status given to human resource experts in want-ads and organizational charts indicates that the importance of human resource management activity is being recognized.

## HUMAN RESOURCE MANAGEMENT IN PERSPECTIVE

Amid historical, external, internal, and professional challenges, it is important to keep human resource management in perspective. Its purpose is to assist in the attainment of organizational objectives with maximum effectiveness. Human resource management only aids other departments. It does not direct operations or decide organizational objectives.

The authority of human resource managers is limited. Although research shows that these managers perceive themselves as having more authority than they really do, their authority is usually viewed as advisory (or staff) authority.[66] That is, human resource managers primarily advise and assist, not decide and direct. In recent years, however, the complexity of the employment environment has meant that these managers get more decision-making (or line) authority.

> James Turner has been personnel manager for B.C. Lumber Yards for seven years. James usually recommended to department managers the best three applicants he could find for each opening. The department managers then made the final hiring decision. But because some of these managers made statements to applicants that could be interpreted as racially or sexually discriminatory, lawsuits resulted. Eventually, therefore, the owners of B.C. Lumber Yards decided to grant James the final hiring authority.

James and many of his peers in other companies now have more decision-making authority as the result of environmental changes. Authority to manage other departments still remains with the managers in those departments, however. In using their advisory and decision-making authority, human resource experts must recognize the priorities of their specific organizations. In a 1987 survey of 251 chief executive officers of organizations, James Walker and Gregory Moorhead found that performance appraisal, recruiting (non-executive staff), and developing human resource strategies were some of the activities in which human resource managers were heavily involved at present (Figure 2-10). Human resource and organization planning and performance appraisal were expected to be some key dimensions of a human resource manager's job in the future.

To be effective, human resource specialists must determine the areas of concern to different levels of management and different departments of the organization.[67] Otherwise, their advisory authority will be less effective and more likely ignored.

The vesting of human resource specialists with authority is important because often the resources of their departments are extremely limited. With no real authority and few resources, the human resource department will be hard put to deal with the burden of its several challenges. These challenges, which result from the historical, external, organization, and professional environment, affect the department's ability to achieve its purpose of contributing to the organization's effectiveness. Moreover, this burden is likely to grow in the future, unless human resource specialists can take proactive measures to meet these challenges.[68]

Perhaps the biggest challenge to the practice of human resource management comes from the need to avoid discrimination in staffing. With the increase of women in the Canadian work force there has been more pressure for affirmative-action programs such as those in the U.S.[69] As well, Murray has pointed out the need for integrating disadvantaged persons into the work force.[70] Today the Canadian human rights program is moving in this direction. While the goals and results of these programs are still somewhat modest, the human rights commissions in various jurisdictions have set up training programs aimed at improving the positions of minorities. Details of these and other programs are given in the next chapter.

FIGURE 2-10   Involvement of Human Resource Specialists in Various
Organizational Activities as Rated by 251 Chief Executives*

(1 = SLIGHTLY INVOLVED, 7 = HEAVILY INVOLVED)

|  | PRESENT (1987) INVOLVEMENT | EXPECTED FUTURE (1992) INVOLVEMENT |
|---|---|---|
| Developing human resource strategies | 6.0 | 6.2 |
| Planning staffing levels | 5.7 | 5.9 |
| Organization planning | 5.4 | 5.9 |
| Recruiting professional/ technical talent | 6.1 | 6.1 |
| Executive recruiting | 5.3 | 5.3 |
| Affirmative action | 5.7 | 5.7 |
| Employee career planning | 4.5 | 5.1 |
| Performance appraisal | 6.0 | 6.1 |
| Incentive pay programs | 5.3 | 5.8 |
| Productivity improvement | 4.7 | 5.3 |

Summarized and adapted from: James W. Walker and Gregory Moorhead, "CEOs: What They Want from HRM," *Personnel Administrator*, December 1987, American Society for Personnel Administration, pp. 50-59.

## SUMMARY

The practice of human resource management is shaped by a variety of environmental challenges. These challenges arise from the historical, external, organizational, and professional demands confronting human resource specialists.

The historical challenges began with the pressures of the Industrial Revolution, which led to the scientific study of work and workers. As the tools available to managers became more sophisticated, the need for specialists in personnel management and human resources grew. Early in this century personnel departments emerged to deal with these demands. Today personnel departments are responsible for meeting the external, organizational, and professional issues that affect employees.

The external challenges to human resource management come from several different sources. The major external concerns are created by changing technologies, economic cycles, demographic developments, cultural changes, and government involvement. The Constitution Act of 1982 which contains a Canadian Charter of Rights and Freedoms is bound to have a very profound impact on several employment-related policies (such as retirement age, hiring, pay equity, and so on) in the years to come. Each of these factors influences the ways in which human resource departments meet their objectives.

Organizational challenges include those elements within the organization that personnel departments cannot ignore if they are to be successful. Unions are one obvious example. They demand that management meet and satisfy their economic objectives within the constraints imposed by labour organizations. Even employers who do not have a union must be aware of actions that can cause workers to unionize. A professionally managed human resource department must develop and maintain a sophisticated data base in order to be effective. The urgency of the need for information and the best way of implementing human resource activities, however, are dependent on unique aspects of the organization involved.

The newest challenge to human resource management is professionalism. The important role that human resource departments and their members play in modern organizations requires a professional approach and professionally trained staff. Although human resource experts face obstacles in reaching the status of professionals, the growing importance of this function requires practitioners to strive for the high standards associated with this status.

If human resource departments can successfully meet the environmental challenges discussed in this chapter, they are more likely to contribute effectively to the goals of the organization and its people.

## TERMS FOR REVIEW

| | |
|---|---|
| Scientific management | Canadian values |
| Paternalism | Government challenges |
| Environmental challenges | Character of an organization |
| Robotics | Professional challenges |
| Computerization | Accreditation/Certification |
| Economic challenges | Authority |
| Demographics | |

## REVIEW AND DISCUSSION QUESTIONS

1. Assuming you do not work in the human resource department, would you prefer to work for a company with a proactive or a reactive department? Why?

2. Identify and briefly describe the major external challenges facing human resource managers. How have the external developments of the 1960s and 1970s influenced human resource management?

3. Would the professionalization of human resource management help personnel experts meet internal and external challenges? How?

4. Find two recent news items and explain how these developments might affect the demands made on the human resource department of some employer.

5. Suppose the birth rate during the 1980s was double the low rates of the 1970s. What implications would this growth have in the years 2000 and 2010 for (a) grocery stores, (b) fast-food restaurants, (c) the Canadian Armed Forces, (d) large metropolitan universities?

6. Why do you think people would want to work in a human resource department, besides ''liking to work with people''? What challenges would most likely appeal to you?

7. Assuming you are entrusted with the responsibility of identifying criteria for accreditation, what qualifications and experience would you prescribe for human resource managers? Why?

8. What items should go into a code of ethics for professional human resource managers?

9. Evaluate the impact of governmental policies on organizations.

## INCIDENT 2-1

### A Possible Technological Scenario

Sometime within the near future electronic technology will advance to the point where the average home will have:

- A computer console and access to several on-line computer systems via satellite communications.
- A television set (with more than 100 working channels fed by cable system) that serves as a visual display for computer outputs and inputs.
- A photocopy machine connected to the television that permits photocopies of screen information.
- A two-way video phone.

At that point, serious people will start asking, ''Why do we still follow the primitive ritual of going to work? Why don't we do our jobs at home, since most workers are now white-collar information handlers?'' And then the practice of going to work, which began with the Industrial Revolution, will end for some workers. Of course, people will still have to work; some will even have to continue to ''go to work.'' But most people will stay at home, plugged into a worldwide information grid.

1. Assuming this scenario comes true during your career, what implications does it hold for our culture and our society? For human resource management?

## INCIDENT 2-2

### Government Intervention

Since the 1930s, federal and provincial governments have increased their regulations of how employers treat employees. Laws have been passed that permit workers to join unions, require employers to pay minimum wages, ensure safe and healthy work environments, prohibit discrimination, and restrict the freedom of employers to make human resource decisions in other areas.

Some futurists believe the trend of increasing government intervention will continue. To support their argument, these thinkers point to Japan and Europe, where government involvement is far more extensive than in Canada. They believe that federal and provincial governments will require employers to provide even greater job security against layoffs, develop more extensive training programs for the disadvantaged and handicapped, and follow other regulations that will further limit human resource decisions.

Other experts think that the trend of growing government involvement is beginning to end. Tax complaints, deregulation of the industries, and the demographic trend towards an older population are the evidence these people cite in support of their position. They also argue that regulation cannot continue if Canadian firms are to remain competitive in international markets.

1. Which trend do you think will manifest itself and why?
2. If government regulation continues to increase, how will human resource departments be affected?

○ ○ ○ ○ ○ ○ ○ ○ ○ ○ ○ ○ ○ ○ ○ ○ ○ ○ ○ ○ ○ ○ ○ ○ ○ ○ ○ ○ ○ ○ ○ ○ ○ ○ ○ ○ ○ ○ ○ ○ ○ ○

## CASE STUDY

### REGINA SHOES LIMITED

Regina Shoes Limited is a medium sized manufacturer of leather and vinyl shoes located in Regina, Saskatchewan. It was started in 1973 and currently employs about 600 persons in its Regina plant and some 250 more in offices and warehouses throughout western Canada.

While Regina Shoes makes shoes of all kinds, descriptions, and sizes, it specializes in the manufacture of women's shoes. The company's designers were successful in producing a product that was stylish yet comfortable to wear and durable. The firm's shoes, marketed under the brand names of Fluffy Puppy, Cariboo, and Madonna, were very popular among ladies in the nineteen to forty-five age group. Its Young Athlete, aimed at boys and girls in the nine to fourteen age group, was a market leader in the children's sports shoes market in British Columbia. Historically, the shoes produced by the firm were cheaper than those of its competitors. This price advantage was a critical aspect of the company's marketing strategy.

Recently, the company has been facing a number of issues and challenges that require immediate attention by its management:

1. Slowly but steadily, the cost of production at Regina Shoes has been rising. Labour costs currently account for over 53% of manufacturing costs and have been increasing rapidly. The productivity levels of the employees have not shown any increase in the last three years. If the present trend continues, the firm is likely to lose its price advantage over its competitors. Already, in two out of six popular brands sold by Regina Shoes, the prices for the firm's products were equal to or higher than its competition.

2. Over 70% of the company's staff are unionized. There are indications that remaining nonmanagerial staff are also about to be unionized. The management believes that this will reduce the already limited autonomy it possesses in hiring, terminating, and managing employees.

3. Contracts with two of the four unions in the company will expire in another eight months. The remaining two unions will not start their contract negotiations for another eighteen months; however, what happens in the negotiations with these two unions could have significant impact on all future contract negotiations. One of the unions with which negotiations are to begin soon, the Leather Workers' Association, had recently elected a leader who is rumoured to be militant and highly results-oriented. A strike in the immediate future could paralyze the firm and it is doubtful whether the firm could recover from its debilitating results for quite some time.

4. Recently, there were two complaints of sex discrimination from women employees. One of these was settled internally in consultation with the concerned union, while the other had to go before the provincial Human Rights Commission. The decision of the commission was in favour of the employee who had grieved.

5. The management of Regina Shoes believes that growth through expanded activities is critical now. The management would like to extend its operations to Ontario and Quebec in the next three years and to the whole of Canada in the next eight to ten years.

6. The need for management training is felt more than ever now. The firm expects the management cadre to grow by roughly 3% each year for the next four to five years. As far as possible, the management would like to achieve this through internal promotions and transfer. From a cost point of view also such a strategy would seem preferable.

Recently, John McAllister, the personnel manager of Regina Shoes, left the firm to take up a similar position in a Toronto firm. McAllister was with the company only for three years. While he was credited with having "run a tight ship," several of his colleagues had complained about his dominating and centralized leadership style. One of the managers went as far as saying that "Regina Shoes would not have been unionized this fast and to this extent but for John." McAllister's predecessor, Tim Donovan, was not a popular personnel manager either. Donovan, who resigned his position after a mere ten-month stay at Regina Shoes, did not have very positive things to say about the company and its management. On the eve of his departure, he is reported to have confided in an associate: "The management system here is primitive. It is as if you are surrounded by forces of darkness. Of course, I could stay here and fight it out — maybe I will win in the end. But then I am not masochistic!"

1. What are the major challenges facing Regina Shoes? List them using the classification provided in your text.

2. Assume you are hired as a consultant to help the firm hire a new personnel manager. What immediate and long-term job responsibilities will you identify for the new job incumbent?

## SUGGESTED READINGS

Cattaneo, R. J. and A. J. Templer, "Determining the Effectiveness of Human Resource Management," *ASAC Personnel and Human Resources Division Proceedings* (edited by T. H. Stone), Halifax: Saint Mary's University, June 1988, pp. 72-82.

*Changing Times*. Twenty-third Annual Review of the Economic Council of Canada, Ottawa: Canadian Government Publishing Centre, 1986, Catalogue No. EC21-1/1986E.

Crispo, John (ed.), *Free Trade: The Real Story*, Toronto: Gage Educational Publishing Co., 1988.

Dickson, N.E., "Personnel Policies Take Form," *Personnel Journal*, Vol. 66, No. 4, April 1987, pp. 52-61.

Flamholtz, E. G., Y. Randle and S. Sackman, "Personnel Management: The Tone of Tomorrow," *Personnel Journal*, Vol. 66, No. 7, July 1987, pp. 42-48.

Kumar, Pradeep, Mary Lou Coates and David Arrowsmith, *The Current Industrial Relations Scene in Canada: 1986*, Kingston, Ontario: Queen's University Industrial Relations Centre, 1986.

MacQueen, Ken, "Opening Doors," *Maclean's*, October 13, 1986, p. 14.

*Women in the Labour Force*. A research report prepared for the Economic Council of Canada, Ottawa: Minister of Supply and Services Canada, 1987, Catalogue No. EC22-141/1987 E.

## REFERENCES

1. Eva Innes, Robert L. Perry and Jim Lyon, *The Financial Post Selects the 100 Best Companies to Work for in Canada*, Toronto: Collins, 1986, p.1

2. Moses was confronted by one of the earliest recorded personnel challenges when Jethro, his father-in-law, advised:

   And thou shalt teach them ordinances and laws, and shalt shew them the way wherein they must walk, and the work they must do.

   Moreover, thou shalt provide out of all the people able men . . . to be rulers. . . . Exod. 18:20-21

3. Margot Gibb-Clark. "Of the Many from Human Resources, Few Get Chosen CEO," The *Globe and Mail*, Sept. 14, 1987, p. B-11.

4. For another view of challenges likely to confront personnel management, see Lawrence A. Wrangler, "The Intensification of the Personnel Role," *Personnel Journal*, February 1979, pp. 111-119; Campbell R. McConnell, "Why Is U.S. Productivity Slowing Down?" *Harvard Business Review*, March-April 1979, pp. 36- 38, 42, 44, 48, 50, 54, 56, 60; and "The Future," *Business Week*, September 3, 1979, pp. 169ff.

5. George L. Whaley, "The Impact of Robotics Technology upon Human Resource Management," *Personnel Administrator*, September 1982, p. 70.

6. Andrew Templer, "The Behavioural Implications of Introducing Robots and Other Forms of New Technology into Canadian Industry," *ASAC Organizational Behaviour Division Proceedings*, Vol. 5, Guelph, Ontario: University of Guelph, 1984, pp. 171-179.

7. P.A. Urban, "Why Automate?" *Innovation*, Supplement to *Canada Commerce*, Fall 1986, p.10.

8. "GM's Ambitious Plans to Employ Robots," *Business Week*, March 16, 1981, p. 31.

9. George L. Whaley, op. cit., pp. 61-63. See also John Dodd, "Robots: The New Steel Collar Workers," *Personnel Journal*, September 1981, pp. 688-695.

10. A.N. Azim, "A Discussion of Quality of Work Life," *ASAC Organizational Behaviour Division Proceedings*, Vol. 5, Guelph, Ontario: University of Guelph, 1984, pp. 26-34.

11. Pyare L. Arya, "Canada in 'No-Win' Situation on Free Trade" The *Mail-Star*, July 15, 1986, p. 7.

12. Sylvia Ostry and Mahmood A. Zaidi, *Labour Economics in Canada*, 2nd ed., Toronto: Macmillan of Canada, 1972.

13. Woods Gordon and Clarkson Gordon, *Tomorrow's Customers*, 20th edition, Toronto, 1986, pp. 1-8.

14. *Financial Times*, "In the Long Run; Good Reasons for Hope," March 26, 1984, pp. 21-25.

15. C. Dumas, "Occupational Trends Among Women in Canada: 1976 to 1985," *The Labour Force*, November 1986.

16. *Maclean's*, August 9, 1982, p. 30.

17. Morton Ritts, "What if Johnny Still Can't Read," *Canadian Business*, May 1986, pp. 54-57, 124.

18. Ibid.

19. "Our Coming Old Age Crisis," *Maclean's*, January 17, 1983, p. 24.

20. Woods Gordon and Clarkson Gordon, *Tomorrow's Customers*, 20th edition, Toronto, 1986; The *Globe and Mail*, January 24, 1987, p. B1, Statistics Canada: *Labour Force Bulletin* No. 71-001, 1987.

21. Edward Harvey, Professor of Sociology, University of Toronto, quoted in *Maclean's*, op. cit., p. 24.

22. S.A. McDaniel, "Demographic Aging as a Guiding Paradigm in Canada's Welfare State," *Canadian Public Policy*, Vol. 13, No. 3, September 1987, pp. 330-336.

23. The *Evening Telegram*, "Part-time Workers: Fastest Growing Element of the Canadian Work Force," December 1, 1986, p. 25.

24. Labour Canada, *Part Time Work in Canada*, Report of the Commission of Inquiry into Part-time work, Ottawa: Ministry of Supply and Services Canada, 1983.

25. Statistics Canada, Catalogue No. 11-003E, Vol. 62, No. 2, March 1987, p. 48.

26. B. Kennedy, "Youth Employment in Canada: A Comment," *Canadian Pacific Policy*, vol. 13, No. 3, 1987, pp. 384-388.

27. Statistics Canada, 1987, op. cit., p. 53.
28. Leandre Desjardins, quoted in *Maclean's*, July 16, 1984, p. 36.
29. Elizabeth Beale, quoted in *Maclean's*, July 16, 1984, p. 37.
30. Woods Gordon and Clarkson Gordon, *Tomorrow's Customers*, 20th Edition, Toronto, 1986, pp. 1-8.
31. Statistics Canada, *The Labour Force*, Bulletin Nos. 71-001 and 94-702, 1970- 1981.
32. John D. Owne, "Workweeks and Leisure: An Analysis of Trends, 1948-75," *Monthly Labour Review*, August 1976, pp. 3-8.
33. Frank G. Vallee and Donald R. Whyte, "Canadian Society: Trends and Perspectives," in Harish C. Jain (ed.), *Contemporary Issues in Canadian Personnel Administration*, Scarborough: Prentice-Hall of Canada, 1974, pp. 29-42.
34. Ibid., p. 31.
35. Ibid.
36. John Porter, *The Vertical Mosaic: An Analysis of Social Class and Power in Canada*, Toronto: University of Toronto Press, 1965. See also V.V. Murray, "Canadian Cultural Values and Personnel Administration," in Harish C. Jain (ed.), *Contemporary Issues in Canadian Personnel Administration*, Scarborough: Prentice-Hall of Canada, 1974.
37. Vallee and Whyte, op. cit., p. 34.
38. Porter, op. cit., pp. 60-63.
39. Mark Nichols, "A Volatile National Mood", Maclean's-Decima Poll Summary, *Maclean's*, Vol. 100, No. 1, January 5, 1987, pp. 26-30.
40. Rae Corelli, "A Turning Away from Policies," Maclean's-Decima Poll Essay, *Maclean's*, vol. 100, No. 1, January 5, 1987, p. 24.
41. Ibid.
42. Ibid.
43. *The Charter of Rights and Freedoms: A Guide for Canadians*, Ottawa: Ministry of Supply and Services of Canada, 1982.
44. *The Charter of Rights and Freedoms*, Section 15(2).
45. P. Scott, "Equality in Employment: A Royal Commission Report," *Current Readings in Race Relations*, Vol. 2, No. 4, Winter 1984-1985.
46. Frank M. Covert, "Bill 98 'Will Protect Employees in the Long Run,'" The *Mail-Star*, December 16, 1980, p. 4.
47. Solomon Barking, "Troubled Worker Militancy: Challenges Confronting Western Industrial Relations Systems," *Relations Industrielles*, 1983, Vol. 38, No. 4, pp. 713-729.
48. A.W.R. Carrothers, "An Outlook on Labour Relations in Canada," *Relations Industrielles*, 1983, Vol. 38, No. 3, pp. 648-657.
49. John Rahiya, "Privacy Protection and Personnel Administration: Are New Laws Needed?" *The Personnel Administrator*, April 1979, pp. 19-21, 28.
50. William B. Wolf, "Organizational Constructs: An Approach to Understanding Organizations," *Journal of the Academy of Management*, April 1968, pp. 7-15. See also Robert Granford Wright, *Mosaics of Organization Character*, New York: Dunellen Publishing Company, Inc.
51. Innes, Perry, and Lyon, *The Financial Post Selects the 100 Best Companies to Work for in Canada*, p. 34.
52. Ibid., pp. 250-251.

53. 1971 figures taken from P. Kumar, *Personnel Management in Canada: A Manpower Profile*, Kingston, Ontario: Industrial Relations Centre, Queen's University, 1975; 1981 and 1991 figures from *Canadian Occupational Projection System*, Reference Growth Scenario, Ottawa: Employment and Immigration Canada, July 1986.
54. P. Kumar, "Personnel Management in Canada — A Manpower Profile," *The Canadian Personnel & Industrial Relations Journal*, 23, 1976, p. 33.
55. J.I.A. Rowney and C.W. Memeth, "Educational Programs for Professionalism," *The Canadian Personnel & Industrial Relations Journal*, 26 (November 1979): 10-14.
56. C.W. Memeth and J.I.A. Rowney, "Professionalize or Perish," *The Canadian Personnel & Industrial Relations Journal*, January 1981, pp. 27-31.
57. Ibid.
58. E.H. Burack and E.L. Miller, "The Personnel Function in Transition," *California Management Review*, Vol. 18, No. 3, Spring 1976, p. 36.
59. Memeth and Rowney, op. cit.
60. J.P. Siegel, D.A. Ondrack, and R.F. Morrison, "Education and Development of Employee Relations Staff: A Survey of Current Practices," *The Canadian Personnel & Industrial Relations Journal*, Vol. 21, March 1974, p. 25-34.
61. Memeth and Rowney, op. cit.
62. Pradeep Kumar, "Professionalism in Canadian Personnel and Industrial Relations," *The Canadian Personnel & Industrial Relations Journal*, October 1980, pp. 34-41.
63. Pradeep Kumar, *Professionalism in the Canadian P/IR Function: Report of a Survey*, Queen's University, Industrial Relations Centre, 1980.
64. D.A. Ondrack, "P/IR Professional Certification in Ontario: The PAO Model," paper presented at a symposium on professional education in P/IR, Canadian Industrial Relations Association (CIRA), Dalhousie University, Halifax, N.S., May 26, 1981.
65. George Ritzer, "The Professionals: Will Personnel Occupations Ever Become Professions?" *The Personnel Administrator*, May-June 1971, pp. 34-36.
66. Wendell French and Dale Henning, "The Authority-Influence Role of the Functional Specialist in Management," *Academy of Management Journal*, September 1966, p. 203.
67. Harold C. White and Robert E. Boynton, "The Role of Personnel: A Management View," *Arizona Business*, October 1974, pp. 17-21; see also Harold C. White and Michael N. Wolfe, "The Role Desired for Personnel Administration," *The Personnel Administrator*, June 1980, pp. 87-97.
68. Robert A. Holmes, "What's Ahead for Personnel Professionals in the '80's?" *The Personnel Administrator*, June 1980, pp. 33-37, 82.
69. Jane Burton, "Studies on the Status of Canadian Women," *The Labour Gazette*, July 1976, pp. 377-380; *Women in the Labour Force: Facts and Figures*, Ottawa: Labour Canada Women's Bureau, 1973.
70. David Murray, "Integration of the Disadvantaged," *The Canadian Personnel & Industrial Relations Journal*, May 1976, pp. 30-31.

# CHAPTER 3 ○○○○○○

# THE CHALLENGE OF DISCRIMINATION

*It is . . . clear . . . that constitutional and legal guarantees will not by themselves be sufficient to bring about equality. We are not going to get there without a genuine and generous commitment on the part of government, business, and the unions — in short, of the leaders without whom paper commitments are just that.*

MAXWELL F. YALDEN
CHIEF COMMISSIONER
CANADIAN HUMAN RIGHTS COMMISSION[1]

○ ○ ○ ○ ○ ○ ○ ○ ○ ○ ○ ○ ○ ○ ○ ○ ○ ○ ○ ○ ○ ○ ○ ○ ○ ○ ○ ○ ○ ○ ○ ○ ○

## CHAPTER OBJECTIVES

After studying this chapter, you should be able to:
1. **Identify** the jurisdictions of Canadian human rights legislation.
2. **List** the major provisions of the Canadian Human Rights Act.
3. **Cite** the remedies for violations.
4. **Explain** the effect of human rights legislation on the role of human resource specialists.
5. **Explain** the Charter of Rights and Freedoms and discuss its impact on Human Resource Management.
6. **Outline** an affirmative-action program.

○ ○ ○ ○ ○ ○ ○ ○ ○ ○ ○ ○ ○ ○ ○ ○ ○ ○ ○ ○ ○ ○ ○ ○ ○ ○ ○ ○ ○ ○ ○ ○ ○

*A* major challenge to human resource management is to provide equal employment opportunities without regard to people's race, religion, sex, national origin, or age. Common sense dictates such a policy, but there are also laws that prohibit certain forms of discrimination. No other laws—perhaps no other single development—rival the impact that these have on human resource management.

COLLEGE INTERN:   What major changes has the human resource field undergone since you started with the company?

H R MANAGER:   Well, when I started in 1960, there was almost no government involvement. You could hire, promote, and fire anyone you wanted.

INTERN:   Can't you still do that today?

MANAGER:   Not really. Today, many companies have affirmative-action plans. These plans set goals for hiring, training, and promoting to ensure that every person has equal-employment opportunities.

INTERN:   Well, since they are the company's plans, I don't see how government is involved.

MANAGER:   The plans are developed to show the government our intention to eliminate discrimination. If we do not meet these goals, we could lose our federal government contracts, or worse.

INTERN:   What could be worse than losing contracts?

MANAGER:   Litigation! Human rights commissions could sue us, and so could those people who thought we had discriminated against them. Suits are tremendously expensive and time consuming, even when we win.

INTERN:   I see. Have there been other changes in human resource management as significant as government involvement?

MANAGER:   Not in my opinion. Sure, there have been many changes. Human resource management is a dynamic field. But government's influence on the employment relationship is the biggest change of all, especially with respect to equal employment opportunity.

As this discussion indicates, many aspects of human resource management (shown in Figure 3-1) are affected by human rights legislation. In fact, few of the challenges discussed in this book affect human resource management as extensively as government. It shapes the role of human resource management through the use of laws aimed at the employment relationship. Government's attention to the employment relationship results from the present nature of society. No longer is Canada primarily a nation of farmers, fishermen, and small proprietors. It is a nation of wage earners. This means that the well-being of society increasingly depends upon the employment relationship.

To avoid flooding the courts with complaints and the prosecution of relatively minor infractions, federal and provincial governments often create special regulatory bodies, such as commissions and boards, to enforce compliance with the law and to aid in its interpretation. Examples are the various human rights commissions and labour relations boards, who evaluate complaints and develop legally binding rules, called regulations. Human resource specialists become involved because legislation and regulations affect the employment relationship. The involvement creates three important responsibilities. First, human resource experts must stay abreast of the laws, their interpretation by regulatory bodies, and court rulings. Otherwise, they will soon find their knowledge outdated and useless to the organization. Second, they must develop and administer programs that ensure company compliance. Failure to do so may lead to the loss of

FIGURE 3-1   A Model of the Human Resource Management System and Its Major Environmental Challenges

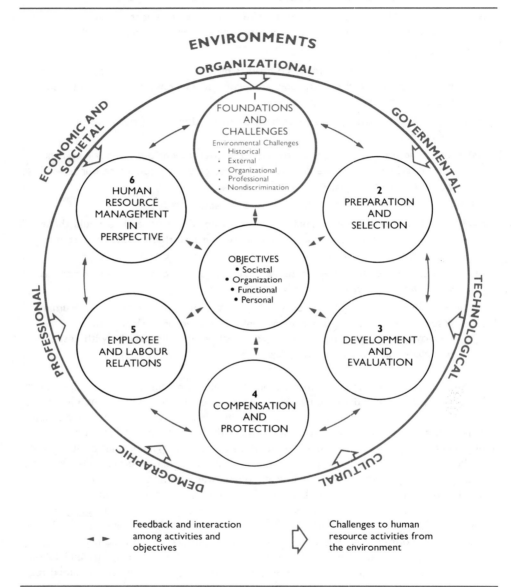

government contracts, poor public relations, and suits by regulatory bodies or affected individuals. Third, they must pursue their traditional roles of obtaining, maintaining, and retaining an optimal work force. No organization benefits from compliance with government constraints at the expense of a well-qualified work force.

## Scope of Employment Laws

Usually, employment-related laws and regulations are limited in scope; their impact on the human resource management process is confined to a single human resource activity. For example, minimum-wage laws specify the lowest amount an employer can pay for each hour worked; in spite of their importance, these laws affect only the compensation management function. Other human resource activities—selection, training, and labour relations—are largely unaffected.

Human rights legislation, however, is an exception. Its role is not limited to a single human resource activity. Instead, human rights legislation affects nearly every human resource function: human resource planning, recruiting, selection, training, compensation, and labour relations. Since these laws are a major challenge to human resource management, this chapter deals exclusively with them.

## HUMAN RIGHTS LEGISLATION: AN OVERVIEW

Human rights legislation is a family of federal and provincial acts that have as a common objective the provision of equal employment opportunity for members of protected groups. These acts outlaw discrimination based on race, colour, religion, national origin, sex, or age. Under special circumstances, they also outlaw discrimination against handicapped persons. Figure 3-2 summarizes these two layers of employment laws. Discrimination between workers on the basis of their effort, performance, or other work-related criteria remains both permissible and advisable.

> Shelly Rossie complained to her provincial Human Rights Commission and charged her former employer with discrimination. When questioned, she insisted to the commission that the "real" reason for her discharge as a welder was that the company discriminated against women in "traditionally" male jobs. Shelly's case was dismissed when the company showed the commission records of her excessive absenteeism and poor productivity. (Undoubtedly, the company's case was strengthened when, later, a woman was hired to replace Shelly.)

Human rights legislation does permit employers to reward outstanding performers and penalize insufficient productivity. Its only requirement is that the basis for rewards

FIGURE 3-2   Types, Sources, Objectives, and Jurisdiction of Canadian Human Rights Legislation

| TYPE | SOURCE | OBJECTIVES AND JURISDICTION |
| --- | --- | --- |
| Federal Law | Passed by Parliament and enforced by federal Human Rights Commission | To ensure equal employment opportunities with employers under federal jurisdiction |
| Provincial Law | Enacted by provincial governments and enforced by provincial human rights commissions | To ensure equal employment opportunities with employers under provincial jurisdiction |

and punishments be work-related — not a person's race, sex, age, or other prohibited criteria.

Despite the fact that only 10% of the Canadian work force falls under federal jurisdiction, the following discussion will focus on federal human rights legislation. To review individual provincial human rights laws would be confusing because of the many, but small differences, often only in terminology, e.g., some provinces use "national" origin, others use "ethnic" origin. The examples used in the discussion of the federal legislation would also be quite typical for provincial situations. By and large, provincial laws mirror the federal law.

## The Canadian Human Rights Act

The Canadian Human Rights Act was passed by Parliament on July 14, 1977, and took effect in March 1978. The act proclaims that

> every individual should have an equal opportunity with other individuals to make for himself or herself the life that he or she is able and wishes to have, consistent with his or her duties and obligations as a member of society, without being hindered in or prevented from doing so by discriminatory practices based on race, national or ethnic origin, colour, religion, age, sex or marital status, or conviction for an offence for which a pardon has been granted or by discriminatory employment practices based on physical handicap.[2]

The act applies to all federal government departments and agencies, and Crown corporations, and to business and industry under federal jurisdiction — such as banks, airlines, and railway companies — in their dealings with the public and in their employment policies.

In areas not under federal jurisdiction, protection is given by provincial human rights laws. Each of the ten Canadian provinces has its own antidiscrimination laws, which are broadly similar to the federal law. Figure 3-3 compares federal and individual provincial human rights legislation as to different grounds of discrimination prohibited.

### Race and Colour

It is sometimes difficult to see which of these two characteristics is the actual basis of discrimination; often both are involved. The discrimination can be intentional or unintentional, subtle or very open, as two examples will show:

> A bank in a small town advertised a position specifying that the applicant should have a pleasing appearance and requested that a recent photograph be submitted. The bank personnel were all Caucasian. A black community leader filed a discrimination complaint, which was settled when the bank agreed to include human rights training in its courses on interviewing, human resource selection, and counselling.
>
> The Western Guard Party of Toronto was operating a tape-recorded message that could be heard by telephone. The message proclaimed the supremacy of the white race and attacked Jews for being determined to destroy the white race by

means of communism. The party refused to withdraw or change the message. The Human Rights Commission therefore held a tribunal, which found the messages to be discriminatory and ordered the respondents to refrain from using this subject matter in any future messages.[3]

## 2) National or Ethnic Origins

It is also illegal for human resource decisions to be influenced by the national or ethnic origins of applicants or of their forebears. Hence the discrimination process can be either direct or indirect. The refusal to hire or promote people because of their national or ethnic origins is a direct and obvious violation:

A Canadian citizen originally from Haiti was refused entrance into the Armed Forces because he was not eligible for security clearance until he had lived in Canada for at least ten years. He had been in this country for six years and was unusually highly qualified in every other respect. During investigation of his complaint, the Armed Forces agreed to invoke a rule already in place which allowed for the ten-year residency requirement to be waived for exceptional candidates. He was cleared and offered enrolment as an officer cadet.[4]

An example of an indirect violation is the following. In one case (which will be detailed later) the hiring requirements for a certain job specified that the candidate had to be 5′8″ (173 cm). But reflection reveals that such a standard disproportionately discriminates against Asian Canadians, who tend to be shorter than descendants of immigrants from European countries. So, although the height rule may not intend to discriminate, the result is discriminatory.

## 3) Religion

A person's religious beliefs and practices should not affect employment decisions. An employer must accommodate an employee's religious practices, unless those practices present undue hardship to the employer.

A Moslem employee of a communications company lost his job over the question of having time off each week to attend prayers at his mosque. After conciliation, a settlement was reached, which did not impose undue hardships on the employer and by which the employee was allowed to take 1 1/2 hours per week of leave without pay. He was reinstated with retroactive pay and benefits.[5]

If an employer does not make a reasonable attempt to accommodate workers' religious practices, he or she can be found guilty of violating the Human Rights Act.

## 4) Age

The use of age as an employment criterion has lately been the object of considerable attention. Many employers consider that the laying-down of minimum or maximum ages for certain jobs is justified, although evidence is rarely available that age is an accurate indication of one's ability to perform a given type of work.

FIGURE 3-3   Prohibited Grounds of Discrimination in Employment

| JURISDICTION | FEDERAL | BRITISH COLUMBIA | ALBERTA | SASKATCHEWAN | MANITOBA | ONTARIO | QUEBEC | NEW BRUNSWICK | PRINCE EDWARD IS. | NOVA SCOTIA | NEWFOUNDLAND | NORTHWEST TERRITORIES | YUKON |
|---|---|---|---|---|---|---|---|---|---|---|---|---|---|
| Race | ● | ● | ● | ● | ● | ● | ● | ● | ● | ● | ● | ● | ● |
| National or ethnic origin[1] | ● | | | | ● | ● | ● | ● | ● | ● | ● | | ● |
| Ancestry | | ● | ● | ● | | ● | ● | | | | | ● | ● |
| Nationality or citizenship | | | | ● | ● | ● | | | | | ● | | |
| Place of origin | | ● | ● | | | ● | | ● | | | ● | | |
| Colour | ● | ● | ● | ● | ● | ● | ● | ● | ● | ● | ● | ● | ● |
| Religion | ● | ● | | ● | ● | | ● | ● | ● | ● | ● | | ● |
| Creed[2] | | | ● | ● | ● | | | | | ● | ● | ● | ● |
| Age | ● | ● | ● | ● | ● | ● | ● | ● | ● | ● | ● | ● | |
| | | (45-65) | (18+) | (18-65) | (18-65) | | (19+) | | | (40-65) | (19-65) | | |
| Sex | ● | ● | ● | ● | ● | ● | ● | ● | ● | ● | ● | ● | ● |
| Pregnancy or childbirth | ● | | ● | ● | | ● | | | | | | | |
| Marital status[3] | ● | ● | ● | ● | ● | ● | ● | ● | ● | ● | ● | ● | ● |
| Family status[3] | ● | | | ● | ● | ● | | | | | ● | | |
| Pardoned offence | ● | | | | | | ● | | | | | ● | |
| Record of criminal conviction | | ● | | | | ● | ● | | | | | | |
| Physical handicap or disability | ● | ● | ● | ● | ● | ● | ● | ● | ● | ● | ● | ● | |
| Mental handicap or disability | ● | ● | | | ● | ● | ● | ● | ● | ● | ● | ● | |
| Dependence on alcohol or drug | ● | | | | | | | | | | | | |
| Place of residence | | | | | | | | | | | | ● | |
| Political belief | | ● | | ● | | | ● | | | ● | ● | | |
| Assignment, attachment or seizure of pay[4] | | | | | | | | | | | | ● | |
| Source of income | | | | | | | | | | | | | |
| Social condition[4] | | | | | | | ● | | | | | | |
| Language | | | | | | | ● | | | | | | |

## FIGURE 3-3   (Continued)

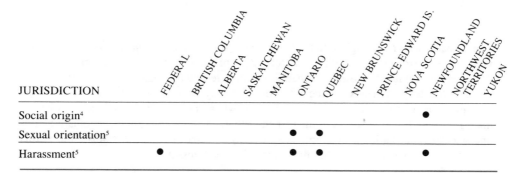

| JURISDICTION | FEDERAL | BRITISH COLUMBIA | ALBERTA | SASKATCHEWAN | MANITOBA | ONTARIO | QUEBEC | NEW BRUNSWICK | PRINCE EDWARD IS. | NOVA SCOTIA | NEWFOUNDLAND | NORTHWEST TERRITORIES | YUKON |
|---|---|---|---|---|---|---|---|---|---|---|---|---|---|
| Social origin⁴ | | | | | | | | | | ● | | | |
| Sexual orientation⁵ | | | | | | ● | ● | | | | | | |
| Harassment⁵ | ● | | | | | ● | ● | | | ● | | | |

1. New Brunswick includes only "national origin."
2. Creed usually means religious beliefs.
3. Quebec uses the term "civil status."
4. In Quebec's charter, "social condition" includes assignment, attachment or seizure of pay and social origin.
5. The federal, Ontario and Quebec statutes ban harassment on all proscribed grounds. Ontario, Nova Scotia and Newfoundland also ban sexual solicitation.

Source: Labour Canada, Worklife Report, March 1987, p. 17. Reproduced with permission of the Minister of Supply and Services Canada.

> The General Pilotage Regulations require that a pilot be removed from the eligibility list after reaching the age of fifty. A special human rights tribunal found that such a regulation was invalid and ordered that pilots affected by this rule be restored into their former positions. An appeal court set aside the tribunal's decision on the basis that the removal of the pilots from the eligibility list because of age was not a discriminatory practice. The Canadian Human Rights Commission appealed to the Supreme Court of Canada, but the appeal was denied.[6]

Age consideration also has important implications for collective bargaining, where seniority rights are often based on the age of an employee (as opposed to seniority based on length of service).

> In the collective agreement between Wardair Canada and the Canadian Association of Passenger Agents, age was the determining factor for ranking of employees on the seniority list when hired on the same day. Following a complaint, the seniority list has been revised and in future, when two or more employees are hired on the same day, their seniority will be determined by company seniority, by starting following completion of training and—if two employees are still tied—by drawing of lots.[7]

The law makes an exception, however, when it comes to retirement age. It is not considered a discriminatory practice if a person's employment is terminated because that person has reached the normal age of retirement for employees working in similar positions.

c) *Sex*

The Canadian Human Rights Act also prevents discrimination on the basis of an individual's sex. Not only is it illegal to recruit, hire, and promote employees because of their sex; it is unlawful to have separate policies for men and women. For example, it is discriminatory to reserve some jobs for men only or women only. It is even illegal to apply similar standards to men and women when such standards arbitrarily discriminate more against one sex than against the other. When standards discriminate against one sex (or race, national or ethnic origin, religion, age, or marital status), the burden is on the employer to prove that the standards are necessary.

> A woman complained that she had been refused an interview for a job as a bus driver because she was under the minimum height requirement of 5'8" (173 cm). She claimed that this height requirement discriminated against women. After conciliation, the case was settled with the company discontinuing the practice of requiring applicants to be 5'8" for drivers' jobs. Two women under 5'8" have since been hired. As part of the settlement, the company agreed that the Canadian Human Rights Commission would monitor the company's driver application records for one year. The complainant was paid $3,500 for lost wages and general damages.[8]

Although the standard did not discriminate against women per se, the arbitrary height requirement tended to exclude most female applicants. To keep the height rule, since it discriminates against women, the employer must show that it is necessary given the nature of the job. If this cannot be shown, the employer can be compelled to drop the requirement.

One issue that falls under the topic of sex discrimination has made headlines lately: that of equal pay for work of equal value. This is not to be confused with the concept of equal pay for equal work. The latter provision was part of the Canadian Labour Code from the beginning. It made it against the law to pay a woman less if she did the same work as a man; the "equal pay for equal work" concept was incorporated into the Canadian Human Rights Act later. But then the act went even further, making it illegal to discriminate against women on the basis of job value (or content).

> A nurse in a federal penitentiary complained that male health care officers, many of whom were less qualified than trained nurses, were being paid at a higher level than nurses performing work of equal value. In the settlement of the complaint, the nurses' salaries in that region will be raised to the level of the health care officers by means of an equalization adjustment.[9]

That the "equal pay for work of equal value" concept can be very costly was shown in the case of 390 federal library science employees — mostly women — who earned less than historical researchers — mostly men — though the library science work was claimed to be of equal value. The settlement, requiring individual salary increases of up to $2,500 a year, cost the federal government $2.4 million. The implication for human resource people is that they had better make very sure their wage and salary system does not subtly discriminate on the basis of sex.

7) *Marital Status*

The idea of what constitutes a family has undergone considerable changes in Canadian society in recent years. Non-traditional families, such as those resulting from so-called "common-law" marriages, or single-parent families, are now far more numerous than in the past. But there is still a strong feeling that the traditional family is a unique institution deserving special consideration.

The Canadian Human Rights Act spells out quite clearly that any discrimination based on marital status is illegal.

> A woman was denied a job with the CBC because her husband was already employed by the corporation at the same station. After a complaint and hearing, the CBC changed its employment practices, which formerly discriminated on the basis of marital status, and placed the woman in a position in the same station in which her husband was employed.

8) *Family Status*

Based on a broad definition of family status, the Canadian Human Rights Commission initiated action against Canadian Pacific Airlines (now Canadian Airlines International). The complaint alleged that CP Air's policy of hiring the children of its employees for summer jobs was discrimination on the prohibited ground of "situation de famille." CP Air's application for a writ of prohibition was dismissed by a federal court.[10]

9) *Pardoned Convicts*

The Canadian Human Rights Act prohibits discrimination against a convicted person if a pardon has been issued for the offence. Pardon may be granted by a parole board after five years following release, parole, or the completion of a sentence. So far only five cases of discrimination of this nature have been brought to the attention of the Canadian Human Rights Commission.

> A person convicted and paroled on a drug offence applied for a job with a government agency dealing with drug abuse. He was denied employment because of his conviction. Subsequently, the National Parole Board granted his request for a full pardon. The government agency maintained, however, that, pardoned or not, he remained a security risk and that being without a criminal record was a bona fide occupational requirement of a correctional service's staff. He appealed to the Canadian Human Rights Commission, and after the commission's investigation, the government agency decided that a criminal record would not, in fact, inhibit the applicant's ability to meet the requirements of the job, and, satisfied that he was suitable, offered him the position.[11]

The Canadian Human Rights Commission has also been approached by several persons who claim to have been refused employment on the basis of their arrest record, even when the arrest did not lead to a conviction. These persons are without legal protection since the Canadian Human Rights Act does not address this type of discrimination. For the human resource manager this does not mean that all applicants can be asked for their arrest record. It must still be shown that it is relevant to the job. For this reason, the commission has advised employees under federal jurisdiction that applicants should not be asked, "Have you ever been convicted of an offence?" It is recommended — if such information is legitimately needed for employment purposes — that the question be phrased: "Have you ever been convicted of an offence for which you have not received a pardon?" (See Recruitment and Interviewing Guide in the appendix to Chapter 3.)

It should be noted, however, that British Columbia, Ontario, and Quebec include record of criminal conviction in their list of prohibited discrimination criteria.

(10)  *Physical Handicap*

No person should be denied employment solely for the reason of his or her being disabled, e.g., blind, deaf, or confined to a wheelchair. Of course, there are exceptions. A blind person cannot be a truck driver, or a deaf person a telephone operator. However, the principle of "reasonable accommodation" has been established. It means that an employer can be expected to take reasonable measures to make available a suitable job to a person with a physical handicap if it does not impose undue hardships on the organization.

> A man was refused a technician's job because he failed a hearing test. However, he had been tested without his hearing aid; he asserted that he could perform the job using a hearing device. Medical advisors for the company claimed that the job required perfectly normal hearing. After conciliation, the company agreed that with a hearing aid the man would be able to do the job. The complaint was settled with the complainant being hired as a technician and paid damages of $750.

Many organizations have established rigid physical standards for certain jobs without being able to show that these standards are truly relevant to the requirements of the job. Some complainants have been refused jobs when their disability might be a problem in a speculative situation, e.g., the firm might argue that a deaf person would be unable to hear a fire alarm. Other complainants have been disqualified for jobs not because they are physically handicapped now, but because they may become so in the future.

> A machinist who had suffered an injury to his leg was refused a position on the hypothesis that at some time in the future he might develop complications that might affect his ability to work, which might in turn lead to a finding against the employer for compensation. After an investigation by the Canadian Human Rights Commission, the company had to agree that its assumptions were highly speculative. In the settlement, the complainant was paid the additional wages, approximately $2,000, that he would have earned if he had not been denied the position, as well as compensation in respect of his feelings and self-respect.[12]

### (1)   *Harassment*

Of importance to employers is a unanimous decision of the Supreme Court of Canada regarding the ultimate responsibility in harassment cases. It ruled that employers are responsible for the actions of their employees. Bonie Robichaud had filed a complaint against her employer, the Department of National Defence. The Supreme Court said that the Department of National Defence must share responsibility for the actions of one of its supervisors who had sexually harassed Robichaud. It means that an employer has to take appropriate steps to prevent sexual harassment and to inform employees of consequences of sexual harassment, e.g., initiate training programs for supervisors and establish policies which open communication channels for harassed employees and which spell out disciplinary measures against offenders.[13]

### (2)   *Exceptions*

An employer is permitted to discriminate against protected groups when a bona fide occupational requirement exists, i.e., when the employer has a justifiable reason for discriminating. For example, a designer of women's fashions, hiring models, would be allowed to discriminate against men. This type of discrimination is also legal in cases involving handicapped people: a trucking company can refuse to hire blind or deaf people as truck drivers. Obviously, discrimination in these situations ought to be permitted — a bona fide occupational requirement certainly exists.

### (3)   *Employer Retaliation*

It is a criminal act to retaliate in any way against those who exercise their rights according to the Human Rights Act. Those who file charges, testify, or otherwise participate in any human rights action, are protected by law. If a supervisor tries to "get even" with an employee who filed charges, he or she violates the act.

### (4)   *Enforcement*

The responsibility for the enforcement of the Canadian Human Rights Act lies in the hands of a specially created Canadian Human Rights Commission. It consists of a Chief Commissioner, a Deputy Chief Commissioner, and from three to six other members — all appointed by the Governor in Council. The chief commissioner and his deputy are full-time members. Full-time members are appointed for a term of not more than seven years, and part-time members for a term of not more than three years.

The commission deals with complaints it receives concerning discriminatory practices covered by the act. The commission may also act on its own when it perceives a possible infraction. It also has the power to issue guidelines interpreting the act. If warranted, the commission can ask the president of the Human Rights Tribunal Panel to appoint a tribunal, which may order cessation of the discriminatory practice and the adoption of measures to ensure that it will not recur, as well as compensation.

Figure 3-4 summarizes the CHRC enforcement procedures. Any individual or group may file a complaint with the commission, given that they have reasonable grounds to believe they have been discriminated against. The commission may refuse to accept the complaint if it is submitted by someone other than the person who allegedly has been discriminated against, unless the alleged victim permits investigation of the claim.

FIGURE 3-4   Canadian Human Rights Commission Enforcement Procedure

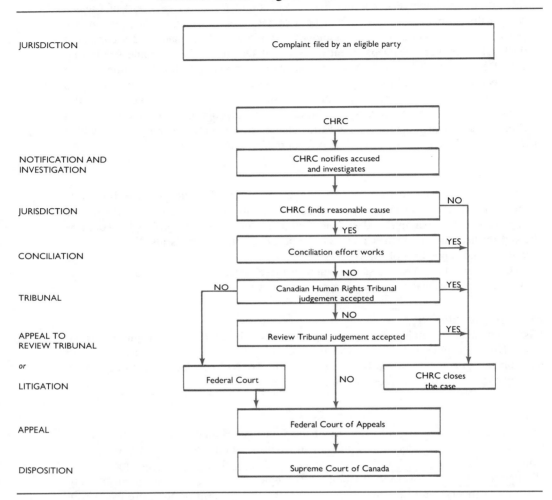

It is also possible for the commission itself to initiate a complaint, if it has reasonable grounds to assume that a party is engaging in a discriminatory practice.

The commission has to deal with any complaint filed with it if it involves a federal government department or agency or any business or industry under federal jurisdiction. The same is true for commissions and organizations at the provincial level. Commissions, however, may refuse to deal with complaints if other procedures seem more appropriate, if the complaint seems trivial or made in bad faith, or if too much time (one year) has elapsed since the alleged discrimination took place.

After a complaint has been accepted by the commission, an investigator is appointed to gather facts about the case. The investigator submits a report to the commission recommending a finding of either substantiation or nonsubstantiation of the allegation. If the allegation is substantiated, a settlement may be arranged in the course of the investigation, or the commission may, after adoption of the investigator's report, appoint a conciliator.

Should the parties involved be unable to reach a conciliation agreement, a Human Rights Tribunal consisting of up to three members — most consist of one — may be appointed to investigate the complaint. Figure 3-5 describes the discretion of the tribunal in settling a complaint.

## FIGURE 3-5  Discretion of a Canadian Human Rights Tribunal

A Canadian Human Rights Tribunal can order a violator to:
- Stop the discriminatory practice.
- Restore the rights, opportunities, and privileges denied the victim.
- Compensate the victim for wages lost and any expenses incurred as a result of the discriminatory practice.
- Compensate the victim for any additional cost of obtaining alternative goods, services, facilities, or accommodation as a result of the discriminatory practice.
- Develop and implement affirmative-action programs to equalize opportunity for certain groups that have suffered from discriminatory practices in the past.

Should the tribunal find that the discriminatory practice was maintained purposely or recklessly, or that the victim's feelings of self-respect have suffered as a result of the practice, it may order the person or organization responsible to compensate the victim appropriately.

A person who obstructs an investigation or a tribunal, or fails to comply with the terms of a settlement, or reduces wages in order to eliminate a discriminatory practice, can be found guilty of an offence punishable by a fine and/or jail sentence. If the guilty party is an employer or any employee organization, the fine might be up to $50,000. For individuals the penalty might be up to $5000.[14]

In the Western Guard Party case mentioned earlier (see under the section "Race and colour") the tribunal had ordered that the party cease preparing recorded telephone messages that expose persons to hatred or contempt because of their religion or race. When the respondents persisted with their messages, the Canadian Human Rights Commission successfully moved in the Court that the respondents be found guilty of contempt. The party's leader, John Ross Taylor, was sentenced to one year in jail and the Western Guard Party was sentenced to a $5,000 fine. The respondents appealed their conviction and sentence to the Federal Court of Appeals and the Supreme Court of Canada, but both let the conviction stand.[15]

## Provincial Human Rights Laws and Human Rights Commissions

Each province and the two territories have their own human rights laws and human rights commissions, with similar discrimination criteria, regulations, and procedures. If a person feels discriminated against, he or she will contact a provincial human rights officer who will investigate the complaint and attempt to reach a settlement that will satisfy all parties. Experience has shown that the majority of cases are settled at this stage. Should there be no agreement, then the case will be presented to the Human Rights Commission. The members of the commission will study the evidence and then submit a report to the minister in charge of administration of the Human Rights Act. The minister may appoint a Board of Inquiry, which has similar powers as a tribunal at the federal level. Noncompliance with the course of action prescribed by the Board of Inquiry may result in prosecution in a provincial court of law. Individuals can be fined between $500 and $1000 and organizations or groups between $1000 and $10,000, depending on the province.

If an issue at hand has Canada-wide implications, any provincial court decision may ultimately be appealed to the Supreme Court of Canada.

The major differences in the activities of the federal and provincial human rights commissions seem to be in the sophistication of cases. While the federal commission deals mainly with government agencies and Crown corporations, which tend to have well-developed human resource policies and experienced human resource professionals, provincial commissions deal mostly with small and medium-sized businesses, whose employees and human resource staff often have little expertise in discrimination cases.

## Affirmative Action

The Canadian Human Rights Act gives the Canadian Human Rights Commission great latitude in pursuing the enforcement of the act. One way for the commission to comply with the intent of the act to improve equal employment opportunities for special groups is for it to encourage what are often called *affirmative-action programs*.

Section 15(1) of the act specifies special programs as a legitimate mechanism for improving the opportunities of a group through the elimination, reduction, or prevention of discrimination.

> It is not a discriminatory practice for a person to adopt or carry out a special program, plan, or arrangement designed to prevent disadvantages that are likely to be suffered by, or to eliminate or reduce disadvantages that are suffered by, any group of individuals when those disadvantages would be or are based on or related to the race, national or ethnic origin, colour, religion, age, sex, marital status, or physical handicap of members of that group, by improving opportunities respecting goods, services, facilities, accommodation, or employment in relation to that group.

Such programs are developed by employers to remedy past discrimination or to prevent discrimination in the future. It usually implies on the part of the organization a self-evaluation with regard to hiring, promotion, and compensation practices. If discrepancies are found, it would be good human resource practice to check the criteria used for different decisions, adjust them if necessary, and make sure that they are consistently applied.

Affirmative-action programs exist for several reasons. From a practice standpoint, employers seldom benefit by excluding people who belong to some particular group. To exclude an entire class of workers, such as women or minorities, limits the labour pool available to the human resource department. Open discrimination can also lead to negative public relations, boycotts by consumers, and government intervention.[16] To ensure that such discrimination does not occur, employers often develop affirmative-action programs voluntarily.

Regardless of the reasons or goals of such programs, human resource departments should adhere to the guidelines discussed below and summarized in Figure 3-6.

 FIGURE 3-6   Major Steps in Affirmative-Action Programs

1. **Exhibit** strong employer commitment.
2. **Appoint** a high-ranking director.
3. **Publicize** commitment internally and externally.
4. **Survey** the work force for underutilization and concentration.
5. **Develop** goals and timetables.
6. **Design** remedial and preventive programs.
7. **Establish** control systems and reporting procedures.

### Exhibit Commitment

No matter how favourably the human resource department is viewed by others in the organization, the president of the company should support the affirmative-action program in writing. Anything less than total backing from top officials raises questions about the sincerity of the organization's commitment in the eyes of government agencies, courts, and employees. To exhibit this commitment forcefully, company officials may make raises, bonuses, and promotions dependent upon each manager's compliance.

### Appoint a Director

Some member of the organization should be responsible for affirmative action. Commonly, the vice president of human resources is appointed director, although day-to-day implementation may be delegated to a compliance specialist in the human resource department.

> Pearl Kays was made the affirmative-action officer for the Daily Times Newspaper. Most department managers at the Times were supportive of Pearl's efforts. But a pressroom supervisor felt affirmative action was "hogwash." Whenever Pearl needed this supervisor's assistance, she would draft an interoffice memo to the supervisor and have the human resource manager sign it.

### Publicize Commitment

Equal employment and affirmative action are meaningless unless publicized externally and internally. Outside the company, sources of potential recruits must be made aware of the new policy. School guidance counsellors, employment agencies, and officers of Canada Employment Centres are likely candidates for notification. The phrase "an equal-opportunity employer" is frequently used on company stationery and in classified ads to further publicize the policy.

Internally, managers at all levels need to be aware of the new commitment. This means more than simply informing them of the policy. Equal employment has to be viewed as their responsibility too. Human resource managers cannot be the only ones responsible for equal opportunity. They must enlist the active support of *all* managers.

### Survey the Work Force

The human resource department needs to know how the composition of the employer's work force compares with the composition of the work force in the labour market. For example, if the employer's mix of male and female employees differs significantly from the labour market from which the employer attracts workers, then it is possible that discrimination has occurred. When a survey of the employer's work force indicates such differences, the employer may find examples of underutilization or concentration. Under-utilization exists when a company or department has a smaller proportion of protected class members than is found in the labour market. For example, when a company has no female managers even though the labour market is 37% female, underutilization exists. Concentration is just the opposite. It occurs when protected class members are concentrated in a few departments out of proportion with their presence in the labour market.

> At Northern Telephone & Telegraph Company 100% of the telephone operators and 25% of the supervisors were female. The labour market was 33% female. Alan Taylor, the human resource manager, realized that the job of operator was an example of concentration and the supervisors' position an example of underutiliza-tion, so he developed a series of goals and timetables to eliminate these problems.

### Develop Goals and Timetables

When, through surveys, underutilization and concentration are found (possibly conse-quences of past discrimination) human resource specialists should set up goals and time-tables to eliminate them. In the case of Northern Telephone & Telegraph, Alan set a three-year goal of 25% male operators and 50% female supervisors. He hoped that in a subsequent five-year plan he could achieve the same male/female ratio in the company's labour force as existed in the local labour market.

### Design Specific Programs

To reach goals, human resource specialists must design both remedial and preventive programs. Remedial programs correct problems that already exist. Alan's remedial pro-gram at the phone company was to train and promote more women into supervisory positions. He also sought more male applicants for operator openings.

Preventive programs are more proactive. They involve an assessment of human resource management policies and practices. Policies that discriminate (such as height rules) or practices that continue past discrimination (such as hiring exclusively from employee referrals) must be eliminated.

### Establish Controls

An affirmative-action program is likely to fail unless controls are established. Human resource specialists and line managers must perceive their rewards as depending upon the success of the affirmative-action plan. To evaluate that success, monthly, quarterly, and yearly benchmarks should be reported directly to the director of the program and to the president or another senior official.

## Affirmative Action in Practice

How do organizations respond to affirmative action programs? How effective are affirmative-action programs? In one research study of 126 firms in the Kitchener-Waterloo area on affirmative action programs for women, it was found that "affirmative-action programs, as they exist today, have failed to transform the employment reality of women." Professor Sandra Burt of the University of Toronto conducted the survey and concluded that:

"(i) few employers know what affirmative action means,
 (ii) many of those who think they understand the term are mistaken,
 (iii) there is little understanding of the barriers to women's employment, and
 (iv) information sent to head offices (of an organization about affirmative action) does not always reach the branch offices."[17]

For example, the respondents "defined" affirmative action in various ways (see Figure 3-7). Several organizations also "thought" they were employing affirmative-action plans when they in fact were not (see Figure 3-8).

FIGURE 3-7   Some Misconceptions of Meaning of Affirmative Action

| "WHAT DOES AFFIRMATIVE ACTION MEAN?" | % OF RESPONDENTS DEFINING IT AS: |
|---|---|
| Special treatment of women/minorities | 23 |
| Equal opportunity | 11 |
| Equal opportunity for women | 11 |
| Other | 7 |
| Don't know or no answer | 47 |

FIGURE 3-8   Description of Self-Defined Affirmative-Action Programs

| SELF DEFINED "AFFIRMATIVE-ACTION PROGRAMS" | % OF RESPONDENTS |
|---|---|
| Skill improvement and education | 12 |
| Hire best person for the job | 28 |
| Employ handicapped persons | 2 |
| Position open to women | 9 |
| Equality in business practices | 5 |
| Expansion and job creation | 5 |
| Job done well | 9 |
| Other | 22 |
| No answer | 5 |

Source: S. Burt, "Voluntary Affirmative Action: Does it Work?" *Relations Industrielles*, 1986, Vol. 41, No. 3, pp. 548-550. Used with permission.

Why don't firms employ affirmative-action plans? Respondents gave varying reasons such as:

They hire on merit:   10%
Respondent unclear about the meaning of affirmative action:   60%
Restrictions on hiring:   17%
Other reasons:   17%

The results of the study—the general lack of interest in affirmative action combined with the feeling that affirmative action is just equal opportunity — are somewhat disappointing. While the findings of the study cannot be generalized to other organizations in Canada, they still provide some indications of the challenge ahead of us. In Burt's words, "This study suggests that it is still considered reasonable, in today's society, for women to work in segregated sectors usually for less money than men. There is a great deal of difference between the argument that women should have the right to work and the argument that women should have equal access to all jobs."[18]

If women do not fare well under affirmative-action programs, how are disabled Canadians treated? Although the recently proclaimed Employment Equity Act (see discussion, pp. 83-84) specifically mentions the physically disabled as a group requiring special considerations, the results one year later are disappointing. In a report submitted to the Canadian Human Rights Commission, the group Disabled People for Employment Equity complained that of the more than 13,000 full-time employees hired in 1987 by the nine largest companies in Canada, fewer than 1% were from among the disabled.[19] It appears that the employment of handicapped persons continues to be not high among the priorities of Canadian companies. Max Yalden, the Chief Human Rights Commissioner, is convinced that by reviewing the hiring records with the chief executive officers of the companies in question and asking them for their cooperation more can be accomplished than by filing complaints.[20]

## Discrimination in Practice

Unfair discrimination may not be an issue just at the workplace. It may be relevant in the sports arena too, according to one study reported by Lavoie, Grenier, and Coloumbe in 1987.[21] In this study, the researchers produced evidence to show that substantial hiring discrimination against francophone hockey players exists in the NHL. For example, the proportion of francophones in all positions in the NHL has fallen over the years. The figures for the various positions in 1977-78 were (1972-1973 figures in brackets):

Defence players:   12.4% (16.0%)
Forward players:   17.5% (20.5%)
Goalie:   28.2% (35.9%)

Nova Scotia would seem to be one of the few Canadian provinces that is determined to discriminate against homosexuals in its police force.

In July 1986, Nova Scotia's Attorney General Ron Giffin stated that the province's police chiefs will not be required to hire homosexuals. Speaking to the annual meeting of the Atlantic Provinces Police Chief's Association in Truro, Mr. Giffin said that if necessary the province will use Section 34 of the Charter of Rights to exempt the province from federal legislation allowing homosexuals to enlist in the RCMP and armed forces.[22]

This clause in the chapter has not been used in Nova Scotia to date. Mr. Giffin's position has, however, sparked a controversy in the province.

Elsewhere in Canada, too, freedom of sexual orientation has been emerging as an important issue in the context of human rights.

In March 1988, the New Democrat MP of B.C., Svend Robinson, revealed that he is a homosexual. He is the first Canadian member of Parliament ever to make such a declaration. "Yes, yes, I am gay and I'm proud to be part of a community of very beautiful men and women," said Robinson.[23]

Indications are that in the years to come, the move to end discrimination on the basis of the sexual orientation of a person may gain momentum.

Mandatory retirement policies are increasingly considered discriminatory by various provinces. In 1985, Professor Olive Dickson, who taught history at the University of Alberta, was asked to retire at the age of sixty-five. Dr. Dickson claimed that mandatory retirement at age sixty-five violated her constitutional rights. The Alberta Human Rights Commission with which she filed a complaint was unable to effect a settlement. The board of inquiry that was appointed to determine the validity of the university's policy of mandatory retirement concluded in October 1987 that the university's policy is contrary to the human rights legislation, as well as the provisions of the Canadian Charter of Rights and Freedoms. While the university plans to appeal the decision, the ruling may have significant implications for all Canadian organizations. The final legal position on the mandatory retirement issue is still unclear. A Supreme Court ruling in the foreseeable future may settle the issue once and for all.[24]

## HUMAN RIGHTS LEGISLATION IN PERSPECTIVE

Equal employment laws have a broad impact on the practice of human resource management in three major areas. One obvious effect is on human resource activities; another is on people who are not directly protected by these laws. The third effect, on line management, may be even more serious.

### Functional Impact

Virtually every human resource function is affected by equal-employment opportunity and affirmative-action plans:
- *Human resource plans* must reflect the organization's affirmative-action goals.
- *Job descriptions* must not contain unneeded requirements that exclude members of protected classes.
- *Recruiting* must ensure that all types of applicants are sought without discriminating.

- *Selection* of applicants must use screening devices that are job-relevant and nondiscriminatory.
- *Training and developmental* opportunities must be made available to workers without discrimination.
- *Performance appraisal* must be free of biases that discriminate.
- *Compensation programs* must be based on skills, performance, and/or seniority and cannot discriminate against jobholders in other respects.

Even when human resource specialists know their intent is not to discriminate, they must carefully review the results of these human resource functions to ensure that the results are not discriminatory. Otherwise, lawsuits may arise and the current affirmative-action plan may need to be revised or scrapped.

## Reverse Discrimination

The use of affirmative-action plans can lead to charges of reverse discrimination against employers. These charges usually arise when an employer seeks to hire or promote a member of a protected group over an equally (or better) qualified candidate who is not a member of the protected group. For example, if an employer has an affirmative-action program that gives preference to women over men when promotions occur, a qualified male may sue the employer and claim that he was discriminated against because of his sex.

Charges of reverse discrimination may place human resource departments in a difficult position. On one hand, the human resource department is responsible for eliminating concentration and underutilization. On the other hand, to give preference to members of a protected class (such as women, for example) raises questions about whether the human resource department is being fair.[25]

For example, if the attitudes expressed in Figure 3-9 are representative of most male employees, it is easy to imagine how special treatment towards women would evoke strongly negative feelings. These negative feelings could easily lead to frustration, tensions, employee turnover, and lower employee satisfaction.[26]

Although preferential treatment will always raise questions of fairness, the Canadian Human Rights Act declares affirmative-action programs nondiscriminatory if they fulfil the spirit of the law as outlined in Section 15(1). So far, reverse discrimination has not been an issue in Canada.

## Line Management

The implementation of an affirmative-action program may cause line managers to feel a loss of authority.[27] Operating managers may lose the right to make final hiring and promotion decisions. To achieve the objectives of the plan, the human resource department may even have to overrule line managers. In time, supervisors may believe that members of protected classes are getting different treatment. If workers also sense an element of reverse discrimination, conflicts may arise that lessen the effectiveness of the work group.

To overcome potentially damaging side effects of affirmative-action plans, human resource specialists must educate line managers — particularly first-line supervisors.

FIGURE 3-9   Reactions of Male Employees Towards Organizational Treatment of Women

| Attitude Expressed | Percentage Agreeing |
| --- | --- |
| **Favouritism towards Women** | |
| Women can get complaints resolved more easily than men. | 19 |
| Women are given too many breaks. | 13 |
| Organizations are forced by law to favour women. | 26 |
| **Promotion and Training** | |
| Promotion opportunities are greater for women than for men. | 50 |
| Recently there has been more emphasis on training women than training men. | 23 |
| Favouritism is shown when it comes to special opportunities for development. | 10 |
| **Women and Power** | |
| Management is afraid of women's liberation. | 27 |
| It would be disastrous if women got much control or power. | 17 |
| I resent women's attempts to get more power. | 14 |
| Women have too much say on policies and decisions. | 5 |
| **Men's and Women's Place** | |
| Some jobs should remain men's jobs and other jobs should remain women's jobs. | 45 |
| A woman's place is in the home. | 26 |
| Men should always be the backbone of the organization. | 21 |

Source: Benson Rosen and Thomas H. Jerdee, "Coping with Affirmative Action Backlash," *Business Horizons*, August 1979, p. 17. Used by permission.

Training programs, seminars, and explanations of human resource decisions affecting protected groups must be given to managers. Otherwise, their support and understanding of affirmative action is likely to be low;[28] and, in turn, the perceived quality of the work environment may decline.

## *A Landmark Decision on Affirmative Action*

In August 1984, a federal human rights tribunal issued its first decision in Canadian history with regard to a mandatory affirmative-action program.[29] The tribunal ordered Canadian National Railways to hire women for one in four nontraditional or blue-collar jobs in its St. Lawrence region until they hold 13% of such jobs. CN was also required to implement a series of other measures, varying from abandoning certain mechanical aptitude tests to modifying the way it publicizes available jobs. The decision arose from a complaint laid against CN in 1979 by a Montreal lobby group, Action Travail de Femmes. The goal of 13% would roughly correspond to the proportion of women in blue-collar jobs in industry generally. Currently, women represent approximately 4% of CN employees.

## *Employment Equity Act*

In August 1987, the Employment Equity Act was proclaimed. Its intent is to remove employment barriers and promote equality for women, aboriginal peoples, persons with disabilities, and visible minorities. The act requires employers with 100 or more employees under federal jurisdiction to develop annual plans setting out goals and timetables and to maintain these plans for three years. The act requires further that each employer submit annual reports describing the progress in attaining the goals set out in the above mentioned plans. The Canada Employment and Immigration Commission will forward employer reports to the Human Rights Commission. Employers who do not comply may be investigated by the Human Rights Commission and, if necessary, prosecuted under the Canadian Human Rights Act.

It is not expected that employers will hire or promote people who are not qualified or to lay off people because they are not members of a target group. However, it is expected that employers will examine and report on: salary ranges, the distribution of employees by occupational groupings, and the number of employees hired, promoted, and terminated by designated group status and occupation.

### Contract Compliance Policy

In addition to the Employment Equity Act, the federal government issued a new policy that requires compliance with the Employment Equity Act for any company doing business with the federal government. Companies with 100 or more employees bidding on contracts for goods and services of $200,000 or more will be subject to the employment equity criteria listed in the act. Under this policy, companies will be required to certify in writing at the tendering stage of a contract their commitment to implement employment equity. Employers will be subject to random reviews to ensure their compliance with the act.

## THE CHARTER OF RIGHTS AND FREEDOMS

Among the government challenges mentioned in Chapter 2, the Canadian Charter of Rights and Freedoms is probably the most far-reaching legal challenge for human resource managers. When it came into effect in 1982, it created high expectations among the collective bargaining partners, unions and management. Both parties hoped that the Charter would strengthen their positions *vis-à-vis* each other. A review of the application of the Charter to human resource and industrial relations issues after six years reveals that the impact has been modest so far. One reason is that it takes considerable time for cases to reach the Supreme Court of Canada, the ultimate interpreter of the Charter. In the following paragraphs, we will have a look at the effects the Charter has had on personnel management and industrial relations in Canada.

### Content and Applicability of the Charter

Section 1 of the Charter guarantees rights and freedoms ''subject only to such reasonable limits prescribed by law as can be demonstrably justified in a free and democratic society.'' Of course, such adjectives as ''reasonable'' and ''demonstrably justified'' will lead to different interpretations by different judges. This is one of the reasons why many cases will eventually end up before the Supreme Court, just to get a final opinion. Every time a court invokes one of the rights or freedoms, it must determine if the infringement is justified.

Section 2 of the Charter guarantees freedom of association, a very important aspect in industrial relations, especially for unions. A key question in this context is whether the freedom to associate carries with it the right to bargain collectively and the right to strike, the main reasons for the existence of unions. As will be shown, these ''rights'' cannot be taken for granted any more.

Section 15—the equality rights part—came into effect on April 17, 1985, delayed for two years in its enactment to allow the federal government and the provinces to create or change laws to ensure compliance with the Charter. It states in its first paragraph:

> Every individual is equal before the law and under the law and has the right to the equal protection and benefit of the law without discrimination and, in particular, without discrimination based on race, national or ethnic origin, colour, religion, sex, age, or mental or physical disability.

This section of the Charter was expected to—and has—caused a flood of litigation which will take many years to resolve.

The Charter of Rights and Freedoms applies only to individuals dealing with federal and provincial governments and agencies under their jurisdiction, but its impact may be far-reaching since potentially every law can be challenged. Courts will have the delicate task of balancing individual and collective rights.

## Areas of Application

Some of the more prominent issues before the courts relate to: the use of compulsory union dues for political causes, the use of closed-shop union security provisions whereby workers must be members of a union in order to be hired, the imposition of first collective agreements designed to help weak unions, the use of union shop arrangements whereby workers must become union members within specified time periods after they are hired, the use of accreditation in the construction industry whereby employer associations bargain on behalf of employers, the right to picket, affirmative-action programs, and mandatory retirement. Even the rights to strike and to bargain collectively have been challenged. Most of these cases are still winding their way through the court system, some have reached the Supreme Court but are still outstanding, and a few have been decided upon.

### The Right to Bargain Collectively and to Strike

On April 9, 1987, the Supreme Court of Canada rendered a long awaited judgement on the impact of the Charter on federal and provincial collective bargaining laws. The three cases in question arose from challenges of the federal public sector laws imposing compulsory arbitration for the right to strike, ''back to work'' legislation, and wage restraint legislation.

In a 4-2 split decision, the Supreme Court held that Section 2 of the Charter does not include the right to bargain collectively and to strike. This judgement was a real blow to Canadian unions, since workers have taken these rights for granted. The Court affirmed that Section 2 protects the freedom to work for the establishment of an association, to belong to an association, to maintain it, and to participate in its lawful activities without penalty or reprisal. However, it also held that the rights to bargain collectively and to strike are not fundamental freedoms but are statutory rights created and regulated by the legislature. Under this ruling, governments can curtail the collective bargaining process by limiting salary increases, legislating strikers back to work, and imposing compulsory arbitration.

### The Use of Union Dues for Political Causes

In a judgement rendered in the case of Lavigne v. Ontario Public Service Employees Union (1986), the Supreme Court held that unions were not entitled to use dues, collected under an agreement with an employer, for purposes other than collective bargaining without the consent of union members. The plaintiff in this case was a community college teacher who was a nonmember paying dues under an agency shop clause. He objected to the use of his dues to make contributions to the New Democratic Party and to nuclear disarmament groups. What is interesting in this ruling is that the Court inferred from the section on freedom of association a right not to associate that is not evident from the wording of this section. It implies also that union expenditures are subject to judicial review.

### The Right to Picket

In another decision, the Supreme Court ruled that the right to picket is not protected under the Charter since it applies only to situations involving government action. It follows that this right is not available to employees in the private sector, where the vast majority of workers are employed. Employers can ask for injunctions to restrict the number of pickets or any other reasonable limitation of picketing activity.

## Discussion

From the rulings of the Supreme Court it can be seen that the effect of the Charter of Rights and Freedoms on human resource management and industrial relations so far has been significant to a certain degree, but not drastic. It appears that the court takes a conservative approach in interpreting the Charter in regard to union activities, meaning that it appears to associate more with employers' interests and the public's interests rather than with unions' and workers' interests. As one law professor put it:

> Anglo-Canadian courts have been dealing with issues of individual and collective labour law for at least 200 years. During that entire period, the courts virtually never, not on any given occasion, created a right which might be asserted by or on behalf of working people. Nor have they since the enactment of the Charter. Nor — I conclude — is it likely that they ever will.[30]

Some very significant cases are before the Supreme Court, one of which is mandatory retirement. Should the court decide that the widely accepted mandatory retirement age of sixty-five is against the Charter, it would have a major impact on human resource management, especially in the areas of employment planning, training, wage and salary administration, and performance appraisal. The performance appraisal process would take on a new and crucial significance, because it would be the only tool available to control the retirement of employees.[31]

## *Testing the Charter of Rights and Freedoms — Anti-Smoking Legislation*

It is estimated that approximately one-third of the employers in North America now have either an outright ban on smoking or restrict smoking in the workplace. The Canadian federal government followed the trend and banned smoking in all federal offices as of January 1, 1989. A restriction on smoking had been in effect since October 1, 1987. Several provincial governments have introduced legislation restricting smoking in public places. Air Canada and Canadian Airlines International have banned smoking on all flights lasting less than two hours. Some companies go so far as to discriminate against smokers when it comes to hiring decisions. The question arises whether this type of discrimination is illegal under the Charter of Rights and Freedoms or the Human Rights Act.

Federal and provincial human rights laws clearly do not mention personal habits like smoking among the prohibited causes for discrimination. It means that an employee cannot appeal to a human rights commission if he or she challenges an employer on this ground. The Charter guarantees equal treatment under the law, "subject to only such reasonable limits prescribed by law as can be demonstrably justified in a free and democratic society." It seems to be unlikely that a smoker or the tobacco industry could challenge restrictions on smoking by using Charter arguments since they would have to show that these restrictions are unreasonable and unjustified. A cursory survey among lawyers by the authors did not turn up a court case related to discrimination based on smoking.

## *SUMMARY*

Government is a significant variable that strongly shapes the role of human resource management. It influences human resources through laws governing the employment relationship. Most of these laws are limited in scope; however, equal-employment laws influence nearly every human resource activity.

The two sources of equal-employment laws are the federal and provincial human rights statutes. The Canadian Human Rights Act of 1978 applies to federal government departments and agencies, Crown corporations, and businesses and industries under federal jurisdiction, such as banks, airlines, and railway companies. Areas not under federal jurisdiction are protected by provincial human rights laws. Each of the ten Canadian provinces has its own antidiscrimination laws that are broadly similar to the federal law.

To eliminate past discrimination and ensure future compliance, many organizations have developed affirmative-action programs. These programs are designed to identify areas of past and present discrimination, develop affirmative goals, and implement corrective programs.

To actively promote the employment of women, aboriginal peoples, persons with disabilities, and visible minorities, the federal government introduced the Employment Equity Act which requires employers with 100 employees or more under federal jurisdiction to develop plans and timetables for the employment of these groups. It also requires annual reports that have to be submitted to the Canada Employment and Immigration Commission. Also, a new policy requires employers with 100 employees or more bidding for government contracts worth $200,000 or more to comply with the above-mentioned guidelines.

The Charter of Rights and Freedoms has been awaited with high expectations from both labour and management. However, the impact on the human resource management field has been modest so far. Three decisions from the Supreme Court of Canada affirmed the right to associate, but found that the right to bargain collectively and to strike is not a fundamental one, but is subject to government regulations. Unions are not allowed to use union dues for purposes other than collective bargaining without the consent of union members. And the Charter does not apply to picketing, which means that employers can ask for injunctions to restrict the number of pickets.

The appendix to this chapter contains a "recruitment and interviewing guide," which describes acceptable and unacceptable questions to ask during job interviews and on application forms.

## TERMS FOR REVIEW

| | |
|---|---|
| Regulations | Conciliation agreement |
| Canadian Human Rights Act | Affirmative-action programs |
| Provincial antidiscrimination laws | Charter of Rights and Freedoms |
| Canadian Human Rights Commission | Employment Equity Act |
| Equal pay for work of equal value | Underutilization |
| Bona fide occupational requirements | Concentration |

## REVIEW AND DISCUSSION QUESTIONS

1. Suppose during your first job interview after graduation you are asked, "Why should a company have an affirmative-action plan?" How would you respond?

2. If you are a supervisor in the production department of a textile mill and an employee demands to be allowed to miss work on Fridays for religious reasons, what would you do? Under what circumstances would you have to let the employee have time off? Under what circumstances could you prohibit it?

3. List the major prohibitions of the Canadian Human Rights Act.

4. Since a human resource department is not a legal department, what role does it play in the area of equal-employment law?

5. Suppose you are told that your first duty as a human resource specialist is to construct an affirmative-action plan. What would you do? What types of information would you seek?

6.  What conditions would have to be met before you could bring suit against an employer who discriminated against you because of your sex?

7.  During the rest of this decade, do you think more groups will receive special legislation to protect them from discrimination? Which groups might get additional protection?

8.  Under the Charter of Rights and Freedoms, the Supreme Court of Canada made three important decisions. What impact do these decisions have on management and unions?

## INCIDENT 3-1

### Metropolitan Hospital's Affirmative-Action Needs

A large metropolitan hospital in Ontario recently developed an affirmative-action program. Under the program the hospital agreed to promote two women into supervisory ranks for each man promoted. This practice was to continue until 40 to 45% of all supervisory jobs in the hospital were held by women.

The need for the first supervisory promotion occurred in the medical records department. The manager of medical records was one of the few female managers in the hospital. Nevertheless, she argued that Roy Biggs should become a medical records supervisor since he was best qualified. Roy had two years of medical school and was a graduate of a medical-records program at the local community college. The assistant director of hospital operations agreed that Roy should get the promotion. The equal-employment compliance specialist in the human resource department argued that Kate VanDam should get the promotion because of the affirmative-action program and because she had more seniority and experience in the department than Roy. The records manager, the assistant administrator, and the compliance specialist decided that the human resource manager should make the final decision.

1.  What weight would you give to (a) Kate's seniority and experience, (b) Roy's superior training, (c) the recommendation of the records manager, (d) the new affirmative-action program?

2.  What are the implications for the affirmative-action program if Roy gets the job? What are the implications for the employees presently taking job-related courses if Kate gets the promotion?

3.  What decision would you make if you were the human resource manager?

*EXERCISE 3-1*

## Carver Jewellery Company

Carver Jewellery Company Ltd. has the following work force composition:

| Job Classes | Male | Female | White | Black | Asian | Native Peoples |
|---|---|---|---|---|---|---|
| Executive | 9 | 1 | 10 | 0 | 0 | 0 |
| Management | 71 | 9 | 79 | 0 | 1 | 0 |
| Salaried/Commission | 43 | 31 | 74 | 0 | 0 | 0 |
| Hourly Paid | 24 | 164 | 168 | 10 | 8 | 2 |

An analysis of the local labour force from which Carver draws its employees is as follows:

| Male | Female | White | Black | Asian | Native Peoples |
|---|---|---|---|---|---|
| 53% | 47% | 84% | 8% | 3% | 5% |

On the basis of this information:
1. Identify which job classes at Carver exhibit underutilization.
2. Identify which job classes at Carver exhibit concentration.

○ ○ ○ ○ ○ ○ ○ ○ ○ ○ ○ ○ ○ ○ ○ ○ ○ ○ ○ ○ ○ ○ ○ ○ ○ ○ ○ ○ ○ ○ ○ ○ ○ ○ ○ ○ ○

*CASE STUDY*

### SORRY, BUT THE JOB IS FILLED

Lorna MacDonald is thirty-two, married, and has one daughter, six years old. Lorna is confined to a wheelchair, the result of a recent automobile accident. She lost the use of her legs, but is able to manoeuvre with her wheelchair very well. She has a Bachelor of Commerce degree with a double major in marketing and finance. She was a good student, was on the Dean's list for the last two years at the university and was quite active in the student government, where she had the position of Entertainment Coordinator, being responsible for organizing bashes, dances, and parties. In addition she played in the university basketball team, which was ranked among the top ten in Canada.

After her graduation she began to work for an investment broker as an investment counsellor. She was quite successful and as a result was promoted after three years to the position of assistant manager.

During her first year with the company, she had met Allistair MacDonald, a high-school teacher. She had advised him on how to invest his money, but her interest in him was more than that to a customer. Since the feelings were mutual they married a year later, just after Lorna had been promoted to assistant manager. When their daughter was born, Lorna took only enough time off to deliver the child and to recover and went back to work within four weeks. Her mother, widowed, moved into her house to take care of the child.

Lorna expected to be soon promoted to the position of manager, since the current job incumbent was scheduled to move up to a recently vacated vice presidential position and she had been told that she was a candidate for the manager's job.

Then disaster struck. When returning late from a visit to a customer, she lost control of her car, drove into a ditch, and overturned. She was trapped for two hours until a passing motorist saw the overturned car and called for help. She had broken her lower back and was not able to move her legs.

She recovered, went through a lengthy physiotherapy program, and learned to cope with life in a wheelchair. Her husband supported her very well and helped her to overcome the initial depression when she realized that she would be confined to her chair for the rest of her life. She even resumed some sports activities and could drive a specially equipped car. She could manage to get into her wheelchair from the driver's seat without assistance.

After a year at home and learning to maintain a house and to raise a daughter — her mother still assisted her — Lorna became restless. She missed the challenge of a job, the activities of an office, the excitement of making decisions. She inquired with her old company whether they had a suitable position available. Her boss was sympathetic, but told her that no position was available and that the outlook was not very good.

She studied the employment ads and found a position advertised that she felt was suitable for her. A local trust company was looking for an investment officer with three years' experi-

ence, for a newly opened branch. She submitted her resumé, but did not mention her disability.

A few days later she received a phone call from the branch of the trust company, inviting her to an interview. She drove to the company's office in her car, got into her wheelchair, and went to the building's entrance. Unfortunately, the entrance was barred by one stair that she was unable to overcome. She had to wait for several minutes until a passer-by could assist her to get over the stair and through the door into the building.

She felt that she must have been the first customer in a wheelchair who came to this branch, because the tellers looked uncomfortable and did not quite know what to do when she struggled through the door. She could not get close to the counters since these were roped off to force customers to form queues. She had to propel herself to the end of the room where she saw some desks and separate offices.

A young woman rose from the first desk and asked what she could do for her. There was a sign at the desk that said: Susan Crandall, loan officer. Lorna introduced herself and explained the purpose of her visit. Susan seemed to be surprised that she was a job applicant, but caught herself and explained that Mr. Ferguson, the branch manager, would conduct the interview himself. She asked Lorna to fill out an application blank and handed her the form (see sample). To be able to write, Lorna had to manoeuvre closer to the desk, which was actually too high for her to write conveniently, but she managed. She wondered about some of the questions, but provided the information anyway since she did not want to start a job interview in a negative atmosphere.

While Lorna wrote, Susan disappeared into one of the offices in the corner. After some time she appeared again and waved to Lorna to come to the office. Lorna wheeled around the other desks; a few women at the desks looked at her with some curiosity. Some of them had

## EMPLOYMENT APPLICATION

Name _____ Telephone (    ) _____
     Print    Last name       First      Middle         Area Code

Present
address _____
      Street and number       City       Province       Postal Code

Last
address _____
      Street and number       City       Province       Postal Code

Date of
birth _____ Sex _____ Height _____ Weight _____
                                                     cm         kg

Are you a Canadian citizen or a permanent resident in Canada?

_____ Soc. Ins. No. _____

## All Questions Must Be Answered

I.    FAMILY STATUS

      Single          Married          Separated          Widowed

      Number of children _____

Spouse working _____ permanently _____ temporarily _____ part time _____

Occupation _____

Father's occupation (present or former) _____

II.    EDUCATION

Give an outline of your education by completing the table below:

| Type of school | Name and location of school | Main field of study | Dates attended From   To | Graduate Yes   No | Average Grades earned |
|---|---|---|---|---|---|
| High School | | | | | |
| Trade or technical College | | | | | |
| Other | | | | | |

If you left school without graduation, what were the reasons?

What were your best liked subjects? _____

Least liked subjects? _____

III.   EMPLOYMENT RECORD

| 1. Name and address of employers (begin with most recent and work backward) | 2. Nature of employer's business | 3. Kind of work you did |
|---|---|---|
| Name | | |
| Address | | |
| City | Province | |
| Name | | |
| Address | | |
| City | Province | |

| 4. Person under whom you worked | 5. Length of service (month and year) | 6. Salary or commission earnings | 7. Why did you leave this employment? |
|---|---|---|---|
| Name | From | First month | |
| Title | To | Last month | |
| Telephone | | | |
| Name | From | First month | |
| Title | To | Last month | |
| Telephone | | | |

(Note: List additional employers on back of form if necessary. Be sure to answer all 7 questions for each employer listed.)

Please indicate any employer you do not wish contacted at this time and why.

_____

IV.   SUPPLEMENTARY INFORMATION

Position applied for _____     Salary expected _____

Date available _____

Length of time you plan to work _____

Have you any friends or relatives employed here? _____

If so give names and relationship _____

Who recommended you apply here? _____

## V. DRIVING STATUS

Do you have a valid driver's license?     Yes     No

What province _____     Operator's number _____

Have you, or any member of your household, ever had your driver's
license revoked?     Yes     No

If yes, what date? _____

Which member and why? _____

Do you have automobile insurance?     Yes     No

Have you ever been cancelled or refused?     Yes     No

If yes, when and why?

_____

Have you ever been convicted for any offense?     Yes     No

If yes, explain.


_____


## VI. PHYSICAL CONDITION

How many days have you lost by reason of illness or injury during the past two years?
_____

For what cause?
_____

Give reasons and cause for any time you have spent in a hospital, sanitarium, or rest
home as a patient.
_____

Give reasons if you have ever been rejected for life insurance _____
_____

Are the members of your immediate family in good health? _____

If not, give age and condition _____

To what extent do you use intoxicating liquor? _____

## VII. MILITARY SERVICE RECORD

Have you served in the Canadian Armed forces? _____     (If yes)

Date active duty started _____

Which branch of service? _____     Starting rank/rate _____

Duties while in service _____

Date of discharge _____

Reasons for discharge (Honourable, Disabled, etc.) _____

Rank/rate at discharge _____

Were you hospitalized while in service?     Yes     No

If yes, from _____ to _____ For what reason?

How much pension or disability compensation are you receiving? _____

For what reason? _____

What special training did you receive, or other usable skills did you acquire, while in
the service that should be considered? _____

Present military classification _____

## VIII. FINANCIAL

| | Value | Amount owed | Monthly payments |
|---|---|---|---|
| Property owned | | | |
| Home _____ | $ _____ | $ _____ | $ _____ |
| Other real estate or property _____ | $ _____ | $ _____ | $ _____ |
| Home furnishings | | | |
| (exclude personal effects) | $ _____ | $ _____ | $ _____ |
| Automobile(s) _____ | $ _____ | $ _____ | $ʼ_____ |

Other obligations

If renting, what rent do you pay?                                      $ _____
Do you pay alimony or child support? _____   $ _____
Amount of outstanding obligations due banks, credit
unions, or finance companies not shown in amounts
owed above                                             $ _____

General information

Spouse's earnings _____ Amount  $ _____
Any independent source of income? _____ Amount  $ _____
Do you have a savings account? _____   Approximate Amount  $ _____

## IX.   MEMBERSHIPS AND ACTIVITIES

Note: Omit the names of organizations which indicate the race, creed, colour, or national origin of members.

| | Name of organization or type of activity | To what extent do you participate? | Hours spent per week | Offices held during past five years |
|---|---|---|---|---|
| Religious | Omit name here | | | |
| Business, honorary, or social | | | | |
| Sports and hobbies | | | | |

## X.   REFERENCES Do not include relatives, former employers, or employees of this company.

| Name | Street and number | City | Occupation | Phone: |
|---|---|---|---|---|
| | | | | |
| | | | | |
| | | | | |

I hereby certify that my answers to all questions herein are true and complete. _____ (company) has my permission to communicate with my present and past employers and the schools I have attended, in determining my qualifications for employment.

Date _____    Applicant's Signature _____

---

to move their chairs to let Lorna pass. Susan introduced Lorna and Mr. Ferguson and left the office.

Mr. Ferguson was in his forties, dressed in a dark suit and a dark blue tie. He came from behind the desk to shake Lorna's hand and it looked as if he wanted to invite her to sit on a sofa which was near the wall, next to a small table and two armchairs. He hesitated and then returned to his chair behind the desk. Two chairs were in front of the desk and prevented Lorna from moving closer. Mr. Ferguson came around the desk again and moved the chairs away.

Ferguson:  You want to apply for the position of investment officer?

Lorna:      Yes. I think that it is a position which would suit me quite well. I have over seven years of experience in a similar position with a broker.

Ferguson:  In your resumé nothing is mentioned about your handicap and your confinement to a wheelchair.

Lorna:      Is that important?

Ferguson:  Well, it is somewhat unexpected. I don't know how it would affect your work. Could you work regular hours?

Lorna:      Sure, there's nothing wrong with me. I just need a desk and you can even save a chair.

Ferguson:  But you would be confined behind the desk. We expect an investment counsellor to visit customers and to be mobile.

Lorna:      I can drive a car and I am capable of visiting customers.

Ferguson:  I don't know what our customers would say if we sent out an investment counsellor in a wheelchair.

Lorna:      I think that they would get used to it, especially if the counsellor knows her stuff. And I am good with customers.

Ferguson:  Hm, I don't know. I have to think about that. We also do not have the facilities to accommodate you. Susan mentioned that you even had difficulties getting through the door.

Lorna:      It should not be too expensive to have a small ramp built to overcome the stair or just to cut something off the stair to make it inclined. With a handle on the wall I could pull myself up. As for the door, I believe that the provincial government assists employers to make changes to accommodate handicapped people. I am sure that you could get the money to make the door self-opening. Besides, it would also make it easier for your disabled customers, would it not?

Mr. Ferguson quickly nodded and changed the subject.

Mr. Ferguson:  But the washroom . . . ?

Lorna:   Could I have a look at it?

Somewhat reluctantly Mr. Ferguson walked ahead of Lorna and showed her the washroom facilities, which turned out to be small, but by changing a partition it was possible to make it accessible for a wheelchair. They returned to

Mr. Ferguson's office where he asked her some questions about her work experience and salary expectations. From his questions, it became obvious that he was not too enthusiastic about Lorna as a candidate for a position in his branch. He promised that he would be in touch with her soon and walked her to the door where he assisted her out and down the stair.

Two weeks went by and Lorna heard nothing from the company. She then called and asked for Mr. Ferguson. Susan came to the telephone and said that the position had been filled and that a letter was in the mail with the company's regrets.

The letter arrived the next day. It had been posted the same day Lorna had called. It read:

Dear Mrs. MacDonald:

We thank you for your interest in the position of Investment Officer at our West District Branch. We regret that we could not accept your application since we found a better qualified person for this position.

It would also have been very difficult for our branch to accommodate somebody in a wheelchair since it had not been planned with that in mind. There would have been substantial modifications necessary which go beyond what we presently can afford given the profitability of this branch. We hope that you will understand our position.

We will keep your application on file in case a suitable position becomes available in a different branch.

Sincerely,

Richard M. Ferguson

Branch Manager

After a few inquiries she found out that the person who got the job was male, with a Bachelor of Commerce degree with a major in accounting, who had worked for two years in a bank as a loans officer and one year as an investment counsellor.

Lorna was sure that she was better qualified than the person who got the job. She was angry and felt that she should do something about the situation. She thought of complaining to the Human Rights Commission, because she had heard of the principle of "reasonable accommodation," which requires an employer to take reasonable measures to accommodate a physically handicapped person if it did not impose an undue hardship on the company. On the other hand, she was reluctant to force the issue because if she won and got the job, she might have to work in a hostile environment.

She wondered what she should do and what her options were.

1. What are the chances that Lorna would get the job in question if she complained to the Human Rights Commission?

2. What factors may the Human Rights Commission take into account in assessing the appropriateness of the selection decision?

3. If it is assumed that the office modifications required to accommodate Lorna would cost approximately $1500, would this constitute a case of "reasonable accommodation"? What if it would cost $5000?

4. If Lorna got the job and subsequently feels that the employer is trying to "get back at her," what options would be open to her? With what potential consequences?

5. What is your opinion on the appropriateness of the employment application? What modifications do you suggest?

## SUGGESTED READINGS

Bayefsky, H. and M. Eberts (eds.), *Equality of Rights and the Canadian Charter of Rights and Freedoms*, Toronto: Carswell Publishers, 1985.

Hunter, I.A., "Human Rights Legislation in Canada: Its Origin, Development, and Interpretation," *University of Western Ontario Law Review*, 1976, vol. 21, p. 25.

Jain, Harish, and Peter Sloane, *Equal Employment Issues*, New York: Praeger Publishers, 1981.

Jain, Harish, "Race and Sex Discrimination in Employment in Canada: Theories, Evidence, and Policies," *Relations Industrielles*, 1982, vol. 37, No. 2, pp. 344-366.

Kelly, John G., *Human Resource Management and the Human Rights Process*, Toronto: CCH Canadian Ltd., 1985.

Kelly, John G., *Equal Opportunity Management — Understanding Affirmative Action and Employment Equity*, Toronto: CCH Canadian Ltd., 1986.

Roberts, Lance W., "Understanding Affirmative Action," in *Discrimination, Affirmative Action, and Equal Opportunity*, Vancouver: Fraser Institute, 1982.

Royal Commission on Equality in Employment (Abella Commission), *Equality in Employment*, Ottawa: Minister of Supply and Services Canada, 1984.

## REFERENCES

1. Maxwell F. Yalden, Chief Commissioner, Canadian Human Rights Commission, in a speech before the Conference Board of Canada, Montreal, February 1988.
2. *Canadian Human Rights Act*, Paragraph 2, Subsection (a).
3. These cases have been taken from either "Summary of Decisions Taken by the Canadian Human Rights Commission," Ottawa: Government of Canada, from 1979 to present, or from the *Annual Reports* of the Canadian Human Rights Commission, Ottawa: Government of Canada, 1980 to 1987. Used with permission.
4. Ibid.
5. Ibid.
6. Ibid.
7. Ibid.
8. Ibid.
9. Ibid.
10. *Annual Report of the Canadian Human Rights Commission*, 1980, p. 33.
11. "Correctional Service Agrees to Hire Ex-Convict," *Release*, a publication of the Canadian Human Rights Commission, Ottawa: Government of Canada, undated.
12. Canadian Human Rights Commission, op. cit.
13. Ibid.
14. *Canadian Human Rights Act*, Paragraph 46, section 2, (a), (b).
15. *Peterborough Examiner*, April 8, 1981.
16. Tove Helland Hanner, "Affirmative Action Programs: Have We Forgotten the First Line Supervisor?" *Personnel Journal*, June 1979, pp. 384-389.
17. S. Burt, "Voluntary Affirmative Action: Does It Work?" *Relations Industrielles*, 1986, Vol. 41, No. 3, p. 548.
18. Burt, op. cit., p. 550.

19. Anne Rauhala, "9 Firms Called Biased against Hiring Disabled," *Globe and Mail*, November 17, 1988, p. 1.
20. Ibid.
21. M. Lavoie, G. Grenier, and S. Coloumbe, "Discrimination and Performance Differences in the NHL," *Canadian Public Policy*, Vol. 13, No. 4, (December 1987) pp. 407-422.
22. "N.S. Police Won't Have to Hire Homosexuals," The *Halifax Mail Star*, July 10, 1986, p. 18.
23. "M.P. Declares Homosexuality," The *Halifax Mail Star*, March 1, 1988, p. 1.
24. "Arbitrator Rejects Mandatory Retirement at U. of A.," *University Affairs*, January 1988, p. 9.
25. Eleanor Homes Norton, "Comment on the Bakke Decision," *The Personnel Administrator*, August 1978, pp. 26-28.
26. Benson Rosen and Thomas H. Jerdee, "Coping with Affirmative Action Backlash," *Business Horizons*, August 1979, pp. 18-19.
27. Hanner, op.cit.
28. Ibid.
29. Margot Gibb-Clark, "CN Ordered to Recruit More Women in Landmark Human Rights Decision," *Globe and Mail*, August 23, 1984, pp. 1-2.
30. H.W. Arthurs, "The Right to Golf: Reflection on the Future of Workers, Unions, and the Rest of Us Under the Charter," paper presented at the Conference on Labour Law Under the Charter, Industrial Relations Centre, Queen's University, September 1987.
31. For a more detailed discussion of the impact of the Charter on Canadian labour relations see S.D. Carter, "Canadian Labour Relations Under the Charter," *Relations Industrielles*, 1988, Vol. 43, No. 2. pp. 305-321.

## APPENDIX TO CHAPTER 3

### Recruitment and Interviewing Guide

| SUBJECT | UNACCEPTABLE PRACTICES | ACCEPTABLE PRACTICES | COMMENTS |
|---|---|---|---|
| NAME | • Asking for maiden name of applicant.<br>• Asking for previous name when name was changed by court order or otherwise. | • Asking for name under which applicant has been educated or employed. | |
| ADDRESS | • Asking for foreign addresses (which may indicate national origin). | • Asking for place and duration of current and previous addresses in Canada. | |
| AGE | • Asking for birth certificate, baptismal record, or any other documents or information regarding age of applicant. | • Asking whether applicant has attained minimum age, or has exceeded maximum age, applying to employment by law. | Verification of age may be obtained after hiring. |
| SEX | • Asking about sex of applicant on the application form.<br>• Using different or coded application forms for males and females. | | Correspondence to applicants may be addressed to their home with or without the prefixes Mr., Mrs., Miss, Ms.; e.g. "Dear Mary Smith." |

| SUBJECT | UNACCEPTABLE PRACTICES | ACCEPTABLE PRACTICES | COMMENTS |
|---|---|---|---|
| MARITAL STATUS | • Asking whether applicant is single, married, remarried, engaged, divorced, separated, widowed, or living common law.<br>• Asking about applicant's spouse, e.g. "Is spouse subject to transfer?"<br>• Asking for number of children or other dependents. | • Asking if applicant is willing to travel or to be transferred to other areas of the province or country, if this requirement is job related. | • Such information, if required for tax or insurance purposes, may be required after hiring. |

| SUBJECT | UNACCEPTABLE PRACTICES | ACCEPTABLE PRACTICES | COMMENTS |
|---|---|---|---|
| NATIONAL OR ETHNIC ORIGIN | • Asking about birthplace.<br>• Asking about nationality of parents, grandparents, relatives, or spouse.<br>• Asking about ethnic or national origin, e.g. requiring birth certificate, asking for mother tongue.<br>• Asking whether applicant is native-born or naturalized.<br>• Asking for date citizenship received.<br>• Asking for proof of citizenship | • Asking if the applicant is legally entitled to work in Canada. | An employer may ask for documentary proof of eligibility to work in Canada after hiring. |

|  | | |
|---|---|---|
| MEDICAL INFORMATION | • Asking about child-care arrangements.<br>• Asking whether applicant is pregnant, on birth control, or has future childbearing plans. | • A medical examination will necessarily reveal prohibited information about an applicant, such as his or her age, race, or sex. For this reason employers should conduct medical examinations after the hiring decision is made. Employers may indicate on application forms that the job offer is conditional on the applicant's passing a medical examination. |
| ORGANIZATIONS | • Asking applicant to list all clubs or organizations he or she belongs to. | • Asking for such a list with the proviso that applicant may decline to list clubs or organizations which may indicate a prohibited ground of discrimination. The request should only be made if membership in organizations is necessary to determine job qualifications. |
| HEIGHT AND WEIGHT | | Height and weight requirements may be discriminatory if they screen out disproportionate numbers of minority-group individuals or women and if they cannot be shown to be essential for the performance of the job. |
| RELATIVES | • Asking for relationship to applicant of next of kin to be notified in case of emergency | Asking for name and address of person to be notified in case of emergency. |

| SUBJECT | UNACCEPTABLE PRACTICES | ACCEPTABLE PRACTICES | COMMENTS |
|---|---|---|---|
| REFERENCES | • Asking any question of a person given as a reference that would not be allowable if asked directly of the applicant. | | |
| CRIMINAL CONVICTION | • Asking whether applicant has ever been convicted of an offence. | • Asking whether applicant has been convicted of an offence for which no pardon has been granted. | The CHRA permits discrimination based on a criminal conviction for which a pardon has not been granted. However, it discourages inquiries into unpardoned criminal convictions unless the particular conviction is relevant to job qualification; e.g., a theft and fraud conviction is relevant to a job requiring honesty, but a conviction for marijuana possession is not. |
| OPTIONAL INQUIRIES | • Making any of the above prohibited inquiries, even if marked "optional" on the application form. | | |
| MILITARY | • Asking about all military service | • Asking about Canadian military service. | Asking about all military service is permissible if military experience directly relates to the job applied for. |
| LANGUAGES | • Asking about mother tongue or where language skills were obtained. | • Asking which languages applicant speaks, reads, or writes, if job-related. | Testing or scoring on applicant in English or French language proficiency is not approved unless English or French language skill is a requirement for the work to be performed. |

| | | |
|---|---|---|
| **RACE OR COLOUR** | • Asking anything which would indicate race, colour, or complexion, including colour of eyes, hair, or skin. | |
| **PHOTOGRAPHS** | • Asking for photograph, or taking of photograph. | Photos may be required after hiring for identification purposes. |
| **RELIGION** | • Asking about religious affiliation.<br>• Asking about willingness or availability to work on a specific religious holiday.<br>• Asking about church attended, religious holidays, customs observed, or religious dress.<br>• Asking for reference or recommendation from pastor, priest, minister, rabbi, or other religious leader. | • Asking about willingness to work a specified work schedule.<br><br>It is the duty of the employer to accommodate the religious observances of the applicant, if it is reasonably possible to do so. After hiring, inquiry about religion to determine when leave of absence might be required for religious observances, is permitted. |
| **PHYSICAL HANDICAP** | • Asking about all physical handicaps, limitations, or health problems which would tend to elicit handicaps or conditions not necessarily related to job performance. | • Asking whether applicant has any physical handicaps or health problems affecting the job applied for.<br>• Inquiry as to any physical handicaps or limitations that the applicant wishes to be taken into consideration when determining job placement.<br><br>A physical handicap is relevant to the job if: (a) the handicap would be hazardous to the applicant, coworkers, clients, or the public; (b) the handicap would prevent the applicant from performing the duties of the job satisfactorily. |

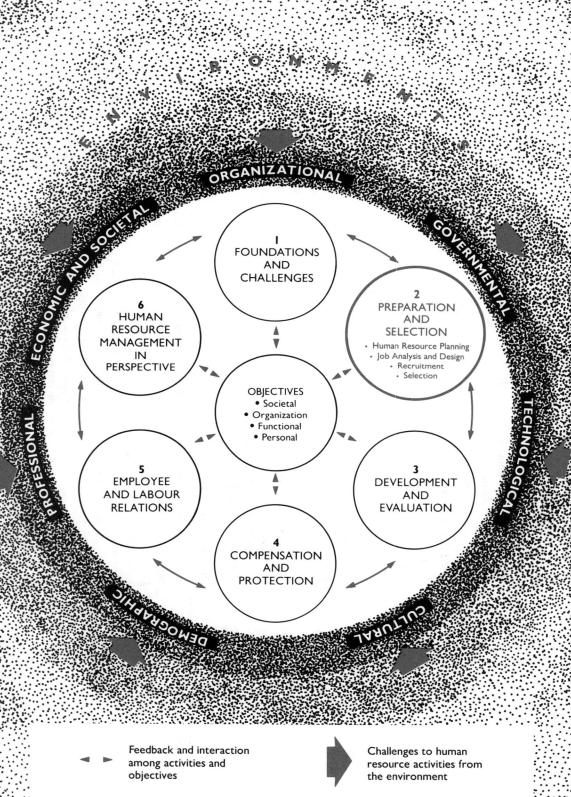

ENVIRONMENTS

ORGANIZATIONAL

ECONOMIC AND SOCIETAL

GOVERNMENTAL

PROFESSIONAL

TECHNOLOGICAL

DEMOGRAPHIC

CULTURAL

**1**
FOUNDATIONS
AND
CHALLENGES

**6**
HUMAN
RESOURCE
MANAGEMENT
IN
PERSPECTIVE

**2**
PREPARATION
AND
SELECTION
• Human Resource Planning
• Job Analysis and Design
• Recruitment
• Selection

OBJECTIVES
• Societal
• Organization
• Functional
• Personal

**5**
EMPLOYEE
AND LABOUR
RELATIONS

**3**
DEVELOPMENT
AND
EVALUATION

**4**
COMPENSATION
AND
PROTECTION

Feedback and interaction
among activities and
objectives

Challenges to human
resource activities from
the environment

# PART 2 ○○○○○○

## *PREPARATION AND SELECTION*

*T*he human resources department hires people to help the organization meet objectives. To staff the organization effectively, the department determines future human resource needs. Then it recruits and selects people to fill job openings. The next four chapters discuss the activities used to select employees. You are affected as either a personnel specialist or a manager because your success depends on the people you hire. Good selection decisions help assure good performance. You also are involved in the selection process each time you look for a job.

# CHAPTER 4 ○○○○○○

# *HUMAN RESOURCE PLANNING*

*Human resource planning can make or break an organization, particularly over the long term. Without effective human resource planning, an organization may find itself with a plant or an office without the people to run it productively.*

SHIMON L. DOLAN AND RANDALL S. SCHULER[1]

*Through human resource planning, management prepares to have the right people at the right places at the right times to fulfill both organizational and individual objectives.*[2]

JAMES W. WALKER

○ ○ ○ ○ ○ ○ ○ ○ ○ ○ ○ ○ ○ ○ ○ ○ ○ ○ ○ ○ ○ ○ ○ ○ ○ ○ ○ ○ ○ ○ ○

## *CHAPTER OBJECTIVES*

After studying this chapter, you should be able to:
1. Explain why large organizations use human resource planning more than small ones do.
2. Identify the factors that change an organization's demand for human resources.
3. Discuss the shortcomings of human resource forecasting techniques.
4. Develop a skills inventory as part of a human resource audit.
5. Recommend solutions to shortages or surpluses of human resources.
6. List the major approaches to accounting for human resources.

○ ○ ○ ○ ○ ○ ○ ○ ○ ○ ○ ○ ○ ○ ○ ○ ○ ○ ○ ○ ○ ○ ○ ○ ○ ○ ○ ○ ○ ○ ○

*P*erhaps, more than any other human resource activity, planning allows the human resource department to be proactive rather than reactive. This, in turn, improves the department's contribution to the organization's objectives.

SY WOLFE:   All I ever seem to do is "put out fires." Every day different department heads tell me they need new employees. Well, we are a service department, so we rush around and try to find someone. And I thought being a city personnel manager would be a snap.

JEAN-MARIE GASSE:   Why don't you do like we do in the police department and develop plans?

SY WOLFE:   Plans? How am I supposed to know who is going to quit?

JEAN-MARIE GASSE:   You don't need to know exactly. Try estimating job vacancies. No one tells us when crimes or accidents are going to happen. We try to anticipate the need for traffic and crime squads for each shift based on past experience.

SY WOLFE:   Your idea would be fine in a police department, but there are too many different jobs in city government to create human resource plans.

## OVERVIEW OF HUMAN RESOURCE PLANNING

Human resource planning systematically forecasts an organization's future demand for and supply of employees.[3] By estimating the number and types of employees that will be needed, the human resource department can better plan its recruitment, selection, training, career planning, and other activities. Human resource planning—or employment planning, as it is also called—allows the department to staff the organization at the right time with the right people. Not only can it help companies meet their equal-employment commitments, but human resource plans also help firms to achieve their overall goals and face environmental challenges more effectively and proactively.

Organizations need short-range and long-range plans for success and coping with change. Long-range strategic plans involve fundamental decisions about the very nature of business. Among other things, it may result in new organizational goals, new business acquisitions, divestiture of current product lines or subsidiaries, new management approaches, and ways of structuring internal activities. Short-range, tactical (or operational) plans deal with current operations and ways of meeting current challenges and using existing opportunities. Purchasing a new personal computing system to improve efficiency, recalling a defective product, managing inventory more effectively are some instances of tactical planning. Whatever type of plan is involved, plans are made and carried out by people. If an organization is not properly staffed with the right numbers and types of people, short- and long-range corporate plans may fail. Of course, production, financial, and marketing plans are important cornerstones of a company's strategic plans. More and more executives realize, however, that well-conceived human resource plans are another cornerstone of company plans.[4] For example, the decision of high-technology firms like Northern Telecom, IBM, and others to develop new products and enter new markets often depends on the availability of qualified technical and support staff. Without sufficient engineering talent, market opportunities can be lost to more appropriately staffed competitors.

At IBM, strategic business planning begins with "top down" revenue and profit targets established by the company's policy committee. Then, executives of the different business areas develop the strategies, product thrusts, and sales volumes needed to reset the policy committee's goals. From here, divisions of IBM create functional strategies for development, manufacturing, marketing, and service. Line managers are responsible for folding the functional plans into divisional ones. The human resource department's role is to review all divisional plans before they are sent to the top management. Although line managers have wide latitude in addressing human resource issues, human resource concerns are injected into the business plans by proactive human resource specialists who work closely with divisional managers. These managers are encouraged to involve human resource staff in decision making because the business plans will be reviewed for human resource considerations before they are finalized. Through their involvement in the strategic business planning process, IBM's human resource planners are better able to develop their corporate and functional human resource plans.[5]

Ideally, all organizations should identify their short-run and long-run employee needs through planning. Short-range plans point out job openings that must be filled during the coming year. Long-range plans estimate the human resource situation two, five, or occasionally ten years into the future. Examples of employment planning are more common in large organizations because it allows them to:

- **Improve** the utilization of human resources.
- **Match** human resource related activities and future organization objectives efficiently.
- **Achieve** economies in hiring new workers.
- **Expand** the human resource management information base to assist other human resource activities and other organizational units.
- **Make** major demands on local labour markets successfully.
- **Coordinate** different human resource management programs such as affirmative-action plans and hiring needs.

General Motors of Canada, Bell Canada Enterprises, Sears Canada, Alcan Aluminum, etc. are some of the largest employers in this country. G.M. of Canada employed about 46,000 persons in 1987 while Bell Canada's work force stood at a whopping 109,900 in the same year! Some of the other big employers in the country: Alcan (67,000), Sears (51,700), Campeau (65,000), Hudson's Bay (40,400) and McDonald's (52,000). The importance of employment planning to these organizations cannot be overemphasized.

Source: Canadian Business, Vol. 60, No. 6, June 1987, pp. 68-73.

A small organization can expect similar advantages, but the gains in effectiveness are often considerably less because its situation is less complex. In fact, the benefits of human resource planning for small firms may not justify the time and costs. Consider the different situations faced by a small- and large-city government.

Rural City employs twenty workers and is growing at a rate of 10% a year. Metropolis has 8,000 employees, and Sy Wolfe estimates it is growing by 5% annually. That means 400 new employees every year plus replacement for those who leave.

> If it costs $400 to find and hire a typical employee, Rural City will spend $800 to hire two more workers. Metropolis will spend $160,000 just to add new employees. If employment planning saves 25%, Rural City's manager cannot justify detailed planning efforts for $200. But for $40,000, Metropolis can afford a specialist and still save thousands of dollars after planning expenses are deducted.

Nevertheless, knowledge of human resource planning is useful to human resource specialists in *both* small and large organizations. It shows small employers the human resource considerations they will face should they expand rapidly. (For example, if Rural City attracted several large factories to its area, expansion of city services would depend partly on the city's human resource planning.) Large organizations can benefit from knowledge of employment planning because it reveals ways to make the human resource function more effective.

This chapter examines the two dimensions of human resource planning. It begins with an explanation of how the human resource department estimates future job openings and ends by showing the methods used by it to isolate potential sources of employees.

## THE DEMAND FOR HUMAN RESOURCES

An organization's future demand for people is central to employment planning. Most firms try to predict their future employment needs (at least informally), but they may not estimate their sources of supply. For example, one study found that employers are two times more likely to estimate demand than supply.[6] The challenges that determine this demand and the methods of forecasting it merit brief review.

*Causes of Demand*

Although countless challenges influence the demand for human resources, changes in the environment, the organization, and the work force are usually involved.[7] These factors are common to both short-range and long-range employment plans. The causes of these changes are summarized in Figure 4-1. Some of these causes are within the organization's control and others are not.

FIGURE 4-1   Causes of Demand for Human Resources in the Future

| EXTERNAL | ORGANIZATIONAL | WORK FORCE |
|---|---|---|
| • Economics | • Strategic plans | • Retirements |
| • Social-political-legal | • Budgets | • Resignations |
| • Technology | • Sales and production forecasts | • Terminations |
| • Competitors | • New ventures | • Deaths |
| | • Organization and job designs | • Leaves of absence |

*External Challenges*

Developments in the organization's environment are difficult for human resource specialists to predict in the short run and sometimes impossible to estimate in the long run. Reconsider the example of the small-city government. City planners seldom know of major factory relocations until shortly before construction begins. Other *economic* developments have a noticeable effect but are difficult to estimate. Examples include inflation, unemployment, and interest rates. High interest rates, for example, often curtail construction and the need for construction workers.

*Social-political-legal* challenges are easier to predict, but their implications are seldom clear. The impact on human resource planning of the Canadian Human Rights Act, passed in 1977, is still somewhat unclear. Although most large firms have established affirmative-action programs, the results of a change from the notion of ''equal pay for equal work'' to that of ''equal pay for work of equal value'' (see Chapter 3), will have profound implications. Likewise, the effect of patriating the Constitution with a Charter of Rights or the Meech Lake Accord will not really be known for many years.

*Technological* changes are difficult to predict and difficult to assess. Many thought the computer would mean mass unemployment, for example. Today it is a major growth industry employing hundreds of thousands directly or indirectly. Very often human resource planning is complicated by technology because it tends to reduce employment in one department while increasing it in another. The increasing popularity of robots in the work place as discussed in Chapter 2 also complicates future employment planning even more. The rapid computerization and automation of many work activities may also necessitate new skills on the part of employees. If there is a reduction in the number of young entry-level job seekers (a scenario that is considered realistic in Canada in the year 2000 and beyond), retraining the existing workers may become critical for most organizations.

*Competitors* are another external challenge that affects an organization's demand for human resources. Employment in the automobile and steel industries barely grows partially because of foreign competition. But in the electronics industry, competition causes lower prices, larger markets, and additional employment.

A major economic challenge facing Canadian organizations today is free trade with the U.S. While the exact form and consequences of free trade are hard to predict, it seems quite likely that in future years, restrictions on trade between these two countries will gradually decrease. If this happens, the effects on the employment situation in Canada could be very significant indeed. Freer trade with the U.S. will mean that more attention will be paid to improving the productivity of Canadian workers—which in turn could have a major impact on the number, quality, and wage levels of workers in different industries. Needless to point out, almost all human resource management functions, and especially human resource planning, will be affected by this proposed change. As mentioned in Chapter 2, free trade will continue to be a major challenge facing the human resource practitioners in this country.

## Organizational Decisions

Major organizational decisions affect the demand for human resources. The organization's *strategic plan* is the most influential decision.[8] It commits the firm to long-range objectives—such as growth rates and new products, markets, or services. These objectives determine the numbers and types of employees needed in the future. If long-term objectives are to be met, personnel specialists must develop long-range human resource plans that accommodate the strategic plan. In the short run, planners find that strategic plans become operational in the form of *budgets*. Budget increases or cuts are the most significant short-run influence on human resource needs.

*Sales and production forecasts* are less exact than budgets, but may provide even quicker notice of short-run changes in human resource demand.

> The human resource manager for a nationwide chain of furniture outlets observed a sharp decline in sales, brought on by a recession. The manager quickly discarded the short-run human resource plan and imposed an employment freeze on all outlets' hiring plans.

*New ventures* mean new human resource demands. When begun internally, the lead time may allow planners to develop short-run and long-run employment plans. But new ventures begun by acquisitions and mergers cause an immediate revision of human resource demands. For example, any one of these decisions can lead to new organization and job designs. A reorganization, especially after a merger or an acquisition, can radically alter human resource needs. Likewise, the redesign of jobs changes the required skill levels of future workers.

### Work-Force Factors

The demand for human resources is modified by employee actions. Retirements, resignations, terminations, deaths, and leaves of absence all increase the need for human resources. When large numbers of employees are involved, past experience usually serves as a reasonably accurate guide. However, reliance on past experiences means that human resource specialists must be sensitive to changes that upset past trends.

> Presently, Jim Santino keeps close track of employees nearing retirement so that his human resource plan remains accurate. Although the establishment of a mandatory retirement age in Canada is not considered discriminatory, as it is in the U.S., the law could change. In such a case, Jim could no longer use his past experience as a guide to predictions when older workers would retire. Such a change would force Jim to seek other ways of forecasting his short-term human resource needs.

### Forecasting Techniques

*Human resource forecasts* are attempts to predict an organization's future demand for employees. As Figure 4-2 shows, forecasting techniques range from the informal to the sophisticated. Even the most sophisticated methods are not perfectly accurate; instead, they are best viewed as approximations. Most firms make only casual estimates about the immediate future. As they gain experience with forecasting human resource needs, they may use more sophisticated techniques (especially if they can afford the specialized staff). Each of the forecasting methods in Figure 4-2 is explained below.

FIGURE 4-2    Forecasting Techniques for Estimating Future
Human Resource Needs

| EXPERT | TREND | OTHER |
|---|---|---|
| • Informal and instant decisions | • Extrapolation | • Budget and planning analysis |
|  | • Indexation |  |
| • Formal expert survey | • Statistical analysis | • New-venture analysis |
| • Delphi technique |  | • Computer models |

### Expert Forecasts

*Expert forecasters* rely on those who are knowledgeable to estimate future human resource needs. At the first level of complexity, the manager may simply be convinced that the work load justifies another employee.

> MANAGER:  Water and gas bills should be mailed by the tenth of each month. How come they haven't gone out?
> WORKER:  I know they should, but we are shorthanded. We used twenty-five hours overtime every week this month. And each billing cycle still takes thirty-four days.
> MANAGER:  Well, we better get human resources to hire us another clerk. We could pay the salary through lower overtime costs.

The example of the billing clerk illustrates an informal and instant forecast. But it is not part of a systematic planning effort. A better method is for planners to *survey* managers, who are the experts, about their department's future employment needs. The centralization of this information permits formal plans that identify the organization's future demand.

The survey may be an informal poll, a written questionnaire, or a focused discussion using the *nominal group technique* (NGT). The NGT presents a group of managers with a problem statement, such as, "What will cause our staffing needs to change over the next year?" Then each of the five to fifteen participants writes down as many answers as he or she can imagine. After about five to ten minutes, these ideas are shared in round-table fashion until all written ideas and any new ones they stimulated have been recorded. The group's ideas are then discussed and ranked by having each member of the group vote for the three to five most important ones.[9]

If the experts cannot be brought together, sophistication can be added to the survey approach with the Delphi technique. The *Delphi technique* solicits estimates from a group of experts, usually managers. Then human resource department planners act as intermediaries, summarizing the various responses and reporting the findings back to the experts. The experts are surveyed again after they get this feedback. Summaries and surveys are repeated until the experts' opinions begin to agree on future developments. (Usually four or five surveys are enough.) For example, the human resource department may survey all production supervisors and managers until an agreement is reached on the number of replacements needed during the next year.

*Trend Projection Forecasts*

①extrapolation
②indexation
③statistical analyses.

Perhaps the quickest forecasting technique is to project past trends. The two simplest methods are extrapolation and indexation. *Extrapolation* involves extending past rates of change into the future. For example, if an average of twenty production workers were hired each month for the past two years, extrapolation indicates that 240 production workers will probably be added during the upcoming year.

*Indexation* is a method of estimating future employment needs by matching employment growth with some index. A common example is the ratio of production employees to sales. For example, planners may discover that for each million-dollar increase in sales, the production department requires ten new assemblers.

Extrapolation and indexation are crude, short-run approximations because they assume that the causes of demand — external, organization, and work-force factors — remain constant, which is seldom the case. They are very inaccurate for long-range human resource projections. The more sophisticated *statistical analyses* make allowances for changes in the underlying causes of demand.[10]

*Other Forecasting Methods*

①budget analysis
②new venture analysis
③computers models

There are several other ways planners can estimate the future demand for human resources. One approach is through *budget and planning analysis.* Organizations that need human resource planning generally have detailed budgets and long-range plans. A study of department budgets reveals the financial authorizations for more employees. These data plus extrapolations of work-force changes (resignations, terminations, and the like) can provide short-run estimates of human resource needs. Long-term estimates can be made from each department or division's long-range plans.

When new ventures complicate employment planning, planners can use new-venture analysis. *New-venture analysis* requires planners to estimate human resource needs by comparison with firms that already perform similar operations. For example, a petroleum company that plans to open a coal mine can estimate its future employment needs by determining them from employment levels of other coal mines.

The most sophisticated forecasting approaches involve computers. *Computer models* are a series of mathematical formulas that simultaneously use extrapolation, indexation, survey results, and estimates of work-force changes to compute future human resource needs. Over time, actual changes in human resource demand are used to refine the computer's formulas.

> In the past, Weyerhaeuser Company, a leading lumber firm, used a sophisticated Markov-type model to plan its human resources. The model analyzed the flow of human resources from the supply point (whether internal or external) to the point of demand (requirements for specific jobs). The model also allowed the company's planners to identify transition rates (rates at which staff moved from one level to the next in the hierarchy) and to use them as constraints in balancing supply and demand for human resources. For instance, under the assumptions of varying transition rates, the company could forecast the work force supply and demand for different levels and different time periods. The Markov-type model enabled the policy makers of the company to analyze the impact of different policies on human resource supply and demand.[11]

FIGURE 4-3    Stages of Complexity and Sophistication in Human Resource Forecasting

| STAGE 1 | STAGE 2 | STAGE 3 |
|---|---|---|
| Managers discuss goals, plans, and thus types and numbers of people needed in the short term.<br>Highly informal and subjective. | Annual planning budgeting process includes human resource needs.<br><br>Specify quantity and quality of talent needs as possible.<br><br>Identify problems requiring action: individual or general. | Using computer-generated analyses, examine causes of problems and future trends regarding the flow of talent. Use computer to relieve managers of routine forecasting tasks (such as vacancies or turnover). |

Source: James W. Walker, "Evaluating the Practical Effectiveness of Human Resource Planning Applications," *Human Resource Management*, Spring 1974, p. 21.

One expert suggests that there are four levels of complexity in human resource forecasting.[12] These stages of forecasting sophistication are summarized in Figure 4-3. As can be seen, they range from informal discussions to highly complex computerized forecasting systems. The more sophisticated techniques are found among large organizations that have had years of experience in human resource planning. Small firms or those just beginning to forecast human resource needs are more likely to start with Stage 1 and progress to other stages as planners seek greater accuracy.

## Human Resource Requirements

Figure 4-4 depicts an overview of the key considerations involved in estimating demand for human resources. It shows that forecasts translate the causes of demand into short-

FIGURE 4-4    Components of the Future Demand for Human Resources

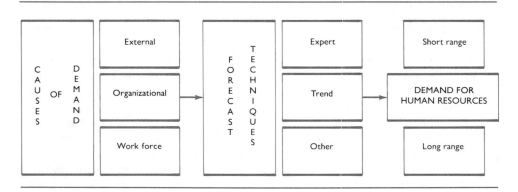

FIGURE 4-3   Stages of Complexity and Sophistication in Human Resource
             Forecasting (Continued)

**STAGE 4**

On-line modelling and computer simulation of talent
needs, flows, and costs to aid in a continuing process of
updating and projecting needs, staffing plans, career
opportunities, and thus program plans.

Provide best possible current information for managerial
decisions.

Exchange data with other companies and with government
(such as economic, employment, and social data).

range and long-range statements of needs. The resulting long-range plans are, of necessity, general statements of *probable* needs. Specific numbers are either omitted or estimated.

Short-term plans are more specific and may be reported as a staffing table, as in Figure 4-5. A *staffing table* lists the future employment needs for each type of job. The listing may be a specific number or an approximate range of needs, depending on the accuracy of the underlying forecast. Staffing tables (also called manning tables) are neither complete nor wholly accurate. They are only approximations. But these estimates allow human resource specialists to match short-run demand and supply. They help operating departments run more smoothly and can enhance the image of the human resource department.

> SY WOLFE:   If you are selected as the city's human resource planner, how will your employment projections help the city?
>
> JEAN-MARIE GASSE:   Earlier you commented that the human resource department spent considerable time reacting to daily requests for new employees. Some requests are for replacements, and others are for new employees for expanding city services. Right?
>
> SY WOLFE:   Yes, but . . .
>
> JEAN-MARIE GASSE:   My employment projections will allow your department to stop reacting to openings after the fact. Instead, people could be found and prepared in anticipation of job openings.
>
> SY WOLFE:   If we could do that, it would really reduce the disruptions managers experience while waiting for replacements to be found, assigned, and taught their jobs.
>
> JEAN-MARIE GASSE:   Yes. And their usual gripes about how long it takes the human resource department to fill jobs would diminish greatly.

With specific estimates of future human resource needs, personnel specialists can become more proactive and systematic. For example, a review of Figure 4-5 shows that

FIGURE 4-5   A Partial Staffing Table for a City Government

METROPOLIS
CITY GOVERNMENT
STAFFING TABLE

Date Compiled: _____

| Budget Code Number | Job Title (As Found) on Job Description | Using Department(s) | Anticipated Openings by Months of the Year | | | | | | | | | | | | |
|---|---|---|---|---|---|---|---|---|---|---|---|---|---|---|---|
| | | | Total | 1 | 2 | 3 | 4 | 5 | 6 | 7 | 8 | 9 | 10 | 11 | 12 |
| 100-32 | Police Recruit | Police | 128 | 32 | | | 32 | | | 32 | | | 32 | | |
| 100-33 | Police Dispatcher | Police | 3 | 2 | | | | | 1 | | | | | | |
| 100-84 | Meter Reader | Police | 24 | 2 | 2 | 2 | 2 | 2 | 2 | 2 | 2 | 2 | 2 | 2 | 2 |
| 100-85 | Traffic Supervisor | Police | 5 | 2 | | | 1 | | | 1 | | | 1 | | |
| 100-86 | Team Supervisor —Police (Sergeant) | Police | 5 | 2 | | | 1 | | | 1 | | | 1 | | |
| 100-97 | Duty Supervisor —Police (Staff Sergeant) | Police | 2 | 1 | | | | | 1 | | | | | | |
| 100-99 | Shift Officer— Police (Inspector) | Police | 1 | 1 | | | | | | | | | | | |
| 200-01 | Car Washer | Motor Pool | 4 | 1 | | | 1 | | | 1 | | | 1 | | |
| 200-12 | Mechanic's Assistant | Motor Pool | 3 | | | | 1 | | | 1 | | | 1 | | |
| 200-13 | Mechanic III | Motor Pool | 2 | 1 | | | | | | | | | 1 | | |
| 200-14 | Mechanic II | Motor Pool | 1 | | | | | | 1 | | | | | | |
| 200-15 | Mechanic I (Working Supervisor) | Motor Pool | 1 | 1 | | | | | | | | | | | |
| 300-01 | Clerk IV | Administration | 27 | 10 | | | 5 | | | 6 | | | 6 | | |

the city's personnel department must hire thirty-two police academy recruits every three months. This knowledge allows recruiters in the personnel department to plan their recruiting campaign so that it peaks about six weeks before the beginning of the next police academy class. The advanced planning allows the department to screen applicants and notify them at least three weeks before the class begins. For those still in school or otherwise unable to be ready that quickly, recruiters can inform them when the following class begins. If the personnel department waited for the police department to notify them, notification might come too late to allow a systematic recruiting and screening process. Staffing tables enable recruiters to be proactive and better plan their activities.

## THE SUPPLY OF HUMAN RESOURCES

Once the human resource department makes projections about future human resource demands, the next major concern is filling projected openings. There are two sources of supply: internal and external. The internal supply consists of present employees who can be promoted, transferred, or demoted to meet anticipated needs. For example, Jean-

Marie Gasse (in the previous dialogue) works in the police department of Metropolis but is applying for a transfer into the personnel department. She is part of the internal supply of human resources to the city government. The external supply consists of people in the labour market who do not work for the city. These include employees of other organizations and those who are unemployed.

Figure 4-6 illustrates the major supply considerations that confront human resource planners. As can be seen, internal and external considerations are intertwined. For ease of explanation, they are discussed separately.

FIGURE 4-6   Factors that Determine the Future Supply of Human Resources

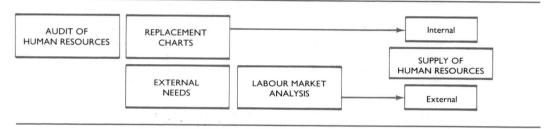

## Internal Supply Estimates

Estimates of the internal supply are more than merely counting the number of employees. As Figure 4-6 implies, planners audit the present work force to learn about the capabilities of present workers. This information allows planners to estimate tentatively which openings can be filled by present employees. These tentative assignments usually are recorded on a replacement chart. Considering present employees for future job openings is important if workers are to have life-long careers with their employer rather than just dead-end jobs. Audits and replacement charts also are important additions to the personnel department's information base. With greater knowledge of employees, the department can more effectively plan recruiting, training, and career-planning activities. A human resource department can also help meet its affirmative-action goals by identifying internal minority candidates for job openings. Since audits and replacement charts are important to proactive human resource work, they are explained more fully below.[13]

### Human Resource Audits

Human resource audits summarize each employee's skills and abilities. When referring to nonmanagers, the audits result in *skills inventories*. Audits of managers are called *management inventories*. Whatever name is used, an inventory catalogues each comprehensive understanding of the capabilities found in the organization's work force.

An example of a skills inventory is found in Figure 4-7. It is divided into four parts. Part I can be completed by the human resource department from employee records. It identifies the employee's job title, experience, age, and previous jobs. Part II seeks information about skills, duties, responsibilities, and education of the worker. From these questions, planners learn about the mix of employee abilities. The human resource department may collect these data through phone or face-to-face interviews. Or the questions may be sent to the employee through the company mail.

FIGURE 4-7   Skills Inventory Form for Metropolis City Government

---

**Part I** (To be completed by human resource department)

1. **Name** _____    2. **Employee Number** _____
3. **Job Title** _____    4. **Experience** _____Years
5. **Age** _____    6. **Years with City** _____
7. **Other Jobs Held:**

    **With City:**    Title _____From _____to _____

                        Title _____From _____to _____

    **Elsewhere:**    Title _____From _____to _____

Title _____From _____to _____

**Part II** (To be completed by employee)

8. **Special Skills.** List below any skills you possess, even if they are not used in your present job. Include types and names of machines or tools with which you are experienced.

        **Skills:** _____

                      _____

  **Machines:** _____
      **Tools:** _____

9. **Duties.** Briefly describe your present duties. _____

---

10. **Responsibilities.** Briefly describe your responsibilities for:

**City Equipment:** _____
**City Funds:** _____
**Employee Safety:** _____
**Employee Supervision:**

11. **Education.** Briefly describe your education and training background:

|  | **Years Completed** | **Year of Graduation** | **Degree and Major** |
|---|---|---|---|
| **High School:** | _____ | _____ | _____ |
| **University:** | _____ | _____ | _____ |
| **Job Training:** | _____ | _____ | _____ |
| **Special Courses:** | _____ | _____ | _____ |

**Part III** (To be completed by human resource department with supervisory inputs)

12. **Overall Evaluation of Performance** _____

13. **Overall Readiness for Promotion** _____
    **To What Job(s):** _____
        **Comments:** _____
14. **Current Deficiencies** _____

15. **Supervisor's Signature** _____    **Date:**_____

**Part IV** (To be completed by human resource department representative)

16. **Are the two most recent performance evaluations attached?**    ___Yes ___No
17. **Prepared by** _____    **Date:** _____

---

The employee's potential is briefly summarized by the immediate supervisor in Part III. Performance, readiness for promotion, and any deficiencies are noted here. The supervisor's signature helps ensure that the form's accuracy is reviewed by someone who knows the employee better than the human resource specialists. Part IV is added as a final check for completeness and for the addition of recent employee evaluations, which give more insight into past performance.

To be useful, inventories of human resources must be updated periodically. Updating every two years is sufficient for most organizations if employees are encouraged to report major changes to the human resource department when they occur. Major changes include new skills, degree completions, changed job duties, and the like. Failure to update skills inventories can lead to present employees being overlooked for job openings within the organization.

Management inventories should be updated periodically, since they also are used for key human resource related decisions. In fact, some employers use the same form for managers and nonmanagers. When the forms differ, the management inventory requests information about management activities. Common topics include:

- Number of employees supervised
- Types of employees supervised
- Total budget managed

- Management training received
- Duties of subordinates
- Previous management duties

### Replacement Charts

Replacement charts are a visual representation of who will replace whom in the event of a job opening. The information for constructing the chart comes from the human resource audit. Figure 4-8 illustrates a typical replacement chart. It shows the replacement status of only a few jobs in the administration of a large city.

Although different firms may seek to summarize different information in their replacement charts, the figure indicates the minimum information usually included. The chart, which is much like an organization chart, depicts the various jobs in the organization and shows the status of likely candidates. Replacement status consists of two variables: present performance and promotability. Present performance is determined largely from supervisory evaluations. Opinions of other managers, peers, and subordinates may contribute to the appraisal of present performance. Future promotability is based primarily on present performance and the estimates by immediate superiors of future success in a new job. The human resource department may contribute to these estimates through the use of psychological tests, interviews, and other methods of assessment. Replacement charts often show the candidates' ages.

Human resource and management decision makers find these charts provide a quick reference. Their shortcoming is that they contain little information.[14] To supplement the chart—and, increasingly, to supplant it—human resource specialists develop replacement summaries. *Replacement summaries* list likely replacements and their relative strengths and weaknesses for each job. As Figure 4-9 shows, the summaries provide considerably more data than the replacement chart. This additional information allows decision makers to make more informed decisions.

Most companies that are sophisticated enough to engage in detailed human resource planning computerize their human resource records, including job analysis information and human resource inventories. Then through a simple computer program, planners can compile replacement summaries each time a job opening occurs. These summaries also show which positions lack human resource backups.

FIGURE 4-8   A Partial Replacement Chart for a Municipal Government

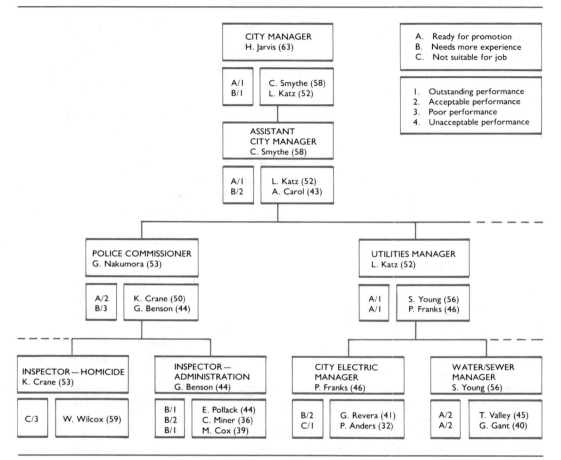

Canada Grocers Ltd., which has a chain of grocery stores in five Canadian provinces, has computerized its search for fast trackers in the organization. Every six months, the organization's managers submit performance appraisals to the human resource department indicating the promotability of their subordinates. By consolidating these reports on a computer, the company has been able to identify the "outstanding" workers. A separate program helps produce career-development plans, pinpointing weaknesses and suggesting solutions — university courses, in-house training on a different job assignment.

In the long run, the human resource department can encourage employees to upgrade their capabilities and prepare for future vacancies. In the short run, an opening without a suitable replacement requires that someone be hired from the external labour market.

FIGURE 4-9   A Replacement Summary for the Position of City Manager

---

**Replacement Summary for the Position of** City Manager

| | |
|---|---|
| **Present Office Holder**   Harold Jarvis | **Age**   63 |
| **Probable Opening**   In two years | **Reason**   Retirement |
| **Salary Grade**   99 ($78,500 yearly) | **Experience**   8 years |

**Candidate 1**   Clyde Smythe

**Current Position**   Assistant City Manager

**Current Performance**   Outstanding          **Explanation**   Clyde's performance evaluations by the City Manager are always the highest possible.

**Promotability**   Ready now for promotion.     **Explanation**   During an extended illness of the City Manager, Clyde assumed all duties successfully, including major policy decisions and negotiations with city unions.

**Training Needs**   None

**Age**   58

**Experience**   4 years

**Candidate 2**   Larry Katz

**Current Position**   Utilities Manager

**Current Performance**   Outstanding          **Explanation**   Larry's performance has kept costs of utilities to citizens 10 to 15% below that of comparable city utilities through careful planning.

**Promotability**   Needs more experience.     **Explanation**   Larry's experience is limited to utilities management. Although successful, he needs more broad administrative experience in other areas. (He is ready for promotion to Assistant City Manager at this time.)

**Training Needs**   Training in budget preparation and public relations would be desirable before promotion to City Manager.

**Age**   52

**Experience**   5 years

---

Whether replacement charts or summaries are used, this information is normally kept confidential. Confidentiality not only guards the privacy of employees, but prevents dissatisfaction among those who are not immediately promotable.

## External Supply Estimates

Not every future opening can be met with present employees. Some jobs lack replacements to fill an opening when it occurs. Other jobs are entry-level positions; that is, they are beginning jobs that are filled by people who do not presently work for the organization. When there are no replacements or when the opening is for an entry-level job, there is a need for external supplies of human resources.

## External Needs

Employer growth and the effectiveness of the human resource department largely determine the need for external supplies of human resources. Growth is primarily responsible for the number of entry-level job openings. Obviously, a fast-growing firm has more beginning-level vacancies. The number of higher-level openings also depends on how well the human resource department assists employees to develop their capabilities. If workers are not encouraged to expand their capabilities, they may not be ready to fill future vacancies. The lack of promotable replacements creates job openings that need to be filled externally.

### Labour Market Analysis

The human resource department's success in finding new employees depends on the labour market. Even when unemployment rates are high, many needed skills are difficult to find.

> In January 1984 the unemployment rate was 12.4%. However, human resource departments that sought managers and administrators had to compete in a labour market with only 4.7% of these people unemployed.[15]

In the short run, the national unemployment rate serves as an approximate measure of how difficult it is to acquire new employees. Personnel specialists realize that this rate varies for different groups as well as from province to province and city to city.

> In 1986 there were some wide variations. The unemployment rate in Ontario during the year was 7%. But in Newfoundland the rate was 20%.[16]

Regardless of the unemployment rate, external needs may be met by attracting employees who work for others. In the long run, local developments and demographic trends have the most significant impact on labour markets.[17] Local developments include community growth rates and attitudes. For example, many farm towns find their population declining. When they attempt to attract new business, employers fear declining population may mean future shortages in the local labour market. So the new businesses often locate elsewhere. The lack of jobs results in still more people leaving the local labour market. Conversely, growing cities are attractive to employers because they promise even larger labour markets in the future.

### Community Attitudes

Community attitudes also affect the nature of the labour market. Antibusiness or no-growth attitudes may cause present employers to move elsewhere. The loss of jobs forces middle-class workers to relocate, and the shrinking work force discourages new businesses from becoming established.

### Demographics

Demographic trends are another long-term development that affects the availability of external supply. Fortunately for planners, these trends are known years in advance of their impact.

> The low birth rates of the 1930s and early 1940s were followed by a baby boom during the late 1940s and 1950s. When the post-World War II babies started to

go to university in the 1960s, the low birth rates of the 1930s led to a shortage of university teachers. These demographic trends were already in motion by 1950. Long-range human resource planning, which was sensitive to demographic developments, could have predicted the shortage soon enough for proactive universities to take corrective action.

Canada Employment and Immigration Commission publishes both short- and long-term labour force projections. One document, *Ford Occupational Imbalance Listing* (FOIL), is a quarterly publication that estimates both labour market demands (by occupation) and supply characteristics. A longer-term projection, typically six years, is provided by the *Canada Occupational Forecasting Program* (COFOR).[18] This document is available in both national and provincial versions, covers more than 500 occupational groups in its projections, but it forecasts only demand requirements. Until recently, COFOR was the major tool used by the federal government to forecast labour market trends.

The Economic Council of Canada has developed another model that is useful in predicting the Canadian economy. The model called CANDIDE—*Canadian Disaggregated Interdepartmental Econometric Model*—which uses over 1500 regression equations to forecast unemployment, real domestic product, etc., is yet another source of information for the human resource planner on the future shape of the Canadian economy.[19]

Yet another source of information on the supply and demand for human resources in Canada is the sophisticated *Canadian Occupational Projection System* (COPS) initiated by Employment and Immigration Canada in 1982.[20] COPS projects the demand for and supply of occupations in Canada and the provinces for up to ten years. Such expanded forecasting capability enables the national planners to identify domestic skill imbalances. For the human resource manager as well such information is invaluable.

*Microelectronics Simulation Model*[21] (or MESIM, as it is popularly known) aims to incorporate the impact of technological change on the occupational composition in this country. The new computer-based technology has changed the fundamental nature of Canadian industry and the skills required in our contemporary society. MESIM is able to incorporate these fundamental shifts in our labour market and forecast the occupational composition in Canada.

Indeed, Canada is one of the few (if not the first) western industrialized countries to adopt industrial human resource planning. The Northern Pipelines Act and the Canada Oil and Gas Act, which contain clauses requiring the partner companies to develop comprehensive human resource plans, is indicative of this country's commitment to human resource planning at the national level.[22]

To build the 2,100 miles of pipeline in Canada, the Alaska Highway Gas Pipeline would require 17,000 person-years. This would necessitate close cooperation among the managements of the firms involved, their labour unions, and the governments (municipal, provincial, and federal) involved. Clearly, a sophisticated human resource plan would be absolutely necessary in this instance.

Statistics Canada also publishes reports on labour-force conditions on a monthly, quarterly, annual, and occasional basis. Information is available on: total labour force projections by geographic, demographic, and occupational variables; labour income;

census data; and population projections by sex and province over various years. For example, Figure 4-10 shows the projected composition of the work force by age for 1990 and 1995. These data have implications for many businesses.

FIGURE 4-10   Changes in the Total Labour Force

| AGE, BOTH SEXES | PROJECTED NUMBERS (Thousands) | |
| | 1990 | 1995 |
| --- | --- | --- |
| 16 years and over: | 20,821 | 22,013 |
| 16 to 24 | 3,569 | 3,557 |
| 25 to 54 | 12,012 | 12,891 |
| 25 to 34 | 4,997 | 4,702 |
| 35 to 44 | 4,201 | 4,705 |
| 45 to 54 | 2,814 | 3,484 |
| 55 years and over: | 5,239 | 5,565 |
| 55 to 64 | 2,308 | 2,340 |
| 65 and over | 2,931 | 3,225 |

Source: Statistics Canada, *Population Projections for Canada and the Provinces 1976-2001*, Catalogue 91-520, Ottawa: Industry, Trade and Commerce, 1979.

> Fast-food restaurants depend on sixteen- to twenty-four-year olds for many jobs. But by 1995 this group will have declined by approximately 500,000 from the 1985 figure of 4,036,000. At the same time, population growth and the trend towards eating more meals away from home will cause an increased demand for fast-food employees.

## IMPLEMENTATION OF HUMAN RESOURCE PLANS

Figure 4-11 summarizes the key concepts discussed throughout the chapter. The left side

FIGURE 4-11   Supply and Demand Consideration in Human Resource Planning

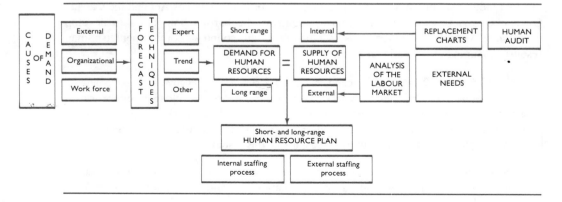

of the figure identifies the major causes of human resource demand, which are external, organizational, and work-force factors. These causes of demand are forecast by experts, trend data, or other methods to determine the short- and long-range demand for human resources. This demand is fulfilled either internally by present employees or externally by newcomers. The internal supply is shown in replacement charts, which are based on audits of the organization's human resources. Sources of external candidates are identified by analysis of the labour market. The results include short- and long-range human resource plans that are fulfilled by an internal and external staffing process.

## OVERSUPPLY OF EMPLOYEES

Once the supply and demand of human resources are estimated, adjustments may be needed. When the internal supply of workers exceeds the firm's demand, a human resource surplus exists. Most employers respond to a surplus with a hiring freeze. This freeze stops the human resource department from filling openings with external applications. Instead, present employees are reassigned. Voluntary departures, called *attrition*, slowly reduce the surplus.[23] Attrition is the normal separation of employees from an organization as a result of resignation, retirement, or death. It is initiated by the individual worker and not by the company. In most organizations, the key component of attrition is resignation, which is a voluntary separation. Although attrition is a slow way to reduce the employment base in an organization, it presents the fewest problems. Voluntary departures simply create a vacancy that is not filled, and the staffing level declines without anyone being forced out of a job.

> Faced with a surplus of employees and a slow-growing economy, a major bank resorted to an employment freeze in the early 1980s. On average, its attrition rate was 4%; within eighteen months, it had reduced its staff level from 40,000 to about 37,600.

A special form of attrition is early retirement. It is one form of separation that the human resource department can actively control. It is used to reduce staffing levels and to create internal job openings. Early retirement plans are designed to encourage long-service workers to retire before the normal retirement age in the organization (say, sixty-five years). Since employees who retire before age sixty-five are going to draw benefits longer, their monthly retirement benefits may be reduced proportionately.

Reducing the number of total work hours through job sharing and part-time work is yet another strategy used by firms to cope with a temporary surplus of workers. *Job sharing* involves dividing duties of a single position between two or more employees.[24] The employees benefit by having more free time at their disposal. From the employer's point of view, this eliminates the need to lay off one employee completely. The use of part-time workers also increases the employer's flexibility to meet peak demands without having to increase the total number of workers on permanent full-time payroll. Indeed, part-time work is growing so much in popularity in Canada that by the year 2000 it is expected to account for about 20% of all employment in this country (currently, 15% of employment time in Canada is worked by part-time employees).

In 1977 the federal government introduced a *work-sharing scheme*, by which the employees worked only for part of the week and received unemployment insurance on other days.[25] This was a layoff-avoidance strategy designed by the government whereby all employees in a work group or unit share part of the lay-off.

> Through work-sharing arrangements, Pratt and Whitney Aircraft of Canada ensured that 300 employees were not completely laid off and that their jobs were saved even during the recession in the late 1970s. In the Motorola Company, 100 employees were asked to work for four days a week (rather than five). The result: the company was able to save twenty jobs.[26]

*Layoffs*, the temporary withdrawal of employment to workers, are also used in cases of a short-run surplus. Layoffs are the separation of employees from the organization for economic or business reasons. The separation may last only a few weeks if its purpose is to adjust inventory levels or to allow the factory to retool for a new product. When caused by a business cycle, the layoffs may last many months or even years. However, if the layoff is the result of a restructuring or rescaling of an industry, the "temporary" layoffs may be permanent.[27]

As unpleasant as layoffs are for both workers and management, they may be required when attrition is insufficient to reduce employment to acceptable levels. In some organizations, each employee who is laid off may receive a supplemental unemployment benefit over and above the Unemployment Insurance benefits. However, during severe economic downturns, the employer's ability to provide these benefits may become seriously jeopardized.

When the layoffs are expected to be of a short duration — as when an automobile plant temporarily closes to change its tooling for a new model — layoffs may not follow the normal pattern of forcing the most recently hired employee to accept unemployment. Rather than following seniority, some contracts have "juniority" clauses. *Juniority* provisions require that layoffs be offered first to senior workers. If the senior worker wants to accept the layoff, that person collects unemployment insurance and the other organizational benefits and the juniors keep their jobs. Senior workers are likely to accept layoffs of short duration because they receive almost the same take-home pay without working. When the layoff is of an unknown duration, the seniors usually decline to exercise their juniority rights and fewer senior employees are put on layoff.

Of course, employees may be separated by termination of the employment relationship. *Termination* is a broad term that encompasses the permanent separation from the organization for any reason. Usually this term implies that the person was fired as a form of discipline. When people are discharged for business or economic reasons, it is commonly, although not always, called a layoff. Sometimes, however, the employer needs to separate some employee for business reasons and has no plans to rehire them. Rather than being laid off, those people are simply terminated. In these cases, the employees may receive severance pay and outplacement assistance.

*Severance pay* is money — often equal to one or more week's salary — that is given to employees who are being permanently separated. Many organizations give severance pay only for involuntary separations and only to employees who have been performing satisfactorily.[28] For example, if a factory is going to close and move operations to another province, employees who are terminated may be given an extra week's salary for each year they have worked for the organization. Some organizations have developed innovative severance pay policies to achieve their human resource objectives, as the following example illustrates:

> Herman Miller, Inc., the world's second largest manufacturer of office furniture, developed a novel approach to severance pay, called a "silver parachute." Unlike the "golden parachutes" offered only to senior executives at firms likely to be targets of a takeover, the "silver parachutes" extend to all 35,000 of the company's employees. "The parachute would be activated in the event of a hostile takeover, and the rip cord would be pulled if a worker's job were eliminated, salary reduced or working conditions or benefits altered."[29]
>
> This unusual form of severance pay would be paid in ten days if terminations occurred. Those employees with between one and five years would receive twice their previous twelve-month compensation. Longer service employees receive 2.5 times their previous twelve months' salary. Besides assuring employees of severance pay should they lose their job in a hostile takeover, this benefit makes the company a less attractive takeover target.[30]

The blow of discharge may be softened through formal *outplacement* procedures, which help present employees find new jobs with other firms. These efforts may include the provision of office space, secretarial services, photocopying machines, long-distance phone calls, counselling, instructions on how to look for work, and even invitations to competitors to meet with employees.[31] Not only do such efforts help the former employee, but they give evidence to the remaining employees of management's commitment to their welfare.

## SHORTAGE OF EMPLOYEES

If the internal supply of human resources can not fulfil the organization's needs, a human resource *shortage* exists. Planners have little flexibility in the short run. Some of the typical actions used are transfer and promotion of employees within the organization; it should, however, be noted that these actions result in the creation of a vacancy in another part of the same organization.

Transfers occur when an employee is moved from one job to another that is relatively equal in pay, responsibility, and/or organizational level. Besides improving the utilization of their human resources, organizations can also make them beneficial to jobholders. The broadening experience of a transfer may provide a person with new skills and a different perspective that makes him or her a better candidate for future promotions. Transfers may even improve an individual's motivation and satisfaction, especially when a person finds little challenge in the old job. The new position, although not a promotion, may offer new technical and interpersonal challenges. In turn, these challenges may prove to be a growth opportunity for the transferee. Even when the challenges are minimal, the transfer at least offers some variety, which may enhance feelings of job satisfaction. However, as Pinder and Das[32] observed, there may be hidden costs associated with transfers, such as the psychological stress and social uprooting of the transferee and his/her family. In the case of two-career families (where both spouses pursue careers), it may be difficult to persuade an employee to move to a place where his/her spouse cannot attain career progress.

A *promotion* occurs when an employee is moved from one job to another that is higher in pay, responsibility, and/or organizational level. It is one of the more pleasant events that happens to people in an organization. Generally, it is given as a recognition of a person's past performance and future promise. Promotions usually are based on merit and/or seniority.[33] Merit-based promotions occur when an employee is promoted because of superior performance in the present job. However, promotion as a "reward" for past efforts and successes may raise two major problems. One problem is whether decision makers can objectively distinguish the strong performers from the weak ones. When merit-based promotions are being used, it is important that the decision reflect the individual's performance and not the biases of the decision maker.[34] An example would be when the best performer is a member of a protected class and the decision maker is prejudiced. The decision maker should not allow personal prejudices to affect promotions. Decisions that are swayed by personal feelings are more common when job performance is not measured objectively. When promotion decisions result from personal biases, the organization ends up with a less competent person in a higher, more important position. The resulting resentment among those not promoted is likely to harm their motivation and satisfaction.

A second problem with merit-based promotions is put forth in the *Peter Principle*.[35] It states that in a hierarchy people tend to rise to their level of *incompetence*. Although not universally true, the "principle" suggests that good performance in one job is no guarantee of good performance in another. For example, if one of the new engineers hired at Bell Canada consistently made major cost-saving design changes, that would be an example of superior performance. However, suppose the engineer were promoted to supervisor. The skills needed to be an effective supervisor are very different from those needed to be a top engineer. As a result of such a promotion, Bell Canada might gain an ineffective supervisor and lose a superior engineer.

In some situations, the most senior employee gets the promotion. "Senior" in this case means the employee who has the longest service with the employer. The advantage of this approach is that it is objective. All one needs to do is compare the seniority records of the candidates to determine who should be promoted.

Part of the rationale for this approach is to eliminate biased promotions and to require management to develop its senior employees since they will eventually be promoted. Seniority-based promotions usually are limited to hourly employees. For example, a promotion from mechanic second class to mechanic first class may occur automatically by seniority whenever an opening for mechanic first class occurs. Labour organizations often seek this type of promotion to prevent employers discriminating among union members.

Most human resource experts express concern about the competency of those promoted solely because of seniority since not all workers are equally capable. Sometimes the person who is the best mechanic, for example, is not the most senior one. Under seniority-based promotions, the best person is denied the job unless the individual happens to be the most senior worker as well. This approach to promotion causes human resource departments to focus their efforts on training senior workers to ensure that they are prepared to handle future promotions.[36] In addition, the human resource department must be concerned with maintaining an accurate seniority list. When promotions are not based solely on seniority, both *merit* and seniority are guiding factors.

## ACCOUNTING FOR HUMAN RESOURCES

Whether staffing needs are met internally or externally, planners must always consider their employer's affirmative action plans. The plan, as discussed in Chapter 3, contains the organization's strategy for undoing past discrimination and guarding against future discrimination. As internal and external candidates are selected to fill job openings, these decisions must match the goals and timetables found in the affirmative-action plan. The human resource plan also indicates how likely it is that the employer's affirmative-action goals will be met. For example, even modest goals of increasing minority representation in a company are unlikely to be met if the human resource plan indicates that no new hiring is planned and the company intends to reduce overall employment through attrition.

The human resource plan does more than serve as a check on the likelihood of the affirmative-action plan's success. It is an important part of an organization's *human resource information system*. The information contained in the plan serves as a guide to recruiters, trainers, career planners, and other human resource specialists. With the knowledge of the firm's internal and external employment needs, human resource specialists, operating managers, and individual employees can direct their efforts towards the organization's future staffing needs. Managers can groom their employees through specific training and development efforts. Even individual employees can prepare themselves for future openings through education and other self-help efforts.

*Human Resource Accounting* (or HRA as it is popularly known) has also been gaining in popularity in recent years. HRA is the process of identifying, measuring, accounting and forecasting the value of human resources in order to facilitate effective management of an organization.[37] HRA attempts to put a dollar figure on the human assets of an organization. In Chapter 1 of this book, it was pointed out that human resources constitute the single most important asset of any organization. However, unless this asset is valued, an organization will not be able to have any idea of the changes in the value and composition of human resources. Besides, HRA enables an organization to receive complete information on the costs of staff turnover; valid estimates of the usefulness of organizational training programs on a regular basis are also available in organizations that implement HRA.[38] It is also suggested by some writers that the ratio of investments in human resources to total assets acts as an indicator of an organization's potential to generate future revenues and profits.[39] Measures of human resources are, thus, likely to be relevant and useful in several phases of human resource planning, development, and compensation decisions.

The various models of HRA currently in vogue can be broadly classified into two groups:[40] *cost* models and *value* models. The cost models attempt to place a dollar value on human assets based on some kind of cost calculation—acquisition, replacement, or opportunity costs. The value-based models, on the other hand, attempt to evaluate human resources on the basis of their economic value to the organization.

Whatever the approach used, most HRA models involve some degree of subjective assignment of a dollar figure to an employee's services and contribution to the organization.[41] Some writers and practitioners feel that the nature of human assets is such that any attempt to quantify them may be unrealistic and fruitless.[42] Investments in people also have been considered more tenuous than investments in physical assets, and accountants have chosen to ignore their investment character. Despite these criticisms, HRA might be a blessing to salary administrators, trainers, human resource planners, and union-management negotiators if it provides them with the kind of objective and reliable information they have long needed to plan these functions.

## SUMMARY

Human resource planning requires considerable time, staff, and financial resources. The return on this investment may not justify the expenditure for small firms. Increasingly, however, large organizations use human resource planning as a means of achieving greater effectiveness. Human resource planning is an attempt by companies to estimate their future needs and supplies of human resources. Through an understanding of the factors that influence the demand for workers, planners can forecast specific short-term and long-term needs.

Given some anticipated level of demand, planners try to estimate the availability of present workers to meet that demand. Such estimates begin with an audit of present employees. Possible replacements are then identified. Internal shortages are resolved by seeking new employees in the external labour markets. Surpluses are reduced by normal attrition, leaves of absence, layoffs, or terminations.

As can be seen in Figure 4-11, both the external and internal staffing processes are used to meet human resource plans. The figure also summarizes the key concepts discussed in this chapter. The usefulness of human resource accounting to human resource specialists was also outlined in this chapter. Chapters 7, 8, and 9 explain the external staffing process in detail. The remaining chapters focus on the various issues involved in the internal staffing process.

## TERMS FOR REVIEW

Strategic plan
Forecasts
Delphi technique
Extrapolation
Indexation
Staffing table
Skills inventories
Replacement charts

Replacement summaries
Labour market analysis
Attrition
Job sharing
Work sharing
Outplacement
Human resource accounting

## REVIEW AND DISCUSSION QUESTIONS

1.  Why is human resource planning more common among large organizations than among small ones? What are the advantages of human resource planning for large organizations?
2.  List and briefly describe the factors that cause an organization's demand for human resources to change.

3. What is a staffing table? Of what use is it to human resource planners?

4. What is the purpose of a human resource audit? Specifically, what information acquired from a human resource audit is needed to construct a replacement chart?

5. Suppose human resource planners estimated that several technological innovations suggested that your firm will need 25% fewer employees in three years. What actions would you take today?

6. Suppose you managed a restaurant in a winter resort area. During the summer it was profitable to keep the business open, but you need only one-half the cooks, table servers, and bartenders. What actions would you take in April when the peak tourist season ended?

7. If your company locates its research and development offices in downtown Windsor, Ontario, the city is willing to forgo city property taxes on the building for ten years. The city is willing to make this concession to help reduce its high unemployment rate. Calgary, Alberta, your company's other choice, has a low unemployment rate and is not offering any tax breaks. Based on just these considerations, which city would you recommend and why?

8. Assume you are the human resource manager in a Canadian university employing approximately 300 faculty members. Since these faculty members constitute a "valuable" resource of your organization, you decided to install an accounting procedure for changes in the value of this asset. How will you go about it. What problems do you anticipate in the process?

## INCIDENT 4-1

### Eastern University's Human Resource Needs

For years Eastern University had operated at a deficit. This loss was made up from the provincial budget, since Eastern was provincially supported. Because of the inflation of the 1970s and 1980s, the drain on the province's budget had tripled to $71 million by 1985.

Several members of the provincial cabinet had heard that university enrolments were to continue to decline during the 1990s. A decline in enrolment would lead to overstaffing and even larger deficits. The president of the university hired Bill Barker to develop a long-range human resource plan for the university. An excerpt from his report stated:

The declining birth rates of the 1960s and 1970s mean that there will be a decline in university-age students at least to the year 2000. If the university is to avoid soaring deficits, it must institute an employment freeze now. Furthermore, a committee should be formed to develop new curricula that appeal to those segments of the work force that are going to experience rapid growth between now and the year 2000.

Zach Taylor, president of Eastern University, argued, "An employment freeze would cut the university off from hiring new faculty members who have the latest training in new areas. Besides, our enrolments have grown by 2 to 4% every year since 1980. I see no reason to doubt that trend will continue."

1. Assuming you are a member of the provincial cabinet, would you recommend that the university implement an employment freeze or not?
2. If Bill Barker had used national birth rate information, what other population information could the president use to support his argument that the university will probably keep growing?
3. Are there any strategies you would recommend that would allow the university to hire newly trained faculty and avoid serious budget deficits in the 1990s if enrolments do drop?

## INCIDENT 4-2

### Human Resource Planning at Western Telephone and Telegraph Company

Western Telephone and Telegraph Company (WT & T) is one of the largest employers in western Canada. At a recent conference, Margot Knox, the vice president of the company, made the following observations about employment in WT & T.

- In 1987, WT & T had to process and interview thirty applicants in order to hire one new employee.
- In 1976 telephone operators represented about 24% of the phone company's work force. Ten years later, operators counted for only 17% of the work force.
- Between 1988 and 1993, about half (180) of the officers of the WT & T will have to be replaced.
- Nearly three-quarters of the company's operating expenses go to people-related costs.
- During the next twenty-five years, WT & T will be serving about 4 million more households — a 50% increase.

1. Assume that WT & T is able to meet its increasing demand for services primarily through automation of clerical, operator, and technical positions without changing its total employment. What implications exist for meeting future staffing needs?
2. How might detailed staffing tables help WT & T reduce the number of applicants that must be processed for each new employee hired?

## INCIDENT 4-3

### Human Resource Consultants*

In October 1988, Human Resource Consultants of Hamilton, Ontario, employed ten consultants (including two trainees), five secretaries, two clerical assistants, an

*This incident was contributed by Professor Terry Wagar of Saint Mary's University.

office manager-cum-accountant, and a marketing representative. Consulting work and secretarial work are both expected to increase by 20% next year. However, a new computer system, which will be operational by January 1, 1989, will do the equivalent of eighty hours of secretarial work per week and forty hours of clerical work per week (but will require maintenance of forty hours per week). As of January 1, 1989, a number of employees are leaving the firm. Bill, a sixty-four-year-old consultant, is planning to retire; John, a Queen's MBA and first-year consultant trainee, has accepted a position with CUSO; Clara, the senior secretary (and supervisor of the secretarial/clerical staff), has agreed to join Ontario Consultants and is taking two other secretaries with her; and Herman, the office manager/accountant, is planning to move to western Canada.

Determine your human resource needs for 1989.

○ ○ ○ ○ ○ ○ ○ ○ ○ ○ ○ ○ ○ ○ ○ ○ ○ ○ ○ ○ ○ ○ ○ ○ ○ ○ ○ ○ ○ ○ ○ ○ ○ ○ ○ ○ ○ ○ ○ ○ ○ ○ ○

*CASE STUDY*

## TIMBER CRAFT LIMITED

Timber Craft Limited, located in southern British Columbia, is a manufacturer of consumer goods relating to sports and recreation activities. It started as a family-controlled organization nine years ago but has since become a private limited company employing professional managers. Timber Craft is currently considering a major expansion of facilities and product lines to take advantage of the rapidly growing sports goods and recreational market. Selected operating figures for the company during 1975-1984 are given in Exhibit I.

The company's plant is located in Midsex near Campbell River, B.C. In 1973, when the company started its operations, it had three sales offices: in Campbell River, Victoria, and Vancouver. However, during 1981-83, Timber Craft had opened four more sales offices to cater to the rapidly rising demand for its products. The company currently employs forty-three managers (excluding the president).

Over the years, the company has built up a reputation for selling quality sports and recreation products. About 70% of the com-

pany's customers are in the eighteen to thirty-five age group and tend to look for new products and the avant-garde. The customers tend to treat price as only one of a number of criteria when buying the firm's products. The company has acquired a solid financial and sales base through a policy of selling credit.

In general, Timber Craft has the reputation of offering competitive salaries and good working conditions. In spite of this, the company had problems in the past in obtaining personnel for key managerial positions, because of the high technical expertise and innovative ability needed on the part of Timber Craft's managers. Basically, the production techniques, the products, and the consumers themselves had grown very sophisticated in the last decade and, to maintain a competitive advantage in the industry, Timber Craft had to be extremely creative in its managerial policies and procedures. By 1980, the company handled two major groups of sports goods; however, this had doubled by 1984. The production process in the company is mainly

---

EXHIBIT I

Operating Figures of Timber Craft, 1975-1984, and Projections 1990-1992 (in thousands of dollars)

|  | 1975 | 1980 | 1984 | 1990 | 1992 |
|---|---|---|---|---|---|
| Net sales values | $17,000 | $17,850 | $21,420 | $27,850 | $30,630 |
| Cash | 49 | 47 | 52 | 56 | 58 |
| Net receivables | 85 | 223 | 450 | 600 | 674 |
| Other assets (excluding paint and facilities) | 212 | 398 | 616 | 1,218 | 1,399 |
| Net plant and equipment | 567 | 756 | 1,161 | 1,625 | 1,628 |
| Accounts payable | 61 | 112 | 312 | 408 | 439 |
| Stock and retained earnings | | | | | |
| Other liabilities | 192 | 216 | 398 | 476 | 492 |
| Percent net income on sales (before taxes) | 10.4% | 11.8% | 12.4% | 13.6% | 14.2% |

Projections based on report of the firm's financial evaluation committee.

---

capital intensive (and not labour intensive). The worker/plant value ratio for managerial personnel in the company is roughly 1:27,000.

## Organizational Structure

In 1984, Timber Craft Limited was organized functionally into four major units: marketing, manufacturing, finance and accounting, and administration. Human resources, public relations, and some aspects of customer relations were grouped under the administration. While no formal organization chart existed, Exhibit 2 shows an approximate chain of command in the organization.

The marketing unit performed essentially two types of functions: sales management at the various branches, and market planning (including market research and advertising). Recently, Timber Craft has been considering a possible switchover to a product manager concept, under which a manager would be responsible for the success or failure of one or more products rather than that of a region of a branch. S. P. Johnson indicated the scope of the responsibilities of a manager under the proposed system:

I am sure Timber Craft can significantly benefit from a product-type of organization structure. Most of the large consumer products companies, General Foods, Kellogg, and Procter & Gamble to mention just

three, are built on the product manager idea. The product manager will be held responsible for the product planning and for constant monitoring of the products' success. Here in Timber Craft we don't believe in lines and arrows to show relationships among people. If problems at the plant are holding up the sales, we expect the sales manager to go down to the plant or call the plant manager or work supervisor to iron out the problems. That is already the way we work here. What we are trying to do is to make it more systematic so that our reward system recognizes responsibility and on-the-job achievement.

W. C. Adams, a fifty-eight-year-old BSc, headed the manufacturing division. Reporting to Adams in 1984 were five managers in production planning, eight supervision and quality control officers, and six R&D managers. Most product development activities were centralized in Midsex, B.C.

Details of the number of managerial employees in Timber Craft are given in Exhibit 3.

## Operations and Future Plans

The company is right now planning a major expansion of its productive capacity. By 1990, sales were targeted at $27,850,000 (for an increase of 30% over 1984 figure). The company hoped to expand its operations to three

EXHIBIT 2

Organization Chart

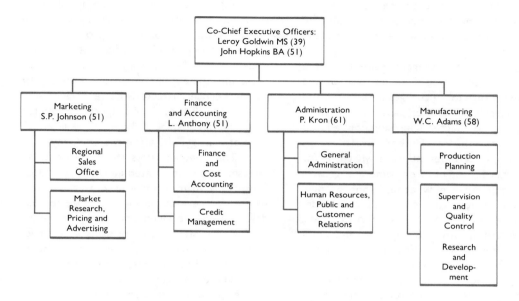

EXHIBIT 3

Details of Managerial Employees in Timber Craft Limited

| | 1975 | 1980 | 1984 |
|---|---|---|---|
| Manufacturing: | | | |
| Production supervising and quality control | 2 | 3 | 5 |
| Research and development | 4 | 6 | 8 |
| Finance and Accounting: | 2 | 3 | 6 |
| Financial accounting | 2 | | |
| Cost and management accounting | 3 | | |
| Credit management | 3 | | |
| Marketing: | 1 | 1 | 1 |
| Sales administration | 1 | 2 | 3 |
| Market research | 4 | 5 | 9 |
| Administration: | 1 | 1 | 2 |
| Personnel and staff relations | 1 | 1 | 2 |
| Labour relations | 1 | 1 | 1 |
| Office management, customer relations, and public relations | 2 | 2 | 3 |
| Total | 21 | 28 | 43 |

more centres in British Columbia and Alberta. Also, Timber Craft was planning to enter the field of water sports by introducing three new products in the fall of 1989. Results of market research and financial analyses showed that the planned expansion was feasible and desirable at that time.

Many of the managers realized that the promise of continued rapid growth of the company would mean changes in the structure and processes of the company. As one manager in the manufacturing division pointed out:

"Growth for Timber Craft means something quite different from what it is for most other firms. For a conglomerate, growth may often mean new acquisitions or new diversified units that will be operating independently. For a company like Timber Craft, however, it means entering new and completely different product-market situations and finding new ways of doing things. This may be the end of our present ways of doing things and the loss of informal relationships. Sure, everybody likes growth; but the associated costs are often not apparent."

Growth also meant identifying new methods of rewarding the employees, more formalization of recruiting and training procedures, identifying newer modes of integration of various operations of the company. The need for managers in the areas of planning, research and development, and selling was expected to increase rapidly in the next few years. The need for supporting sources, like finance, human resource department, market research, and credit management, was also expected to increase, although not to the same extent as in the case of above functions.

### Human Resource Policies

Timber Craft has had a policy of promoting qualified personnel from within before seeking outside candidates. The policy further implies consideration of the best-qualified people from all departments within Timber Craft, rather than simply promoting only from within

the department in which the opening occurs (unless the skill needed is very specific and cannot be acquired in a relatively short period of time, e.g., design engineer, computer programmer, financial accountant). Typically, the human resource department provides assistance in locating qualified candidates and takes pride in its "skills inventory" of all managerial personnel. The skills inventory consists of names, certain characteristics (e.g., age, education), and skills of the managers working for Timber Craft. Exhibit 4 shows the skills inventory of managerial staff in the company.

The company uses the services of an assessment centre located in Vancouver, B.C. Periodically, managers were sent to this centre where, for periods ranging from two to four days, they were given tests and interviews. During their stay, the participants also participated in management games, group discussions, in-basket exercises, and other role-plays. These managers were later rated by the centre for their leadership potential. Exhibit 4 also gives the details of the assessment centre report on leadership abilities of Timber Craft managers.

The salaries offered by Timber Craft are slightly higher than the ruling market rates for similar positions. Despite this, the company had problems in attracting qualified managers. The salaries of the supporting staff are comparable to the market rates. The bonus system for sales staff, however, has been criticized by several employees as being unfair. Several instances of salesmen's territories being taken away after they have cultivated them have been pointed out. Timber Craft has no pension or stock option plan for its employees. Despite these shortcomings, Timber Craft has built up a good name for giving equal and fair opportunities to minority groups.

The mandatory retirement age at Timber Craft is sixty-five. The company is committed to the development of its employees and, in the past, has sent many of its employees for training to the University of British Columbia,

EXHIBIT 4

"Skills Inventory" of Managerial Staff at Timber Craft Limited

| Employee | Dept. | Current Performance Level (1-lowest, 5-highest) | Highest Educational Level* | Age | Present Managerial Level (1-lowest, 7-highest) | Assessment Centre Report Rating on Potential Leadership Skill (1-low, 10-high) | Time in Present Job (mos.) |
|---|---|---|---|---|---|---|---|
| W.C. Adams | Mfg. | 5 | BS | 58 | 6 | 10 | 90 |
| S.R. Allen | Acc. | 4 | CGA | 31 | 5 | 9 | 29 |
| P.T. Anderson | Mfg. | 5 | MS | 63 | 6 | 8 | 92 |
| L. Anthony | Acc. | 4 | CA | 51 | 6 | 8 | 100 |
| R. Arnesen | Acc. | 5 | BComm | 59 | 6 | 4 | 108 |
| L. Belcheff | Mktg. | 4 | MBA | 28 | 4 | 8 | 20 |
| R. Bensoff | Acc. | 5 | RIA | 58 | 6 | 7 | 105 |
| R.K. Bloom | Mfg. | 4 | BSc | 37 | 5 | 7 | 26 |
| M.T. Barberton | Mktg. | 4 | BSc | 49 | 7 | 7 | 39 |
| M.P. Burke | Mktg. | 3 | BA | 24 | 4 | 5 | 24 |
| T.P. Buyer | Mfg. | 4 | MS | 29 | 5 | 9 | 16 |
| D. Caroon | Mktg. | 4 | BSc | 28 | 5 | 6 | 22 |
| N.T. Cayon | Mfg. | 4 | HS | 28 | 3 | 4 | 17 |
| R. Chapman | Mfg. | 3 | HS | 24 | 2 | 6 | 13 |
| E.S. Conway | Mfg. | 3 | BS | 29 | 4 | 7 | 36 |
| R.T. Dickoff | Pers. | 5 | MBA | 47 | 6 | 8 | 49 |
| P. Frost | Mktg. | 5 | BComm | 48 | 6 | 9 | 24 |
| W.K. Goodwin | Mktg. | 4 | MBA | 38 | 5 | 7 | 20 |
| K.N. Griggs | Pers. | 4 | MBA | 33 | 5 | 7 | 16 |
| R. Groster | Mktg. | 4 | MBA | 31 | 5 | 5 | 34 |
| P. Hack | Mktg. | 5 | BComm | 44 | 6 | 8 | 62 |
| K. Heneman | Mfg. | 4 | MS | 44 | 6 | 8 | 43 |
| S. Hickory | Mfg. | 5 | BSc | 64 | 6 | 10 | 108 |
| T. Hitronf | Pers. | 4 | BLit | 29 | 3 | 7 | 32 |
| S. Inckson | Mfg. | 4 | BSc | 37 | 5 | 8 | 79 |
| P. Jackson | Mfg. | 3 | HS | 47 | 5 | 5 | 60 |
| S.P. Johnson | Mktg. | 5 | BA | 51 | 6 | 9 | 64 |
| T. Kennelly | Mfg. | 5 | BS | 62 | 5 | 9 | 58 |
| S. Kiefel | Mktg. | 4 | HS | 58 | 5 | 7 | 69 |
| P.Q. Kimble | Mfg. | 4 | BSc | 27 | 4 | 8 | 14 |
| S. Kirton | Mktg. | 5 | BA | 51 | 6 | 8 | 39 |
| T. Knoll | Mfg. | 5 | MS | 29 | 4 | 7 | 19 |
| P. Kron | Adm. | 5 | HS | 61 | 6 | 8 | 31 |
| J.H. Laboy | Mfg. | 4 | MS | 43 | 5 | 6 | 42 |
| E.F. Pederson | Mfg. | 4 | MS | 47 | 5 | 6 | 19 |
| N. T. Potler | Mfg. | 5 | BTech | 31 | 5 | 7 | 60 |
| A. Ranallo | Adm. | 4 | BA | 39 | 5 | 5 | 29 |
| H.C. Reeves | Mfg. | 5 | BSc | 60 | 6 | 8 | 63 |
| T. Reitman | Mfg. | 4 | BSc | 28 | 4 | 9 | 20 |
| R.E. Smith | Acc. | 4 | BComm | 29 | 5 | 7 | 19 |
| J. Sorenson | Acc. | 5 | HS | 42 | 6 | 7 | 41 |
| N.F. Trandt | Adm. | 4 | BSc | 28 | 5 | 8 | 17 |
| H. Walden | Acc. | 4 | HS | 49 | 4 | 4 | 69 |

*Almost everyone in this list has undergone special training programs at some time during their stay at Timber Craft Limited.

## EXHIBIT 5

Current and Projected Employment Data for Selected Job Classes in Western Canada*

| Job Class | Latest Employment Data | Predicted Annual Average Job Openings for Next Decade | Predicted Annual Average Supply of Personnel in Job Class in Next Decade |
|---|---|---|---|
| Accountants | 94,316 | 8,390 | 8,120 |
| Aerospace engineers | 11,205 | 345 | 410 |
| Agricultural engineers | 1,900 | 120 | 431 |
| Architects | 7,300 | 1,122 | 692 |
| Carpenters | 8,940 | 3,860 | 1,760 |
| Chemists | 11,216 | 4,127 | 1,673 |
| City managers | 512 | 36 | 62 |
| Computer programmers | 6,382 | 4,230 | 3,190 |
| Credit officers | 1,700 | 430 | 416 |
| Employment counsellors | 857 | 362 | 118 |
| Lawyers | 6,988 | 636 | 739 |
| Office managers | 12,108 | 430 | 378 |
| Other engineers | 72,300 | 16,120 | 14,002 |
| Human resource managers | 6,381 | 1,785 | 1,123 |
| Photographers | 21,300 | 9,020 | 9,108 |
| Physicians and medical personnel | 42,130 | 13,000 | 9,368 |
| Research and design personnel | 9,180 | 2,127 | 730 |
| Sales managers | 51,320 | 4,362 | 2,930 |
| Sales persons | 149,346 | 16,300 | 17,360 |
| Technicians | 231,700 | 19,216 | 16,390 |

*Fictitious data.

Simon Fraser University, Vancouver Institute of Technology, and the University of Alberta. Current and projected employment data for selected job classes in Western Canada for the next decade is shown in Exhibit 5. The reader may assume that the company recruits only from Western Canada. (This is more or less true, since currently 91% percent of Timber Craft's managerial personnel come from Western Canada.)

1. Assume you are Ron Dickoff, the human resource manager of Timber Craft. You have been asked to prepare a staffing forecast for the years 1990 and 1992. Assume the current expansion plans of the company will be implemented by 1989.

2. What are some specific environmental, task, organizational, and human variables that should be considered in making such a forecast?

3. For an organization like Timber Craft, which is poised for a fast growth, what policy related and operational problems do you foresee?

4. What is your evaluation of the human resource policies at Timber Craft Limited?

This case was prepared by Professor Hari Das, Saint Mary's University, Halifax, Nova Scotia. All rights reserved by the author.

○ ○ ○ ○ ○ ○ ○ ○ ○ ○ ○ ○ ○ ○ ○ ○ ○ ○ ○ ○ ○ ○ ○ ○ ○ ○ ○ ○ ○ ○ ○ ○ ○ ○ ○ ○ ○ ○ ○ ○ ○ ○ ○ ○ ○ ○

## SUGGESTED READINGS

Bloom, E. P., ''Creating an Employee Information System,'' *Personnel Administrator*, November 1982, pp. 67-75.

Das, Hari and Mallika Das, ''One More Time: How Do We Place a Value Tag on Our Employees? Some Issues in Human Resource Accounting,'' *Human Resource Planning*, Vol. 2, No. 2, 1979, pp. 91-101.

Enderle, R. C., ''HRIS Models for Staffing,'' *Personnel Journal*, Vol. 66, No. 11, November 1987, pp. 72-79.

Frantzreb, R. B., ''Human Resource Planning: Forecasting Manpower Needs,'' *Personnel Journal*, Vol. 60, No. 11, November 1981, pp. 850-857.

Lapointe, J., ''How to Calculate the Cost of Human Resources,'' *Personnel Journal*, Vol. 67, No. 1, January 1988, pp. 34-45.

Nelsen, R. E., ''Common Sense Staff Reduction,'' *Personnel Journal*, Vol. 67, No. 8, pp. 50-57.

## REFERENCES

1. Sherman L. Dolan and Randall S. Schuler, *Personnel and Human Resource Management in Canada*, St. Paul, Minn.: West Publishing Co., 1987, page 65.

2. Bernard Taylor and Gordon L. Lippitt, *Management Development and Training Handbook*, New York: McGraw-Hill Book Company, 1975, p. ix.

3. George T. Milkovich and Thomas A. Mahoney, ''Human Resource Planning Models: A Perspective.'' in James W. Walker (ed.), The Challenge of Human Resource Planning: Selected Readings, New York: Human Resource Planning Society, 1979, pp. 73-84.

4. Eddie C. Smith, ''Strategic Business Planning and Human Resources: Part I,'' *Personnel Journal*, August 1982, pp. 606-610(Part II appears in *Personnel Journal*, September 1982, pp. 680-682.). See also Stella M. Nkomo, ''The Theory and practice of HR Planning: The Gap Still Remains,'' *Personnel Administrator*, August 1986, pp. 70-73; Matt Hennecke, ''The 'People' Side of Strategic Planning,'' *Training*, November 1984, pp. 25-32; Anil Gupta, ''Matching Managers to Strategies: Points and Counterpoints,'' *Human Resource Management*, Vol. 25, No. 2, Summer 1986, pp. 215-234.

5. Lee Dyer, ''Human Resource Planning at IBM,'' *Human Resource Planning*, Spring 1984, pp. 111-125.

6. Herbert Heneman and G. Seltzer, *Employer Manpower Planning and Forecasting* (Manpower Research Monograph No. 19), Washington: U.S. Department of Labor, 1970, p. 42.

7. Elmer H. Burack, *Strategies for Manpower Planning and Programming*, Morristown, N.J.: General Learning Press, 1982, pp. 1-8. See also Raymond E. Miles and Charles C. Snow, ''Designing Strategic Human Resources Systems,'' *Organizational Dynamics*, Summer 1984, pp. 36-52.

8. James W. Walker, ''Linking Human Resources Planning and Strategic Planning,'' *Human Resource Planning*, Spring 1978, pp. 1-18. See also Harold L. Angle, Charles C. Manz and Andres H. Van de Ven, ''Integrating Human Resource Management and Corporate Strategy: A Preview of the 3M Story,'' *Human Resource Management*, Spring 1985, pp. 51-68.

9. A.L. Delbecq, A.H. Van de Ven, and D.H. Gustafson, *Group Techniques for Progress Planning: A Guide to Nominal and Delphi Process*, Glenview, Ill.: Scott, Foresman & Co., 1975; J.M. Bartwrek and J.K. Muringhan, ''The Nominal Group Technique: Expanding the Basic Procedure and

Underlying Assumptions,'' *Group and Organization Studies*, Vol. 9, 1984, pp. 417-432.

10. Don Bryant, ''Manpower Planning Models and Techniques,'' *Business Horizons*, April 1973, pp. 69-73. See also David J. Bartholomew, ''Statistics in *Human Resource Planning*,'' *Human Resource Planning*, November 1978, pp. 67-77.

11. P.F. Buller and W.R. Maki, ''A Case History of a Manpower Planning Model,'' *Human Resource Planning*, Vol. 4, No. 3, 1981, pp. 129-137.

12. James W. Walker, ''Evaluating the Practical Effectiveness of Human Resource Planning Applications,'' *Human Resource Management*, Spring 1974, p. 21. See also Paul Pakchan, ''Effective Manpower Planning,'' *Personnel Journal*, October 1983, pp. 826-830.

13. David L. Chicci, ''Four Steps to an Organizational/Human Resource Plan,'' *Personnel Journal*, June 1979, p. 392. See also George S. Odiorne, ''For Successful Succession Planning . . . Match Organizational Requirements to Corporate Human Potential,'' *Management Review*, November 1982, pp. 49-54.

14. James W. Walker, ''Human Resource Planning: Managerial Concerns and Practices,'' *Business Horizons*, June 1976, pp. 56-57. See also George S. Odiorne, ''The Crystal Ball of HR Strategy,'' *Personnel Administrator*, December 1986, pp. 103-106; John A. Byrne and Alison L. Cowan, ''Should Companies Groom New Leaders Or Buy Them?'' *Business Week*, September 22, 1986, pp. 94-96.

15. Statistics Canada, *The Labour Force*, Catalogue No. 71-001, January 1984, Ottawa: Minister of Supply and Services, p. 70.

16. Statistics Canada, Catalogue # 11-003E, Vol. 62, No. 2, March 1987, p. 48.

17. Eli Ginzberg, *The Manpower Connection*, Cambridge, Mass.: Harvard University Press, 1975. See also George S. Odiorne, op. cit., December 1986.

18. Pierre Paul Proulx, Luce Bourgault and Jean-Francois Manegre, ''CANDIDE-COFOR and Forecasting Manpower Needs by Occupation and Industry in Canada,'' in Larry F. Moore and Larry Charach, (eds.), *Manpower Planning for Canadians*, 2nd Edition, Institute of Industrial Relations, University of British Columbia: Vancouver, B.C., 1979.

19. Ibid. See also ''The Candide Model,'' in *Manpower Review*, Vol. 10, 1977, pp. 31-33.

20. ''Notions and Numbers — The Canadian Occupational Projection System,'' Ottawa: Employment and Immigration Canada, WH-3-418 undated. See also these publications by Employment and Immigration Canada: ''The Canadian Occupational Projection System — Supply Issues and Approaches,'' WH 3-335E, January 1983 and ''Demand Methodology,'' WH 3-341, January, 1983.

21. *Innovation and Jobs in Canada*, A research report prepared for the Economic Council of Canada, Chapter 4, Ottawa: Minister of Supplies and Services Canada, 1987, Catalogue No. EC22-141/1987E.

22. *Human Resource Planning: A Challenge for the 1980s*, Ottawa: Minister of Supply and Services, 1983, Cat. No. MP 43-125/83.

23. Kendrith M. Rowland and Scott L. Summers, ''Human Resource Planning: A Second Look,'' *Personnel Administration*, December 1981, pp. 73-80. See also William H. Hoffman and L. L. Wyatt, ''Human Resource Planning,'' *Personnel Administrator*, January 1977, pp. 19-23.

24. David A. Bratton, ''Moving Away From Nine to Five,'' *Canadian Business Review*, Spring 1986, pp. 15-17; *Globe and Mail*, ''Job-Sharing: Good Outweighs Bad,'' July 26, 1985, p. B-1; Lesley Krueger, ''When Half Job Is Better Than None,'' *Maclean's*, November 15, 1982,; pp. 61-64; Julianne LaBreche, ''Two Can Work As Cheaply As One,'' *Financial Post Magazine*, October 31, 1981, p. 226.

25. Frank Reid, ''Combatting Unemployment Through Work Time Reductions,'' *Canadian Public Policy*, Vol. 12, No. 2, 1986, pp. 275-285; Noah M. Meltz, Frank Reid, and G. Swartz, *Sharing the Work*, Toronto: University of Toronto Press, 1981.

26. Heywood Klem, ''Interest Grows in Worksharing,'' *The Wall Street Journal*, April 7, 1983, p. 4.

27. ''AT & T. Hangs Up on 24,000 of Its Workers,'' *Business Week*, September 2, 1985,` pp. 35-36; Angelo J. Kinicki, ''Personnel Consequences of Plant Closure,'' Working Paper, Arizona State University, 1987.

28. ''Most Firms Have Severance Pay Programs,'' *Resource*, October 1986, p. 2.

29. ''Silver Parachute Protects Work Force,'' *Resource*, January 1987, p. 3.

30. Ibid.

31. Dane Henriksen, ''Outplacement: Guidelines that Ensure Success,'' *Personnel Journal*, August 1982, pp. 583-589. See also Joel A. Bearak, ''Termination Made Easier: Is Outplacement Really the Answer?'' *Personnel Administrator*, April 1982, pp. 63-71, 99; Jack Mendleson, ''Does Your Company Really Need Outplacement?'' *SAM Advanced Management Journal*, Winter 1975, pp. 4-12; Jack Mendleson, ''What's Fair Treatment for Terminated Employees?'' *Supervisory Management*, November 1974, pp. 25-34; and Donald H. Sweet, *Recruitment: A Guide for Managers*, Menlo Park, Calif.: Addison-Wesley Publishing Company, 1975.

32. Craig C. Pinder and Hari Das, ''The Hidden Costs and Benefits of Employee Transfers,'' *Human Resource Planning*, Vol. 2, No. 3, 1979. See also Craig C. Pinder, ''Employee Transfer Studies — Summary,'' Faculty of Commerce and Business Administration, University of British Columbia: Vancouver, B.C., November, 1985; Jeanne M. Brett, ''Job Transfer and Well Being,'' *Journal of Applied Psychology*, Vol. 67, No. 4, 1982, pp. 450-463; Jeanne M. Brett and James Werbel, *The Effect of Job Transfer on Employees and Their Families*, Washington, D.C.: Employer Relocation Council, 1980.

33. Alfred W. Swimyard and Floyd A. Bond, ''Who Gets Promoted?'' *Harvard Business Review*, September-October, 1980, pp. 6-8, 12, 14, 18.

34. Ronald W. Clement, George E. Stevens, and Daniel Brenenstuhl, ''Promotion Practices in American Business Colleges: A Comprehensive Investigation,'' *Manhattan College Journal of Business*, Spring 1986, pp. 9-15.

35. Laurence J. Peter and Raymond Hull, *The Peter Principle*, New York: William Morrow, 1969.

36. Larry Reibstein, ''The Not-So-Fast Track: Firms Try Promoting Hotshots More Slowly,'' *The Wall Street Journal*, Western Edition, March 24, 1986, p. 21.

37. Hari Das and Mallika Das, ''One More Time: How Do We Place a Value Tag on Our Employees? Some Issues in Human Resource Accounting,'' *Human Resource Planning*, Vol. 2, No. 2, 1979, pp. 91-101.

38. Ibid.

39. For example, see R.L. Brummet, E.G. Flamholtz, and W.C. Pyle, ''Human Resource Measurement — A Challenge for Accountants,'' *The Accounting Review*, 1968, Vol. XLIII, No. 2, pp. 217-224.

40. For a discussion of the various models, see Das and Das, op. cit., 1979.

41. Ibid.

42. For example, see D.A. Dittman, H.A. Juris, and L. Revsine, ''For the Existence of Unrecorded Human Assets: An Economic Perspective,'' Working Paper, Graduate School of Management, North Western University, 1975. See also Das and Das, op. cit., 1979.

# CHAPTER 5 ○○○○○○○

## *JOB ANALYSIS AND DESIGN*

*The data generated by job analyses have significant use in nearly every phase of human resource administration: designing jobs and reward systems; staffing and training; performance control and more. Few other processes executed by organizations have the* potential *for being such a powerful aid to management decision making.*

PHILIP C. GRANT[1]

○ ○ ○ ○ ○ ○ ○ ○ ○ ○ ○ ○ ○ ○ ○ ○ ○ ○ ○ ○ ○ ○ ○ ○ ○ ○ ○ ○ ○ ○ ○ ○ ○ ○ ○ ○
## *CHAPTER OBJECTIVES*

After studying this chapter, you should be able to:
1. *Explain* why human resource departments must have job analysis information.
2. *List* the major methods of collecting job analysis information.
3. *Describe* the content of a job description.
4. *Identify* the efficiency and behaviourial considerations in job design.
5. *Explain* how job specialization affects productivity, satisfaction, and turnover.
6. *Discuss* the different job-redesign techniques used to improve the quality of work life.

○ ○ ○ ○ ○ ○ ○ ○ ○ ○ ○ ○ ○ ○ ○ ○ ○ ○ ○ ○ ○ ○ ○ ○ ○ ○ ○ ○ ○ ○ ○ ○ ○ ○ ○ ○

*F*or a human resource department to be proactive, it needs information. The information needed is about the external challenges facing the organization (for example, changes in technology, labour force, government regulations) and factors internal to the organization. The present chapter explains how human resource specialists discover the *actual* characteristics that presently exist in each job. This knowledge forms the beginnings of a human resource information system that helps human resource specialists perform effectively. The need for this information is made clear by the following dialogue:

SERVICE MANAGER:  Before we had a human resource department, we took care of people matters pretty well. Now we have a human resource department, and there is too much paperwork on each job. I wonder if it is a help or a hindrance.

H.R. MANAGER:  I can sympathize with your views. Before the department was set up, you probably had complete authority for people matters. Right?

SERVICE MANAGER:  I sure did! And I did it without a lot of paperwork.

H.R. MANAGER:  Sure you did. You know every job in the service department, in and out. You had all the information you needed stored in your experiences.

SERVICE MANAGER:  That is my point. If I got along without all this paperwork, why can't your department?

H.R. MANAGER:  Why? Because you deal with those jobs every day. You've probably done most of them yourself. But my department is also responsible for jobs in sales, production, warehouse, supervision, and others. Without the paperwork describing these jobs, we would have no idea of their requirements.

Jobs are at the core of every organization's productivity. If they are designed well and done right, the organization makes progress towards its objectives. Otherwise, productivity suffers, profits fall, and the organization is less able to meet the demands of society, customers, employees, and others with a stake in its success. The importance and implications of well-designed jobs are perhaps best illustrated by an example:

Rapid growth in a Calgary construction company led to an increase in the number of invoices and a decrease in the quality and timeliness of its departments' performance. Consultants who were hired to look into the problems faced by the company conducted workshops and taught organizational members to apply job diagnostic tools to their activities. The result of all these activities was a 12.3% increase in the number of invoices processed, a saving of $15,200 in salaries and overtime, and a better understanding among the workers of the importance of their work roles.

Not all attempts to restructure jobs succeed as well as this example. However, improvements in productivity, quality, and cost often begin with the jobs employees do. For a human resource department to be effective, its members must have a clear understanding of the jobs found throughout organizations. But with hundreds—or even thousands — of jobs, it is nearly impossible for the human resource professionals in large companies to know the details of every job. The solution is an effective human resource information system that contains detailed information about every job in the organization. With this written or electronically stored information, human resource specialists can quickly learn the details of any job. This knowledge is crucial to the success of a human resource department, especially in large corporations, because it enables human resource specialists to be more proactive in their efforts to assist the organization. Without this information base, the human resource department would be less able to redesign jobs, recruit new employees, train present employees, determine appropriate compensation, and perform many other human resource functions.

Where there is no human resource department, all employee related matters are handled by individual managers. Since operating managers are familiar with the jobs they supervise, they do not need recorded job information. They already know the characteristics, standards, and human abilities required of every job.

After a human resource department is created, however, knowledge about jobs and their requirements must be collected through job analysis. *Job analysis* systematically collects, evaluates, and organizes information. It is done by specialists called *job analysts*, who gather data about each position (though not necessarily about the individual jobs available).

> One insurance company has 150 clerical employees who process incoming premium payments. Each job is the same. Therefore, job analysis requires only a random sample of these positions. Data collection on a few of these jobs generates an accurate information base for all 150 positions. Job analysts can then understand the premium clerk's job without studying each clerk's individual characteristics.

Recorded job information plays a crucial role in human resource departments. It supplies the minimum data to do many human resource activities. Figure 5-1 lists major human resource actions that are affected by job analysis information. For example, without job analysis information, human resource specialists would find it difficult to evaluate how environmental challenges or specific job requirements affect workers' quality of work life. To match job applicants to openings, human resource specialists must have an understanding of what each job requires. Similarly, compensation analysts could not be expected to determine a fair salary without detailed knowledge of what a job requires. Even before a human resource department exists, successful managers consider the informal job information they have acquired. Human resource departments merely formalize the collection, evaluation, and organization of this information.

This chapter describes the specific information sought by job analysis and the

FIGURE 5-1    Major Human Resource Management Actions That Rely on
Job Analysis Information

1. **Evaluate** how environmental challenges affect individual jobs.
2. **Eliminate** unneeded job requirements that can cause discrimination in employment.
3. **Discover** job elements that help or hinder the quality of work life.
4. **Plan** for future human resource requirements.
5. **Match** job applicants and job openings.
6. **Determine** training needs for new and experienced employees.
7. **Create** plans to develop employee potential.
8. **Set** realistic performance standards.
9. **Place** employees in jobs that use their skills effectively.
10. **Compensate** jobholders fairly.

techniques used to collect it. The chapter also examines how the data are converted into useful tools that form the basis of a human resource information system.

## COLLECTION OF JOB ANALYSIS INFORMATION

Job analysts gather information about jobs and jobholder characteristics. The function of job analysis is to provide information not only about the job itself, but also about what it calls for in employee behaviour.[2] Before studying jobs, analysts typically study the organization — its purpose, design, inputs (people, materials, and procedures), and outputs (products or services). They may also study industry and government reports about the jobs to be analyzed. In all cases, however, the major aim of job analysis is to provide the basic clues for identifying predictors and measures of job behaviour.[3] Armed with a general understanding of the organization and its work, job analysts:

- Identify the jobs to be analyzed.
- Develop a job analysis questionnaire.
- Collect job analysis information.

### Job Identification

Analysts identify every different job in the organization before they collect job information. This process is simple in small organizations because there are few jobs to uncover. In large companies analysts may have to construct lists of jobs from payroll records, organization charts, or discussions with workers and supervisors. If job analysis has been done before, previous records may be used. Moreover, existing job descriptions, process specifications, and various records and reports relating to organizational performance may also help in establishing the nature of the various jobs.[4]

### Questionnaire Development

To study jobs, analysts develop checklists or questionnaires that are sometimes called job analysis schedules. These questionnaires seek to collect job information uniformly. They uncover the duties, responsibilities, human abilities, and performance standards of the jobs investigated.

It is important to use the same questionnaire on similar jobs. Analysts want differences in job information to reflect differences in the jobs, not differences in the questions asked. Uniformity is especially hard to maintain in large organizations: when analysts study similar jobs in different departments, only a uniform questionnaire is likely to result in usable data.

After two appliance producers merged, each initially retained its separate human resource departments and separate job analysis schedules. As a result, all the production supervisors evaluated by one form had their jobs and pay substantially upgraded. The supervisors in the other plant had identical jobs, but they received only modest pay raises.

As the example points out, similar jobs should be studied with identical checklists. Otherwise, job analysis adds confusion. This does *not* mean that the human resource department is limited to one questionnaire. Job analysts often find that technical, clerical, and managerial jobs require different checklists. Different checklists, however, should never be applied to similar jobs.

What are the questions asked in a job analysis questionnaire? Figure 5-2 shows an abbreviated sample form.

FIGURE 5-2   A Job Analysis Questionnaire

---

**BREVARD GENERAL HOSPITAL**
**Job Analysis Questionnaire**
**(Form 110-JAQ)**

**A.  Job Analysis Status**

   **1.** Job analysis form revised on _____
   **2.** Previous revisions on _____
   **3.** Date of job analysis for specified job _____
   **4.** Previous analysis on _____
   **5.** Job analysis is conducted by _____
   **6.** Verified by _____

**B.  Job Identification**

   **1.** Job title _____   **2.** Other titles _____
   **3.** Division(s) _____   **4.** Department(s) _____
   **5.** Title of supervisor(s) _____

**C.  Job Summary**

   Briefly describe purpose of job, what is done, and how. _____
_____

**D.  Duties**

   **1.** The primary duties of this job are best classified as:
      _____Medical     _____Technical     _____Managerial
      _____Clerical     _____Professional
   **2.** List **major** duties and the proportion of time each involves:
      **a.** _____ . _____ %
      **b.** _____ . _____ %
      **c.** _____ . _____ %
   **3.** List other duties and the proportion of time each involves:
      **a.** _____ . _____ %
      **b.** _____ . _____ %
      **c.** _____ . _____ %
   **4.** What constitutes successful performance of these duties? _____
_____

   **5.** How much training is needed for normal performance of these duties?
_____
_____
_____

**E.  Responsibility**

   **1.** What are the responsibilities involved in this job and how great are these responsibilities?

---

FIGURE 5-2 (continued)   A Job Analysis Questionnaire

| Responsibility for: | Extent of Responsibility | |
|---|---|---|
| | Minor | Major |
| a.  Equipment operation | _____ | _____ |
| b.  Use of tools | _____ | _____ |
| c.  Materials usage | _____ | _____ |
| d.  Protection of equipment | _____ | _____ |
| e.  Protection of tools | _____ | _____ |
| f.  Protection of materials | _____ | _____ |
| g.  Personal safety | _____ | _____ |
| h.  Safety of others | _____ | _____ |
| i.  Others' work performance | _____ | _____ |
| j.  Other (Specify _____) | _____ | _____ |

**F.  Human Characteristics**

 1. What physical attributes are necessary to perform the job? _____
_____
_____

 2. Of the following characteristics, which ones are needed and how important are they?

| Characteristic | Unneeded | Helpful | Essential |
|---|---|---|---|
| 1.  Vision | _____ | _____ | _____ |
| 2.  Hearing | _____ | _____ | _____ |
| 3.  Talking | _____ | _____ | _____ |
| 4.  Sense of smell | _____ | _____ | _____ |
| 5.  Sense of touch | _____ | _____ | _____ |
| 6.  Sense of taste | _____ | _____ | _____ |
| 7.  Eye-hand coordination | _____ | _____ | _____ |
| 8.  Overall coordination | _____ | _____ | _____ |
| 9.  Strength | _____ | _____ | _____ |
| 10.  Height | _____ | _____ | _____ |
| 11.  Health | _____ | _____ | _____ |
| 12.  Initiative | _____ | _____ | _____ |
| 13.  Ingenuity | _____ | _____ | _____ |
| 14.  Judgement | _____ | _____ | _____ |
| 15.  Attention | _____ | _____ | _____ |
| 16.  Reading | _____ | _____ | _____ |
| 17.  Arithmetic | _____ | _____ | _____ |
| 18.  Writing | _____ | _____ | _____ |
| 19.  Education (Level _____) | _____ | _____ | _____ |
| 20.  Other (Specify _____) | _____ | _____ | _____ |

 3. Experience for this job:
   _____a.  Unimportant
   _____b.  Includes_____ (months) as (job title)_____
 4. Can training be substituted for experience?
   _____Yes   How: _____
   _____No    Why: _____

**G.  Working Conditions**

 1. Describe the physical conditions under which this job is performed. _____
_____

FIGURE 5-2 (continued)   A Job Analysis Questionnaire

**2.** Are there unusual psychological demands connected with this job? _____

_____

**3.** Describe any unusual conditions under which the job is performed.

_____

_____

_____

**H. Health or Safety Features**

**1.** Describe fully any health or safety hazards associated with this job. _____

_____

_____

**2.** Is any safety training or equipment required? _____

_____

**I.  Performance Standards**

**1.** How is the performance of this job measured? _____

_____

**2.** What identifiable factors contribute most to the successful performance of this job? _____

**J.  Miscellaneous Comments**

Are there any aspects of this job that should be especially noted?_____

_____

_____

| | |
|---|---|
| **Job Analyst's Signature** | **Date Completed** |

## Status and Identification

The first two headings in the figure show how current the information is and identify the job being described. Without these entries, users of job analysis data may rely on out-of-date information or apply it to the wrong job. Since most jobs change over time, outdated information may misdirect other human resource activities.

> At Brevard General Hospital, new job analysis information had not been collected for two years on the job of billing clerk. The outdated information indicated that bookkeeping experience was the major skill needed by billing clerks. But once the hospital's entire billing system had been computerized, bookkeeping skills became unimportant; instead, billing clerks needed typing skills to process billing information into the computer.

## Duties and Responsibilities

Many job analysis schedules briefly explain the purpose of the job, what the job accomplishes, and how the job is performed. This summary provides a quick overview. The specific duties and responsibilities are also listed to give more detailed insight into the position. Questions on responsibility are expanded significantly when the checklist is applied to management jobs. Additional questions map areas of responsibility for decision making, controlling, organizing, planning, and other management functions.

### Human Characteristics and Working Conditions

Besides information about the job, analysts need data about the people who do the work. This section of the checklist uncovers the particular skills, abilities, training, education, experience, and other characteristics that jobholders need. It is invaluable when filling job openings or advising workers about new job assignments.

Information about the job environment improves understanding of the job. Working conditions may explain the need for particular skills, training, knowledge, or even a particular job design. Likewise, jobs must be free from recognizable health and safety hazards. Knowledge of hazards allows the human resource department to redesign the job or protect workers through training and safety equipment. Unique working conditions also influence hiring, placement, and compensation decisions.

> During World War II, one airplane manufacturer had problems installing fuel tanks inside the wings of the bombers it was building. The crawl space was extremely narrow and cramped. These tight conditions caused considerable production delays. When the human resource department learned about this situation, it recruited welders who were less than 5 feet tall and weighed less than 100 pounds.

### Performance Standards

The job analysis questionnaire also seeks information about job standards, which are used to evaluate performance. This information is collected on jobs with obvious and objective standards of performance. When standards are not readily apparent, job analysts may ask supervisors or industrial engineers to develop reasonable standards of performance.

## Data Collection

There is no one best way to collect job analysis information. Analysts must evaluate the trade-offs between time, cost, and accuracy associated with each method.[5] Once they decide which trade-offs are most important, they use interviews, questionnaires, employee logbooks, observations, or some combination of these techniques.

### Interviews

Face-to-face interviews are an effective way to collect job information. The analyst has the job checklist as a guide, but can add other questions where needed. Although the process is slow and expensive, it allows the interviewer to explain unclear questions and probe into uncertain answers. Both jobholders and supervisors typically are interviewed. The analyst usually talks with a limited number of workers first. Then interviews with supervisors verify the information. This pattern ensures a high level of accuracy.

## Mail Questionnaires

A fast and less costly option is a mail questionnaire developed from the job analysis checklist. This approach allows many jobs to be studied at once and at little cost. However, there is less accuracy because of misunderstood questions, incomplete responses, and unreturned questionnaires. Supervisors can also be given mail questionnaires to verify employee responses.

## Employee Log

An employee log or diary is a third option. Workers periodically summarize their tasks and activities in the log. If entries are made over the entire job cycle, the diary can prove quite accurate. It may even be the only feasible way to collect job information.

> New Brunswick Brokers' three dozen account executives each handled a bewildering array of activities for clients. Since interviews and questionnaires often overlooked major parts of the job, the human resource department suggested a logbook. Most account executives initially resisted, but eventually they agreed to a one-month trial. The human resource department obtained the information it wanted, and account executives learned how they actually spent their days.

Logs are not a popular technique. They are time-consuming for jobholders and personnel specialists. This makes them costly. Managers and workers often see them as a nuisance and resist their introduction. Moreover, after the novelty wears off, accuracy tends to decline as entries become less frequent.

## Observation

Another approach is direct observation. It is slow, costly, and potentially less accurate than other methods. Accuracy may be low because the analysts may miss irregularly occurring activities. But observation is the preferred method in some situations. When analysts question data from other techniques, observation may confirm or remove doubts. The existence of language barriers may also necessitate the observation approach, especially in cases involving foreign-language workers.

## Combinations

Since each method has its faults, analysts often use two or more techniques concurrently.

> A lumber company had six facilities scattered throughout Canada and the United States. To interview a few workers and supervisors at each facility was considered prohibitively expensive; to rely only on questionnaire data was thought to be too inaccurate. So the human resource department both interviewed selected employees at the home office and sent questionnaires to other facilities.

Combinations can ensure high accuracy at minimum cost, as the example implies. Human resource departments may even use combined methods when all employees are at the same location. Regardless of the technique used, the job analysis information is of little value until analysts convert it into more usable forms.

## USES OF JOB ANALYSIS INFORMATION

Through the preparation and collection phases of job analysis shown in Figure 5-3, human resource departments obtain information about jobs. Then this information is put into such usable forms as job descriptions, job specifications, and job standards. Together, these applications of job analysis information provide a minimum human resource information system. The remainder of this chapter discusses these applications.

**FIGURE 5-3** The Three Phases of Job Analysis Information

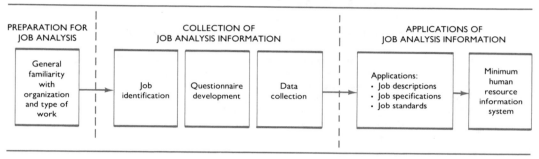

## Job Descriptions

A *job description* is a written statement that explains the duties, working conditions, and other aspects of a specified job. Within a firm, all the job descriptions follow the same style, although between companies, form and content may vary. One approach is to write a narrative description that covers the job in a few paragraphs. Another typical style breaks the description down into several subparts, as shown in Figure 5-4.[6] This figure shows a job description that parallels the job analysis checklist which originally generated the data.

In a job description, the section on job identity may include a *job code*. Job codes use numbers, letters, or both to provide a quick summary of the job. These codes are useful for comparing jobs. Figure 5-5 explains the code used in the *Canadian Classification and Dictionary of Occupations* (CCDO). It is an alphanumeric code that helps arrange jobs into occupational groups. This classification is based on, among other things, the kind of work performed, the materials or equipment used or produced, the standards to be met, the education or training required, the working conditions, and the relationship to coworkers of the jobholder.[7]

The job identity section contains other useful information.
- *Date*. The date is essential. It tells subsequent users how old the description is. The older the description, the less likely it is to reflect the job as now done.
- *Author*. The writer of the description is identified so that questions or errors can be brought to the attention of the author.
- *Location*. The department (or departments) where the job is located helps identify the job for future reference. Location references may include division, plant, or other organization breakdowns.

FIGURE 5-4   A Job Description

---

**BREVARD GENERAL HOSPITAL**
Job Description

| | | | |
|---|---|---|---|
| Job Title: | Job Analyst | Job Code: | 166.088 |
| Date: | January 3, 19–– | Author: | John Doakes |
| Job Location: | Human Resource Department | Job Grade: | |
| Supervisor: | Harold Grantinni | Status: | Exempt |

Job Summary:     Collects and develops job analysis, information through interviews, questionnaires, observation, or other means. Provides other personnel specialists with needed information.

Job Duties:     Designs job analysis schedules and questionnaires.
Collects job information.
Interacts with workers, supervisors, and peers.
Writes job descriptions and job specifications.
Reports safety hazards to area manager and safety department.
Verifies all information through two sources.
Performs other duties as assigned by supervisors.

Working Conditions:     Works most of the time in well-ventilated modern office. Data collection often requires on-site work under every working condition found in company. Works standard 8 a.m. to 5 p.m., except to collect second-shift data and when travelling (one to three days per month).

The above information is correct as approved by:

(Signed) _____     (Signed) _____
                  Job Analyst                                          Department Manager

---

FIGURE 5-5   Explanation of Job Codes in the Canadian Classification and Dictionary of Occupations (CCDO)

---

Each occupational definition in the *Canadian Classification and Dictionary of Occupations* (CCDO) has a seven-digit code number, a title, and an industry designation; for example, 9173-110 TAXI DRIVER (motor trans.). The first four digits of the code number represent the major, minor, and unit groups which categorize occupations in successively finer detail; for example, 11 represents managerial, administrative, and related occupations (major group), 111 officials and administrations unique to government (minor group), and 1111 members of legislative bodies (unit group). The last three digits provide a code number within the classification structure for each occupation; for example 4133-110 TELLER (bank and finance) and 6191-110 JANITOR (any industry).

Occupational descriptions include five selected occupational characteristics and appear as coded digits or letters. These are: the general educational development needed for the job (GED), the specific vocational preparation needed (SVP), the environmental conditions within which the work is performed (EC), the physical activities involved in the work (PA), and the demands made on the worker and the worker's function in relation to data, people, and things (DPT). The codes GED and SVP reflect the training-time requirements of occupations independently of years of schooling (or other standards commonly used) of job incumbents; they also arrange occupations in each unit group in order of complexity. The EC code indicates the relevant physical surroundings of a worker; noise, mechanical hazards, fumes, and dust are examples of the kind of factors considered. The PA code expresses both the physical requirements of the occupation and the physical capacities (or traits) a worker must have to meet those requirements; for example, seeing, lifting, climbing, etc. The DPT code indicates the worker's functional relationships to data (for example, analyzing, synthesizing), people (negotiating, supervising), and things (handling, tending).

Aptitudes required for each job (APT), apart from the above, are also coded. The factors included are intelligence (G), verbal ability (V), numerical ability (N), spatial ability (S), form perception or the ability to perceive pertinent details in objects (P), clerical perception ability (Q), eye-hand motor coordination (K), finger dexterity (F), manual dexterity (M), eye-hand-foot coordination (E), and colour discrimination (C). Five levels, i.e., five codes, are used for every aptitude except intelligence, for which only four levels are used.

The interest factors (INT) required for the particular job are also shown in the CCDO coding. Five pairs of interest factors are provided such that a positive concern for one factor of a pair usually implies rejection of the other factor (for example, routine, concrete, organized work vs. abstract, creative work). Finally, the temperament or personality requirements (TEMP) are shown against each job. Twelve such factors are used in CCDO.

Given below is an example of CCDO job coding.

---

8739-170                                          Tree Trimmer (elec. power, telecom.)

Trims trees to clear right-of-way for communication and electric power lines to minimize storm and short-circuit hazards:

Climbs trees to reach branches interfering with wires and transmission towers, using climbing equipment. Prunes treetops and branches, using saws and pruning shears. Trims damaged trees and paints stumps to prevent bleeding of sap. Removes broken limbs from wires, using extension pole. Fells trees interfering with power service, using chain-saw.

Works from bucket of extended truck boom to reach branches as required.

GED: 2     SVP: 3     PA: M 2 4     EC: 0 4 6     DPT: 687

|        APT        |  INT  |  TEMP  |
|-------------------|-------|--------|
| G V N S P Q K F M E C | | |
| 4 4 5 4 4 5 4 4 3 3 5 | 3 1 | 2 3 Y |

---

Source: *Canadian Classification and Dictionary of Occupations*, Vols. 1-2, Canada Employment and Immigration, 1971.

- *Job grade.* Job descriptions may have a blank for later addition of the job grade or level. This information helps rank the job's importance for pay purposes.

- *Supervisor.* The supervisor's title may be listed to help identify the job and its relative importance.

- *Status.* Analysts may identify the job as exempt or not from overtime laws.

## Job Summary and Duties

After the job identification section, the next part of the description is the job summary. It is a written narrative that concisely summarizes the job in a few sentences. It tells what the job is, how it is done, and why. Most authorities recommend that job summaries specify the primary actions involved. Then in a simple, action-oriented style, the job description lists the job duties. Figure 5-4 provides an example of this style.

This section is important to human resource specialists. It explains what the job requires. The effectiveness of other human resource actions depends upon this understanding, because each major duty is described in terms of the actions expected. Tasks and activities are identified. Performance is emphasized. Even responsibilities are implied or stated within the job duties. If employees are in a union, the union may want to narrow the duties associated with specific jobs.

> Before the union organized, the employee job descriptions contained the phrase "or other work as assigned." The union believed supervisors abused this clause by assigning idle workers to do unrelated jobs. With the threat of a strike, management removed the phrase, and supervisors lost much of their flexibility in assigning work.

## Working Conditions

A job description also explains working conditions. It may go beyond descriptions of the physical environment. Hours of work, safety and health hazards, travel requirements, and other features of the job expand the meaning of this section.

## Approvals

Since job descriptions affect most human resource decisions, their accuracy should be reviewed by selected jobholders and their supervisors. Then supervisors are asked to approve the description. This approval serves as a further test of the job description and a further check on the collection of job analysis information. Neither human resource specialists nor managers should consider approval lightly. If the description is in error, the human resource department will become a source of problems, not assistance.

> In explaining the job of foundry attendant to new employees, human resource specialists at one firm relied on an inaccurate job description. Many new employees quit the job during the first two weeks. When asked why, most said the duties were less challenging than they were led to believe. When analysts checked, it was found the job description had never been verified by the supervisors.

## Job Specifications

The difference between a job description and a job specification is one of perspective. A job description defines what the job does; it is a profile of the job. A *job specification* describes what the job demands of employees who do it and the human factors that are required.[8] It is a profile of the human characteristics needed by the job. These requirements include experience, training, education, physical demands, and mental demands.

FIGURE 5-6   A Job Specification Sheet

---

**BREVARD GENERAL HOSPITAL**
Job Description

Job Title:    Job Analyst                    Job Code:   166.088

Date:         January 3, 19--               Author:     John Doakes

Job Location: Human Resource Department      Job Grade:

Supervisor:   Harold Grantinni              Status:     Exempt

Skill Factors
  Education:        College degree required.
  Experience:      At least one year as job analyst trainee, recruiter, or other
                   professional assignment in human resource area.
  Communication:   Oral and written skills should evidence ability to capsulize job data
                   succinctly.

Effort Factors
  Physical Demands:  Limited to those normally associated with clerical jobs: sitting,
                     standing, and walking.
  Mental demands:    Extended visual attention is needed to observe jobs. Initiative and
                     ingenuity are mandatory since job receives only general supervision.
                     Judgement must be exercised on job features to be emphasized, jobs
                     to be studied, and methods used to collect job data.
                     Decision-making discretion is frequent.
                     Analyzes and synthesizes large amounts of abstract information into
                     job descriptions, job specifications, and job standards.

Working Conditions
Travels to hospital clinics in municipality from one to three days per month.
Travels around each work site collecting job information.
Works mostly in an office setting.

---

Since the job description and specifications both focus on the job, they are often combined into one document. The combination is simply called a job description. Whether part of a job description or a separate document, job specifications include the information illustrated in Figure 5-6. The data to compile specifications also come from the job analysis checklist.

Job specifications contain a job identification section if they are a separate document. The subheadings and purpose are the same as those found in the job identification section of the job description.

A job specification should include *specific* tools, actions, experiences, education, and training, i.e., the *individual* requirements of the job. For example, it should describe "physical effort" in terms of the special actions demanded by the job. "Lifts 40-kilogram bags" is better than "Lifts heavy weights."[9] Clear behaviour statements give a better picture than vague generalities.[10] Specifications of mental effort help human resource experts determine the intellectual abilities that are needed. Figure 5-6 contains several examples of the kind of information about physical and mental efforts needed by job analysts for a hospital.

Do the working conditions make any unusual demands on jobholders? The working conditions found in job descriptions may be translated by job specifications into demands faced by workers. Figure 5-7 provides examples for the job of hospital orderly. It shows that a simple statement of working conditions found in the job description can hold significant implications for jobholders. For example, compare points 2 and 3 under the job description column with points 2 and 3 under job specifications.

FIGURE 5-7   Translation of Working Conditions for Job Description to Job Specification

| HOSPITAL ORDERLY | |
| --- | --- |
| JOB DESCRIPTION STATEMENT OF WORKING CONDITIONS | JOB SPECIFICATIONS INTERPRETATION OF WORKING CONDITIONS |
| 1. Works in physically comfortable surroundings. | 1. (Omitted. This item on the job description makes no demands on jobholders.) |
| 2. Deals with physically ill and diseased patients. | 2. Exposed to unpleasant situations and communicable diseases. |
| 3. Deals with mentally ill patients. | 3. May be exposed to verbal and physical abuse. |

## JOB PERFORMANCE STANDARDS

Job analysis has a third application, *job performance standards*. These standards serve two functions. First, they become objectives or targets for employee efforts. The challenge or pride of meeting objectives may serve to motivate employees. Once standards are met, workers may feel accomplishment and achievement. This outcome contributes to employee satisfaction. Without standards, employee performance may suffer.

Second, standards are criteria against which job success is measured. They are indispensable to managers or human resource specialists who attempt to control work performance. Without standards, no control system can evaluate job performance.[11]

All control systems have four features: standards, measures, correction, and feedback. The relationship between these four factors is illustrated in Figure 5-8. Job performance standards are developed from job analysis information, and then actual employee performance is measured. When measured performance strays from the job standard, corrective action is taken. That is, human resource experts or line managers intervene. The corrective action serves as feedback to the standards and actual performance. This feedback leads to changes in either the standards (if they were inappropriate) or actual job performance.

FIGURE 5-8    Diagram of a Job Control System

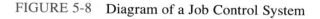
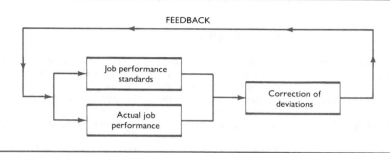

In the Toronto Trust Company, current standards dictated that each loan supervisor review 250 mortgage-loan applications per month. Yet the actual output averaged 210. When more recent job information was collected, analysts discovered that since the standards had been first set, several new duties had been added for each supervisor. Corrective action resulted in new job designs, revised job descriptions, and more realistic standards.

Job standards are a key part of any control system. When the standards are wrong, as in the trust company example, they alert managers and human resource specialists to problems that need correction. The example also underscores the need for keeping job analysis information current.

Job standards are obtained either from job analysis information or from alternative sources. Job analysis information is usually sufficient for jobs that have the following features:

- Performance is quantified.
- Performance is easily measurable.
- Performance standards are understood by workers and supervisors.
- Performance requires little interpretation.

Jobs with short work cycles often exhibit these features. An example is an assembly-line job. For these jobs, questions on the job analysis checklist may generate specific, quantitative answers. When confirmed by supervisors, this information becomes the job performance standard. Figure 5-9 shows the job dimensions for professors teaching organizational behaviour courses in Canada. Figure 5-10 elaborates some "effective" and "ineffective" behaviours associated with one performance dimension, "teaching style." Clear behavioural descriptions of job performance such as these facilitate a more accurate appraisal of the performer.[12] More details of behaviourally oriented performance appraisals will be discussed in Chapter 11.

FIGURE 5-9   Empirically Derived Performance Dimensions of Professors Teaching Behavioural Sciences in Canada

| PERFORMANCE DIMENSION | KEY ASPECTS COVERED |
|---|---|
| 1. Course outlining and structuring | Definition of the course objectives; inclusion of student needs and expectations into the outline; provision of detailed schedule for lectures and assignments in class. |
| 2. Coverage of material | Nature, relevance, scope, and depth of course content and readings; linkage to other disciplines. |
| 3. Teaching style | Actual behaviour within the classroom, including leadership style used within classroom. |
| 4. Teaching methods | Variety, relevance, and usefulness of various teaching methods and aids used. |
| 5. Evaluation | Objective definition of evaluation criteria; extent of feedback given to students about their performance; flexibility displayed in evaluation methods. |
| 6. Interaction outside class | Instructor being available for consultation outside class; friendliness, interest, and help given by him/her to students. |
| 7. Flexibility and responsiveness | Flexibility and responsiveness displayed by instructor. Sensitivity to student needs. |

Source: Hari Das, Peter J. Frost, and J. Thad Barnowe, "Behaviourally Anchored Scales for Assessing Behavioural Science Teaching," *Canadian Journal of Behavioural Science*. Vol. II, No. 1, January 1979, p. 82.

FIGURE 5-10   Scale Scores and "Effective" and "Ineffective" Behavioural Anchors for "Teaching Style" Performance Dimension of University Professors

| SCALE SCORE | BEHAVIOURAL ANCHOR |
|---|---|
| 6.73 | Could be expected to provide real-life and personal examples to explain a concept. |
| 5.81 | Could be expected to speak with considerable energy and enthusiasm. |
| 2.10 | Could be expected to give dull lectures which are repetitive of the textbook. |
| 1.70 | Could be expected to use abstract and difficult language in his/her lectures. |
| 5.39 | Could be expected to lay emphasis on many students participating in class discussions rather than students only giving right answers. |
| 3.71 | Could be expected to spend considerable class time in stating his/her personal views on different matters. |
| 6.44 | Could be expected to encourage students to ask questions and answer their questions without "putting them down." |
| 5.89 | Could be expected to take considerable effort to learn names of students and engage in conversations. |
| 5.46 | Could be expected to treat his/her students as equals within class. |
| 4.39 | Could be expected to secure participation of individual students by asking them specific questions. |

Source: Hari Das, Peter J. Frost, and J. Thad Barnowe, "Behaviourally Anchored Scales for Assessing Behavioural Science Teaching," *Canadian Journal of Behavioural Science*, Vol. II, No. 1, January 1979, p. 83.

## ALTERNATIVE SOURCES OF STANDARDS

Although job analysis information does not always provide a source of job standards, it is necessary even if analysts use other means to develop reasonable standards. The most common alternative sources of job standards are work measurement and participative goal setting.

### Work Measurement

*Work measurement* techniques estimate the normal performance of average workers; the results dictate the job performance standard. Such techniques are applied to nonmanagerial jobs and are created from historical data, time study, and work sampling. They may be used by the human resource department, line management, or industrial engineering. Regardless of who applies work measurement techniques, however, job analysis information is also needed.

### Historical Data

*Historical data* can be obtained from past records if job analysis does not supply performance standards. For example, the number of shirts produced per month by a clothing manufacturer indicates how many sleeves, collars, and buttons should be sewn on by each worker. One weakness of this approach is that it assumes past performance is average performance. Another weakness is that historical data are useless on new jobs. However, if production records are reviewed for long-standing jobs, historically based standards may be more accurate than standards drawn from a job analysis checklist.

### Time Study

*Time studies* produce standards when jobs can be observed and timed. Time studies identify each element within a job. Then each element is timed while being repeated by an average worker using the standard method of doing the job. The average times for each element of the job are summed up to yield the *rated job time*. Allowances for rest breaks, fatigue, or equipment delays are added to produce a *standard time*. The standard time allows human resource specialists to compute performance standards.

> Assume a secretary can type a page of straight copy on a word processor in an average of four minutes, based on several direct observations. To this rated job time of four minutes, allowances for changing disks, replacing printer paper, taking rest breaks, etc., are added. The total is a standard time of five minutes. This means that the secretary's standard of performance should be an average of one page of word processing per five minutes, or twelve an hour.

### Work Sampling

How does the analyst know the number of minutes to add for allowances? Allowances are usually set through *work sampling*. By making 300 observations of typists at different times during the day over a two-week period, for example, analysts might discover that the typists were actually typing two-thirds of the time. If eight minutes of uninterrupted typing are required to type a page, then the standard time can be computed by dividing the rated time of eight minutes by the fraction of time spent working, or two-thirds in this example. The result is a standard time of twelve minutes. Mathematically, the computation is:

$$\text{Rated time} \div \text{observed proportion of work time used} = \text{standard time}$$

$$\text{OR}$$

$$8 \text{ minutes} \div \tfrac{2}{3} = 12 \text{ minutes}$$

Standards for some jobs cannot be determined by either job analysis information or work measurement. In service or managerial jobs, output may reflect changing trade-offs. For example, the number of customers handled by a grocery checkout clerk depends on how busy the store is and on the size of each customer's purchases. But standards are still useful, even though they are difficult to set. In some cases, mutual agreement between the worker and the manager — participative goal setting — is more likely to be effective.

## *Participative Goal Setting*

When a job lacks obvious standards, managers may develop them participatively through discussions with subordinates. These conversations discuss the purpose of the job, its role in relation to other jobs, the organization's requirements, and the employee's needs. The employee gains insight into what is expected. Implicit or explicit promises of future rewards may also result. From these discussions, the manager and the employee reach some jointly shared objectives and standards.[13] The process may even lead to greater employee commitment, morale, satisfaction, and motivation. Since objectives are usually for individual positions (instead of jobs), they are seldom included in job descriptions.

Performance standards sometimes are set participatively with union leaders. Labour leaders understand the important role of job analysis information, and they may insist on negotiating performance standards for jobs. These negotiated agreements are written into legally enforceable contracts.

> In one paper products company, management decided to increase production rates by 5% to meet customer demand. After this was done, the union threatened legal action because the new standards conflicted with those in the labour contract. Management was forced to retain the old standard.

## THE HUMAN RESOURCE INFORMATION SYSTEM

Job descriptions, job specifications, and job standards are the minimum data base needed by human resource departments. Together, these outputs of job analysis information explain each job. Supported with this information, human resource specialists can make intelligent decisions concerning jobs and human resources.[14] But there are three problems with the minimum human resource information system as it has been explained so far: organization, legal considerations, and the scope of the data base.

## Organization of the Data Base .

Whether job information is on written forms or in computer memories, it is organized around individual jobs. Although this is useful, human resource departments also need job analysis information that is organized around job families. *Job families* are groups of jobs that are closely related by similar duties, responsibilities, skills, or job elements. The jobs of clerk, typist, clerk-typist, and secretary constitute a job family, for example. These groups allow human resource departments to facilitate job rotation programs, permanent job transfers, and other human resource decisions.

Job families can be constructed in several ways. One way is by careful study of existing job analysis information. Matching of the data in job descriptions can identify jobs with similar requirements. A second method is to use the codes in the *Canadian Classification and Dictionary of Occupations* (Figure 5-5). Similarities in the job codes indicate similarities in the jobs.

The third approach is the *position analysis questionnaire*. The position analysis questionnaire (also called the PAQ) is a standardized, preprinted form that collects specific information about job tasks and worker traits. Through statistical analysis of the PAQ responses, related jobs are grouped into job families.

## Legal Considerations

For the most part, job analysis information is an internal matter that is affected little by external challenges. But when human resource specialists rely on job analysis information to pursue other external activities, such as hiring, legal considerations arise in the area of compliance with Human Rights Legislation. For example, charges of discrimination may result from the unequal impact of some needless job requirement:

> In one instance, an employer required a high school diploma for nearly all jobs within the company except those in the labour pool. When the need for a diploma was challenged, the employer could not show that it was absolutely necessary to perform many of the jobs for which it was officially required and although this requirement was applied equally to all applicants, it had an unequal impact on minority-group applicants. As a result, many persons belonging to such groups were offered labour-pool jobs only.

Further, needless job requirements exclude potentially qualified individuals from consideration, which may reduce the effectiveness not only of hiring but of other human resource activities.

## Scope of the Data Base

Job descriptions, job specifications, and job standards provide only a narrow data base. Arranging these data into job families helps, but more information is demanded for the purpose of some human resource management activities. Thus job analysis information is only the first part of a sophisticated human resource information system. Additions to this information system are made through other human resource activities discussed throughout the book.

## DESIGNING SATISFYING JOBS

Worldwide competition, expensive technology, and worker expectations demand jobs that are more productive and more satisfying. The computer—which barely existed when many of today's retirees began their careers — is estimated to have changed the jobs of 50 million people in North America.[15] While some jobs have grown more challenging, others have become less skilled or have even been eliminated. And yet, for all the talk of computerization and automation, people are more, not less, important.

> For example, the cost of a human error in a nuclear plant or in flying a supersonic jet can be enormous. Whether it is the high-speed computers or the traditional auto assembly plant now run by robots, the contribution of the human beings continues to be critical. Indeed, the new technologies may be dangerous or unforgiving when operated by uncommitted or poorly skilled persons.

How well people perform is shaped, at least in part, by the characteristics designed into their jobs.[16] Not only is productivity affected, but quality of work life is also tied to job design. Jobs are the central link between employees and the organization. Job openings are why organizations need human resources. If human resource departments are going to help the organization obtain and maintain a desired work force, people specialists must have a thorough understanding of job designs.

Figure 5-11 illustrates a systems view of job design. The design of a job reflects the organizational, environmental, and behavioural demands placed on it. Job designers attempt to consider these elements and create jobs that are both productive and satisfying. However, trade-offs among these elements of job design mean that some jobs are more or less satisfying than others. Employee productivity and satisfaction provide feedback on how well designed a job is. Poorly designed jobs not only lead to low productivity, but they can also cause employee turnover, absenteeism, complaints, sabotage, unionization, resignations, and other problems.

> In General Life and Home Insurance Company, each clerk had narrowly defined responsibilities. Each did a specific function and moved the "paperwork" on to someone else. The result was that no one had responsibility for handling an application for a policy conversion. In fact, no one department had responsibility since activities were spread over three departments.
>
> The job redesign grouped the clerks into teams of five to seven employees. Each team was trained to do the functions of all three departments. Members learned new skills, job satisfaction went up, and pay improved since each team member now had greater skills and responsibilities.

In this instance, the company did consider the various environmental, organizational, and behavioural elements before redesigning the jobs. The result was better customer service, higher work productivity, and overall improved worker morale.

FIGURE 5-11    The Job Design Input-Output Framework

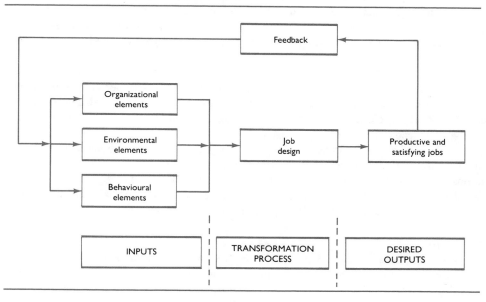

It should be noted that job redesign does have some trade-offs. Under the new structure in General Life and Home Insurance Company, each clerk needs to have knowledge of several activities. Therefore, more training for these clerks is necessary. And, as they become more qualified, the company will need to pay them higher salaries. To explain these trade-offs more fully, a review of the organizational, environmental, and behavioural elements of job design follows. Then the chapter will conclude with a discussion of job-redesign techniques.

## Organizational Elements of Job Design

Organizational elements of job design are concerned with efficiency. Efficiently designed jobs allow a highly motivated and capable worker to achieve maximum output. This concern for efficiency was formalized by the management scientists around the turn of the century. They devoted much of their research to finding the best ways to design efficient jobs. Their success with stopwatches and motion pictures even gave rise to a new discipline, industrial engineering. They also contributed to the formal study of management as a separate discipline. From their efforts, we have learned that specialization is a key element in the design of jobs. When workers are limited to a few repetitive tasks, output is usually higher. The findings of these early researchers are still applicable today. They can be summarized under the heading of the mechanistic approach.

### Mechanistic Approach
The mechanistic approach seeks to identify *every* task in a job so that tasks can be arranged to minimize the time and effort of workers. Once task identification is complete, a limited number of tasks is grouped into a job. The result is *specialization.* Specialized jobs lead to short *job cycles,* the time to complete every task in the job. For example:

> An assembly-line worker in Windsor, Ontario, might pick up a headlight, plug it in, twist the adjustment screws, and pick up the next headlight within thirty seconds. Completing these tasks in thirty seconds means this worker's job cycle takes one-half a minute. The job cycle begins when the next headlight is picked up.

Headlight installation is a specialized job. It is so specialized that training takes only a few minutes. And the short job cycle means that the assembler gains much experience in a short time. Said another way, short job cycles require small investments in training and allow the worker to learn the job quickly. Training costs remain low because the worker needs to master only one job.

This mechanistic approach stresses efficiency in effort, time, labour costs, training, and employee learning time. Today, this technique is still widely used in assembly operations. It is especially effective when dealing with poorly educated workers or workers who have little industrial experience. But the efficient design of jobs also considers such organizational elements as work flow, ergonomics, and work practices.

### Work Flow

The flow of work in an organization is strongly influenced by the nature of the product or service. The product or service usually suggests the sequence of and balance between jobs if the work is to be done efficiently. For example, the frame of a car must be built before the fenders and doors can be added. Once the sequence of jobs is determined, then the balance between jobs is established.

> Suppose it takes one person thirty seconds to install each headlight. In two minutes, an assembler can put on four headlights. If, however, it takes four minutes to install the necessary headlight receptacles, then the job designer must balance these two interrelated jobs by assigning two people to install the receptacles. Otherwise, a production bottle-neck results. Since the work flow demands two receptacle installers for each headlight installer, one worker specializes on the right-side receptacles and another specializes on the left side.

### Ergonomics

Optimal productivity requires that the physical relationship between the worker and the work be considered in designing jobs. *Ergonomics* is the study of how human beings physically interface with their work. Although the nature of job tasks may not vary when ergonomics are considered, the location of tools, switches, and the work product itself are evaluated and placed in a position for ease of use. On an automobile assembly line, for example, a car frame may actually be elevated at a work station so the worker does not become fatigued from stooping. Similarly, the location of dashboard instruments in a car is ergonomically engineered to make driving easier.

### Work Practices

Work practices are set ways of performing work. These methods may arise from tradition or the collective wishes of employees. Either way, the human resource department's flexibility to design jobs is limited, especially when such practices are part of a union-management relationship. Failure to consider work practices can have undesired outcomes.

> General Motors decided to increase productivity at one of its American plants by eliminating some jobs and adding new tasks to others. These design changes caused workers to stage a strike for several weeks because traditional practices at the plant had required a slower rate of production and less work by the employees. The additional demands on their jobs by management were seen as an attempt by the company to disregard past work practices.[17]

## Environmental Elements of Job Design

A second aspect of job design concerns environmental elements. As with most human resource activities, job designers cannot ignore the influence of the external environment. In designing jobs, human resource specialists and managers should consider the ability and availability of potential employees. At the same time, social expectations have to be weighed.

### Employee Abilities and Availability

Efficiency considerations must be balanced against the abilities and availability of the people who are to do the work. For example, since workers lack any automobile-making experience, jobs are designed to be simple and require little training. Thought must be given to who will actually do the work. An extreme example underlines this point.

> Governments of less developed countries often think they can "buy" progress. To be "up to date," they seek the most advanced equipment they can find. Leaders of one country ordered a computerized oil refinery. This decision dictated a level of technology that exceeded the abilities of the country's available work force. As a result, these government leaders have hired Europeans to operate the refinery.

In less developed nations, the major risk is jobs that are too complex. Jobs that are too simple can produce equally disturbing problems in industrial nations with highly educated workers. For example, even when unemployment rates are high, many simple and overly specialized jobs are sometimes hard to fill, as long-standing newspaper want ads for dishwashers and janitors attest.

### Social Expectations

The acceptability of a job's design is also influenced by the expectations of society. For example, working conditions that would have been acceptable to some early Canadian immigrants are no longer suitable to our present generation. At the time when rail lines were being laid across Canada, many persons had to work long hours of hard labour. Often, they had fled countries where jobs were unavailable. This made a job—any job —acceptable to them. Today, industrial workers are much better educated and have higher expectations about the quality of work life. Although work flow or work practices may suggest a particular job design, the job must meet the expectations of workers. Failure to consider these social expectations can create dissatisfaction, low motivation, hard-to-fill job openings, and low quality of work life.

## Behavioural Elements of Job Design

Jobs cannot be designed by using only those elements that aid efficiency. To do so overlooks the human needs of the people who are to perform the work. Instead, job designers draw heavily on behavioural research to provide a work environment that helps satisfy individual needs. In particular, individuals by and large prefer jobs that have high autonomy, variety, task identity, and feedback.

### Autonomy

*Autonomy* is having responsibility for what one does. It is the freedom to control one's response to the environment. Jobs that give workers the authority to make decisions provide added responsibilities that tend to increase the employee's sense of recognition and self-esteem. The absence of autonomy, on the other hand, can cause employee apathy or poor performance.[18]

> A common problem in many production operations is that employees develop an "I don't care attitude" because they believe they have no control over their jobs. On the bottling line of a small brewery, teams of workers were allowed to speed up or slow down the rate of the bottling line as long as they met daily production goals. Although total output per shift did not change, there were fewer cases of capping machines jamming or breaking down for other reasons. When asked about this unexpected development, the supervisor concluded, "Employees pride themselves on meeting the shift quota. So they are more careful to check for defective bottle caps before they load the machine."

### Variety

A lack of variety may cause boredom. Boredom in turn leads to fatigue, and fatigue causes errors. By injecting variety into jobs, human resource specialists can reduce fatigue-caused errors. Being able to control the speed of the bottling line in the brewery example added variety to the pace of work and probably reduced both boredom and fatigue.

One research study found that diversity of work was partially responsible for effective performance.[19] And another study found that autonomy and variety were major contributors to employee satisfaction.[20]

### Task Identity

One problem with some jobs is that they lack any *task identity*. Workers cannot point to some complete piece of work. They have little sense of responsibility and may lack pride in the results. After completing their job, they may have little sense of accomplishment. When tasks are grouped so that employees feel they are making an identifiable contribution, job satisfaction may be increased significantly.[21] Returning to our General Life and Home Insurance Company example, we saw that productivity and satisfaction increased when employees became responsible for an identifiable and sensible group of tasks.

### Feedback

When jobs do not give the workers any feedback on how well they are doing, there is little guidance or motivation to perform better. For example, by letting employees know how they are doing relative to the daily production quota, the brewery gives workers feedback that allows them to adjust their efforts. Providing feedback leads to improved motivation.[22]

Closely related to the above dimensions is *task significance.* Doing an identifiable piece of work makes the job more satisfying. Task significance, knowing that the work is important to others in the organization or outside it, makes the job even more meaningful for incumbents. Their personal sense of self-importance is enhanced because they know that others are depending on what they do. Pride, commitment, motivation, satisfaction, and better performance are likely to result.

## BEHAVIOURAL AND EFFICIENCY TRADE-OFFS

Behavioural elements of job design tell human resource specialists to add more autonomy, variety, task identity, task significance, and feedback. But efficiency elements point to greater specialization, less variety, and minimum autonomy. Thus, to make jobs more efficient may cause them to be less satisfying. Conversely, satisfying jobs may prove to be inefficient. What should human resource specialists do? There is no simple solution. Instead, human resource experts often make trade-offs between efficiency and behavioural elements. Figure 5-12 depicts the most significant trade-offs faced by job designers in the human resource department.

### Graph A: Productivity versus Specialization

The assumption that additional specialization means increased output is true only up to some point. As jobs are made more specialized, productivity climbs until behavioural elements such as boredom offset the advantages of further specialization. In Figure 5-12A, additional specialization beyond point *b* causes productivity to drop. In fact, jobs that are between *b* and *c* can have their productivity *increased* by reducing the degree of specialization.

### Graph B: Satisfaction versus Specialization

Another interesting relationship exists between satisfaction and specialization. Here satisfaction first goes up with specialization, and then additional specialization causes satisfaction to drop quickly. Jobs without any specialization take too long to learn; frustration is decreased and feedback is increased by adding some specialization. However, when specialization is carried past point *b* in Figure 5-12B, satisfaction drops because of a lack of autonomy, variety, and task identification. Notice that even while satisfaction is falling in graph B, productivity may still increase in graph A, from *a* to *b*. Productivity continues to go up only if the advantages of specialization outweigh the disadvantages of dissatisfaction.

### Graph C: Learning versus Specialization

When a job is highly specialized, there is less to learn. Therefore, it takes less time to learn a specialized job than a nonspecialized one. Graphically, this means that the rate of learning reaches an acceptable standard more quickly (shown as a dashed line).

FIGURE 5-12   Efficiency versus Behavioural Trade-offs in Job Design

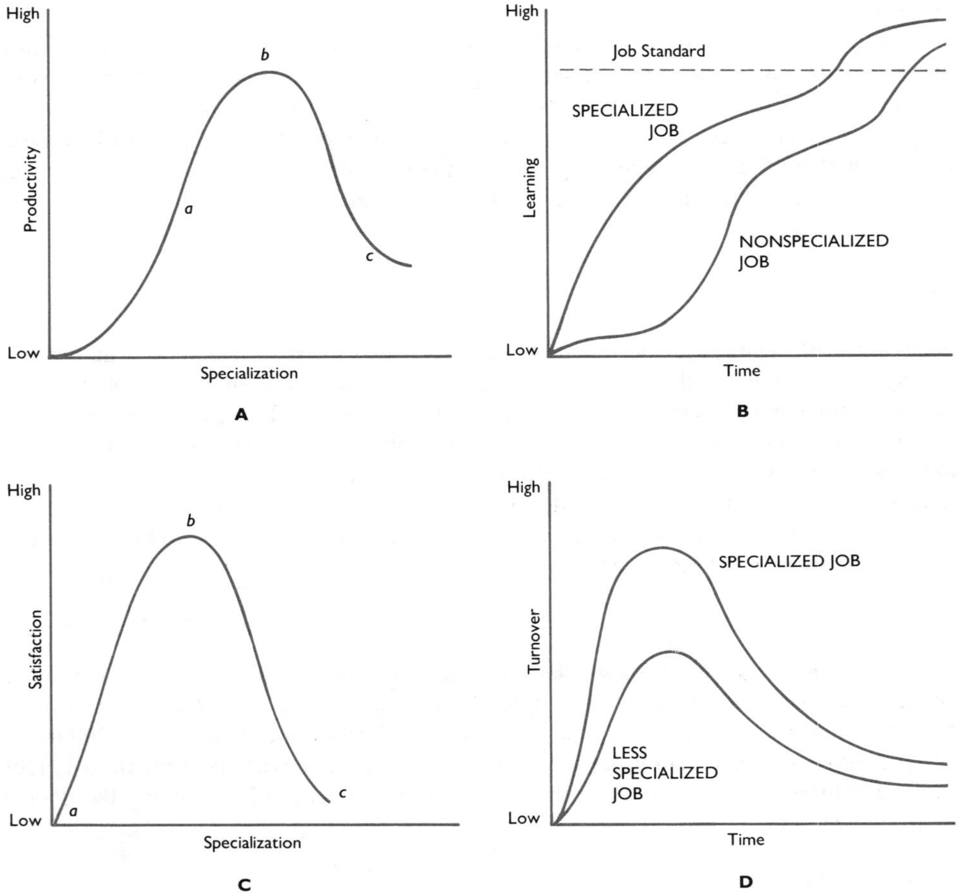

## Graph D: Turnover versus Specialization

Although overspecialized jobs are quicker to learn, the lower levels of satisfaction generally associated with them can lead to higher turnover rates. When turnover rates are high, redesigning the job with more attention to behavioural elements may reduce this quit rate.

## TECHNIQUES OF JOB REDESIGN

The central question often facing job designers is whether a particular job should have more or less specialization. As can be seen in graph A in Figure 5-12, the answer depends on whether the job is near point *a*, *b*, or *c*. Jobs near point *a* may need more specialization to become more effective. Analysis and experimentation are the only sure ways to determine where a particular job is located on the graph.

## Underspecialization

When human resource specialists believe jobs are not specialized enough, they engage in *work simplification.* That is, the job is simplified. The tasks of one job may be assigned to two jobs. Unneeded tasks are identified and eliminated. What is left are jobs that contain fewer tasks.

> When the Yukon Weekly Newspaper operated with its old press, Guy Parsons could catch the newspapers as they came off the press, stack them, and wrap them. But when a new high-speed press was added, he could not keep up with the output. So the circulation manager simplified Guy's job by making him responsible for stacking the newspapers. Two part-time high school students took turns catching and wrapping.

The risk with work simplification is that jobs may be so specialized that boredom causes errors or resignations. This potential problem is more common in advanced industrial countries that have a highly educated work force. In less developed countries, highly specialized factory jobs may be acceptable and even appealing because they provide jobs for workers with limited skills.

## Overspecialization

As the labour force in advanced industrial societies becomes more educated and affluent, routine jobs that are very specialized, such as assembly-line positions, hold less and less appeal for many people. These jobs seldom offer opportunities for accomplishment, recognition, psychological growth, or other sources of satisfaction. To increase the quality of work life for those who hold such jobs, human resource departments can use a variety of methods to improve jobs through redesign. The most widely practised techniques include job rotation, job enlargement, and job enrichment.

### Job Rotation

*Job rotation* moves employees from job to job. Jobs themselves are not actually changed; only the workers are rotated. Rotation breaks the monotony of highly specialized work by calling on different skills and abilities. The organization benefits because workers become competent in several jobs rather than only one. Knowing a variety of jobs helps the worker's self-image, provides personal growth, and makes the worker more valuable to the organization.

Human resource experts should caution those who desire to use job rotation. It does not improve the jobs themselves; the relationships between tasks, activities, and objectives remain unchanged. It may even postpone the use of more effective techniques while adding to training costs. Implementation should occur only after other techniques are considered.

## Job Enlargement

*Job enlargement* expands the number of related tasks in the job. It adds similar duties to provide greater variety. Enlargement reduces monotony by expanding the job cycle and drawing on a wider range of employee skills. According to one summary of job design research:

> IBM reported job enlargement led to higher wages and more inspection equipment, but improved quality and worker satisfaction offset these costs.
>
> Maytag Company claimed that production quality was improved, labour costs declined, worker satisfaction and overall efficiency were increased, and management production schedules became more flexible.[23]

## Job Enrichment

*Job enrichment* adds new sources of need satisfaction to jobs. It increases responsibility, autonomy, and control. Adding these elements to jobs is sometimes called *vertical loading*. *Horizontal loading* occurs when the job is expanded by simply adding related tasks, as with job enlargement. Job enrichment sees jobs as consisting of three elements: plan, do, and control.[24] Job enlargement (or horizontal loading) adds more things to *do*. Enrichment (or vertical loading) attempts to add more *planning* and *control* responsibilities. These additions to the job coupled with rethinking the job itself often lead to increased motivation and other improvements.

> In a pilot project with one unit of the Data Capture section of Statistics Canada, job enrichment and other changes resulted in increased employee satisfaction, lower absentee rates, increases in the quality and quantity of work done, and improved relationships between the union and management.
>
> One employee recalled that prior to the changes, "we were watched every second. We weren't able to talk. We had no responsibility or variety in our work. We'd just go to the basket and take the job that was on top." The changes implemented included more variety and more worker responsibility, both for completing the work and for attendance, hiring, training, appraisals, and discipline. Aside from the success indicators already mentioned, when the rest of the section was asked whether they were interested in being involved in similar changes for their units, 171 of the remaining 177 employees were in favour.[25]

Job enrichment, however, is not a cure-all; if it were, this book could end here. Job enrichment techniques are merely tools, and they are not applied universally. When the diagnosis indicates jobs are unrewarding and unchallenging and limit the motivation and satisfaction of employees, human resource departments *may* find job enrichment to be the most appropriate strategy. Even then, however, job enrichment faces problems.

One author has listed twenty-two arguments against job enrichment.[26] The most compelling points are the existence of union resistance, the cost of design and implementation, and the scarcity of research on long-term effects. Another criticism of job enrichment is that it does not go far enough. To enrich the job and ignore other variables that contribute to the quality of work life may simply increase dissatisfaction with the unimproved aspects of the job environment. There is a need to go beyond job enrichment in some work situations.[27]. Last but not least, the cultural values and social expectations surrounding the organization have to be carefully considered before any job redesign attempts are made.[28]

## SUMMARY

Job analysis information provides the foundations of an organization's human resource information system. Analysts seek to gain a general understanding of the organization and the work it performs. Then they design job analysis questionnaires to collect specific data about jobs, jobholder characteristics, and job performance standards. Job analysis information can be collected through interviews, juries of experts, mailed questionnaires, employee logs, direct observation, or some combination of these techniques. Once collected, the data are converted into such useful applications as job descriptions, job specifications, and job standards.

Job analysis information is important because it tells human resource specialists what duties and responsibilities are associated with each job. This information then is used when human resource specialists undertake other human resource management activities such as job design, recruiting, and selection. Jobs are the link between organizations and their human resources. The combined accomplishment of every job allows the organization to meet its objectives. Similarly, jobs represent not only a source of income to workers but also a means of fulfilling their needs. However, for the organization and its employees to receive these mutual benefits, jobs must provide a high quality of work life.

To achieve a high quality of work life requires jobs that are well designed. Effective job design seeks a trade-off between efficiency and behavioural elements. Efficiency elements stress productivity. Behavioural elements focus on employee needs. The role of human resource specialists is to achieve a balance between these trade-offs. When jobs are underspecialized, job designers may simplify the job by reducing the number of tasks. If jobs are overspecialized, they must be expanded or enriched.

## TERMS FOR REVIEW

Job analysis
Job description
Job code
*Canadian Classification and Dictionary
   of Occupations* (CCDO)
Job specification
Job performance standards
Work measurement
Time studies
Work sampling
Job families

Position analysis questionnaire
Specialization
Ergonomics
Autonomy
Task variety
Task identity
Task significance
Work simplification
Job rotation
Job enrichment

*REVIEW AND DISCUSSION QUESTIONS*

1.  What types of raw data do the questions on a job analysis checklist seek to obtain? Are there other data you should seek for management jobs?
2.  What are the different methods of collecting job analysis information, and what are the advantages and disadvantages of each technique?
3.  What is the purpose of (a) job descriptions, (b) job specifications, (c) job performance standards?
4.  How can performance standards be set for production jobs when job analysis information is insufficient? How would you set standards of performance for a research scientist if you were chief scientist?
5.  Describe three ways jobs can be grouped into job families.
6.  Suppose that you were assigned to write the job descriptions for a shirt factory in Toronto employing mostly Chinese immigrants who spoke little English.
    (a)  What methods would you use to collect job analysis data?
    (b)  If a manager in the shirt factory refused to complete a job analysis questionnaire, what reasons would you use to persuade that individual to complete it?
    (c)  If, after your best efforts at persuasion failed, you still wanted job analysis information on the manager's job, how would you get it?
7.  What are some of the problems you would expect to arise in an organization that had carefully designed its jobs for maximum efficiency without careful consideration of each employee's individual priority of needs?
8.  Suppose you have been assigned to design the job of ticket clerk for a regional airline. How would you handle the following trade-offs?
    (a)  Would you recommend highly specialized job designs to minimize training or very broad jobs with all clerks cross-trained to handle multiple tasks? Why?
    (b)  Would you change your answer if you knew that employees tended to quit the job of ticket clerk within the first six months? Why or why not?
9.  Assume you are told to evaluate a group of jobs in a boat-building business. After studying each job for a considerable amount of time, you identify the following activities associated with each job. What job-redesign techniques would you recommend for these jobs, if any?
    (a)  *Sailmaker.* Cuts and sews material with very little variety in the type of work from day to day. Job is highly skilled and takes years to learn.
    (b)  *Sander.* Sands rough wood and fibreglass edges almost continuously. Little skill is required in this job.
    (c)  *Sales representative.* Talks to customers, answers phone inquiries, suggests customized additions to special-order boats.
    (d)  *Boat preparer.* Cleans up completed boats, waxes fittings, and generally makes the boat ready for customer delivery. Few skills are required for this job.

## INCIDENT 5-1

### Hedges Electronics Computerized Job Data

Hedges Electronics is a small manufacturer of remote access consoles, cathode-ray-tube display terminals, and other on-line computer equipment. The remote consoles and cathode displays are widely used within the company. Through the consoles, most managers can store and retrieve data from the company's main-frame computer. This information appears on cathode-ray displays, which are similar to small television screens.

One day, since most line and staff managers were familiar with on-line equipment, it was decided to store the human resource information system on the main computer. Then when managers or human resource specialists needed a job description, they could simply secure one from the computer.

After computerizing all human resource information, job analysts began to notice that job descriptions, job specifications, and job standards were constantly being changed by jobholders. It seemed that whenever a manager or worker reviewed a job description or job specification that seemed outdated, he or she would "write in" a correction on the computer's memory.

Thus although in the beginning human resource specialists were glad that workers were showing an interest by updating the computerized job analysis information, they eventually became worried because workers with the same job titles had different views of their jobs. Changes would come from almost anyone, and there was no consistency in style or content.

To eliminate this problem, a subroutine was programmed into the computer that prevented unauthorized changes. Job analysts then reviewed the job descriptions and job specifications to ensure uniformity of style. Line and staff managers could still obtain copies of job analysis information.

1. Assume that you are the human resource manager at Hedges. What procedures would you lay down that would ensure that the restudied job analysis information was correct?
2. Given the ability of most managers to "communicate" directly with the computer, does Hedges Electronics have a new way to collect job analysis information? Explain.

## INCIDENT 5-2

### Western Canada Insurance Services Limited

Western Canada Insurance Services Limited, with its head office in Calgary, Alberta, is a large insurance company offering personal, auto, fire, home and business, and fidelity insurance services. It currently has offices in B.C., Alberta, Saskatchewan, and Manitoba and is planning to open new branches in Ontario and Quebec.

Recently, it began a pilot project in job redesign. Called work effectiveness, Western's innovative approach to restructuring office jobs has led to increased productivity, lower costs, improved quality of services, and greater job satisfaction among workers.

The job-redesign effort resulted from an increase in the number of invoices and a decrease in the quality and timeliness of the department's performance. Consultants conducted workshops and taught members of a task force to apply job diagnostic tools to the department's work. Interviews and surveys of incumbents provided additional inputs. As a result, the work effectiveness program redesigned jobs and helped the department achieve (1) an increase of 13% in invoices processed, (2) cost savings (in salaries and overtime) of approximately $18,000, (3) job restructuring to meet the growth needs of workers by permitting them to fully utilize their capabilities, and (4) the creation of better understanding among workers of the role they play in helping the department reach its objectives.

In the central accounts payable department at Western, the jobs were perceived as important by the people who did them, but these incumbents did not feel their personal growth needs were being met. Part of the problem stemmed from employees not knowing where their jobs fit into the overall flow of work. In addition, employees felt that they had little autonomy and received little performance feedback.

At the time the job analysis interviews were conducted, the accounts payable jobs were broken down into three phases: processing invoices, handling correspondence over payment discrepancies, and providing general information to agents and other Western employees about the status of invoices. No one clerk handled all three phases. Each person had important tasks to perform, but no one had entire responsibility for all phases of accounts payable.

The redesign of the jobs gave individual employees full responsibility for groups of accounts. This meant an accounts payable clerk would process invoices, resolve discrepancies, and handle inquiries from agents and Western employees about ''his'' or ''her'' group of accounts. The environmental and organizational demands by those outside agents and Western employees were better met through the redesigned jobs. Feedback was especially affected because now one clerk dealt with an agent and its in-house counterpart. Perhaps the biggest improvements occurred in the behavioural elements such as autonomy, variety, and task identity. With their broader responsibilities, the employees had a greater sense of autonomy in resolving issues. They also felt that their jobs had more variety, significance, and, of course, more feedback. Since they could identify with a set of accounts, they also received a greater sense of task identity because they could point to a completed set of accounts as theirs.

1. Although the changes made at Western's central accounts payable department sound effective, what trade-offs do you think management encountered?
2. Why might some employees prefer the previous job design?

## EXERCISE 5-1

### Preparation of a Job Description

As discussed in the chapter, there are several ways to collect job analysis information. One way is through observation. Using the form in Figure 5-2, complete parts C through J for the job of professor. After you have completed those sections of the job analysis questionnaire, use the format in Figure 5-4 and write a job description for the job of professor. When you are finished, look up the definition of professorprovided in the Canadian Classification and Dictionaryof Occupations.

1. How does the description in the *Canadian Classification and Dictionary of Occupations* vary in format and content from the one you wrote?
2. What parts of a professor's job are most important, in your opinion?

○ ○ ○ ○ ○ ○ ○ ○ ○ ○ ○ ○ ○ ○ ○ ○ ○ ○ ○ ○ ○ ○ ○ ○ ○ ○ ○ ○ ○ ○ ○ ○ ○ ○ ○ ○ ○ ○ ○ ○ ○ ○ ○

## CASE STUDY

### REGINA SHOES LIMITED: An Exercise in Job Analysis and Design

Regina Shoes Limited, a medium-sized manufacturer of leather and vinyl shoes located in Regina, Saskatchewan, currently employs about 600 persons in its plants and some 250 more in offices and warehouses throughout Western Canada. In recent months, the company has been experiencing a number of challenges and problems (see the Case Study on page 58 of this text). Added to these was the departure of John McAllister, the company's human resource manager, two weeks ago. McAllister had been with the company for a little over three years and was reputed to have "run a tight ship."

Robert Clark, president and a major shareholder of Regina Shoes, decided to re-evaluate the role of the company's human resource manager before hiring a new person. Tim Lance, a graduate of the University of Manitoba and now the chief executive and owner of Productivity Systems, a management consulting operation located in Saskatoon, was hired to "look into the present and future role of Regina's human resource department and suggest appropriate action plans to improve its contribution to the organization and help the company meet its future challenges."

#### Views of the Senior Managers

Lance began his assignment by interviewing the senior managers of Regina Shoes. He prepared a short checklist of questions to prepare for his interview with the managers (see Figure 1). He was, however, determined not to restrict his interview to these questions. By keeping an informal and free-flowing format, he felt that he could gain a better understanding of the structure, processes, and culture of the organization. His intent, therefore, was to use these questions as a springboard for letting the interviewee speak out and pursue any point that he or she might consider relevant. Lance was able to meet three of the five "key" managers in the company. Figure 2 shows an approximate chain of command in the company in 1988. At the time Lance conducted his study, André Cardin, manager (Design & Research), was away on holidays. Lance was also not able to have an interview with the

---

FIGURE I

Checklist prepared by Lance for interviewing the senior managers.

- What do you expect from the human resource department in this company?
- What is your evaluation of the human resource department's contributions in the past?
- What activities should the human resource department of this company carry out?
- Which of these are done now? How well are you satisfied with the performance of the department in those fields?

- Overall, are you happy with the human resource staff? Why?
- What are the major challenges facing Regina Shoes in the next five years?
- What are the unique needs of your department?
- What new services or information should the human resource department provide you?

---

production manager as he was on trips to Montreal and Winnipeg investigating the potential of expanding the company's operations to those cities. Lance felt that the half-hour interview with Robert Clark (interrupted by three or four phone calls "on urgent matters which unexpectedly arose") was totally inadequate for his purpose. However, Clark was due to leave town the next day and Lance could not wait until Clark's return to proceed with his study.

Going through his notes, Lance realized that the human resource function was viewed very differently by the three senior managers to whom he talked. "I believe that we need a mover and a shaker here," Clark told him. "McAllister was all right, but he did not have the time or inclination to have a good system in place. He made most of the human resource decisions himself. I'm not saying that they weren't the correct decisions for those occasions; but he wasn't a popular man with either the workers or several managers here. And as you know, this is one job where you need a lot of rapport with people at all levels."

Some of the excerpts from Lance's interview with Clark are given below:

"I believe that the new person should be able to work with the people. In fact, not simply working with the people but *leading* them.

He or she should be able to look beyond today's needs . . . into the technological and other challenges that face this company and our managers in 1990s and beyond. . . .

"The future of Regina Shoes? I would say that we can go almost as high in the list of successful Canadian firms as we want. Shoes are something that everyone needs — every day, every week, and all through their lives. Also, most persons don't mind buying an extra pair if the price is right. But there's the catch. It's a pretty competitive market and what we do here and how well we do it depends quite a bit on how good our competitors are. To succeed, we need to have a clear market segment, control our costs, and meet our customer's needs. Two of our brands are already leaders in the Western Canada shoe market. I am confident that we can do much better than this in the years to come. . . .

"The most immediate problem? I should say we have two pressing issues: first, we have to upgrade our production processes if we are to improve our efficiency and competitiveness. I personally believe that we have more employees than we need. If we could automate many of the production processes, we could improve the efficiency and reduce costs. But that is easier said than done. We have strong unions and firing someone is going to be awfully hard in

## FIGURE 2

An Approximate Chain of Command in Regina Shoes in Early 1988

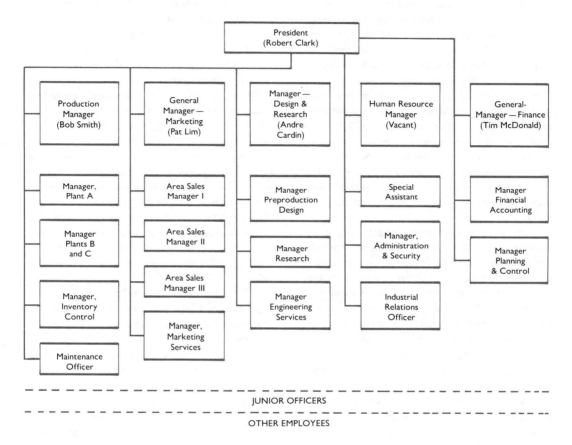

future. At the same time, the reality is that no customer is going to pay 15 or 20% extra for our shoes if we cannot give a damn good reason for that. With the free trade agreement on now, the market is going to be flooded with American products. Our survival may very well depend on technological upgrading and improving worker productivity.

"A second and related issue is dealing with unions. We have four major unions and I would term two of them as militant. Actually, our workers are pretty good—many of them have been with us for several years now — it is the union leadership that is causing much of the problem. The new human resource manager hired has to be tough with the unions yet caring and understanding. In the last three or four years, the union-management relations have gone from bad to worse. We have to turn a new leaf now or else all of us will sink."

The responses to Lance's questions from the other two senior managers at Regina Shoes were varied. Excerpts from his interview with Tim McDonald, general manager, Finance, are given below:

"I don't think human resource management is the most critical activity in the management of a shoe company," McDonald had told him. "True, we have to pay the employees adequately and there must be a system for keeping employee records. But, beyond that, I don't think that the human resource department has anything major to offer that has a significant impact on an organization's working. What we really should focus on now is how to control our costs and come out with a sound marketing program. We especially need a good advertising campaign; we need to hire competent sales staff and upgrade the skills of the present sales force. . . .

"The human resource department here hasn't done much, if you ask me. They haven't had any input into job design or organizational planning. Part of the problem stems from the fact that there has been little continuity in that department. A typical manager in the human resource department stays for a maximum of three years before he moves out. Neither McAllister nor his predecessor stayed in the company for five years. Tony Rezkov, the manager in charge of administration and security, is new; so are several of the other junior officers and staff in the department. . . . I do believe that there is a problem there. . . .

"Oh, don't get me wrong. The human resource department staff are very friendly and cooperative. McAllister had a few rough edges, but overall, he was someone whom I grew to like. He was one of those tough guys — straight out of a John Wayne movie. He made fast decisions and was sort of a trouble-shooter here. . . .

"The big challenge? Free trade, of course. We'd better be prepared to meet the Americans — and in a sense the South Koreans and Chinese since the Americans get much of their cheap materials from those places now. Unless we maintain our competitiveness, we are just not going to survive. It is as simple as that. . . .

"Of course, free trade also brings with it a great opportunity. We have access to a market now that is several times the size of our local market. But can we make use of this opportunity? That is the big question."

Pat Lim, general manager, Marketing, had a somewhat different vision of the role of the human resource department.

"It is probably one of the most important functions in this company," Lim had told Lance. "In my university days, I was taught that human resources are the single most important asset of any organization. After working for nearly twenty-five years in the management area, I have grown to realize how true that statement is. In my mind, people make all the difference. You can have all the resources you want, but in the absence of good employees, all those resources are worthless. The human resource department is the backbone of our employee relations. . . .

"What do I expect from the human resource department? Quite a lot, I should say. I believe that the department can play a leadership and developmental role. Until now, it has played a somewhat low-key, record-keeping, staff role. It is time that the department got involved seriously in employee planning, job redesign, career planning, organizational design, and other developmental activities. Gone are the times when it could simply play a support role. Look at all the successful companies in this country and the U.S., especially those that are listed in books such as *In Search of Excellence*. It is the people and people management that differentiate them from the common crop. . . .

"The new human resource manager should be an expert — an expert on systems and people. We need new ideas here and with a growing work force, we need more formal procedures and systems, whether it is orientation or performance appraisal. Right now, many of the human resource activities are done on an ad hoc basis.

"Above everything else, I believe that the

new human resource manager needs to bring a new philosophy to deal with the unions. In the last several months, there has been an increasing degree of hostility between the unions and management. I am not blaming anyone for this. But I do believe that we, as part of the management team, have the responsibility to solve some of these problems. It is up to us to take the initiative to improve the situation. Isn't that the essence of good management?''

### View from the Human Resource Department

As part of the study, Lance met with the three key staff members in the human resource department: Jane Reynold, special assistant to the human resource manager; Tony Rezkov, manager of administration and security; and Joseph McDonald, the industrial relations officer. Rezkov, being new on the job, was not able to tell Lance very much about his position or the human resource function. In Lance's opinion, his two meetings (lasting approximately an hour each) with Jane Reynold were more productive.

Lance studied the various comments made by Reynold:

''The possibilities here are simply enormous. With a little determination and the right type of resources, we can make this one of the best human resource departments in this country. To be really effective, I believe that human resource management has to be well-integrated with the strategic and operational planning in a firm. That has not occurred here yet. . . .

''When I joined this company two years back, it didn't have any system — at least, not anything that is worth mentioning. My job since I arrived here has been to introduce new procedures and decision support systems. For example, recently, we started a formal orientation program for all plant workers. We are also in the process of developing two performance appraisal instruments — one for the plant employees and the other for administrative

staff. We introduced an improved job evaluation procedure last year, but obviously, there are many weaknesses still in the system. We are also beginning to provide absenteeism and turnover data in the various departments to the respective managers. But I want to emphasize that these are just the beginnings. With the right support, we can do wonders here. . . .

''Why do I sound pessimistic? Well, look at our department's staff strength compared to human resource departments in similar-sized organizations in this part of the country. We probably employ 50 or 60% of the number you would see elsewhere. We also do not have the computer hardware or software support and the necessary number of PCs to do an adequate job. . . .

''Sure, despite everything, we could have still done better if we had the will to do it. I will be totally frank with you — you will keep my observations confidential, won't you? Not that I mind too much if someone comes to know about it. It is as if we are a poor cousin here. Being in human resource is just not considered to be important or very useful. We are looked at by many others as an unnecessary appendage.''

Lance found that Joseph McDonald (''call me Joe, everyone does'') the industrial relations officer, was the toughest to handle. McDonald was very friendly and supportive, but did not give a direct or coherent answer to any of Lance's questions. McDonald was one of those persons (reflected Lance) who talked to you for half an hour nonstop without giving any useful information. Lance realized that he got only two points of information out of his forty-five-minute meeting with McDonald. First, one of the unions in the company was very militant and might go on strike when its contract expired in the next few months, and secondly, McDonald's son was planning to go to medical school — Lance knew the former fact already and didn't care to know about the latter.

In less than ten days, Lance was scheduled to meet Robert Clark to give a summary of his findings and recommendations. Already, Lance had received a call from his office in Saskatoon informing him that one of his consultants had been injured in an automobile accident and would not be back to work for the next several weeks. This meant that Lance had to return to his office soon to complete that project himself. Given the time constraints, Lance was wondering how he should proceed from here.

1. What is your evaluation of Lance's approach to the project?
2. What would you do if you were in Lance's position right now?

## SUGGESTED READINGS

Buford, J.A., Jr., B.B. Burkhalter and G.T. Jacobs, "Link Job Descriptions to Performance Appraisals," *Personnel Journal*, Vol. 67, No. 6, June 1988, pp. 132-140.

Gael, Sydney, *Job Analysis*, San Francisco, California: Jossey Bass, 1983.

Grant, P.C., "Why Job descriptions Don't Work," *Personnel Journal*, Vol. 67, No. 1, January 1988, pp. 52-59.

McCormick, Ernest J., *Job Analysis: Methods and Applications*, New York: AMACOM, 1979.

Pati, G.C., R. Salitone and S. Brady, "What Went Wrong with Quality Circles?" *Personnel Journal*, Vol. 66, No. 11, November 1987, pp. 82-87.

## REFERENCES

1. Philip C. Grant, "What Use Is a Job Description?" *Personnel Journal*, Vol. 67, No. 2, February 1988, p. 50.
2. Harish C. Jain (ed.), *Contemporary Issues in Canadian Personnel Administration*, Scarborough: Prentice-Hall of Canada Limited, 1974, pp. 54-55.
3. Marvin D. Dunnette, "Studying Jobs and Job Behaviour," in Jain (ed.), op. cit.
4. Dunnette, op. cit., p. 60.
5. J.D. Dunn and Frank M. Rachel, *Wage and Salary Administration: Total Compensation Systems,* New York: McGraw-Hill Book Company, 1971, pp. 139-141; Ernest J. McCormick, "Job Information: Its Development and Applications" in D. Yoder and H.G. Heneman III (eds.), *Handbook of Personnel and Industrial Relations*, Washington, D.C.: Bureau of National Affairs, 1979; Paul Sparks, "Job Analysis" in K. Rowland and G. Ferris (eds.), *Personnel Management*, Boston: Allyn & Bacon, 1982; Edward L. Levine, Ronald A. Ash, and Frank Sistrunk, "Evaluation of Job Analysis Methods by Experienced Job Analysts," *Academy of Management Journal*, Vol. 26, No. 2, 1983, pp. 339-348, E.J. McCormick, *Job Analysis: Methods and Applications*, New York: AMACOM, 1979; Luis R. Gomez-Mejia, Ronald C. Page, and Walter W. Tormow, "A Comparison of the Practical Utility of Traditional, Statistical and Hybrid Job Evaluation Approaches," *Academy of Management Journal* Vol. 25, No. 4, 1982, pp. 790-809; Ronald A. Ash and Edward C. Levine, "A Framework for Evaluating Job Analysis Methods," *Personnel*, November-December 1980, pp. 53-59.
6. Herbert G. Zollitsch and Adolph Langsner, *Wage and Salary Administration*, 2nd ed., Dallas: South-Western Publishing Co., 1970, pp. 290-301. See also Grant, op. cit., pp. 44-53; Philip C. Grant, "Why Job Descriptions Don't Work," *Personnel Journal*, Vol. 67, No. 1, January, 1988, pp. 52-59; Roger J. Plachy, "Writing Job Descriptions That Get Results," *Personnel*, October 1987, pp. 56-63.
7. Canada Employment and Immigration, *Canadian Classification and Dictionary of Occupations 1971*, Vols. 1-2, Ottawa: Information Canada, 1971. See also Canada Employment and Immigration, *Updates on CCDO*, Ottawa: Information Canada (published for major groups annually); *CCDO: Occupations in Major Groups*, Employment and Immigration Canada, 1986.
8. Zollitsch and Langsner, op. cit., pp. 301-311. See also Allan N. Nash and Stephen J. Carroll Jr., *The Management of Compensation*, Monterey, Calif.: Brooks/Cole Publishing Company, 1975, pp. 116-117.
9. Paul Sheibar, "A Simple Selection System Called 'Job Match,'" *Personnel Journal*, January 1979, p. 26.
10. Dunnette, op. cit.
11. Tom Laufer, "A Practical Tool For Evaluating Clerical Jobs," *The Canadian Personnel & Industrial Relations Jour-*

*nal*, Vol. 25, No. 2, March 1978, pp. 10-16.

12. Tom Janz, "Estimating the Standard Deviation of Job Performance: A Behavioural Approach," *Administrative Sciences Association of Canada (Organizational Behaviour Division) Meeting Proceedings*, Vol. 2, Part 5, 1981, pp. 70-78. See also Tom Janz, "Behaviour Relationship Scales: Behaviour Observation Scales for Small Samples," Simon Fraser Discussion Series 80.6.3, Department of Business Administration, Simon Fraser University, B.C., 1980; Hari Das, Peter J. Frost, and J. Thad Barnowe, "Behaviourally Anchored Scales for Assessing Behavioural Science Teaching," *Canadian Journal of Behavioural Science*, Vol. 11, No. 1, January 1979, pp. 79-88.

13. William B. Werther, Jr. and Heinz Weihrich, "Refining MBO through Negotiations," *MSU Business Topics*, Summer 1975, pp. 53-59.

14. William P. Anthony, "Get to Know Your Employees—The Human Resource Information System," *Personnel Journal*, April 1977, pp. 179-183, 202-203.

15. Hoerr, Pollock, and Whiteside, op. cit., pp. 70-82. See also John Diebold, "How New Technologies Are Making the Automated Office More Human," *Management Review*, November 1984, pp. 9-17.

16. William H. Glick, G. Douglas Jenkins, Jr., and Nina Gupta, "Method Versus Substance: How Strong Are Underlying Relationships Between Job Characteristics and Attitudinal Outcomes?" *Academy of Management Journal*, Vol. 29, No. 3, 1985, pp. 441-464. See also Daniel A. Ondrack and Martin Evans, "Job Enrichment and Job Satisfaction in Quality of Working Life and Nonquality of Working Life Work Sites," *Human Relations*, Vol. 39, No. 9, 1986, pp. 871-889; A. Campbell, "Management Styles Are Changing to Include Employee Participation," *The Globe and Mail*, October 7, 1985; W. List, "When Workers and Managers Act as a Team," *Report on Business Magazine*, October 1985, pp. 60-67.

17. Barbara Garson, "Luddites in Lordstown," *Harpers*, June 1972, pp. 68-73.

18. Frederick Herzberg, Bernard Mausner, and Barbara Snyderman, *The Motivation to Work*, New York: Wiley, 1959. See also E.F. Stone and L. W. Porter, "Job Characteristics and Job Attitudes: A Multivariate Study," *Journal of Applied Psychology*, Vol. 59, 1975, pp. 57-64. David J. Cherrington and J. Lymme England, "The Desire for an Enriched Job as a Moderator of the Enrichment-Satisfaction Relationship," *Organizational Behaviour and Human Performance*, February 1980, pp. 139-159; Kae H. Chung and Monica F. Ross,

"Differences in Motivational Properties Between Job Enlargement and Job Enrichment," *Academy of Management Review*, January 1977, pp. 113-121; George H. Dreher, "Individual Needs or Correlates of Satisfaction and Involvement with a Modified Scanlon Plan Company," *Journal of Vocational Behaviour*, August 1980, pp. 89-94; J. Richard Hackman, June L. Pearce and Jane Caminis Wolfe, "Effects of Changes in Job Characteristics on Work Attitudes and Behaviours: A Naturally Occurring Quasi-Experiment," *Organizational Behaviour and Human Performance*, Vol. 21, No. 2, 1978, pp. 289-304.

19. G. E. Farris, "Organizational Factors and Individual Performance: A Longitudinal Study," *Journal of Applied Psychology*, 1969 Vol. 53, pp. 87-92.

20. Stone and Porter, op. cit.

21. J.R. Hackman and E.E. Lawler, III, "Employee Reactions to Job Characteristics," in W.E. Scott and L.L. Cummings (eds.), *Readings in Organizational Behavior and Human Performance*, Homewood, Ill.: Richard D. Irwin, 1972.

22. Edward E. Lawler, III, "Job Attitudes and Employee Motivation: Theory, Research, and Practice," *Personnel Psychology*, Summer 1970, p. 234.

23. Richard W. Woodward and John J. Sherwood, "A Comprehensive Look at Job Design," *Personnel Journal*, August 1977, p. 386.

24. M. Scott Myers, *Every Employee a Manager*, New York: McGraw-Hill Book Company, 1970.

25. Myers, *op. cit.*

26. Jennifer Trapnell, "Quality of Working Life at Statistics Canada," *Quality of Working Life: The Canadian Scene*, Vol. 2, No. 3, 1979, pp. 11-14.

27. Robert H. Schappe, "Twenty-Two Arguments against Job Enrichment," *Personnel Journal*, February 1974, pp. 116-123.

28. William B. Werther, Jr., "Beyond Job Enrichment to Employment Enrichment," *Personnel Journal*, August 1975, pp. 438-442.

29. Natalie Lam, "Work Orientations: A Crosscultural Comparison and Relevance for Participative Management," Working Paper No. 84-21, Ottawa: University of Ottawa, 1984. Also see R.N. Kanungo, G.J. Graen, and H.J. Dauderis, "Motivational Orientation of Canadian Anglophone and Francophone Managers," *Canadian Journal of Behavioural Science*, 1976, 8, 107-121. See also Gary L. Cooper, "Humanizing the Workplace in Europe: An Overview of Six Countries," *Personnel Journal*, June 1980, pp. 488-91.

# C H A P T E R *6* ○ ○ ○ ○ ○ ○ ○

# *RECRUITMENT*

*The recruitment process plays a major role in ensuring a match between the employer's needs for qualified employees and the individual's needs for challenging and rewarding work.*

GEORGE T. MILKOVICH, WILLIAM F. GLUECK, RICHARD T. BARTH, AND
STEVEN L. MCSHANE[1]

○ ○ ○ ○ ○ ○ ○ ○ ○ ○ ○ ○ ○ ○ ○ ○ ○ ○ ○ ○ ○ ○ ○ ○ ○ ○ ○ ○ ○ ○ ○ ○ ○

## *CHAPTER OBJECTIVES*

After studying this chapter, you should be able to:
1.  **Explain** the constraints under which the recruitment process occurs.
2.  **Identify** the appropriate recruiting methods for finding and attracting different types of recruits.
3.  **Describe** the major employment-related services provided by Canada Employment Centres.
4.  **Develop** an appropriate job application form.
5.  **Diagram** the major features of the recruitment process.
6.  **Describe** the major measures used for evaluating the effectiveness of the recruitment function.

○ ○ ○ ○ ○ ○ ○ ○ ○ ○ ○ ○ ○ ○ ○ ○ ○ ○ ○ ○ ○ ○ ○ ○ ○ ○ ○ ○ ○ ○ ○ ○ ○

*F*inding new employees for the organization is a continuing challenge for most human resource departments. Sometimes the need for new workers is known well in advance because of detailed human resource plans. At other times, the human resource department is faced with urgent requests for replacements that must be filled as quickly as possible. In either case, finding qualified applicants is a key activity.

Shirley Dodd was a junior mechanical engineer for Blakely Electronics when she quit to work for a competitor. Her resignation created a problem for the head of the mechanical engineering department, Sid Benson. As he expressed it, "She was doing an important job of developing the mechanical tolerances for our new electronic scale. It was all theoretical work, but it was going to save three months' worth of product development time. We must have a bright junior engineer to complete her work. I hope someone can be recruited."

*Recruitment* is the process of finding and attracting capable individuals to apply for employment. The process begins when new recruits are sought and ends when their applications are submitted. The result is a pool of jobseekers from which new employees are selected.

Responsibility for recruitment usually belongs to the human resource department. This responsibility is important because the quality of an organization's human resources depends upon the quality of its recruits. Since large organizations recruit almost continuously, their human resource departments use specialists in the recruiting process. These specialists are called *recruiters*.

Recruiters work to find and attract capable applicants. Their methods depend on the situation, since there is no one best recruiting technique. Normally, recruiters follow several steps. As Figure 6-1 illustrates, recruiters identify job openings through human resource planning or requests by managers. Then recruiters learn about the job's requirements from job analysis information and talks with the requesting manager. The job's requirements influence the recruiter's methods of finding satisfactory applicants.

FIGURE 6-1   An Overview of the Recruitment Process

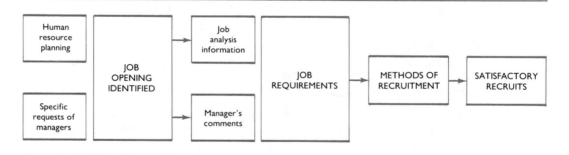

In the last several years, primarily as a result of the recession, employers have found that it is much easier to attract potential employees. In education, for example, it is not uncommon to have hundreds of applicants for a vacancy. However, this situation can lull the human resource department into a false sense of security, for two reasons. First, the Canadian economy has been fairly robust in recent years. As a result of the past ease of attracting applicants, some human resource departments have become very lax in their recruitment efforts and may well end up paying the price for this laxness in years to come. Second, recruitment, as will be discussed in this chapter, involves far more than just getting people to apply for jobs. An effective recruitment process involves all the aspects shown in Figure 6-1; therefore, success in recruiting is not simply measured by the number of applications received. The right type of applicants are far more important than the number of applicants.

> Sid Benson, head of mechanical engineering at Blakely Electronics, requested that the human resource department find a new junior engineer. Charles Shaw, a recruiter, reviewed the job's requirements and discovered that applicants should have a basic understanding of mechanical engineering concepts. No experience was required. This requirement of knowledge but not experience led Charles to seek applicants from among the graduating class of a small engineering-oriented university in the area.

This illustration makes several assumptions about Charles's role as a recruiter. It assumes that he knows the organizational and environmental constraints under which recruiting occurs at Blakely. It also assumes that he is aware of other sources of recruits but rejects those alternatives as inferior. Lastly, it assumes he will find people who are interested in applying for a job at Blakely Electronics.

These assumptions outline the key issues covered in this chapter: the constraints encountered in recruitment, the channels through which recruits are found and attracted, and the nature of application forms.

## CONSTRAINTS ON RECRUITMENT

A successful recruiter must be sensitive to the constraints on the recruitment process. These limits arise from the organization, the recruiter, and the external environment. Although the emphasis may vary from situation to situation, the following list includes the most common constraints:

- Organizational policies
- Human resource plans
- Affirmative-action programs
- Recruiter habits

- Environmental conditions
- Job requirements
- Costs
- Inducements

### Organizational Policies

Organizational policies are a potent source of constraints. Policies seek to achieve uniformity, economies, public relations benefits, and other objectives unrelated to recruiting. Those policies that may affect recruitment are highlighted below.

#### Promote-from-Within Policies

Promote-from-within policies are intended to give present employees the first opportunity for job openings. These policies are widespread. In a U.S. study, 76% of the organizations reported that they fill a majority of their openings internally.[2] Promote-from-within policies aid employee morale, attract recruits looking for jobs with a future, and help retain present employees. Although these policies reduce the flow of new people and ideas into different levels of the organization, the alternative is to pass over employees in favour of outsiders. Bypassing current employees can lead to employee dissatisfaction and turnover. In the junior engineer example, Charles Shaw, the recruiter, should check with present employees—such as technicians who have been studying engineering at night school—before a new engineer is recruited.

## Compensation Policies

A common constraint faced by recruiters is pay policies. Organizations with human resource departments usually establish pay ranges for different jobs. If Charles Shaw finds a promising candidate, the pay range will influence the jobseeker's desire to become a serious applicant. Recruiters seldom have the authority to exceed stated pay ranges. For example, when the market rate for junior engineers is $2400 to $2600 per month, satisfactory applicants will be few if Charles can offer only $2000 to $2200 per month.

## Employment Status Policies

Some companies have policies restricting the hiring of part-time and temporary employees. Although there is growing interest in hiring these types of workers, such policies are common and can cause recruiters to reject all but those seeking full-time work. Limitations against part-time and temporary employees exclude many individuals from consideration. Likewise, policies against hiring employees who "moonlight" by having second jobs also inhibit recruiters. Prohibitions against holding extra jobs are intended to ensure a rested work force.

## International Hiring Policies

Policies in some countries, including Canada, may also require foreign job openings to be staffed with local citizens. The use of foreign nationals, however, does reduce relocation expenses, lessen the likelihood of nationalization, and, if top jobs are held by local citizens, minimize charges of economic exploitation. Moreover, unlike relocated employees, foreign nationals are more apt to be involved in the local community and understand local customs and business practices.

## Human Resource Plans

The human resource plan is another factor recruiters consider. Through skills inventories and promotion ladders, the plan outlines which jobs should be filled by recruiting and which should be filled internally. The plan helps recruiters because it summarizes future recruiting needs. This foresight can lead to economies in recruiting.

At Blakely Electronics, Charles Shaw checked the human resource plan before recruiting a junior mechanical engineer. The plan indicated a projected need for five junior electrical engineers during the next three months. So Charles decided to recruit electrical engineering candidates at the same time he was looking for a junior mechanical engineer. If advertisements were to be placed in the university newspaper, there would be no additional cost for seeking both types of engineers. Travel costs, advertising costs, and the time devoted to a second recruiting trip would be saved. Since junior engineer is the lowest-level engineering position, it is unlikely that there would be any internal candidates identified in the human resource plan. However, if the opening had been for a more experienced worker, the human resource planning process may have identified potential candidates from within the company.

## Affirmative-Action Programs

Before recruiting for any position, Charles also checked the organization's voluntary affirmative-action program. The plan indicated a desire to recruit more women and minorities into professional jobs. So Charles had to consider what actions were needed to achieve these goals.

> Blakely Electronics never pursued policies that intentionally discriminated against any group. But over the years, its sources of engineering recruits had been mostly white males who attended the small local university. To fulfil the intent of the affirmative-action plan, Charles decided to recruit engineering technicians at a large metropolitan university.

## Recruiter Habits

A recruiter's past success can lead to habits. Admittedly, habits can eliminate time-consuming deliberations that reach the same answers. However, habits may also perpetuate past mistakes or obscure more effective alternatives. So although recruiters need positive and negative feedback, they must guard against self-imposed constraints.

Consider again the recruitment of the junior engineer at Blakely Electronics. Suppose that the engineering department expresses satisfaction with recruits from the nearby university. Such positive feedback encourages recruiters to make a habit of using this source for beginning engineers. Since all these engineers have a similar curriculum, they may also share strengths and weaknesses. As a result, the engineering department may suffer because of the educational uniformity of new recruits.

## Environmental Conditions

External conditions strongly influence recruitment. Changes in the labour market and the challenges mentioned in Chapter 2 affect recruiting. The unemployment rate, the pace of the economy, spot shortages in specific skills, projections of the labour force by Statistics Canada, labour laws, and the recruiting activities of other employers—all of these affect the recruiter's efforts. Although these factors are considered in human resource planning, the economic environment can change quickly after the plan is finalized. To be sure that the plan's economic assumptions remain valid, recruiters can check three fast-changing measures:

### Leading Economic Indicators
Each month Statistics Canada announces the direction of the leading indicators. These economic indexes suggest the future course of the national economy. If these indexes signal a sudden downturn in the economy, recruiting plans may have to be modified.

### Predicted Versus Actual Sales
Since human resource plans are partially based upon the firm's predicted sales, variations between actual and predicted sales may indicate that these plans also are inaccurate. Thus recruiting efforts may need to be changed accordingly.

### Want-Ads Index

Statistics Canada and the Technical Service Council report the volume of want ads in major metropolitan newspapers. An upward trend in this index indicates increased competition for engineers and managers who are recruited on a nationwide basis. For clerical and production workers, who are usually recruited on a local basis, the human resource department may want to create its own index to monitor local changes in want ads.

As the economy, sales, and want ads change, recruiters also must adjust their efforts accordingly. Tighter competition for applicants may require more vigorous recruiting. When business conditions decline, an opposite approach is called for—as the following example illustrates.

> As a major recreation centre was opening in Quebec, the leading economic indicators dropped. Although the human resource plan called for recruiting 100 workers a week for the first month, the employment manager set a revised target of 75. Lower recruiting and employment levels helped establish a profitable operation even though first-year admissions fell below the projections used in the human resource plan.

## Job Requirements

Of course, the requirements of each job are a constraint. Highly specialized workers, for example, are more difficult to find than unskilled ones. Recruiters learn of a job's demands from the requesting manager's comments and job analysis information. Job analysis information is especially useful because it reveals the important characteristics of the job and applicants. Knowledge of a job's requirements allows the recruiter to choose the best way to find recruits, given the constraints under which the recruiter must operate.

"Find the best and most experienced applicant you can" is often a constraint that is imposed on recruiters as though it were a job requirement. At first this demand seems reasonable: All managers want to have the best and most experienced people working for them. But several potential problems exist with this innocent-sounding request. One problem in seeking out the "best and most experienced" applicant is cost. People with greater experience usually command higher salaries than less experienced people. If a high level of experience is not truly necessary, the recruit may become bored soon after being hired. Moreover, if the human resource department cannot show that a high degree of experience is needed, then experience may be an artificial requirement that discriminates against some applicants. Another point about experience is worth remembering: For some people in some jobs, ten years of experience is another way of saying one year of experience repeated ten times. Someone with ten years of experience may not be any better qualified than an applicant with only one year.[3]

## Costs

Like all other members of an organization, recruiters must also operate within budgets. So, the cost of identifying and attracting recruits is an ever-present limitation.[4]

Manitoba Engineering Company Limited found that the average cost of recruiting engineers in the company was more than $3300 per hire. To hire senior engineers and managers, the cost was even higher. To fill a $70,000-a-year position, the company often had to pay $5000—$6000 to search firms. To monitor and control costs, the human resource manager of the company was asked to assess the effectiveness of the company's recruitment programs and costs of recruitment under alternative recruitment methods.

Careful human resource planning and forethought by recruiters can minimize these expenses. For example, recruiting for several job openings simultaneously may reduce the cost per recruit. Of course, a better solution would be to take actions to reduce employee turnover, thus minimizing the need for recruiting. Pro-active human resource management actions go far in achieving this objective.

## Inducements

The recruiter is very much like a marketer—he or she is selling the company as a potential place of work to all eligible recruits. As with any marketing effort, inducements may be necessary to stimulate a potential recruit's interest. Inducements may be monetary or non-monetary in nature (e.g., flextime), but can also be a constraint, as when other employers are using them. In such an instance, a firm needs to meet the prevailing standards. Inducements may be a response to overcoming other limitations faced by the recruiter.

The fast-food industry, which employs a large percentage of young workers, typically experiences high employee turnover. To reduce turnover and thereby its recruiting costs, one fast-food chain introduced an educational assistance program. Under the program, an employee could accrue up to $2000 worth of tuition credits over a two-year period. Result? Turnover among participants in the program is a mere 22% compared to 97% turnover of those who were not part of the plan.[5] Needless to point out, this significantly reduced the firm's recruitment efforts and costs.

The inducements used by an organization need not always be economic in nature but may be emotional or intangible.

A university in Atlantic Canada takes all its potential faculty recruits to the scenic areas for a day's car tour in an effort to "sell" the location (and through that the institution). Faced with severe constraints on the compensation package it can offer, the university decided to use its "intangible" assets to assist in its recruitment and selection process.

## CHANNELS OF RECRUITMENT

The ways of finding recruits are sometimes referred to as *channels*. Recruiters and applicants have historically contacted each other through a few typical channels, which are summarized in Figure 6-2. As can be seen from the research reported in the figure, applying directly to the employer was the most popular job search method for both males and females in the country. However, people tend to use several methods in their search for employment. Past research evidence shows that persons with higher educational qualifications tend to use more methods to find a job than those with lower educational levels.

FIGURE 6-2   Popular Job Search Methods in Canada

| METHOD | % OF MALES WHO USE | % OF FEMALES WHO USE | TOTAL |
|---|---|---|---|
| Contacted employers directly | 75.0 | 68.9 | 72.5 |
| Canada Employment Centres | 51.0 | 46.0 | 49.0 |
| Answered advertisements | 41.9 | 48.5 | 44.5 |
| Other methods | 38.2 | 32.4 | 35.8 |

Source: *Discussion Paper No. 156*, Economic Council of Canada, Ottawa, 1980.

### Walk-ins and Write-ins

*Walk-ins* are jobseekers who arrive at the human resource department in search of a job. *Write-ins* are those who send a written inquiry. They normally are asked to complete an application form to determine their interests and abilities. Suitable applications are kept in an active file until an appropriate opening occurs or until the application is too old to be considered valid—usually six months.

### Employee Referrals

Present employees may refer jobseekers to the human resource department. Employee referrals have several unique advantages. First, employees with hard-to-find job skills may know others who do the same work. For example, a shortage of oilfield workers in Alberta during the oil boom in the early 1980's was partially counteracted by having employees ask their friends to apply for the unfilled openings. Second, new recruits already know something about the organization from those employees who referred them. Thus referred applicants may be more strongly attracted to the organization than are walk-ins. Third, employees tend to refer friends who are likely to have similar work habits and work attitudes. Even if work values are different, these candidates may have a strong desire to work hard so that they do not let down the person who recommended them.

Employee referrals are an excellent and legal recruitment technique. However, recruiters must be careful that this method does not intentionally or unintentionally discriminate. The major problem with this recruiting method is that it tends to maintain the racial, religious, sex, and other features of the employer's work force. Such results can be viewed as discriminatory.

### Advertising

Advertising is another effective method of seeking recruits. Since it can reach a wider audience than employee referrals or unsolicited walk-ins, many recruiters use it as a key part of their efforts

*Want ads* describe the job and the benefits, identify the employer, and tell those who are interested how to apply. They are the most familiar form of employment advertising. For highly specialized recruits, ads may be placed in professional journals or out-of-town newspapers located in areas with high concentrations of the desired skills. For example, recruiters in finance often advertise in Vancouver, Toronto, Montreal, and Halifax newspapers because these cities are major banking centres.

Want ads have some severe drawbacks. They may lead to thousands of jobseekers for one popular job opening. Often the ideal recruits are already employed and not reading want ads. Finally, secretly advertising for a recruit to replace a current employee cannot easily be done with traditional want ads.

These problems are avoided with *blind ads*. A blind ad is a want ad that does not identify the employer. Interested applicants are told to send their résumé to a box number at the post office or to the newspaper. The *résumé* (or *vita*), which is a brief summary of the applicant's background, is then forwarded to the employer. These ads allow the opening to remain confidential, prevent countless telephone inquiries, and avoid the public relations problem of disappointed recruits.

As one writer observed, "Recruitment advertising should be written from the viewpoint of the applicant and his or her motivations rather than exclusively from the point of view of the company."[6] Since the cost of most classified advertising is determined by the size of the advertisement, short blurbs are the norm. These ads usually describe the job duties, outline minimum job qualifications, and tell interested readers how to apply. Short phrases and sentences, sometimes written in the second person, are the usual format. Figure 6-3 provides an example. However, some experts doubt that traditional approaches will remain sufficient, particularly when recruiting people with hard-to-find skills or whenever labour markets are tight. As one researcher suggested, want ads

> must contain not only information about the job but also information presented in a way that effectively portrays a message about the job and the company. This can't be done if the ad contains information that explains only what responsibilities the job includes, who can be qualified, where it is located, and how and when to apply. . . . [7]
> More important, in today's labour market, where increasing demands are being made for job relevance, quality of work life, and other job satisfaction factors, . . . the need for more descriptive job information and information concerning working environment, supervisory style and organizational climate are necessary.[8]

Advertisements for recruits through other media—billboards, television, and radio, for example—are seldom used because the results seldom justify the expense. However, these approaches may be useful when unemployment is low and the target recruits are not likely reading want ads.[9]

Whatever media are used, the layout, design, and copy of an advertisement should reflect the image and character of the company and departments that are being represented.[10] This includes dimensions such as the size of the organization, the degree of decentralization seen in the firm, the degree of dynamism and progressive policies typical

FIGURE 6-3   Sample Want Ad

### ENGINEERING GRADUATES

Blakely Electronics seeks junior mechanical and electrical engineering trainees for our growing team of engineering professionals. You will work with senior engineers in designing state-of-the-art electronic equipment for home and industry. Qualified applicants will be engineers graduating by the end of this term and wanting immediate employment. Send your résumé and transcripts to: Charles Shaw, Employment Office, Blakely Electronics, P.O. Box 473, Halifax, Nova Scotia, B3H 3C3. Do it today for an exciting career tomorrow.

of the unit, and so on. This, in turn, means that an ad should emphasize the nature of the organization and the benefits of the package that it offers to attract the applications of qualified people, but at the same time be specific enough to screen the wrong persons.

## Canada Employment Centres

Canada Employment Centres (CECs), through the ten regional offices of the Canadian Employment and Immigration Commission (CEIC) and a national network of about 800 CECs, offer a variety of programs and services for both employers and prospective employees.[11]

To match candidates with job openings, the process works as follows: When an employer has a job opening, the human resource department voluntarily notifies the CEC of the job and its requirements. Typically, the job opening information is then posted at the CEC's Job Information Centre. Here prospective employees can scan the job openings and discuss any vacancy with one of the centre's counsellors. When an applicant expresses interest in some particular job, the counsellors interview that person. Qualified applicants are then referred to the firm.

In larger metropolitan areas (e.g., Vancouver or Toronto) a Metropolitan Order Processing System (MOPS) has recently been established. This is a computerized system that automatically conveys information about vacancies listed with one centre to all other centres in the area. It allows employers to have their vacancy posted easily and quickly in more centres, thus improving their range of selection. On a national basis, CECs are linked via a telephone-computer system into the National Job Bank. Thus employers can make job information available across Canada. For workers who are willing to relocate or employers needing skills not available in their area, such a system provides yet another avenue for achieving their objectives.

Aside from the services already mentioned, most CECs also provide career and vocational counselling services, aptitude and skill assessments, training referrals, special services for women, native peoples, and the handicapped, and numerous other employment-related activities. They have also been involved with many ''grant-type'' programs such as Local Employment Assistance Programs (LEAP), Summer Youth Employment Programs (SYEP), and Canada Community Services Projects. These programs typically involved a cost-sharing arrangement between employers and the government; thus through them, organizations were able to obtain funding to support employment of certain kinds of persons.

Canada Employment Centres provide a virtually no-cost recruitment source for employers, yet their use has been somewhat limited. Most employers in the past have used CECs for recruiting white collar, blue collar, or technical employees rather than managerial and professional persons.[12] There is, however, no reason why the CEC's cannot play an active role in these fields.

## Private Employment Agencies

Private employment agencies—which now exist in every major metropolitan area—arose to help employers find capable applicants. Placement firms take an employer's request for recruits and then solicit jobseekers, usually through advertising or from walk-ins. Candidates are matched with employer requests and then told to report to the employer's human resource department. The matching process conducted by private agencies varies widely. Some placement services carefully screen applicants for their client. Others simply provide a stream of applicants and let the client's human resource department do most of the screening.

In most provinces it is either illegal for private employment agencies to charge the applicant a fee for placing him or her, or the fees charged are regulated. Most fees are paid by the agencies' clients, i.e., the prospective employers. The fees commonly equal either 10% of the first year's salary or one month's wages, but the fraction may vary with the volume of business provided by the client and the type of employee sought.

## Professional Search Firms

Professional search firms are much more specialized than placement agencies. *Search firms* usually recruit only specific types of human resources for a fee paid by the employer. For example, some search firms specialize in executive talent, while others use their expertise to find technical and scientific personnel. Perhaps the most significant difference between search firms and placement agencies is their approach. Placement agencies hope to attract applicants through advertising, but search firms actively seek out recruits from among the employees of other companies. Although they may advertise, the telephone is their primary tool for locating and attracting prospective recruits.

> The Nelson Radar Company needed a quality control manager for its assembly line. After several weeks of unsuccessful recruiting efforts, the human resource manager hired a search firm. The search firm reviewed the in-house phone directories of competing firms and telephoned the assistant quality control manager at one of Nelson's competitors. The phone call was used to encourage this assistant manager to apply for the position at the Nelson Company.

This brief example illustrates several important points. First, search firms have an in-depth experience that most human resource departments lack. Second, search firms are often willing to undertake actions that an employer would not do, such as calling a competitor. Third, it can be seen that some human resource professionals would consider search firms unethical because these firms engage in "stealing" or "raiding" among their clients' competitors. This last example shows why search firms are sometimes called "headhunters."[13]

In the past few years, the number of executive recruiting firms in Canada has been growing fast. While most of them are located in large metropolitan cities such as Toronto and Montreal, an increasing number of these firms are making an appearance in smaller cities and towns.

What is the reason for the growing popularity of executive search firms? According to one writer, the use of a search firm leads to more objectivity, less cost per recruit, and an overall higher success rate in recruiting the right quality personnel.[14] However, when choosing a search firm, care has to be taken to test the "fit" between the firm and the client organization. Some of the search firms, especially the smaller ones, are often highly specialized and may not be able to meet the general needs of a client. Checking the recruiting record of the firm and its reputation is, consequently, very important.

## *Educational Institutions*

For beginning-level openings, educational institutions are another common source of recruits. Many universities, community colleges, and technical schools offer their current students and alumni placement assistance. This assistance helps employers and graduates to meet and discuss employment opportunities and the applicant's interest. Counsellors and teachers also may provide recruiters with leads to desirable candidates in high schools.

A view of what one group of university students sought in a recruiter is found in Figure 6-4. It shows that students desire well-informed and skilled campus recruiters. It also shows that candour among recruiters is an important characteristic.[15] Another study reports that the recruiter's title and age are important factors in creating a favourable impression on recruits.[16]

## FIGURE 6-4   A Profile of the Ideal Recruiter

From a survey of second-year students in a university MBA program, the following profile of the ideal recruiter emerged.

The ideal recruiter:
1. was actually hiring for a specific position.
2. was very knowledgeable about and close to the job that was open.
3. knew the company well and could discuss both good and bad points.
4. didn't try to oversell the company.
5. had read the résumé before the interview.
6. found out how much the candidate knew about the job and the company.
7. was interested in the student as an individual.
8. was happy with the company and felt he or she was going places.
9. was personable, polite, on time, and sincere.
10. asked thought-provoking questions without being too direct or personal.
11. followed up promptly with feedback and evaluation.

Source: John E. Steele, "A Profile of the Ideal Recruiter," *Personnel Journal*, February 1977, pp. 58-59. Used by permission.

## *Professional Associations*

Recruiters find that professional associations also can be a source of jobseekers. Many associations conduct placement activities to help new and experienced professionals get jobs; some have publications that accept classified advertisements. Professionals who belong to the appropriate associations are considered more likely to remain informed of the latest developments in their field, and so this channel of recruitment may lead to higher-quality applicants. Another advantage of this source of applicants is that it helps recruiters zero in on specific specialties, especially in hard-to-fill technical areas.

## Labour Organizations

When recruiters want people with trade skills, local labour organizations have rosters of those people who are looking for employment. The local union of plumbers, for example, keeps a list of plumbers who are seeking jobs. In the construction industry, many contractors get their skilled workers from the local labour organizations. Since contractors often hire on a per-project basis, a union hiring hall is a convenient channel for attracting large numbers of pretrained recruits for new projects.

## Military Personnel

Trained personnel leave the armed forces every day. Some veterans, such as those who have been trained as mechanics, welders, or pilots, have hard-to-find skills. Human resource departments that need skills similar to those found in the military often find nearby military installations a valuable source of recruits. Many of the technicians who maintain commercial jet airliners were first trained in the military, for example.

## Canada Manpower Training Program

The Canada Manpower Training Program, a service provided under CEIC, supports both institutional (classroom) and industrial (on-the-job) training. In order to qualify for institutional training, an individual needs to be at least one year beyond the provincial school-leaving age (except for apprentices) and have been out of school for at least one year. Counsellors at the CECs are responsible for selecting people for this program. Persons selected for such training typically receive a training allowance or unemployment insurance benefits.

CEIC also assists employers with the training needs of their employees. Under the General Industrial Training Program, CEIC reimburses selected employers for a portion of the training costs and trainee wages. There are also other programs that encourage employers to train and hire women for jobs that have traditionally been held by men and, as well, one that supports training in high-level blue-collar skills.[17]

## Temporary-Help Agencies

Most large cities have temporary-help agencies that can respond quickly to an employer's need for help. These agencies do not provide recruits. Instead, they are a source of supplemental workers. The temporary help actually work for the agency and are "on loan" to the requesting employer. For temporary jobs—during vacations, peak seasons, illnesses, etc.—these agencies can be a better alternative than recruiting new workers for short periods of employment. Besides handling the recruiting and bookkeeping tasks caused by new employees, these agencies can often provide clerical and secretarial talent on short notice—sometimes less than a day.[18] And when the temporary shortage is over, there is no need to lay off surplus workers, because "temporaries" work for the agency, not the company. Occasionally, temporary help are recruited to become permanent employees.

## Departing Employees

An often overlooked source of recruits is among departing employees. These workers might gladly stay if they could rearrange their schedules or change the number of hours worked. Family responsibilities, health conditions, or other circumstances may lead a worker to quit when a transfer to a part-time job may retain valuable skills and training.[19] Even if part-time work is not a solution, a temporary leave of absence may satisfy the employee and some future recruiting need of the employer.

Buy-backs are a channel worthy of mention, although human resource specialists and workers tend to avoid them. A *buy-back* occurs when an employee resigns to take another job and the original employer outbids the new job offer. The following dialogue provides an example:

> EMPLOYEE:   I quit. I am going to work as a computer programmer for International Plastics.
>
> MANAGER:   You are too valuable for us to just let you walk out the door. How much is International offering?
>
> EMPLOYEE:   They are offering me $3000 a year more!
>
> MANAGER:   Stay and I'll make it $4000.
>
> EMPLOYEE:   No. I'm going.
>
> MANAGER:   How about $5000?
>
> EMPLOYEE:   Well, okay.

Even when the authority to enter into a bidding war exists, the manager may discover that other workers expect like raises. Employees may reject a buy-back attempt because of the ethical issue raised by not reporting to a job that has already been accepted. Besides, what is to prevent the manager from using a blind ad to find a replacement? Then after International has filled its job in the example above, the employee is terminated.

## Open House

A relatively new technique of recruiting involves holding an open house. People in the adjacent community are invited to see the company facilities, have refreshments, and maybe view a film about the company. This method has proved successful for recruiting clerical workers when people with office skills are in tight supply.

## Recruitment Process Summary

Figure 6-5 summarizes the recruiting process and identifies each of the commonly used channels of recruitment. As the figure indicates, the recruitment process ends when a recruit makes formal application, usually by completing an application form.

FIGURE 6-5   Summary of Recruiting Process

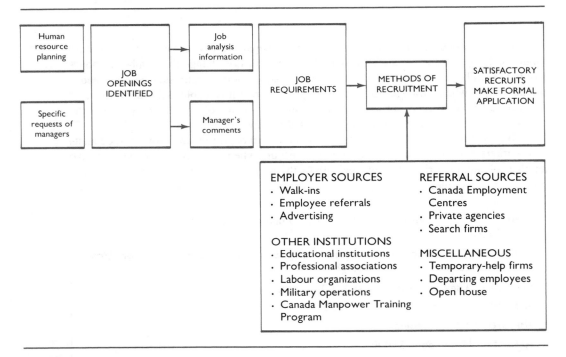

## JOB APPLICATION FORMS

The *job application form* collects information about recruits in a uniform manner. Even when recruits volunteer detailed information about themselves, applications are often required so that the information gathered is comparable. Each human resource department generally designs its own form. Nevertheless, certain common features exist. Figure 6-6 provides a typical example of an application form and its major divisions.

FIGURE 6-6   A Typical Application Form

**BLAKELY ELECTRONICS, INC.**
**"An Equal-Opportunity Employer"**
**Application for Employment**

**Personal Data**

1. **Name** _____

2. **Address** _____   3. **Phone Number** _____

FIGURE 6-6 (continued)   A Typical Application Form

**Employment Status**

4. Type of employment sought _____ Full-time _____ Part-time
   _____ Permanent _____ Temporary
5. Job or position sought _____
6. Date of availability, if hired _____
7. Are you willing to accept other employment if the position you seek is unavailable?
   _____ Yes _____ No
8. Approximate wages/salary desired $_____ per month

**Education and Skills**

9. Circle the highest grade or years completed.

       9  10  11  12  13           1  2  3  4            1  2  3  4
        **High School**           **University**       **Graduate School**

10. Please provide the following information about your education. (Include high school, trade or vocational schools, and colleges.)
    a. School name _____ Degree(s) or diploma _____
       School address _____
       Date of admission _____ Date of completion _____
    b. School name _____ Degree(s) or diploma _____
       School address _____
       Date of admission _____ Date of completion _____
11. Please describe your work skills. (Include machines, tools, equipment, and other abilities you possess.) _____
    _____
    _____
    _____
    _____

**Work History**

Beginning with your most recent or current employer, please provide the following information about each employer. (If additional space is needed, please use an additional sheet.)

12. a. Employer _____ Dates of employment _____
       Employer's address _____
       Job title _____ Supervisor's name _____
       Job duties _____
       Starting pay _____ Ending pay _____
    b. Employer _____ Dates of employment _____
       Employer's address _____
       Job title _____ Supervisor's name _____
       Job duties _____
       Starting pay _____ Ending pay _____

**Military Background**

If you were ever a member of the Canadian Armed Forces, please complete the following:

13.    Branch of service _____ Rank at discharge _____
       Dates of service _____ to _____

FIGURE 6-6 (continued)   A Typical Application Form

Responsibilities _____
Type of discharge _____

**Memberships, Awards, and Hobbies**

14. What are your hobbies? _____
15. List civic/professional/social organizations to which you have belonged. _____
_____

16. List any awards you have received. _____
_____

**References**

In the space provided, list three references who are not members of your family.
17. **a.** Name _____    Address _____
    **b.** Name _____    Address _____
    **c.** Name _____    Address _____
18. Please feel free to add any other information you think should be considered in evaluating
    your application. _____
    _____

By my signature on this application, I:
   **a.** Authorize the verification of the above information and any other necessary inquiries that
       may be needed to determine my suitability for employment.
   **b.** Affirm that the above information is true to the best of my knowledge.

_____    **Date** _____
                **Applicant's Signature**
_____

## Personal Data

Most application forms begin with a request for personal data. Name, address, and
telephone number are nearly universal. But requests for some personal data such as place
of birth, marital status, number of dependants, sex, race religion, or national origin may
lead to charges of discrimination. Since it is illegal to discriminate against applicants,
an unsuccessful applicant may conclude that rejection was motivated by discrimination
when discriminatory questions are asked. The human resource department must be able
to show that these questions are job-related if it asks them.

Applications may solicit information about health, height, weight, handicaps that
relate to the job, major illnesses, and claims for injuries. Here again, there may be legal
problems. Discriminating against handicapped individuals is prohibited under the Canadian Human Rights Act of 1977. The burden of proof that such questions are job related
falls on the employer.

## Employment Status

Some questions on the application form concern the applicant's employment objective
and availability. Included here are questions about the position sought, willingness to
accept other positions, date available for work, salary or wages desired, and acceptability
of part-time and full-time work schedules.

This information helps a recruiter match the applicant's objective and the organization's needs. Broad or uncertain responses can prevent the application from being considered. An example follows:

INEXPERIENCED RECRUITER:   Under "position sought," this applicant put "any available job." Also, under "wages desired" the applicant wrote "minimum wage or better." What should I do with this application?

EMPLOYMENT MANAGER:   You are not a career counsellor. You are a recruiter. Put that application in the inactive file and forget about it.

### Education and Skills

The education and skills section of the application form is designed to uncover the jobseeker's abilities. An understanding of the applicant's personality may be gained from this section too. Traditionally, education has been a major criterion in evaluating jobseekers. Educational attainment does imply certain abilities and is therefore a common request on virtually all applications. Questions about specific skills are also used to judge prospective employees. More than any other part of the application form, the skills section reveals the suitability of a candidate for a particular job.

### Work History

Jobseekers must frequently list their past jobs. From this information, a recruiter can tell whether the applicant is one who hops from job to job or is likely to be a long-service employee. A quick review of the stated job title, duties, responsibilities, and ending pay also shows whether the candidate is a potentially capable applicant.[20] If this information does not coincide with what an experienced recruiter expects to see, the candidate may have exaggerated job title, duties, responsibilities, or pay.

### Military Background

Some applications request information on military experience. Questions usually include date of discharge, area of service, rank at discharge, and type of discharge. Such information clarifies the applicant's background and ability to function in a structured environment.

### Memberships, Awards, and Hobbies

Recruits are more than potential workers. They are also representatives of the employer in the community. For managerial and professional positions, off-the-job activities may make one candidate preferable over another. Memberships in civic, social, and professional organizations indicate the recruit's concern about community and career. Awards show recognition for noteworthy achievements. Hobbies may reinforce important job skills and indicate outlets for stress and frustrations, or opportunities for further service to the company.

When handed a pile of completed applications for manager of the car- and truck-leasing department, Frank Simmons (the human resource manager for a Toronto Ford dealership) sorted the completed applications into two piles. When asked what criteria were being used to sort the applications, he said, "I'm looking for golfers. Many of our largest car and truck accounts are sold on Saturday afternoons at the golf course."

## References

Besides the traditional references from friends or previous employers, applications may ask for other "referencelike" information. Questions may explore the jobseeker's criminal record, credit history, friends and relatives who work for the employer, or previous employment with the organization. Criminal record, credit history, and friends or relatives who work for the company may be important considerations if the job involves sensitive information, cash, or other valuables. Job-relatedness must be substantiated if these criteria disproportionately discriminate against some protected group. Previous employment with the organization means there are records of the applicant's performance.

## Signature Line

Candidates are usually required to sign and date their applications. Adjacent to the signature line, a blanket authorization commonly appears. This authorization allows the employer to check references; verify medical, criminal, or financial records; and undertake any other necessary investigations. Another common provision of the signature line is a statement that the applicant affirms the information in the application to be true and accurate as far as is known. Although many people give this clause little thought, falsification of an application form is grounds for discharge in most organizations.

> Jim LaVera lied about his age to get into the police officers' training program. As he neared retirement age, Jim was notified that he would have to retire in six months, instead of thirty months as he had planned. When Jim protested, the lie he made years before came to the surface. Jim was given the option of being terminated or taking early retirement at substantially reduced benefits.

When the application is completed and signed, the recruitment process is finished. Its unanswered questions and implications continue to affect human resource management, as the Jim LaVera example illustrates.[21] In fact, the end of the recruitment process marks the beginning of the selection process, which is discussed in the next chapter.

## EVALUATING THE RECRUITING FUNCTION

Like most other important functions, the recruiting activity in an organization should also be subjected to periodic evaluation. Typically, the recruitment process is expensive;[22] unless efforts are made to identify and control these costs, the potential benefits from the activity may end up being lower than the costs. Past research studies have indicated that recruitment costs can run as high as 50% of the yearly salary for professionals and managers.[23] Further, recruitment can reflect a firm's overall human resource policy and focus.[24]

How can the effectiveness of the recruiting function be evaluated? Several indices have been suggested:

*1. Cost per hire.* The dollar cost per person recruited is one possible measure of the effectiveness of the recruiting function. The costs should include not only the direct costs (e.g., recruiters' salaries, costs of advertisement, consultants' fees, etc.), but also apportioned costs and overheads (e.g., time of operating personnel, stationery, rent). However, often cost data are either not collected at all or are not interpreted so as to facilitate the evaluation of recruiting. Cost data collected from previous recruiting activities could serve as useful bench-marks for comparison.[25]

*2. Quality of hires and cost.* A major criticism of using a simple dollar cost per hire as a measure of effectiveness is that it ignores the quality of the people hired. The performance, absenteeism, and motivation levels of employees recruited from one source (or using one media) will differ from those of other sources.[26] For example, Breaugh found that recruits selected through advertisements in professional journals and professional conventions were qualitatively superior (on performance, absenteeism, job involvement, etc.) than those who were selected through newspaper advertisements or college recruitment programs.[27] The number and quality of résumés by source or method gives an indication of the overall effectiveness of a recruitment method or source.

*3. Offers:Applicants ratio.* A somewhat better index is the ratio between the number of job offers extended and the total number of applicants calculated for each recruitment method or media. Even if a recruiting source brings in better quality résumés, this may not be translated finally to job offers; an offer:applicants ratio gives a better picture of the overall quality of the applicant pool.

The ratio of number of offers accepted to total number of job offers extended to applicants gives an indication of the overall effectiveness of the recruiting. Caution is, however, in order. The acceptance of a job offer is dependent on a number of extraneous variables including the labour market situation, the compensation package offered by the organization and its competitors, the firm's location, and so on. However, when used judiciously, it can point up weaknesses such as lack of professionalism and long delays in the recruiting process that could encourage a prospective employee to go elsewhere.[28] This is particularly true of good candidates, who may get multiple job offers from employers.

*4. Time lapsed per hire.* The number of days, weeks, or months taken to fill a position provides yet another measure of the effectiveness of the recruitment system. Clearly, a firm that took a week to fill a position when the industry average is ten days or two weeks is, in comparison, more efficient. Once again, several external and uncontrollable factors (including the nature of the job, labour market conditions, location, etc.) affect the time for recruiting; consequently, this index should be used in conjunction with other information.

Figure 6-7 shows some of the more popular measures used to evaluate the recruiting function. Naturally, many of these measures are influenced by a firm's selection, training, and compensation systems. Indeed, an evaluation system that explicitly considers various factors related to the selection process and that contains job performance information (including tenure and value of job to the organization) may be very useful in several organizational settings.[29] The next chapter will look at the various steps involved in the selection of personnel from the pool of applicants identified during recruiting.

FIGURE 6-7   Popular Measures Used for Evaluating Effectiveness of
            Recruitment Function

1. Total number of applicants received
2. Time required to get applications
3. Time elapsed before filling positions
4. Costs per hire
5. Offers extended:Number of applicants
6. Offers accepted: Number of offers extended
7. Number of qualified applicants: Total number of applicants
8. Performance rating of hires
9. Turnover of hires

## SUMMARY

Recruitment is the process of finding and attracting capable applicants for employment. This responsibility normally is associated with specialists in the human resource department called recruiters. Before recruiters can solicit applicants, they should be aware of the constraints under which they operate. Of particular importance are such limitations as organizational policies, human resource plans, affirmative-action plans, recruiter habits, environmental conditions, and the requirements of the job.

At the recruiter's disposal are a variety of methods to find and attract jobseekers. Employer sources include walk-ins, write-ins, employee referrals, and direct solicitations through want-ads and other forms of advertisement. Applicants can be found through the referrals of Canada Employment Centres, private placement agencies, or search firms. Of course, recruits can be found through a variety of institutions, such as educational, professional, and labour organizations, the military, and government training programs. Some firms have reported success in converting temporary employees into permanent ones, on a full-time or part-time basis, and in inducing departing employees to remain. An open house may bring people into the facility and prompt them to submit applications.

The end of recruiting is a completed application form from ready, willing, and able candidates. Application forms seek a variety of answers from recruits, including personal, employment, educational, and work history information. Questions may be asked about hobbies, memberships, awards, and personal interests. References are usually solicited on the application form too.

Like all other human resource functions, the recruitment activity also needs to be evaluated for its degree of effectiveness and efficiency. This is to ensure that the recruitment function achieves both organizational and individual objectives. A number of indices for evaluating the recruitment activity were suggested in the chapter. Bear in mind that all these indices are affected by a firm's selection, training, compensation, and general human resource related policies. With a pool of recruits and the information contained in completed application forms, the human resource department is now ready to assist line managers in the process of selecting new employees.

## TERMS FOR REVIEW

Recruitment

Walk-ins

Blind ads

Résumé

Canada Employment Centres
  (CECs)

Metropolitan Order Processing
  Systems (MOPS)

National Job Bank

Search firms

Canada Manpower Training Program

Buy-back

Cost per hire

Time lapse per hire

## REVIEW AND DISCUSSION QUESTIONS

1.  What background information should a recruiter have before beginning to recruit jobseekers?

2.  Give three examples of how organizational policies affect the recruitment process. Explain how these influence a recruiter's actions.

3.  Under what circumstances would a blind ad be a useful recruiting technique?

4.  After months of insufficient recognition (and two years without a raise), you accept an offer from another firm that involves a $1500-a-year raise. When you tell your boss that you are resigning, you are told how crucial you are to the business and are offered a raise of $3250 per year. What do you do? Why? What problems might exist if you accept the buy-back?

5.  Suppose you are a manager who has just accepted the resignation of a crucial employee. After you send your request for a replacement to the human resource department, how could you help the recruiter do a more effective job?

6.  If at your company the regular university recruiter became ill and you were assigned to recruit at six universities in two weeks, what information would you need before leaving on the trip?

7.  In small businesses, managers usually handle their own recruiting. What methods would you use in the following situations? Why?

    (a)  The regular janitor is going on vacation for three weeks.

    (b)  Your secretary has the flu.

    (c)  Two more salespeople are needed: one for local customers and one to open a sales office in Victoria, B.C.

    (d)  Your only chemist is retiring and must be replaced with a highly skilled person.

8. "If a job application omits important questions, needed information about recruits will not be available. But if a needless question is asked, the information can be ignored by the recruiter without any other complications." Do you agree or disagree? Why?

9. You are the human resource manager in a large auto-assembly unit employing 1700 blue-collar and white-collar workers. Each year, you recruit dozens of full-time and part-time workers. Recently, the vice-president, Finance, pointed out that recruitment costs in your firm are going up steadily. He was proposing a freeze in the recruitment budget. What kind of information will you provide in an effort to change his mind on the matter?

## INCIDENT 6-1

### Blakely Electronics Expansion

Blakely Electronics developed a revolutionary method of storing data electronically. The head of research and development, Guy Swensen, estimated that Blakely could become a supplier to every computer manufacturer in the world. The future success of the company seemed to hang on securing the broadest possible patents to cover the still-secret process.

The human resource director, Carol Kane, recommended that Swensen become a project leader in charge of developing and filing the necessary patent information. Swensen and Kane developed a list of specialists who would be needed to rush the patent applications through the final stages of development and the patent application process. Most of the needed skills were found among Blakely's present employees. However, after a preliminary review of skills inventories and staffing levels, a list of priority recruits was developed. It required the following:

- An experienced patent attorney with a strong background in electronics technology.
- A patent attorney familiar with the ins and outs of the patent process and the patent office in Hull, Quebec.
- Twelve engineers. Three had to be senior engineers with experience in the latest computer technology and design. Four had to be senior engineers with experience in photographic etching reduction. Five junior engineers were also requested in the belief that they could handle the routine computations for the senior engineers.
- An office manager, ten keyboard operators, and four secretaries to transcribe the engineering notebooks and prepare the patent applications.

Swensen wanted these twenty-nine people recruited as promptly as possible.

1. Assuming you are given the responsibility of recruiting these needed employees, what channels would you use to find and attract each type of recruit sought?

2. What other actions should the human resource department take now that there is the possibility of very rapid expansion?

*INCIDENT 6-2*

## *The Ethics of "Headhunting"*

Darrow Thomas worked as a professional placement specialist for L. A. and D., Inc., an executive search firm. For the last three months Darrow had not been very successful in finding high-level executives to fill the openings of L. A. and D.'s clients. Not only did his poor record affect his commissions, but the office manager at L. A. and D. was not very pleased with Darrow's performance. Since Darrow desperately needed to make a placement, he resolved that he would do everything he could to fill the new opening he had received that morning.

The opening was for a director of research and development at a major food processor. Darrow began by unsuccessfully reviewing the in-house telephone directories of most of the large companies in this industry. Finally, he stumbled across the directory of a small food processor in the West. In the directory he found a listing for Suzanne Derby, assistant director of product development. He called her, and the following conversation took place.

SUZANNE:   Hello. P.D. Department, Suzanne Derby speaking.

DARROW:   Hello. My name is Darrow Thomas, and I am with L. A. and D. One of my clients has an opening for a director of research and development at a well-known food processor. In discussions with people in the industry, your name was recommended as a likely candidate. I was . . .

SUZANNE:   Who recommended that you call me?

DARROW:   I'm awfully sorry, but we treat references and candidates with the utmost confidentiality. I cannot reveal that name. But rest assured, he thought you were ready for a more challenging job.

SUZANNE:   What company is it? What does the job involve?

DARROW:   Again, confidentiality requires that the company name go unmentioned for now. Before we go any further, would you mind answering a few questions? Once I feel confident you are the right candidate, I can reveal my client.

SUZANNE:   Well, okay.

DARROW:   Good. How many people do you supervise?

SUZANNE:   Three professionals, seven technicians, and two clerks.

DARROW:   Approximately how large a budget are you responsible for?

SUZANNE:   Oh, it's about half a million dollars a year.

DARROW:   What degree do you hold, and how many years have you been assistant director?

SUZANNE:   My undergraduate degree and master's are in nutrition science. After I graduated in 1980, I came to work here as an applications researcher. In 1985, I was promoted to chief applications researcher. In 1987, I was appointed assistant director of product development.

DARROW:   Good career progress, two degrees, and managerial experience. Your background sounds great! This is a little personal, but would you tell me your salary?

SUZANNE:   I make $42,500 a year.

DARROW:   Oh, that is disappointing. The opening I have to fill is for $56,500. That would be such a substantial jump that my client would probably assume your past experience and responsibility are too limited to be considered.

SUZANNE:   What do you mean?

DARROW:   Well, the ideal candidate would be making about $50,000 a year. That figure would indicate a higher level of responsibility than your low salary. We could get around that problem.

SUZANNE:   How?

DARROW:   On the data sheet I have filled out I could put down that you are making, oh, say $50,000. That sure would increase my client's interest. Besides, then they would know a salary of $56,500 was needed to attract you.

SUZANNE:   Wow! But when they checked on my salary history, they'd know that $50,000 was an inflated figure.

DARROW:   No, they wouldn't. They wouldn't check. And even if they did, companies never reveal the salary information of past employees. Besides, my client is anxious to fill the job. I'll tell you what, let me send them the data sheet; I'm sure they'll be interested. Then we can talk about more of this. Okay?

SUZANNE:   Well, if you think it would mean a raise to $56,500, and they really need someone with my background, I guess I'd be interested.

1.   Although ''headhunters'' do not necessarily engage in the practice of ''inflating'' an applicant's wage, it does happen occasionally. What would you do in Suzanne's place? Would you allow your name to be used?

2.   Since most ''headhunters'' receive a commission that is a percentage of the successful applicant's starting salary, what safeguards would you suggest to prevent ''headhunters'' from inflating salaries?

3.   If Suzanne goes along with Darrow's inflated salary figure and she is hired, what problems may she face?

○ ○ ○ ○ ○ ○ ○ ○ ○ ○ ○ ○ ○ ○ ○ ○ ○ ○ ○ ○ ○ ○ ○ ○ ○ ○ ○ ○ ○ ○ ○ ○ ○ ○ ○ ○ ○ ○ ○ ○ ○ ○ ○ ○ ○ ○ ○ ○ ○

## CASE STUDY

### TIMBER CRAFT LIMITED

Timber Craft Limited, a manufacturer of sports and recreation goods located in Midsex, British Columbia, is considering a major expansion. It is expected that the number of employees in the organization will increase by almost 30% in the foreseeable future to meet the needs of expansion. Though capital intensive, much of this increase in labour force will happen in the production and sales division of the organization. Over the years, the company has built up a reputation for offering competitive salaries and good working conditions (see Case Study on page 133 of this text for more details on Timber Craft and its structure and processes). Despite this, the company had problems in the past in obtaining personnel for key managerial positions and other skilled jobs. The company has been keeping records of its experiences with various recruiting methods and sources until now. The following table shows a summary of relevant data in this regard for production and sales work force.

| | | | **Recruiting method used** | | | | |
| | WALK-IN | WRITE-IN | CANADA EMPLOY-MENT CENTRE | ADVER-TISE-MENTS | UNION | REFERRAL FROM EMPLOYEES | HIGH SCHOOL |
|---|---|---|---|---|---|---|---|
| **Total number of applications** | | | | | | | |
| Production | 90 | 170 | 40 | 230 | 30 | 30 | 170 |
| Sales | 30 | 60 | 130 | 420 | 20 | 40 | 90 |
| **Total yield (%) (i.e., of the applications from this method)** | | | | | | | |
| Production | 12 | 22 | 5 | 31 | 4 | 4 | 22 |
| Sales | 4 | 8 | 16 | 53 | 3 | 5 | 11 |
| **Ratio of acceptance to applications (%)** | | | | | | | |
| Production | 30 | 40 | 60 | 50 | 50 | 60 | 70 |
| Sales | 30 | 80 | 70 | 50 | 40 | 50 | 60 |
| **Ratio of acceptance to job offers (%)** | | | | | | | |
| Production | 50 | 60 | 70 | 75 | 60 | 75 | 80 |
| Sales | 70 | 80 | 80 | 50 | 50 | 60 | 70 |
| **Cost of recruiting per person hired ($)** | | | | | | | |
| Production | 2 | 4 | 3 | 11 | 2 | 2 | 14 |
| Sales | 2 | 3 | 3 | 14 | 2 | 3 | 13 |
| **Employee turnover within a three-year period (% of hired)** | | | | | | | |
| Production | 14 | 15 | 10 | 12.5 | 10 | 7.5 | 19 |
| Sales | 10 | 5 | 7.5 | 15 | 15 | 14 | 18 |

Make your recommendation on the best recruitment method(s) for each type of work force.
© Hari Das, 1988.

## SUGGESTED READINGS

Gerson, Herbert E., and Louis P. Britt III, "Hiring—The Dangers of Promising Too Much," *Personnel Administrator*, March 1984, pp. 5-8, 112.

Hochheiser, R.M., "Recruitment: A Prescription for Hiring Headaches," *Personnel Journal*, 1982, pp. 578, 580-582.

Magnus, M., "Is Your Recruitment All It Can Be?" *Personnel Journal*, Vol. 66, No. 2, 1987, pp. 54-63.

Wanous, J.P., *Organizational Entry: Recruitment, Selection and Socialization of Newcomers*, Reading, Mass.: Addison-Wesley Publishing, 1980.

## REFERENCES

1. George T. Milkovich, William F. Glueck, Richard T. Barth, and Steven L. McShane, *Canadian Personnel/Human Resource Management: A diagnostic approach*, Plano, Texas: Business Publications Inc., 1988, p. 352.

2. Herbert J. Sweeney and Kenneth S. Teel, "A New Look at Promotion from Within," *Personnel Journal*, August 1979, p. 535.

3. Gene E. Burton and Dev S. Pathak, "101 Ways to Discriminate Against Equal Employment," *Personnel Administrator*, August 1977, pp. 42-45.

4. Jeffrey J. Hallett, "Why Does Recruitment Cost So Much?" *Personnel Administrator*, November 1986, p. 22.

5. Annetta Miller, "Burgers: The Heat Is On," *Newsweek*, June 1986, p. 53.

6. Van M. Evans, "Recruitment Advertising in the '80's," *Personnel Administrator*, 1978, p. 23.

7. James W. Schreier, "Deciphering Messages in Recruitment Ads," *Personnel Administrator*, March 1983, p. 35.

8. Ibid., p. 39.

9. Jo Bredwell, "The Use of Broadcast Advertising for Recruitment," *Personnel Administrator*, February 1981, pp. 45-49.

10. Cathy Edwards, "Aggressive Recruitment: The Lessons of High-Tech Hiring," *Personnel Journal*, January 1986, pp. 41-48; see also Margaret Magnus, "Is Your Recruitment All It Can Be?" *Personnel Journal*, February 1987, pp. 54-63.

11. Employment and Immigration Canada, *Employment Programs and Services for Canadians*, Catalogue No. WH-7-092, Ottawa: Minister of Supply and Services Canada, 1981, p. 1.

12. Sunder Magnum, "The Placement Activity of the Canadian Employment Agency," *Relations Industrielles*, Vol. 38, No. 1, 1983, pp. 72-94.

13. John D. Erdlen, "Ethics and the Employee Relations Function," *The Personnel Administrator*, January 1979, pp. 41-43, 68.

14. John J. Wypich, "The Head Hunters Are Coming," *Canada Commerce*, Fall 1986, pp. 27-28.

15. Madalyn Freund and Patricia Somers, "Ethics in College Recruiting: Views from the Front Lines," *The Personnel Administrator*, April 1979, pp. 30-33. See also Joe Thomas, "College Recruitment: How to Use Student Perceptions of Business," *Personnel Journal*, January 1980, pp. 44-46.

16. Donald P. Rogers and Michael Z. Sincoff, "Favorable Impression Characteristics of the Recruitment Interviewer," *Personnel Psychology*, Autumn 1978, pp. 495-504.

17. Employment and Immigration Canada, op. cit., pp. 3-5.

18. Martin J. Gannon, "A Profile of the Temporary Help Industry and Its Workers," *Monthly Labor Review*, May 1974, pp. 44-49.

19. Barney Olmsted, "Job Sharing—A New Way to Work," *Personnel Journal*, February 1977, pp. 78-81. See also William B. Werther, Jr., "Part-Timers: Overlooked and Undervalued," *Business Horizons*, February 1975, pp. 13-20.

20. Bernard M. Bass, "Interface between Personnel and Organizational Psychology," in W. Clay Hamner and Frank L. Schmidt (eds.), *Contemporary Problems in Personnel*, Chicago: St. Clair Press, 1974, pp. 44-45.

21. Robert W. Ericson, "Recruitment: Some Unanswered Questions," *Personnel Journal*, February 1974, pp. 136-140, 147. See also Stephen J. Wilhelm, "Is On-Campus Recruiting on Its Way Out?" *Personnel Journal*, April 1980, pp. 302-304, 318.

22. Robert Sibson, "The High Cost of Hiring," *Nation's Business*, February 14, 1975, pp. 85-88; Margaret Magnus, "Is Your Recruitment All It Can Be?" *Personnel Journal*, Vol. 66, No. 2, February 1987, pp. 54-63.

23. Ibid.

24. J. Scott Lord, "How Recruitment Efforts Can Elevate Credibility," *Personnel Journal*, Vol. 66, No. 4, April 1987, pp. 102-106.

25. R. Stoops, "Recruitment Strategy," *Personnel Journal*, February 1982, p. 102.

26. M.J. Gannon, "Source of Referral and Employee Turnover," *Journal of Applied Psychology*, Vol. 55, 1971, pp. 226-228; also see P.J. Decker and E.T. Cornelius, "A Note on Recruiting Sources and Job Survival Rates," *Journal of Applied Psychology*, Vol. 64, 1979, pp. 463-464.

27. J.A. Breaugh, "Relationships between Recruiting Sources and Employee Performance, Absenteeism, and Work Attitudes," *Academy of Management Journal*, Vol. 24, 1981, pp. 142-147.

28. George T. Milkovich, William F. Glueck, Richard T. Barth, and Steven L. McShane, *Canadian Personnel/Human Resource Management: A Diagnostic Approach*, Plano, Texas: Business Publications Inc., 1988, p. 344.

29. J.T. Janz, "Exploring the Implications of the Utility Equation for Selection, Recruitment, and Turnover Reduction Programs," *Proceedings of the 1982 Administrative Sciences Association of Canada Meeting*, University of Ottawa, 1982, pp. 18-28.

# CHAPTER 7 OOOOOO

## SELECTION

*Two realities face Canadian personnel managers. . . . First, they must manage human resources more productively. Second, they must be prepared to defend their employment tests on the grounds of business necessity before human rights commissions and courts. Reliable, valid employment tests . . . fulfill both functions.*

STEVEN F. CRANSHAW[1]

o o o o o o o o o o o o o o o o o o o o o o o o o o o o o o o o o
## CHAPTER OBJECTIVES

After studying this chapter, you should be able to:
1. **Explain** the dependency of human resource management activities on the selection process.
2. **Describe** the role of employment testing in the selection process.
3. **List** and explain each step in the selection process.
4. **Explain** the importance of validity and reliability in employee selection.
5. **Outline** the importance of a realistic job preview.
6. **Avoid** major pitfalls in conducting an employment interview.
7. **List** the factors to be considered when assessing the utility of a selection device.

o o o o o o o o o o o o o o o o o o o o o o o o o o o o o o o o o

$O$nce a pool of suitable applicants is created through recruiting, the process of selecting applicants begins. This process involves a series of steps that add time and complexity to the hiring decision. Although important, it should be recognized that this time and complexity can lead to frustration among applicants who need jobs and operating managers who need their job openings filled. By way of introduction, consider an overview of the hiring process at Merrill Lynch Canada Inc., one of the larger securities firms.

Applicants for the position of account executive at Merrill Lynch complete an application, take a written test, and undergo an interview. But none of these steps prepare them for the account-executive simulation test, which is just one step in Merrill Lynch's selection process. As described by a reporter for The Wall Street Journal, the test can be unnerving.

"Welcome to the Merrill Lynch account-executive simulation exercise, or, as dubbed by some, the Merrill Lynch stress test. It's a nail-biting three hours . . . that leaves many longing for the good old days of calculus finals.

"The stakes are high, too. Those taking part in the simulation, except me, are applicants for the job of account executive, or stockbroker. . . . The simulation exercise is designed to gauge how they will perform under conditions similar to those that a real stockbroker faces.[2]

The test works by telling each applicant that he or she is replacing a stockbroker who has gone to another office. The stockbroker left the client book, which describes the accounts of each client. In addition, the applicants are given a variety of unanswered memos, letters, and telephone messages that they must sort through and decide how to treat. In the background, recorded sounds of a brokerage office are played to add an air of confusing noises, shouts, telephone rings, and other unexpected distractions. During the three hours, fictitious clients call and other messages and reports are dropped on the applicant's "desk." As one applicant commented an hour after the simulation was over, "I just can't calm down. It was a real high."[3]

The point of this illustration is simply that the simulation exercise is only one part of Merrill Lynch's selection process. Other steps precede and follow it. Although most employers do not use this elaborate a screening device, all but the smallest employers put applicants through a variety of steps called the selection process. The *selection process* is a series of specific steps used to decide which recruits should be hired. The process begins when recruits apply for employment and ends with the hiring decision. The steps in between match the employment needs of the applicant and the organization. When these steps are not understood, selection seems like a stressful time and a bureaucratic process rather than the important function it is.

In many human resource departments, recruiting and selection are combined and called the *employment function*. In large human resource departments, the employment function is the responsibility of the employment manager. In smaller departments, human resource managers handle these duties.[4] Perhaps more than any other function, employment is associated closely with the human resource department. It is often the primary reason for creating the human resource department, since the selection process is central to human resource management. Improper selection causes the human resource department to fail at the objectives set forth in Chapter 1 and the challenges discussed in Chapter 2. Even worse, improper selection can crush individual hopes and violate antidiscrimination laws. Subsequent human resource activities (discussed later in the book) lose much of their effectiveness when they must contend with improperly selected workers. Therefore, it is not an exaggeration to say that selection is central to the success of human resource management and even to the success of the organization.

## INPUTS TO SELECTION

Employment managers use the selection process to find new workers. As Figure 7-1 reveals, the selection process relies on three helpful inputs. Job analysis information provides the description of the jobs, the human specifications, and the performance standards each job requires. Human resource plans tell employment managers what job openings are likely to occur. These plans allow selection to proceed in a logical and effective manner. Finally, recruits are necessary so that the employment manager has a group of people from which to choose. These three inputs largely determine the effectiveness of the selection process. If job analysis information, human resource plans, and recruits are of high quality, the selection process should function well. At the same time, there are other inputs into the selection process that limit its success. To succeed, employment managers must grapple with a limited supply of labour, ethical considerations, and organizational and equal-opportunity policies.

FIGURE 7-1   Dependency of Human Resource Management Activities on the Selection Process

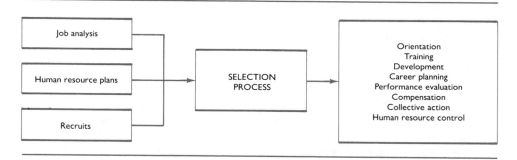

### Supply Challenges

It is important to have a large, qualified pool of recruits from which to select applicants. But some jobs are so hard to fill that there are few applicants per opening. For example, Canadian business schools currently have about 200 vacancies that they are unable to fill, due to a shortage of qualified personnel. Thus when hiring, they have small selection ratios. A *selection ratio* is the relationship between the number of applicants hired and the total number of applicants available. A large selection ratio is 1:25; a small selection ratio is 1:2. A small selection ratio means there are few applicants from which to select. In many instances a small selection ratio also means a low quality of recruits. The ratio is computed as follows:

$$\frac{\text{Number of applicants hired}}{\text{Total number of applicants}} = \text{selection ratio}$$

> Wes Klugh, an employment manager for a chain of motels, faced a low selection ratio for the third-shift desk clerk's job. Although it paid 25 cents an hour more than the day or evening clerk jobs, few people applied for it. Wes decided to redesign the job by enriching it. The job was expanded to include responsibility for completing the daily financial report and other bookkeeping tasks. The additional duties justified the substantial raise and new title — night auditor. The result was more applicants.

## Ethical Challenges

Since employment specialists strongly influence the hiring decision, that decision is shaped by their ethics.[5] Hiring a neighbour's relative, accepting gifts from a placement agency, and taking bribes all challenge the employment specialist's ethical standards. If those standards are low, new employees may not be properly selected.

> Every summer, Athena Klemmer was told to find jobs for some of the executives' children. To disobey would affect her career. On the other hand, hiring some of them would be an admission that she selected people on criteria other than merit. Although many of her peers in the local human resource association thought employing the bosses' children was merely a benefit of the executive suite, Athena felt it was improper. Accordingly, she found summer jobs for them in other companies.

## Organizational Challenges

The selection process is not an end; it is a means through which the organization achieves its objectives. Naturally, the organization imposes limits, such as budgets and policies, that may hinder the selection process. Without budget limitations, recruiting efforts and selection techniques could be refined. But without limits, employment expenses may be so high that organizational effectiveness would suffer.

Policies may expand existing challenges or simply add more constraints. Policies against discrimination reinforce external prohibitions, for example. Internal decrees may exceed legal demands from outside. For example, policies to hire ex-convicts further societal objectives but are not legally required. Yet such internal policies add still another challenge for employment specialists.

## SELECTION: AN OVERVIEW

The selection process is a series of steps through which applicants pass. Sometimes the process can be made simple and effective, especially when selecting employees to fill internal openings.

> At Citibank the selection process has been simplified and computerized in order to match present employees with internal openings. The "Jobmatch" selection system

rests upon matching a profile of candidates for nonprofessional jobs and the jobs' task requirements. The specific tasks required of the job are programmed into the computer along with the specific abilities of employees. Those employees with the highest match for a given opening are then considered for the job. A major shortcoming of this computerized approach is that the matching process largely ignores behaviours not directly related to the job, such as attitudes, personality, and the like.[6]

To ensure that both task and nontask factors are considered, human resource departments commonly use a more involved sequence of steps, as shown in Figure 7-2. For internal applicants, there is seldom a need to provide a preliminary reception of applicants, verify references, or do a medical evaluation. But with external applicants, the steps in Figure 7-2 are common.

FIGURE 7-2   Steps in the Selection Process

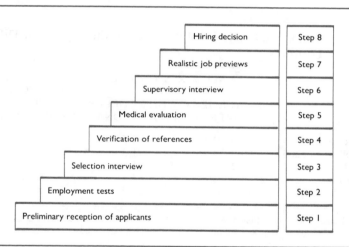

The type of selection procedure used by an organization also depends on the size of the organization and the jobs involved. In a survey of 581 Canadian organizations by James Thacker and Julian Cattaneo, of the University of Windsor, letters of reference and weighted application blanks are most popular for the selection of white-collar professional workers, and biographical information blanks were most frequently used for white-collar nonprofessional jobs.[7] Personality tests were popular for selecting middle-management employees, and aptitude tests were most common for white-collar nonprofessional jobs. Further, the survey showed that half of the respondents used at least one paper-and-pencil test. A summary of the selection practices in the organizations that Thacker and Cattaneo surveyed is shown in Figure 7-3; Figure 7-4 shows the major predictions used by the same organizations in selecting personnel for different positions.

FIGURE 7-3  Selection Practices in Canadian Organizations (n = 581)

| SELECTION TOOL | % OF RESPONDENTS WHO USE THIS SELECTION TOOL IN ORGANIZATIONS OF | | |
| --- | --- | --- | --- |
| | SMALL SIZE | MEDIUM SIZE | LARGE SIZE |
| Application blank | 93 | 94 | 100 |
| Letters of reference | 76 | 69 | 63 |
| Weighted application blanks | 4 | 3 | 5 |
| Biographical information blanks | 24 | 25 | 26 |
| Personality tests | 20 | 16 | 28 |
| Aptitude tests | 35 | 43 | 57 |
| Honesty tests | 2 | 0.4 | 0.8 |
| Interests inventories | 14 | 10 | 23 |

Source: Adapted from J.W. Thacker, and R.J. Cattaneo, *Survey of Personnel Practices in Canadian Organizations*, Unpublished manuscript, University of Windsor, February 1987, pp. 13-14.

FIGURE 7-4  Major Predictors Used in Selecting Employees for Different Positions

| | ALL % RESPONDING FIRMS SAYING "YES" | | | |
| --- | --- | --- | --- | --- |
| | MANAGEMENT STAFF | WHITE COLLAR (PROFESSIONAL) | WHITE COLLAR (NON-PROFESSIONAL) | BLUE COLLAR |
| Letters of reference | 73.0–80.5 | 83.5 | 76.5 | 48.5 |
| Weighted application blanks | 60.9–73.9 | 91.3 | 78.2 | 69.6 |
| Biographical blanks | 65.2–79.2 | 81.9 | 83.3 | 70.1 |
| Tests (personality) | 68.4–82.5 | 54.4 | 50.0 | 23.7 |
| Assessment centres | 42.3–60.6 | 22.5 | 11.3 | 9.9 |

Source: J.W. Thacker and R.J. Cattaneo, *Survey of Personnel Practices in Canadian Organizations*, Unpublished manuscript, Faculty of Business Administration, University of Windsor, February 1987, pp. 13–16.

## STEPS IN SELECTION

### Preliminary Reception: Step 1

The selection process is a two-way street. The organization selects employees, and *applicants select employers*. From both views, selection begins with a visit to the human resource office or with a written request for an application. How this initial reception is handled affects the applicant's opinion of the employer.

When the applicant appears in person, a preliminary interview may be granted as a courtesy. This "courtesy interview," as it is often called, is simply a matter of good public relations. It also helps the human resource department screen out obvious misfits and get background information on potential recruits. A completed application is usually requested during this initial meeting. Later steps in the selection process verify this application information.

## Employment Tests: Step 2

Employment tests are useful for obtaining relatively objective information, which can be compared with that pertaining to other applicants and present workers. *Employment tests* are devices that assess the match between applicants and job requirements. Some are paper-and-pencil tests; others are exercises that simulate work conditions. A math test for a bookkeeper is an example of a paper-and-pencil test, and a manual dexterity test for an assembly worker is an example of a simulation exercise. These tests are used more frequently for jobs that pay an hourly wage than for salaried positions because hourly jobs usually call for a limited number of skills or activities that can be tested easily. Management and professional jobs are often too complex to be tested fairly and economically in this manner.

In Thacker and Cattaneo's study, it was found that tests were popular in Canada for selecting white-collar and managerial positions, but not for blue-collar jobs (see Figure 7-3). Personality tests were particularly popular for selecting managers. The use of personality and aptitude tests became more and more popular with the increase in an organization's size. In contrast, honesty tests were not very popular at all and, even if used, were restricted to mostly small firms (see Figure 7-3 for details).[8]

## Test Validation

Testing became popular on a large scale during World War I when intelligence tests were given to army recruits. During the following sixty years, tests were developed for a wide range of employment uses, but many of these tests were assumed to be valid without sufficient proof.

For a test to be relied upon, it must be valid. *Validity* requires that the test scores significantly relate to job performance or some other relevant criterion. The stronger the relationship between test results and performance, the more effective the test is as a selection tool. When scores and performance are unrelated, the test is invalid and should not be used for selection.

> An Ontario trucking company once gave all its applicants an extensive reading test. However, because the drivers received their instructions orally and were shown on a map where to go, the reading test had no relationship to job performance; it did not distinguish good drivers from bad ones. It only distinguished between those who could read English well and those who could not.

When an invalid test rejects people of a particular race, sex, religion, or national origin, it violates the Canadian Human Rights Act or related provincial legislation. However, test validity as it is related to discrimination has not received a great deal of attention in Canada. Given that many of the tests we use were developed in the United States, one wonders whether they are particularly valid, since they were developed for a different group of workers. A Toronto-based industrial psychologist has estimated that "only 3% of firms use properly validated selection tests."[9] If this estimate is correct, then an increased scrutiny of testing and its relationship to discrimination may well be a future trend in the human resource area.

To assure that its tests are valid, human resource departments should conduct *val-*

*idation studies.*[10] These studies compare test results with performance or traits needed to perform the job. Figure 7-5 summarizes the most common approaches to validation.

Empirical approaches rely on predictive or concurrent validity. Both methods attempt to relate test scores to some criterion, usually performance. The higher the correlation between test scores and the criterion, the more effective the test is. Empirical approaches are generally preferred because they are less subjective than rational methods.

Rational approaches include content and construct validity. These techniques are used when empirical validity is not feasible because the small number of subjects does not permit a reasonable sample upon which to conduct the validation study.

Regardless of which approach is used, testing experts advise separate validation studies for different subgroups, such as women and minorities. These separate studies for different subgroups are called *differential validity*. Without differential validity, a test may be valid for a large group (white male applicants) but not for subgroups of minorities or women.

FIGURE 7-5    An Explanation of Common Approaches to Test Validation

---

### EMPIRICAL APPROACHES

---

Empirical approaches to test validation attempt to relate test scores with a job-related criterion, usually performance. If the test actually measures a job-related criterion, the test and the criterion exhibit a positive correlation between 0 and 1.0. The higher the correlation, the better the match.
- **Predictive validity** is determined by giving a test to a group of applicants. After these applicants have been hired and have mastered the job reasonably well, their performance is measured. This measurement and the test score are then correlated.
- **Concurrent validity** allows the human resource department to test present employees and correlate these scores with measures of their performance. This approach does not require the delay between hiring and mastery of the job.

---

### RATIONAL APPROACHES

---

When the number of subjects is too low to have a reasonable sample of people to test, rational approaches are used. These approaches are considered inferior to empirical techniques, but are acceptable validation strategies when empirical approaches are not feasible.
- **Content validity** is assumed to exist when the test includes reasonable samples of the skills needed to successfully perform the job. A typing test for an applicant that is being hired simply to do typing is an example of a test with content validity.
- **Construct validity** seeks to establish a relationship between performance and other characteristics that are assumed to be necessary for successful job performance. Tests of intelligence and scientific terms would be considered to have construct validity if they were used to hire researchers for a chemical company.

---

Yet even when tests have been validated, the type of validation used is still important. Faulty procedures, no matter how well intentioned, cannot be relied on to prove a test's validity. An example of this point follows:

The Albemarle Paper Company, a U.S. firm, gave several black workers a battery of tests that had not been validated. The workers sued Albemarle, so the company then implemented a validation study. But the study had several weaknesses, and the court ruled the tests as invalid and discriminatory.

The problem was that Albemarle:

- Used the tests that had been validated for advanced jobs, not the entry-level positions to which tests were being applied. Such validation does not prove tests are valid for entry-level jobs. Tests must be validated on those jobs to which tests are being applied.

- Validated the test on one group (white workers) and then applied the test to another group (black workers). Tests must be validated for all the groups to whom the test applies.[11]

Besides being valid, a test should also be reliable. *Reliability* means that the test yields consistent results. For example, a test of manual dexterity for assembly workers should give a similar score each time the same person takes the test. If the results vary widely with each retest because good scores depend on luck, the test is not reliable. When tests are not reliable, they may also be invalid.

## Testing Tools and Cautions

There are a wide variety of employment tests. But each type of test has only limited usefulness. The exact purpose of a test, its design, the directions for its administration, and its applications are recorded in the test manual, which should be reviewed before a test is used. The manual also reports the test's reliability and the results of validation efforts by the test designer. Today many tests have been validated on large populations. But human resource specialists should conduct their own studies to make sure a particular test is valid for its planned use. Each type of test has a different purpose. Figure 7-6 lists examples and a brief explanation of each of several different types of tests.

*Psychological tests* are those that measure personality or temperament. They are among the least reliable. Validity suffers because the exact relationship between personality and performance is unknown and perhaps nonexistent.

*Knowledge tests* are more reliable because they determine information or knowledge. Math tests for an accountant and a weather test for a pilot are examples. But human resource specialists must be able to demonstrate that the knowledge is needed to perform the job. The Ontario trucking company example is a case wherein the tested knowledge (reading at an advanced level) was not needed. Figure 7-7 shows an example of a knowledge test.

*Performance tests* measure the ability of applicants to do some parts of the work for which they are to be hired. A typing test for typists is an obvious example. Validity is often assumed when the test includes a representative sample of the work the applicant is to do when hired. However, if the test discriminates against some minority group, human resource's assumption must be backed by detailed validation studies.

A popular procedure used for identifying managerial potential is the assessment centre (AC).[12] Currently assessment centres are popular at Alcan, Northern Telecom, B.C. Forest Products, Steinberg Ltd., to mention a few organizations in the private sector. AC is also becoming very popular in several municipal, provincial, and federal

FIGURE 7-6   Examples of Applications of Employment-Related Tests

## PSYCHOLOGICAL TESTS

| NAME | APPLICATION (SUBJECTS) |
|---|---|
| Minnesota Multiphasic Personality Inventory | Measures personality or temperament (executives, nuclear power security) |
| California Psychological Inventory | Measures personality or temperament (executives, managers, supervisors) |
| Guilford-Zimmerman Temperament Survey | Measures personality or temperament (sales personnel) |
| Watson-Glaser Critical Thinking Appraisal | Measures logic and reasoning ability (executives, managers, supervisors) |
| Owens Creativity Test | Measures creativity and judgement ability (engineers) |

## KNOWLEDGE TESTS

| | |
|---|---|
| How to Supervise? | Measures knowledge of supervisory practices (managers and supervisors) |
| Leadership Opinion Questionnaire | Measures knowledge of leadership practices (managers and supervisors) |
| General Aptitude Test Battery | Measures verbal, spatial, numeric, and other aptitudes and dexterity (jobseekers at unemployment offices) |

## PERFORMANCE TESTS

| | |
|---|---|
| Stromberg Dexterity Test | Measures physical coordination (shop workers) |
| Revised Minnesota Paper Form Board Test | Measures spatial visualization (draftsman and draftswoman) |
| Minnesota Clerical Test | Measures ability to work with numbers and names (clerks) |
| Job Simulation Tests, Assessment Centres | Measures a sample of ''on-the-job'' demands (managers, professionals, supervisory, and nonsupervisory employees) |

## GRAPHIC RESPONSE TESTS

| | |
|---|---|
| Lie Detector | Honesty and truthfulness (police, retail store workers) |

## ATTITUDE TESTS

| | |
|---|---|
| Honesty Test | Measures attitudes about theft and related subjects (retail workers, securities employees, banks) |
| Work Opinion Questionnaire | Measures attitudes about work and values (entry level, low-income workers) |

## MEDICAL TESTS

| | |
|---|---|
| Drug Tests | Measures the presence of illegal or performance-affecting drugs (athletes, government employees, equipment operators) |
| Genetic Screening | Identifies genetic predispositions to specific medical problems |
| Medical Screening | Measures and monitors exposure to hazardous chemicals (miners, factory workers, researchers) |

FIGURE 7-7   A Segment of a Verbal Ability Test

*Directions:* Each of the following questions consists of a word printed in capital letters followed by four words or phrases, lettered A through D. Choose the word that is most nearly IDENTICAL in meaning to the word in capital letters.
1. AFFECT: (a) to insult (b) to move, stir, or have influence upon (c) to imitate or pretend (d) the impression or result produced
2. INANE: (a) humorous (b) careless (c) dejected (d) silly
3. SOPORIFIC: (a) soapy (b) sleep inducing (c) unsophisticated (d) saturated
4. LATENT: (a) backward (b) dormant (c) extreme (d) obvious

Source: Hari Das and Nathan Kling, *Verbal Ability and Composition Test*, Faculty of Commerce, Saint Mary's University, Halifax, 1981.

government units. ACs use several methods of assessment, including paper-and-pencil tests, job simulations, in-basket exercises, projective tests, interviews, personality inventories, and/or leaderless group discussions (LGD). Typically, the tests are used to measure intellectual ability, work orientation, and career orientation, and LGD, role playing, and in-basket exercises measure an applicant's administrative skill. However, assessment centres do more than simply test applicants. Through the use of multiple assessment techniques and multiple assessors (or panel judges), ACs are able to predict a candidate's future job behaviour and managerial potential. The assessment process itself may vary in length from a few hours to several days depending on an organizations's needs and objectives. A typical AC evaluation for a first-level supervisory job lasts one to two days. In recent years, the AC technique has been becoming popular for nonsupervisory and skilled labour as well.[13] General Motors, for example, uses an eighteen-hour assessment centre procedure for all its production workers in Autoplex.[14] Research studies evaluating the validity of the assessment centre technique have, by and large, come out with positive conclusions indicating a median 0.40 correlation coefficient between AC ratings and such criteria as career progress, salary advances, supervisor ratings, and evaluations of potential progress.[15] This has led to a phenomenal growth in the number of organizations using the AC technique. Currently, more than 20,000 organizations in North America use the AC techniques; and more are doing so each year. More details on AC procedures will be given in Chapter 11 on Performance Appraisal.

*Graphic response tests* are a more recent development that seek information about applicants in ways that cannot be distorted easily. The *polygraph* (or lie detector) is the most common.[16] It measures physiological changes as a person responds to questions. When a person tells a lie, the conscience usually causes involuntary physiological reactions that are detected by the polygraph. At $30 to $60 per test, it is more economical than a detailed background check on applicants. In addition to ethical and public relations considerations, there are serious questions about the ability of most lie detector operators validly to administer and interpret the results.[17] Despite this, Canadian companies continue to use them.[18] In the U.S., 50% of all retail firms and 20% of all corporations and banks are reported to be using polygraph tests.[19]

*Attitude tests* are being used in some circumstances to learn about the attitudes of applicants and employees on a variety of job-related subjects. As polygraph tests draw criticisms about their accuracy and appropriateness, attitude tests are being used to assess attitudes about honesty and, presumably, on-the-job behaviours.[20] Attitude tests also reveal employee attitudes and values about work. The *Work Opinion Questionnaire*, for example, has been effectively used in predicting job performance of entry-level, low-income workers.[21]

*Medical tests* in recent years have grown in popularity. Through the analysis of urine or blood samples, laboratories are able to screen for the presence of drugs. More than 30% of *Fortune* 500 firms now test applicants and employees for drugs according to the National Institute of Drug Abuse in the United States.[22] Professional and amateur inter-collegiate athletes have been tested for many years to assure the absence of steroids, stimulants, and other chemicals that may yield short-term advantages. Drug testing for employment purposes, however, primarily developed in the mid-1980s as a response to the growing use of illegal drugs.

> The controversy surrounding Canada's ace sprinter, Ben Johnson, in the 1988 Seoul Olympics drew the public's attention to the possible widespread use of drugs among athletes. Although drug abuse among workers in Canada is still quite moderate when compared to the state of affairs in the U.S., it warrants serious attention in major centres such as Toronto, Vancouver, and Montreal.
>
> In the U.S., concern about employee drug abuse has spurred IBM, American Airlines, and many other organizations to require all job applicants to pass a urinalysis test for marijuana and cocaine.[23]

As technology has improved, genetic and other forms of testing have become technically and financially feasible. Genetic screening may alert employers to those with higher chances of developing specific diseases.[24] Likewise, medical monitoring of diseases such as Acquired Immune Deficiency Syndrome (AIDS) or the build-up of toxic chemicals such as lead or mercury poisoning among workers may alert employers to high-risk employees or shortcomings in health standards at the workplace.

Graphic response and medical tests present human resource specialists with an inherent dilemma. On the one hand, these methods do offer some additional screening tools to better assure an optimal work force. On the other hand, such tests are subject to errors. When they are inaccurate, needless discrimination results. Similarly, when tests discriminate against members of a protected class disproportionately, human rights violations may occur. In the U.S., in some jurisdictions, for example, carriers of the AIDS virus are protected by new laws or ordinances or by coverage under laws intended to protect the handicapped. In Canada, a clear national policy on this issue is yet to emerge, so that each province has its own policies and standards on these tests. To many applicants and employees these tests are an invasion of their privacy.[25]

> In 1987, in Nova Scotia, a school teacher who was diagnosed as infected with AIDS was not allowed to keep his job; demands from parent and community groups led to his removal from the position.

Besides specific cautions associated with individual tests, human resource specialists should realize that testing is not always feasible. Even when tests can be developed or bought, their cost may not be justified for jobs that have low selection ratios or that are seldom filled. Examples include technical, professional, and managerial jobs.

Even when feasible, the use of tests must be flexible. They need not always be the first or last step in the selection process. Instead, human resource experts use tests during the selection process at the point they deem appropriate. Consider the comments of an experienced human resource manager for a chain of grocery stores.

> Many human resource managers in other industries use testing only after other steps in the selection process. In the grocery business you must test first. Why waste time interviewing a grocery clerk who doesn't know that three for 88 cents is 30 cents apiece? Besides, when we take applications on Tuesdays, we may have 300 of them. Interviews would take seventy-five hours a week, and my staff consists of a clerk and myself. But through testing, we can test the entire group in an hour. Then we interview only those who score well.

Lastly, the employment test is only one of several techniques used in the selection process, because it is limited only to factors that can be tested and validated easily. Other items, not measurable through testing, may be equally important.

## Selection Interview: Step 3

The *selection interview* is a formal, in-depth conversation conducted to evaluate the applicant's acceptability. The interviewer seeks to answer two broad questions: Can the applicant do the job? How does the applicant compare with others who are applying for the job?

Selection interviews, or in-depth interviews as they are also known, are the most widely used selection technique. One study reports that 90% of all companies surveyed had more confidence in interviews than in any other source of selection information.[26] Their popularity stems from their flexibility. They can be adapted to unskilled, skilled managerial, and staff employees. They also allow a two-way exchange of information: interviewers learn about the applicant and the applicant learns about the employer.

Interviews do have shortcomings. The most noticeable flaw is their varying reliability and validity. Some early studies reported an average validity coefficient (i.e., the correlation between the interview assessment of candidates and their actual performance) of 0.10, or virtually nil.[27] In a more recent review of the interview technique, Maurer and Russell[28] found a validity coefficient of 0.24—still not high enough to allow a supervisor to make accurate predictions as far as job performance is concerned. Why then are they still so widely used? Schwind provides several reasons:[29]

- An interview allows a personal impression. Besides assessing a candidate's ability to perform well on the job, an interviewer also wants to make sure that there is a match between the person's personality and the team he/she has to work with. An interview provides an opportunity to do this.
- An interview offers the firm an opportunity to sell a job to a candidate. In high-demand areas such as engineering and business administration, this "selling" assumes great importance.
- An interview offers the organization an opportunity to answer the candidate's questions regarding the job, career opportunities, and company policies.

• An interview is an effective public relations tool. Interviewees are potential consumers, clients, or voters; their perception of fair treatment could have important consequences.

Good reliability means that the interpretation of the interview results should not vary from interviewer to interviewer. But it is common for different interviewers to form different opinions. Reliability is improved when identical questions are asked, especially if interviewers are trained to record responses systematically.[30] Validity is questionable because few human resource departments conduct validation studies on their interview results. However, proactive human resource departments are beginning to realize this problem and are comparing interview results with actual performance or other criteria, such as stability of employment.[31] More validation of interviews is needed because they may relate more to personal features of candidates than to the candidates' potential performance. For example, one study reported that two of the most important variables that influence an interview are fluency of speech and composure.[32] If these findings are applicable to most employment interviews, the results of the interviews may correlate with fluency and composure, instead of potential performance. Maurer and Russell's study (referred to earlier), which found a validity coefficient of 0.24 for interviews, still makes it a *weak* predictor of future performance. (A validity coefficient of 0.24 means that less than 6% of future performance can be predicted by an interview alone.) This means that human resource practitioners should always combine interviews with other predictors while selecting personnel. Carefully structured interviews based on a thorough job analysis may be more useful and valid than unstructured interviews that dwell on applicant opinions about topics not directly related to the job.[33] Also, interviews that probe what the applicant has actually done in the past in situations similar to those described in the job analysis may be better predictors of future performance.[34]

## Types of Interviews

Interviews are commonly conducted between the interviewer and the applicant on a one-to-one basis. Group interviews, however, are sometimes used. Variations of group interviews appear in Figure 7-8.

FIGURE 7-8   Different Combinations of Interviewers and Applicants

| NUMBER OF INTERVIEWERS | NUMBER OF APPLICANTS |
|---|---|
| INDIVIDUAL INTERVIEW | |
| 1 | 1 |
| GROUP INTERVIEWS | |
| 2 or more | 1 |
| 1 | 2 or more |
| 2 or more | 2 or more |

One form of group interview is to have applicants meet with two or more interviewers. This allows all interviewers to evaluate the individual on the same questions and answers. Since the interviewers are more apt to reach the same conclusion, reliability is improved. Another major variation in the figure is to have two or more applicants interviewed together, by one or more interviewers. This saves time, especially for busy executives. It also permits the answers of different applicants to be compared immediately.

Whether a group interview or not, there are different interview formats that depend on the type of questions that are asked. Questions can be structured, unstructured, mixed, problem-solving, or stress-producing. Figure 7-9 compares these different formats. And although the mixed format is most common in practice, each of the others has an appropriate role to play.

**FIGURE 7-9**  Different Question Formats in Interviews

| INTERVIEW FORMAT | TYPES OF QUESTIONS | USEFUL APPLICATIONS |
| --- | --- | --- |
| **Unstructured** | Few if any planned questions. Questions are made up during the interview. | Useful when trying to help interviewees solve personal problems or understand why they are not right for a job. |
| **Structured** | A predetermined checklist of questions, usually asked of all applicants. | Useful for valid results, especially when dealing with large numbers of applicants. |
| **Mixed** | A combination of structured and unstructured questions, which resembles what is usually done in practice. | Realistic approach that yields comparable answers plus in-depth insights. |
| **Problem-Solving** | Questions are limited to hypothetical situations. Evaluation is on the solution and the approach of the applicant. | Useful to understand applicant's reasoning and analytical abilities under modest stress. |
| **Stress-Producing** | A series of harsh rapid-fire questions intended to upset the applicant. | Useful for stressful jobs, such as handling complaints. |

## Unstructured Interviews

As the summary in Figure 7-9 indicates, the unstructured interview allows human resource specialists to develop questions as the interview proceeds. The interviewer goes into topic areas as they arise, and the end result is more like a friendly conversation. Unfortunately, this unstructured method lacks the reliability of a structured interview because each applicant is asked a different series of questions. Even worse, this approach may overlook key areas of the applicant's skills or background.

## Structured Interviews

Structured interviews rely on a predetermined set of questions. The questions are developed before the interview begins and are asked of every applicant. This approach improves the reliability of the interview process, but it does not allow the interviewer to follow up interesting or unusual responses. Here, the end result is an interview that seems quite mechanical to all concerned. The rigid format may even convey lack of interest to applicants who are used to more flexible interviews.

### Mixed Interviews

In practice, interviewers typically use a blend of structured and unstructured questions. The structured questions provide a base of information that allows comparisons between candidates. But the unstructured questions make the interview more conversational and permit greater insights into the unique differences between applicants. Community college and university recruiters, for example, use mixed interviews most of the time.

### Problem-Solving Interviews

Problem-solving interviews focus on a problem or series of problems that the applicant is expected to solve. Often these are hypothetical interpersonal situations and the applicant is asked what should be done. Both the answer and the approach used by the applicant are evaluated. This interview technique has a very narrow scope. It primarily reveals the applicant's ability to solve the types of problems presented. Validity is more likely if the hypothetical situations are similar to those found on the job. The actual interview might consist of ten situations similar to the following:

> Suppose you had to decide between two candidates for a promotion. Candidate A is loyal, cooperative, punctual, and hard-working. Candidate B is a complainer and is tardy and discourteous, but is the best producer in your department. Whom would you recommend for promotion to supervisor? Why?

The way the applicant reacts to the questions is noted. Since this type of interview produces modest amounts of stress, it gives an indication of how the applicant can function under moderately stressful situations.

### Stress Interviews

When the job involves much stress, a stress interview attempts to learn how the applicant will respond. Originally developed during World War II to see how selected recruits might react under stress behind enemy lines, these interviews have useful application in civilian employment. For example, applicants for police work are sometimes put through a stress interview to see how they might react to problems they encounter on the job. The interview itself consists of a series of harsh questions asked in rapid succession and in an unfriendly manner. Since stressful situations are usually only part of the job, this technique should be used in connection with other interview formats. Even then, negative public relations is likely to result among those who are not hired.

### The Interview Process

The five stages of a typical employment interview are listed in Figure 7-10. These stages are interviewer preparation, creation of rapport, information exchange, termination, and evaluation. Regardless of the type of interview used, each of these steps must occur for a successful interview to result. They are discussed briefly to illustrate how the actual interview process occurs.[35]

### Interviewer Preparation

Obviously, before the interview begins, the interviewer needs to prepare. This preparation requires that specific questions be developed by the interviewer. It is the answers

FIGURE 7-10    Stages in the Typical Employment Interview

to these questions that the interviewer will use in deciding the applicant's suitability. At the same time the interviewer must consider what questions the applicant is likely to ask. Since the interview is used to persuade top applicants to accept subsequent job offers, the interviewer needs to be able to explain job duties, performance standards, pay, benefits, and other areas of interest. A list of typical questions asked by recruiters and other interviewers appears in Figure 7-11. As can be seen from that list, these questions are intended to give the interviewer some insight into the applicant's interests, attitudes, and background. Specific or technical questions are added to the list according to the type of job opening.

Another action the interviewer should undertake before the interview is to review the application form. Research shows that the quality of the interviewer's decision is significantly better when the application form is present.[36] With or without the application form, interviewers seem to take about the same length of time to reach a conclusion— from four to ten minutes.[37] The longer the interview is scheduled to last and the better the quality of the applicants, the longer it takes interviewers to reach a decision.[38]

With the average cost of hiring new employees estimated to be as high as $4000 for managerial and professional employees, the interviewer's preparation should be aimed at making the interview process efficient and comfortable for the applicant.[39] Often the interviewer is one of the first representatives of the company with whom the applicant has had an opportunity to talk. A strong and lasting impression of the company is likely to be formed at this stage.[40] If the interviewer does not show courtesy to the applicant, that impression is certain to be negative. If the applicant is a promising candidate for the job, he or she likely has other job prospects.[41]

### Creation of Rapport

Once the interview begins, the burden is on the interviewer to establish a relaxed rapport with the recruit. Without a relaxed rapport, the interviewer may not get a clear picture of the applicant's potential. Rapport is aided by beginning the interview on time and starting with nonthreatening questions such as, "Did you have any parking problems?"

FIGURE 7-11    Sample Questions Used in Employment Interviews

1. How do you spend your spare time? What are your hobbies?
2. What community or school activities have you been involved in?
3. Describe your ideal job. In what type of work are you interested?
4. Why do you want to work for our company?
5. What were your favourite classes? Why?
6. Do you have any geographic preferences?
7. What do you think a fair salary would be?
8. What do you think your salary should be in five years? Ten?
9. Why did you select your university major?
10. What do you know about our company's products or services?
11. Describe the ideal boss.
12. How often do you expect to be promoted?
13. What is your major weakness? Strength?
14. Why do you think your friends like you?
15. Do you plan to take additional university courses? Which ones?
16. What jobs have you had that you liked most? Least?
17. Describe your least favourite boss or teacher.
18. What are your career goals?
19. If you could go back five years, what would you do the same? Differently?
20. Why should you be hired by our company?
21. Describe your last job.
22. How many hours do you think you will have to work at your job?
23. What job skills do you have?
24. Do you have a sample of your writing?
25. What is your favourite sport?

At the same time, the interviewer may use body language to help relax the applicant. A smile, a handshake, relaxed posture, and moving paperwork aside all communicate without words; such nonverbal communications maintain rapport throughout the interview session.[42] As one writer pointed out, the interviewer has to act the perfect host or hostess, greet the candidate with a warm smile showing him/her into the office, make small talk, and reduce the nervousness of the applicant by friendly conversation.[43] Only in a relationship of mutual trust and comfort will a candidate talk freely. By projecting an image of confidence, competence, and concern, especially in the early stages of the interview, an interviewer can create trust.[44]

*Information Exchange*
The heart of the interview process is the exchange of information. To help establish rapport, some interviewers may begin by asking the applicant if there are any questions. This establishes two-way communication and lets the interviewer begin to judge the recruit by the type of questions asked. Consider the following dialogue. Which response creates the most favourable impression?

INTERVIEWER:  Well, let's start with any questions you may have.
APPLICANT 1:  I don't have any questions.

APPLICANT 2: I have several questions. How much does the job pay? Will I get two weeks' vacation at the end of the first year?

APPLICANT 3: What will the responsibilities be? I am hoping to find a job that offers me challenges now and career potential down the road.

Each response creates a different impression on the interviewer. But only Applicant 3 appears concerned about the job. The other two applicants appear to be either unconcerned or interested only in what benefits they will receive.

In general, an interviewer will ask questions worded to learn as much as possible. Questions that begin with how, what, why, compare, describe, expand, or "Could you tell me more about . . . " are likely to solicit an open response, while questions that can be answered with a simple "yes" or "no" do not give the interviewer much insight.[45] As noted earlier, specific questions and areas of interest to an interviewer are suggested in Figure 7-11. Besides those questions, the interviewer may want more specific information about the applicant's background, skills, and interests.

### Termination

As the list of questions dwindles or available time ends, the interviewer must draw the session to a close. Here again, nonverbal communication is useful. Sitting erect, turning towards the door, glancing at a watch or clock all clue the applicant that the end is near. Some interviewers terminate the interview by asking, "Do you have any final questions?" At this point, the interviewer informs the applicant of the next step in the interview process, which may be to wait for a call or letter.

### Evaluation

Immediately after the interview ends, the interviewer should record specific answers and general impressions. Figure 7-12 shows a typical checklist used to record these impressions of the interviewee. Use of a checklist like the one in the figure can improve the reliability of the interview as a selection technique. As the checklist shows, the interviewer is able to obtain a large amount of information even from a short interview.

## Interviewer Errors

Caution must be exercised to avoid some common pitfalls of the interviewer, summarized in Figure 7-13, that lower the effectiveness of the interview. When the applicant is judged according to the "halo effect" or personal biases, the results of the interview are misinterpreted. Applicants are accepted or rejected for reasons that may bear no relation to their potential performance. Likewise, leading questions and domination do not allow the interviewer to learn of the applicant's potential either. The evaluation of the applicant then becomes based on a guess with little or no substantiation. No matter which pitfall is involved, it reduces the validity and reliability of the interview. All the interview does when biases are presented is waste organizational resources and the applicant's time. Figure 7-14 summarizes some major dos and don'ts in the employment interview.

FIGURE 7-12   A Postinterview Checklist

---

**EMPIRE INC.**
**"An Equal-Opportunity Employer"**
**Postinterview Checklist**

Applicant's Name _____   Date _____
Position Under Consideration _____   Interviewer _____

**Interviewer's Comments**

A.   Rate the applicant on the following (1 = low; 10 = high):

_____ Appearance                 _____ Ability to perform job
_____ Apparent interest          _____ Education/training
_____ Experience/background      _____ Timely availability
_____ Reasonable expectations    _____ Past employment stability

B.   List specific comments that reveal the candidate's strengths and weaknesses for the job being
considered:

1. Attitude towards previous job _____
2. Attitude towards previous boss _____
3. Expectations about job duties _____
4. Career or occupational expectations _____
5. Other specific comments about applicant _____
_____

**Follow-up Actions Required**

_____ None                       _____ Follow-up interview with personnel
_____ Testing                    _____ Applicant unacceptable (file)
_____ Supervisory interview      _____ Notify applicant of rejection
_____ Applicant unacceptable for job under consideration. Reconsider for job as
_____

---

## Interviewee Errors

Interviewees make errors too. Some may be to cover up job-related weaknesses. Others
may emerge from simple nervousness. Although interviewers — especially those in the
human resource department — may conduct hundreds of job interviews in a year, most
applicants never experience that many in a lifetime. Common interviewing mistakes made
by job candidates are:

· Playing games
· Talking too much
· Boasting
· Not listening
· Being unprepared

Playing games, for example, acting nonchalant, are often taken at face value: the

FIGURE 7-13 A Summary of Typical Interviewer Errors

---

### "HALO EFFECT"

Interviewers who use limited information about an applicant to bias their evaluation of that person's other characteristics are subject to the *halo effect*. In other words, some information about the candidate erroneously plays a disproportionate part in the final evaluation of the candidate.

**Examples:**
- An applicant who has a pleasant smile and firm handshake is considered a leading candidate before the interview begins.
- An applicant who wears blue jeans to the interview is rejected mentally.

### LEADING QUESTIONS

Interviewers who "telegraph" the desired answer by the way they frame their questions are using leading questions.

**Examples:**
- "Do you think you'll like this work?"
- "Do you agree that profits are necessary?"

### PERSONAL BIASES

Interviewers who harbour prejudice against specific groups are exhibiting a personal bias.

**Examples:**
- "I prefer sales personnel who are tall."
- "Some jobs are for men and others for women."

### INTERVIEWER DOMINATION

Interviewers who use the interview to oversell the applicant, brag about their successes, or carry on a social conversation instead of an interview are guilty of interviewer domination.

**Examples:**
- Spending the entire interview telling the applicant about the company plans or benefits.
- Using the interview to tell the applicant how important the interviewer's job is.

---

candidate is not interested. The candidate may be excited or nervous and talk too much, especially about irrelevant topics such as sports or weather. Instead applicants should stick to the subject at hand. Likewise, boasting also is a common mistake. Applicants need to "sell themselves," but credential distortion — even if just "embellishments" — about responsibilities and accomplishments or simply bragging too much can turn off the interviewer's interest. Failure to listen may result from anxiety about the interview. Unfortunately, it usually means missing the interviewer's questions and failing to maintain rapport. And, of course, being unprepared means asking poorly thought-out questions and even conveying disinterest, neither of which are likely to land the job being sought.[46]

## References and Background Checks: Step 4

What type of person is the applicant? Is the applicant a good, reliable worker? To answer these questions, employment specialists use references.

FIGURE 7-14   Some Dos and Don'ts of Conducting Employment Interviews

___

DO:

___

1. collect only job-related information and not information on general personality traits.
2. concentrate on securing information about the applicant's past job behaviour.
3. use several interviewers (to interview each candidate) to increase the reliability of interview process.
4. treat all interviewees equally and impartially.
5. have a checklist of questions to ask each job applicant.
6. attempt to create a relaxed setting by asking easy, nonthreatening questions first and showing support to the applicant.
7. provide job-related information to the candidate.
8. compare your evaluations of each candidate with other interviewers and find out why discrepancies exist.

DO NOT:

___

1. attempt to predict personality traits from a single interview.
2. be guided by initial impressions (or nonverbal cues) and generalize them to all relevant work and nonwork behaviour of the applicant.
3. allow your evaluation of the candidate's job performance to be influenced by a single characteristic (such as how well the applicant dresses).
4. be tempted to make ''snap'' judgements of the candidate early in the interview, thus blocking out further information.
5. ask leading questions that communicate the correct or desired answer to the applicant (e.g., ''Do you believe that women workers should be treated equally with males?'').
6. exhibit personal biases (''In my experience, good sale managers have all been men'').
7. dominate the interview; rather use the interview to collect relevant information about the candidate.

___

Source: Based on Mallika Das and Hari Das, ''Selection Interview,'' Unpublished manuscript, Saint Mary's University, April 1986.

Many professionals have a very sceptical attitude towards references. *Personal references*—those that attest to the applicant's sound character—are usually provided by friends or family. Their objectivity and candour are certainly questionable. When a reference is in writing, the author usually emphasizes only positive points. Thus personal references are not commonly used.

*Employment references* differ from personal references because they discuss the applicant's work history. Many human resource specialists doubt the usefulness of these references because former supervisors or teachers may not be completely candid, especially with negative information. As a result, many employment references are little more than confirmation of prior employment.

This lack of candour has caused some human resource specialists to omit this step entirely from the selection process. Other specialists have substituted telephone inquiries for written references. Besides getting a faster response, often at lower cost, telephone inquiries have the advantage of directness: voice inflections or hesitation over blunt questions may tip off the interviewer to underlying problems. In practice, however, less than 22% of all reference checks seek negative information, according to one study.[47] The same study revealed that 48% of reference checks are used to verify application information and 30% are used to gather additional data.

John Adams impressed his interviewers a few minutes after the interview began. The position was that of a store manager in a large building supplies chain. His ready wit, ability to think on the spot, and keen mind appealed to the interviewers. Equally attractive was what his previous employers had to say about him. One of the references called him a young dynamo because of his drive and enthusiasm; another commented on John's ability to "come out with totally creative ideas" and his "methodical approach to problems." John Adams, who was hired for the position by the firm, did perform true to these statements for the first three months. It was by sheer accident that one day a colleague noted a shortfall in the cash register. On investigation, it was found that Adams had been systematically stealing money from his employers. Even worse, he had a history of embezzling accounts with his three previous employers. One of the previous employers admitted being aware of a couple of incidents where Adams had received kickbacks from vendors. None of the references, however, made any mention of these facts in their letters.[48]

Das and Das concluded that such lack of candour in reference letters was due to a variety of reasons including: fear of legal reprisal, legal requirements (as in the U.S.) to show reference letters to an applicant, desire to get rid of an employee, and reluctance to pass judgement on a fellow human being.[49] Given this state of affairs, an employer can get to the truth about a potential employee's character and work performance in a number of ways. Some of the possible strategies are shown in Figure 7-15. In all cases, the references should be combined with the information coming from other predictors such as biographical data, tests, and interviews.

FIGURE 7-15   How to Get the Truth Out of References

1. **Use the phone:** Most references are more likely to be honest over the phone or in person rather than in a formal letter.
2. **Seek information on job-related behaviour:** Ask for details on job behaviours, such as tardiness and absenteeism, rather than on personality traits, such as ambition and intelligence, which are hard to evaluate reliably.
3. **Ask direct questions:** Questions such as "Would you re-hire this employee now?" or "How is this person's behaviour in a group setting?" would result in more honest answers than when a person is asked to write a paragraph on the strengths and weaknesses of the employee.
4. **Combine references with other predictors:** Reference letters are no substitute for application blanks, tests, and interviews.
5. **Use credible sources only:** Former work supervisors are, typically, the most useful reference sources. Letters from acquaintances and friends are usually worthless.
6. **Note frequency of job changes:** A person who has not stayed in any organization for more than a few months may be either an extremely successful employee or a problem employee. Persons who have been moving laterally across organizations without any apparent change in job challenge, rewards, or working conditions should be carefully watched.
7. **Watch out for phrases with hidden meanings:** Most references do not blatantly lie; they simply don't tell the whole truth. A person who is described as "deeply committed to his family and friends" may be someone who will not work beyond five o'clock; an "individualist" may be a person who cannot work with others.

Adapted and summarized from: Hari Das and Mallika Das, "But He Had Excellent References: Refining the Reference Letter," *The Human Resource*, June-July 1988, pp. 15-16.

## Medical Evaluation: Step 5

The selection process may include a medical evaluation of the applicant before the hiring decision is made. Normally, the evaluation is a health checklist that asks the applicant to indicate health and accident information. The questionnaire is sometimes supplemented with a physical examination by a company nurse or physician. The medical evaluation may:

- Entitle the employer to lower health or life insurance rates for company-paid insurance.
- Be required by provincial or local health officials—particularly in food-handling operations where communicable diseases are a danger.
- Be useful to evaluate whether the applicant can handle the physical or mental stress of a job.

Many employers have done away with this step because of the costs involved. Also, if an applicant is rejected, charges of discrimination under the Canadian Human Rights Act or related provincial legislation may be brought. A congenital health condition may be considered a disability, and failure to hire may be seen as discrimination against the qualified applicant. If the employer wants a medical evaluation, it may be scheduled after the hiring decision.

One noteworthy exception to the trend of fewer medical evaluations is drug testing. A small but growing number of organizations, both in the private and public sectors, include drug screening as part of their employment process, either before or immediately after the hiring decision. These organizations seek to avoid the economic and legal risks associated with drug users. Increases in mortality rates, accidents, theft, and poor performance affect the employer's economic performance. And, if the drug user's performance carries negative consequences for customers or fellow employees, lawsuits are likely.[50]

## Supervisory Interview: Step 6

The immediate supervisor is ultimately responsible for newly hired workers. Since that responsibility is ever-present, supervisors should have input into the final hiring decision. The supervisor is often better able to evaluate the applicant's technical abilities than is the human resource department. Likewise, the immediate supervisor can often answer the interviewee's specific job-related questions with greater precision. As a result, one study reported that in more than three-quarters of the organizations surveyed, the supervisor had the authority to make the final hiring decision.

When supervisors make the final decision, the role of the human resource department is to provide the supervisor with the best applicants available. From these two or three applicants, the supervisor decides whom to hire. Some organizations leave the final hiring decision to the human resource department, especially when applicants are hired into a training program instead of for a specific job. If supervisors constantly reject particular groups of applicants, such as minorities or women, the human resource department may be given final hiring authority to avoid future charges of discrimination.

Regardless of who has the final hiring authority, the personal commitment of supervisors is generally higher when they participate in the selection process. Their participation is best obtained through the supervisory interview. Through a variety of structured and nonstructured questions, the supervisor attempts to assess the technical competency, potential, and overall suitability of the applicant. The supervisory interview also allows the recruit to have technical, work-related questions answered. Often, the supervisory interview is supplemented with a realistic job preview that better enables the employee to comprehend the job before being hired. A review of realistic job previews caused one writer to conclude that there are effective ways to minimize turnover among employees who are eventually hired.[51]

When the supervisor recommends hiring an individual, he or she has made a psychological commitment to assist the new employee. If the candidate turns out to be unsatisfactory, the supervisor is then more likely to accept some of the responsibility for failure.

## *Realistic Job Previews: Step 7*

Often, the supervisory interview is supplemented with a realistic job preview. A *realistic job preview* (RJP) allows the potential employee to understand the job setting before the hiring decision is made—often by showing him or her the type of work, equipment, and working conditions involved.

Unmet expectations about a job probably contribute to initial job dissatisfaction. The realistic job preview attempts to prevent job dissatisfaction by giving the newcomer an insight into the job.[52] Recently hired employees who have had a realistic job preview are less likely to be shocked by the job or the job setting on the first day they report to work after being hired. Two writers concluded the following:

> The RJP functions very much like a medical vaccination. . . . The typical medical vaccination injects one with a small, weakened dose of germs, so that one's body can develop a natural resistance to that disease. The RJP functions similarly by presenting job candidates with a small dose of "organizational reality." And, like the medical vaccination, the RJP is probably much less effective after a person has already entered a new organization.[53]

Research on the effectiveness of realistic job previews has shown that in nine out of ten studies, employee turnover was higher when the job previews were not used. The average of these studies was 28.8% higher.[54]

> In one organization, a film was used to "warn" potential employees about the unpleasant aspects of a job. The job was that of a telephone operator. The film made it clear that the work was repetitive and closely supervised and sometimes required dealing with rude or unpleasant customers. Use of realistic job preview (RJP) was found to be related to decreased turnover rates, but RJP has no effect on job performance.[55]

The adverse effect of RJP may be more candidates refusing to accept job offers. Jick and Greenhalgh suggest that although RJP results in less turnover of recruits, the general reduction in turnover is often offset by a tendency for the job offer acceptance rate to decline.[56] Many of the RJPs may also be focusing unduly on extrinsic and job-context factors rather than on job content (or intrinsic) factors.[57] Also, RJPs are no substitute for continuous monitoring of working conditions and in-depth job analysis. As two researchers concluded:

> Telling prospective employees about unpleasant working conditions may improve the probability that they will remain on the job in comparison to those who are not told about the conditions. However . . . those who are told about less pleasant conditions will be no more satisfied with them once they are experienced than will those who are not told. To improve satisfaction and the quality of work, ultimately some changes must be made in those aspects of the work environment with which employees are dissatisfied.[58]

## Hiring Decision: Step 8

Whether made by the supervisor or the human resource department, the final hiring decision marks the end of the selection process. From a public relations standpoint, other applicants should be notified that they were not selected. Employment specialists may want to consider rejected applicants for other openings, since these recruits have already gone through various stages of the selection process. Even if no openings are available, applications of candidates not hired should be kept on file for future openings. Retaining these applications can be useful if the employer is charged with employment discrimination.

The applications of those hired should be retained also. The application form begins the employee's personnel file and contains useful information for studies that the human resource department may conduct to learn about the source of its applicants, their age, sex, race, or other work-related characteristics. If some recruits prove unsatisfactory after they are hired, for example, human resource specialists may be able to reconstruct the selection process beginning with the application. In their reconstruction, they may uncover invalid tests, improperly conducted interviews, or other flaws in the selection process.

## OUTCOMES AND FEEDBACK

The final outcome of the selection process is the people who are hired. If the preselection inputs are considered carefully and the major steps of the selection process have been followed correctly, then new employees are likely to be productive. And productive employees are the best evidence of an effective selection process.

To evaluate both new employees and the selection process requires feedback. Feedback on successful employees is sometimes hard to find for employment managers, since supervisors usually claim responsibility for their successes. Feedback on failures is ample. It can include displeased supervisors, growing employee turnover and absenteeism, poor performance, low employee satisfaction, union activity, and legal suits.

More constructive feedback is obtained through specific questions. How well does the new employee adapt to the organization? To the job? To the career of which the job is a part? And lastly, how well does the employee perform? Answers to each of these questions provide feedback about the employee and the selection process. The following section provides some guidelines for evaluating the selection function.

## EVALUATING THE SELECTION FUNCTION

How do you know whether the selection procedures in your organization are effective? How can you evaluate whether they achieved your organization's goals? Even if the procedures are effective (namely, they achieve the objective of hiring the right candidates), are they efficient and worth the costs and trouble? In Chapter 1 of this book, it was pointed out that all human resource activities have to meet the functional objective. This means that the department's contribution in various areas should be at levels appropriate to an organization's needs. If the selection system is more or less sophisticated than the organization requires, then resources are wasted. This necessitates continuous monitoring of the effectiveness and efficiency of selection procedures.

In the ultimate sense, the utility of a selection procedure is decided by looking at the quality and productivity of the work force hired and the costs incurred in the process. The costs include not only the out-of-pocket costs (such as costs of testing, interviewing, postage, and stationery) but also costs associated with errors in the decisions made.[59] If the wrong candidate is hired or promoted, the costs are particularly high.[60] However, an exhaustive look at all costs (actual and potential) associated with a selection system may be very difficult in real life.

In all instances, however, the utility of a selection procedure should be assessed only after considering a number of factors. The more important ones among these are: 1) the validity of the predictor; 2) the variability in job performance; 3) the selection ratio; 4) the base rate of job success; and 5) selection costs.

*1. The validity of the predictor.* Different predictors have differing validity coefficients. One study by Hunter and Hunter[61] showed that predictors such as tests and assessment centres had average validities in the range of 0.43 to 0.54, while others such as reference checks (0.26) and interviews (0.14) were much lower. Of course, when choosing between predictors with equal validity, the cost of the predictor becomes an important consideration; however, as one writer noted, the trade-off between the cost of a predictor and its validity should almost always be resolved in favour of validity.[62] This is because the potential cost of an error in the case of the test is extremely high.

*2. The variability in job performance.* A useful measure of a job's value to the organization is the variability of job performance for a job expressed in dollar terms. For some jobs, the differences in performance ranges (example: "outstanding" to "totally incompetent") have relatively little effect in terms of dollar value to the organization. For example, the variability in performance of a receptionist or window cleaner is relatively less significant to the organization than that of a production planner or marketing manager. Thus, a "good" receptionist may contribute, say, $6000 over his/her salary and benefits to the organization, while a "poor" one may cost the firm, say, $2000 in terms of lost sales because of disgruntled customers who had bad experiences when paying visits to the organization. In the case of a marketing manager, the effects or outcomes may be far more serious. A good marketing manager may contribute $500,000 above his/her salary and benefits, while a poor one may cost the firm $200,000 in lost sales or decreased market share. The variability in performance in dollar terms for the receptionist is about $8000; for the marketing manager's position, the corresponding figure may be $700,000. The statistical index used for computing this type of variability is the standard deviation of performance. Hunter and Schmidt's[63] research led them to conclude that a "40-percent rule" prevails for most common job positions — namely, the variability in job performance is typically 40% of the average annual salary of a position. Clearly, in the above example, an organization is more likely to spend $5000 on improving the selection procedures for its marketing manager than for the receptionist.

3. *Selection ratio.* As already mentioned in this chapter, a large selection ratio (such as 1:25) means that the firm can afford to be choosy, while a small ratio of 1:2 does not give much freedom to the organization to make selection decisions. On the one hand, a ratio such as 1:25 means that a large number of applicants have to be tested and screened (thus adding to the selection costs). On the other hand, it also means that only the "cream" of the applicant group will be selected, thus implying that even a predictor with relatively low validity can be employed.

4. *The base rate of job success.* The base rate denotes the relative incidence of any given attribute or behaviour in the total population.[64] If 70% of the people between 22 and 40 years old are married, then the base rate for marriage for that segment of the society is 70. A low base rate of job success in an organization indicates that few employees reach an acceptable level of job performance. Typically, base rates of success tend to be high for easy and simple jobs. For complex jobs requiring many skills and years of training, the base rates tend to be lower. Generally, the usefulness of a selection procedure increases when it is able to increase the base rate of success for a job. If the base rate is already high at 80 or 90, it is very difficult to find a predictor that will improve on it as the typical validity coefficients for various predictors currently in use range from 0.15 to 0.60.

5. *Selection costs.* Selection costs may be actual or potential. Actual costs include costs of administering standardized tests, collecting and processing biographical blanks, conducting selection interviews, and offering money and other benefits to job candidates who are selected. The potential costs include cost of selection errors as when the wrong person is hired for a job. The benefits of a selection process should also be defined broadly to include not only current benefits but also likely future events (e.g., potential of an employee to hold additional responsibility).

Clearly, a thorough evaluation of all the above variables is a very complex and difficult task. In the past, several writers have offered somewhat different algorithms and formulas to assess the usefulness of the selection procedure.[65] One formula suggested by Cascio to calculate the utility of selection procedure is:[66]

$$\Delta U = n \, t \, \gamma_{xy} \, SD_y \, \bar{z}$$

Where $\Delta U$ = increase in productivity in dollars
       $n$ = number of persons hired
       $t$ = average job tenure in years of those hired
       $\gamma_{xy}$ = the correlation between a selection predictor and job performance (or validity coefficient)

SD$_y$ = variability in job performance (measured by standard deviation of job performance in dollars, roughly 40% of annual wage)[67]

$\bar{z}$ = the average predictor score of those selected (in standard score form)

As an illustration, consider the job position of a marketing manager in a consumer goods organization. Let us assume that the organization used an assessment centre technique (which had an estimated validity of 0.6) to hire ten managers who are paid a salary of $80,000 each year. Further, let us assume that each manager will stay with the organization for five years. Assuming an average predictor score (standardized) of 1.4, it can be shown that the assessment centre procedure would increase productivity by $1.344 million over five years or an average of $268,800 each year of their tenure.

Utility analysis such as the above has been successfully used in a number of organizations and different work settings.[68] It should be noted that utility analysis does not require reducing all selection-decision outcomes to a dollar figure; indeed, what is more important may be identifying all possible outcomes of a decision and weighing their relative importance systematically.[69] The factors identified earlier in this section (namely, selection ratio, base rate of success, etc.) interact; hence they must be considered together. For example, typically the utility is higher with a low base rate of job success or when the variability in job performance is high. However, given identical base rates of job success, different selection ratios can make a major difference in the context of selection. For example, it can be mathematically shown that with a base rate of 50% and a validity coefficient of 0.40, a selection ratio of 70% will yield 58% successful employees. Keeping the other things the same, if the selection ratio is changed to 40%, the proportion of successful employees climbs to 66% while for a 10% selection ratio, the corresponding figure is a whopping 78%![70] Such interdependence among the relevant selection variables makes utility analysis a very complex procedure indeed. Yet, its contribution to an effective human resource management system should not be underestimated.

## SUMMARY

The selection process depends heavily upon inputs such as job analysis, human resource plans, and recruits. These inputs are used within the challenges of the external environment, ethics, and guidelines established by the organization.

With these inputs and challenges, the selection process takes recruits and puts them through a series of steps to evaluate their potential. These steps vary from organization to organization and from one job opening to another. In general, the selection procedure relies on testing for many hourly jobs and on interviews for virtually every opening that is to be filled. References and medical evaluations are steps commonly found in the selection process of most employers.

The supervisor's role should include participation in the selection process, usually through an interview with job candidates. Through participation, the supervisor is more likely to be committed to the new worker's success.

Growing research evidence supports the use of realistic job previews (RJPs). After considerable expense and effort to recruit and select employees, the use of realistic job previews seems well advised as a means of reducing turnover among new employees.

Like all other human resource functions, the costs and benefits of the selection process also have to be compared periodically to evaluate the utility of various predictors. However, this is a very complex activity, often requiring fairly advanced mathematical skills. Notwithstanding this, all human resource management systems have to implement evaluation studies to maintain their effectiveness and efficiency.

## TERMS FOR REVIEW

| | |
|---|---|
| Selection process | Structured interviews |
| Employment function | Stress interviews |
| Selection ratio | "Halo effect" |
| Employment tests | Employment references |
| Validity | Realistic job preview (RJP) |
| Reliability | Utility analysis |
| Selection interview | |

## REVIEW AND DISCUSSION QUESTIONS

1. What information should the employment specialist review before beginning the selection process?

2. Suppose you are an employment specialist. Would you expect to have a large or small selection ratio for each of the following job openings?
   (a) Janitors
   (b) Nuclear engineers with five years' experience designing nuclear reactors
   (c) Clerk-typists
   (d) Supervisors
   (e) Elementary school teachers in the Yukon
   (f) Elementary school teachers in the Atlantic provinces

3. List and briefly describe each of the steps in the selection process.

4. If an employment manager asked you to streamline the firm's selection process for hourly paid workers, which steps described in this chapter would you recommend cutting? Why?

5. The typical employment interview has five stages to it. What are those stages? Briefly explain each.

6. Why should employment tests be validated?

7. As you begin interviewing a job applicant, you notice this person is very nervous. Yet your evaluation of the applicant indicates that this applicant is highly qualified. What should you do to put the person at ease in order to establish rapport?

8. Some people believe that the human resource department should have the authority to decide who is hired because human resource are the experts on hiring. Others say that the immediate supervisor, being responsible for employee performance,

should have the final authority. Explain your reasons for accepting one argument or the other.

9. A Canadian university has been experiencing high student dropout rates in recent years. One calculation showed that although the first-year enrolment in commerce courses increased from 650 to 980 students in the last four years, the dropout rate for first-year students has also worsened from 9% to 15%. The university has been using uniform admission standards during the years and has not made any significant changes in the grading or instructional procedures. The university is currently thinking of making a short film that will be shown in major recruitment areas. Given your knowledge of recruitment, selection, and realistic job preview procedures, what items would you recommend being included in the film? Why?

## INCIDENT 7-1

### A Selection Decision at Empire Inc.

At Empire Inc., the turnover rate is very high among assembly workers. Supervisors in the production department have told the human resource department that they do not have time to conduct a supervisory interview with the large number of applicants who are processed to fill assembly-line openings. As a result, the human resource department's employment specialists make the final hiring decisions.

The profiles of three typical applicants are presented below.

|  | APPLICANT A | APPLICANT B | APPLICANT C |
|---|---|---|---|
| **Years of Experience** | 4 | 7½ | 1 |
| **Education** | 1 year of university | Finished eighth grade | High school diploma |
| **Age** | 24 | 43 | 32 |
| **Test Score** | 76/100 | 73/100 | 85/100 |
| **Medical Evaluation** | OK | OK | OK |
| **Job Knowledge** | Very good | Excellent | Fair/good |
| **Work History** | Limited data | Stable | Stable |
| **Ranking by:** | | | |
| Interviewer 1 | 1 | 2 | 3 |
| Interviewer 2 | 3 | 2 | 1 |
| **Apparent Eagerness** | Moderate | Strong | Weak/average |
| **Availability** | 4 weeks | 2 weeks | Immediately |

The nature of the assembly jobs is rather simple. Training seldom takes more than an hour or two. Most people master the job and achieve an acceptable level of production during the second full day on the job. The tasks involve very little physical or mental effort. The test is valid, but has only a weak relationship between scores and actual performance.

1. What information would you consider irrelevant in the preceding selection profiles?

2. Are there any changes you would recommend in the selection process?

3. Which of the three candidates would you select, given the limited knowledge you possess? Why?

## INCIDENT 7-2

### National Food Brokers Selection Process

> National Food Brokers buys carload orders of nonperishable food products for resale to food wholesalers. Phone-sales personnel take orders from major food wholesalers, write up the orders, and send them to the appropriate food producers. Nearly 90 of National's 130 employees work in the phone-sales department. Since the job requires long hours on the phone to different accounts, the work is not very pleasant and turnover is high.
>
> The manager of the phone-sales department Carol Decinni, made the following observations in the presence of the human resource manager, Craig Reems:
>
> "Most of the people who work in the department fall into two groups. There are those who have been here for two or more years. They seem reasonably content and are the top sellers we have. The other group consists of people who have been here for less than two years. Most of our turnover comes from this group. In fact, we lose one of every three new employees during the first two months. When I talk with the people who are quitting, most of them tell me that they had no idea how much time they had to spend on the phone. I am generally pleased with the quality of recruits the human resource department provides. But we cannot continue with this high turnover. My supervisors are spending most of their time training new workers. Is there anything the human resource department can do to hire more stable workers?"

1. Suppose you are asked by the human resource manager to suggest some strategies for improving the selection process in order to hire more stable workers. What suggestions do you have for (a) preemployment testing and (b) reference checks?

2. Do you believe an interview with a supervisor in the department would help applicants understand the work better?

3. What do you think the supervisors should do to give the applicants a realistic understanding of the job before they are hired?

## CASE STUDY

### REGINA SHOES LIMITED: SELECTION OF A HUMAN RESOURCE MANAGER

Robert Clark, president and key shareholder of Regina Shoes, knew that he had a tough situation on hand. In less than a month, Regina Shoes will have to negotiate a contract with a newly formed union in its plant covering approximately 23% of the nonmanagerial work force. A second and a more militant union is up for contract negotiations a few months later. Recently, the firm's human resource manager, John McAllister, left Regina Shoes for a better position in Toronto. Despite its best recruitment efforts, Regina Shoes has not been able to fill the vacancy. The firm had run want ads in major Canadian dailies, including the Globeand Mail, Financial Post, VancouverSun, and the Halifax Herald. The ads yielded only eighteen potential candidates, out of which a preliminary screening had reduced the number to eight. All eight were interviewed and five were eliminated from further consideration after this preliminary interview. One of Regina Shoes' present employees, Jane Reynold, is also under consideration. Summaries of the résumés submitted by the four candidates are given in Figures 1 through 4.

FIGURE 1

Michael Anderson

| | |
|---|---|
| Personal data: | Age 54 years; widower, two children — Ken (26 years) and Maggie (23 years) |
| Education: | Grade 12, Belvedere High School, Vancouver. |
| | Two years in B. Comm. University of B.C. |
| | Extension courses in Personnel Management in B.C. and Ontario |
| Experience: | 5 years in Canadian Armed Forces; honorary discharge; outstanding record |
| | 4 years, Production Scheduler, Corner Brook Arts and Crafts, Newfoundland |
| | 5 years, Production Supervisor, Hamilton Steel Manufacturing, Ontario |
| | 12 years, Administrative Manager, De-Brook Safety Glasses Limited, Mississauga, Ontario |
| | 4 years, Assistant Personnel Manager, U-Save Groceries Limited, Ontario |

FIGURE 2

Arthur Dougherty

| | |
|---|---|
| Personal: | Age 49 years; married for the last 23 years, three children, Jack (22), John (20), and Martha (17) |
| Education: | Grade 12 from St. Matthew's High School, Sudbury, Ontario |
| | Dale Carnegie course |
| | Public Speaking workshop |
| | 2 Personnel Management courses (non-credit) at McMaster University, Ontario |
| Experience: | 2 years, Clerical (accounting), Great West Insurance Company, Saskatoon, Saskatchewan |
| | 6 years, Sales Assistant, Classic Leather Shoes and Accessories, Winnipeg, Manitoba |
| | 5 years, Sales Supervisor, Winnie's Auto Trades, Winnipeg, Manitoba |
| | 6 years, Sales Supervisor, Safe and Fun Toys, Mississauga, Ontario |
| | 3 years, Senior Personnel Assistant, Maritime Agro Industries, Fredericton, New Brunswick |
| | 2 years, Senior Personnel Assistant, Light Engineering Works, Hamilton, Ontario |
| | 1 year, Assistant Personnel Manager, Madman McIsac's Carpets, Hamilton, Ontario |

FIGURE 3

Jane Reynold

| | |
|---|---|
| Personal: | Age 31 years; single, one child, John (8 years) |
| Education: | B.A. Sociology, University of New Brunswick (Dean's Honour List) |
| | 3 courses in Personnel Management, Saint Mary's University, Halifax, Nova Scotia |
| | 1 course on Stress Management, Ontario Personnel Association |

Experience:  1 year, Employment Recruiter, Atlantic Crafts and Toys, New Brunswick

3 years, Recruiter, Atlantic Brewery, Nova Scotia

3 years, Administrative Assistant, Ontario Steel and Metal Extracting Limited, Ontario

2 years, Personnel Assistant, Regina Shoes Limited, Regina, Saskatchewan

FIGURE 4

Steven Robinson

Personal:  Age 29 years; divorced, one child under Robinson's custody, Melanie (7 years)

Education:  B.A. (Political Science), University of Saskatchewan

Experience:  2 years, Correspondent for The Bugle, a small-town newspaper in Ontario

2 years, Guidance Counsellor, St. Xavier High School, Moncton, New Brunswick

2 years, Personnel Assistant, St. Xavier High School, Moncton, New Brunswick

1 year, Assistant Personnel Manager, Bedford Town, Nova Scotia

Based on their résumés and on his impressions of the interviews with the four candidates, Robert Clark made the following mental evaluations of the applicants, Michael Anderson, Arthur Dougherty, Jane Reynold, and Steven Robinson. Clark felt that each applicant had a few strong points but also possessed major weaknesses.

MICHAEL ANDERSON: Anderson was the oldest of the lot (observed Clark). A widower with two grown-up children, he had the most diverse background. Anderson impressed Clark as a very interesting, if somewhat reserved, person. He had five years' experience in the Canadian Armed Forces (with an outstanding record there) and knew several trades ("Jack of all trades"?). During the interview, Anderson came through as a results-oriented individual. As a previous employer noted, Corner Brook Arts and Crafts, where Anderson worked in the past, had been about to be declared bankrupt at the time Anderson entered the company ("for peanuts money") and turned it around to become a successful firm by refining its planning and control systems. In Clark's mind, Anderson was someone who could take charge, but one of the referees had warned about Anderson's "need for autonomy in his work place." Clark felt that personally he would get along better with someone else (for example, Dougherty) than with Anderson. But then, his personal feelings should not play that important a role in the hiring decision. Or should they?

ARTHUR DOUGHERTY: Dougherty impressed Clark as the most gregarious of the four he interviewed. He was totally at ease with the interviewers and displayed the best interpersonal skills among the four. He not only was comfortable in the presence of others but seemed to have the knack of making others feel comfortable as well. It was true that Dougherty's past experience was mostly in sales — he had moved to human resources only four years ago ("I wanted bigger things to do; there is only so much you can do in selling a toy duck to toddlers"). His references called Dougherty a "very pleasant person to work with" and "always having the time for others." Clark, however, has serious doubts about Dougherty's knowledge of human resource management systems. This would be crucial for Regina Shoes, where the human resource function is going to play a key role in the next few years (one reason why the title "personnel manager" was changed to "human resource manager"). In favour of Dougherty was another fact: his children had all grown up — so, he should be able to devote extra time to the new position. This job, with all these union contract negotiations ahead, is going to require a lot of eighteen-hour workdays!

JANE REYNOLD: The first thing that struck Clark about Reynold was the way she dressed. She was so meticulously dressed and had impeccable manners (she reminded him of his German aunt — so nice and pleasant yet very formal and methodical). Reynold was very popular among her colleagues, except for the finance manager, Jim Potovisky, who didn't like her at all ("I can't stand that pushy female"). Considered a real "mover," Reynold had been active in Regina Shoes, always working on some project or other. John McAllister, the previous personnel manager and Reynold's boss, had, however, mixed evaluations of Reynold's job performance ("She is darn efficient and very competent, I will say that; but she is also so aggressive that she will alienate some people"). Clark has his own doubts about the wisdom of hiring a female for the position. He feels that given the challenges facing Regina Shoes, a woman simply can't handle the job. Can Reynold really face up to Steven Mathews, the new leader of the Leather Worker's Association? Mathews has the reputation of being a tough, militant leader who is out to get results for his union. And while Clark doesn't consider himself prudish, he still can't accept a woman who had a child out of wedlock. The references from Reynold's previous employers had given her consistently very high to outstanding ratings. There is a rumour that Reynold has been offered a better position in an Ontario firm and may move East. Reynold impressed Clark as very career-minded.

STEVEN ROBINSON: The first thing that struck Clark about Robinson was what hiring him would do to the public's and employees' image of the company. Hiring a black is just the thing to do right now — no one can criticize you any more about not being sensitive to the multicultural mosaic of Canada. Just by hiring Robinson, you could create the impression of being a "progressive employer." Regina Shoes has been facing a barrage of criticisms about Human Rights Law violations; now just by a single act of hiring Robinson, the firm could eliminate all those negative impressions. During the interview, Clark had received good "vibes" from Robinson. Robinson, who is divorced, has a small child. Robinson's mother lives with him to take care of the child. Robinson's referees gave him satisfactory recommendations, although not outstanding. Robinson was the youngest of all the four applicants and seemed full of energy and enthusiasm.

Clark knew that he had a difficult decision to make. To complicate matters, there was not very much agreement among the three managers who interviewed the four job applicants. The rankings given by the finance, marketing, and production managers to the four candidates are shown below (1 = first; 4 = last).

Clark realized that he didn't approve of any one of the four applicants completely. He also knew that he urgently needed an energetic, results-oriented person. The person selected should be able to deal with the unions, redesign jobs to cut down costs, handle the growing number of employee complaints, and manage the challenges posed by the firm's growth. In the next three years, the firm was planning to expand its operations to Ontario and Quebec and in eight to ten years, Regina Shoes will

| INTERVIEWER | APPLICANT | | | |
|---|---|---|---|---|
| | Anderson | Dougherty | Reynold | Robinson |
| Finance manager | 2 | 1 | 3 | 4 |
| Marketing manager | 2 | 4 | 1 | 3 |
| Production manager | 1 | 3 | 2 | 4 |

have operations in all ten Canadian provinces. The firm's management cadre is expected to grow by roughly 3% each year for the next four to five years and the need for management training exists now more than ever before. This meant that the new person who is hired should be a mover and shaker but at the same time be able to work with people without offending them. The previous personnel manager, John McAllister, was reported to have "run a tight ship," but several of his colleagues had complained about his domineering and centralized leadership style.

"A tough problem to resolve," murmured Clark to himself as he sipped the seventh cup of coffee of the day. His doctor had warned him against having too much caffeine in his system due to his heart condition; but this was going to be one of those long, dreary days. In less than an hour, Clark had a meeting with Sam Polliani, shop steward of the Vinyl and Leather Worker's Union, who wanted to talk about a "serious problem that exists in Plant I of Regina Shoes." How much he wished he had a manager who could do all these thankless jobs!

Case prepared by Dr. Hari Das of Saint Mary's University, Halifax, Nova Scotia. This case may be used for regular university class room instruction or other non-profit purposes by writing to the author prior to its use. © Hari Das, 1988.

○ ○ ○ ○ ○ ○ ○ ○ ○ ○ ○ ○ ○ ○ ○ ○ ○ ○ ○ ○ ○ ○ ○ ○ ○ ○ ○ ○ ○ ○ ○ ○' ○ ○

*CASE STUDY*

## TIMBER CRAFT LIMITED

Timber Craft Limited, located in southern British Columbia, is a manufacturer of consumer goods relating to sports and recreation activities. It started as a family-controlled organization nine years ago but since then has become a private limited company employing professional managers. Timber Craft is currently considering a major expansion of its facilities and product lines to take advantage of the rapidly growing sports goods and recreation market. Although the company is capital intensive, the proposed expansion is still expected to lead to the hiring of forty production workers in the next year alone. The firm's past selection practice has been to use biographical blanks, interview scores, and reference letters as predictors of job success. However, the selection procedures employed until now have not been totally satisfactory. For one thing, so far, there has been only a 50% success rate in the procedure. This meant that typically, only one-half of the persons chosen through the selection process

became "successful" employees in terms of quantity and quality of production. The firm's analysis of the inter-judge reliability figures also had led to somewhat disappointing conclusions. Presently, all selected candidates are put through an orientation and training program that costs Timber Craft $300 per employee.

Recently, Ron Dickoff, the human resource manager of Timber Craft, went to a conference in Toronto where he came across a selection test that appeared to have considerable promise. The Engineering Aptitude Test, designed by a Toronto firm, had a good validation record for job positions similar to those found in Timber Craft. Initial concurrent validation studies in Timber Craft using two groups of employees also indicated the test's potential usefulness to the organization. The cost of the test per applicant was $30, which included all costs associated with the administration, scoring, and interpretation of test results.

Timber Craft added the test as an additional

FIGURE 1
Engineering Aptitude Test
Scores of "Successful" and "Unsuccessful" Job Candidates (n = 100)

| Score in the test | Number of persons who received this score | Number of persons who are considered successful on the job | Number of persons who are considered unsuccessful on the job |
|---|---|---|---|
| 10 | 4 | — | 4 |
| 20 | 5 | — | 5 |
| 30 | 9 | — | 9 |
| 40 | 12 | 2 | 10 |
| 50 | 14 | 5 | 9 |
| 60 | 13 | 6 | 7 |
| 70 | 15 | 9 | 6 |
| 80 | 13 | 13 | — |
| 90 | 8 | 8 | — |
| 100 | 7 | 7 | — |
| Total | 100 | 50 | 50 |

predictor in its selection kit. Figure 1 shows the scores received by 100 applicants on the test with a breakdown of number of applicants who are expected to be "successful" or a "failure" on the job. The firm will continue to use its orientation and training program for all its selected employees. At present the firm wants to use these test results to fill forty existing vacancies in the Production Division.

1. Calculate the cut-off test score that will minimize the overall cost of testing plus training.
2. To get forty "successful" employees, how may persons will have to be hired who have:
   (a) a score of 70 or higher on the test?
   (b) a score of 60 or higher on the test?

Case prepared by Dr. Hari Das of Saint Mary's University, Halifax, Nova Scotia. This case may be used for regular university class room instruction or other non-profit purposes by writing to the author prior to its use. © Hari Das, 1988.

○ ○ ○ ○ ○ ○ ○ ○ ○ ○ ○ ○ ○ ○ ○ ○ ○ ○ ○ ○ ○ ○ ○ ○ ○ ○ ○ ○ ○ ○ ○ ○ ○ ○ ○

## SUGGESTED READINGS

Cranshaw, Steven, F., "The State of Employment Testing in Canada: A Review and Evaluation of Theory and Professional Practice," *Canadian Psychology*, Vol. 27, No. 2, 1986, pp. 183-195.

Das, Hari and Mallika Das, "But He Had Excellent References: Refining the Reference Letter," *The Human Resource*, June-July 1988, pp. 15-16.

Guion, Robert M., *Personnel Testing*, New York: McGraw-Hill Book Company, 1965.

44. John W. Cogger, "Are You a Skilled Interviewer?" *Personnel Journal*, November 1982, pp. 840-843.

45. Michael H. Frisch, *Coaching and Counselling Handbook*, New York: Resource Dynamics, 1981.

46. John A. Byrne, "Interviews: The Best Face Is Your Own," *Business Week*, February 1987, p. 122.

47. George M. Beason and John A. Belt, "Verifying Applicants' Backgrounds," *Personnel Journal*, July 1976, p. 346. See also Jeremiah Bogert, "Learning the Applicant's Background through Confidential Investigations," *Personnel Journal*, May 1981, pp. 376-377.

48. Das and Das, op. cit., 1988, pp. 15-16.

49. Das and Das, 1988, op. cit. See also Bruce D. Wonder and Kenneth S. Keleman, "Increasing the Value of Reference Information," *Personnel Administrator*, March 1984, pp. 98-103; Bogert, 1981, op. cit.; Richard D. Broussard and Dalton E. Brannen, "Credential Distortions: Personnel Practitioners Give Their Views," *Personnel Administrator*, June 1986, p. 129; Carlo Sewell, "Pre-Employment Investigations: The Key to Security in Hiring," *Personnel Journal*, May 1981, pp. 376-377.

50. Chapman, 1985, op. cit.

51. John P. Wanous, "Realistic Job Previews: Can a Procedure to Reduce Turnover Also Influence the Relationship between Abilities and Performance?" *Personnel Psychology*, Summer, 1978, pp. 249-258.

52. Lyman Porter and Richard Steers, "Organizational, Work, and Personal Factors in Employee Turnover and Absenteeism," *Psychological Bulletin*, Vol. 80, 1973, pp. 151-176.

53. Paula Popovich and John P. Wanous, "The Realistic Job Preview as a Persuasive Communication," *Academy of Management Review*, October 1982, p. 571.

54. Ibid., p. 572.

55. J.P. Wanous, *Organizational Entry: Recruitment, Selection and Socialization of Newcomers*, Reading, Mass.: Addison-Wesley Publishing, 1980.

56. Todd D. Jick and Leonard Greenhalgh, "Realistic Job Previews: A Reconceptualization," paper presented at The Academy of Management National Meeting, August 1980, Detroit, Michigan.

57. Wayne F. Cascio, *Applied Psychology in Personnel Management*, second edition, Reston, Va.: Reston Publishing, 1982; see also Steven L. Premack and John P. Wanous, "A Meta-Analysis of Realistic Job Preview Experiments," *Journal of Applied Psychology*, Vol. 70, 1985, pp. 706-719; James A. Breaugh, "Realistic Job Previews: A Critical Appraisal and Future Research Directions," *Academy of Management Review*, Vol. 8, No. 4, 1983, pp. 612-619; Roger A. Dean and John P. Wanous, "Effects of Realistic Job Previews on Hiring Bank Tellers," *Journal of Applied Psychology*, Vol. 69, No. 1, 1984, pp. 61-68.

58. Bernard L. Dugoni and Daniel R. Ilgen, "Realistic Job Preview and the Adjustment of New Employees," *Academy of Management Journal*, September 1981, p. 590; see also Breaugh, op. cit., pp. 612-619.

59. Marvin D. Dunnete, *Personnel Selection and Placement*, Belmont, Calif.: Wadsworth Publishing Co., 1966, p. 174.

60. W.F. Cascio and V. Silbey, "Utility of the Assessment Centre as a Selection Device," *Journal of Applied Psychology*, 64, 1979, pp. 107-118; see also Wayne F. Cascio and N. Philips, "Performance Testing: A Rose among Thorns?" *Personnel Psychology*, 32, 1979, pp. 751-766.

61. J.E. Hunter and R.E. Hunter, "Validity and Utility of Alternative Predictors of Job Performance," *Psychological Bulletin*, 96, 1984, pp. 72-98; see also Schwind, 1987, op. cit.

62. Wayne F. Cascio, *Managing Human Resources*, New York: McGraw-Hill, 1986, p. 199.

63. J.E. Hunter and F.L. Schmidt, "Quantifying the Effects of Psychological Interventions on Employee Job Performance and Work Force Productivity," *American Psychologist*, 38, 1983, pp. 473-478; see also J.E. Hunter and F.L. Schmidt, "Fitting People to Jobs: The Impact of Personnel Selection on National Productivity," in Marvin D. Dunnette and E.A. Fleishman (eds.) *Human Capability Assessment*, Hillsdale, N.J.: Lawrence Erlbaum Associates, 1982.

64. Dunnette, 1966, op. cit.

65. Hunter and Schmidt, 1982, op. cit.; F.L. Schmidt, J.E. Hunter, R.C. McKenzie, and T.W. Muldrow, "Impact of Valid Selection Procedures on Work Force Productivity," *Journal of Applied Psychology*, 64, 1979, pp. 609-626; Ralph B. Alexander and Murray R. Barrick, "Estimating the Standard Error of Projected Dollar Gains in Utility Analysis," *Journal of Applied Psychology*, 72, 1987, pp. 463-474; J.E. Hunter, *The Economic Benefits of Personnel Selection Using Ability Tests: A State of the Art Review Including a Detailed Analysis of the Dollar Benefit of U.S. Employment Service Placement and a Critique of the Low Cutoff Method of Test Use*, Washington, D.C.: U.S. Employment Service, U.S. Department of Labor, January 15, 1981; F.L. Schmidt, J.E. Hunter and K. Pearlman, "Assessing the Economic Impact of Personnel Programs on Work Force Productivity," *Personnel Psychology*, Vol. 35, No. 3, 1982, pp. 333-343; Wayne F. Cascio, *Costing Human Resources: The Financial Impact of Behaviour in Organizations*, Boston: Kent Publishing, 1982; Cascio and Silbey, 1979, op. cit.; Cascio and Philips, 1979, op. cit.

66. Cascio, 1987, op. cit., p. 199.

67. See Hunter and Schmidt, 1983 op. cit., pp. 474-477.

68. For example, see Schmidt, Hunter, McKenzie, and Muldrow, 1979, op. cit.; Cascio, 1982, op. cit.; Schmidt, Hunter, and Pearlman, 1982, op. cit.; Steven F. Cranshaw, "The Utility of Employment Testing for Clerical/Administrative Trades in the Canadian Military," *Canadian Journal of Administrative Sciences*, Vol. 3, No. 2, 1986, pp. 376-385; Steven F. Cranshaw, Ralph A. Alexander, Willi H. Weisner, and Murray R. Barrick, "Incorporating Risk into Selection Utility: Two Models of Sensitivity Analysis and Risk Simulation," *Organizational Behaviour and Decision Processes*, Vol. 40, 1987, pp. 270-286.

69. Dunette, 1966, op. cit., p. 174

70. H.C. Taylor and J.T. Russell, "The Relationship of Validity Coefficients to the Practical Effectiveness of Tests in Selection: Discussion and Tables," *Journal of Applied Psychology*, 23, 1939, pp. 565-578.

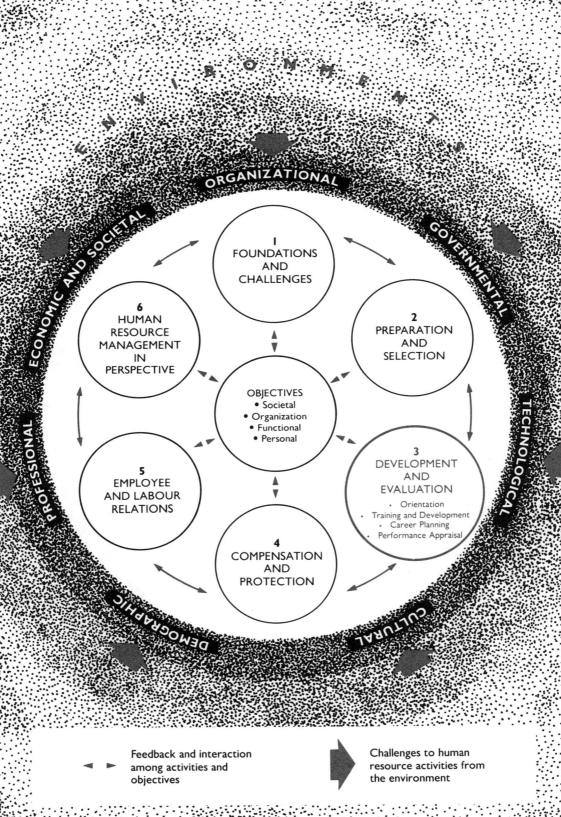

ENVIRONMENTS

ORGANIZATIONAL

GOVERNMENTAL

TECHNOLOGICAL

CULTURAL

DEMOGRAPHIC

PROFESSIONAL

ECONOMIC AND SOCIETAL

1
FOUNDATIONS
AND
CHALLENGES

2
PREPARATION
AND
SELECTION

3
DEVELOPMENT
AND
EVALUATION
• Orientation
• Training and Development
• Career Planning
• Performance Appraisal

4
COMPENSATION
AND
PROTECTION

5
EMPLOYEE
AND LABOUR
RELATIONS

6
HUMAN
RESOURCE
MANAGEMENT
IN
PERSPECTIVE

OBJECTIVES
• Societal
• Organization
• Functional
• Personal

Feedback and interaction
among activities and
objectives

Challenges to human
resource activities from
the environment

# PART 3 ○○○○○○

# DEVELOPMENT AND EVALUATION

*E*mployees need help if they are to grow and be successful. The employer wants to help for its own benefit as well as theirs. It trains and develops them. It also helps them plan their careers for promotion and helps them learn to adjust to change. Finally, it appraises their performance so that both they and the company know how they are doing.

The next four chapters are about employee development and evaluation. As a student, you need to understand the human resource department's role in these activities. They affect you whether you work in a human resource department or elsewhere in an organization. Knowledge of these activities assists you to be a better employee or manager.

# CHAPTER $8$ ○○○○○○

# ORIENTATION

*Effective socialization means an* internal commitment *to the organization, rather than just compliance with organization practices.*

JOHN P. WANOUS[1]

○ ○ ○ ○ ○ ○ ○ ○ ○ ○ ○ ○ ○ ○ ○ ○ ○ ○ ○ ○ ○ ○ ○ ○ ○ ○ ○ ○ ○ ○ ○ ○ ○

## CHAPTER OBJECTIVES

After studying this chapter, you should be able to:
1. **Describe** the content and scope of a two-tier orientation program.
2. **Explain** the impact of a new employee orientation program on turnover and learning.
3. **Identify** the human resource department's and the supervisor's responsibilities in employee orientation.

○ ○ ○ ○ ○ ○ ○ ○ ○ ○ ○ ○ ○ ○ ○ ○ ○ ○ ○ ○ ○ ○ ○ ○ ○ ○ ○ ○ ○ ○ ○ ○ ○

*H*uman resource management is much more than simply hiring people. Once employee selection is completed, a proactive human resource department should still help the new employees to become productive and satisfied. The process of becoming a productive and satisfied employee is important to the organization and to the employee. As the last two chapters on recruitment and selection have shown, organizations devote considerable time and resources to hiring people. By the first day of work, the employer already has an investment in the new worker. And there is a job—or at least a potential job—that the organization needs to have done. At the same time, the newcomer has needs that may hinder the transition from recruit to worker. Anxieties leading to questions such as "Will I be able to do the job?" or "Will I fit in around here?" or "Will the boss like me?" are common among new employees. These "first day jitters" may be natural, but they reduce both the employee's ability to learn and the employee's satisfaction with the organization. Psychologists tell us that initial impressions are strong and lasting because newcomers have little else by which to judge the organization and its people. As a first step to helping the employee become a satisfied and productive member of the organization, the human resource department must make those initial impressions favourable.

> MANAGER:  Maybe you can tell me why our company needs a fancy orientation program and such a large training budget? The human resource department follows a very detailed selection process. Why can't we hire people who can be put right to work?
>
> HUMAN RESOURCE MANAGER:  No matter how well-qualified applicants are when we hire them, they need to know the people with whom they work. They also need to understand our company's procedures and policies. And most need to be trained to do their job properly.
>
> MANAGER:  But that shouldn't require a half-day orientation program . While these people are in the orientation sessions, they are getting paid but do not contribute anything to the company.
>
> HUMAN RESOURCE MANAGER:  You're right. But the half-day orientation program speeds up the training process, and it lowers turnover among new recruits. It is more effective to spend a half-day in orientation and reduce training time by nearly two days.
>
> MANAGER:  I do not see how an orientation session speeds up training. What is the connection?
>
> HUMAN RESOURCE MANAGER:  The connection is that well-oriented employees can grasp what will be important to their job success. They spend less time trying to figure out if they will fit in, if they will like the company, if they will like the job, if they will be accepted by others, and if they have any future with our company.

The gap between a new employee's abilities and the job's demands may be substantial. As Figure 8-1 suggests, orientation and training supplement the new worker's

FIGURE 8-1   The Balance Between New Employee Capabilities and Job Demands

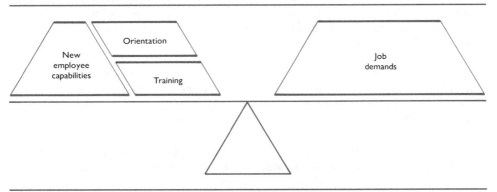

abilities. The hoped-for result is a balance between what the new employee can do and what the job demands. Although these efforts are time consuming and expensive, they reduce employee turnover and help new employees to be productive sooner. This part of the chapter will discuss the key steps involved in the orientation process, and the next part will discuss the training and development of an organization's work force.

## PURPOSE OF ORIENTATION

*[handwritten: (1) reduces turnover (2) reduces errors + saves time (3) develops clear job + org'l expectations]*

Orientation programs familiarize new employees with their roles, with the organization, and with other employees. Orientation, if properly done, can serve several purposes.

**1.** *Reduces employee turnover.* Employees are more likely to quit during their first few months than at any other time in their employment. The difference between what a person expects to find at the work place and what one actually finds is referred to as cognitive dissonance. If the dissonance is too high, employees take action. For new employees, that action may mean quitting.

Other potential causes of dissonance exist besides the job itself. New employees may not like work-related policies, coworkers, supervision, or other aspects of their employment relationship. And until the newcomer reports to work, neither the employee nor the human resource department can tell which areas will be of concern. Nevertheless, a proactive human resource department can help employees fit into the organization by anticipating these concerns and addressing them during an orientation program.

> At IBM, the annual turnover averages 3% of its North American work force. While this at first glance looks reasonable and almost insignificant, the size of IBM's work force warrants action to reduce it. One estimate shows IBM's domestic work force to be about 242,000, which means that more than 7000 employees leave IBM annually in North America alone.[2]

To a large firm, a few thousand dollars may seem inconsequential. But if thousands of employees leave each year, the costs of turnover can quickly escalate into the millions of dollars. And when experienced, long-service employees quit, the loss may be incalculable because of the training, knowledge, and skills that these workers take with them.[3] In general, the human resource department can reduce turnover by meeting the personal objectives of employees. When that happens, both the employee and the organization can benefit. The experience of Texas Instruments, a worldwide producer of micro electronics and electronic equipment is a good example in this context.[4]

> At Texas Instruments — or TI, as it is called by the employees — the orientation program was superficial at best. New employees went to a large room where they were quickly told about the company and its fringe benefits. They completed forms about benefits and other job-related matters and then were sent to their supervisor to report for work.
>
> Most supervisors took a few minutes to introduce the newcomer to the other assemblers. The supervisor often "assigned" the new employee to a work station with instructions for nearby workers to show the newcomer what to do. After being

put through a superficial orientation program and quickly introduced to coworkers, the employee found himself or herself (most of the employees were female) sitting between two other employees trying to learn the job of assembling electronic components.

As many groups of workers do, the experienced assemblers had developed a little ritual for newcomers to endure. It was mild hazing. The trainees were told that Texas Instruments treated employees unfairly and that their present supervisor was one of the worst in the company. The newcomers' anxieties were greatly increased, to say the least. Their ability to learn and do the job suffered and some of the new employees would even go on a break or go to lunch and never return — not even to pick up their one-half day paycheque.

The human resource department reacted by recruiting an even larger number of new employees to offset the high initial turnover. After an internal investigation into the causes of this turnover, the department revamped its entire orientation process. New employees were given an extended orientation. The session, which lasted nearly all morning, explored the background and human resource policies of the company. Some forms were completed at the session, but the thrust of the orientation was to create a more positive attitude about TI among the recently hired recruits. Newcomers also were told that they had a high probability of success. Shortly before lunch, the new employees were taken to a roped-off section of the cafeteria where they had lunch with their future supervisors.

Following lunch, the supervisor would take the new employee back to the department and provide introductions to the other assemblers. Although the hazing went on for some time, the new employees had a more wholesome understanding of the company and were apparently better able to recognize the hazing for what it was, a ritualized introduction to the work group.

The revised orientation approach led to some significant benefits to both the organization and the employees. For one thing, turnover among recently hired employees dropped significantly. It was also found that recipients of the new orientation program learned their jobs more quickly. That is, the more fully oriented employees mastered their jobs more quickly than those employees who had the short orientation. This outcome was unexpected since the workers in the new program were off the job for four hours while the workers in the shorter program missed only an hour or so of work. It would seem, particularly since this job was not very skilled, that a short orientation would get newcomers on the job quicker so they might learn their jobs faster. But the more fully oriented employees probably had fewer anxieties. They probably felt more at ease with the organization and hence were more motivated to stay with it.

**2.** *Reduces errors and saves time*. A well-oriented employee knows exactly what is expected of him or her and, hence, is likely to make fewer mistakes. Typically, a new employee is less efficient than an experienced employee. This factor combined with other additional costs involved in getting a new employee started (e.g., supervisor's time and attention) makes the "start-up" costs of new employees very significant.[5] Effective orientation can reduce these start-up costs as well as the number of mistakes committed by the inexperienced employees.

**3.** *Develops clear job and organizational expectations*. For some jobs, the duties and job expectations are clear. However, for a majority of other jobs, this is simply not the case. There are no clear-cut lists of "desirable" behaviours, outcomes, and job attitudes. Most new employees would like to know "what it takes to survive and get ahead in this organization." In the absence of clear guidelines from their employer, they may have to find answers to their questions informally through the grapevine and by gossiping with others. Unfortunately, in the latter instance, there is no guarantee that they will find the right answers. To tell employees what the organization expects of them and what they can expect in return, effective orientation is absolutely necessary. Orientation is thus a part of the larger socialization of the employee.[6]

In summary, the orientation program helps the individual understand the social, technical, and cultural aspects of the workplace. As new employees are accepted, they become part of the social fabric of the organization. Orientation programs help speed up the socialization process and benefit both the employee and the organization.

## CONTENT OF ORIENTATION PROGRAMS

A variety of approaches to orienting new employees is available, although all are not popular to the same extent. Most organizations conduct orientation on an individual basis, although group orientation programs are also used in large organizations where several employees are hired at the same time.

Most orientation programs introduce new employees to their jobs, colleagues, and the organization's policies. Figure 8-2 lists the topics typically covered during orientation. The program usually explains the organizational issues that new employees need to know. Often a film or slide show describes the history, products, services, and policies of the organization. Commonly, workers are given an *employee handbook* that explains key benefits, policies, and general information about the company. Human resource experts may also discuss pay rates as part of the program. The human resource department's role in the program often ends when the employees meet their future supervisors or trainers.

Trainers or supervisors continue the orientation program by introducing the new employee to the other trainees and coworkers. Introductions are usually followed by a tour of the facilities and an explanation of the job, its objectives, and related information.

In organizations that hire large numbers of employees, the orientation program may take a half or even a whole day to discuss the topics in Figure 8-2. For employers that hire workers only occasionally and in small numbers, there may be no formal orientation program. Instead the employee is introduced to a senior worker who shows the new person around. These highly informal "buddy systems" are also used in large companies to help orient the new employee.

Formal programs explain orientation topics systematically. These programs are also more likely to create a favourable impression on new employees, which may explain why in a U.S. survey 72% of firms had formal programs.[7] A Canadian study showed that roughly 10% of orientations lasted one hour, but 51% took a day or longer. The same study reported that more than two-thirds of the firms conducted the orientation immediately after the employee reported to work.[8] Of course, the experiences of employ-

FIGURE 8-2  Topics Often Covered in Employee Orientation Programs

### ORGANIZATIONAL ISSUES

| | |
|---|---|
| History of employer | Product line or services provided |
| Organization of employer | Overview of production process |
| Names and titles of key executives | Company policies and rules |
| Employee's title and department | Disciplinary regulations |
| Layout of physical facilities | Employee handbook |
| Probationary period | Safety procedures and enforcement |

### EMPLOYEE BENEFITS

| | |
|---|---|
| Pay scales and paydays | Insurance benefits |
| Vacations and holidays | Retirement program |
| Rest breaks | Employer-provided services to employees |
| Training and education benefits | Rehabilitation programs |
| Counselling | |

### INTRODUCTIONS

| | |
|---|---|
| To supervisor | To coworkers |
| To trainers | To employee counsellor |

### JOB DUTIES

| | |
|---|---|
| Job location | Overview of job |
| Job tasks | Job objectives |
| Job safety requirements | Relationship to other jobs |

ees during orientation can differ greatly. Here is an example of how an orientation can affect new employees:

CAROLINE MATHAU:   I reported to the human resource department ten minutes early. I was told to have a seat and that someone would "show me around." An hour later I was led to an interview room. After a few minutes the interviewer realized that I was not an applicant but a new employee. After apologies, I was taken to meet my supervisor. The supervisor screamed for a claims processor to show me around. While I was being introduced to other people, the claims processor, Irv Porter, complained about what a grouch the supervisor was all the time. At lunch, I asked if I could get a transfer to another claims department. They told me that transfers were not permitted until after the three-month probation period. I am thinking about finding another job.

HARVEY JACKSON:   My orientation was really super! When I arrived, I was shown to the auditorium. After coffee and pastry, we were given an employee handbook that explained most of the company's benefits and policies. We also received some forms to complete and a brief lecture about company policies. The lecture was followed by a really interesting film that explained the company's history, facilities, and how different jobs related to one another. The following hour was spent on questions and answers. We had a tour of the plant and then we were treated to lunch by the company. At lunch, our

> supervisors joined us to answer questions and tell us about their departments. Afterward, the supervisors introduced us to the people in my department and training began.

If Caroline's experience is a typical one in her company, employees probably begin work with low motivation, poor morale, and a lot of anxiety. The company is "saving" the cost of orientation, but it is paying a high cost in employee attitudes and performance.

## Responsibility for Orientation

Responsibility for orientation is shared between the human resource department and the immediate supervisor.[9] Human resource departments usually explain to employees the broad organizational concerns and benefits. Supervisors handle introductions and on-the-job training and help employees "fit in" with the work group.

A research study carried out by McShane and Baal in Western Canada indicates that human resource departments play the key role in conducting formal orientations, typically followed by the new employee's supervisor.[10] Other senior executives seem to play a minor role. Other persons who participate in the orientation process include heads of various departments, representatives of the firm's public relations department, safety officers, and union officials. In recent years, some organizations have also been using the services of experienced workers who have already retired to orient new employees. These social interactions and the "buddy system" of orientation give the newcomers an introduction to the organization and its people in a more relaxed setting.[11]

It should be emphasized that the buddy system is a *supplement* to the supervisor's orientation efforts. If the buddy system is *substituted* for the supervisory orientation, the supervisor loses an excellent opportunity to establish open communications with new employees. Very soon, newcomers may find it more comfortable to ask coworkers, rather than the supervisor, about job-related issues. Supervisors who pass up the opportunity to spend some time with new employees miss a chance to create a favourable relationship before the employee becomes influenced by what other people think about the supervisor and the organization.

## Orientation Follow-up

Successful orientation programs include a built-in follow-up procedure. Follow-up is needed because new employees are often reluctant to admit that they do not recall everything they were told in the initial orientation. As one writer pointed out, "The worst mistake a company can make is to ignore the new employee after orientation."[12] Even if the organization has an "open-door" policy, very rarely are new employees assertive enough to seek out new information by meeting their supervisors or the human resource staff. Systematic follow-up of the orientation after a week, a month, and probably a quarter of a year helps to assess the information needs of the new employee. It also tells the employee that the organizations cares. The follow-up can be a prescheduled meeting or a simple checklist that asks the employee to assess the weaknesses of the orientation program. Weak areas, presumably, are topics about which an employee needs more information. The checklist also serves as feedback to the human resource department so that it can identify parts of the program that are good or bad. Poor orientation efforts by supervisors will also become apparent through feedback. A research study indicates that Canadian organizations typically follow up orientation within three months — one-third of the organizations studied having such follow-up sessions within one month and another third doing it between one and three months.[13]

Many supervisors believe they follow up with the new hire frequently, but many new employees often do not perceive their supervisor's actions as true follow-ups. One problem may be the supervisor's body language, for example. A supervisor may ask, "Is everything okay? Let me know if you have any questions." But if this is stated as the supervisor continues to walk past the employee, the body language received by the employee is, "My supervisor really doesn't want to stop and talk." Instead of raising questions, the employee responds with some affirmative indication that all is okay. Or the supervisor appears and disappears so quickly that even an assertive employee may not think of appropriate questions before the supervisor is gone.

Sometimes the supervisor cannot answer an employee's question and must refer it to someone else. Even though a referral may be the best answer, the employee may feel that the supervisor does not really care about the problem. An even worse situation occurs when the supervisor says, "I'll find out" and never gets back to the employee with the correct answer. That *is* indifference. Consider how Exxon attacked this problem of weak follow-up by supervisors at its Research and Engineering Division.

At Exxon Research and Engineering Division, 50 to 150 engineers have been hired each year for several years. In recognition of the need for a smooth entry into the organization, Exxon had an action guide and reference manual developed for supervisors to help them do a better job with newcomers. The manual outlines actions the supervisor should take before the employee arrives, such as arranging for work space, telephones, office supplies, and the like. It also describes the actions a supervisor should take after the new employee arrives.

The particularly innovative parts of the program are the follow-up meetings that supervisors are supposed to have with their new engineers. These sessions are called "How's It Going" meetings. They are intended to open up communications between the newcomer and the supervisor. Information is shared, concern is shown, and matters of interest are discussed. To make these sessions as effective as possible, they are held separately from meetings that give work assignments or review performance. Supervisors also are trained to conduct these meetings. The objectives of the training are to increase the supervisor's awareness of the new employee's needs, introduce the supervisors to the company's socialization procedures, and improve the supervisor's skills at communicating with new employees.

Internal company research showed that after the training, supervisors were 40% more likely to hold initial orientation discussions with newcomers and were 20% more likely to hold follow-up sessions at the end of three months.[14]

## Evaluating the Effectiveness of Orientation

Orientation programs, however systematically done, can be ineffective in some instances.

The human resource manager and the immediate supervisor should recognize several common pitfalls that detract from successful orientation programs.[15] Both are responsible for seeing that the employee is not:

- Overwhelmed with too much information to absorb in a short time.
- Given only menial tasks that discourage job interest and company loyalty.
- Overloaded with forms to fill out and manuals to read.
- Pushed into the job with a sketchy orientation under the mistaken philosophy that "trial by fire" is the best orientation.
- Forced to fill in the gaps between a broad orientation by the human resource department and a narrow orientation at the department level.

As Thorp pointed out, a good employee orientation program focuses on various aspects of an employee's life in the organization, both on the job and off the job.[16] *On the job*, the new recruits should be sponsored and guided by an experienced supervisor or colleague who can respond to questions and keep in close touch. The orientation program should introduce new employees to their colleagues and coworkers *gradually* rather than give a superficial introduction to all of them on the first day itself. Also, a good orientation program will ensure that employees have sufficient time to get their feet on the ground before job demands on them are increased. *Off the job*, an effective orientation program will provide the most relevant and immediate information on the company first. Above all, it will emphasize the human side — it will tell the employees what supervisors and coworkers are like and encourage them to seek help and advice when needed. Orientation is also an occasion to communicate the culture of the organization. Indeed, the available research evidence indicates a growing emphasis on corporate culture during orientation in Canadian companies.[17]

> Organizational stories and folklore are important for the newcomer to an organization in understanding the prevailing culture. At a large Canadian telecommunications company, there is a story about prospective employees being asked to come for a job interview at 9 A.M. on a Sunday. The intent is to weed out undedicated employees who do not want long hours and are not prepared to make sacrifices when necessary. At Digital Equipment of Canada Limited, new employees often hear stories that highlight the first rule in the company, namely, "When dealing with a customer or an employee, do what is 'right'." "Doing right" often may mean turning down business that is profitable for the company but that is not right for the customer.[18]

How does one evaluate the effectiveness of orientation programs? A few of the approaches are discussed below.

**1.** *Reactions from new employees.* Probably the single most useful method of evaluating the effectiveness of orientation is getting the reactions of new employees who went through the process. The feedback itself can be obtained through in-depth interviews with randomly selected employees and through questionnaire surveys. Questionnaires are particularly useful if the organization wants responses from a large number of recently hired employees. They also allow the identity of the respondent to be kept anonymous, thus increasing the overall truthfulness and validity of responses. Whether an interview or survey format is used, the questions included should measure the appropriateness and effectiveness of the orientation procedures used. Questions on the readability of the literature supplied to employees during orientation, the appropriateness of the lectures and other presentations, the degree of structure visible in the program, the ease of understanding various ideas and organizational policies, etc., should form part of the feedback checklist used.

**2.** *Effects of socialization on job attitudes and roles.* "Socialization" is the continuing process by which an employee begins to understand and accept the values, norms, and beliefs held by others in the organization. The socialization process may be an effective method to change employee values and beliefs to make them conform with an organization's requirements. According to Feldman, it is through socialization that major shifts in a new employee's values take place.[19] On entering an organization, a new recruit encounters the reality of the organization—he or she sees what the organization is really like. Some initial shifting of values, attitudes, and skills occurs soon, along with a definition of his or her role in the organization, the work group, and the task. If the newcomers survive the initial change process, relatively long-lasting changes take place within the new employees: they master the job skills, successfully perform their new roles, and make adjustments to their work group's and organization's values and culture. The progress in a person's socialization can be measured attitudinally (e.g., overall satisfaction with the organization and the job, work motivation, etc.) and behaviourally (e.g., labour turnover, ability to carry out roles effectively, spontaneity visible in job performance, etc.). Ideally, an orientation program should hasten this socialization process by enabling a recruit to interact with new colleagues extensively. Measures of job satisfaction, work motivation, and job performance may be some useful indications of the effectiveness of the program to achieve this end.

**3.** *Degree to which the program is economical.* In Chapter 1, the functional objective of human resource departments was discussed. This means that all human resource activities should be at a level appropriate to the organization's needs. If the orientation program in an organization is more or less sophisticated than the firm's needs, then resources are wasted. Cost-benefit studies on orientation activities should be carried out continually. The costs of an orientation program typically include cost of materials, salaries of instructors and human resource department staff, rent, lost work time of other employees and supervisors, and the cost of training tools such as films, slides, tours, etc. The monetary benefits emerging from an orientation program include lower labour turnover, shorter time to learn a job, lower scrap rates and wastage, reduced re-work, etc. Obviously, the cost-benefit analysis should take into consideration the unique needs of a business and an organization.

## SUMMARY

After workers are selected, they are seldom ready to perform successfully. They must be integrated into the social and work environment of the organization.[20] Orientation programs help a worker begin this socialization process. The organization benefits because training time and costs are lowered, employee satisfaction is higher, and initial turnover is lower.

A variety of orientation programs are currently available, although all are not popular to the same degree. Typically, orientation is done on an individual basis and consists of introductions to a person's job, colleagues, and the organization's policies. The responsibility for orientation is usually shared between the human resource department and the recruit's immediate boss. Whatever the method used, an orientation program to be successful should include a built-in follow-up procedure. The criteria employed in evaluating the orientation function may vary from one organization to another depending on their unique needs; however, measures of employee satisfaction with the job and the orientation program, the turnover among new recruits, measures of job-related attitudes, etc., should be included. All successful orientation programs enhance and strengthen the socialization process by which the new employee and the organization are bonded, resulting in mutual acceptance and trust of one another.

## TERMS FOR REVIEW

Start-up costs                    Orientation programs
Employee handbook                 Buddy systems
Orientation follow-up             Pitfalls in orientation
Socialization

## REVIEW AND DISCUSSION QUESTIONS

1.  "If employees are properly selected, there should be no need for an orientation or training." Do you agree or disagree? Why?
2.  What are the employee benefits from orientation programs? The organization benefits?
3.  What are the common pitfalls of an informal orientation program?
4.  Suppose your organization hired six new clerical workers. What types of orientation program would you design to help these workers become productive and satisfied?
5.  Before you entered your college or university, you had certain ideas about what your values and expectations would be as a student. How did the institution's socialization process change those values and expectations?
6.  If the Student Services office of this institution asked you to evaluate the effectiveness of the orientation programs, what measures would you use? Why?

## INCIDENT 8-1

### The Follow-up Orientation at Chever's Carpets

During the first six months with Chever's Carpets, Oliver Talbot was promoted from supervisor to assistant warehouse manager. He also received two pay increases during that time. Thus Leslie Coulter expected the follow-up orientation session with Oliver to be a short and pleasant experience. But when she asked Oliver what questions he had about Chever's operations, he replied:"For a business employing nearly 200 people, I am dumbfounded by the orientation and training new employees are provided with or, more correctly, the lack of orientation and training. My orientation program consisted of being shuffled in to see Mr. Chever for fifteen minutes, over ten of which he spent on the phone. My encounters with other managers around here were equally unimpressive. Most spent the few minutes I had with them complaining of all of their problems. If the warehouse manager had not taken a couple of hours with me after work the first day to explain procedures and my job, I would have failed as a supervisor or quit.

"The training I received was essentially nonexistent. I was thrown in with drivers, forklift operators, and sales clerks and shown how to complete the necessary ordering and shipping forms. Three-quarters of that training applied to office procedures the sales people are supposed to follow, not I.

"I do not let new warehouse supervisors go to the training or orientation sessions. I may be new and have a narrow perspective, but I know they get a better orientation and better training from me than I was given when I came here. This follow-up orientation is a nice idea, but it is six months too late. I hope my criticisms have been useful to you. I sure do not have any compliments about orientation and training around here."

1. On the basis of what Oliver Talbot said, what changes would you suggest in the orientation program? In the training program?

2. If you were Leslie Coulter, what specific questions would you want to ask Oliver Talbot?

3. What problems do you see in Oliver Talbot's conducting his own orientation and training programs?

*CASE STUDY*

## HICKLING ASSOCIATES LTD.

### Introduction

For almost seven years prior to June 1983, Tony Azzara had been employed by Pisces Exporters Ltd. The company, located in Vancouver, was a subsidiary of a U.S. food products conglomerate headquartered in Los Angeles. Pisces was one of the largest exporters for fresh and frozen seafood on Canada's west coast and had generated revenues between $40 million and $60 million annually, depending on the quality of the fishing season and market demand. The company's major markets were primarily in Europe as well as several areas of Asia and Japan. Pisces also traded other food products, which, over the years, overtook seafood as the main revenue producer for the firm.

At the age of twenty-seven, Tony Azzara began his career with Pisces as a sales person where he learned the complexities of exporting both fresh and frozen sea products to various countries. Within two and one-half years he was promoted to the position of sales manager responsible for all seafood exports to Europe. This was an exciting job and a respected position. He was given a comfortable office and a very acceptable compensation package. There was an annual bonus based on group sales, which was as high as 100% of Tony's base salary in the best years. Even in the poorest years, the bonus was about 20% of base salary. He also received a generous car allowance. The work required Tony to develop contacts with other people in the seafood industry in Canada as well as with the major customers in Europe. He was able to take several trips to Europe to expand the market there and develop better relations with Pisces' existing customers. The job was also a constant challenge because of the increasing international competition in seafood sales and the need to closely coordinate the sales group with the buyers in Pisces. Tony learned early in his career that product quality and delivery time were just as important as price in this market, and only by keeping in touch with the company's seafood buyers could he make those guarantees to his overseas customers.

After about two years as sales manager, it became increasingly clear that Pisces' products were being priced out of the European market. The competition from Asia and Scandinavia was increasing dramatically as they improved their export marketing practices to Europe. Equally important was the appreciation of the Canadian dollar against most European currencies. This dramatically increased the price of Canadian goods in most European countries, whereas the seafood products entering from the Pacific Rim did not experience these fluctuations. By the end of 1982, European seafood sales from Pisces and all other North American exporters had dropped both in volume and market share. Only in the higher end of the market—the expensive seafood products — did the price have a modest effect on European market share.

Unfortunately, the American parent company of Pisces Exporters Ltd. was also experiencing serious financial problems for several different reasons and, combined with the depressed export market in seafood, the entire fresh and frozen seafood export division of Pisces Exporters Ltd. was discontinued in the second week of June 1983. Consequently, the vice-president, six sales managers (including Tony Azzara), ten sales people, and five support staff lost their jobs. The notices of permanent layoff were given in March, and all laid-off staff were given reasonable severance payments in June in amounts that corresponded to their position and length of service. For Tony, this was equivalent to about four months' salary.

### An Opening at Hickling Associates Ltd.

In the weeks leading up to the final day of work at Pisces Exporters Ltd., Tony Azzara began telephoning around to the people he knew in the Vancouver area in order to let it be known that he was looking for a job in the industry. He had the right experience and had become fairly well known in the city as a good trader in the canned and frozen seafood business. The president of Pisces even approached Tony before he left to say that he would be pleased to write a letter of reference if it would help Tony's search for alternative employment. Tony was flattered by the gesture. In spite of these factors, however, Tony Azzara did not expect to find another job in the seafood exporting business in the near future. With a depressed seafood market and high unemployment throughout British Columbia, securing alternative employment was not going to be easy. In fact, Tony entertained the possibility of changing industries and even began to look through newspapers for sales positions in other products.

In early June, Mr. James Hickling telephoned

Tony Azzara at his office and invited him to lunch the next day. Mr. Hickling owned Hickling Associates Ltd., a medium-sized trading organization in Vancouver that specialized in the import and export of several types of canned and frozen foods. In addition, the company traded a few other commodities such as grains and finishing nails. Tony had met Mr. Hickling in two joint ventures between the two companies a few years earlier. However, Tony worked mainly with Thomas Siu who was the export seafood trader at Hickling Associates.

Following the call from James Hickling, Tony tried to recall what else he knew about Hickling Associates Ltd. and later in the day made several inquiries regarding the firm. He knew that the company was mainly an importer of canned foods such as mushrooms and oriental foods from several Asian countries. Seafood trading was restricted mainly to the export of canned salmon and represented a very small factor in the business. As far a Tony knew, Thomas Siu was the only person responsible for this part of the operation and had been employed by Hickling Associates for about five years. Tony also learned from one of his contacts in the industry that Hickling Associates was financially very strong and well established. It was founded by James Hickling's father in 1934 and grew steadily throughout the years. When the elder Hickling retired in the late 1960's, James Hickling took over the company and is given a lot of credit for the company's current success.

James Hickling was considered by many people in the import-export industry to be something of a maverick and was generally respected for his business sense and solid understanding of the international merchant business. Tony had heard a rumour of a disenchanted trader in canned foods who left Hickling Associates Ltd. a few years ago. The trader joined a rival importer and took with him a few Asian accounts whose contracts with Hickling Associates Ltd. were about to expire. Nevertheless, James Hickling subsequently won back some of those customers and further expanded his business in the import of mushrooms, bamboo shoots, and other canned goods.

### The Meeting with James Hickling

Tony Azzara arrived early at the posh restaurant where Mr. Hickling had made reservations and ordered a glass of white wine while he waited. Precisely at 12:15, the time of the scheduled meeting, James Hickling arrived. He was conservatively dressed in a dark blue suit and looked to be in his early fifties. He introduced himself as he arrived at the table and ordered a double scotch on the rocks. After a few initial pleasantries and acknowledgements of the troubles in the European market, Mr. Hickling got right to the point.

"Tony, I'm looking for a man like you to take charge of the seafood export trading in Hickling Associates. It's been a small part of the company for too long, in my opinion. The market is down in a few areas such as Europe and that's knocked the wind out of some of the competition. I believe that you could help me to get a bigger share of the canned salmon market and even get into the export of fresh fish over the next few years as the market rebounds."

Tony took a quick sip of his wine. He was sure that this meeting was about a possible job opening, but he was surprised by the sudden offer. These jobs were rare in Vancouver in 1983, and there were a lot of good traders around.

"This sounds like the sort of challenge that I'd like," Tony replied, trying to sound calm and interested in the position at the same time. "As you know, I've been in this business for a few years now and have developed several contacts in Europe and other markets. I've also worked with Tom Siu on occasion, as you'll recall." Tony was hoping to find out how he and Tom Siu would be working together.

"Yes, indeed," Hickling continued. "Those

ventures turned out very well. Siu told me that the two of you worked well together. That's why I think you can do an excellent job in this market.''

"What do you have in mind, Mr. Hickling?'' It was a risky question but worth asking. Tony had seen situations at Pisces Exporters where two traders clashed because the vice president neglected to clarify their respective duties. He also wanted to avoid stepping on Tom Siu's toes by taking his job away from him.

Hickling took a final bite of his sole florentine and ordered another double scotch. ''Siu's done a good job as a trader for me, but his strength is as a buyer, not as a seller,'' he explained. ''He came to us about five years ago from (the Department of) Fisheries in the Canadian government and really knows the quality of seafood. His knowledge of the processing industry on the West Coast has been a real plus. My intention is to bring you in as the export seller and Siu will be primarily responsible as the buyer.''

Tony felt satisfied. The job looked challenging and the setup would take advantage of both Tom Siu's and his talents.

Hickling continued. ''Tony, there's a lot of opportunity at Hickling Associates if you decide to join our team. I'll start you at $40,000 per year and, depending on your contribution, you'll receive a bonus with no ceiling. That means virtually unlimited earnings potential if you boost our export seafood business. And I know you will.''

The offer was quite satisfactory to Tony, especially considering his employment alternatives. The salary was slightly lower than his current $42,000 salary, but this could be made up in bonuses. He was curious about the bonus plan, but felt that this was not diplomatically the right time to go into details on compensation matters. It was not a large company, and written employment contracts were rarely seen in the industry, even at the senior executive level.

''That sounds reasonable.'' Tony didn't want to sound too enthusiastic. ''Of course, I'll have to give this some thought. Could you tell me more about the company's facilities for export trading?''

James Hickling explained the computer system that had recently been introduced to keep track of client accounts as well as purchase inventories. Tony would have complete access to the support staff and would have freedom to develop fresh and frozen seafood sales. In order to develop these sales, Tony would be free to travel as required. In addition, traders at Hickling Associates Ltd. have a company car up to a certain value. This value was about $3,000 lower than Tony's car because Pisces had a higher limit. However, Hickling agreed to raise this limit for as long as Tony had his present automobile. The limit would then be lowered for any subsequent car purchase.

The conversation wandered into the quality of recent salmon catches and the opportunities for international merchants with the rapid growth of fish farms along British Columbia's coast. Tony saw these farms as an excellent source for fresh salmon exports, particularly in competition with the Norwegians, who had been taking an increasing percentage of market share in several areas of the world.

About one and one-half hours after the lunch began, Tony Azzara and James Hickling shook hands and left the restaurant. Tony promised to get back to Hickling within the next couple of days with an answer. That evening, Tony discussed the offer with his wife, and the next day he accepted Mr. Hickling's offer. Tony would start work on July 18, 1983, giving Tony and his wife a few weeks of vacation on Vancouver Island in early July.

### The Start of a New Job

Promptly at 8 A.M. on Monday, July 18, Tony Azzara walked into the office of Hickling Associates Ltd. in downtown Vancouver eager to accept his new challenge. Mr. Hickling had not arrived yet, but the receptionist had just sat down at her desk. Tony could hear that other people were already at work behind the partition that separated the receptionist from the rest of the offices.

When Tony introduced himself to the receptionist, she answered in an apologetic way that she knew nothing of this arrival. It was evident from her awkwardness that the receptionist wasn't quite sure how to deal with this situation, so Tony let himself into the general office and wandered through the various areas (see Exhibit 1). There were five secretarial workstations directly behind the reception area and, along the hallway to the left, another larger, open section of the office

where several men and a few women were working. As Tony entered this area, an oriental gentleman in his late thirties approached him. It was Thomas Siu. Tom looked genuinely pleased to meet Tony as the two men shook hands. After short introductions, Tom walked Tony over to a far corner of the room and pointed to two of the large desks butted up against each other.

"This is where you'll be working, Tony," Tom said with a smile. "Mr. Hickling likes to have the traders who work together near each other. Since I'm doing the buying and you're doing the selling, I'll be right here." Tom put his hand on the other desk.

The proximity of the work areas was some-

EXHIBIT 1    Office layout of Hickling Associates

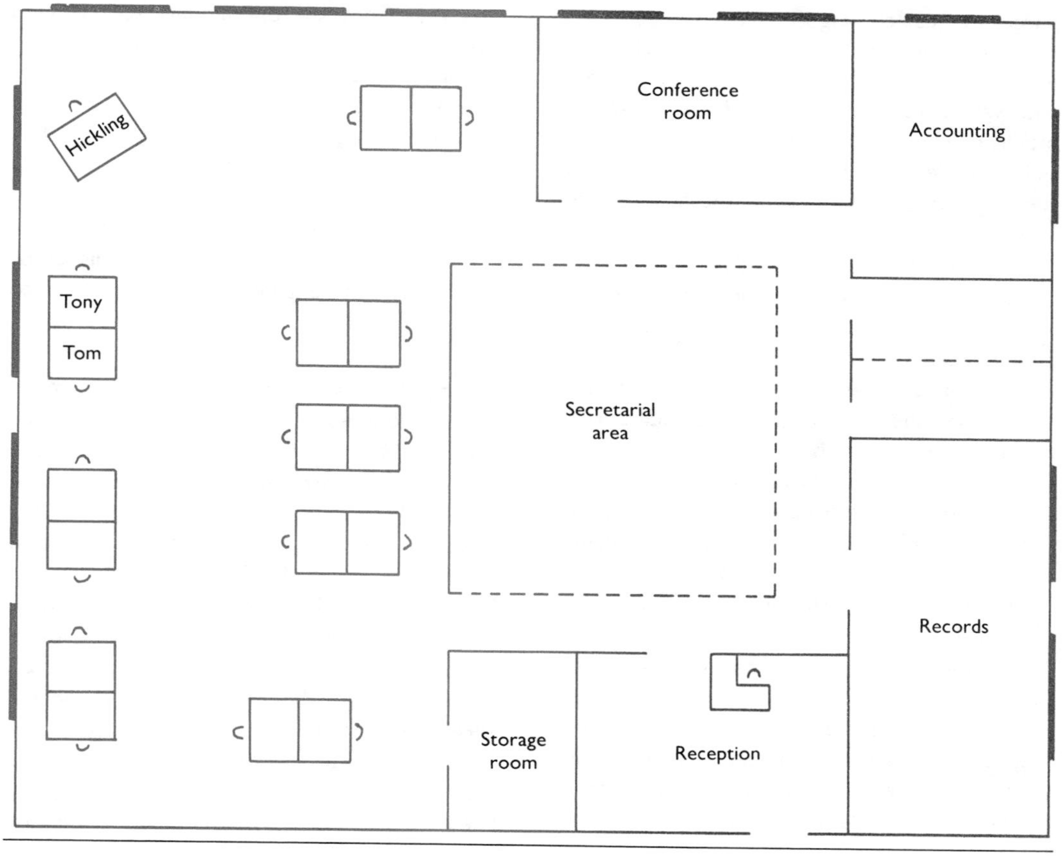

thing of a shock to Tony. He was accustomed to his own office and, although aware that Hickling Associates had an open office arrangement, he did not expect to be so physically close to the other traders. Tony looked around the large room. It was an older building with high ceilings and large arched windows. The offices of Hickling Associates took up half of the fourth floor of the ten-storey office building. The clerical workstations he had passed earlier were very modern while the trader desks were large oak pieces with wooden swivel rockers. Except for the carpeting and fixtures, the room looked much like it would have thirty years earlier. It was actually rather appealing to Tony except for the physical arrangements. The other traders were at their desks, most of them on the telephone, or just coming in to work.

At that moment James Hickling walked in from the entrance of the far side of the room and walked towards Tony and Tom. "Good morning, Tony. I see that you're getting yourself all settled in." He shook Tony's hand and then sat down at the desk at the head of the room.

Tony's heart sank. Hickling's desk was only five feet from his, allowing Hickling to literally look over Tony's shoulder. He sat down and looked around the room again. It then dawned on him that he was the only person wearing a suit. The other traders were dressed casually in slacks and open shirts. Some were even wearing blue jeans. Tony glanced back to Hickling who was on the telephone and looking out the window. He was dressed in corduroy pants and a plaid sport shirt — a sharp contrast from Tony's three-piece dark grey pinstripe suit with white shirt and tie.

Not knowing quite what to do, Tony rummaged through his desk to discover what supplies were available. He jotted down the supplies he needed and made a short list of his goals for the next few weeks. Unfortunately, this didn't take very long, and Tony was soon left with the task of finding something else to do. It wasn't a good idea to ask Tom about work procedures yet, with Hickling just a few feet away. That wouldn't leave a good impression. Instead, Tony walked around the office, introducing himself to the other traders and staff in the firm. In a casual manner, he observed some of the forms and procedures the other traders were using while asking them about their product area. After about half an hour, Tony returned to his desk. His watch said it was only 9:30 A.M. It was going to be an awkward morning. For the next few hours, Tony made telephone calls to some of his contacts to inform them that he was now employed at Hickling Associates Ltd.

James Hickling left the office before lunch and didn't return until late in the afternoon. This gave Tony the opportunity to talk with Tom and learn more about the firm's buy and sell procedures. Tom was very helpful as the two discussed matters over lunch. They also formed a fairly good understanding of how they could coordinate the work. Tom was quite pleased that he was now handling only the purchases of seafood, but Tony felt that Tom wasn't very enthusiastic either about his job or the possibility of expanding the product line to fresh fish exports.

### Settling In

During the first month, Tony Azzara made several successful foreign sales of canned salmon and other fish products and was able to use the records and inventory system at Hickling Associates Ltd. with minimal difficulty. Having previous experience in the industry was a definite help. Much of the job could be performed in a similar manner no matter where he worked. However, there was still a lot of uncertainty about some of the more technical procedures and the extent of his authority. Hickling hadn't given Tony any idea about this. The office layout was also difficult to get used to. It was quite clear that Mr. Hickling had tried to overhear some of Tony's telephone conversations. The records people also were putting pressure on Tony to sign all correspondence with the company name rather than his own. This made him feel very uncomfortable because these were contacts and customers that he had established. It was certainly common for traders to sign their own names in other trading firms. For several weeks, these factors took their toll as Tony felt quite worn out by the end of the day.

At the end of the third week, Tony decided to approach Mr. Hickling about a few company policies so that he would have a clearer idea about how to approach certain items on his agenda. For example, Tony was still unsure about the limit of his signing authority for shipments to new customers. There was also the question of the firm's approach to selling odd-sized lots. On both issues, Tony had received conflicting opinions from the other traders. This may have been because they were in such diverse product lines and company policy might vary with the product. So Tony approached James Hickling directly for the answers.

Hickling's reply was hostile. "For God's sake, Tony!" he barked. "Can't you figure these things out for yourself? I haven't time for that trivia!"

Tony's initial feeling was that of embarrassment. Hickling spoke loud enough for all of the traders to hear, and several of them turned to find out what was going on. Embarrassment turned to anger, however, as Tony realized that his questions were not unreasonable. He turned on his heel and, without replying to Hickling, marched out of the room towards the records office. Hopefully, some of the answers might be found there in old invoices and other documents. Later that day, Tom Siu apologized to Tony for not warning him earlier about Hickling. Tom pointed out that most of the traders had received the same dress-down at one time or another and therefore avoided Hickling whenever possible. Tom

said, "Hickling may be one of the best traders in the city, but he isn't easy to get along with."

The only exception was when Hickling had been drinking. It became increasingly apparent to Tony that Hickling and several of the traders were heavy drinkers. They almost always drank copious amounts of liquor at lunch. There was also a ritual of sharing a large bottle of rye or scotch whenever a major deal was finalized. Tony figured that at least one bottle was consumed openly in the office each week. Every trader had his or her own glass. Both an ice machine and liquor store were conveniently located around the block from the Hickling Associates offices. It was during these celebrations that Hickling became more personable with the traders, although the traders still watched what they said to him. Tony wasn't much of a drinker, but went along with the ritual and even broke out a bottle of scotch for the group one day in September when he signed up a major European customer. This office behaviour was quite different from Pisces Exporters Ltd. where drinking on the job was strictly forbidden.

The drinking habits of Hickling and the office staff (mainly the traders) paled against a more startling observation that Tony made after about a month on the job. James Hickling was married with three children, but Tony noticed him on several occasions leave for lunch with a female employee in the accounting group and not return until late in the afternoon. He quietly asked Tom Siu about this one day and was told that Hickling was having an affair with the woman. Tony was surprised at how casually Tom said this. Over the next few months, Tony learned about two other relationships in the office between traders and support staff. In both cases, one or both of the employees were married. All three affairs were generally known of and accepted throughout the firm. Apparently, other relationships had formed in the past, and when they dissolved one or both of the employees involved had left the company within a few months. Tony had difficulty accepting the moral standards of the office and couldn't understand how these affairs were conducted so easily by the other members of Hickling Associates Ltd.

After three months, Tony Azzara was beginning to feel a little more comfortable in his position at Hickling Associates Ltd. He hadn't received any feedback from Hickling, but had a fairly good idea that he was doing well by industry standards. The other traders were in diverse product areas and it was difficult to compare performance. Nevertheless, several of them congratulated Tony on the number of new customers he had signed up for the export of canned salmon and other seafood products. Tom Siu's excellent buying skills helped considerably, but in the tough European market, the traders knew that export sales would be the more difficult task.

Tony felt that his earlier contacts had really helped to increase sales. But he was not receiving the industry mail that used to come across his desk at Pisces Exports Ltd. This mail was important because it would inform Tony of upcoming functions in Vancouver and abroad. Instead, the mail was going directly to James Hickling's desk. On several occasions, Hickling attended these functions and Tony would not find out until after the event. In fact, Tony attended only two industry functions during the first year compared with the five or six events he had formerly attended annually.

Another major setback occurred in late November. Hickling had planned a trip to Europe and made arrangements to visit several of Tony's new customers. Tony was angry and frustrated. But when he approached his boss about this, Hickling replied, "It doesn't make sense for both of us to travel." Two more trips were made in February and April 1984. On both of these occasions, Tony was told that he would be able to make these trips in the future. Meanwhile, Tony had to rely on the telephone and other forms of communi-

cation to make his important contacts for new business. On none of the trips that Hickling took did any new seafood export sales materialize.

### The Bonus and the Final Straw

At the end of six months of work, Tony Azzara had contributed over $425,000 in net profits to Hickling Associates Ltd. Seafood exports had more than doubled, and several new customers had been established in spite of the limitations that were placed on Tony. Hickling still hadn't provided any performance feedback but Tony had high expectations of the bonus, which was paid at the end of the year. In his final pay cheque for 1983, Tony found a bonus in the amount of $10,000. It was a disappointment. He had worked harder than ever before and had personally generated record sales for the company. A few days later, when Hickling had returned from lunch and was in high spirits, Tony confronted Hickling about how the bonus was decided. Hickling looked rather awkward as he explained that it was based on a combination of overall company profitability and individual performance. He then promised Tony that if he sold as well in 1984, the bonus for that year would reflect this performance.

In February, when Hickling was out of town, Tony had the opportunity to talk about the bonus system with a few of the other traders. To his surprise, many of the traders had gone through a similar reaction to their first bonus. Most were still disappointed, but had resigned themselves to the fact that salaries would not be much higher than the base rate. As long as they avoided James Hickling and did their jobs, the traders accepted the situation. It was quite clear that they were doing enough to survive in the job and nothing more.

After a year on the job, Tony was feeling increasingly antagonistic to Hickling and the firm. He still had not been given the opportunity to visit his customers and make new contacts abroad. Tony even began rummaging through Hickling's mail to find out about upcoming industry events. He continued to sign his own name rather than the company's to most telex correspondence, but it was clear that Hickling wanted the customers to identify with him, not the traders. It was fairly easy at first to accept the drinking ritual. However, Tony later separated himself more from Hickling and the other traders when he realized how much alcohol he was drinking. In fact, it was his wife who first noticed this as Tony began to consume more liquor at home.

As the end of 1984 approached, Tony felt somewhat confident that his bonus would be at least as high as last year's. Sales had continued to climb and the seafood export component of Hickling Associates Ltd. represented a larger proportion of the business than ever before. The 1984 bonus was

$5,000. Tony Azzara was shocked and upset. Neglecting the possibility of a loud confrontation, Tony again confronted Hickling. Hickling indicated that several other parts of the organization were not producing the expected levels of profit and, as a result, all bonuses were lower. He added that it was important to be part of the team at Hickling Associates Ltd. and share the profits and losses throughout the firm.

A few weeks later, Tony learned from sales records that none of the other trading areas in the company had suffered any serious drop in sales. In February 1985, Tony Azzara submitted his resignation at Hickling Associates Ltd. He accepted a position with a competing international merchant in Vancouver at a lower salary.

Hickling Associates has hired you as a human resource management consultant following Tony Azzara's resignation.

1.   Identify the problems that you see in this case.

2.   Recommend human resource activities that would solve the problems at Hickling Associates Ltd.

*© 1985. Steven L. McShane, Faculty of Business Administration, Simon Fraser University. All names and locations have been changed. Any similarity to current names and places is purely coincidental. Reprinted with the permission of Richard D. Irwin Inc. and Steven McShane.

## SUGGESTED READINGS

Feldman, Daniel C., ''A Socialization Process that Helps New Recruits Succeed,'' in K. Rowland, A. Ferris and J. Sherman (eds.), *Current Issues in Personnel Management*, Boston: Allyn & Bacon, 1985.

Jones, David F., ''Developing a New Employee Orientation Program,'' *Personnel Journal*, March 1984, pp. 86-87.

McShane, Steven L., and Trudy Baal, ''Employee Socialization Practices on Canada's West Coast: A Management Report,'' Faculty of Business Administration, Simon Fraser University, Burnaby, B.C., December 1984.

St. John, Walter D., ''The Complete Employee Orientation Program,'' *Personnel Journal*, May 1980, pp. 377-378.

Wanous, J.P., *Organizational Entry: Recruitment, Selection and Socialization of Newcomers*, Reading, Mass.: Addison-Wesley Publishing, 1980.

# REFERENCES

1. John P. Wanous, *Organization Entry: Recruitment, Selection and Socialization of Newcomers*, Reading, Mass.: Addison-Wesley, 1979, p. 171.
2. Carl J. Loomis, "IBM's Big Blues: A Legend Tries to Remake Itself," *Fortune*, January 19, 1987, p. 52.
3. William H. Mobley, "Some Unanswered Questions in Turnover and Withdrawal Research," *Academy of Management Review*, January 1982, pp. 111-116.
4. Earl A. Gomersall and M. Scott Myers, "Breakthrough in on-the-job Training," *Harvard Business Review*, July-August 1966, pp. 66-72.
5. Hari Das, "Organizational Engagement: Recruitment, Selection, and Orientation," in Kalburgi M. Srinivas (ed.), *Human Resource Management*, Toronto: McGraw-Hill Ryerson, 1984, p. 186.
6. John Van Maanen, "Breaking In: Socialization to Work," in Robert Dubin (ed.), *Handbook of Work, Organization and Society*, Chicago: Rand McNally, 1976.
7. "ASPA-BNA Survey No. 32: Employee Orientation Programs," *Bulletin to Management* No. 1436, Washington: Bureau of National Affairs, Inc., August 25, 1977, p. 1; see also R. Zenke, "U.S. Training Census and Trends Report, 1982," *Training*, 19, October 1982, p. 16; John M. Ivancevich and William F. Glueck, *Foundations of Personnel/Human Resource Management*, 3rd. Edition, Plano, Texas: Business Publications, 1986.
8. Steven L. McShane and Trudy Baal, "Employee Socialization Practices on Canada's West Coast: A Management Report," Faculty of Business Administration, Simon Fraser University, Burnaby, B.C., December 1984.
9. Robert W. Hollmann, "Let's Not Forget about New Employee Orientation," *Personnel Journal*, May 1976, pp. 244-247, 250; see also Thomas LaMott, "Making Employee Orientation Work," *Personnel Journal*, January 1974, pp. 35-37, 44; and Walter D. St. John, "The Complete Employee Orientation Program," *Personnel Journal*, May 1980, pp. 373-378.
10. McShane and Baal, 1984, op. cit.
11. "Companies Calling Retirees Back to Work Place," *Management Review*, February 1982, p. 29; see also Kenneth Oldfield and Nancy Ayers, "Avoid the New Job Blues," *Personnel Journal*, August 1986, pp. 49-56.
12. Wayne F. Cascio, *Managing Human Resources*, N.Y.: McGraw-Hill, 1986, p. 216.
13. McShane and Baal, 1984, op. cit.
14. Thomas K. Meier and Susan Hough, "Beyond Orientation: Assimilating New Employees," *Human Resource Management*, Spring 1982, pp. 27-29.
15. For example, see Hollman, 1976, op. cit.; Walter D. St. John, 1980, op cit.; Ronald E. Smith, "Employee Orientation: 10 steps to success," *Personnel Journal*, December 1984, pp. 46-48.
16. Cary Thorp, Jr., quoted in George T. Milkovich, William F. Glueck, Richard T. Barth, and Steven L. McShane, *Canadian Personnel/Human Resource Management*, Plano, Texas: Business Publications Inc., 1988, p. 439.
17. McShane and Baal, 1984, op cit.
18. M. Lubliner, "Employee Orientation," *Personnel Journal*, April 1978, pp. 207-208.
19. Daniel C. Feldman, "The Multiple Socialization of Organization Members," *Academy of Management Review*, 6, 1981, pp. 309-318; see also J. Van Maanen, "People Processing: Strategies of Organizational Socialization," *Organizational Dynamics* 7, 1978, pp. 18-36; Edgar H. Schein, *Career Dynamics: Match Individual and Organizational Needs*, Reading, Mass.: Addison-Wesley, 1978.
20. Meier and Hough, 1982, op. cit., pp. 27-29; see also Donald B. Summers, "Understanding the Process by which New Employees Enter Work Groups," *Personnel Journal*, August 1977, pp. 394-397, 416.

# CHAPTER 9 ○○○○○○○

# *TRAINING AND DEVELOPMENT*

*It is no longer a question of whether we want to develop our human resources or whether we should develop our human resources . . . It is a matter of survival for our society that we develop human resources.*

JAMES L. HAYES[1]

*Our refusal to spend money on investing in a skilled work force shows up in large numbers of people who are unemployable.*

HERBERT E. STRINER[2]

○ ○ ○ ○ ○ ○ ○ ○ ○ ○ ○ ○ ○ ○ ○ ○ ○ ○ ○ ○ ○ ○ ○ ○ ○ ○ ○ ○ ○ ○ ○ ● ● ●

## *CHAPTER OBJECTIVES*

After studying this chapter, you should be able to:
1. **Distinguish** between training and development of human resources.
2. **Explain** different approaches to needs analysis in designing training and development programs.
3. **Describe** the major learning principles associated with each training technique.
4. **Discuss** the steps necessary to implement organization development.
5. **Develop** an evaluation procedure to assess the results of a training and development program.
6. **Do** a cost benefit analysis of a training program.
7. **Discuss** the dimensions of cross-cultural management training.

○ ○ ○ ○ ○ ○ ○ ○ ○ ○ ○ ○ ○ ○ ○ ○ ○ ○ ○ ○ ○ ○ ○ ○ ○ ○ ○ ○ ○ ○ ○ ○ ○

## *EMPLOYEE TRAINING AND DEVELOPMENT*

Even long-service employees need training to avoid obsolescence and to do their present jobs better. When management wants to prepare employees for *future* job responsibilities, this activity is called human resource development. This distinction between training and development is primarily one of intent. *Training* prepares people to do their *present* jobs. *Development* prepares them for *future* jobs. Both training and development teach employees needed skills, knowledge, and attitudes. These activities are usually the responsibility of the human resource department and the immediate supervisor. The rest of this chapter explains the major types of training and development programs, along with the underlying learning principles involved.

New employees seldom perform satisfactorily. They must be trained in the duties they are expected to perform. And experienced employees may need training to reduce poor work habits or to learn new skills that improve their performance.

Although *training* seeks to help employees do their present job, the benefits of training may extend throughout a person's entire career and help *develop* that person for future responsibilities.[3] Developmental activities, on the other hand, aim to help the individual handle future responsibilities with little concern for present job duties. As a result, the distinction between training and development often is blurred. What starts out as training commonly develops people into better workers or managers. Since the distinction between training and development is primarily one of intent, both are discussed together throughout the chapter with significant differences noted where important. To illustrate the developmental impact of training, consider one human resource director's observations.

> When I was first promoted to head all the job analysts in 1974, I did not know the first thing about supervising. So I was sent to a training program for new supervisors. In that seminar I learned a lot of things. But the section on delegation really impressed me. I have relied on that knowledge ever since. Probably the reason I head the human resource department today is because that training helped to develop me into a manager.

When looked at from the overall perspective of a corporate training and development effort, the distinction between training for a present job and development for future ones blurs even further.

Consider the description of one company's training policy. Lloyds Bank of Canada makes training count. Its training program is closely linked with the bank's career advancement policy. Simply taking the bank's training courses is not enough to assure promotion. "The main criteria for promotion is performance, so the training must develop skills that give us a competitive edge," explains Frank Pasquill, the bank's assistant general manager of HRD. The competitive-edge aspect ties in with training profitability. Pasquill mentions the "virtuous circle" as opposed to the "vicious circle." The virtuous circle denotes increased training leading to increased profits, which pays for further training, and so forth. The bank developed the following guidelines:

1. Analyze the strategic context of your training. Identify closely with the mission, strategy, goals, and objectives of our organization.
2. Define the role of human resource development broadly. Integrate your training into other HR functions, like career development.
3. Measure the profitability of training.

4. Focus on "critical skills," the ones that impact heavily on the bottom line of our organization. Avoid getting on the bandwagon with the latest training fads.

5. Concentrate your efforts on achieving excellence in program design. Make it entertaining as well as instructive.

6. Involve line management in the implementation of training programs. The design and coordination is more difficult, but the payoff is much greater in terms of speed, cost-benefit, and skills transfer.

7. Dedicate time and effort to the evaluation of our programs and link it back to the training needs analysis.

Lloyds Bank of Canada obviously has a well-integrated strategy for the training of its employees and their career development. Both are tied in with the strategic vision of the organization: training must lead to improved profits and greater effectiveness of the company, which in turn makes it easier to pay for better training and development of the bank's employees. Management of the bank demands that its trainers make employees aware of how training relates to the bottom line, which requires creating an awareness among bank employees of how training fits into their career development and how it helps the organization as a whole to move ahead. Making employees aware of this demands dealing with strategy and structure and the part training and development play; in short, it requires the services of a training and development professional.[4]

Figure 9-1 summarizes some of the more common benefits of training and development. As can be seen in the figure, training helps the organization, the individual, and the human relations of the work group. Perhaps the easiest way to summarize these benefits is to consider training and development as an investment the organization makes in employees. That investment pays dividends to the employee, the organization, and other workers.

FIGURE 9-1   The Benefits of Employee Training

---

### BENEFITS TO THE ORGANIZATION

---

- Leads to improved profitability and/or more positive attitudes towards profit orientation.
- Improves job knowledge and skills at all levels of the organization.
- Improves the morale of the work force.
- Helps people identify with organizational goals.
- Helps create a better corporate image.
- Fosters authenticity, openness, and trust.
- Improves the relationship between boss and subordinate.
- Aids in organizational development.
- Learns from the trainee.
- Helps prepare guidelines for work.
- Aids in understanding and carrying out organizational policies.
- Provides information for future needs in all areas of the organization.
- Promotes more effective decision making and problem solving.
- Aids in developing promotions from within.
- Aids in developing leadership skill, motivation, loyalty, positive attitudes, and other traits that successful workers and managers usually display.

FIGURE 9-1 (continued)   The Benefits of Employee Training

- Aids in increasing productivity and/or quality of work.
- Helps keep costs down in many areas, e.g., production, staffing, administration, etc.
- Develops in employees a sense of responsibility for being competent and knowledgeable.
- Improves labour-management relations.
- Reduces outside consulting costs by utilizing competent internal consulting.
- Stimulates preventive management, as opposed to ''putting out fires.''
- Eliminates suboptimal behaviour (such as hiding tools).
- Creates an appropriate climate for growth and communication.
- Aids in improving organizational communication.
- Helps employees adjust to change.
- Aids in handling conflict, thereby helping to prevent stress and tension.

### BENEFITS TO THE INDIVIDUAL, WHICH IN TURN BENEFIT THE ORGANIZATION

- Helps the individual towards better decision making and effective problem solving.
- Fosters a sense of recognition, achievement, growth, responsibility, and desire for advancement.
- Aids in encouraging and achieving self-development and self-confidence.
- Helps in handling stress, tension, frustration, and conflict.
- Provides information for improving leadership knowledge, communication skills, and attitudes.
- Increases job satisfaction and recognition.
- Moves the individual towards personal goals while improving interaction skills.
- Satisfies personal needs of the trainer (and trainee!).
- Provides the trainee an avenue for growth and a say in his/her own future.
- Develops a sense of growth in learning.
- Helps a person develop speaking and listening skills—and writing skills when exercises are required.
- Helps eliminate fear of attempting new tasks.

### BENEFITS IN H.R. MANAGEMENT AND HUMAN RELATIONS, INTRA- AND INTERGROUP RELATIONS, AND POLICY IMPLEMENTATION

- Improves communication between groups and individuals.
- Aids in orientation for new employees and those taking new jobs through transfer or promotion.
- Provides information on equal opportunity and affirmative action.
- Provides information on other governmental laws and administrative policies.
- Improves interpersonal skills.
- Makes organizational policies, rules, and regulations viable.
- Improves morale.
- Builds cohesiveness in groups.
- Provides a good climate for learning, growth, and coordination.
- Makes the organization a better place in which to work.

Source: From M.J. Tessin, ''Once Again, Why Training?'' *Training*, February 1978, p.7. Reprinted by permission.

To receive the benefits listed in Figure 9-1, human resource specialists and managers must assess the needs, objectives, content, and learning principles associated with training. Figure 9-2 plots the sequence of events to be followed before training and development begin. First, the person who is responsible for the training or development (usually a trainer) must assess the needs of the employee and the organization in order to learn what objectives should be sought. Once objectives are set, the specific content and learning principles are considered. Whether the learning process is to be guided by trainers in the human resource department or by first-level supervisors, these preliminary steps should be undertaken to create an effective program.

FIGURE 9-2    Preliminary Steps in Preparing a Training and Development Program

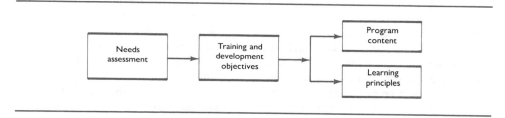

## Needs Assessment

Although precise figures are not available, it is estimated that the cost of training and development in government and industry in Canada is between $10 and $12 billion annually.[5] An estimate of similar costs in the U.S. puts the figure at $100 billion.[6] If organizations are to get maximum benefit from this staggering expenditure, then efforts must concentrate on people and situations that can benefit most.[7] To decide what approach to use, the trainer assesses the needs for training and development. *Needs assessment* diagnoses present problems and environmental challenges that can be met through training, or the future challenges to be met through long-term development. For example, changes in the external environment may present an organization with new challenges. To respond effectively, employees may need training to deal with the change. The comments of one training director illustrate the impact of the external environment.

> After enactment of the human rights legislation, we had to train every interviewer in the human resource department. This training was needed to ensure that our interviewers would not ask questions that might violate federal or provincial laws. When managers in other departments heard of the training, they, too, wanted to sign up. What was to be a one-time seminar became a monthly session for nearly three years. We evaluated the requests of these other managers and decided that they interviewed recruits and that they should be trained also.

Sometimes a change in the organization's strategy can create a need for training. For example, new products or services usually require employees to learn new procedures. Xerox encountered this challenge when it decided to produce computers. Sales personnel, programmers, and production workers had to be trained to produce, sell, and service this new product line. Training can also be used when high accident rates, low morale and motivation, or other problems are diagnosed. Although training is not an organizational cure-all, undesirable trends may be evidence of a poorly prepared work force.

Regardless of these challenges, needs assessment must consider each person.[8] Needs may be determined by the human resource department, supervisors, or self-nomination. The human resource department may find weaknesses among those who are hired or promoted. Supervisors see employee performance daily, and so they are another source of recommendations for training. But their suggestions may be made to banish troublemakers, "hide" surplus employees who are temporarily expendable, or reward good workers. Since these are not valid reasons, the human resource department often reviews supervisory recommendations to verify the need for training. Likewise, the department also reviews self-nominations to determine whether the training is actually needed. In one research study, supervisors selected attendees for training programs more frequently than self-nominations.[9] Self-nomination appears to be less common for training situations but more common for developmental activities, such as getting an MBA under the employer's tuition reimbursement program.

Even when employees are allowed to nominate themselves for available training programs, training directors have little assurance that they are offering the correct mix of courses or that the courses have the right content. To better narrow the range of courses and define their content, more refined approaches to needs assessment are used. One approach is through task identification. Trainers begin by evaluating the job description to identify the salient tasks that the job requires. Then with an understanding of these tasks, specific plans are developed to provide the necessary training so that jobholders can perform the tasks.[10]

Another approach is to survey potential trainees to identify specific topical areas that they want to learn more about.[11] The advantage of this method is that trainees are more likely to see the subsequent training programs as relevant, and thus they are more likely to be receptive to them. Of course, this approach to assessing training needs presumes that those surveyed know what training they need. For new employees needing specific individual or departmental training, this method is unlikely to be successful. In the case of more general training needs, however, group recommendations may be the best way to identify training needs. The groups' expertise may be tapped through a group discussion, questionnaire, a Delphi procedure (see Chapter 4, Human Resource Planning), or through a nominal group meeting.

The *Nominal Group Technique* (NGT) is a method of drawing out the ideas of a group of people on a specified topic.[12] It asks a group of ten to fifteen trainers, managers, or potential trainees to privately list on a piece of paper all the training needs they can think of. After the group has gone through this silent idea-generation phase, each person is asked to give one idea in round-robin fashion. This process of soliciting an idea from each person continues until each person has exhausted his or her ideas and "passes" when asked for another idea. The moderator (or scribe) lists every idea, without comment, until all ideas are listed. Comments are then clarified and duplications, if any, eliminated. Participants then vote for the five most important training needs. The votes are tabulated to determine which needs are regarded by the group as most pressing.

Unlike brainstorming (where some people may not offer their ideas), NGT taps everyone's ideas and encourages the suggestions of others during the round-robin session, to stimulate even more ideas among the group members. The final "voting" ensures that the outcome reflects the group's collective wisdom.

Trainers are alert to other sources of information that may indicate a need for training. Production records, quality control reports, grievances, safety reports, absenteeism and turnover statistics, and exit interviews among departing employees may indicate problems that should be addressed through training and development efforts. Training needs may also become apparent from career planning and development discussions or performance appraisal reviews — both of which are treated in subsequent chapters.[13] Regardless of how needs assessment takes place, it is important because the success of the remaining steps in Figure 9-2 depends on an accurate assessment. If the trainer's assessment of need is not correct, it is unlikely that training objectives and program content will be appropriate.

## Training and Development Objectives

An evaluation of training needs results in training and development objectives. These objectives should state:

1. The desired behaviour.
2. The conditions under which it is to occur.
3. The acceptable performance criteria.

These statements serve as the standard against which individual performance and the program can be measured. For example, the objectives for an airline reservation agent might be stated as follows:

1. Provide flight information to call-in customers within thirty seconds.
2. Complete a one-city, round-trip reservation in 120 seconds after all information is obtained from the customer.

Objectives like these give the trainer and the trainee specific goals that can be used by both to evaluate their success. If these objectives are not met, failure gives the human resource department feedback on the program and the participants.

## Program Content

The program's content is shaped by the needs assessment and the learning objectives. This content may seek to teach specific skills, provide needed knowledge, or try to influence attitudes. Whatever the content, the program must meet the needs of the organization and the participants. If company goals are not furthered, resources are wasted. And participants must view the content as relevant to their needs, or their motivation to learn may be low.

## Learning Principles

Although it is widely studied, little is known about the learning process. Part of the problem is that learning cannot be observed; only its results can be measured. From studies of learning, however, researchers have sketched a broad picture of the learning process and have developed some tentative principles of learning.

Perhaps the best way to understand learning is through the use of a *learning curve*, pictured in Figure 9-3. As the curve illustrates, learning takes place in bursts (from points *A* to *B*) and in plateaus (from points *B* to *C*). Trainers have two goals related to the shape of each employee's learning curve. First, they want the learning curve to reach a satisfactory level of performance. This level is shown as a dashed line in the figure. Second, they want the learning curve to get to the satisfactory level as quickly as possible. Although the rate at which an individual learns depends upon the person, the use of various learning principles helps speed up the learning process.

*Learning principles* are guidelines to the ways in which people learn most effectively. The more they are included in training, the more effective training is likely to be. The principles are: participation, repetition, relevance, transference, and feedback.

### FIGURE 9-3   A Typical Learning Curve

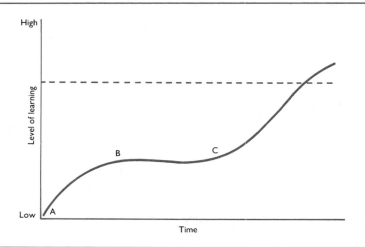

### Participation

Learning is usually quicker and more long-lasting when the learner can participate actively. Participation improves motivation and apparently engages more senses that help reinforce the learning process. As a result of participation, we learn more quickly and retain that learning longer. For example, once they have learned, most people never forget how to ride a bicycle or drive a car.

### Repetition

Although it is seldom fun, repetition apparently etches a pattern into our memory. Studying for an examination, for example, involves memorization of key ideas to be recalled during the test. Likewise, most people learned the alphabet and the multiplication tables by repetition.

### Relevance

Learning is helped when the material to be learned is meaningful. For example, trainers usually explain the overall purpose of a job to trainees before explaining specific tasks. This explanation allows the worker to see the relevance of each task and the importance of following the given procedures.

### Transference

The closer the demands of the training program match the demands of the job, the faster a person learns to master the job.[14] For example, pilots are usually trained in flight simulators because the simulators very closely resemble the actual cockpit and flight characteristics of the plane. The close match between the simulator and the plane allows the trainee to transfer quickly the learning in the simulator to actual flight conditions.

### Feedback

Feedback gives learners information on their progress. With feedback, motivated learners can adjust their behaviour to achieve the quickest possible learning curve. Without feedback, learners cannot gauge their progress and may become discouraged. Test grades are feedback on the study habits of test takers, for example.

## TRAINING AND DEVELOPMENT TECHNIQUES

Before reviewing the various training and development techniques, it is important to remember that any method may be applied to both training and development. For example, a class on management techniques may be attended by supervisors and workers who are likely to be promoted to those positions.[15] For supervisors, the class covers how to do their present job better. In the case of workers who have no management responsibilities, the classes are intended to develop them into supervisors. The classroom instruction would be identical for both groups, but it has two different purposes: training for supervisors and development for workers.

In selecting a particular technique to use in training or development, there are several trade-offs. That is, no one technique is always best; the best method depends upon:

· Cost-effectiveness
· Desired program content
· Appropriateness of the facilities
· Trainee preferences and capabilities
· Trainer preferences and capabilities
· Learning principles

The importance of these six trade-offs depends upon the situation. For example, cost-effectiveness may be a minor factor when training an airline pilot in emergency manoeuvres. But whatever method is selected, it has certain learning principles associated with it. Figure 9-4 lists the most common training and development techniques and the learning principles each includes. As the figure reveals, some techniques make

FIGURE 9-4   Learning Principles in Different Training and Development
Techniques

|  | PARTICIPATION | REPETITION | RELEVANCE | TRANSFERENCE | FEEDBACK |
|---|---|---|---|---|---|
| **On-the-Job Techniques** | | | | | |
| Job instruction training | Yes | Yes | Yes | Yes | Sometimes |
| Job rotation | Yes | Sometimes | Yes | Sometimes | No |
| Apprenticeships | Yes | Sometimes | Yes | Sometimes | Sometimes |
| Coaching | Yes | Sometimes | Yes | Sometimes | Yes |
| **Off-the-job Techniques** | | | | | |
| Lecture | No | No | No | Sometimes | No |
| Video presentation | No | No | No | Yes | No |
| Vestibule training | Yes | Yes | Sometimes | Yes | Sometimes |
| Role playing | Yes | Sometimes | Sometimes | No | Sometimes |
| Case study | Yes | Sometimes | Sometimes | Sometimes | Sometimes |
| Simulation | Yes | Sometimes | Sometimes | Sometimes | Sometimes |
| Self-study | Yes | Yes | Sometimes | Sometimes | No |
| Programmed learning | Yes | Yes | No | Yes | Yes |
| Laboratory training | Yes | Yes | Sometimes | No | Yes |
| Computer-based training | Yes | Yes | Sometimes | Yes | Yes |

Source: From *Training in Industry: The Management of Learning*, by B. M. Bass and J. A. Vaughn. Copyright
© 1966 by Wadsworth Publishing Company, Inc. Reprinted by permission of the publisher, Brooks/Cole
Publishing Company, Monterey, Calif.

more effective use of learning principles than others. Even those approaches that use
few learning principles, such as the lecture, are valuable tools because they may satisfy
one of the other five trade-offs listed above. For example, lectures may be the best way
to communicate some academic content in the most cost-effective manner, especially if
the classroom is large and the room does not lend itself to other approaches. Although
these six trade-offs affect the methods used, human resource specialists must be familiar
with all the techniques and learning principles found in Figure 9-4.

## Job Instruction Training

*Job instruction training* (also called on-the-job training) is received directly on the job
and is used primarily to teach workers how to do their present job. A trainer, supervisor,
or coworker serves as the instructor. This method includes each of the five learning
principles (participation, repetition, relevance, transference, and feedback) in a series
of carefully planned steps.

First, the trainee receives an overview of the job, its purpose, and its desired outcomes, which emphasizes the relevance of the training. Then the trainer demonstrates the job to provide the employee with a model to copy. Since the employee is being shown the actions that the job actually requires, the training is transferable to the job. Next, the employee is allowed to mimic the trainer's example. Demonstrations by the trainer and the practice by the trainee are repeated until the job is mastered by the trainee. Repeated demonstrations and practice provide the advantage of repetition and feedback. Finally, the employee performs the job without supervision, although the trainer may visit the employee to see if there are any lingering questions.

## Job Rotation

To cross-train employees in a variety of jobs, some trainers will move the trainee from job to job. Each move is normally preceded by job instruction training. Besides giving workers variety in their jobs, cross-training helps the organization when vacations, absences, and resignations occur. Learner participation and high job transferability are the learning advantages to job rotation.

## Apprenticeships and Coaching

Apprenticeships involve learning from a more experienced employee or employees. This approach to training may be supplemented with off-the-job classroom training. Most tradespeople, such as plumbers and carpenters, are trained through formal apprenticeship programs. Assistantships and internships are similar to apprenticeships. These approaches use high levels of participation by the trainee and have high transferability to the job.

Coaching is similar to apprenticeships in that the coach attempts to provide a model for the trainee to copy. Most companies use some coaching. It tends to be less formal than an apprenticeship program because there are few formal classroom sessions, and the coaching is provided when needed rather than being part of a carefully planned program. Coaching is almost always handled by the supervisor or manager and not the human resource department. Participation, feedback, and job transference are likely to be high in this form of learning.[16]

Someone who receives coaching by another person to assume that person's specific job is called an *understudy.* A senior executive may designate a replacement well before retirement so that that person can serve as an understudy.

Assignments to task forces or committees can also help to develop people in much the same way that apprenticeships and coaching do. Through periodic staff meetings or work with task forces and committees, a manager develops interpersonal skills, learns to evaluate information, and gains experience in observing other potential models.

## Lecture and Video Presentations

Lecture and other off-the-job techniques tend to rely more heavily on communications rather than modelling, which is used in on-the-job programs. These approaches are applied in both training and development. Lecture is a popular approach because it offers relative economy and a meaningful organization of materials. However, participation, feedback, transference, and repetition are often low. Feedback and participation can be improved when discussion is permitted after the lecture.

Television, films, slides, and filmstrip presentations are comparable to lectures. A meaningful organization of materials and initial audience interest are potential strengths of these approaches. Interestingly, one survey of training directors revealed that they thought films were superior to lectures with questions.[17]

## Vestibule Training

So that training does not disrupt normal operations, some organizations use *vestibule training*. Separate areas or vestibules are set up with the same kind of equipment that will be used on the job. This arrangement allows transference, repetition, and participation. The meaningful organization of materials and feedback are also possible.

> At the corporate training facilities of Best Western motels and hotels, vestibules exist that duplicate a typical motel room, a typical front counter, and a typical restaurant kitchen. This allows trainees to practise housekeeping, front counter service, and kitchen skills without disrupting the operations of any one property.

## Role Playing

*Role playing* is a device that forces trainees to assume different identities. For example, a male worker and a female supervisor may trade roles. Then both may be given a typical work situation and told to respond in their new roles. The result? Usually participants exaggerate each other's behaviour. Ideally, they both get to see themselves as others see them. The experience may create greater empathy and tolerance of individual differences. This technique seeks to change attitudes of trainees, such as to improve racial understanding. It also helps to develop interpersonal skills.[18] Although participation and feedback are present, the inclusion of other learning principles depends on the situation.

Many companies employ role playing to train supervisors to give performance feedback, a crucial managerial skill in motivating employees. Supervisors often avoid giving negative feedback, because they feel uneasy about it. However, since it is normal for an employee to exhibit ineffective job behaviour, managers have to learn to provide their employees with constructive criticism. During the role-play exercise, two supervisors assume the roles of a rater, who gives feedback, and of a ratee, who is at the receiving end. Once the role play is over, observers (usually trainers) give both comments about their effectiveness as feedback provider and receiver. Then the roles are reversed. Through the exercises and subsequent discussions, supervisors can learn about their attitudes towards negative feedback and how to change it into constructive criticism.

> The RCMP in British Columbia uses role-playing exercises to reduce tensions between members of the force who are of Caucasian and Indian (mainly Sikh) origin. Friction between members of the different cultures on the force caused breakdowns in communication between officers on extended patrol duties, especially when they were in the confinement of a patrol car.

The role-playing exercises required a small number of members of the two groups to assume the role of the other race. The role-playing leader gave each group an assignment and then directed them to carry it out as they thought members of the other race would do it. With the other group watching, each group in turn acted out the behaviour of the other. Through these exercises and the subsequent discussions, members of the different cultural groups were able to learn how their behaviour and attitudes affected each other. These role-playing exercises were an important step in reducing racial tensions.

Closely related to this form of role playing is behaviour modelling. *Behaviour modelling* was described by two writers as follows:

Modeling is one of the fundamental psychological processes by which new patterns of behaviour can be acquired, and existing patterns can be altered. The fundamental characteristic of modeling is that learning takes place, *not* through actual experience, but through observation or imagination of another individual's experience. Modeling is a "vicarious process," which implies sharing in the experience of another person through imagination or sympathetic participation.[19]

Whether behaviour modelling is referred to as "matching" or "copying," "observational learning" or "imitation," " . . . all of these terms imply that a behaviour is learned or modified through the observation of some other individual . . . ."[20] Employees may learn a new behaviour through modelling by observing a new or novel behaviour and then imitating it. The re-creation of the behaviour may be videotaped so that the trainer and trainee can review and criticize the behaviour. Often, when watching the ideal behaviour, the trainee also gets to see the negative consequences of not behaving in the ideal way. Observing both the positive and negative consequences of the taped behaviour gives the employee vicarious reinforcement to adopt the right behaviour. One area where this approach has been used successfully is in teaching supervisors the correct way to discipline employees.

In the supervisory training program of a large, unionized steel company, supervisors were put through a half-day disciplinary training session that used videotape-based behaviour modelling. After a short lecture on the principles of discipline, trainees were shown a brief tape of a supervisor conducting a disciplinary interview incorrectly and another where the discipline was handled properly. Then the supervisors were paired off and each one was told to "discipline" his or her partner using the correct method they just observed. These mock discipline sessions were filmed and played back—often to the horror of the participants. Each saw how others saw him or her when they conducted a disciplinary interview. After a brief and largely positive critique from the trainer, each supervisor conducted a second and a third "discipline session" that was followed by a critique. By the end of the morning, each supervisor was able to conduct a disciplinary interview in the correct manner. Whether this training was actually transferred to their day-to-day behaviour on the job was not evaluated by the training department nor the shop manager.

## Case Study

By studying a case, trainees learned about real or hypothetical circumstances and the actions others took under those circumstances. Besides learning from the content of the case, trainees can develop decision-making skills. When cases are meaningful and similar to work-related situations, there is some transference. There also is the advantage of participation through discussion of the case. Feedback and repetition are usually lacking. Research indicates that this technique is most effective for developing problem-solving skills.[21]

## Simulation

Simulation exercises are in two forms. One form involves a mechanical simulator that replicates the major features of the work situation. Driving simulators used in driver's education programs are an example. This training method is similar to vestibule training, except that the simulator more often provides instantaneous feedback on performance.

Computer simulations are another technique. For training and development purposes, this method is often employed in the form of games. Players make a decision and the computer determines the outcome of the decision, given the conditions under which it was programmed. This technique is used most commonly to train managers, who otherwise might have to use trial and error in decision making.

## Self-study and Programmed Learning

Carefully planned instructional materials can be used to train and develop employees. These are particularly useful when employees are dispersed geographically or when learning requires little interaction. Self-study techniques range from manuals to prerecorded cassettes or videotapes. Unfortunately, few learning principles are included in this type of training.

> Pepsi Cola Management Institute is responsible for training bottlers all over the world. To contend with this dispersion, it created a network of videotape recorders and supplied bottlers with videotaped materials. The institute also uses other techniques.

Programmed learning materials are another form of self-study. Commonly, these are printed booklets that contain a series of questions and answers. After a question is read, the answer can be uncovered immediately. If the reader was right, he or she proceeds. If wrong, the reader is directed to review accompanying materials. Of course, computer programs with visual displays may be used instead of printed booklets.[22] Programmed materials do provide learner participation, repetition, relevance, and feedback; transference, however, tends to be low.

## Laboratory Training

*Laboratory training* is a form of group training used primarily to enhance interpersonal skills. It, too, can be used to develop desired behaviours for future job responsibilities.

Participants seek to improve their human relations skills by better understanding themselves and others. It involves sharing their experiences and examining the feelings, behaviour, perceptions, and reactions that result. Usually a trained professional serves as a facilitator. The process relies on participation, feedback, and repetition. One popular form of laboratory training is sensitivity training, which seeks to improve a person's sensitivity to the feelings of others.

## Computer-based Training

*Computer-based training* (CBT) has been gaining prominence in Canada in recent years. CBT offers the student control over the pace of learning and even other training contents in modular-type training programs and offers the benefits of interactive learning, participation, and positive reinforcement during training.

Current available CBT courses fall into three main categories: off-the-shelf courses on generic topics, support courses with software packages, and custom courseware.

### Off-the-shelf Courses

Courses available in this category are typically in the areas of personal or professional skills. A number of topics ranging from business writing and time management on the one end to complex statistical techniques on the other end currently exist. The quality of these courses "ranges from excellent to abysmal, with everything in between."[23]

### Support Courses

Increasingly, courses on a number of topics are making their appearance on diskettes with supplementary tutorial packages. Many of these courses are on simple skills development (e.g., learning how to use a spreadsheet), but training on more complex skills and management topics can be found in complete tutorial packages (e.g., strategic planning).

### Custom Courseware

Here the focus is on producing customized courses for a particular type of employee or organization. An increasing number of Canadian organizations is using customized CBT techniques for their staffs. Figure 9-5 illustrates the use of computerized training in the Edmonton Police Department.

CBT is unlikely to be very beneficial unless:

1.  It meets the specific needs of the individual,
2.  it is supported by other material that facilitates or reinforces learning,
3.  the skill learned is usable in the organization's context, and
4.  the students do not have a mental block against the use of computers.

Some employees may need to change their attitude towards computers and their relevance for the work place. Unless the human resource manager understands the "fear" or "awe" of employees towards computers and works to eliminate it, gaining wide acceptance for computer-based training may be impossible. Also, there are some skills which can never be effectively communicated through computers.[24]

FIGURE 9-5  Use of Computerized Training in the Edmonton Police
Department

One of Canada's most successful examples of computer-based training is the program developed by the Edmonton Police Department (EPD).

The program, referred to as Decentralized, Individualized, Inservice Training (DIIT), uses modern forms of training delivery: a powerful combination of video-based training, for realism and accuracy, plus computer-based training for efficiency, cost effectiveness, and record-keeping.

The EPD implemented CBT in 1983 following dissatisfaction with other training methods, such as roll-call, lecture, and video-based training. Thirty-two CBT modules were developed in the areas of criminal law and specialized investigations, such as handling bomb threats, vehicle thefts, and high-risk incidents. The courseware was developed using Control Data's PLATO Learning Management and the OMNISIM Authoring Systems. Officers are required to achieve 100% mastery of all topics.

"Not only was the department dissatisfied with conventional training methods, but it realized that training a large group of 1100 people was not possible with those methods," says William Wosar of the Learning Resources Unit, Training Section, EPD. The department's commitment to CBT appears to be years ahead of most Canadian organizations. "Much of the credit," Wosar says, "goes to former Police Chief Lunney, who was very progressive in training matters."

The new training message is clear, consistent, and validated by actual measures of performance. A recent study shows superior performance by DIIT trainees (relative to classroom-based instruction) as measured by both on-the-job performance and traditional paper-and-pencil measures.

### EFFICIENT RESULTS

Training efficiency at the EPD has increased and skill maintenance (refresher training) occurs monthly rather than yearly. In on-the-job performance measures (for the first six months after CBT was implemented, compared to the previous six-month period), the number of scenes attended by the canine unit increased by 27%, and the number of apprehensions by the canine unit rose by 45%.

In the area of criminal law, the number of incorrectly written warrant notices decreased by 49.8% after the first year CBT was implemented, saving four worker-months of paperwork.

The previously used method of instruction consisted of a two-week classroom course offered every five years and lasting eighty hours. DIIT training now requires only sixty hours and provides training on a monthly basis.

The net training cost to the EPD has been reduced by $70,000 per year for five years due to reductions in student hours devoted to training and reduced delivery costs, improved job performance, a decrease in the number of failures on promotional exams for upgrades, and an increase in the average score of participants.

In addition to its record-keeping abilities, CBT is considered by the EPD to be an effective means of increasing retention, improving motivation, and providing standardized information.

### HOW DIIT WORKS

The first part of DIIT is individually administered and scored diagnostic tests, determining which objectives have been mastered and which require further training. The computer handles all details of testing, including recording the performance of each trainee.

Once the set of mastered objectives for each trainee is known, they are given a list of study assignments to prepare them to meet their objectives. The trainees then study the materials until they are confident of mastery.

At this point, trainees are retested by the computer and the cycle is repeated until all objectives are mastered. The time spent testing is more than made up in time saved by not having trainees study assignments they already know. Testing time is brief because retesting is done only on the unmastered objectives, and each retest is terminated as soon as mastery is or isn't possible.

FIGURE 9-5 (continued)   Use of Computerized Training in the Edmonton
Police Department

Since the lessons, video, and testing components of DIIT are self-contained, the program is highly individualized and interactive and can be delivered in a decentralized fashion.

The instructor can examine the extensive performance records of each trainee with the push of a few buttons. This information enables the instructor to provide further assistance or motivation if needed.

A learning station consists of a terminal (or microcomputer), modem, and videotape player. One learning station is required for every 100 to 150 trainees and another is recommended for the instructor.

Trainees learn to sign on in less than three minutes. Computer-managed training automatically routes or directs trainees through the correct lesson sequence.

Source: "CBT a Success with Edmonton Police Department," *The Human Resource*, April-May 1987, p.9. Used with permission.

## HUMAN RESOURCE DEVELOPMENT

The long-term development of human resources—as distinct from training for a specific job—is of growing concern to human resource departments. Through the development of present employees, the human resource department reduces the company's dependence on hiring new employees. If workers are developed properly, the job openings found through human resource planning are more likely to be filled internally. Promotion and transfers also show employees that they have a career, not just a job. The employer benefits by increased continuity in operations and by employees who feel a greater commitment to the firm.

Human resource development is also an effective way to meet several challenges faced by most large organizations. These challenges include employee obsolescence, socio-technical changes, and employee turnover.[25] By meeting these challenges, the human resource department can help maintain an effective work force.

### Reducing Obsolescence

*Obsolescence* results when an employee no longer possesses the knowledge or abilities to perform successfully. In fast-changing and highly technical fields, such as engineering and medicine, obsolescence can occur quickly. Among managers, the change may take place more slowly and be more difficult to determine. Other people in the organization may not notice obsolescence until it is advanced. Too often, favourable opinions about a manager, which are formed over years of association, prevent others from seeing telltale signs of obsolescence — such as inappropriate attitudes, poor performance, or incorrect or outdated procedures.

Although obsolescence may develop from some change in the individual, it is more likely to result from that person's failure to adapt to new technology, new procedures, or other changes. The more rapidly the environment changes, the more likely it is that employees will become obsolete.[26]

Some employers are reluctant to take strong action and fire obsolete employees, particularly those who have been with the company for a long time. Instead, they may be given a job where their obsolescence does not matter as much or where their skills are not as obsolete. For example, when top executives fail to perform satisfactorily, they sometimes are "promoted" to chair the board, where their primary role is to attend ceremonial functions such as banquets for retiring employees. For lower-level employees, the solution is often additional development programs.

To avoid the problem of obsolescence before it occurs is a major challenge for the human resource department. By periodically assessing the needs of employees and giving them programs to develop new skills, the department is using development programs proactively. If programs are designed reactively, after obsolescence occurs, they are likely to be less effective and more costly. For example, consider the situation faced by a human resource department of a regional airline:

> Sam Oliver had been a ground crew chief in the Armed Forces for many of his twenty years in the service. After retirement, he joined a regional airline as a mechanic. Since he had extensive supervisory experience, he was promoted to ground crew chief with the airline. Sam had been successful in the Armed Forces by giving direct orders with little explanation, and he followed the same leadership style in his civilian job.
>
> The human resource department realized something was wrong when an unusually large number of grievances were filed with the union by Sam's ground crew. To correct the problems, Sam was enrolled in an intensive sixteen-week supervisory training program at the local community college. Although he changed his approach after the program, Sam now showed resentment against those of his subordinates who had filed the grievances.

Had the human resource department undertaken proactive supervisory development before Sam was promoted rather than reacting to his obsolescence after problems arose, his resentment might have been avoided.

When an employee reaches a career plateau, obsolescence may set in. A *career plateau* occurs when an employee is in a position that he or she does well enough not to be demoted or fired, but not so well as to be promoted.[27] When the employee realizes that he or she is at this plateau, the motivation to keep up with the times as a manager, professional, or technician may be reduced.[28]

One attempt to deal with obsolescence has been the continuing education offered by many companies to middle- and upper-level management. In one survey of more than 10,000 companies in Canada, 26% reported having training programs for executives, professionals, and managerial personnel.[29] Some large companies, like Alcan, Bell Canada, or Ontario Hydro, have their own programs, but most other firms allow their managers to attend continuing education courses offered by colleges and universities. Most of these companies pay all or part of the costs involved, usually depending on the degree of job relevance of the particular course.

Approximately 10% of the companies surveyed above offer extended leave of absence for educational purposes, often to acquire a university or professional degree or designation.[30]

## Socio-technical Changes

Social and technological changes also challenge the human resource department to maintain an effective work force. For example, cultural attitudes about women in the work force have caused many companies to redesign their development programs in order to meet societal pressures for equal employment:

> Bell Canada redesigned an existing program for outside technicians to enable more women to qualify for outside jobs that previously had been dominated by men.

Likewise, rapid changes in technology require technology-based firms to engage in near-continuous development. Consider the technological change that occurred during Frank T. Carey's career with IBM, from sales representative to chairman of the board:

> Mr. Carey joined IBM in 1948 "because he liked its bright prospects in the office-equipment business."[31] Although IBM is a major producer of office equipment, most people think of IBM as the giant computer manufacturer. While Mr. Carey's career at IBM progressed up to chairman of the board, technology radically transformed IBM into the largest computer manufacturer in the world. Undoubtedly, his career, like many others' at IBM, was marked by near-continuous development activities in order to keep up with rapid technological change.

## Employee Turnover

*Turnover* — the movement of employees from one organization to another — creates a special challenge for human resource development. Since these departures are largely unpredictable, development activities must prepare present employees to succeed those who leave. Although research shows that leaders of very large industrial companies spend nearly all of their careers with one firm, the same research found that mobility is widespread among other managers.[32] Therefore, development programs must prepare other employees to replace departing managers. Sometimes an employer with excellent development programs finds that these programs actually *contribute* to employee turnover.

> Ironically, the widely recognized development programs of such companies as the Royal Bank, Air Canada, Bell Canada, IBM Canada, and others partially cause some employee mobility. Their programs produce such high-quality results that recruiters from other companies are attracted to these employees.

## EVALUATION OF TRAINING AND DEVELOPMENT

The implementation of training and development serves as a transformation process. Untrained employees are transformed into capable workers, and present workers may be developed to assume new responsibilities. To verify the program's success, human resource managers increasingly demand that training and development activities be evaluated systematically.

The lack of evaluation may be the most serious flaw in most training and development efforts.[33] Simply stated, human resource professionals too seldom ask, "Did the program achieve the objectives established for it?" They often assume it had value because the content seemed important. Or trainers may rely on the evaluations of trainees who comment on how enjoyable the experience was for them but who cannot yet determine how valuable it is.

FIGURE 9-6   Steps in the Evaluation of Training and Development

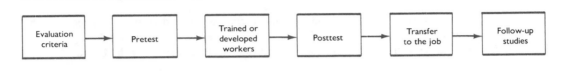

Evaluation of training and development should follow the steps in Figure 9-6. First, evaluation criteria should be established before training begins.[34] There are five types of criteria:

1. Reaction
2. Knowledge
3. Attitudes
4. Behaviour
5. Organizational results

Which of the criteria is the most suitable? This depends on the training objectives. If the objective is to increase the knowledge of the participants, the obvious choice would be the knowledge criterion; if it is behaviour change, the behaviour criterion would be the most appropriate measure. The ideal criterion, however, is organizational results, because this is the ultimate objective of every training program. However, each criterion has its advantages and disadvantages, described in the following discussion.

**1.** *Reaction.* This is undoubtedly the most widely used criterion in training evaluation, although it is rarely stated as an objective. Its measurement does not pose any problem; its interpretation does. Reaction responses are given to the questions "How did you like the program?" "Do you think you got something useful out of it?" "Would you recommend it to a colleague?" etc. What do the answers tell us about the effectiveness of the training program? Almost nothing. A positive answer may indicate that the set-up was well done or that the instructor was popular. However, the measurement is not useless. It is certainly good to know that the participants liked the program. The point is that it says so little about whether the program achieved its objectives. An absolutely ineffective program may receive a top rating because it was executed in a pleasant environment.

**2.** *Knowledge.* A change in knowledge is relatively easy to measure provided that a pretest and a post-test are used. But again, as in the case of the reaction criteria, training programs rarely state increase in knowledge as their prime objective. If the latter is something else, e.g., attitudes or behaviour, the measurement of knowledge is of not much help in assessing the effectiveness of a program. A knowledge test simply asks items that the program conveys. A well-planned and executed program results in a low pre-test and high post-test outcome.

**3.** *Attitudes.* Attitudes are more difficult to measure because they cannot be observed and have to be assessed through self-reports, a sometimes doubtful approach. Instead of a true attitude we often get what researchers call a "social desirability response"; i.e., people respond in a way they think they *should* respond. But we don't have anything better. For this reason we have to make sure that the respondents know that it is safe for them to tell the truth.

**4.** *Behaviour.* For the measurement of behaviour change we can use self-reports and observations by others, e.g., neutral observers, superiors, peers, and subordinates. With self-reports we encounter, of course, the same response problems we discussed with attitude measurements. In addition, research has shown that respondents over-estimate the degree of their (perceived) behaviour change. Supervisor observations are the most widely used measurements, but this approach has some inherent weaknesses. In many, if not most cases, the supervisor recommended the subordinate for or advised him or her to participate in the training program. If the supervisor does not report a behaviour change, then his or her judgement could be questioned. The judgement may also be biased by the personal relationship with the subordinate. For these reasons, behaviour measurements are more reliable when they are based on observations by different people, e.g., an employee is rated by his or her supervisor, some peers, and some subordinates (where applicable). This approach should balance personal biases.

In the opinion of many experts, behaviour criteria are the most useful ones to measure training effectiveness, especially when the behaviour to be observed is specific and well-defined. And behaviour change is what most training programs are about. Don't we want to change ineffective behaviour into more effective behaviour? Even if the explicit objective of a training program is "increase in knowledge" we still hope that this will lead to improved performance; otherwise we would not undertake the training.

**5.** *Organizational results.* This criterion would be—as mentioned above—the ideal one were it not so difficult to determine a cause-effect relationship between a training program and organizational outcomes. The ultimate objective of all our training efforts is to improve the results of an organization as a whole. It takes a certain period of time until an effective training program has a strong enough impact on an organization so that such factors as profits, costs, waste, absenteeism, turnover, etc., improve significantly. Who dares to say that when profits go up and costs down that the training is to be credited for the change? Undoubtedly we will develop ways to link training with organizational results, but so far the attempts have been less than satisfactory.

## Evaluation Methodology

Experts in the field of evaluation research are divided on their answer to the question "Should the methodological design of an evaluation study be *strictly scientific* or can it be adjusted for practical purposes?'' One group says that without adherence to stringent scientific research methodology studies on evaluation are without value. Other practitioners suggest that anything will do as long as it adds to our knowledge and provides useful feedback. What is really at issue here is the value of feedback on one hand, and the strength of conclusions on the other. The first approach will yield strong evidence of cause-and-effect relationships, and the other approach results in weaker evidence because it uses less rigorous controls that are often difficult to apply in organizational settings.

"*Strictly scientific*" means *systematic and controlled*. Systematic implies a logical order, and controlled means that the investigator tries to rule out other causes than the ones being studied.

If the effects of different training methods on the outcome of a program are being studied, the investigator has to make sure that changes in outcomes are truly attributable to different methods and not to a different instructor, a different group, or a different environment.

Practical, on the other hand, means feasible, economical, reasonable. Practical and scientific are not necessarily mutually exclusive but it is often the case. Let us look at some examples to illustrate the problems.

A still very popular design is the one-shop case study where the instructor applies just one test at the end of a program.

Group 1:          T                O
              (treatment    (observation
              or training)   or outcome)

This approach is certainly systematic but it is not controlled. How does the instructor know that T really caused O? Perhaps the participants were already experienced enough and did not need the training in the first place. Of course, the instructor *assumes* that the participants did not know the subject of the course but the point is: how sure can he or she be? Of what value is this kind of "evaluation"?

A better approach is the one-group, pre-test-post-test design where the instructor applies a test at the beginning of the course to measure the precondition of the participants and, at the end of the course, to measure the change (hopefully improvement).

Group 1:          $O_1$          T          $O_2$

As an example: we measure the participants' knowledge prior to and after the training, but it could be attitudes, behaviour, or other criteria we are interested in. The important point is that we establish the exact conditions of the participants before we apply the treatment. Any change occurring can now be attributed to the training. Can it?

Let us look at a "realistic" situation and let us assume that we are dealing with a one- or two-week training program. During this time the following events take place:

1.  a new boss takes over the department where the participants are employed;
2.  several employees return from another seminar;
3.  a thousand workers are laid off in the plant;
4.  it was announced in the company newsletter that inflation hit a new high and that the company's market is in deep trouble.

It is agreed that these are strong assumptions. But we would like to make a point. Actually, we may add a dozen or more events and other factors of lesser impact that in one way or another shape employees' attitudes and behaviour.

If we look now at the outcome of the program we may have second thoughts. What really caused the observed change? If we want to determine cause and effect precisely or with a high degree of accuracy we have to control for these factors, i.e., eliminate other explanations.

In order to "control" for other factors we need a control group. Such a group consists of persons who are selected on the same basis — ideally at random — as the training group, the only difference being that the control group does not undergo training. An arrangement that offers a certain degree of control is the pre-test post-test control group design.

| Group 1: | $O_1$ | T | $O_2$ |
|---|---|---|---|
| Group 2: | $O_3$ | | $O_4$ |

Here we select the two groups (ideally on a random basis) before the training takes place; both will take the pre-test and the post-test, but only group 1 will undergo training.

Let us look at the possible outcomes. Observations No. 1 and No. 3 should indicate no or insignificant differences. If differences show up then the selection was probably biased, i.e., persons with certain abilities were assigned to a certain group. If the training program is effective $O_1$ and $O_2$ will indicate large differences, as will $O_2$ and $O_4$. If $O_1$ and $O_2$ are not very different, then the training manager had better review the program or check the effectiveness of the instructor. What if ($O_1$ and $O_2$) and ($O_3$ and $O_4$) are significantly different and $O_2$ and $O_4$ very little? Then we have the situation where factors other than the training program caused the change, e.g., the four events mentioned above.

There are more explanations. It is possible that the pre-test is a so-called sensitizer. When we ask supervisors about their attitudes towards authoritarian and democratic leadership, the questions alone may cause the supervisors to change their attitudes to a significant degree. (Whether they change their behaviour is a different matter.)

In order to control for this factor — sensitization — and others we need more sophisticated designs, e.g., the Solomon-four-group (developed by Professor Solomon).

| Group 1: | $O_1$ | T | $O_2$ |
|---|---|---|---|
| Group 2: | $O_3$ | | $O_4$ |
| Group 3: | | T | $O_5$ |
| Group 4: | | | $O_6$ |

We don't want to discuss the merits of this very effective research design here; they can be found elsewhere.[35] However, by now it is clear to every practitioner that this design is out of the question for most practical applications. In any organization it is already difficult enough to find one control group, let alone four. Only where a "captive audience" is available (students, soldiers, prisoners, patients) is it easier to use the Solomon design, and even there it is rarely done.

Besides the implication that the above described design is for most practical purposes not feasible (and even uneconomical) a second conclusion can be drawn: to be "scientific," i.e., systematic and controlled, is a matter of degree. The Solomon-four-group design is much more rigorous than the simpler pre-test post-test control group design; both are systematic and controlled, but controlled to a different degree.

Do we have to rely on control groups in order to get meaningful results? Not necessarily. In the following part, we will discuss so-called quasi-experimental designs that can be used with good results where control groups are difficult to find or are unavailable. These approaches offer less control of an evaluation study, but are more flexible with regard to which factors the investigator wants to control.

One very useful method for the practitioner undoubtedly is the time-series design (see Figure 9-7) which involves several periodic measurements after training without a control group.

$$O_1 \quad O_2 \quad O_3 \quad T \quad O_4 \quad O_5$$

This approach has the advantage that, for example, sensitization is controlled; e.g., if a test has a sensitizing effect it will show up as a difference between the measurements $O_1$ and $O_2$. Any additional effect should come from the training program. However, there

FIGURE 9-7

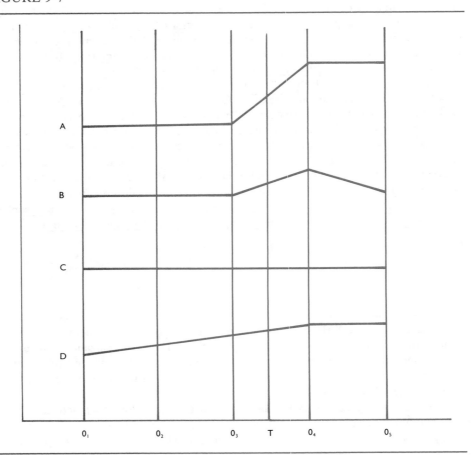

is still the possibility that at the same time that training was performed something happened in the organization which could have caused a change between $O_3$ and $O_4$, e.g., a new boss took over. Only if the investigator can rule out with "good conscience" any other explanation for an observed change the conclusion can be drawn that the effect was caused by the training program.

It may be helpful to look at the graphical illustration of the above described process and at different possible outcomes.

The pattern of outcome "A" indicates a strong effect, very likely attributable to the training program. "B" seems to demonstrate a weak and short-lasting result, while "C" shows no training impact at all. "D" may illustrate a sensitization process with training outcome being inconclusive. There are still other patterns possible and interpretation of the results must be left to the investigator.

If a program is repeated several times it may be possible to use a group of future participants as a control group. This is not the previously described pre-test post-test control group design where both, training and control group, are selected on a random basis. For the quasi-experimental approach — called the nonequivalent control group design — we just take any other group available, even a group from another department.

| Group 1: | $O_1$ | T | $O_2$ |
|---|---|---|---|
| Group 2: | $O_3$ | | $O_4$ |

It can easily be seen that this approach is not tightly controlled because very likely the groups will differ because of selection effects and the outcomes may be influenced by environmental effects, e.g., when a group begins training it may already be affected by those who completed the program. Still, it is much better than having no control group at all.

There are several other quasi-experimental designs that may be useful for certain situations, but a discussion of them in this chapter would go too far. However, if other approaches are needed it may be preferable for the uninitiated to ask an expert for advice.

It has been shown that there are more or less rigorous approaches to training evaluation studies. In turn this also implies more or less feasible, economical and reasonable designs. What does it mean to the evaluator in terms of what type of approach should be selected? We suggest choice of the method according to the purpose of the evaluation:

1.  If the results of the evaluation are to be used to develop a new theory, to support or reject an existing theory or model, or the publication of the outcome in a scholarly journal, then we should try to be as scientific as possible. The more rigorously controlled the study, the more valid and reliable are the results and conclusions based on it.

2.  If the goal is only feedback to the training manager and if he or she is reasonably sure that other factors are controlled — if other causes can be ruled out "with good conscience" — then less rigorous methods can be used. However, the less controlled a study is, the weaker is the basis for any conclusions.

    The conclusions that can be drawn from the discussion so far are:

1.  To be scientific, i.e. systematic and controlled, is a matter of degree.

2.  There are more or less useful designs for evaluators.

3.  It is possible to get useful and valid results with quasi-experimental designs without control groups.

4.  Evaluators should choose an evaluation design according to the *purpose of the results* and not according to rigid "scientific" standards.[36]

## Cost-Benefit Analysis

A training investment should be treated like any other investment decision. No manager worth his or her salt would invest a significant amount of money without an appropriate *cost-benefit analysis*. Such an analysis assesses the cost-effectiveness of a project or program. It also assists a trainer or human resource manager in demonstrating the contributions the training or human resource management department makes to the organization's profit.

Contributions to profit can be made through increasing revenues or by decreasing expenditures according to the formula:

$$\text{revenue} - \text{costs} = \text{profit}$$

Training can contribute to increased revenue by improving the performance of revenue-producing employees, either by increasing output or by reducing production costs or both. If training is used to increase productivity, then training costs have to be included in the pricing of the product. Figure 9-8 presents factors associated with different training activities.

FIGURE 9-8   Contributing Factors to Training Costs

| ACTIVITIES | COSTS |
|---|---|
| Needs analysis | Labour: consultant, clerical staff |
| Program development | Labour: consultant, clerical staff<br>Material: office material; video films |
| | Equipment rental |
| | Other potential costs: travel; accommodation; per diem expenses |
| Course delivery | Equipment<br>Room rental<br>Food<br>Trainers' salaries<br>Trainees' salaries<br>Lost production |
| Program evaluation | Evaluator's fee |
| | Travel and accommodation<br>(assuming external evaluator) |
| | Overhead costs: staff and clerical support, office space, utilities |

## Calculation of Costs

Let's assume that an auto repair shop employs twenty mechanics who earn $15 per hour. Benefits are calculated at $5 per hour, producing a total cost of $20 per hour. There is one master mechanic who is not involved in repair work. The average mechanic repairs three cars a day, generating a potential profit of $50 a car. However, because of faulty workmanship, one in three cars comes back for warranty work which takes an additional two hours to perform on the average, resulting in only two profitable repairs per mechanic a day. It is assumed that the workshop is open 250 days a year and that each mechanic works eight hours a day.

The owner learned that another repair shop had implemented a training program that reduced the cost of faulty repairs by 30%. Further inquiries revealed that such savings through training were actually quite common. He asked his master mechanic to develop an appropriate training program.

To assess the potential return on the training investment, it is necessary to determine the additional income resulting from training. We must calculate the increase in profit due to the reduction in faulty repairs. First we calculate the potential profit.

$$3 \text{ repairs} \times 20 \text{ mechanics} \times 250 \text{ days} = 15,000 \text{ repairs/year}$$

$$15,000 \text{ repairs} \times \$50 \text{ profit} = \$750,000 \text{ profit}$$

If all repairs were without fault, the auto repair shop would generate $750,000 in profit. Actually, one-third of a mechanic's time was used for rework, which did not allow him to generate profitable repairs; in other words, he performed one repair work per day for free. These costs must be subtracted from the profit. In addition, the profit that could have been generated if the mechanic had used his time fully for repairs must also be subtracted. These costs are calculated as follows (assuming two hours of repair time and that no new material is used and neglecting depreciation):

$$1 \text{ faulty repair} \times 20 \text{ mechanics} \times (2 \text{ hours repair time @ } \$20 + \$50 \text{ lost profit}) \times$$
$$250 \text{ days} = \$450,000$$

Close to 60% of the potential annual profit is lost due to faulty repairs.

To calculate the possible annual savings through training, subtract the post-training costs from the pre-training costs. The pre-training costs are calculated by multiplying the costs of bad repairs by the potential 30% savings due to less rework.

$$\$450,000 \times 30\% = \$135,000$$

Subtracting the post-training costs from the pre-training costs provides the additional gross income resulting from training.

$$\$450,000 - \$135,000 = \$315,000$$

If we assume a 50% tax on this additional income, the net income is $157,500 that could be generated through training.

Of course, the cost of the training program has to be taken into account also.

Cost of developing the program:

| | |
|---|---:|
| 30 days of the master mechanic's time at $60,000/year | $ 7,200 |
| Training material (handouts, manuals, films) | $ 5,000 |
| | Subtotal $12,200 |

Actual training (assuming 2 days for groups of 4 mechanics = 10 days):

| | |
|---|---:|
| 10 days of master mechanic's time | $ 2,400 |
| Materials and equipment | $ 4,200 |
| 20 mechanics for 16 hours at $20/hour | $6,400 |
| Lost profit (potential profit — cost of faulty repairs for two days) (20 mechanics × 2 × 3 repairs × $50 profit) − (20 mechanics × 2 × $50 in lost profits)* = $6,000 − $2,000 | $ 4,000 |
| Meals, coffee, juice, muffins | $ 1,000 |
| | Subtotal $18,000 |

Overhead:

| | |
|---|---:|
| Using company formula | $ 5,500 |
| | Total Training Costs $35,700 |

*20 mechanics would have generated at least one faulty repair each per day.

Looking at these figures, it appears that the owner of the auto repair shop has invested $35,700 and received a $157,500 return. This amounts to a 441% return on a one-year investment. This figure is not as unrealistic as it sounds. Improvements in performance or reductions in costs of 10 or 20% through training is not unusual, depending on the complexity of the job. A training department worth its money should have no problem in accomplishing performance improvements of this magnitude.

## CROSS-CULTURAL MANAGEMENT TRAINING

One would expect, given the increased importance of international business and the worldwide expansion of international trade, that cross-cultural management training would be a common practice in multinational companies. Several studies have shown that this is not the case. One study found that only 50% of the fifty largest multinational corporations in North America provided some type of predeparture training. The percentage dropped to 33 when a larger number of companies was investigated (127).[37] One Canadian study revealed that none of twenty-five multinational companies did offer any preparation for their employees for working abroad.[38] This is the more surprising since the cost of inadequate training has been well documented, ranging from the loss of business deals worth millions of dollars, the break-up of profitable joint-ventures, and the loss of valuable local employees, to high turnover rates and premature returns among maladjusted overseas employees.[39]

There are several reasons for the lack of proper cross-cultural management training:

1.  The temporary nature of many such assignments.
2.  Lack of time because of the immediacy of the need for the employee overseas.
3.  The trend towards employment of local nationals.
4.  Doubt about the need for special training.
5.  Parallel doubt about the effectiveness of existing training programs.[40]

## Methods of Cross-Cultural Training

### Sensitivity Training

Several organizations have used *sensitivity training* as a method to prepare managers for overseas assignments. The aims of sensitivity training seem to be well-suited for that purpose since they include:

1.  Increased self-insight or self-awareness perceiving one's own behaviour and its meaning in a social context.
2.  Increased sensitivity to the behaviour of others.
3.  Increased awareness and understanding of the types of processes that facilitate or inhibit group functioning and the interaction between different groups.
4.  Heightened diagnostic skills in social, interpersonal, and intergroup situations.
5.  Increased action skill (referring to ability to intervene successfully in inter- and intragroup situations).
6.  Learning how to learn.[41]

### Culture Assimilators

*Culture assimilator* is a training method that consists of a series of episodes dealing with interpersonal issues in a cross-cultural situation. By responding to the individual episodes and referring to the explanations describing why their responses were appropriate or not, trainees have an opportunity to test their cross-cultural effectiveness and to learn about the appropriate responses in a specific culture. The method has one drawback: each culture requires a different assimilator, which makes it costly. Studies have shown that assimilator-trained subjects generally perform better in another culture than subjects who did not receive training.[42]

### Critical Incidents

Closely related to the culture assimilator method is the use of *critical incidents*. Consisting of a collection of short cases, they can be used to illustrate and to provide valuable insight into problems that might confront a visitor in a foreign culture.[43]

### Cases

Somewhat similar to critical incidents is the case method. The difference lies in the greater detail and complexity of cases. A variety of cross-cultural problems in management can be described in a single case. The trainee is asked to interpret, analyze, discuss, and find solutions to the problem. Cases in different functional management areas (e.g., marketing, finance, human resource management) and from many countries are available from different sources, notably from the Intercollegiate Case Clearinghouse of Harvard University and the University of Western Ontario.

### Role Playing

The *role play* method is a semi-structured activity. Participants are given a description of a certain situation with specific role instructions, but no script. The participants have to improvise. The results usually reveal personal values and biases that can be analyzed and discussed. A significant learning experience can be achieved if participants are asked to advocate a position that is contrary to their own beliefs.[44] Studies indicate that this method is relatively effective in changing a person's attitudes.[45]

### Simulation

A popular cross-cultural training method is *simulation*, the best known simulation game being Ba Fa' Ba Fa'. Participants are divided into two cultures, Alpha and Beta. After learning the "rules" of their own culture, participants have to interact with members of the other culture. Since the interaction rules for each culture are different, confusion and frustration, even hostility, result. These experiences are discussed at a debriefing session.[46]

It is unlikely that any single method will be sufficient to prepare an employee for the complex experiences that lie ahead when going abroad. More likely, a combination of the methods described will be most effective, as people react differently to different methods.

## Dimensions of Cross-Cultural Behaviour

Perhaps one of the reasons why so little cross-cultural management training is offered may be that there is no clear understanding of what the objectives and the content of such training should be. What is really required of a manager in order to be effective in a job in a foreign country? We certainly want the manager to develop effective job behaviour; that is, communication patterns, ways of decision making, information gathering and dispensing, giving orders, cooperation and coordination with native managers, interpersonal relationships, and others. But behaviour change is probably not enough. Trainers have to look at changes at three levels:

1. *Cognitive*: This stage emphasizes knowledge about another culture; for example, customs, values, and social institutions through reading books, observing films, etc.

2. *Affective*: At this stage an attempt is made to change the attitudes of trainees towards another culture by exposing them to stimuli from this culture and being asked to respond to it; for example, through critical incidents, culture assimilator, case studies.

3. *Behavioral*: This is the applied stage. Trainees are expected to behave appropriately

under certain conditions in different situations; for example, through role playing, simulation, experiential exercises.[47]

An analysis of the data from many cross-cultural studies results in the following list of widely accepted dimensions of cross-cultural management training:

1. *Cultural sensitivity*: understanding one's own culture and its impact on own behaviour.
2. *Sensitivity* towards others' behaviour.
3. *General knowledge about target culture*: historical development, values, customs, social institutions.
4. *Tolerance*: acceptance of different values, customs, behaviours.
5. *Ability to adapt*: that is, to adapt behaviour appropriately; understand social relations, such as superior-subordinate relationships, relations between sexes, and different age groups; willingness to eat local food; willingness to develop social ties with natives.
6. *Ability to translate and apply newly acquired insights and skills in an organizational environment*: that is, to relate the parent company's system to that of the local organization and vice versa.[48]

These six dimensions should serve as the key learning principles in any cross-cultural management training, regardless of target group. Executives and blue-collar workers going abroad need these characteristics to be effective in a different cultural environment.

Knowing about these training objectives should enable training managers to determine the appropriate training methods by which these objectives can be accomplished. As mentioned before, it is likely that no single approach will be sufficient, but a combination of different methods, e.g., reading books and articles, participating in sensitivity training, doing some case analyses, experiencing role playing, and perhaps going through some simulations. Each method will accomplish something different, thus providing a trainee with a better overall cross-cultural preparation.

## SUMMARY

After workers have gone through an orientation program, they still may lack the necessary skills, attitudes, or knowledge to perform their jobs successfully. This deficiency is remedied through training, which begins with needs assessment. Then specific training objectives can be set. These objectives give direction to the training program and serve to evaluate the training program at its completion.

The content of the program depends upon the training objectives. The design of the training should consider such learning principles as participation, repetition, relevance, transference, and feedback.

Once training is completed, it should be evaluated. Evaluations include a pretest, a posttest, measurement of how well the training content has been transferred to the actual job, and some form of follow-up studies to ensure that the learning has been retained.

A cost-benefit analysis should be conducted whenever possible to assess the contributions any training program makes to the profits of the company.

Cross-cultural management training is an essential part of a company's plans to conduct business abroad. A combination of methods will ensure that trainees will get a minimum exposure to the many pitfalls they will encounter when they assume a position in another culture. Knowing about the objectives of cross-cultural training allows trainers to choose the most appropriate training methods for a predeparture program.

## TERMS FOR REVIEW

Needs assessment
Nominal Group Technique (NGT)
Learning curve
Learning principles
Repetition
Transference
Feedback
Job instruction training
Vestibule training

Role playing
Behaviour modelling
Laboratory training
Obsolescence
Career plateau
Turnover
Cost-benefit analysis
Cross-cultural management
   training

## REVIEW AND DISCUSSION QUESTIONS

1.  For each of the following occupations, which training techniques do you recommend? Why?
    (a)  A cashier in a grocery store
    (b)  A welder
    (c)  An assembly-line worker
    (d)  An inexperienced supervisor

2.  If you were directed to design a development program for managers that made use of all five learning principles, which two training techniques would you combine? Why?

3.  Suppose you were a supervisor in an accounting department and the training manager wanted to implement a new training program to teach bookkeepers how to complete some new accounting forms. What steps would you recommend to evaluate the effectiveness of the training program?

4.  Assume you were hired to manage a research and development department. After a few weeks you noticed that some researchers were more effective than others, and that the less effective ones received little recognition from their more productive counterparts. What forms of development would you consider for both groups?

5.  What is the purpose of a cost-benefit analysis?

6.  What factors do you take into account for a cost-benefit analysis?

7.  Explain the dimensions of cross-cultural management training.

8. What method(s) would you recommend to train a supervisor destined to go to Japan for a three-year assignment on a joint venture with mainly Japanese employees? Why?

## INCIDENT 9-1

### Development of Human Resources at General Hospital

Clayton Dahl was appointed director of human resource development at General Hospital. The hospital director, Andrea Hess, suggested that Clayton could best familiarize himself with the hospital's development needs by compiling a report about past development efforts.

In gathering the information for the report, Clayton made several interesting observations:

- Development activities had been limited to preparing nonprofessionals to assume supervisory positions.

- Most department managers and staff directors took the attitude that it was easier to hire staff as it was needed than to develop present employees.

- Those managers who supervised professional hospital employees took the attitude that development is the responsibility of each professional.

- Most other managers viewed development programs as an admission of inability by those who took them voluntarily.

- During each of the last three years, the development budget had been cut by about 10%.

1. What would you recommend if you were in Clayton's position?
2. What type of support should Clayton seek from the hospital administrator?
3. If a new development program is offered, what type of attendance policy should Clayton set? Why? What types of problems will that policy cause?

## INCIDENT 9-2

### Perils of Process Evaluations

Carl Treadway, an experienced instructor in a provincial community college system, has filed a grievance through the instructors' union against his department chairman, dean, college, and the administration of the community college system. His grievance alleges that he was denied a reasonable salary increase for the past three years because the quality of his teaching was wrongfully evaluated as substandard. His complaint alleges (and the college officials admit) that teaching performance at Treadway's college is based solely upon the evaluation forms students fill out in classes. The evaluations use a standardized questionnaire, on which the students mark such items as the instructor's attendance, enthusiasm, knowledge of the subject, teaching effectiveness, organization, fairness in marking, and similar items. Treadway's argument is that students' evaluations are helpful to the instructor in improving the course and making the students who enrol more satisfied, but that they are an inaccurate and unreliable measure for purposes of salary increment decisions.

Because the case has nationwide implications (nearly every college and university uses essentially the same system), the provincial department of education has retained your services as a consultant. They would like you to examine the following issues.

1. What is good or bad teaching performance?
2. In what ways might student evaluations misrepresent the actual teaching performance of an instructor by making it look better or worse?
3. Student evaluations are fundamentally a process measure of effectiveness. If an instructor disagreed with the results of his/her student evaluations, what other process or outcome information could he/she introduce to give his/her side of the story?

○ ○ ○ ○ ○ ○ ○ ○ ○ ○ ○ ○ ○ ○ ○ ○ ○ ○ ○ ○ ○ ○ ○ ○ ○ ○ ○ ○ ○ ○ ○ ○ ○ ○ ○ ○ ○ ○ ○ ○

*CASE STUDY*

### HIRING, ORIENTATION, AND TRAINING AT FUJI COMMUNICATIONS INTERNATIONAL, INC., AND CANADIAN TELECOMMUNICATIONS INTERNATIONAL, INC.

Fuji Communications International (FCI) is a joint venture between Canadian Telecommunications International (CTI) and Fuji Electronics (FE), a Japanese company. The Canadian partner holds a 51% share of the joint venture. Its headquarters is in Sagamihara, a suburb of Tokyo. It has several manufacturing plants across Japan, one near Osaka, a second one in Sagamihara, and a third near Sapporo in Hokkaido, the northernmost island.

The joint venture employs approximately 22,000 employees, 600 of whom are employed at its headquarters in Sagamihara. The president of the joint venture is Japanese, as are most vice presidents and directors. The highest ranking Canadian is the senior vice president, who is in charge of finance.

The human resource management department (HRMD) at FCI is the largest of all departments, with a staff of sixty-two at headquarters alone, or approximately one full-time staff for every 350 employees. If one adds to this the HRM staff at all three plants, it amounts to 115, or one full-time staff member for every 190 employees. This compares with approximately one full-time HRM staff for every 250 to 300 employees with large Western employers.

The executive of FCI will not make any important decisions without input from its vice president of human resource management. As a result, the HR department is always up to date on the long-range objectives of top management and can plan accordingly.

The top management of the joint venture feels that hiring decisions are one of the most crucial decisions management has to make. If the wrong person is chosen, the company will feel the effects for years to come, especially because FCI follows the Japanese tradition of lifetime employment for its permanent work force.

FCI also follows the traditional Japanese way of hiring employees, by going directly to colleges and universities to hire candidates without any business experience. Japanese employers prefer inexperienced new employees because of the danger of "contamination," meaning being indoctrinated by a different business philosophy.

The joint venture is in constant contact with instructors and professors at high schools, colleges, and universities. These contacts are maintained through small research grants or other "amenities," mainly to get referrals of good students from the instructors.

Each year FCI hires between 100 and 200 white-collar employees, most of them as management trainees. For this purpose, the joint venture solicits about 1000 applications from its contacts at high schools, colleges, and universities. All applicants will be run through a procedure that weeds out about half of them: a careful analysis of school records; a battery of tests that ask mainly factual material, such as historical, political, geographical, or international information; and an essay-type test that reflects both common sense and business sense.

The remaining applicants are invited to the company's headquarters in Sagamihara where they will undergo multi-tier personal interviews with junior and senior executives. This process eliminates another 50%.

The surviving 200 or 250 are screened again. Does anybody in the family work for a competitor? Did the candidate belong to a radical student organization? Has the candidate ever had any encounter with the law? Has anybody in the family been convicted of a crime? Out go the applicants who answer yes to any one of these questions. That leaves about the required number of employees the company planned to hire.

The new employees will undergo a rigorous orientation and indoctrination program that lasts approximately three months. The first day is spent mainly in the auditorium, listening to speeches by top executives who discuss the history of the company (in this case the parent company), extol the virtues and accomplishments of the company's past leaders, and explain the current status of the company in the Japanese and world market. The rest of the week they will be shown around the plant, meet with their supervisors, and be introduced to their work teams.

The main purpose of the indoctrination program is to instil pride in the new employee and make him* identify with the company (Japanese employees proudly wear the company button in their lapels and introduce themselves as "Tanaka from Fuji Computer"), and to create commitment and loyalty in him. It is now easier to understand why an employee who has undergone an indoctrination program in another company will have difficulties adjusting to a different company philosophy and spirit.

This process shows to what extraordinary length FCI goes to insure that the right hiring decision is made. And FCI is not an exception among Japanese companies. Once an employee is hired, there is no backing out of the implicit contract. Even if it turns out that a hiring decision was wrong, the employee will not be let go. He may progress a little more slowly and will not rise as high as his peers, but he will have job security.** And the commitment is mutual.

After the orientation and indoctrination

---

*"His" and "him" are used throughout this case because very few, if any, permanent female employees are hired.

**Of course in extreme cases there are ways to get rid of undesirable employees. One typical Japanese way to get rid of an employee is to give him the "window desk," a desk in a separate room, with no telephone and no in and out basket. The employee is virtually ignored until he quits voluntarily. A Westerner may think that this would be an easy way to make a living, but for the group-dependent Japanese employee, it is living hell.

program, the actual training begins. Employees are hired with little regard to their study topics because it is not expected that they will have any job-related experiences and training (the exception being an engineer). The first two years on the job are usually spent rotating through the organization, under constant training, until the trainee has had experiences in many different departments.

A "godfather," usually a senior employee, will track the progress of the trainee. He will be in touch with the various supervisors under whose direction the trainee will learn the ropes, will monitor his progress, and will be available to the trainee for help if problems arise.

Annual evaluations will look at two main characteristics of the trainee: business ability and work attitudes. The former contains such items as ability to administer staff, ability to work harmoniously within a team, decisiveness, prejudices, perception, judgement, concentration, planning, negotiating ability, and business knowledge. Work attitudes are measured by such criteria as following proper reporting procedures, keeping apart personal and professional matters, accepting responsibility, maintaining required office hours, and obeying company regulations.

After two years of constant training under close supervision and monitoring, the godfather, managers, and the trainee jointly will decide for which position he is best suited. As mentioned, this may not be related to what the employee has studied. To the Japanese, it is much more important how motivated the employee is and how he fits into the organization rather than what his skills are.

This orientation and training program ensures that the employee has a thorough knowledge of all aspects of the organization and is a true generalist. When needed, the employee can take on any job in the organization. He will take into account the needs of other departments when he makes decisions in his own realm. Here we see the systems approach applied in a way it rarely happens in a Western company.

There is another interesting aspect of the Japanese attitude towards training. Japanese companies are not afraid to invest heavily in training because they are assured that the employee will be with them for the rest of his life.

For example, FCI sends some of its most promising trainees to a special management training program lasting three months, offered by a management training centre set up by Keidanren (the Japanese equivalent to the Canadian Manufacturers Association, but much more powerful and influential). The cost for the program is $12,000 for each participant. Not many North American companies would be willing to risk such an amount as an investment into the training of one employee.

### Training in the Canadian Parent Company

The Canadian partner, Canadian Telecommunications International (CTI), conducts its training programs in the typical North American way. CTI hires its management trainees mainly from Canadian universities through advertisements and campus screening interviews. Candidates are then invited for an interview at corporate headquarters where the human resource manager does the initial job interview and provides a short list to department managers who conduct a hiring interview and make the final hiring decision.

Hiring criteria are based on (in descending order of priority):

1. University grades, especially in field of specialization;
2. Extra-curricular activities (whether the candidate played any leadership role during his/her study period, e.g., in student organizations);
3. Relevant job experiences (desirable, but not essential);

4. Language skills (especially second official language);

5. Personal impression during interview.

Candidates are hired according to their specialties, e.g., marketing, finance, accounting, engineering. They go through a two-day orientation program during which executives explain company policies and goals and HRM specialists talk about career paths and the benefit package. Following the orientation, employees are introduced by their supervisors to their work teams and given their first assignment. After six months the new employees have their first performance review. If supervisors identify specific shortcomings,

they will recommend either available internal training programs or, if not, relevant outside programs for which CTI will pay the fees if the employee completes them successfully.

CTI has a training department (TD) with a manager and three instructors. The TD conducts annual training needs analyses by asking supervisors to make suggestions as to what topics should be offered during the following year. The training manager then decides whether it is feasible to develop an internal training program or whether it will be less costly to send employees to programs offered elsewhere.

1. Analyze the strengths and weaknesses of the two approaches to training.

2. The Japanese educational system emphasizes personal development and a broad education and leaves the training of job-related skills to employers. The Canadian system emphasizes a more narrow specialized education and focuses on job-related skills (marketing, finance, etc.). In your opinion, which system is more suitable to produce effective managers? Why?

3. Which system is more costly? Which system is more cost efficient? Which system provides the better long-range training investment for the company? For the employees? For the industry? For the country?

4. Could both companies benefit from looking at each other's training approach? What could they learn that would be to their advantage?

○ ○ ○ ○ ○ ○ ○ ○ ○ ○ ○ ○ ○ ○ ○ ○ ○ ○ ○ ○ ○ ○ ○ ○ ○ ○ ○ ○ ○ ○ ○ ○ ○ ○ ○ ○ ○ ○ ○ ○ ○ ○ ○

## SUGGESTED READINGS

Camp, Richard R., P. N. Blanchard and G. E. Huszczo, *Toward a More Organizationally Effective Training Strategy and Practice*, Reston, Va.: Reston Publishing Company, 1986

Cascio, Wayne F., *Costing Human Resources: The Financial Impact of Behavior in Organizations*, Belmont, California: Kent Publishing Company, 1982.

Harris, Philip R., and Robert T. Moran, *Managing Cultural Differences*, Houston, Texas: Gulf Publishing Company, 1979.

Kearsley, Greg, *Costs, Benefits and Productivity in Training Systems*, Reading, Mass.: Addison-Wesley Publishing Company, 1982.

Laird, Dugan, *Approaches to Training and Development*, 2nd ed., Reading, Mass.: Addison-Wesley Publishing Company, 1985.

Moran, Robert T., and Philip R. Harris, *Managing Cultural Synergy*, Houston, Texas: Gulf Publishing Company, 1982.

Tung, Rosalie L., *The New Expatriates: Managing Human Resources Abroad*, Philadelphia, Penn.: Ballinger Publishing, 1988.

Wesley, Kenneth N. and Gary P. Latham, *Developing and Training Human Resources in Organizations*, Dallas, Texas: Scott, Foresman and Company, 1981.

# REFERENCES

1. James L. Hayes, "Human Resources—The Last Resource of a Frontier Society," *Training and Development Journal,* June 1976, p. 9.

2. Herbert E. Striner, "Retraining Displaced Workers: Too Little, Too Late?" *Business Week,* July 19, 1982, p. 178.

3. Gale E. Newell, "How to Plan a Training Program," *Personnel Journal,* May 1976, pp. 220-224. See also Bonnye L. Matthes and Virginia Sweet Lincoln, "Try S.T.A.R.T.: The Systematic Training Aid Resource Tool," *Training,* January 1978, pp. 32-33; and S. D. Inderlied and D. L. Bates, "A Practical Approach to Determining Training Solvable Problems," *Personnel Journal,* January 1980, pp. 121-125. See also Donald B. Miller, "Training Managers to Stimulate Employee Development," *Training and Development Journal,* February 1981, pp. 47-53.

4. Linda Gutvi, "Trainers Must Tie in to Strategic Visions," *Canadian HR Reporter,* October 3, 1988, p. 10.

5. This figure is a composite derived from the following sources: Labour Canada, *Education and Working Canadians: Report of the Commission of Inquiry on Educational Leave and Productivity,* Ottawa, June 1979, and Employment and Immigration Canada, *Labour Market Development in the 1980's: Report of the Task Force on Labour Market Development,* Ottawa, 1981, p. 153. See also Ian Morrison and Paul Belanger (eds.), "Manpower Training at the Crossroads," proceedings of A Conference on Adult Education in Canada, Canadian Association for Adult Education, January 1976; and Roy T. Adams, "Toward a More Competent Labour Force," *Relations Industrielles,* Vol. 35, No. 3, 1980, pp. 422-436.

6. Thomas F. Gilbert, "The High Cost of Knowledge," *Personnel,* March 1976, p. 23.

7. William C. Byham and James Robinson, "Building Supervisory Confidence—A Key to Transfer of Training," *Personnel Journal,* May 1977, pp. 248-250,253.

8. John W. Lawrie, "A Guide to Customized Leadership Training and Development," *Personnel Journal,* September 1979, pp. 593-596.

9. "Employee Training," *Personnel Management: Policies and Practices,* Englewood Cliffs, N.J.: Prentice-Hall, 1979, p. 9.

10. Kenneth N. Wexley and Gary P. Latham, *Developing and Training Human Resources in Organizations,* Dallas, Texas: Scott, Foresmann and Company, 1981, p. 35.

11. Mariless S. Niehoff and M. Jay Romans, "Needs Assessment as Step One toward Enhancing Productivity," *Personnel Administrator,* May 1982, pp. 35-39.

12. Andre Delbecq and A. Van de Ven, "A Group Process Model for Problem Identification and Program Planning," *Journal of Applied Behavioral Science,* August 1971, pp. 78-83. See also Mark Martinko and Jim Gepson, "Nominal Grouping and Needs Analysis," in Francis L. Ulschak (ed.), *Human Resource Development: The Theory and Practice of Needs Assessment,* Reston, Va.: Reston Publishing Company, 1983, pp. 101-110.

13. Martinko and Gepson, op. cit.

14. Byham and Robinson, op. cit.

15. Ernest D. Jobe, W. Randy Boxx, and D. L. Howell, "A Customized Approach to Management Development," *Personnel Journal,* March 1979, pp. 150-153.

16. Joseph Yeager, "Coaching the Executive: Can You Teach an Old Dog New Tricks?" *Personnel Administrator,* November 1982, pp. 37-42.

17. Stephen J. Carroll, Frank T. Paine, and John M. Ivancevich, "The Relative Effectiveness of Training Methods — Expert Opinion and Research," *Personnel Psychology,* Autumn 1972, p. 499.

18. Ibid.

19. Henry P. Sims, Jr., and Charles C. Manz, "Modeling Influences on Employee Behavior," *Personnel Journal,* January 1982, p. 58.

20. Ibid.

21. See also John W. Newstrom, "Evaluating the Effectiveness of Training Methods," *The Personnel Administrator,* January 1980, pp. 55-60.

22. John R. Hinrichs, "Personnel Training," in Marvin D. Dunnette (ed.). *Handbook of Industrial and Organizational Psychology,* Chicago: Rand McNally, 1976, pp. 850-851.

23. M. Williams, "The Current Acceptance of CBT," *The Human Resource,* April-May 1987, pp. 10-11.

24. Williams, 1987, op. cit., p. 10.

25. Edward J. Mandt, "A Basic Model of Manager Development," *Personnel Journal,* June 1979, pp. 395-400. See also Alfred W. Hill, "How Organizational Philosophy Influences Management Development," *Personnel Journal,* February 1980, pp. 118-120,148.

26. Elmer Burack and Gopal Pati, "Technology and Managerial Obsolescence," *MSU Business Topics,* Spring 1970, pp. 49-56. See also Herbert Kaufman, *Obsolescence and Professional Career Development,* New York: AMACOM, 1974.

27. Christopher M. Dawson, "Will Career Plateauing Become a Bigger Problem?" *Personnel Journal,* January 1983, pp. 78-81.

28. Morley D. Glicken, "A Counseling Approach to Employee Burnout," *Personnel Journal,* March 1983, pp. 222-228. See also Jack Brewer and Carol Dubnicki, "Relighting the Fire with an Employee Revitalization Program," *Personnel Journal,* October 1983, pp. 812-818.

29. Labour Canada, "Education and Working Canadians," Report of the Commission of Inquiry on Educational Leave and Productivity, June 1979.

30. K. Weiermair, "Industrial Training and Industrial Excellence: Canada's Record in International Perspective," paper presented at the Ninth Annual Management Research Forum, Wilfrid Laurier University, September 1978.

31. "In the News," *Fortune,* February 27, 1979, pp. 15-16.

32. William B. Werther, Jr., "Management Turnover Implication of Career Mobility," *The Personnel Administrator,* February 1977, pp. 63-66. See also Simeon J. Touretzky, "Changing Attitudes: A Question of Loyalty," *The Personnel Administrator,* April 1979, pp. 35-36.

33. Hermann F. Schwind, "Thoughts on Training Evaluation," *Canadian Training Methods,* Vol. 7, No. 1, June 1975, pp. 14-15.

34. Hermann F. Schwind, "Issues in Training Evaluation: The Criterion," *Canadian Training Methods,* Vol. 7, No. 4, October 1975, pp. 14-15.

35. D. T. Campbell and J. C. Stanley, *Experimental and Quasi-*

*Experimental Design,* Chicago: Rand McNally College Publishing Co., 1963.

36. Hermann F. Schwind, "Issues in Training Evaluation: The Methodology," *Canadian Training Methods,* Vol. 7, No. 3, August 1975, pp. 22-25.

37. John Baker and John Ivancevich, "The Assignment of American Executives Abroad: Systematic, Haphazard, or Chaotic?" *California Management Review,* Spring 1971, pp. 39-44.

38. P. W. L. Wong, "An Investigation of Cross-Cultural Preparatory Programs Offered by Canadian Companies for Managers Posted Overseas," unpublished Master's Thesis, Saint Mary's University, 1987.

39. Philip R. Harris, "Cultural Awareness Training for Human Resource Development," *Training and Development Journal 33,* 1979, pp. 64-74; see also Philip R. Harris and Dorothy L. Harris, "Training for Cultural Understanding," *Training and Development Journal,* May 9, 1972, pp. 8-10; A. R. Lanier, "Planning for the Human Factor in Your Overseas Moves," *International Business,* May-June 1977; H. F. Schwind, "Personnel Problems in International Companies and Joint Ventures in Japan," Unpublished Master's Thesis, Seattle: University of Washington, 1972; W. O. Shabaz, "Cross-Cultural Orientation for Overseas Employees," *The Personnel Administrator,* 23, 1978. pp. 54-57.

40. R. D. Robinson, *International Business Management,* Hinsdale, Ill.: Dryden Press, 1973.

41. J. P. Campbell and M. D. Dunnette, "Effectiveness of T-Group Experiences in Managerial Training and Development," *Psychological Bulletin,* 70, 1968, pp. 73-104.

42. M. M. Chemers, F. E. Fiedler, D. Lekhyananda, and L. M. Stolusow, "Some Effects of Cultural Training on Leadership in Hetero-Cultural Task Groups," *International Journal of Psychology, 1,* 1966, pp. 301-314.

43. R. N. Farmer, *Incidents in International Business* (3rd ed.), Bloomington, Indiana: Cedarwood Press, 1980.

44. F. M. Culberson, "Modification of an Emotionally Held Attitude Through Role-Playing," *Journal of Abnormal and Social Psychology, 54,* March 1957, pp. 230-233.

45. B. T. King and I. L. Janis, "Comparison of the Effectiveness of Improvised versus Non-Improvised Role-Playing in Producing Opinion change," *Human Relations* May 1956, pp. 177-186; see also W. A. Scott, "Attitude Change through Reward of Verbal Behavior," *Journal of Abnormal and Social Psychology,* 55, July 1957, pp. 72-75.

46. R. G. Shirts, *Ba Fa' Ba Fa', a Cross-Culture Simulation.* Del Mar, Calif.: Sirrile, 1977.

47. G. R. Smith and G. G. Otero, *Teaching about Cultural Awareness.* Denver, Co.: Center for Research and Education, 1977.

48. H. F. Schwind, "The State of the Art in Cross-Cultural Management Training," *International HRD Annual,* Vol. 1, R. Doktor (ed.), American Society for Training and Development, Washington, D.C., 1985.

# CHAPTER *10* ○○○○○○

# *CAREER PLANNING*

> *Organizations are in a position to provide assessment and career planning programs for their employees so that more realistic and realizable aspirations are developed. These programs must also give due consideration to the personal life needs and goals. . . .*
> RONALD J. BURKE AND TAMARA WEIR[1]

> *In the search for miracle workers to turn their firms into giants, some crazed executives often hire and fire employees with great regularity.*
> DR. SRULLY BLOTNICK[2]

○ ○ ○ ○ ○ ○ ○ ○ ○ ○ ○ ○ ○ ○ ○ ○ ○ ○ ○ ○ ○ ○ ○ ○ ○ ○ ○ ○ ○ ○

## *CHAPTER OBJECTIVES*

After studying this chapter, you should be able to:
1. **Advise** someone about the major points in career planning.
2. **Describe** how human resource departments encourage and assist career planning.
3. **Identify** the major advantages of career planning.
4. **Explain** the relationship between career planning and career development.
5. **List** the major actions that aid career development.

○ ○ ○ ○ ○ ○ ○ ○ ○ ○ ○ ○ ○ ○ ○ ○ ○ ○ ○ ○ ○ ○ ○ ○ ○ ○ ○ ○ ○ ○

*A career* is all the jobs that are held during one's working life. For some people, these jobs are part of a careful plan. For others, their career is simply a matter of luck. These two extremes are illustrated in the following dialogue between a retired bank executive and an assistant manager of a branch bank.

JOE:    I didn't make it to executive vice president of a major bank by chance. I wanted to be a banking executive since I was a customer service clerk trainee. Sure I worked hard, but I also tried to plan my career.

JOAN:    Career planning is a waste of time. There are too many variables. Who knows which openings will occur? Besides, promotions are largely a matter of luck, a matter of being in the right place at the right time.

JOE:    I agree, luck plays a part. But you would not be an assistant branch manager if you didn't have some university education.

JOAN:    Well, sure, that's true. But whether I make branch manager is mostly luck.

JOE:    Is it? Don't you think you can control your future to some extent? Don't you believe that a promotion is more likely if you develop the background needed to function as a branch manager? If your performance as a branch manager is superior to other branch managers, don't you think that your chances of promotion will be better? There are many things you can do to increase your changes of career success.

But merely planning a career does not guarantee success. Superior performance, experience, education, and some occasional luck play an important part. But when people like Joan rely almost wholly on luck, they seldom are prepared for opportunities that arise. To be ready for career opportunities, successful people develop career plans and then take action to achieve their plans. Simply stated, a successful career needs to be managed through careful planning. If it is not, employees are seldom ready for career opportunities, and human resource departments find it extremely difficult to meet their internal staffing needs.[3]

Some people fail to manage their careers because they are unaware of the basic concept of career planning described in Figure 10-1. They do not realize that goals can shape their career and yield greater success. As a result, their planning is left to fate and their development rests in the hands of others. Awareness of the concepts in the figure is no guarantee of action. But when awareness leads to goal setting, career planning is more likely to occur. For example, if Joan set a goal of becoming a branch bank manager in two years, that goal would lead her to the next question: How do I achieve the goal? If Joan answers that question by taking a special bank management course, she becomes better prepared to be a branch manager and her chances for promotion increase.

## FIGURE 10-1    Selected Career Planning Terms

- **Career.** A career is all the jobs that are held during one's working life.
- **Career path.** A career path is the sequential pattern of jobs that forms one's career.
- **Career goals.** Career goals are the future positions one strives to reach as part of a career. These goals serve as benchmarks along one's career path.
- **Career planning.** Career planning is the process by which one selects career goals and the path to those goals.
- **Career development.** Career development is the process by which one undertakes personal improvements to achieve a personal career plan.

FIGURE 10-2   Career Path for a Retired Senior Vice President in the Banking Industry

| JOB NUMBER | JOB LEVEL | JOB TITLE | TYPE OF CHANGE | YEARS ON JOB | ENDING AGE |
|---|---|---|---|---|---|
| 1 | Worker | Customer Service Clerk Trainee | | ½ | 22 |
| 2 | Worker | Customer Service Clerk | Promotion | 5 | 27 |
| 3 | Supervising | Supervisor Customer Service | Promotion | 2 | 29 |
| 4 | Supervising | Loan Officer | Change in duties only | 2 | 31 |
| 5 | Management | Accounts Manager | Promotion and transfer | 2 | 33 |
| 6 | Management | Branch Manager | Promotion and transfer | 2 | 35 |
| 7 | Management | Branch Manager | Transfer | 3 | 38 |
| 8 | Management | District Manager | Promotion | 5 | 43 |
| 9 | Management | District Manager | Transfer (CGA) | 6 | 49 |
| 10 | Executive | Vice President (Finance) | Resignation and promotion | 6 | 55 |
| 11 | Executive | Senior V.P. (Finance) | Promotion | 10 | 65 |

Although every person's career is unique, a review of Joe's career in the banking industry shows how career planning works in practice. Joe's progress is summarized in Figure 10-2 and explained below.

- Four years after graduating from high school, Joe joined the Bank of New Brunswick as a customer service clerk trainee. At that point in his career his goal was to become a banking executive. He had no idea of the *career path* he would follow. But Joe realized that his first step would be to become a supervisor. This *career planning* caused him to enrol in the evening degree-program of a nearby university. During the next nine years he also entered some training programs organized by the local Board of Trade. These *career development* actions were the first of many that Joe undertook. He received two promotions and then at the age of thirty was made a loan officer.

- After he completed his degree, Joe was promoted to accounts manager and was transferred. Although the new job did not give him much of a salary raise in real terms (since the cost of living in the new city where he was to go was comparatively very high), Joe knew that some diversification in his background would increase his chances of becoming a senior manager someday.

- Two years after he became accounts manager, Joe was promoted to branch manager and transferred to a small branch in a suburban area. After two years, he was again transferred to a major city branch as its manager.

- Joe realized that without further qualifications his future career progress was likely to be quite slow. He therefore enrolled in the Certified General Accountant's Program. At the same time he began attending executive development seminars conducted by a nearby university. Three years later he was promoted to district manager, and five years later he was again transferred to a larger district.

- At the end of his fifth year in the new district, he had completed his Certified General

Accountant's diploma. Since no promotion was forthcoming immediately, Joe left the Bank of New Brunswick a year later and joined the Ontario Dominion Bank as its vice president of finance. Six years later he was promoted to senior vice president (finance), in which position he remained for ten years.

As a review of Figure 10-2 indicates, Joe's career plan involved well-timed transfers and an educational leave. Figure 10-3 superimposes Joe's career changes on the organization charts of the two banks for which he worked. As the organization chart shows, career progress is seldom straight up in an organization. Lateral transfers, leaves, and even resignations are used. When Joe started as a customer service clerk trainee at age twenty-one, there was no way he could have predicted the career path he would follow. But through periodic career planning, he reassessed his career progress and then

FIGURE 10-3   A Career Path Diagram for an Executive Vice President in the Banking Industry

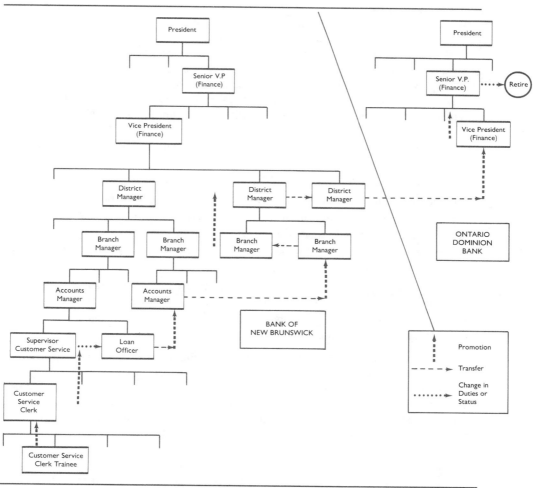

undertook development activities to achieve intermediate career goals, such as becoming a supervisor. As a result of career planning and development, Joe's career consisted of a path that led him to his goal of becoming an executive in the banking industry.

## CAREER PLANNING AND DEVELOPMENT OVERVIEW

During the forty years of Joe's career, human resource departments in banks and other large organizations gave relatively little support to career planning. When promotable talent was scarce, human resource departments usually reacted with crash training programs or additional recruitment. Human resource planning and career planning seldom occurred. Instead, organizations and employees reacted to new developments rather than seeking proactive solutions.

Viewed historically, this limited role for human resource departments was understandable, because career plans were seen largely as a personal matter.[4] Even when managers wanted their department to provide assistance in career planning, they often lacked the resources to become involved. As a result, only a few (mostly large) organizations encouraged career planning by employees.

Today, an increasing number of human resource departments see career planning as a way to meet their internal staffing needs.[5] When employers encourage career planning, employees are more likely to set goals. In turn, these goals may motivate employees to pursue further education, training, or other career development activities. These activities then improve the value of employees to the organization and give the human resource department a larger pool of qualified applicants from which to fill internal job openings.

But what do employees want? A study of one group of employees revealed five areas of concern. These include:

- *Career equity.* Employees want to perceive equity in the organization's performance/ promotion system with respect to career advancement opportunities.
- *Supervisory concern.* Employees want their supervisors to play an active role in career development and provide timely performance feedback.
- *Awareness of opportunities.* Employees want knowledge of the career advancement opportunities that exist in their organization.
- *Employee interest.* Employees need different amounts of information and have different degrees of interest in career advancement depending on a variety of factors.
- *Career satisfaction.* Employees have different levels of career satisfaction depending on their age and occupation.

Effective career planning and development programs must consider these different perceptions and wants of employees. What employees expect from the career programs developed by the human resource department will vary according to age, sex, occupation, and other variables. In short, whatever approach the human resource department takes towards career planning and development, it must be a flexible, proactive approach. As one human resource manager in a large corporation concluded:

Flexibility in career development programs is paramount if the goals of improved productivity, increased personal satisfaction, growth and ultimately increased organizational effectiveness are to be achieved. In many cases, this will require the modification of basic existing programs to address the specific needs of a particular group of employees.

## HUMAN RESOURCE DEPARTMENTS AND CAREER PLANNING

Human Resource departments should, and increasingly do, take an active interest in employee career planning.[6] Planning and managing human resources is emerging as an increasingly important determinant of organizational effectiveness.[7]

Human resource departments often handle career planning because their human resource plans indicate the organization's future employment needs and related career opportunities. In addition, human resource experts are more likely to be aware of training or other developmental opportunities. Of course, individual managers also should encourage career planning, as Joe did in the opening dialogue. But if human resource specialists leave career planning to managers, it may not get done. Not all managers take as strong an interest in their employees' careers as Joe appears to.

The involvement of human resource managers in career planning has grown during recent years because of its benefits. Here is a partial list of those benefits:

· *Develops promotable employees.* Career planning helps to develop internal supplies of promotable talent.
· *Lowers turnover.* The increased attention to and concern for individual careers generate more organizational loyalty and therefore lower employee turnover.
· *Taps employee potential.* Career planning encourages employees to tap more of their potential abilities because they have specific career goals.
· *Furthers growth.* Career plans and goals motivate employees to grow and develop.
· *Reduces hoarding.* Without career planning, it is easier for managers to hoard key subordinates. Career planning causes employees, managers, and the human resource department to become aware of employee qualifications.
· *Satisfies employee needs.* With less hoarding and improved growth opportunities for employees, individual needs for recognition and accomplishment are more readily satisfied, and self-esteem is boosted.
· *Assists affirmative-action plans.* Career planning can help members of protected groups prepare for more important jobs.

To realize these benefits, more human resource departments are following the lead of a few pioneers and supporting career planning. In practice, human resource departments encourage career planning in three ways: through career education, information, and counselling.

### Career Education

Surprisingly, many employees know very little about career planning. Often they are unaware of the need for and advantages of career planning. And once made aware, they often lack the necessary information to plan their careers successfully. Human resource departments are suited to solve both of these shortcomings.

Human resource departments can increase employee awareness through a variety of educational techniques. For example, speeches, memoranda, and position papers from senior executives stimulate employee interest at low cost to the employer. If executives communicate their belief in career planning, other managers are likely to do the same.

Workshops and seminars on career planning increase employee interest by pointing out the key concepts associated with career planning.[8] Workshops help the employee set career goals, identify career paths, and uncover specific career development activities. These educational activities may be supplemented by printed or taped information on career planning.

> Most of the employees in Trans Canada Harvester company had thirty or more years of service. Rapid growth caused many newcomers to join the company. These new employees had not developed the loyalty of their senior colleagues and were more prone to ask, "What is the company doing for my career?"
>
> The human resource department of the company had taken the view that career planning and development is the responsibility of the employee. With this philosophy, a voluntary, four-hour career planning workshop was developed. Employees had to sign up to go to the workshop on their own time and did not receive any pay for attending. Instructors from the human resource department were not paid either; they volunteered to do the sessions, which helped to reinforce the perspective that the department was interested in the participants as people, not just as employees.
>
> The workshops typically began with participants being assigned to teams. This was followed by introductions and a discussion about the confidentiality of what they learn about each other's career interests. The groups then listed enjoyable and unpleasant activities as the first step in creating a personal inventory and identifying alternatives. Usually, discussion followed, centring on an internal staffing decision in which the teams were asked to fill a hypothetical job opening. These discussions were found to be extremely helpful in promoting acceptance of the management perspective on internal selection and promotion. Many participants realized for the first time that being passed over meant only that someone else was slightly better qualified — not that they were in disfavour with the company's management.

When the human resource department lacks the necessary staff to design and conduct educational programs, public programs conducted by local institutions or consultants may help.

> One worldwide consulting firm, Towers, Perrin, Forster & Crosby, provides its clients with a four-step package. The package program develops (1) a strategy for the organization to solve its unique needs, (2) support systems based upon the present human resource management information systems to give employees the data they need to plan their careers, (3) workbooks that allow employees to engage in career planning, and (4) a career resource centre that offers employees assistance with their career planning.

## Information on Career Planning

Regardless of the educational strategy the human resource department selects, it should provide employees with other information they need to plan their careers. Much of this information is already a part of the human resource department's information system. For example, job descriptions and specifications can be quite valuable to someone who is trying to estimate reasonable career goals. Likewise, human resource departments can identify future job openings through the human resource plan. Human resource specialists can also share their knowledge of potential career paths. For example, they are often keenly aware of the similarities between unrelated jobs. If this information is given to employees, it may reveal previously unseen career paths.

> For example, consider the possible career paths faced by Leslie Stevens, who works in a newspaper. In this type of work, the jobs of typist, Linotype operator, and Teletype operator call for a similar characteristics: finger dexterity. But Leslie, a clerk-typist in the advertising department, may not realize that this skill applied to a Linotype machine may earn her three times as much as the other jobs.

When different jobs require similar skills, they form *job families*. Career paths within a job family demand little additional training since the skills of each job are closely related.[9] If human resource departments make information about job families available, employees can find feasible career paths. They can then assess these career paths by talking with those who already hold jobs along the path.

One problem with job families is that employees may want to skip over less pleasant jobs. To prevent employees from rejecting some jobs in a job family, the human resource department may establish a sequential progression of jobs. A *job progression ladder* is a partial career path where some jobs have prerequisites, as shown in Figure 10-4. The job progression ladder shown in the figure requires Leslie to become a Teletype operator before moving to the better-paying job of Linotype operator. This requirement assures the human resource department of an ample internal supply of Teletype operators because this job is a prerequisite for the well-paying position of Linotype operator.

FIGURE 10-4   Three Jobs with Similar Requirements Grouped Into a Job
Family — different jobs which require similar skills

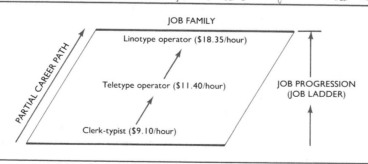

The human resource department can also encourage career planning by providing information about alternative career paths. Figure 10-5 shows that Leslie and other clerk-

FIGURE 10-5    Alternative Career Paths Available to a Clerk-Typist in a
Newspaper Company

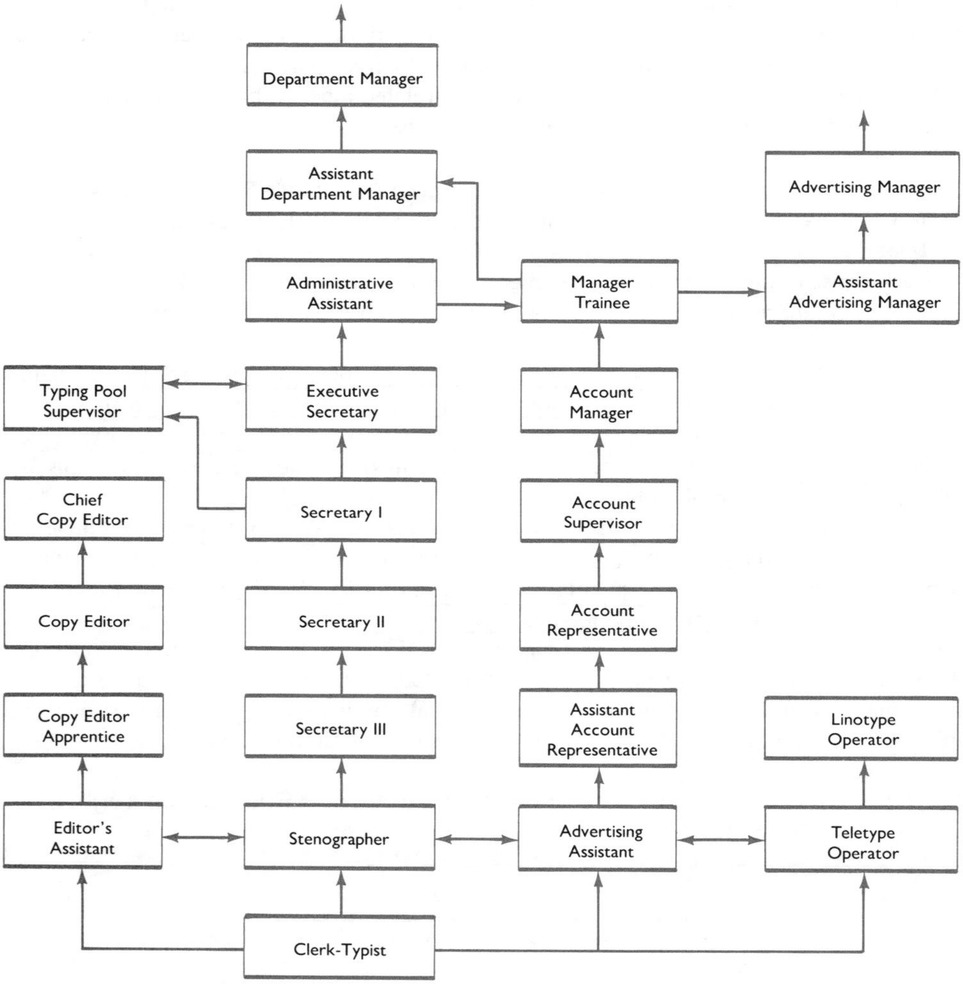

typists face several possible career paths. If a particular clerk-typist does not want to become a Teletype operator, human resource specialists can provide information about alternative careers not considered by the clerk-typist. In the newspaper example, Leslie might prefer a career in editorial, secretarial, or advertising fields because those careers offer more long-term potential.

## Career Counselling

To help employees establish career goals and find appropriate career paths, some human resource departments offer career counselling by counsellors who are a source of competent advice. The counsellor may simply be someone who has the employee's interests in mind and provides the specific job-related information.[10] Or the counsellor may help employees discover their interests by administering and interpreting aptitude and skill tests.[11] Two tests in particular—the *Kuder Preference Record* and the *Strong Vocational Interest Blank*—are useful for guiding people into occupations that are likely to be of interest. Other tests are also available to measure individual abilities and interests in specific types of work. But to be truly successful, career counsellors must get employees to assess themselves and their environment.

### Employee Self-Assessment

Career counsellors realize that a career is not the entirety of one's life. It may be a large part or even a central part; but career planning is only a part of one's *life plan*. A life plan is that often ill-defined series of hopes, dreams, and personal goals each person carries through life. For example, broad objectives to be happy, healthy, and successful combine with specific goals to be a good spouse, parent, student, citizen, neighbour, and manager. Together, these roles form one's life plan. Ideally, a career plan is an integral part of one's life plan. Otherwise, career goals become ends (sometimes dead ends!) rather than means toward fulfilling a life plan. An example can be drawn from an overworked movie plot:

> The husband struggles for decades to achieve a degree of success. When that success is within reach, he realizes that his personal life—friendships, marriage, and paternal relationships—is in shambles. It is in shambles because career plans were pursued to the exclusion of all else; there was no integral life plan.

Why should people who are very successful in their careers develop feelings of personal failure? One research study[12] has suggested the following factors:

- *Contradictory life demands*. The realization that one has strived throughout one's life to attain goals that were irreconcilable.
- *Failure of expectations.* The realization that things one expected to happen will not ever happen and that one's beliefs about the work environment (e.g., the belief that rising in the organizational hierarchy will make one personally satisfied) are wrong.
- *Sense of external control.* The realization that one has been making too many of life's decisions in order to please others rather than oneself.
- *Loss of affiliative satisfactions.* A feeling of loneliness both at the workplace and at home.

In order to avoid this sense of personal failure, self-assessment coupled with life planning at the beginning of a career and at every major crossroads is crucial. Self-assessment includes a self-inventory. Components of a self-inventory are listed in Figure 10-6. If a career counsellor can get employees to complete a detailed and honest self-evaluation, it helps to focus their thinking about themselves. Then employees can match their interests and abilities on the self-inventory with the career information available to them from the human resource department. Likewise, they can match better their attitudes and career paths with their personal life plan.

FIGURE 10-6   A Self-Inventory for Career Planning

| WORK INTERESTS AND APTITUDES | LOW 1 | 2 | 3 | 4 | HIGH 5 |
|---|---|---|---|---|---|
| Physical work (fixing, building, using hands) | ___ | ___ | ___ | ___ | ___ |
| Written work (writing, reading, using words) | ___ | ___ | ___ | ___ | ___ |
| Oral work (talking, giving speeches, using words) | ___ | ___ | ___ | ___ | ___ |
| Quantitative work (calculating, doing accounting, using numbers) | ___ | ___ | ___ | ___ | ___ |
| Visual work (watching, inspecting, using eyes) | ___ | ___ | ___ | ___ | ___ |
| Interpersonal work (counselling, interviewing) | ___ | ___ | ___ | ___ | ___ |
| Creative work (inventing, designing, ideas) | ___ | ___ | ___ | ___ | ___ |
| Analytical work (doing research, solving problems) | ___ | ___ | ___ | ___ | ___ |
| Managerial work (initiating, directing, coordinating) | ___ | ___ | ___ | ___ | ___ |
| Clerical (keeping records) | ___ | ___ | ___ | ___ | ___ |
| Outdoor work (farming, travelling, doing athletics) | ___ | ___ | ___ | ___ | ___ |
| Mechanical (repairing, fixing, tinkering) | ___ | ___ | ___ | ___ | ___ |

WORK SKILLS AND ABILITIES

| List below specialized skills, unique personal assets, enjoyable experiences, and major accomplishments. Then evaluate. | Physical | Written | Oral | Quantitative | Visual | Interpersonal | Creative | Analytical | Managerial | Clerical | Outdoor | Mechanical |
|---|---|---|---|---|---|---|---|---|---|---|---|---|
| _____ | _ | _ | _ | _ | _ | _ | _ | _ | _ | _ | _ | _ |
| _____ | _ | _ | _ | _ | _ | _ | _ | _ | _ | _ | _ | _ |
| _____ | _ | _ | _ | _ | _ | _ | _ | _ | _ | _ | _ | _ |
| _____ | _ | _ | _ | _ | _ | _ | _ | _ | _ | _ | _ | _ |
| _____ | _ | _ | _ | _ | _ | _ | _ | _ | _ | _ | _ | _ |
| _____ | _ | _ | _ | _ | _ | _ | _ | _ | _ | _ | _ | _ |
| _____ | _ | _ | _ | _ | _ | _ | _ | _ | _ | _ | _ | _ |

*Environmental Assessment*

A career plan that matches employee interests with likely career paths may actually do a disservice to the employee if environmental factors are overlooked. Returning to the choices faced by Leslie Stevens at the newspaper provides an example.

> The job family of clerk-typist, Teletype operator, and Linotype operator may appear to be a reasonable career path for Leslie since she already has the basic typing skills needed for all three jobs. But technological changes in the newspaper industry may reduce the need for Linotype operators in the future. Photographic and computer developments are quickly replacing the use of Linotype machines in newspaper printing. If career counsellors in the human resource department do not point out this development to Leslie, she may find her career stalled in the job of Teletype operator.

Regardless of the match between one's skills and the organization's career paths, counsellors need to inform employees of likely changes that will affect their occupational choices. Occupational information is readily available from publications of Employment and Immigration Canada and Statistics Canada. For example, Employment and Immigration Canada periodically publishes information relating to the demand and supply of various jobs in the *Ford Occupational Imbalance Listing* (FOIL). In another annual (sometimes biannual) publication entitled *Canada Occupational Forecasting Program* (COFOR), Employment and Immigration Canada provides forecasts on the demand for various types of jobs in the country. Some of the national daily newspapers and business magazines also provide useful information in this context. Figure 10-7 shows some of the trends in the Canadian job market in the late 1980s and early 1990s. As can be seen, companies are increasingly looking for specific experience and skills in their employees (in contrast to general skills several years ago). Traditional occupations such as dentists, lawyers, doctors, and engineers have "flooded" the markets, which are fast becoming saturated. Fortunately for students in business administration, management positions show no signs of drying up.

**FIGURE 10-7**   Some Trends in the Canadian Labour Market

| TWENTY OCCUPATIONS CONTRIBUTING MOST TO EMPLOYMENT GROWTH FROM 1986-1995<br><br>OCCUPATIONAL TITLE | INCREASE IN EMPLOYMENT LEVEL (1986-95) |
|---|---|
| Food and beverage serving occupations | 89 000 |
| Sales workers, commodities | 64 000 |
| Secretaries and stenographers | 52 000 |
| Bookkeepers and accounting clerks | 51 000 |
| Chefs and cooks | 51 000 |
| Tellers and cashiers | 38 000 |
| Janitors, charworkers, and cleaners | 38 000 |
| Truck drivers | 26 000 |
| Accounting, auditors, and other financial officers | 23 000 |
| Elementary and kindergarten teachers | 22 000 |
| Supervisors, food and beverage preparation and related service occupations | 21 000 |
| Sales and advertising management occupations | 20 000 |
| Motor-vehicle mechanics and repairers | 18 000 |
| Nurses, graduate, except supervisors | 18 000 |
| Secondary school teachers | 18 000 |
| Services management occupations | 18 000 |
| Occupations in labouring and other elemental work, services | 17 000 |
| Occupations in labouring and other elemental work, other construction trades | 15 000 |
| Welding and flame cutting occupations | 15 000 |
| Supervisors: sales occupations, commodities | 14 000 |
| Total for all occupations | 1 660 317 |

Note: Based on the C.O.P.S. 1987 Reference Scenario. Levels are rounded off to the nearest thousand.
Source: Employment and Immigration, Canada, 1988.

## CAREER DEVELOPMENT

The implementation of career plans requires career development. *Career development* comprises those personal improvements one undertakes to achieve a career plan. These actions may be sponsored by the human resource department or undertaken independently by the employee. The section reviews tactics that employees may use to achieve their career plans and then discusses the department's role in career development.

## Individual Career Development

The starting point for career development is the individual. Each person must accept his or her responsibility for career development, or career progress is likely to suffer. Once this personal commitment is made, several career development actions may prove useful. These actions involve:

- Job performance
- Exposure
- Resignations
- Organizational loyalty

- Mentors and sponsors
- Key subordinates
- Growth opportunities

### Job Performance

The most important action an individual can undertake to further his or her career is good job performance. The assumption of good performance underlies all career development activities. When performance is substandard, regardless of other career development efforts, even modest career goals are usually unattainable. Individuals who perform poorly are excluded quickly by the human resource department and management decision makers. *Career progress rests largely upon performance.*

### Exposure

Career progress also is furthered by exposure.[13] Exposure means becoming known (and, it is hoped, held in high regard) by those who decide on promotions, transfers, and other career opportunities. Without exposure, otherwise good performers may not get a chance at the opportunities needed to achieve their career goals. Managers gain exposure primarily through their performance, written reports, oral presentations, committee work, community service, and even the hours they work. Simply put, exposure makes an individual stand out from the crowd—a necessary ingredient in career success, especially in large organizations. For example, consider how one management trainee gained some vital exposure early in her career:

> Paula Dorsey noticed that two executives worked on Saturday mornings. As one of twelve new management trainees, she decided that coming to work on Saturday mornings would give her additional exposure to these key decision makers. Soon these two executives began greeting her by name whenever they passed in the halls. While still in the training program, she was assigned to the product introduction committee, which planned strategy for new products. At the end of the training program, Paula was made an assistant product manager for a new line of video recorders. The other eleven trainees received less important jobs.

In small organizations, exposure to decision makers is more frequent and less dependent upon reports, presentations, and the like. In some situations—especially in other nations — social status, school ties, and seniority can be more important than exposure.

## Resignations

When a person sees greater career opportunities elsewhere, a resignation may be the only way to meet one's career goals. Some employees—managers and professionals in particular—change employers as part of a conscious career strategy. If this is done effectively, they usually get a promotion, pay increase, and new learning experience. Resigning in order to further one's career with another employer has been called *leveraging*.[14] Astute managers and professionals use this technique sparingly because too many moves can lead to the label of "job hopper." Those who leave seldom benefit their previous organization, because they almost never return with their new experiences.

> In a study of 268 mobile executives conducted by one of the authors, only 3% (seven of the executives) ever returned to an organization they left during their careers.[15] This finding means that organizations seldom benefit from the return of managers who quit and go elsewhere.

## Organizational Loyalty

In many organizations, people put career loyalty above organizational loyalty. Low levels of organizational loyalty are common among recent university graduates (whose high expectations often lead to disappointment with their first few employers) and professionals (whose first loyalty is often to their profession).[16] Career-long dedication to the same organization complements the human resource department's objective of reducing employee turnover. However, if the following findings are applicable to other organizations, there may be few rewards for such dedication:

> In a study conducted by one of the authors, it was found that a bare majority (51%) of the chief executives in the 100 largest industrial companies spent their entire careers with the same organization. The minority (49%) of presidents who changed employers at least once became chief executive officers at a younger age than those who spent their entire career with the same organization.[17]

## Mentors and Sponsors

Many employees quickly learn that a mentor can aid their career development. A *mentor* is someone who offers informal career advice. Neither the mentor nor the employee always recognizes that such a relationship exists; the junior worker simply knows that here is someone who gives good advice; the mentor sees the employee as simply someone who wants advice.

If the mentor can nominate the employee for career development activities, such as training programs, transfers, or promotions, the mentor becomes a sponsor. A *sponsor* is someone in the organization who can create career development opportunities for others. Often an employee's sponsor is the immediate supervisor, although others may serve as nominators.[18]

> Many Japanese firms rely on senior managers to use their store of insight and wisdom

to help junior managers with career development. In a relationship based on school ties or some other net-work-related factor, the senior manager serves as a career counsellor, mentor, and sponsor for the junior employee, who often works in a different department. In return, the senior manager's actions are reinforced by the respect he receives from other managers.

### Key Subordinates

A successful manager relies on subordinates who aid his or her development and performance. The subordinates may possess highly specialized knowledge or skills that the manager may learn from them. Or the employees may perform a crucial role in helping a manager achieve good performance. In either case, employees of this type are *key subordinates.* They exhibit loyalty and dedication to their boss. They gather and interpret information, offer skills that supplement their manager's, and work unselfishly to further their manager's career. They benefit when the manager is promoted by also moving up the career ladder. Key subordinates also benefit by receiving important delegations that serve to develop their careers. These people complement human resource department objectives through their teamwork, motivation, and dedication. But when a manager resigns and takes a string of key subordinates along, the results can be devastating.

> A small Ontario research firm had ten months' lead in developing a new type of memory component for computers. A major electronics company hired away the project manager, the chief engineer, and their key subordinates. With this loss, the small firm was forced to recruit replacements at a higher salary and at a cost of several months' delay.

As a career strategy, perceptive subordinates are careful not to become attached to an immobile manager. One researcher calls such immobiles "shelf-sitters."[19] Not only do shelf-sitters block promotion channels, but their key subordinates can become unfairly labelled as shelf-sitters too. Although working for a shelf-sitter may develop an employee's skills, it can also arrest one's career progress.

### Growth Opportunities

When employees expand their abilities, they complement the organization's objectives. For example, enrolling in a training program, taking noncredit courses, pursuing an additional degree, or seeking a new work assignment can contribute to employee growth. These growth opportunities aid both the human resource department's objective of developing internal replacements and the individual's personal career plan.

> Rachael Holmes was the chief recruiter in the employment department of Brem Paper Products. Her department manager was sixty years old and had indicated that he planned to retire at age sixty-five. At thirty-seven with three years of experience as a recruiter, Rachael felt she was in a dead-end job. She obtained a transfer to the wage and salary department. Two years later the company planned a new facility and made Rachael the human resource manager for it. She was selected because of her broad experience in recruiting and compensation—two major concerns in starting the new operation.

Rachael initiated the transfer through self-nomination because she wanted to further her career development. But the real opportunity she obtained from the transfer was a chance to grow—a chance to develop new skills and knowledge.

Besides self-nomination to pursue growth opportunities, other groups outside the organization may help. For years, men have used private clubs and professional associations to form "old-boy networks," which afforded growth opportunities and often a fair amount of interaction among organizational decision makers. Now, however, many of these clubs have been forced to admit women, and increasingly, women are forming their own associations.

> Halifax Women's Network aims to facilitate interaction among career-oriented women in the Halifax metropolitan area. Members of the network meet regularly in informal settings to disseminate professional and career-related information to other members. The network also holds sessions on a variety of job-related topics including money management, career search for women, etc.

## Human Resource Supported Career Development

Career development should not rely solely on individual efforts, because they are not always in the organization's best interests. For example, employees may move to another employer, as in the Ontario research example. Or employees may simply be unaware of opportunities to further their careers and the organization's staffing needs. To guide career development so that it benefits the organization and employees, a human resource department often provides a variety of training and development programs for employees. In addition, departments should enlist the support of managers, provide feedback to employees, and create a cohesive work environment to improve the ability and desire of workers to undertake career development.

### Management Support

Efforts by the human resource department to encourage career development have little impact unless supported by managers. Commitment by top management is crucial to gain the support of other managers. When support is lacking, managers are likely to ignore career development and devote their attention to their other responsibilities. Unlike Japanese employees, for example, North American and other Western employers do not have a tradition of giving meaningful peer recognition to managers who voluntarily support employee development.

### Feedback

Without feedback about their career development efforts, it is difficult for employees to sustain the years of preparation sometimes needed to reach career goals. Human resource departments can provide this feedback in several ways. One way is to periodically tell employees how well they are performing their present job. To do this, many human resource departments develop performance evaluation procedures. If performance is poor, this feedback allows a worker to adjust his or her efforts or career development plan.

Another type of feedback concerns job placement. An employee who pursues career development activities and is passed over for promotion may conclude that career development is not worth the effort. Unsuccessful candidates for internal job openings should be told why they did not get the job they sought. This feedback has three purposes:

1. *To assure* bypassed employees that they are still valued and will be considered for further promotions, if they are qualified. Otherwise, valuable employees may resign because they think the organization does not appreciate their efforts.

2. *To explain* why they were not selected.

3. *To indicate* what specific career development actions should be undertaken. Care should be exercised not to imply that certain career development actions will automatically mean a promotion. Instead, the individuals *candidacy* for selection will be influenced by appropriate career development actions.

### Cohesive Work Groups

For employees who want to pursue a career within an organization, they must feel that the organization is a satisfying environment. When they are a part of a cohesive work group, their career development efforts are more likely to be directed towards improving their opportunities within the organization.[20] But to create such a satisfying environment, human resource departments must deal with change and organizational development, the subject of the next chapter.

### SUMMARY

Career planning and development are relatively new concepts to human resource specialists. In recent years, human resource departments have begun to recognize the need for more proactive efforts in this area. As a result, some (mostly large) departments provide career education, information, and counselling. But the primary responsibility for career planning and development rests with the individual employee.

Figure 10-8 illustrates an overview of career planning and development.

FIGURE 10-8　**The Career Planning and Development Framework**

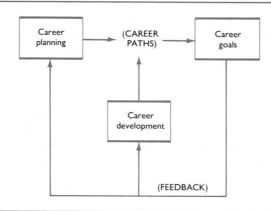

The planning process enables employees to identify career goals and the paths to those goals. Then through developmental activities the workers seek ways to improve themselves and further their career goals.

Even today, most developmental activities are individual and voluntary. Individual efforts include good job performance, favourable exposure, leveraging, building of alliances, and other actions. Human resource departments become involved by providing information and obtaining management support. The human resource department helps make career planning and development a success for both the employees and the organization.

Career planning does not guarantee success. But without it employees are seldom ready for career opportunities that arise. As a result, their career progress may be slowed and the human resource department may be unable to fill openings internally.

## TERMS FOR REVIEW

| | |
|---|---|
| Career | Career counselling |
| Career path | Life plan |
| Career planning | Exposure |
| Career development | Leveraging |
| Job families | Mentors and sponsors |
| Job progression ladder | Key subordinates |

## REVIEW AND DISCUSSION QUESTIONS

1. Why should a human resource department be concerned about career planning, especially since employee plans may conflict with the organization's objectives? What advantages does a human resource department expect to receive from assisting career planning?

2. In what ways can a human resource department assist career planning?

3. If you were interested in making a career out of your own ability to play a musical instrument, what types of career goals would you set for yourself? How would you find out about the career prospects for musicians before you took your first job?

4. Suppose you are in a management training position after completing university. Your career goal is not very clear, but you would like to become a top manager in your firm. What types of information would you seek from the human resource department to help you develop your career plan?

5. After you develop your first career plan while employed by a bank, what career development activities would you pursue? Why?

6. Suppose you are assigned to develop a career planning and development program for the employees of a large city. How would you go about developing employee interest in career planning? How would you enlist the support of managers throughout the organization?

7. Why is employee feedback an important element of any organization's attempt to encourage career development?

8.  Suppose a hard-working and loyal employee is passed over for promotion. What would you tell this person?

## INCIDENT 10-1

### Career Planning and Development at Immobile Ltd.

Long-term employees at Saskatchewan Electric Company Ltd. nicknamed the company "Immobile Ltd." It seemed that the only time anyone received a promotion was when a manager retired or died. Even when job vacancies did occur, the human resource department frequently hired a replacement from some other electric utility, so that few employees received a promotion. Employee turnover was low partially because the jobs paid very well, provided high job security, and offered outstanding fringe benefits.

Top management became concerned about the negative attitude reflected by the nickname "Immobile Ltd." and hired a large Toronto consulting firm to develop a career planning program. After several months, the consultants revealed a detailed plan, complete with a special office of career counselling in the human resource department. Initially, employees responded favourably and made extensive use of the counselling and career information services available to them. But by the fourth month, the chief career counsellor asked the human resource manager for a transfer into any other part of the human resource department. When asked why, the counsellor said that employees were not using the service and the job of counsellor had become lonely and boring. The human resource manager gave the counsellor an assignment to discover why the program had failed and what might be done to revitalize it.

1.  What explanations can you offer to explain the initial enthusiasm for career planning assistance followed by an almost total avoidance by employees?
2.  Assuming part of the problem was a lack of support by middle and first-level management, what recommendations would you make? Could this company learn a lesson from the approach used by the Japanese?

## INCIDENT 10-2

### Moosehead Transportation System

Moosehead Transportation System had been through some bad times. Year after year, losses had piled up. Finally, management decided that it must close down many of its operations in small towns that were not profitable. To ease the burden on long-term employees, a decision was made that no one with ten years of experience or more was to be laid off.

The human resource department developed a plan and notified each long-service employee in towns where the service was to be discontinued. Since many of the jobs were those of Depot Master and Assistant Depot Master, not enough comparable openings existed in other cities. While the human resource department sought a permanent solution, these long-service employees were transferred into any other openings that were available.

Many of the transferees complained that they were being demoted. The union thought it unfair that these workers were paid their old salary when other workers on the same jobs received considerably less.

1.  Under these circumstances, would career planning be a useful tool for the human resource department to reduce the ill feelings of these long-service workers?

2.  How do you think these long-term employees might react to career planning efforts by the human resource department? How do you think unaffected employees might react to a new career planning effort?

*CASE STUDY*

## AT THE CROSSROAD

Gerald Squamish was Director of Engineers at Canadian Oil Refinery (COR), a Best Service subsidiary. It seemed that it never rained but it poured! First, there were the two previous incidents. And now the suicide.

A month ago, two teenagers were drowned cleaning out the sludge in the holding pond. Squamish had told his subordinates to get the pond clean, but he did not realize that proper safety precautions would not be taken. And two weeks ago, they had to close the plant down — at a cost of $7,000,000. That had prompted a visit and a "chewing out" from Head Office personnel. Yesterday, he had fired one of the shift supervisors, Clarence Iruck — a man who drank continuously and was absent excessively. Squamish had not realized that Iruck's wife had left him and that he would commit suicide.

Squamish had almost made up his mind to leave COR. It was a good job, paying in six figures and with generous profit-sharing and benefit plans. His wife enjoyed her prestigious position within the Edmonton social community. They had a large, expensive, and beautiful home located on the Crescent, and their three older children would be able to live at home while attending the University of Alberta.

At the same time, he doubted that he was being paid enough to continually make the type of life-and-death decisions that his job demanded. He wondered, too, if, because of the shut-down, his future with COR was at a dead end. He thought back. He had worked very hard and looked forward to this promotion. Somehow, actually receiving it was almost anti-climactic. His job had not changed significantly, but the decisions that had to be made and the responsibility that had to be assumed increased. And they were always short-staffed.

If he left the company, he had two alternatives. First, the American Oil Refinery, in Calgary, had offered him a position heading their power plant construction program. There he would be a member of senior management and be able to have a considerable impact on company decisions regarding safety, costs, and new technology within the power plants. His wife and children would have to make an adjustment, however. Perra (his wife) would have to change positions, build new friends, and re-establish herself in the company social hierarchy. For his older children, there should be little difference between the University of Alberta and the University of Calgary. The change in high schools might present a problem to the two youngest children — particularly Rona, who was a shy, reserved child. She had been ill for a number of years when she was younger and found it difficult to make friends. Willis would be fine as long as he could play hockey and basketball.

He was not sure that his wife would like the second alternative. All his life, he had dreamed of going back to farming. He could retire now, sell his house, and take his pension and profit-sharing money and buy a combination farm and cattle ranch and the necessary equipment. Indeed, there was just such a place for sale. This would alleviate the severe stress that he was under, and his health would probably improve. His doctor had been warning him for

some time that he had to slow down. And he looked at his brother, also a farmer. Willard did not seem to have a care in the world. Sure, there were droughts and bills to be paid, but things seemed to look after themselves somehow. And the farm/ranch that was for sale was very near Willard's. It would be like the old days when they were growing up. They would share equipment and work together again.

But could their wives get along? Perra's parents had been highly paid professionals and she had grown up amid luxury and learning. Willard's wife, on the other hand, had limited education. She had been abandoned by both her mother and father at an early age. In many ways, she was a typical hard-working farm woman—extremely competent running a tractor but impatient with the politicking and social niceties at which his own wife was so adept.

Squamish wondered what he should do. It would help if he could find some type of career decision-making model to assist him.

1.  As a human resource manager at COR responsible for career planning, what specific recommendations would you make to assist Squamish in his decision making?

2.  Assuming Squamish decides to remain with COR, draw up a career development plan to assist him in his future career plans.

From Olga Crocker, *Incidents and Cases in Canadian Personnel Administration*, 1986, pp. 54-55. © Nelson Canada, 1986, A Division of International Thomson Limited, 1120 Birchmount Road, Scarborough, Ontario M1K 5G4.

○ ○ ○ ○ ○ ○ ○ ○ ○ ○ ○ ○ ○ ○ ○ ○ ○ ○ ○ ○ ○ ○ ○ ○ ○ ○ ○ ○ ○ ○ ○ ○ ○ ○ ○ ○ ○ ○ ○ ○ ○

## SUGGESTED READINGS

Hall, D. *Careers in Organizations*, Santa Monica, California: Goodyear Publishing, 1976.

Rush, J., A. Peacock and G. Milkovich, "Career Stages: A Partial Test of Levinson's Model of Life/Career Stages," *Journal of Vocational Behaviour*, Vol. 16, 1980, pp. 347-359.

Schein, E. G., *Career Dynamics: Matching Individual and Organizational Needs*, Reading, Mass.: Addison-Wesley Publishing, 1978.

Super, D., D. T. Hall, "Career Development: Exploration and Planning," in M. R. Rosenzweig and L. W. Porter (eds.), *Annual Review of Psychology*, Palo Alto, California: Annual Reviews, 1978.

Van Maanen, J., E. G. Schein, "Career Development," in J. R. Hackman and J. L. Suttle (eds.), *Improving Life at Work*, Santa Monica, California: Goodyear Publications, 1977.

## REFERENCES

1.  Ronald J. Burke and Tamara Weir, "Career Success and Personal Failure Part II," *The Canadian Personnel & Industrial Relations Journal*, November 1980, p. 36.

2.  Dr. Srully Blotnick, "How to Change Jobs and Live to Enjoy

it," *Canadian Business*, August 1984, p. 83.

3.  Harvey A. Thomson and Claude A. Guay, "Tapping Human Potential," *The Canadian Personnel & Industrial Relations Journal*, September 1978, pp. 21-26; Stephen L. Cohen,

"Toward a More Comprehensive Career Planning Program," *Personnel Journal*, September 1979, pp. 611-615.

4. This individual/organizational dichotomy is useful for distinguishing between the role of the person and the role of the human resource department. For a more detailed discussion of this distinction, see Elmer H. Burack, "Why All the Confusion about Career Planning?" *Human Resource Management*, Summer 1977, pp. 21-23. See also B. A. Keys, F. A. Thompson, and M. Heath, "Managerial Training and Development Practices of Selected Firms in Canada," *Meeting Managerial Manpower Needs*, Ottawa: Economic Council of Canada, 1971.

5. T. F. Hercus, "A Survey of Responses to Current Manpower," *The Canadian Personnel & Industrial Relations Journal*, January 1979, pp. 19-30. See also *The Financial Post*, "Urgent Priority to Job Training," January 16, 1982, p. 3.

6. William F. Rothenbach, "Career Development: Ask Your Employees for Their Opinions," *Personnel Administration*, November 1982, pp. 43-46, 51. See also J. Thad Barnowe, "Influences of Personality, Organizational Experience, and Anticipated Future Outcomes on Choice of Career," Working Paper No. 537, Faculty of Commerce, University of British Columbia, December 1977.

7. C. W. Memeth and J. I. A. Rowney, "Professionalize or Perish," *The Canadian Personnel & Industrial Relations Journal*, January 1981, pp. 27-31.

8. Donald D. Bowen and Douglas T. Hall, "Career Planning for Employer Development: A Primer for Managers," *California Management Review*, Winter 1977, pp. 29-30. See also Douglas T. Hall, *Careers in Organizations*, Pacific Palisades, Calif.: Goodyear Publishing Company, Inc., 1976.

9. Elmer H. Burack and Nicholas Mathys, "Career Ladders, Pathing and Planning: Some Neglected Basics,"*Human Resource Management*, Summer 1979. pp. 2-8. See also Philomena D. Warihay, "The Climb to the Top: Is the Network the Route for Women?" *The Personnel Administrator*, April 1980, pp. 55-60.

10. Ted R. Gambilll, "Career Counseling: Too Little, Too Late?" *Training and Development Journal*, February 1979, pp. 24-29.

11. Hall, op. cit., pp. 27-28.

12. Ronald J. Burke and Tamara Weir, "Career Success and Personal Failure Part I," *The Canadian Personnel and Industrial Relations Journal*, October 1980, pp. 7-17. See also Laird W. Mealiea and Swee C. Goh, "An Empirical Evaluation of the Fear of Success Construct for Women Working in a Sex Stereotyped Job," *ASAC (Organizational Behaviour Division) Meeting Proceedings*, Vol. 2, Part 5, 1981, pp. 112-123.

13. Eugene E. Jennings, *The Mobile Manager*, New York: McGraw-Hill Book Company, 1967.

14. Jennings, op. cit.

15. William B. Werther, Jr., "Management Turnover Implications of Career Mobility," *The Personnel Administrator*, February 1977, pp. 63-66.

16. Simeon J. Touretzky, "Changing Attitudes: A Question of Loyalty," *The Personnel Administrator*, April 1979, pp. 35-38.

17. Werther, op. cit.

18. Verne Walter, "Self-Motivated Personnel Career Planning: A Breakthrough in Human Resource Management (Part I)," *Personnel Journal*, March 1976, pp. 112-115, 136. See also Part II in the April 1976 issue of *Personnel Journal*, pp. 162-167, 185-186.

19. Jennings, op. cit.

20. William A. Westley, "The Role of the Supervisor," *The Canadian Personnel & Industrial Relations Journal*, November 1980, pp. 10-23. See also Larry Earwood, "Employee Satisfaction through Career Development," *The Personnel Administrator*, August 1979, pp. 41-44; Kalburgi M. Srinivas, "The Superior-Subordinate Interface," Chapter 7 in K. M. Srinivas (ed.) *Human Resource Management: Contemporary Perspectives in Canada*, Toronto: McGraw-Hill Ryerson, 1984; Ron J. Burke and D. S. Wilson, "Effects of Different Patterns and Degrees of Openness in Superior-Subordinate Communication on Subordinate Job Satisfaction." *Academy of Management Journal*, 12, 3, 1969, pp. 319-326; Manfred F. R. Kets de Vries, "Crossed Signals: Dysfunctional Superior Subordinates Interaction Patterns," Working Paper No. 7911, Faculty of Management, Montreal: McGill University, Spring 1979; Ronald J. Burke, "Mentors in Organizations," *ASAC (Organizational Behaviour Division) Meeting Proceedings*, Vol. 3, Part 5, 1982, pp. 41-47.

# CHAPTER *11* ○○○○○○

# *PERFORMANCE APPRAISAL*

*The performance appraisal concept is central to effective management.*

HARRY LEVINSON[1]

○ ○ ○ ○ ○ ○ ○ ○ ○ ○ ○ ○ ○ ○ ○ ○ ○ ○ ○ ○ ○ ○ ○ ○ ○ ○ ○ ○ ○

## *CHAPTER OBJECTIVES*

After studying this chapter, you should be able to:

1. **Identify** the issues that influence selection of a performance appraisal system.
2. **Explain** the uses of performance appraisals.
3. **Discuss** rater biases in performance appraisals.
4. **Describe** commonly used appraisal methods.
5. **Explain** how the results of performance appraisal affect human resource management.

○ ○ ○ ○ ○ ○ ○ ○ ○ ○ ○ ○ ○ ○ ○ ○ ○ ○ ○ ○ ○ ○ ○ ○ ○ ○ ○ ○ ○

*P*revious chapters discussed how employees are selected, developed, and formed into cohesive work groups. These are important activities. But the ultimate measure of a human resource department's success is employee performance. Both the human resource department and employees need feedback on their efforts. Unfortunately, managers in other departments may not understand the need for evaluating employee performance. Too often, they see performance appraisals as unnecessary conversation. The following discussion between Ellen, a line manager, and Sam, a human resource specialist, high- lights these different views of performance appraisals:

> ELLEN:  Don't you think I know who the good performers are in my department? I know the strengths and weaknesses of every employee who works for me. So why do we need to have a formal performance evaluation program?
>
> SAM:  No one in the human resource department is questioning whether you know who the good performers are. In fact, we in human resource management

334

hope that all managers know who their best workers are. But we need a formal appraisal system to compare employees in different departments.

ELLEN:  Why is that so important?

SAM:  We need that information for many reasons. We need to know who should receive additional training and development, who should be promoted, and who should get pay raises. Besides, employees need formal feedback on how they are doing their job.

ELLEN:  Well, I let my employees know how they are doing. And I do it without all the formality of a performance appraisal program.

SAM:  Good managers, like yourself, always give employees feedback. The human resource department merely wants to formalize the process so that there is a written record of performance. Without such a record, we in the human resource department have no consistent way to compare employees when staff-related decisions are made.

*Performance appraisal* is the process by which organizations evaluate employee job performance. As the dialogue between Ellen and Sam indicates, appraisals expand the human resource department's information base. This knowledge can improve human resource decisions and the feedback employees receive about their performance.

The uses of performance appraisals are described in Figure 11-1. Accurate per-

## FIGURE 11-1   Uses of Performance Appraisals

- **Performance improvement.** Performance feedback allows the employee, the manager, and human resource specialists to intervene with appropriate actions to improve performance.
- **Compensation adjustments.** Performance evaluations help decision makers determine who should receive pay raises. Many firms grant part or all of their pay increases and bonuses on the basis of merit, which is determined mostly through performance appraisals.
- **Placement decisions.** Promotions, transfers, and demotions are usually based on past or anticipated performance. Often promotions are a reward for past performance.
- **Training and development needs.** Poor performance may indicate the need for retraining. Likewise, good performance may indicate untapped potential that should be developed.
- **Career planning and development.** Performance feedback guides career decisions about specific career paths one should investigate.
- **Deficiencies in staffing process.** Good or bad performance implies strengths or weaknesses in the human resource department's staffing procedures.
- **Informational inaccuracies.** Poor performance may indicate errors in job analysis information, human resource plans, or other parts of the human resource management information system. Reliance on inaccurate information may have led to inappropriate hiring, training, or counselling decisions.
- **Job design errors.** Poor performance may be a symptom of ill-conceived job designs. Appraisals help diagnose these errors.
- **Avoidance of discrimination.** Accurate performance appraisals that actually measure job-related performance ensure that internal placement decisions are not discriminatory.
- **External challenges.** Sometimes performance is influenced by factors outside the work environment, such as family, finances, health, or other personal matters. If such influences are uncovered through appraisals, the human resource department may be able to provide assistance.

formance evaluations show employees where they are deficient. For the human resource department, appraisals make compensation, placement, training, development, and career guidance decisions more effective. At the same time, the department obtains feedback on its development activities, staffing process, job designs, and external challenges. In short, performance appraisals serve as a quality control check on employee and human resource department performance.

Without an effective appraisal system, promotions, transfers, and other employee-related decisions become subject to trial and error. Career planning and human resource development suffer because there is no systematic performance feedback. And the human resource department lacks adequate information to evaluate its performance objectively. This lack of feedback can cause the human resource department to miss its objectives. Sometimes the consequences of this failure are severe:

> A large agricultural cooperative association in the western provinces rated employees twice a year. But employees were evaluated on personality characteristics, such as attitude, cooperation, and other factors that were related only indirectly to actual performance. Employees that were well liked by their managers received higher ratings than others. As a result, promotions, pay raises, and other employee-related decisions were biased by personalities. Eventually, several employees filed charges against the cooperative, alleging racial and sexual discrimination. When company lawyers defended past decisions as unbiased, they lost the case because they could not show how the ratings related to job performance.

As this example emphasizes, an organization cannot have just any performance appraisal system. Figure 11-2 shows the elements of an acceptable appraisal system. The approach must identify performance-related criteria, measure those criteria, and then give feedback to employees and the human resource department. If performance measures are not job-related, the evaluation can lead to inaccurate or biased results.[2] Not only is performance feedback distorted, but errors in employee records can lead to incorrect human resource decisions, as happened in the example of the agricultural cooperative.

The human resource department usually develops performance appraisals for employees in all departments. One U.S. study found that the development of appraisal systems is the responsibility of the human resource department in more than 80% of the firms surveyed.[3] This centralization is meant to ensure uniformity. With uniformity in design and implementation, results are more likely to be comparable among similar groups of employees. Although the human resource department may develop different approaches for managers and workers, uniformity within each group is needed to ensure useful results.

Even though the human resource department usually designs the appraisal system, it seldom does the actual evaluation of performance. Instead, research shows that the employee's immediate supervisor performs the evaluation 95% of the time.[4] Although others could rate performance, the immediate supervisor is often in the best position to make the appraisal.

So important is the evaluation of performance that 75% of large companies and 55% of medium-sized companies in one Canadian study used appraisals for the clerical, professional, supervisory, and management employees.[5] To explain the importance of

FIGURE 11-2   Key Elements of Performance Appraisal Systems

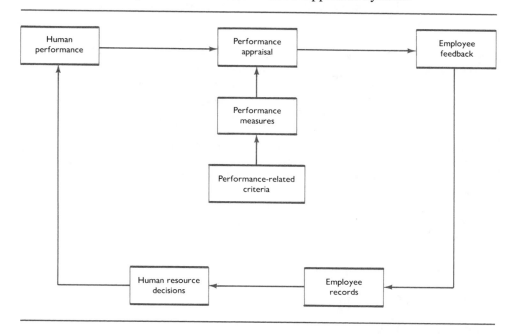

this widely used tool of human resource management, the rest of this chapter examines the preparation, methods, and implications of performance appraisals.

## PERFORMANCE APPRAISAL PREPARATION

The appraisal should create an accurate picture of an individual's job performance. To achieve this goal, appraisal systems should be job-related, be practical, have standards, and use dependable measures. Job-related means that the system evaluates critical behaviours that constitute job success. If the evaluation is not job-related, it is invalid and probably unreliable. Without validity and reliability, the system may discriminate in violation of antidiscrimination laws. Even when discrimination does not occur, appraisals are inaccurate and useless if they are not job-related.

But a job-related approach also must be practical. A practical system is one that, first of all, is understood by evaluators and employees; a complicated, impractical approach may cause resentment and nonuse. The confusion can lead to inaccuracies that reduce the effectiveness of the appraisal. To be practical the procedure should also be standardized.

### Performance Standards

Performance evaluation requires *performance standards*. They are the benchmarks against which performance is measured. To be effective they should relate to the desired results of each job. They cannot be set arbitrarily. Knowledge of these standards is collected through job analysis. As discussed in Chapter 5, job analysis uncovers specific performance criteria by analyzing the performance of existing employees. As one pair of writers has observed:

> It is important that management carefully examine the characteristics of effective performance. Job analysis coupled with a detailed performance analysis of existing employees should begin to identify what characteristics are required by a job and which of those are exhibited by "successful" employees. It is possible that such an investigation may reveal that what management has used in the past to define successful performance is inadequate or misleading. This should not deter management from the task of defining the criteria, but should reinforce management for the "house cleaning" which is being undertaken. This must be a careful scrutiny with an eye to what the performance criteria should be in the future, rather than what criteria have been used in the past.[6]

From the duties and standards listed in the job description, the analyst can decide which behaviours are critical and should be evaluated. If it should happen that this information is lacking or unclear, standards may be developed from observation of the job or discussion with the immediate supervisor.

## PERFORMANCE MEASURES

Performance evaluation also requires dependable *performance measures*. They are the ratings used to evaluate performance. To be useful, they must be easy to use, be reliable, and report on the critical behaviours that determine performance. For example, a telephone company supervisor must observe each operator's:

- Use of company procedures—staying calm, applying tariff rates for phone calls, and following company rules and regulations.
- Pleasant phone manners—speaking clearly and courteously.
- Call-placement accuracy—placing operator-assisted calls accurately.

These observations can be made either directly or indirectly. *Direct observation* occurs when the rater actually sees the performance. *Indirect observation* occurs when the rater can evaluate only substitutes for actual performance. For example, a supervisor's monitoring of an operator's calls is direct observation; a written test on company procedures for handling emergency calls is indirect observation. Indirect observations are usually less accurate because they evaluate substitutes for actual performance. Substitutes for actual performance are called *constructs*. Since constructs are not exactly the same as actual performance, they may lead to errors.

> To test how well operators might respond to emergency calls, a provincial telephone company developed a paper-and-pencil test. The test was intended to determine if each operator knew exactly how to proceed when emergency calls were received for such requests as police, ambulance, or fire equipment. After several hundred operators were tested, it was noticed that fast readers scored better. The human resource department decided to scrap the test and use false emergency calls to evaluate the operators.

Another dimension of performance measures is whether they are objective or subjective. *Objective performance measures* are those indications of job performance that are verifiable by others. For example, if two supervisors monitor an operator's calls, they can count the number of misdialed ones. The results are objective and verifiable since each supervisor gets the same call-placement accuracy percentage. Usually, objective measures are quantitative. They typically include items such as gross units produced, net units approved by quality control, scrap rates, number of computational errors, number of customer complaints, or some other mathematically precise measure of performance.

*Subjective performance measures* are those ratings that are not verifiable by others. Usually, such measures are the rater's personal opinions. Figure 11-3 compares the accuracy of objective and subjective measures. It shows that subjective measures are low in accuracy. When subjective measures are also indirect, accuracy becomes even lower. For example, measurement of an operator's phone manners is done subjectively since supervisors must use their personal opinions of good or bad manners. Since the evaluation is subjective, accuracy is usually low even if the supervisor directly observes the operator. Accuracy is likely to be even lower when the rater uses an indirect measure, such as an essay test of phone manners. Whenever possible, human resource specialists prefer objective and direct measures of performance.

FIGURE 11-3   Types and Accuracy of Performance Measures

| TYPES OF PERFORMANCE MEASURES | RELATIVE DEGREE OF ACCURACY | |
|---|---|---|
| | DIRECT | INDIRECT |
| OBJECTIVE | Very high | High |
| SUBJECTIVE | Low | Very Low |

## Rater Biases

The problem with subjective measures is the opportunity for bias. *Bias* is the (mostly unintentional) distortion of a measurement. Usually it is caused by raters who fail to remain emotionally detached while they evaluate employee performance. The most common rater biases include:

- The halo effect
- The error of central tendency
- The leniency and strictness biases
- Personal prejudice
- The recency effect

### The Halo Effect

The halo effect (discussed in Chapter 7) occurs when the rater's personal opinion of the employee sways the rater's measurement of performance. For example, if a supervisor likes an employee, that opinion may distort the supervisor's estimate of the employee's performance. The problem is most severe when raters must evaluate their friends.

### The Error of Central Tendency

Some raters do not like to judge employees as "effective" or "ineffective," so they avoid checking extremes — very poor or excellent — and instead place their marks near the centre of the rating sheet so that employees appear to be "average."[7] Thus the term *error of central tendency* has been applied to this bias. Human resource departments sometimes unintentionally encourage this behaviour by requiring raters to justify extremely high or low ratings.

### The Leniency and Strictness Biases

The *leniency bias* occurs when raters are too easy in evaluating employee performance. The *strictness bias* is just the opposite; it results from raters' being too harsh in their evaluation of performance. Both errors more commonly occur when performance standards are vague.

### Personal Prejudice

A rater's dislike for a person or group may distort the ratings. For example, some human resource departments notice that male supervisors give undeservedly low ratings to women who hold "traditionally male jobs." Sometimes raters are unaware of their prejudice, which makes such biases even more difficult to overcome. Nevertheless, human resource specialists should pay close attention to prejudice in appraisals since it prevents effective evaluations and violates antidiscrimination laws.

### The Recency Effect

When using subjective performance measures, ratings are affected strongly by the employee's most recent actions. Recent actions — either good or bad — are more likely to be remembered by the rater.

When subjective performance measures must be used, human resources specialists can reduce the distortion from biases through training, feedback, and the proper selection of performance appraisal techniques. Training for raters should involve three steps. First, biases and their causes should be explained. Second, the role of performance appraisals in employee decisions should be explained to stress the need for impartiality and objectivity. Third, raters should be allowed to apply subjective performance measures as part of their training. For example, classroom exercises may require evaluation of the trainer or videotapes of various workers. Mistakes uncovered during simulated evaluations then can be corrected through additional training or counselling.

Once the use of subjective performance measures moves out of the classroom and into practice, raters should get feedback about their previous ratings.[8] When ratings prove relatively accurate or inaccurate, feedback helps raters adjust their behaviour accordingly.

Human resource departments also can reduce distortion through the careful selection of performance appraisal techniques.[9] For ease of discussion, these techniques are grouped into those that focus on past performance and those that focus on future performance.

## PAST-ORIENTED APPRAISAL METHODS

The importance of performance evaluations has led academics and practitioners to create many methods to appraise past performance. Most of these techniques are a direct attempt to minimize some particular problem found in other approaches. None is perfect; each has advantages and disadvantages.

Past-oriented approaches have the advantage of dealing with performance that has already occurred and, to some degree, can be measured. The obvious disadvantage is that past performance cannot be changed. But by evaluating past performance, employees can get feedback about their effects. This feedback may then lead to renewed efforts at improved performance. The most widely used appraisal techniques that have a past orientation include:

- Rating scale
- Checklist
- Forced choice method
- Critical incident method
- Behaviourally anchored rating scales

- Field review method
- Performance tests and observations
- Comparative evaluation methods

## Rating Scale

Perhaps the oldest and most widely used form of performance appraisal is the *rating scale*, which requires the rater to provide a subjective evaluation of an individual's performance along a scale from low to high. An example appears in Figure 11-4. As the figure indicates, the evaluation is based solely on the opinions of the rater. In many

FIGURE 11-4   A Sample of a Rating Scale for Performance Evaluation

**WESTERN FARM COOPERATIVE ASSOCIATION**
**Rating Scale**

**Instructions:** For the following performance factors, please indicate on the rating scale your evaluation of the named employee.

**Employee's Name** _____    **Department** _____
**Rater's Name** _____    **Date** _____

| | Excellent 5 | Good 4 | Acceptable 3 | Fair 2 | Poor 1 |
|---|---|---|---|---|---|
| 1. **Dependability** | ____ | ____ | ____ | ____ | ____ |
| 2. **Initiative** | ____ | ____ | ____ | ____ | ____ |
| 3. **Overall Output** | ____ | ____ | ____ | ____ | ____ |
| 4. **Attendance** | ____ | ____ | ____ | ____ | ____ |
| 5. **Attitude** | ____ | ____ | ____ | ____ | ____ |
| 6. **Cooperation** | | | | | |
| • • | • | • | • | • | • |
| • • | • | • | • | • | • |
| • • | • | • | • | • | • |
| 20. **Quality of Work Results** | ____ | ____ | ____ | ____ | ____ |
| **Totals** | ____ + | ____ + | ____ + | ____ + | ____ = ____ |

**Total Score**

cases, the criteria are not directly related to job performance. Although subordinates or peers may use it, the immediate supervisor usually completes the form.

The form is completed by checking the most appropriate response for each performance factor. Responses may be given numerical values to enable an average score to be computed and compared for each employee. The advantages of this method are that it is inexpensive to develop and administer, raters need little training or time to complete the form, and it can be applied to a large number of employees.

Disadvantages are numerous. A rater's biases are likely to be reflected in a subjective instrument of this type. Specific performance criteria may be omitted to make the form applicable to a variety of jobs. For example, "maintenance of equipment" may be left off because it applies to only a few workers. But for some employees, that item may be the most important part of their job. This and other omissions tend to limit specific feedback. Also, these descriptive evaluations are subject to individual interpretations that vary widely. And when specific performance criteria are hard to identify, the form may rely on irrelevant personality variables that dilute the meaning of the evaluation. The result is a standardized form and procedure that is not always job related.

## Checklist

The *checklist* rating method requires the rater to select statements or words that describe the employee's performance and characteristics. Again, the rater is usually the immediate superior. But unknown to the rater, the human resource department may assign weights to different items on the checklist, according to each item's importance. The result is called a *weighted checklist*. The weights allow the rating to be quantified so that the total scores can be determined. Figure 11-5 shows a portion of a checklist. The weights for each item are in parentheses here but are usually omitted from the actual form. If

FIGURE 11-5   An Example of a Weighted Performance Checklist

**HATHAWAY DEPARTMENT STORES LTD.**
**Performance Checklist**

**Instructions:** Check each of the following items that apply to the named employee's performance.

Employee's Name _____   Department _____
Rater's Name _____   Date _____

| Weights | | Check here |
|---|---|---|
| (6.5) | **1.** Employee works overtime when asked. | _____ |
| (4.0) | **2.** Employee keeps workstation or desk well organized. | _____ |
| (3.9) | **3.** Employee cooperatively assists others who need help. | _____ |
| (4.3) | **4.** Employee plans actions before beginning job. | _____ |
| • | •        • | • |
| • | •        • | • |
| • | •        • | • |
| (0.2) | **30.** Employee listens to others' advice but seldom follows it. | _____ |
| 100.0 | **Total of All Weights** | |

the list contains enough items, it may provide an accurate picture of employee perform-ance. Although this method is practical and standardized, the use of general statements reduces its job-relatedness.

The advantages of a checklist are economy, ease of administration, limited training of raters, and standardization. The disadvantages include susceptibility to rater biases (especially the halo effect), use of personality criteria instead of performance criteria, misinterpretation of checklist items, and use of improper weights by the human resource department. Moreover, it does not allow the rater to give relative ratings. On item 1 in the figure, for example, employees who gladly work overtime get the same score as those who do so unwillingly.

## Forced Choice Method

The *forced choice method* requires the rater to choose the most descriptive statement in each pair of statements about the employee being rated. Often both statements in the pair are positive or negative. For example:

1. Learns quickly . . . . . . . . . . . . . . . . . . Works hard
2. Work is reliable and accurate . . . . . . . Performance is a good example to others
3. Absent too often . . . . . . . . . . . . . . . Usually tardy

Sometimes the rater must select the best statement (or even pair of statements) from four choices. However the form is constructed, human resource specialists usually group the items on the form into predetermined categories, such as learning ability, performance, interpersonal relations, and the like. Then effectiveness can be computed for each category by adding up the number of times each category is selected by the rater. The results in each category can be reported to show which areas need further improvement. Again, the supervisor is usually the rater, although peers or subordinates may make the evaluation.

The forced choice method has the advantages of reducing rater bias, being easy to administer, and fitting a wide variety of jobs. Although practical and easily stand-ardized, the general statements may not be specifically job-related. Thus it may have limited usefulness in helping employees to improve their performance. Even worse, an employee may feel slighted when one statement is checked in preference to another. For example, if the rater checks "learns quickly" in number 1 above, the worker may feel that his or her hard work is overlooked.[10] This method is seldom liked by either the rater or ratee because it provides little useful feedback.

## Critical Incident Method

The *critical incident method* requires the rater to record statements that describe extremely good or bad employee behaviour related to performance. The statements are called critical incidents. These incidents are usually recorded by the supervisor during the evaluation period for each subordinate. Recorded incidents include a brief explanation of what happened. Several typical entries for a laboratory assistant appear in Figure 11-6. As shown in the figure, both positive and negative incidents are recorded. Incidents are classified (either as they occur or later by the human resource department) into

FIGURE 11-6   Critical Incidents Record for a Lab Assistant

## HARTFORD CHEMICALS LTD.
## Critical Incidents Worksheet

**Instructions:** In each category below, record specific incidents of employee behaviour that were either extremely good or extremely poor.

Employee's Name   Kay Watts (lab assistant)          Department   Chemistry Lab

Rater's Name   Nat Cordoba                           Rating Period of   10/1   to   12/31

**Control of Safety Hazards**

| Date | Positive Employee Behaviour | Date | Negative Employee Behaviour |
|------|-----------------------------|------|-----------------------------|
| 10/12 | Reported broken rung on utility ladder and flagged ladder as unsafe | 11/3 | Left hose across storeroom aisle |
| 10/15 | Put out small trash fire promptly | 11/27 | Smoked in chemical storeroom |

**Control of Material Scrap**

| Date | Positive Employee Behaviour | Date | Negative Employee Behaviour |
|------|-----------------------------|------|-----------------------------|
| 10/3 | Sorted through damaged shipment of glassware to salvage usable beakers | 11/7 | Used glass containers for strong bases ruining glass |
| | | 11/19 | Repeatedly used glass for storage of lye and other bases |
| | | | Poured acid into plastic container ruining counter top |

categories such as control of safety hazards, control of material scrap, and employee development.

The critical incident method is extremely useful for giving employees job-related feedback. It also reduces the recency bias. Of course, the practical drawback is the difficulty of getting supervisors to record incidents as they occur. Many supervisors start out recording incidents faithfully, but lose interest. Then, just before the evaluation period ends, they add new entries. When this happens, the recency bias is exaggerated and employees may feel that the supervisors are building a case to support their subjective opinion. Even when the form is filled out over the entire rating period, employees may feel that the supervisor is unwilling to forget negative incidents that occurred months before.

## Behaviourally Anchored Rating Scales

*Behaviourally anchored rating scales* (BARS) attempt to reduce the subjectivity and biases of subjective performance measures.[11] From descriptions of good and bad performance provided by incumbents, peers, and supervisors, job analysts or knowledgeable employees group these examples into performance-related categories such as employee knowledge, customer relations, and the like. Then specific examples of these behaviours are placed along a scale (usually from 1 to 7). Actual behaviours for a bank branch manager are illustrated on the rating scale shown in Figure 11-7. Since the positions on the scale are described in job-related behaviour, an objective evaluation along the scale is more likely. And the form cites specific behaviours that can be used to provide performance feedback to employees. The BARS are job-related, practical, and standardized for similar jobs. But the rater's personal biases may still cause ratings to be high or low, although the specific behaviours that "anchor" the scale provide some criteria to guide the sincere rater.[12] If the rater collects specific incidents during the rating period, the evaluation is apt to be more accurate and more legally defensible, besides being a more

FIGURE 11-7   Behaviourally Anchored Rating Scale for Bank Branch Manager

Job Part: Human Resource Management          Bank of Ontario

| | | |
|---|---|---|
| Outstanding Performance | 7 | Can be expected to praise publicly for tasks completed well, and constructively criticizes in private those individuals who have produced less than adequate results. |
| Good Performance | 6 | Can be expected to show great confidence in subordinates, and openly displays this with the result that they develop to meet expectations. |
| Fairly Good Performance | 5 | Can be expected to ensure that human resource management records are kept right up to date, that reports are written on time, and that salary reviews are not overlooked. |
| Acceptable Performance | 4 | Can be expected to admit a personal mistake, thus showing that he is human too. |
| Fairly Poor Performance | 3 | Can be expected to make "surprise" performance appraisals of subordinates. |
| Poor Performance | 2 | Can be expected not to support decisions made by a subordinate (makes exceptions to rules). |
| Extremely Poor Performance | 1 | Can be expected not to accept responsibility for errors and to pass blame to subordinates. |

effective counselling tool.[13] One serious limitation of BARS is that they only look at a limited number of performance categories, such as customer relations or human resource management. Also, each of these categories has only a limited number of specific behaviours. Like the critical incident method, most supervisors are reluctant to maintain records of critical incidents during the rating period, which reduces the effectiveness of this approach when it comes time to counsel the employee.[14]

Whenever subjective performance measures are used, differences in rater perceptions cause bias. To provide greater standardization in reviews, some employers use the *field review method*. In this method, a skilled representative of the human resource department goes ''into the field'' and assists supervisors with their ratings. The human resource specialist solicits from the immediate supervisor specific information about the employee's performance. Then the expert prepares an evaluation based on this information. The evaluation is sent to the supervisor for review, changes, approval, and discussion with the employee who was rated. The human resource specialist records the rating on whatever specific type of rating form the employer uses. Since a skilled professional is completing the form, reliability and comparability are more likely. But the need for the services of skilled professionals may make this approach impractical for many firms.

## Performance Tests and Observations

With a limited number of jobs, performance appraisal may be based upon a test of knowledge or skills. The test may be of the paper-and-pencil variety or an actual demonstration of skills. The test must be reliable and valid to be useful. In order for the method to be job-related, observations should be made under circumstances likely to be encountered. Practicality may suffer when the cost of test development is high.

> Pilots of all major airlines are subject to evaluation by airline raters and Transport Canada. Evaluations of flying ability are usually made both in a flight simulator and while being observed during an actual flight. The evaluation is based on how well the pilot follows prescribed flight procedures and safety rules. Although this approach is expensive, public safety makes it practical, as well as job-related and standardized.

## Comparative Evaluation Methods

*Comparative evaluation methods* are a collection of different methods that compare one person's performance with that of coworkers. Usually, comparative evaluations are conducted by the supervisor. They are useful for deciding merit pay increases, promotions, and organizational rewards because they can result in a ranking of employees from best to worst. The most common forms of comparative evaluations are the ranking method, forced distributions, point allocation method, and paired comparisons. Although these methods are practical and easily standardized, they too are subject to bias and offer little job-related feedback.

Many large companies use an elaborate group evaluation method. This method reduces biases because multiple raters are used, and some feedback results when managers and professionals learn how they compared with others on each critical factor.

However, these comparative results are often not shared with the employee because the supervisor and the human resource department want to create an atmosphere of cooperation among employees. To share comparative rankings may lead to internal competition instead of cooperation. Nevertheless, two arguments in favour of comparative approaches merit mention before discussing specific methods.

Arguments for a comparative approach are simple and powerful. The simple part of it is that organizations do it anyway, all the time. Whenever human resource decisions are made, the performance of the individuals being considered is ranked and compared. People are not promoted because they achieve their objectives, but rather because they achieve their objectives *better* than others.

The second reason (the powerful one) for using comparative as opposed to non-comparative methods is that they are far more reliable. This is because reliability is controlled by the rating process itself, not by rules, policies, and other external constraints.[15]

### Ranking Method

The *ranking method* has the rater place each employee in order from best to worst. All the human resource department knows is that certain employees are better than others. It does not know by how much. The employee ranked second may be almost as good as the one who was first or considerably worse. This method is subject to the halo and recency effects, although rankings by two or more raters can be averaged to help reduce biases. Its advantages include ease of administration and explanation.

### Forced Distributions

*Forced distributions* require raters to sort employees into different classifications. Usually a certain proportion must be put in each category. Figure 11-8 shows how a rater might classify ten subordinates. The criterion shown in the figure is for overall performance (but this method can be used for other performance criteria, such as reliability and control of costs). As with the ranking method, relative differences among employees are unknown, but this method does overcome the biases of central tendency, leniency,

FIGURE 11-8   The Forced Distribution Method of Appraisal of Ten Subordinates

CAPTONE FISHERIES LTD.
Forced Distribution Rating

CLASSIFICATION: OVERALL PERFORMANCE

| BEST 10% OF SUBORDINATES | NEXT 20% OF SUBORDINATES | MIDDLE 40% OF SUBORDINATES | NEXT 20% OF SUBORDINATES | LOWEST 10% OF SUBORDINATES |
|---|---|---|---|---|
| A. Wilson | G. Carrs<br>M. Lopez | B. Johnson<br>E. Wilson<br>C. Grant<br>T. Valley | K. McDougal<br>L. Ray | W. Smythe |

and strictness. Some workers and supervisors strongly dislike this method because employees are often rated lower than they or their supervisor/rater think to be correct. However, the human resource department's forced distribution requires some employees to be rated low.

### Point Allocation Method

The *point allocation method* requires the rater to allocate a fixed number of points among the employees in the group, as shown in Figure 11-9. Better employees are given more points than poor performers. The advantage of the point allocation method is that the rater can recognize the relative differences between employees, although the halo effect and the recency bias are disadvantages that remain.

FIGURE 11-9   The Point Allocation Method of Appraisal

**CAPTONE FISHERIES LTD.**
**Point Allocation Rating**

**Instructions:** Allocate all **100** points to all employees according to their relative worth. The employee with the maximum points is the best employee.

| Points | Employee |
|--------|----------|
| 17 | A. Wilson |
| 14 | G. Carrs |
| 13 | M. Lopez |
| 11 | B. Johnson |
| 10 | E. Wilson |
| 10 | C. Grant |
| 9 | T. Valley |
| 6 | K. McDougal |
| 5 | L. Ray |
| 5 | W. Smythe |
| 100 | |

### Paired Comparisons

*Paired comparisons* require raters to compare each employee with all other employees who are being rated in the same group. An example of paired comparisons appears in Figure 11-10. The basis for comparison is usually overall performance. The number of times each employee is rated superior to another can be summed up to develop an index. The employee who is preferred the most is the best employee on the criterion selected. In the figure, A. Wilson is selected nine times and is the top-ranked employee. Although subject to halo and recency effects, this method counteracts the leniency, strictness, and central tendency errors because some employees must be rated better than others.

## FUTURE-ORIENTED APPRAISALS

The use of past-oriented approaches is like driving a car by looking through the rearview mirror: you only know where you have been, not where you are going. Future-oriented appraisals focus on future performance by evaluating employee potential or setting future performance goals. Included here are four techniques used:

- Self-appraisals
- Psychological appraisals
- Management-by-objectives approach
- Assessment centre technique

## *Self-appraisals*

Getting employees to conduct a self-appraisal can be a useful evaluation technique if the goal of evaluation is to further self-development. When employees evaluate themselves, defensive behaviour is less likely to occur. Thus self-improvement is more likely. When self-appraisals are used to determine areas of needed improvement, they can help users set personal goals for future improvement.

Obviously, self-appraisals can be used with any evaluation approach, past- or future-oriented. But the important dimension of self-appraisals is the employee's involvement and commitment to the improvement process.

FIGURE 11-10   The Paired Comparison Method of Evaluating Employees

**CAPTONE FISHERIES LTD.**
**Paired Comparison Rating**

**Instructions:** Compare each employee on overall performance with every other employee. For each comparison, write the number of the employee who is best in the intersecting box. Each time an employee is found superior to another employee, the better employee receives one point. Employees then can be ranked according to the number of times each is selected as best by the rater.

| Employee | 2 | 3 | 4 | 5 | 6 | 7 | 8 | 9 | 10 |
|---|---|---|---|---|---|---|---|---|---|
| **1** G. Carrs | 1 | 1 | 4 | 1 | 1 | 1 | 1 | 9 | 1 |
| **2** C. Grant | | 3 | 4 | 2 | 2 | 2 | 2 | 9 | 2 |
| **3** B. Johnson | | | 4 | 3 | 3 | 3 | 3 | 9 | 3 |
| **4** M. Lopez | | | | 4 | 4 | 4 | 4 | 9 | 4 |
| **5** K. McDougal | | | | | 6 | 5 | 8 | 9 | 10 |
| **6** L. Ray | | | | | | 6 | 8 | 9 | 10 |
| **7** W. Smythe | | | | | | | 8 | 9 | 10 |
| **8** T. Valley | | | | | | | | 9 | 10 |
| **9** A. Wilson | | | | | | | | | 9 |
| **10** E. Wilson | | | | | | | | | |

At the Bechtel Company, the largest privately held construction and engineering firm in the world, their performance planning system involves the employee in a process of self-appraisal. The process starts with the supervisor telling the employee what is expected. Then the employee gets a worksheet and writes down his or her understanding of the job. Then, ten to fifteen days before a performance evaluation is done, the employee completes the worksheet by filling in the portions that relate to job accomplishments, performance difficulties, and suggestions for improvement. Not only does it get the employee involved in forming a self-appraisal of improvement areas, but the completed sheet indicates to the supervisor what he or she needs to do to " . . . eliminate roadblocks to meeting or exceeding job standards."[16]

## Psychological Appraisals

Some, mostly very large, organizations employ full-time psychologists. When psychologists are used for evaluations, their role is primarily to assess an individual's future potential. The appraisal normally consists of in-depth interviews, psychological tests, discussions with supervisors, and a review of other evaluations. The psychologist then writes an evaluation of the employee's intellectual, emotional, motivational, and other work-related characteristics that may help predict future performance. The estimate by the psychologist may be for a specific job opening for which a person is being considered, or it may be a global assessment of an employee's future potential. From these evaluations, placement and development decisions may be made to shape the person's career. Because this approach is slow and costly, it is usually reserved for bright young managers who are thought to have considerable potential with the organization. The quality of these appraisals depends largely on the skills of the psychologists, and some employees object to evaluations by company psychologists.

## Management-by-Objectives Approach

The heart of the management-by-objectives (MBO) approach is that each employee and superior jointly establish performance goals for the future.[17] Ideally, these goals are mutually agreed upon and objectively measurable. If both conditions are met, employees are apt to be more motivated to achieve the goal since they have participated in setting it. Moreover, they can periodically adjust their behaviour to ensure attainment of the objectives if they can measure their progress towards the objective. But to adjust their efforts, performance feedback must be available on a regular basis.

When future objectives are set, employees gain the motivational benefit of a specific target to organize and direct their efforts. Objectives also help the employee and supervisor discuss specific developmental needs of the employee. When done correctly, performance discussions focus on the job's objectives and not personality variables. Biases are reduced to the extent that goal attainment can be measured objectively.

In practice, MBO programs have encountered difficulties. Objectives are sometimes too ambitious or too narrow. The result is frustrated employees or overlooked areas of performance. For example, employees may set objectives that are measured by quantity rather than quality because quality, while it may be equally important, is often more difficult to measure. When employees and managers do focus on subjectively measured objectives, special care is needed to ensure that biases do not distort the manager's evaluation.

## Assessment Centre Technique

*Assessment centres* are another method of evaluating future potential, but they do not rely on the conclusions of one psychologist. Assessment centres are a standardized form of employee appraisal that relies on multiple types of evaluation and multiple raters. The assessment centre technique is usually applied to groups of middle-level managers who appear to have potential to perform at more responsible levels in the organization. Often the members of the group first meet at the assessment centre. During a brief stay at the facility, candidates are individually evaluated. The process subjects selected employees to in-depth interviews, psychological tests, personal background histories, peer ratings by other attendees, leaderless group discussions, ratings by psychologists and managers, and simulated work exercises to evaluate future potential. The simulated work experiences usually include in-basket exercises, decision-making exercises, computer-based business games, and other job-like opportunities that test the employee in realistic ways.

These activities are usually conducted for a few days at a location physically removed from the jobsite. During this time, the psychologists and managers who do the rating attempt to estimate the strengths, weaknesses, and potential of each attendee.[18] They then pool their estimates to arrive at some conclusion about each member of the group being assessed.

Assessment centres were first applied in business in 1956, by the director of human resources research at American Telephone and Telegraph. By the 1980s, more than 2000 corporate-operated assessment centres were in existence in North America. This approach is both time consuming and costly: candidates are away from their jobs, travel and accommodation must be paid for, and evaluators are often company managers assigned to the assessment centre for short durations.[19] These managers are often supplemented by psychologists and human resource professionals who run the centre and make evaluations.[20] Some critics question whether the procedures used are objective and job-related, especially since rater biases are possible in forming the subjective opinions of attendees.[21] Nevertheless, assessment centres have gained widespread use and human resource researchers are finding ways to validate the process.

The results can be extremely useful for aiding management development and placement decisions. From the composite ratings, a report is prepared on each attendee. This information goes into the human resource management information system to assist human resource planning (particularly the development of replacement charts) and other human resource management decisions. Interestingly, research indicates that the results of assessment centres are a good prediction of actual on-the-job performance in 75% of all cases.[22] Unfortunately, this accurate method is expensive since it usually requires a separate facility and the time of multiple raters. Consider how the process works at Johnson Wax:

For years, the Consumer Products Division of S.C. Johnson & Son, Inc. ran a traditional assessment centre. Twice a year, selected managers from all over Johnson Wax attended the assessment centre for five days and were evaluated on a variety of skills. On the fourth day, the candidates attended a debriefing and career development session while the raters wrote their final evaluations. On the fifth day, attendees received a report of their performance and counselling. The assessment process was successful in helping management select sales representatives. However, the results of the centre tended to be overemphasized: people were seen to have "passed" or "failed" the process. Those who "failed" became dissatisfied because they believed their career potential had been severely limited. Many people who attended the centre "failed" because field management had few guidelines as to who should be sent and at what stage of career development. Likewise, few programs existed to prepare people for the assessment centre process and no formal program existed to train people in management skills.

To overcome these shortcomings, a project group was formed that included people in human resource management, field sales management, and a consultant. The group changed the thrust of Johnson Wax's assessment centre by recommending that the centre's results be given less importance and that they be used to identify strengths and weaknesses in individual skills. The group also recommended that field management become more involved in assisting management candidates with career planning and development activities. The project group also made sure that field management knew what the purpose of the centre was and gave them guidelines for recommending people to attend the centre. A voluntary program for skill development was also undertaken. Even the name of the centre was changed to the Management Skill Identification Center.[23]

Today, the MSI Center results are but one element in the "management promotion equation." This equation consists of four weighted elements which are used by management to make a promotion determination: 1) the individual's record of performance on the job; 2) the individual's sales experience level; 3) the individual's previous job-related experience (i.e., previous employment experience, education experience, etc.); and 4) the individual's MSI Center results.[24]

As the Johnson Wax example illustrates, the assessment centre results must be kept in perspective. If they are the sole determinant of future career progress in the organization, people will see the assessment process as threatening. However, if they are used to appraise an individual's strengths and weaknesses, and if the person has a way of improving areas of deficiency, then the centre can be a positive force for developing future talent within the organization.

To reduce the expense but still capture some of the benefits associated with assessment centres, some companies use "mail-in" assessments. A package of tests, exercises, and required reports are mailed to the individual, who mails them to the raters for subsequent evaluation.[25] Not only are costs lower, but raters and employees do not spend time going to a centralized location.

## Validity of Assessment Centres

The assessment centre is used for a variety of purposes, such as selection, placement, identification of management potential, promotion, development, career management and training. The popularity of the assessment centre concept has spawned a number of research studies that tried to assess its validity. The results of these studies were somewhat confusing, since the validity coefficients (the correlation between results originating from the assessment centre and the actual performance as measured by performance evaluations) ranged from -.25 to +.78.

One recent study looked at fifty investigations on assessment centres to find out what the reasons for this wide range were. They found that some of the studies used improper methodology or came to false conclusions, but when taking everything into account their conclusion was that the average validity for the assessment centre approach was .37, a sufficiently high correlation to suggest that the use of this method is justified.[26]

## IMPLICATIONS OF THE APPRAISAL PROCESS

Design of the appraisal system and its procedures are usually handled by the human resource department. The specific approach is influenced by previous procedures and the purpose of the new appraisal. If the goal is to evaluate past performance to allocate rewards, comparative approaches may be preferred. Similarly, other past-oriented methods may be best if the appraisal system exists primarily to give employees counselling about their behaviour. Future-oriented appraisals may focus on specific goals, as is the case with MBO techniques. Self-appraisals or assessment centres may seek to uncover specific weakness or help with internal placement. Regardless of the technique selected by the human resource department, however, the approach must be converted into an ongoing practice among the line managers. Except in the field review or psychological appraisal methods, raters are often unfamiliar with the procedures or the forms. And they may not be very interested in self-study to learn more, because the evaluation process may be seen as a project imposed by the human resource department and not something of immediate concern to those who supervise others.

Evaluation systems that involve others in their design may gain greater acceptance. Human rights legislation supports having employees involved in the design of the appraisal system. Involvement may increase interest and understanding of whatever performance appraisal system the human resource department eventually administers. However, to operate the performance appraisal system may require training for those who serve as raters.

### Training Raters

Whether a simple comparative method or a sophisticated assessment centre is used, raters need knowledge of the system and its purpose. Just knowing whether the appraisal is to be used for compensation or placement recommendations may change the rater's evaluation of those being rated.

A major problem is rater understanding and consistency of evaluations. Some human resource departments provide raters with a rater's handbook that describes the employer's approach. Guidelines for conducting the evaluation or for providing ratees with feedback are often included in the handbook. Key terms—such as "shows initiative" or "provides leadership"—may also be defined in the handbook.

Companies like The Royal Bank, Air Canada, and others solve this knowledge gap through training. Training workshops are usually intended to explain to raters the purpose of the procedure, the mechanics of it, likely pitfalls or biases they may encounter, and answers to their questions. The training may even include trial-runs of evaluating other classmates just to gain some supervised experience. The Royal Bank and Air Canada use videotapes and role-playing evaluation sessions to give raters both experience and insight into the evaluation process. During the training, the timing and scheduling of evaluations are discussed. Typically, most companies do formal evaluations annually, around the time

of the individual's employment anniversary. For new employees or those having performance problems, evaluations may be done more frequently as part of the human resource
department's formal program or as the supervisor sees fit. Consider how one vice president
and manager of human resources viewed the implementation of his firm's program:

> With the new appraisal process and related forms in place, the next major step
> was educating managers and supervisors in the use of the program. Mandatory
> one-day training workshops were given, providing each manager an opportunity
> to review, discuss and understand the objectives of the program. The appraisal
> forms were reviewed in detail with an explanation of how to use the various sec-
> tions in each form. A videotaped appraisal discussion was presented to demonstrate
> how performance appraisal worked. And finally, during the workshops, managers
> were given role-play situations using the new appraisal forms.[27]
>
> Then on the bi-weekly payroll sheets that included everyone in the department
> or branch, the manager received a notification of who was due to be evaluated
> during the next month. If the review date was passed, a reminder would appear
> on the payroll sheets showing that the review date for the indicated employee was
> past due. As a result, managers know how to complete the forms and few delin-
> quencies occur. The human resource department also has valuable data that allow
> it to anticipate and respond to training needs and employee concerns.[28]

Although in the past rater training has focused on rating errors such as the halo
effect, leniency bias, and central tendency, the emphasis has shifted now to the cognitive
aspect of the rating process, i.e., the ability of raters to make valid judgements based
on relatively complex information. One model divides the performance-appraisal process
into four steps: attention, categorization, recall, and information integration.

### Attention
The rater consciously or subconsciously records certain stimuli because they are relevant
to a task performed, e.g., the rater is a supervisor and as part of her duty observes an
employee performing his job. The more deviant the observed behaviour is from the
expected norm, the more strongly the attention-arousing stimuli work. If, for example,
the employee does something very wrong, the supervisor is much more likely to pay
attention to the observed behaviour than if it were mildly off the mark.

### Categorization
This is the process of classifying and storing data. Several studies have shown that human
beings have a limited capability of perceiving and processing information simultaneously,
the upper limit being approximately seven items. Categorization helps us to make quick
judgements with limited information about something. Stereotyping is one type of categorization that, as we all know, may result in biased conclusions.

### Recall
When we have to make a judgement we try to remember all the relevant information
we stored in our memory about the event or person in question. Depending on the

strength of an impression we recorded, we will be able to recall some items more easily than others (see recency effect). When supervisors are asked to do a performance appraisal once a year, the probability is low that they recall all the important information about an employee's work. Only if a conscious effort to record such information is made, by writing down critical incidents, for example, will raters be able to do an accurate evaluation.

### Information Integration

Once a judgement is called for, such as the annual performance appraisal, the rater tries to recall as much information as possible and to generate an integrated picture of the employee. However, due to the attention-arousing process (only strong stimuli are recorded), the categorization process (limited information is stored), and the recall process (a limited number of events is remembered) the final picture that emerges will be understandably biased.

Several measures can be taken to improve the validity of supervisory ratings:

- Use of behaviour-based scales, e.g., the use of critical incidents to categorize effective and ineffective job behaviour;
- Training in the use of these scales;
- Familiarization of raters with performance definitions, e.g., what constitutes outstanding performance (with practical examples);
- Use of several raters (more eyes see more, and more eyes see different things, resulting in a more balanced judgement);
- Use of quantitative criteria whenever possible (measurable results);
- Use of job samples for important evaluation decisions, e.g., promotion and transfers;
- Training of raters to make behaviour sampling a routine part of a supervisor's job to avoid memory-related biases;
- Avoidance of trait ratings; and
- Creation of positive consequences for both the rater and ratee.[29]

One can easily see that the new focus of rater training makes the job of an instructor in performance appraisal much more difficult. On the other hand, it makes less likely such comments as this, offered by a human resource manager: "Of all the performance appraisal systems I have worked with in fifteen years as a supervisor, not one really worked!"[30] Such experiences are as much the result of using invalid criteria as they are the outcome of inadequate rater training.[31]

Once raters are trained, the appraisal process can begin. But the results of the appraisal process do little to improve employee performance unless employees receive feedback on their appraisals. This feedback process is called evaluation interviews.

### Evaluation Interviews

*Evaluation interviews* are performance review sessions that give employees feedback about their past performance or future potential. The evaluator may provide this feedback through several approaches: tell and sell, tell and listen, and problem solving.[32] The *tell-*

*and-sell approach* reviews the employee's performance and tries to convince the employee to perform better. It is best used on new employees. The *tell-and-listen method* allows the employee to explain reasons, excuses, and defensive feelings about performance. It attempts to overcome these reactions by counselling the employee on how to perform better. The *problem-solving approach* identifies problems that are interfering with employee performance. Then through training, coaching, or counselling, efforts are made to remove these deficiencies, often by setting goals for future performance.

Regardless of which approach is used to give employees feedback, the guidelines listed in Figure 11-11 can help make the performance review session more effective.[33] The intent of these suggestions is to make the interview a positive, performance-improving dialogue. By stressing desirable aspects of employee performance, the evaluator can give the employee renewed confidence in her or his ability to perform satisfactorily. This positive approach also enables the employee to keep desirable and undesirable performance in perspective, because it prevents the individual from feeling that performance review sessions are entirely negative. When negative comments are made, they focus on work performance and not the individual's personality. Specific, rather than general and vague, examples of the employee's shortcomings are used, so that the individual knows exactly what behaviours need to be changed. The review session concludes by focusing on actions that the employee can take to improve areas of poor performance. In that concluding discussion, the evaluator usually offers to provide whatever assistance the employee needs to overcome the deficiencies discussed.

FIGURE 11-11    Guidelines for Effective Performance Evaluation Interviews

1. **Emphasize** positive aspects of employee performance.
2. **Tell** each employee that the evaluation session is to improve performance, not to discipline.
3. **Conduct** the performance review session in private with minimum interruptions.
4. **Review** performance formally at least annually and more frequently for new employees or those who are performing poorly.
5. **Make** criticisms specific, not general and vague.
6. **Focus** criticisms on performance, not on personality characteristics.
7. **Stay** calm and do not argue with the person being evaluated.
8. **Identify** specific actions the employee can take to improve performance.
9. **Emphasize** the evaluator's willingness to assist the employee's efforts and to improve performance.
10. **End** the evaluation sessions by stressing the positive aspects of the employee's performance.

Since the evaluation interview provides employees with performance-related feedback, it is not surprising that 95% of the firms in one study require managers to discuss the appraisal with employees.[34] The study also reports that nearly 40% of these employers use appraisals at least annually.[35]

## Human Resource Management Feedback

The performance appraisal process also provides insight into the effectiveness of the human resource management function. Figure 11-12 summarizes the major concepts discussed so far in this book. As can be seen, performance appraisal serves as a "quality-

FIGURE 11-12   The Personnel Management Process

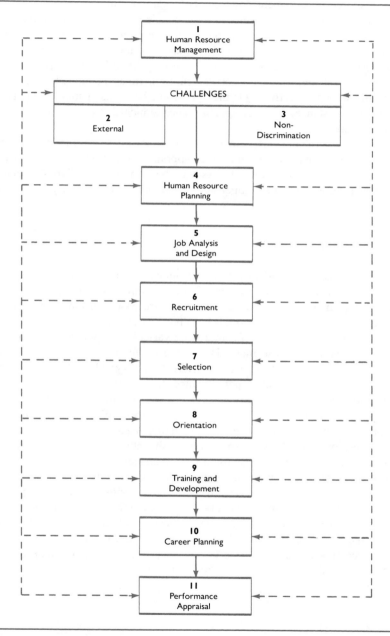

control check.'' If the appraisal process indicates that poor performance is widespread, many employees are excluded from internal placement decisions. They will not be promoted or transferred. In fact, they may be excluded from the organization through termination.

Unacceptably high numbers of poor performers may indicate errors elsewhere in the human resource management function. For example, human resource development may be failing to fulfil career plans because the people who are hired during the selection process are screened poorly. Or the human resource plan may be in error because the job analysis information is wrong or the affirmative-action plan seeks the wrong objectives. Likewise, the human resource department may be failing to respond to the challenges of the external environment or job design. Sometimes the human resource function is pursuing the wrong objectives. Or the appraisal system itself may be faulty because of management resistance, incorrect performance standards or measures, or a lack of constructive feedback.[36]

Wherever the problem lies, human resource specialists need to monitor carefully the results of the organization's performance appraisal process. It can serve as a barometer of the entire personnel function. As will be explained in Part 4, performance appraisal serves as a guide to compensation and other human resource management activities too.

## SUMMARY

Performance appraisal is a critical activity of human resource management. Its goal is to provide an accurate picture of past and/or future employee performance. To do this, performance standards are established. Standards are based on job-related criteria that best determine successful job performance. Where possible, actual performance then is measured directly and objectively. From a wide variety of appraisal techniques, human resource specialists select those methods that most effectively measure employee performance against the previously set standards. Techniques can be selected both to review past performance and to anticipate performance in the future.

The appraisal process is usually designed by the human resource department, often with little consultation from other parts of the organization. When it is time to implement a new appraisal approach, those who do the rating usually have little idea about the appraisal process or its objectives. To overcome this shortcoming, the department may design and deliver appraisal workshops to train managers.

A necessary requirement of the appraisal process is employee feedback through an evaluation interview. The interview tries to balance positive areas of performance and those areas where performance is deficient, so that the employee receives a realistic view of performance. Perhaps the most significant challenge raised by performance appraisals is the feedback they provide about human resource department performance. Human resource specialists need to be keenly aware that poor performance, especially when it is widespread, may reflect problems with previous human resource management activities that are malfunctioning.

## TERMS FOR REVIEW

Performance standards  
Performance measures  
Halo effect

Error of central tendency  
Leniency and strictness  
biases

Recency effect
Rating Scale
Weighted checklist
Forced choice method
Critical incident method
Behaviourally anchored rating scales

Field review method
Comparative evaluation methods
Management by objectives approach
 (MBO)
Assessment centres
Evaluation interviews

## REVIEW AND DISCUSSION QUESTIONS

1. What are the uses of performance appraisals?

2. Suppose a company for which you work uses a rating scale. The items on the scale are general personality characteristics. What criticisms would you have of this method?

3. If you were asked to recommend a replacement for the rating scale, what actions would you take before selecting another appraisal technique?

4. If the dean of your faculty asked you to serve on a committee to develop a performance appraisal system for evaluating the faculty, what performance criteria would you identify? Of these criteria, which ones do you think are most likely to determine the faculty members' success at your school? What standards would you recommend to the dean, regardless of the specific evaluation instrument selected?

5. Why are direct and objective measures of performance usually considered superior to indirect and subjective measures?

6. If your organization were to use subjective measures to evaluate employee performance, what instructions would you give evaluators about the biases they might encounter?

7. Describe how you would conduct a typical performance evaluation interview.

8. How do the results of performance appraisals affect other human resource management activities?

## INCIDENT 11-1

### Multiple Appraisal Failures at Roget's Waterworks

For two years, the employees at Roget's Waterworks were evaluated with the same performance appraisal method as other employees of the Roget Municipal Services Corporation (a company-operated city utility). The human resource manager decided that the duties at the waterworks were sufficiently different that a specially designed appraisal should be developed. A weighted checklist was decided on and was used for about one year. The human resource manager left, and the replacement disliked weighted checklists. Specialists then implemented behaviourally anchored rating scales. But no sooner was the method installed than top management decided to shift all evaluations at the Roget corporation to the critical incident method.

The critical incident method worked well in all phases of the corporation's operations except the waterworks. Supervisors in the waterworks would not keep a record of critical incidents until about a week before the incidents were due to be submitted to the human resource department. Training sessions were held for these supervisors, but little change in their behaviour resulted. To evaluate the supervisors, the company conducted a survey of employees at the waterworks. Most employees thought the supervision was fair to good in all dimensions except that supervisors showed too much favouritism. Thought was being given to other methods.

1. How would you suggest overcoming the resistance of the supervisors to using the critical incident method?
2. Should another evaluation method be tried?
3. What method would you recommend and why?

## INCIDENT 11-2

### The Malfunctioning Regional Human Resource Department

For one month the corporate human resource department of Universal Insurance Ltd. had two specialists review the operations of their regional human resource department in Vancouver. The review of the regional office centred on the department's human resource information base. A brief summary of their findings listed the following observations:

**A.** Each employee's performance appraisal showed little change from the previous year. Poor performers rated poor year in and year out.

**B.** Nearly 70% of the appraisals were not initialled by the employee even though company policy required employees to do so after they had discussed their review with the rater.

**C.** Of those employees who initialled the evaluations, several commented that the work standards were irrelevant and unfair.

**D.** A survey of past employees conducted by corporate office specialists revealed that 35% of them believed performance feedback was too infrequent.

**E.** Another 30% complained about the lack of advancement opportunities because most openings were filled from outside, and no one ever told these workers they were unpromotable.

The corporate and regional human resource directors were dismayed by the findings. Each thought the problems facing the regional office were different.

1. What do you think is the major problem with the performance appraisal process in the regional office?
2. What problems do you think exist with the regional office's (a) job analysis information, (b) human resource planning, (c) training and development, (d) career planning?

○ ○ ○ ○ ○ ○ ○ ○ ○ ○ ○ ○ ○ ○ ○ ○ ○ ○ ○ ○ ○ ○ ○ ○ ○ ○ ○ ○ ○ ○ ○ ○ ○ ○ ○ ○ ○ ○

*CASE STUDY*

## SASKATOON POWER: I

A large electric power plant in Saskatoon, Saskatchewan, has been having difficulty with its performance evaluation program. The organization has an evaluation program by which all operating employees and clerical employees are evaluated semiannually by their supervisors. The form that they have been using is given in Exhibit I. It has been in use for ten years. The form is scored as follows: Excellent = 5, above average = 4, average = 3, below average = 2, and poor = 1. The scores for each question are entered in the right-hand column and are totalled for an overall evaluation score.

The procedure used has been as follows: Each supervisor rates each employee on July 30 and January 30. The supervisor discusses the rating with the employee. The supervisor

---

EXHIBIT I

PERFORMANCE EVALUATION FORM OF SASKATOON POWER

### PERFORMANCE EVALUATION

*Supervisors*: When you are asked to do so by the human resource department, please complete this form for each of your employees. The supervisor who is responsible for 75% or more of an employee's work should complete this form for him or her. Please evaluate each facet of the employee separately.

| Quantity of work | Excellent | Above average | Average | Below average | Poor | Score |
|---|---|---|---|---|---|---|
| Quality of work | Poor | Below average | Average | Above average | Excellent | |
| Dependability at work | Excellent | Above average | Average | Below average | Poor | |
| Initiative at work | Poor | Below average | Average | Above average | Excellent | |
| Cooperativeness | Excellent | Above average | Average | Below average | Poor | |
| Getting along with co-workers | Poor | Below average | Average | Above average | Excellent | |

Total _____

Supervisor's signature _____

Employee name _____

Employee number _____

sends the rating to the human resource department. Each rating is placed in the employee's file. If promotions come up, the cumulative ratings are considered at that time. The ratings are also supposed to be used as a check when raises are given.

The system was designed by the human resource manager who retired two years ago, Joanna Kyle. Her replacement was Eugene Meyer. Meyer is a graduate in commerce from the University of Alberta at Edmonton. He graduated fifteen years ago. Since then, he's had a variety of experiences, mostly in utilities like the power company. For about five of these years he did human resource work.

Meyer has been reviewing the evaluation system. Employees have a mixture of indifferent and negative feelings about it. An informal survey has shown that about 60% of the supervisors fill the forms out, give about three minutes to each form, and send them to human resources without discussing them with the employees. Another 30% do a little better. They spend more time completing the forms but communicate about them only briefly and superficially with their employees.

Only about 10% of the supervisors seriously try to do what was intended.

Meyer found out that the forms were rarely retrieved for promotion or pay-raise analyses. Because of this, most supervisors may have felt the evaluation program was a useless ritual.

Where he had been previously employed, Meyer had seen performance evaluation as a much more useful experience, which included giving positive feedback to employees, improving future employee performance, developing employee capabilities, and providing data for promotion and compensation.

Meyer has not had much experience with design of performance evaluation systems. He feels he should seek advice on the topic.

*Requirement.* Write a report summarizing your evaluation of the strengths and weaknesses of the present evaluation system. Recommend some specific improvements or data-gathering exercises to develop a better system for Meyer.

## SASKATOON POWER: II

Maurice Botswick, a consultant specializing in human resource administration, has come to Saskatoon from his office in Calgary to examine the power plant's evaluation system. It is expected that he will propose an alternative system to Eugene Meyer for approval by his superiors. Normally, Ross Flamholtz, the top manager of the power plant, goes along with Meyer's suggestions.

Flamholtz is fifty-nine years old, an engineer by training. His interest has always been in direct operations of the plant. He has shown little interest in the people or money side of the utility. He pays more attention to equipment maintenance and replacement and the

purchase of materials used to produce the electricity. Flamholtz is a conservative person, always addressing everyone as Mr. or Mrs. or Miss. He is quiet, retiring, and an introvert. In his period of top management (the last two years), he has introduced no major changes in policy. His health is not good, and he has made it known that he would like to retire in three years and go to live with his daughter in Victoria, British Columbia.

After examining Meyer's data and interviewing persons around the plant, Botswick is sitting in Meyer's office. Botswick says:

Gene, before I go any further, I thought I might bounce my present thinking off you.

Your program lacks employee involvement. It involves one-way communication — supervisor to subordinate, or no communication at all.

Many of your supervisors have many persons to supervise. Typically, they have fifteen to twenty to oversee. They can't possibly observe this many people and evaluate them well. What would you think of this three-pronged improvement program?

1. Improve your supervisory rating program by getting a better form, training the supervisors in the importance of its use and how to use it, and increasing the number of reviews from two to four annually.

2. Institute a peer evaluation system to give the supervisors more data. That is, the people in each section rate each other (except for themselves) 1-15 best to worst. There is evidence that this is a good addition to the supervisor's information.

3. Introduce a "rate your supervisor" program. When the supervisor rates the employees, they rate him or her. This gets dialogue going and improves performance of both employees and supervisors.

*Requirement:* You are Meyer. Evaluate these suggestions for your power plant and decide how to proceed before giving Botswick the go ahead. How do you think Flamholtz will react to these suggestions? If you were Meyer, how would you convince Flamholtz to implement some or all of them?

From William F. Glueck, *Cases and Exercises in Personnel,* Second Edition, 1978, pp. 56-58. Reproduced with permission of Richard D. Irwin Inc., Homewood, Illinois.

○ ○ ○ ○ ○ ○ ○ ○ ○ ○ ○ ○ ○ ○ ○ ○ ○ ○ ○ ○ ○ ○ ○ ○ ○ ○ ○ ○ ○ ○ ○ ○ ○ ○ ○ ○ ○ ○ ○ ○ ○ ○ ○ ○ ○ ○ ○ ○

## SUGGESTED READINGS

Bernardin, H.J., and R.W. Beatty, *Performance Appraisal: Assessing Human Behavior at Work,* Belmont, Calif.: Wadsworth, 1984.

Cardy, R.L., and G.H. Dobbins, "Affect and Appraisal Accuracy: Liking as an Integral Dimension in Evaluating Performance," *Journal of Applied Psychology,* Vol. 71, 1986, pp. 672-678.

De Nisi, A.S., T.P. Cafferty and B.M. Meglino, "A Cognitive View of the Performance Appraisal Process: A Model and Research Propositions," *Organizational Behavior and Human Performance,* Vol. 33, 1984, pp. 360-396.

Ilgen, D.R., and J. Feldman, "Performance Appraisal: A Process Focus," in B. Staw (ed.), *Research in Organizational Behavior,* Vol. 5, pp. 151-197, Greenwich, Conn.: JAI Press, 1983.

Latham, G.P., and K.N. Wexley, *Increasing Productivity through Performance Appraisal,* Reading, Mass.: Addison-Wesley Publishing Company, 1981.

## REFERENCES

1. Harry Levinson, "Appraisal of *What* Performance?" *Harvard Business Review,* July-August 1976, pp. 30-32, 34, 36, 40, 44, 46, 160.

2. John B. Miner, "Management Appraisal: A Review of Procedures and Practices," in W. Clay Hamner and Frank L. Schmidt (eds.), *Contemporary Problems in Personnel,* Chicago: St. Clair Press, 1977, p. 228.

3. Robert I. Lazer and Walter S. Wilkstrom, *Appraising Managerial Performance: Current Practices and Future Directions,* New York: The Conference Board, 1977, p. 20.

4. Ibid., p. 26.

5. Royal Commission on Corporate Concentration, *Personnel Administration in Large and Middle-sized Business,* Study No. 25, Ottawa: November 1976, p. 61.

6. James M. McFillen and Patrick G. Decker, "Building Meaning into Appraisal," *The Personnel Administrator,* June 1978, pp. 78-79.

7. Miner, op. cit.

8. McFillen and Decker, op. cit., p. 80.

9. Bruce McAfee and Blake Green, "Selecting a Performance Appraisal Method," *The Personnel Administrator,* June 1978, pp. 78-79.

10. John B. McMaster, "Designing an Appraisal System That Is Fair and Accurate," *Personnel Journal,* January 1979, pp. 38-40.

11. L. Fogli, C.L. Hulin, and M.R. Blood, "Development of First-Level Behavioural Job Criteria," *Journal of Applied Psychology,* January 1979, pp. 3-8.

12. Craig Eric Schneir and Richard W. Beatty, "Developing Behaviourally-Anchored Rating Scales (BARS)," *The Personnel Administrator,* August 1979, pp. 59-68. See also Hermann F. Schwind, "Behavior Sampling for Effective Performance Feedback," in Judith W. Springer (ed.), *Job Performance Standards and Measures,* Madison: American Society for Training and Development, 1980, pp. 11-39.

13. Latham and Wexley, op. cit., pp. 52-54.

14. Ibid. See also Craig Eric Schneir and Richard W. Beatty, "Developing Behaviorally-Anchored Rating Scales (BARS)," *Personnel Administrator,* August 1979, pp. 59-68; Aaron Tziner, "A Fairer Examination of Rating Scales When Used for Performance Appraisal in a Real Organizational Setting," unpublished paper, 1982.

15. J. Peter Graves, "Let's Put Appraisal Back in Performance Appraisal: II," *Personnel Journal,* December 1982, p. 918.

16. Milan Moravec, "How Performance Appraisal Can Tie Communication to Productivity," *Personnel Administrator,* January 1981, pp. 51-52.

17. William B. Werther, Jr., and Heinz Weihrich, "Refining MBO through Negotiations," *MSU Business Topics,* Summer 1975, pp. 53-58.

18. John P. Bucalo, Jr., "The Assessment Center — A More Specified Approach," *Human Resource Management,* Fall 1974, pp. 2-13. See also William C. Byham, "Starting an Assessment Center," *Personnel Administrator,* February 1980, pp. 27-32.

19. Ibid.

20. "How to Spot the Hotshots," *Business Week,* October 8, 1979, pp. 62, 67.

21. Hubert S. Field and William H. Holley, "The Relationship of Performance Appraisal System Characteristics to Verdicts in Selected Employment Discrimination Cases," *Academy of Management Journal,* June 1982, pp. 392-406. See also George F. Dreher and Paul S. Sackett, "Some Problems with Applying Content Validity Evidence to Assessment Center Procedures," *Academy of Management Review,* October 1981, pp. 551-560; Steven D. Norton, "The Assessment Center Process and Content Validity: A Reply to Dreher and Sackett," *Academy of Management Review,* October 1981, pp. 561-566; Paul R. Sackett and George F. Dreher, "Some Misconceptions about Content-Oriented Validation: A Rejoinder to Norton," *Academy of Management Review,* October 1981, pp. 567-568.

22. Bucalo, op. cit., p. 11.

23. Leland C. Nichols and Joseph Hudson, "Dual-Role Assessment Center: Selection and Development, *Personnel Journal,* May 1981, pp. 380-386.

24. Ibid., p. 382.

25. "How to Spot the Hotshots," *Business Week,* October 8, 1979, pp. 62, 67.

26. B.B. Gaugler, D.B. Rosenthal, G.C. Thornton, and C. Bentson, "Meta-Analysis of Assessment Center Validity," *Journal of Applied Psychology,* 1987, Vol. 72, No. 3, pp. 493-511.

27. William J. Birch, "Performance Appraisal: One Company's Experience," *Personnel Journal,* June 1981, pp. 456-460.

28. Ibid.

29. J.M. Feldman, "Beyond Attribution Theory: Cognitive Processes in Performance Appraisal," *Journal of Applied Psychology,* 1981, Vol. 66, pp. 127-148.

30. Comment made by a human resource manager during a guest lecture in one of the authors' classes. He had worked for fifteen years with a number of U.S. and Canadian department stores.

31. H.F. Schwind, "Performance Appraisal: The State of the Art," in Dolan and Schuler (eds.) *Personnel and Human Resources Management in Canada,* Toronto West Publishing, 1987, pp. 197-209.

32. Norman R.F. Maier, *The Appraisal Interview: Three Basic Approaches,* La Jolla, Calif.: University Associates, 1976.

33. Miner, op. cit., p. 249.

34. Lazer and Wikstrom, op. cit., p. 31.

35. Ibid., p. 24.

36. Kenneth S. Teel, "Performance Appraisal: Current Trends, Persistent Progress," *Personnel Journal,* April 1980, pp. 296-301. See also "Appraising the Performance Appraisal," *Business Week,* May 19, 1980, pp. 153-154.

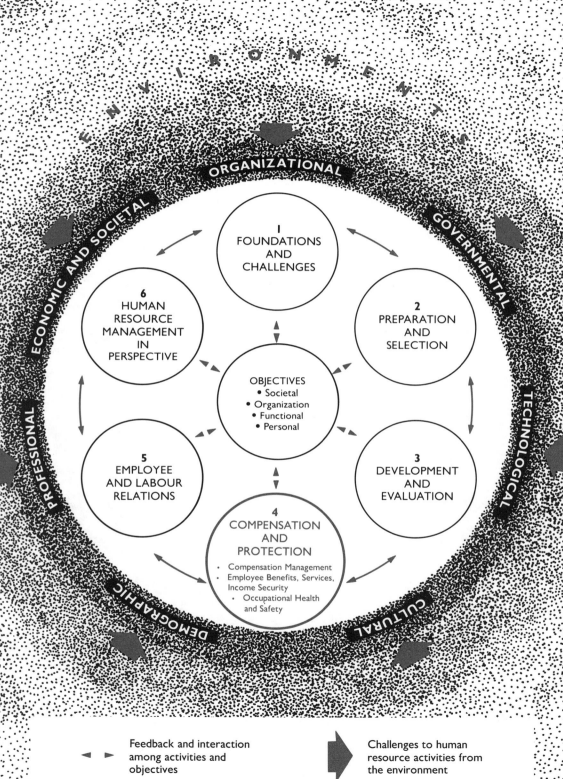

ENVIRONMENTS

ORGANIZATIONAL

ECONOMIC AND SOCIETAL

GOVERNMENTAL

PROFESSIONAL

TECHNOLOGICAL

DEMOGRAPHIC

CULTURAL

**1**
FOUNDATIONS
AND
CHALLENGES

**2**
PREPARATION
AND
SELECTION

**6**
HUMAN
RESOURCE
MANAGEMENT
IN
PERSPECTIVE

**3**
DEVELOPMENT
AND
EVALUATION

**5**
EMPLOYEE
AND LABOUR
RELATIONS

OBJECTIVES
• Societal
• Organization
• Functional
• Personal

**4**
COMPENSATION
AND
PROTECTION

• Compensation Management
• Employee Benefits, Services, Income Security
• Occupational Health and Safety

Feedback and interaction among activities and objectives

Challenges to human resource activities from the environment

# P A R T 4 ○○○○○○

## *COMPENSATION AND PROTECTION*

*A* successful company needs a motivated and satisfied work force. This responsibility is part of every manager's job. But the human resource department can help. It can advise managers about useful motivation techniques. It can also help indirectly with compensation, benefits, and services. Often the department assists managers with safety and communications programs. When employee problems do recur, the human resource department helps with counselling and discipline.

Each of these topics is discussed in Part 4. They are important management tools for human resource specialists and managers alike. Regardless of your job, you will find that these tools are helpful ways to ensure effective performance.

# CHAPTER *12* ○ ○ ○ ○ ○ ○ ○

## *COMPENSATION MANAGEMENT*

*Management's challenge is to create an environment which stimulates people in their jobs and fosters company growth, and a key aspect of the environment is compensation.*

MILTON L. ROCK[1]

*. . . something happened on the road to the 20th century. Employees became "wage earners"—pure and simple—not concerned about the overall success of the business because they did not have a direct stake in profits or ownership.*

BERT L. METZGER[2]

○ ○ ○ ○ ○ ○ ○ ○ ○ ○ ○ ○ ○ ○ ○ ○ ○ ○ ○ ○ ○ ○ ○ ○ ○ ○ ○ ○ ○ ○ ○ ○ ○ ○ ○ ○ ○ ○

## *CHAPTER OBJECTIVES*

After studying this chapter, you should be able to:

1. **Discuss** the consequences of mismanaged compensation programs.
2. **Explain** the objectives of effective compensation management.
3. **Describe** how wages and salaries are determined.
4. **Identify** the major issues that influence compensation management.
5. **Explain** the differences between "equal pay for equal work" and "equal pay for work of equal value."
6. **Evaluate** the advantages and disadvantages of incentive systems.
7. **Explain** the major approaches to group incentive plans.

○ ○ ○ ○ ○ ○ ○ ○ ○ ○ ○ ○ ○ ○ ○ ○ ○ ○ ○ ○ ○ ○ ○ ○ ○ ○ ○ ○ ○ ○ ○ ○ ○ ○ ○ ○ ○ ○

*O*ne way the human resource department improves employee performance, motivation, and satisfaction is through compensation. *Compensation* is the money employees receive in exchange for their work. Whether it be in the form of hourly wages or periodic salaries, the human resource department usually designs and administers employee compensation. When compensation is done correctly, employees are more likely to be satisfied and motivated towards organizational objectives. And the department is more likely to achieve its objective of an effective work force. But when employees perceive their compensation to be inappropriate, performance, motivation, and satisfaction may decline dramatically, as the following dialogue illustrates.

> Joan Swensen walked into Al Jorgeson's office, slammed down her clipboard, and said, "I quit!"
>
> "What is the matter, Joan?" Al questioned. "You've been here two years, and I've never seen you so mad."
>
> "That's just the problem. I've been here two years, and this morning I found out that the new man you hired last week, Kurt, is making the same pay that I am," Joan said.
>
> "Well, he does the same work, he works the same hours, and he has the same responsibilities. Would it be fair to pay him less?" Al asked.
>
> "Doesn't experience count for anything around here? When you brought him into the shop, you told me to show him the ropes. So not only did I have more experience, but I am also responsible for training him," Joan responded.
>
> "Okay, okay, I'll talk with Human Resources this afternoon and see if I can get you a raise," Al conceded.
>
> "Don't bother. I'm quitting," Joan asserted. "If this company doesn't want to do what is right voluntarily, I'd rather work someplace else."

Compensation programs maintain an organization's human resources. When wages and salaries are not administered properly, the firm may lose employees and the money spent to recruit, select, train, and develop them. Even if workers do not quit, as Joan did in the opening illustration, they may become dissatisfied with the company.

Dissatisfaction arises because employee needs are affected by absolute and relative levels of pay, as shown in Figure 12-1. When the total, or *absolute*, amount of pay is too low, employees cannot meet their physiological or security needs. In industrial societies, the absolute level of pay usually is high enough to meet these basic needs, at least minimally. A more common source of dissatisfaction centres on *relative pay*, which is an employee's pay compared with that of other workers. For example, Joan's concern was over the *relative* amount of her salary in comparison with the new, less experienced employee, Kurt. Her additional experience and training responsibilities were not reflected in her pay as compared with Kurt's pay. Her esteem needs were affected because she did not get the recognition she thought she deserved.

Absolute and relative pay levels also may hold negative consequences for the organization.[3] The implications of pay dissatisfaction are diagrammed in Figure 12-2. In

FIGURE 12-1   Absolute and Relative Pay Levels in Relation to Employee Needs

| PAY LEVELS | EMPLOYEE NEEDS PRIMARILY SERVED |
| --- | --- |
| Absolute | Physiological and security needs |
| Relative | Social and esteem needs |

severe cases, the desire for more pay can lower performance, increase grievances, or lead employees to search for new jobs. The lower attractiveness of their jobs can cause job dissatisfaction, absenteeism, or other undesirable outcomes. Even overpayment of wages and salaries can harm the organization and its people. Overpaid employees may feel anxiety, guilt, and discomfort.[4] High compensation costs can reduce the firm's competitiveness and lessen its future ability to provide attractive jobs. This balance between pay satisfaction and the organization's competitiveness underlies most of the human resource department's compensation efforts.

**FIGURE 12-2** Model of the Consequences of Pay Dissatisfaction

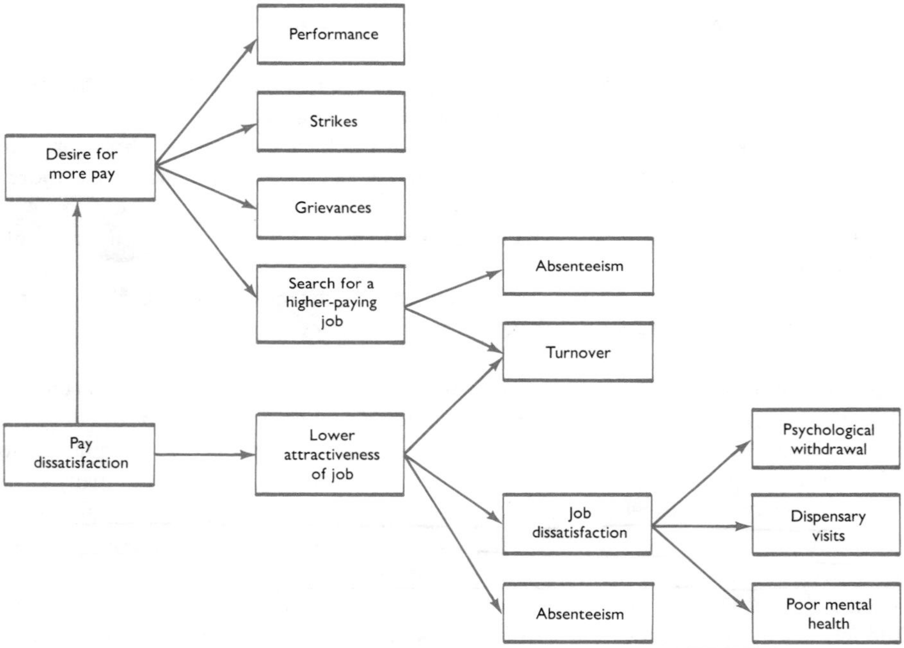

Source: Edward E. Lawler, III, *Pay and Organizational Effectiveness: A Psychological View,* New York: McGraw-Hill Book Company, 1971, p. 233. Used with permission of the McGraw-Hill Book Company.

Since compensation affects the organization and its employees, this chapter examines the requirements for an effective compensation system.[5] The chapter also discusses the objectives and procedures used to administer compensation. Then it concludes with a review of financial incentives.

## OBJECTIVES OF COMPENSATION ADMINISTRATION

The administration of compensation must meet numerous objectives. Sometimes the ones listed in Figure 12-3 conflict with each other and trade-offs must be made.[6] For example, to retain employees and ensure equity, wage and salary analysts pay similar amounts for similar jobs. But a recruiter may want to offer an unusually high salary to attract a qualified recruit. At this point the human resource manager must make a trade-off between the recruiting and the consistency objectives.

FIGURE 12-3   Objectives Sought Through Effective Compensation Administration

- **Acquire qualified personnel.** Compensation needs to be high enough to attract applicants. Since companies compete in the labour market, pay levels must respond to the supply and demand of workers. But sometimes a premium wage rate is needed to attract applicants who are already employed in other firms.
- **Retain present employees.** When compensation levels are not competitive, some employees quit. To prevent employee turnover, pay must be kept competitive with that of other employers.
- **Ensure equity.** The administration of wages and salaries strives for internal and external equity. **Internal equity** requires that pay be related to the relative worth of jobs. That is, similar jobs get similar pay. **External equity** involves paying workers at a rate equal to the pay that similar workers receive in other companies.
- **Reward desired behaviour**. Pay should reinforce desired behaviours. Good performance, experience, loyalty, new responsibilities, and other behaviours can be rewarded through an effective compensation plan.
- **Control costs.** A rational compensation program helps an organization to obtain and retain its work force at a reasonable cost. Without a systematic wage and salary structure the organization could overpay or underpay its employees.
- **Comply with legal regulations.** As with other aspects of human resource management, wage and salary administration faces legal constraints. A sound pay program considers these constraints and ensures compliance with all government regulations that affect employee compensation.
- **Further administrative efficiency.** In pursuing the other objectives of effective compensation management, wage and salary specialists try to design the program so that it can be efficiently administered. Administrative efficiency, however, should be a secondary consideration compared with other objectives.

Other objectives of compensation are to reward desired behaviour and to control costs. These objectives can conflict, too. For example, a department manager may want to reward outstanding performance with a raise, but every raise adds to costs. Here again, the human resource manager must decide between two conflicting goals.

Regardless of the trade-offs, an overriding objective is to maintain legal compliance. For example, the Canada Labour Code requires employers to pay minimum wages and time and a half for overtime. Periodically, federal and provincial governments raise minimum wages, and employers must comply regardless of other objectives being sought.

Compensation objectives are not rules. They are guidelines. but the less these guidelines are violated, the more effective wage and salary administration can be. To meet these objectives, compensation specialists evaluate every job, conduct wage and salary surveys, and price each job. Through these steps, the appropriate pay level for each job is determined.

Figure 12-4 depicts these three major phases of compensation management. Each phase is discussed in the following sections.

FIGURE 12-4   Major Phases of Compensation Management

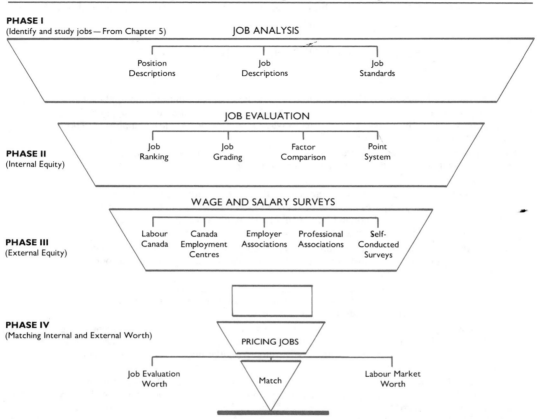

## JOB EVALUATION

*Job evaluations* are systematic procedures to determine the relative worth of jobs. Although there are several different approaches, each one considers the duties, responsibilities, and working conditions of the job. The purpose of job evaluation is to identify which jobs should be paid more than others.

Since evaluation is subjective, it is conducted by specialists, or a group of specialists called a *job evaluation committee.*[7] They begin with a review of job analysis information to learn about the duties, responsibilities, and working conditions that shape their evaluation. With this knowledge, the relative worth of jobs is determined by selecting a job evaluation method. The most common ones are job ranking, job grading, factor comparison, and the point system.

### Job Ranking

The simplest and least precise method of job evaluation is *job ranking*. Specialists review the job analysis information for each job. Then each job is ranked subjectively according to its importance in comparison with other jobs. These are overall rankings, although raters may consider the responsibility, skill, effort, and working conditions of each job. It is quite possible that important elements of some jobs may be overlooked while unimportant items are weighted too heavily. What is even more damaging, these rankings do not differentiate the relative importance of jobs. For example, the job of janitor may be ranked as 1, the secretary's job may get a 2, and the office manager is ranked as a 3. But the secretarial position may be three times as important as the janitorial job and half as important as the job of office manager. The job ranking approach does not allow for these relative differences between jobs. Pay scales based on these broad rankings ensure that more important jobs are paid more. But since the rankings lack precision, the resulting pay levels may be inaccurate.

## Job Grading

*Job grading,* or job classification, is a slightly more sophisticated method than job ranking, but it, too, is not very precise. It works by having each job assigned a grade, as explained in Figure 12-5. The standard description in the figure that most nearly matches the job description determines the grade of the job. Once again, more important jobs are paid more. But the lack of precision can lead to inaccurate pay levels. The largest user of this approach has been the Canadian Public Service Commission, which is gradually replacing this approach with more sophisticated methods.

FIGURE 12-5   A Job Classification Schedule for Use with the Job Grading Method

---

**EMPIRE MACHINE SHOP**
**Job Classification Schedule**

**Directions:** To determine appropriate job grade, match standard description with job description.

| Job Grade | Standard Description |
|---|---|
| I | Work is simple and highly repetitive, done under close supervision, requiring minimal training and little responsibility or initiative. **Examples:** Janitor, file clerk |
| II | Work is simple and repetitive, done under close supervision, requiring some training or skill. Employee is expected to assume responsibility or exhibit initiative only rarely. **Examples:** Clerk-typist I, machine cleaner |
| III | Work is simple, with little variation, done under general supervision. Training or skill required. Employee has minimum responsibilities and must take some initiative to perform satisfactorily. **Examples:** Parts expediter, machine oiler, clerk-typist II |
| IV | Work is moderately complex, with some variation, done under general supervision. High level of skill required. Employee is responsible for equipment or safety; regularly exhibits initiative. **Examples:** Machine operator I, tool and die apprentice |
| V | Work is complex, varied, done under general supervision. Advanced skill level required. Employee is responsible for equipment and safety; shows high degree of initiative. **Examples:** Machine operator II, tool and die specialist |

## Factor Comparison

The *factor comparison* method requires the job evaluation committee to compare critical job components. The critical components are those factors common to all jobs being evaluated. The most widely used ones are responsibility, skill, mental effort, physical effort, and working conditions.[8] Each of these factors is compared, one at a time, against the same factor for other jobs. This evaluation allows the committee to determine the relative importance of each job. The factor comparison method involves five steps, as follows:

### Step 1: Determine the Critical Factors

Analysts must first decide which factors are common and important in a broad range of jobs. The critical factors shown in Figure 12-6 are most commonly used. Some organizations use different factors for managerial, professional, sales, or other types of jobs if the factors in the figure are considered inappropriate.

FIGURE 12-6   The Apportionment of Wages for Key Jobs

| CRITICAL FACTORS | KEY JOBS | | | | |
|---|---|---|---|---|---|
| | MACHINIST | FORKLIFT DRIVER | SECRETARY | JANITOR | FILE CLERK |
| Responsibility | $ 4.40 | $ 3.60 | $ 2.40 | $ .80 | $1.90 |
| Skill | 8.00 | 3.00 | 3.20 | 1.20 | 2.40 |
| Mental Effort | 4.00 | 1.60 | 2.60 | .60 | 1.80 |
| Physical Effort | 4.00 | 2.20 | 1.40 | 3.40 | 1.40 |
| Working Conditions | 1.40 | 1.20 | 1.20 | 3.00 | 1.20 |
| Total | $21.80 | $11.60 | $10.80 | $9.00 | $8.70 |
| Wage Rate | $21.80 | $11.60 | $10.80 | $9.00 | $8.70 |

### Step 2: Determine Key jobs

*Key jobs* are those that are common in the organization and are common in the employer's labour market. Common jobs are selected because it is easier to discover the market rate for them. Ideally, these jobs should include those with a wide variety of critical factors to be evaluated.

### Step 3: Apportion Present Wages for Key Jobs

The job evaluation committee then allocates a part of each key job's wage rate to each critical factor, as shown in Figure 12-6. The proportion of each wage assigned to the different critical factors depends on the importance of the factor.

> For example, a janitor receives $9. This amount is apportioned in Figure 12-6 as follows: $.80 for responsibility, $1.20 for skill, $.60 for mental effort, $3.40 for physical effort, and $3.00 for working conditions. In apportioning these wage rates, two comparisons must be made. First, the amount assigned to each factor should reflect its importance when compared with the other factors of that job. For exam-

ple, if $8 is assigned to skill and $4 to physical effort for the machinist, this implies that the skill factor is two times as important as physical effort. Second, the amount allocated to a single factor should reflect the relative importance of that factor among different jobs. For example, if responsibility of the secretary is three times that of the janitor, then the money allocated to the secretary for responsibility ($2.40) should be three times that of the janitor ($.80).

FIGURE 12-7   Factor Comparison Chart

| RATE | RESPONSI-BILITY | SKILL | MENTAL EFFORT | PHYSICAL EFFORT | WORKING CONDITIONS |
|---|---|---|---|---|---|
| 8.00 — | — | — Machinist | — | — | — |
| — | — | — | — | — | — |
| — | — | — | — | — | — |
| — | — | — | — | — | — |
| 7.00 — | — | — | — | — | — |
| — | — | — | — | — | — |
| — | — | — | — | — | — |
| — | — | — | — | — | — |
| — | — | — | — | — | — |
| 6.00 — | — | — **Mechanic** | — | — | — |
| — | — | — | — **Mechanic** | — | — |
| — | — | — | — | — | — |
| 5.00 — | — | — | — | — | — |
| — | — | — | — | — | — |
| — | — | — | — | — | — |
| — | — Machinist | — | — | — | — |
| 4.00 — | — | — | — Machinist | — Machinist | — |
| — | — Forklift | — | — | — | — |
| — | — | — | — | — Janitor | — |
| — | — | — Secretary | — | — | — |
| 3.00 — | **Mechanic** | — Forklift | — | — **Mechanic** | — Janitor |
| — | — | — | — Secretary | — | — **Mechanic** |
| — | — Secretary | — File clerk | — | — | — |
| — | — | — | — | — Forklift | — |
| 2.00 — | — File clerk | — | — | — | — |
| — | — | — | — File clerk | — | — |
| — | — | — | — Forklift | — | — |
| — | — | — | — | — {Secretary / File clerk | — Machinist |
| — | — | — Janitor | — | — | — {Forklift / Secretary / File clerk |
| 1.00 — | — Janitor | — | — | — | — |
| — | — | — | — | — | — |
| — | — | — Janitor | — | — | — |
| — | — | — | — | — | — |
| 0.00 — | — | — | — | — | — |

*Step 4: Place Key Jobs on Factor Comparison Chart*

Once the wage rates are assigned to the critical factors of each key job, this information is transferred to a factor comparison chart like the one in Figure 12-7. The titles of key jobs are placed in the columns according to the amount of wages assigned to each critical factor. In the responsibility column, for example, the secretary title is placed next to the $2.40 rate to reflect how much the secretary's responsibility is worth to the organization. This job also appears under the other critical factors according to the relative worth of those factors in the job of secretary. The same assignment process takes place for every other key job.

*Step 5: Evaluate Other Jobs*

The titles of key jobs in each column of Figure 12-7 serve as benchmarks. Other non-key jobs are then evaluated by fitting them on the scale in each column.

> For the job of senior maintenance mechanic to be evaluated, the job evaluation committee compares the responsibility of the mechanic with that involved in other key jobs already on the chart. It is decided subjectively that the mechanic's responsibility is between that of the forklift driver and the secretary. And since the mechanic's job requires about three-quarters of the machinist's skills, the skill component of this job is placed below that of the machinist in the skill column. This procedure is repeated for each critical factor. When completed, the committee can determine the worth of the mechanic's job, which is:
>
> | | |
> |---|---:|
> | Responsibility | $2.90 |
> | Skill | 6.00 |
> | Mental effort | 5.40 |
> | Physical effort | 2.80 |
> | Working conditions | 2.60 |
> | | $19.70 |

By using the same procedure applied to the mechanic's job, every other job in the organization is then evaluated. When the evaluations are completed, the job evaluation committee can rank every job according to its relative worth as indicated by its wage rate. These rankings should be reviewed by department managers to verify their appropriateness.[9]

## Point System

Research shows that the *point system* is used more than any other method.[10] It evaluates the critical factors of each job. But instead of using wages, as the factor comparison method does, points are used. Although it is more difficult to develop initially, it is more precise than the factor comparison method because it can handle critical factors in more detail. This system requires six steps to implement. It is usually done by a job evaluation committee or an individual analyst.

## Step 1: Determine Critical Factors

The point system can use the same factors as the factor comparison method, but it usually adds more detail by breaking those factors down into subfactors. For example, Figure 12-8 shows how the factor of responsibility can be broken down into:

**a.** Safety of others
**b.** Equipment and materials

**c.** Assisting trainees
**d.** Product/service quality

FIGURE 12-8   Point System Matrix

| CRITICAL FACTORS | MINIMUM I | LOW II | MODERATE III | HIGH IV |
|---|---|---|---|---|
| **1. Responsibility** | | | | |
|   **a.** Safety of others | 25 | 50 | 75 | 100 |
|   **b.** Equipment and materials | 20 | 40 | 60 | 80 |
|   **c.** Assisting trainees | 5 | 20 | 35 | 50 |
|   **d.** Product/service quality | 20 | 40 | 60 | 80 |
| **2. Skill** | | | | |
|   **a.** Experience | 45 | 90 | 135 | 180 |
|   **b.** Education/training | 25 | 50 | 75 | 100 |
| **3. Effort** | | | | |
|   **a.** Physical | 25 | 50 | 75 | 100 |
|   **b.** Mental | 35 | 70 | 105 | 150 |
| **4. Working conditions** | | | | |
|   **a.** Unpleasant conditions | 20 | 40 | 60 | 80 |
|   **b.** Hazards | 20 | 40 | 60 | 80 |
| Total points | | | | 1000 |

## Step 2: Determine Levels of Factors

Since the extent of responsibility, or other factors, may vary from job to job, the point system creates several levels associated with each factor. Figure 12-8 shows four levels, although more or fewer may be used. These levels help analysts to reward different degrees of responsibility, skills, and other critical factors.

## Step 3: Allocate Points to Subfactors

With the factors listed down one side and the levels placed across the top of Figure 12-8, the result is a point system matrix. Points are then assigned to each subfactor to reflect the relative importance of different subfactors. Analysts start with level IV and weight each subfactor with the number of points they think it deserves. This allocation allows them to give very precise weights to each element of the job. For example, if safety is twice as important as assisting trainees, it is assigned twice as many points (100) as assisting trainees (50).

## Step 4: Allocate Points to Levels

Once the points for each job element are satisfactory under column IV, analysts allocate points across each row to reflect the importance of the different levels. For simplicity, equal point differences are usually assigned between levels, as was done for "Safety of others" in Figure 12-8. Or point differences between levels can be variable, as shown for "assisting trainees." Both approaches are used depending on how important each level of each subfactor is.

### Step 5: Develop the Point Manual

Analysts then develop a point manual. It contains a written explanation of each job element, as shown in Figure 12-9 for responsibility of equipment and materials. It also defines what is expected for the four levels of each subfactor. This information is needed to assign jobs to their appropriate level.

FIGURE 12-9    Point Manual Description of "Responsibility: Equipment and Materials"

---

1. **Responsibility**
   **b. Equipment and Materials.** Each employee is responsible for conserving the company's equipment and materials. This includes reporting malfunctioning equipment or defective materials, keeping equipment and materials cleaned or in proper order, and maintaining, repairing, or modifying equipment and materials according to individual job duties. The company recognizes that the degree of responsibility for equipment and material varies widely throughout the organization.

   **Level I.** Employee reports malfunctioning equipment or defective materials to immediate superior.

   **Level II.** Employee maintains the appearance of equipment or order of materials and has responsibility for the security of such equipment or materials.

   **Level III.** Employee performs preventive maintenance and minor repairs on equipment or corrects minor defects in materials.

   **Level IV.** Employee performs major maintenance or overhauls of equipment or is responsible for deciding type, quantity, and quality of materials to be used.

---

### Step 6: Apply the Point System

When the point matrix and manual are ready, the relative value of each job can be determined. This process is subjective. It requires specialists to compare job descriptions with the point manual for each subfactor. The match between the job description and the point manual statement reveals the level and points for each subfactor of every job. Once completed, the points for each subfactor are added to find the total number of points for the job. An example of this matching process for Machine Operator I appears below:

> The job description of Machine Operator I states " . . . operator is responsible for performing preventive maintenance (such as cleaning, oiling, and adjusting belts) and minor repairs." The sample point manual excerpt in Figure 12-9 states "Level III: . . . performs preventive maintenance and minor repairs . . . ." Since the job description and the point manual match at Level III, the points for the equipment subfactor are 60. Repeating this matching process for each subfactor yields the total points for the job of Machine Operator I.

After the total points for each job are known, the jobs are ranked. As with the job ranking, job grade, and factor comparison systems, this relative ranking should be reviewed by department managers to ensure that it is appropriate.

Beyond the four job evaluation methods discussed in this section, many other variations exist. Large organizations often modify standard approaches to create unique in-house variations.

The "Hay Plan," for example, is one variation widely used by Canadian and U.S. firms. This proprietary method is marketed by a large consulting firm, Hay and Associates, and relies on a committee evaluation of critical job factors to determine each job's relative worth. Although other job evaluation approaches exist, all effective job evaluation schemes attempt to determine a job's relative worth to ensure internal equity.

## WAGE AND SALARY SURVEYS

All job evaluation techniques result in a ranking of jobs based upon their relative worth. This assures *internal* equity. That is, jobs that are worth more will be paid more. But how much should be paid? What constitutes *external* equity?

To determine a fair rate of compensation, most firms rely on *wage and salary surveys*. These surveys discover what other employers in the *same* labour market are paying for specific key jobs. The *labour market* is the area from which the employer recruits. Generally, it is the local community in which the employer is located. However, the firms may have to compete for some workers in a labour market that extends beyond the local community. Consider how the president of one large university viewed the market:

> Our labour market depends on the type of position we are trying to fill. For the hourly paid jobs such as janitor, clerk, typist, and secretary, the labour market is the surrounding metropolitan community. When we hire professors, our labour market is Canada. We have to compete with universities in other provinces to get the type of faculty member we seek. When we have the funds to hire a distinguished professor, our labour market is the whole world.

### Sources of Compensation Data

Wage and salary data are benchmarks against which analysts compare compensation levels. This survey information can be obtained in several ways. One source is Labour Canada. It conducts surveys in major metropolitan labour markets periodically. Sometimes, these surveys are out of date in a fast-changing labour market, and so other sources may be needed. Many consultants provide this service for their clientele. Canada Employment Centres also compile wage and salary information for distribution to employers. When compiled frequently by the centre consulted, this information may be current enough for use by compensation analysts. A fourth source of compensation data may be an employer association, which surveys member firms. Employer associations — or a fifth source, professional associations — may be the only source of compensation data for highly specialized jobs.

The major problem with all these published surveys is their varying comparability.

Analysts cannot always be sure that their jobs match those reported in the survey. Matching just job titles may be misleading. Federal, provincial, and association job descriptions may be considerably different, even when the jobs have the same title. Since most published surveys rely on the *Canadian Classification and Dictionary of Occupations* (CCDO), any job description should be compared with descriptions in the CCDO.

## Survey Procedure

To overcome the limitations of published surveys, some human resource departments conduct their own wage and salary survey.[11] Since surveying all jobs is cumbersome and expensive, usually only key jobs are used. Then a sample of firms from the labour market is selected. Finally, these organizations are contacted by phone or mail to learn what they are paying for the key jobs. Most companies are willing to cooperate since they, too, need this information. Contracts through professional associations, such as the Canadian Manufacturers' Association and its local affiliates or provincial human resource associations, can further aid this process. Again, it is important to make sure that the comparisons are between similar jobs and not just similar titles.

At this point, all jobs are ranked according to their relative worth, as a result of the job evaluation process. Through wage and salary surveys, the rate for key jobs in the labour market is also known. This leaves the last phase of wage and salary administration, pricing the jobs.

## PRICING JOBS

Pricing jobs includes two activities: establishing the appropriate pay level for each job and grouping the different pay levels into a structure that can be managed effectively.

## Pay Levels

The appropriate pay level for any job reflects its relative and absolute worth. A job's relative worth is determined by its ranking through the job evaluation process. The absolute worth of a job is controlled by what the labour market pays similar jobs. To set the right pay level means combining the job evaluation rankings and the survey wage rates.

This information is combined through the use of a graph called a *scattergram*. As Figure 12-10 shows, its vertical axis is pay rates. If the point system is used to determine the ranking of jobs, the horizontal axis is in points. The scattergram is created by plotting the total points and wage level for each *key job*. Thus each dot represents the intersection of the point value and the wage rate for a particular key job. For example, Key Job A in Figure 12-10 is worth 500 points and is paid $8 an hour.

Through the dots that represent key jobs, a *wage-trend line* is drawn as close to as many points as possible. (This line can be done freehand, or more accurately, by a statistical technique called the *least squares method*.)[12]

The wage-trend line helps to determine the wage rates for non-key jobs. There are two steps. First, the point value for the non-key job is located on the horizontal axis. Second, a line is traced vertically to the wage-trend line, then horizontally to the dollar

FIGURE 12-10   The Development of a Wage-Trend Line

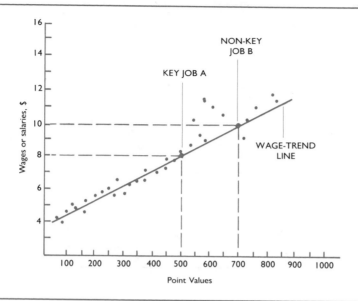

scale. The amount on the vertical scale is the appropriate wage rate for the non-key job. For example, non-key job B is worth 700 points. By tracing a vertical line up to the wage-trend line and then horizontally to the vertical (dollar) scale, it can be seen in Figure 12-10 that the appropriate wage rate for job B is $10 per hour.

## The Compensation Structure

A medium-sized organization with 2000 workers and 325 separately identifiable jobs would present the wage and salary analyst with complex problems. The existence of 325 separate wage rates would be meaningless because the differences in wages between each job might be no more than a few cents.

Compensation analysts find it more convenient to lump jobs together into *job classes.* In the job grade approach, jobs are already grouped into predetermined categories. With other methods, the grouping is done by creating job grades based on the previous ranking, pay, or points. In the point system, for example, classifications are based on point ranges: 0 to 100, 101 to 150, 151 to 200, and so forth. This grouping causes the wage-trend line to be replaced with a series of ascending dashes, as shown in Figure 12-11. Thus all jobs in the same class receive the same wage rate. A job valued at 105 points, for example, receives the same pay as a job with 145 points. Too many grades defeat the purpose of grouping; too few groupings result in workers with jobs of widely varying importance receiving the same pay.

The problem with flat rates for each job class is that exceptional performance cannot be rewarded. To give a worker a merit increase requires moving the employee

FIGURE 12-11    The Impact of Job Classes on the Wage-Trend Line

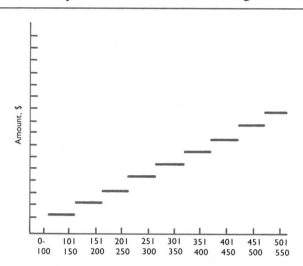

into a higher job class. This upsets the entire balance of internal equity developed through job evaluations. To solve these problems, most firms use rate ranges for each class.[13]

*Rate ranges* means simply a pay range for each job class. For example, suppose the wage-trend line indicates that $10 is the average hourly rate for a particular job class. Every employee in that class gets $10 if a flat rate is paid. With a rate range of $2 for each class, a marginal performer can be paid $9 at the bottom of the range, as indicated in Figure 12-12. Then an average performer is placed at midpoint in the rate range, $10. When performance appraisals indicate above-average performance, the employee may be given a *merit raise* of, say, $.50 per hour for the exceptional performance.[14] If this performance continues, another merit raise of $.50 can be granted. Once the employee reaches the top of the rate range, no more wage increases will be forthcoming. Either a promotion or a general across-the-board pay raise needs to occur for this worker's wages to exceed $11. An across-the-board increase moves the entire wage-trend line upward.[15]

As new jobs are created, the wage and salary section performs a job evaluation. From this evaluation, the new job is assigned to an appropriate job class. If the rate ranges are used, the new employee will start at the bottom of the range and receive raises, where appropriate, to the top of the rate range.

## CHALLENGES AFFECTING COMPENSATION

Even the most rational methods of determining pay must be tempered by several challenges. The implications of these contingencies may cause wage and salary analysts to make further adjustments to employee compensation.

FIGURE 12-12   Varying Wage Rates for Job Classes

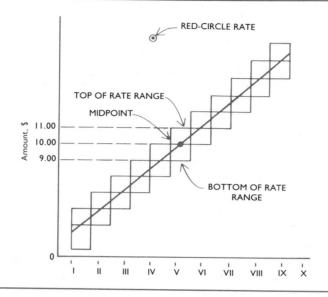

## Prevailing Wage Rates

Some jobs must be paid more than is indicated by their relative worth because of market forces. In the late 1960s, there was a scarcity of computer specialists. Fitting these jobs onto a wage-trend line often resulted in a wage rate below their prevailing wage rate. Since demand outstripped supply, market forces caused wage rates for these specialists to rise above their relative worth when compared with other jobs. Firms that needed these talents were forced to pay a premium. Diagrammatically, these rates appear on a wage chart as a *red-circle rate,* as seen in Figure 12-12. The term arises from the practice of marking out-of-line rates with a red circle on the chart.

## Union Power

When unions represent a portion of the work force, they may be able to use their power to obtain wage rates out of proportion to their relative worth. For example, wage and salary studies may determine that $14 an hour is appropriate for a truck driver. But if the union insists on $18, the human resource department may believe paying the higher rate is less expensive than a strike. Sometimes the union controls most or all of a particular skill, such as carpentry or plumbing. This enables the union actually to raise the prevailing rate for those jobs.

## Productivity

Companies must make a profit to survive. Without it, the company cannot attract the investors necessary to remain competitive. Therefore, a company cannot pay workers more than they contribute back to the firm through their productivity. When this happens (because of scarcity or union power), companies usually redesign those jobs, train new workers to increase their supply, or automate.

## Wage and Salary Policies

Most organizations have policies that cause wages and salaries to be adjusted. One common policy is to give nonunion workers the same raise as that received by unionized workers. Some companies have a policy of paying a premium above the prevailing wages to minimize turnover or to recruit the best workers. Also, some companies have automatic cost-of-living clauses that give employees automatic raises when the Statistics Canada cost-of-living index increases. Raises or policies that increase employee compensation move the wage-trend line upward.

## Government Constraints

Canada is a nation of wage earners. What people earn bears a direct relationship to the economy and general welfare of the population. Since the 1930s, the federal government has regulated some aspects of compensation.

The Canada Labour Code in its revised version of 1971 is the most comprehensive law affecting compensation rights for organizations under federal jurisdiction. It sets requirements for minimum wage, overtime pay, equal pay, child labour, and record-keeping. The minimum-wage and over-time provisions require employers to pay at least a minimum hourly rate of pay regardless of the worth of the job. (When the minimum is increased by law, it may mean adjusting upward the wages of those who already earn above the minimum. If those just above minimum wage do not also get raises, wage differentials will be squeezed together.[16] This is called *wage compression*.) For every covered job, the organization must pay one and a half times the employee's regular pay rate for all hours over forty per week. Executive, administrative, professional, and other employees are exempt from the overtime provisions. Laws involving similar regulations have been enacted by each province for organizations under their jurisdiction.

In 1977 the Canada Labour Code, Part I, was repealed and replaced by the Canadian Human Rights Act. Since this act prohibits, among other things, discrimination because of sex, it is illegal for companies to pay women less than men if their jobs involve equal skills, effort, responsibilities, and conditions.[17] As explained more fully in chapter 3, the government enforces these provisions by requiring wrongdoers to equalize pay and make up past discrepancies:

> The Ste. Anne de Bellevue Veterans Hospital near Montreal had to increase a woman's salary by $10,000 and pay $14,262 in back wages for past discrimination.[18]

The law also creates standards for employment of children. These regulations apply to minors under the age of seventeen and limit the use of children in hazardous occupations. They also determine the minimum wages for children.

The record-keeping requirements mean that employers must maintain detailed records of hours worked, pay rates, amounts of overtime, deductions and additions to pay, and other information related to compensation. These records must be kept for at least thirty-six months after the work is performed and must be available at all reasonable times for examination by an inspector.

## PAY EQUITY

> Donna Fleury, a forty-five-year-old mother of two children had worked for fifteen years as a secretary in a Toronto school. A high-school graduate, Fleury earned $10.98 an hour in 1986. Frank Sousa, fifty-nine, a custodian in the same school, mows the lawn in the summer and clears the parking lot in winter. Sousa has only an elementary school education and a poor grasp of English. Sousa supports a wife and two children. After more than sixteen years on the job, his hourly wage was $12.33 in 1986.
>
> "Is there any justification for the wage difference in terms of the value of each of them to the job?" asks Ontario Attorney General Ian Scott.[19]

As first mentioned in Chapter 3, an important issue in compensation management and equal opportunity is *equal pay for work of equal value*. Equal pay for work of equal value is the concept that jobs of comparable worth to the organization should be equally paid (referred to as *pay equity*). The idea goes beyond *equal pay for equal work* (referred to as *equal pay*). The latter concept has been part of the Canada Labour Code since 1971. It requires an employer to pay men and women the same wage or salary when they do the same work. Exceptions to equal pay are allowed when a valid seniority or merit system exists. Employers can pay more for seniority or to workers who perform better and merit higher pay. Exceptions are also allowed when pay is determined by the employee's production, such as sales commissions.

The pay equity concept, however, takes a different perspective. It became law in an amendment to the Canadian Human Rights Act in 1978. It makes it illegal to discriminate on the basis of job *value* (or content). For example, if a nurse and an electrician both received approximately the same number of job evaluation points under the point system, they would have to be paid the same wage or salary, regardless of market conditions. This approach to compensation is sought by governments as a means of eliminating the historical gap between the income of men and women, which results in women in Canada earning about 60% as much as men.[20] This gap exists in part because women have traditionally found work in lower-paying occupations—teaching, retailing, nursing, secretarial work, and in such positions as receptionist and telephone operator.

It should be emphasized, however, that the above mentioned figure of 60% as the earning gap between men and women is misleading although it is widely used by proponents of equal pay to point to the "discrimination" in pay against women. This figure emerges if one compares all men and women wage earners regardless of job tenure and skill level. But this is not an appropriate comparison. If a woman chooses to leave the labour force to have children and to bring them up and then returns to continue her career, she will have missed many training and advancement opportunities in her organization as compared to her husband who presumably continued to grow and advance in his career.

By using comparable groups, the pay gap decreases to between 15% and 25%, depending on the group studied.[21] This difference is most likely "true" discrimination, because it cannot be accounted for by education, tenure, or skill level. However, there is no evidence that there is a conspiracy among entrepreneurs and managers to keep the wages of women-dominated jobs down.*

Then what keeps women's wages below comparable men's wages? Society's expectations about the role of women in our culture determine to a large degree women's job choices. Traditionally, it was the son who, after high school, would go on to study for a profession and pursue a career, while the daughter had to be content to learn some household skills, like cooking and sewing, or, at the most, secretarial skills, such as typing and shorthand. However, this attitude has changed, as the enrolments in our business and engineering schools demonstrate. But even today a woman's job choice is often influenced by her role as a housewife and mother, as evidenced in the following study.

Two researchers were asked to examine a manufacturing company whose management wanted to find out why in some jobs there were so few women despite the company's sincere affirmative-action program. They found that some of the higher paying jobs were not attractive to women because of overtime requirements, shift work, and heavy lifting. Women felt that they had a stronger responsibility towards the family and could not afford to work overtime or do shift work. This—and other studies—shows that some contextual factors such as family considerations, which do not enter the job evaluation process, have a strong impact on job choices.[22]

What makes the issue of equal pay for work of equal value very tricky is the lack of any generally acceptable definition of "equal value" and how it can be measured. The definition offered in the guidelines issued by the Canadian Human rights Commission is not of much help:

> Value of work is the value which the work performed by an employee in a given establishment represents in relation to the value of work of another employee, or group of employees, the value being determined on the basis of approved criteria, without the wage market or negotiated wage rates being taken into account.[23]

The approved criteria referred to above are: skill, effort, responsibility, and working conditions. These criteria will be considered together, i.e., they will form a composite measure. This does not mean that employees must be paid the same salary, even if their jobs are considered equal. The Equal Wage Guidelines define seven "reasonable factors" that can justify differences in wages:

1. Different performance ratings (ratings must be based on a formal appraisal system and be brought to the attention of each employee).
2. Seniority (based on length of service).
3. Red-circling (because of job re-evaluation).
4. Rehabilitation assignment (e.g., after lengthy absence because of sickness).
5. Demotion pay procedures (because of unsatisfactory work performance, or re-assignment because of labour force surplus).

*A job is seen as gender dominated if, depending on jurisdiction, 60 or 70% of the job occupants are from one sex.

6.  Procedure of phased-in wage reductions.

7.  Temporary training positions.[24]

These factors justify a difference in wages only if they are applied consistently and equitably. It must be clearly demonstrable that existing wage differences are not based on sex.

Where does this leave the human resource manager? The Canadian Human Rights Act applies only to organizations under federal jurisdiction, such as federal government departments and Crown agencies, RCMP, armed forces, banks, airlines, most railway companies, and communication firms. However, three provinces now have pay equity legislation enacted, which means all organizations under their jurisdiction have to comply with these laws. Fortunately, these pay equity laws are modelled after the federal law and use similar criteria.

A human resource manager has to make sure that the company's pay system is in line with the province's or the federal government's legislation. The following measures are suggested:

- Review the organization's human resource policies, procedures, and practices with the objective of determining relevance and consistency of application.

- Review recruiting and promotional decisions and track career trends, particularly with respect to compensation levels; examine how the organization has "treated" employees in the past.

- Review human resource planning techniques and procedures to determine consistency of application throughout the organization.

- Review the underlying philosophy and rationale of the job evaluation plan(s) currently used (e.g., are they appropriate for the organization today; has the evaluation process been as objective as possible; what "groups" fall under which plan, and is this appropriate?).

- By specific positions, examine the differential between earnings of men and women in the organization.

- By salary grade, examine the differential between earnings of men and women.

- For groups of positions performing work of "relative importance," examine the differential between earnings of men and women.

- Examine all employee benefits practices across the organization, including those in place for plant and hourly rated employees to determine if inequalities exist (e.g., to determine if overtime, vacation, and other benefit levels are consistently applied).[25]

Should inequalities be found, it would be advisable to eliminate them, or, if the organization is large, it may be useful to implement an affirmative-action program. The initiation of such a program does not imply any past wrongdoing on the part of the organization, but it is actually encouraged by federal and provincial Human Rights Commissions.

## Provincial Legislation

At the time of this writing (fall 1989) only three provinces had enacted pay equity legislation: Quebec (1975, Charter of Human Rights and Freedoms, covering public and private sectors), Manitoba (1985, Pay Equity Act, covering the public sector), and Ontario (1987, An Act to Provide for Pay Equity, covering public and private sectors). Other provinces have laws on the drawing boards (Prince Edward Island, Nova Scotia).

The Manitoba and Ontario legislators took a new approach to pay equity legislation by creating Pay Equity Bureaus that are responsible for the administration and implementation of the laws. Both also take a proactive approach by requiring employers to evaluate all jobs in an organization under a single, gender-neutral job evaluation scheme, and to apply the scheme to classes of work where one sex predominates. In contrast, the federal and Quebec laws are reactive, since they deal with inequities only if the latter are brought to the attention of the appropriate Human Rights Commissions.

Since the Ontario pay equity legislation is the most recent one and seems to be the most comprehensive, a synopsis is shown in Figure 12-13.

### FIGURE 12-13 Synopsis of Bill 154 Ontario Pay Equity Act

The Pay Equity Act, which was passed by the Ontario legislature on June 15, 1987, and became effective January 1, 1988, provides for: "the redressing of systemic gender discrimination in compensation for work performed by employees in female job classes, in the establishments of all employers in the broader public sector and those in the private sector who employ 10 or more employees."

This Bill will require a thorough review of compensation practices to ensure that there are no compensation differences between men in male-dominated job classes and women in female-dominated job classes who have work which is judged to be equivalent through a systematic evaluation process.

The Act is far-reaching. It will require:
- formulating a pay equity plan for each "establishment,"
- formulating and negotiating a pay equity plan with unions,
- posting the pay equity plan (or plans) for employees to examine and approve, and
- cost up to 1% per year of total Ontario employee payroll (pay and benefits).

With Bill 154, Ontario is the third jurisdiction in Canada to require pay equity in the private sector. Federally regulated private sector employers as well as employers in the Province of Quebec are also covered by pay equity requirements.

It is important to note that all public sector organizations and all private sector organizations with over 100 employees in Ontario *must* prepare a pay equity plan and post this plan for employees to examine.

### BROAD CONCEPT

The broad concepts of the bill include:
- Employers must equalize compensation for females in jobs or female-dominated job classes that are deemed of equivalent value to male-dominated job classes
- Employees' compensation will be compared within one establishment.
- Establishment is defined as geographic area, such as Metropolitan Toronto, a county or a regional municipality.
- Employees may be in full-time and part-time jobs, but work under one-third of the normal work period is not included unless regular and continuing.
- Jobs or classes will be composed of positions with similar duties and responsibilities, qualifications, recruiting procedures and pay schedules.
- Comparisons will be done only when job classes of 60% female incumbents and 70% male incumbents are deemed to be of equal or comparable value.
- Comparisons will be made across an establishment (non-union), within a bargaining unit, between bargaining units and non-union positions if there are no male job class comparisons within a bargaining unit.
- Comparisons will be made of the job rates. Job rate is the highest rate of compensation for a job class.

FIGURE 12-13 (continued)   Synopsis of Bill 154 Ontario Pay equity Act

- Comparable value is determined by a job evaluation process. The method must include skill, effort, responsibility, and working conditions and be free of any bias based on gender.
- Employers must adjust for inequities in compensation (pay and benefits) between female-dominated job classes and male-dominated job classes if they are found to be comparable, unless one of these allowed exclusions applies: seniority, temporary training, merit pay, red circling, skills shortage.
- A pay equity plan will be negotiated with unions as part of the collective bargaining process but not necessarily at the same time as contract renegotiation.
- Where a pay equity plan is not mandatory, the employer and union may choose to negotiate a plan.
- A Pay Equity Commission will be established. The Pay Equity Hearings Tribunal will hear cases where agreement cannot be reached. The Pay Equity Office will provide information, and resolve complaints.

## WHAT YOU MUST DO TO COMPLY WITH LEGISLATION
- Conduct a *pay equity audit,* following the guidelines in Bill 154 and the steps outlined in this article.
- Develop a *pay equity plan* for each establishment.
- *Adjust pay* to achieve pay equity overtime.

## CONTENTS OF A PAY EQUITY PLAN
A pay equity plan must:
—describe the evaluation system.
—provide the results of evaluations and comparisons.
—set out dates when pay adjustments are to begin and when pay equity is to be achieved.

## TIMETABLE FOR A PAY EQUITY PLAN
A plan must be developed and posted for each establishment by these dates:

| Establishment | Employees In Ontario | Years After Proclamation |
|---|---|---|
| Broader public sector | | 2 |
| Private sector | 500 + | 2 |
| | 100 – 499 | 3 |
| | 50 – 99 | 4 (voluntary posting |
| | 10 – 49 | 5 (voluntary posting) |

The plan must provide for greater adjustments for lower job classes needing increases to achieve pay equity.

## TIMETABLE FOR PAY ADJUSTMENTS
Pay equity adjustments must begin according to these dates:

| Establishment | Employees In Ontario | Years After Proclamation |
|---|---|---|
| Broader public sector | | 2 |
| Private sector | 500 + | 3 |
| 100 – 499 | 4 | |
| | 5 – 99 | 5 |
| | 10 – 49 | 6 |

A private sector organization must make pay adjustments up to the maximum cost allowed each year. For public sector employers, inequities must be adjusted within five years.

FIGURE 12-13 (continued)   Synopsis of Bill 154 Ontario Pay equity Act

---

### IMPLEMENTATION CONCLUSIONS

- Every broader public sector organization must have a pay equity plan two years after proclamation.
- Eventually, every private sector organization over 100 employees must have a pay equity plan.
- Smaller private sector organizations (10-99) should have pay equity plans. Complaints can be made by employees to the Commission whether or not a plan has been developed.
- Pay increases start for the private sector *one year after the plan* is required to be posted. For the public sector, pay increases start at the same time as the plan is required to be posted, i.e., two years after proclamation.

---

Prepared by Jim Keyser, Partner Human Resources, Coopers & Lybrard Consulting Group.


## *FINANCIAL INCENTIVE SYSTEMS*

Incentive systems provide the clearest link between compensation and performance. Employees who work under a financial incentive system find that their performance determines, in whole or part, their income.

One of the most significant benefits of financial incentives is that better performance is reinforced on a regular basis. Unlike raises and promotions, the reinforcement is generally quick and frequent—usually with each paycheque. Since the worker sees the results of the desired behaviour quickly, that behaviour is more likely to continue. The employer benefits because wages are given in proportion to performance, not for the indirect measure of time worked. And if employees are motivated by the system to expand their output, recruiting expenses for additional employees and capital outlays for new work stations are minimized. As one economist observed:

> With fixed wages individual workers also have little incentive to cooperate with management or to take the initiative in suggesting new ideas for raising productivity. At the level of the individual worker, higher productivity has no immediate payoff — wages are fixed for the length of the contract. The immediate effect of higher productivity is, in fact, negative. Less labour is needed, and the probability of layoffs rises.
>
> The higher productivity growth rates of the Japanese may also be due to their bonus system that encourages labour to take a direct interest in raising productivity.[26]

Offsetting these advantages are significant problems. The administration of an incentive system can be complex. As with any control system, standards have to be established and results measured. For many jobs, the standards and measures are too imprecise or too costly to develop. This means that the incentive system may result in inequities. Some incentive systems require less effort than other systems that pay the same. Sometimes workers make more than their supervisors, who are on salary. Another problem is that the employee may not achieve the standard because of uncontrollable forces, such as work delays or machine breakdowns.

Unions often resist incentive systems because they fear management will change the standard and workers will have to work harder for the same pay. This fear of a speedup often leads to peer pressure against anyone who exceeds the group's output norms. The advantages of the incentive system are essentially lost when group pressures restrict output. And incentives tend to focus efforts on only one aspect (output, sales, or stock prices), sometimes to the exclusion of other dimensions (quality, service, and long-term objectives).

Some of the more common incentive systems follow.

## Piecework

Piecework is an incentive system that compensates the worker for each unit of output. Daily or weekly pay is determined by multiplying the output in units times the piece rate per unit. For example, in agricultural labour, workers are often paid a specific amount per bushel of produce picked. Piecework does not always mean higher productivity, however. Group norms may have a more significant impact if peer pressure works against higher productivity. And in many jobs, it may be difficult to measure the person's productive contribution (for example, a receptionist), or the employee may not be able to control the rate of output (for example, an assembly-line worker).

## Production Bonuses

Production bonuses are incentives paid to workers for exceeding a specified level of output. They are used in conjunction with a base wage rate or salary. Under one approach, the employee receives a predetermined salary or wage. Through extra effort that results in output above the standard, the base compensation is supplemented by a bonus, usually figured at a given rate for each unit of production over the standard. Another variation rewards the employee for saving time. For example, if the standard time for replacing an automobile transmission is four hours and the mechanic does it in three, the mechanic may be paid for four hours. A third method combines production bonuses with piecework by compensating workers on an hourly basis, plus an incentive payment for each unit produced. In some cases, the employee may get a higher piece rate once a minimum number of units are produced. For example, the employee may be paid $6 an hour plus $.25 per unit for the first thirty units each day. Beginning with the thirty-first unit, the bonus may become $.35.

## Commissions

In sales jobs, the salesperson may be paid a percentage of the selling price or a flat amount for each unit sold. When no base compensation is paid, the salesperson's total earnings come from commissions. Real estate agents and car salespeople are often paid this form of straight commission.

## Maturity Curves

What happens when technical or scientific employees reach the top of their rate range? Generally, still higher increases can be achieved only by promotion into a management position. To provide an incentive for technical people, some companies have developed

FIGURE 12-14    Maturity Curves for Professionals with Varying Degrees of
Performance

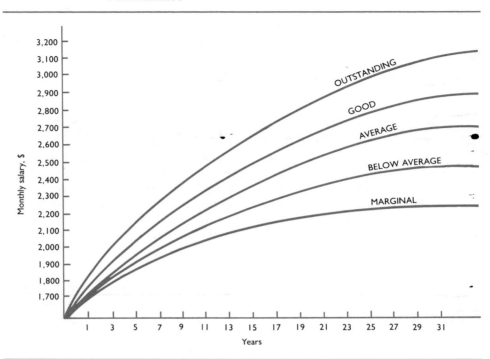

*maturity curves*. Employees are rated on productivity and experience. Outstanding contributors are assigned to the top curve in Figure 12-14. Good, but less outstanding,
performers are placed on the next-to-top curve. Through this technique, high-performing
professionals continue to be rewarded for their efforts without being forced into a management position to keep increasing their earnings.

## Executive Incentives

Executive incentives vary widely. Young and middle-aged executives are likely to want
*cash bonuses* to meet the needs of a growing or maturing family. As they get older, the
need for present income is offset by retirement considerations. Here, bonuses may be
deferred until the executive reaches the lower tax rates of retirement.

Executives are sometimes granted stock options—the right to purchase the company's stock at a predetermined price. This price may be set at, below, or above the
market value of the stock. Thus the executive has an incentive to improve the company's
performance in order to enhance the value of the stock options. Generally, it is considered
appropriate to give stock options only to those executives who can have a significant effect
on company profits.

Other forms of executive incentives exist, including incentive systems that allow executives to design their own compensation package. The common element in most executive incentive plans, however, is their relation to the performance of the organization. When these systems do not relate the incentive to performance, no matter what they are called, they are not incentive plans. Besides, executive incentives are increasingly being geared to promote long-term performance.[27]

## Group Incentive Plans

Performance is often a group effort. In recognition of this fact, several plans have been developed to provide incentive for teamwork. Most fall into one of the following categories: production incentives, profit sharing, stock ownership, or cost-reduction plans.

### Production Incentive Plans

These plans allow groups of workers to receive bonuses for exceeding predetermined levels of output. They tend to be short-range and related to very specific production goals. A work team may be offered a bonus for exceeding predetermined production levels. Or it may receive a per-unit incentive which results in group piece rate.

### Profit-Sharing Plans

Profit-sharing plans share company profits with the workers. The effectiveness of these plans may suffer because profitability is not always related to the employee's performance; a recession or new competitors may have a more significant impact. Even when outside sources do not seriously affect results, it is difficult for employees to perceive their efforts as making much difference. Some companies further reduce the effectiveness of the incentive by diverting the employee's share of profits into retirement plans. Thus the immediate reinforcement value of the incentive is reduced because the incentive is delayed. However, when these plans work well they can have a dramatic impact on the organization, because profit-sharing plans can create a sense of trust and a feeling of common fate among workers and management. One example comes from a leading Canadian producer of steel, Dofasco Inc.

Located in Hamilton, Ontario, Dofasco is the largest manufacturer of steel in Canada. Within a very competitive and technologically fast-changing industry Dofasco has become a model of economic efficiency and effectiveness through the development of a "people-oriented" organization.

The company has experienced great success through the mechanisms of a profit-sharing plan (on top of high wages relative to the industry average) and open, sincere, personal communications based upon a healthy and cooperative management-employee relationship. Since the company was founded in 1912 it has never unionized, despite several efforts by the United Steelworkers of America, and since the introduction of its profit-sharing plan in 1938 it has never had an unprofitable year. Employees contribute a maximum of $200 a year to the Employees Savings and Profit-Sharing Fund. The company contributes 11% of its pretax profits, paid out in two ways:

1. For every $1 the employee contributes to the fund, Dofasco pays in $3. This

contribution is made even if the company must exceed the 11% ceiling, but the deficit is made up from the fund the following year.

2. Once the three-for-one payout is made, any funds remaining up to that ceiling of 11% of pretax profits are divided equally among all fund members. Employees can take the money as cash or put it in a deferred profit-sharing plan to postpone paying tax until retirement. Most opt for cash. Since 1977 the average cash payout has been $1536. In 1987 it was $1948. Some long-service blue collar workers who let the savings accumulate collected over $400,000 upon retirement.

John Sheppard, executive vice president, concedes that in terms of costs per employee Dofasco is not better off than other steelmakers. If the cost of all the frills are added (recreation program, the famous Christmas party for 35,000 employees and their families) the costs are probably higher. But according to Sheppard, the benefits outweigh the costs. The benefits include the absence of work stoppages, a lower turnover rate than the industry average, and no fear of strikes. In addition, there are no union demarcation rules. "There is nothing that stops our people from pitching in and helping with something that is not their particular defined job," says Sheppard. "An electrician is allowed to hammer a nail into a piece of wood."[28]

Robert J. Swenor, vice president of human resources, puts the profit-sharing concept into perspective. "Profit sharing alone," he says, "will not do it. There has to be a compatible atmosphere, trust between management and employees, and a good line of communication. Then it works."[29]

## Stock Ownership

A report by the Toronto Stock Exchange (TSE) shows a rapid increase in employee share ownership in Canada in recent years.[30] According to this study, as of July 1986, 63% of the companies listed on the TSE offered at least one form of employee ownership plan. Of the TSE listed companies, 23% offered share purchase plans, and 54% offered stock option plans. Roughly 80% of the plans were introduced in the 1980s, more than 60% of them since 1983. The report further indicates that companies with employee ownership plans dramatically outperform their competitors on profit margins, growth, and return on equity.

## Cost-Reduction Plans

Some critics of group incentive plans argue that profit-sharing schemes, such as those found at Dofasco, do not always reward the employees' efforts if profits fall for reasons beyond the employees' control. For example, the average bonus received by workers at Lincoln Electric, a company with a cost-reduction plan, fell from $22,690 one year to $15,460 the next because of a slow-down in the economy during the early 1980s. Although $15,460 is a considerable bonus, the bonus is influenced by forces outside the employees' control.

Another approach is to reward employees for something they can control: labour costs. Most cost-reduction plans seek to tap employee effort and ideas for ways to reduce costs. Many times, a committee of employees will be formed to open new lines of communications that allow employee ideas to be heard, while the plan allows greater psychological and financial participation in the firm's day-to-day operations. Perhaps the best known of these approaches is the *Scanlon Plan,* which bases bonuses on improvements in labour costs, as compared with historical norms.[31] Under a Scanlon Plan group incentive, employees aim to reduce costs and then they share in those savings. If, for example, employee productivity increases at the Canadian Valve and Hydrant Manufacturing Company, the ratio of payroll costs to net sales revenue improves. These savings are then shared with employees in the form of a bonus. *Rucker* and *Improshare* Plans are similar to the Scanlon approach, but they differ in how bonuses are calculated and in other administrative matters. All three of these approaches differ from profit-sharing in that they focus on something the employee can influence (costs), and not on something that the employees may control only indirectly (profitability).

Compensation consists of more than wages, salaries, and bonuses. Remuneration includes an ever-growing list of fringe benefits and services. Although these benefits are referred to as non-cash compensation, they are a significant part of most employee's total labour costs. The next chapter describes the range of fringe benefits and services offered by employers.

## SUMMARY

Employee compensation, if properly administered, can be an effective tool to improve employee performance, motivation, and satisfaction. Pay programs that are mismanaged may lead to high turnover, high absenteeism, more grievances, poor performance, and job dissatisfaction.

For compensation to be appropriate, it must be internally and externally equitable. Through job evaluation techniques, the relative worth of jobs is determined. This assures internal equity. Wage and salary surveys are used to determine external equity. With knowledge of the relative worth of jobs and external pay levels, each job can be properly priced.

The process of wage and salary administration is influenced by several challenges, including union power, the productivity of workers, the company's compensation policies, and government constraints on pay. The Canada Labour Code is the major federal law affecting compensation management. It regulates minimum wages, overtime, and child labour. The Human Rights Act seeks to eliminate sex-based pay differentials. All provinces have similar laws, i.e., labour codes and human rights legislation, for their jurisdictions. (A good example of government constraints on pay is wage and price controls. In 1975 the federal government introduced such a program in order to fight inflation. Pay and price increases were limited to a certain percentage and were controlled by an anti-inflation board. The program was abolished in 1978.[32]

Pay equity has become a major issue during the last few years. When the Canadian Human Rights Act was passed in 1977, it introduced the new concept of "equal pay for work of equal value," which requires employers to compare the content of jobs when determining pay scales and to pay equal wages for jobs of comparable value. The Canadian Human Rights Commission specifies four criteria by which jobs can be evaluated: skill, effort, responsibility, and working conditions. Provincial equal pay legislation is usually modelled after the federal law.

Another dimension of compensation management is financial incentives. Individual incentives attempt to relate pay to productivity. Group plans have the same objectives, but the relationship is often not as direct or obvious to workers. Some approaches pay a bonus for reaching a production target, others share the company's profits with workers, and still others share savings in labour costs.

## TERMS FOR REVIEW

| | |
|---|---|
| Job evaluations | Red-circle rate |
| Job ranking | Canada Labour Code |
| Job grading | Pay Equity |
| Factor comparison method | Equal pay for work of equal value |
| Key jobs | Piecework |
| Point system | Production bonuses |
| Wage and salary surveys | Maturity curves |
| Rate range | Profit sharing |
| Merit raise | Scanlon Plan |

## REVIEW AND DISCUSSION QUESTIONS

1. Suppose you manage a small business with thirty employees. You discover that some people are much motivated by money and others by security. For those who want more money you provide an incentive plan in which their income is determined by their results. The other employees have a fair salary. What problems might arise?

2. Why is job analysis information, discussed in Chapter 5, necessary before job evaluations can be performed?

3. Suppose that when you interview new employees, you ask them what they think is a fair wage or salary. If you hire them, you pay them that amount as long as it is reasonable and not below minimum-wage laws. What problems would you expect?

4. Assume your company has a properly conducted compensation program. If a group of employees asks you why they receive different hourly pay rates even though they perform the same job, how would you respond?

5. Why are the factor comparison method and the point system more widely used than the job ranking or the job grading approaches to job evaluation?

6. If you are told to find out what competitors in your area are paying their employees, how would you get this information without conducting a wage and salary survey?

7. Even after jobs are first priced using a wage-trend line, what other challenges might cause you to adjust some rates upward?

8. Since financial incentives give employees feedback for good performance and they relate pay to performance, why do most companies pay wages and salaries rather than financial incentives?

9. Explain the difference between "equal pay for equal work" and "equal pay for

work of equal value'' and the implications of the difference for a human resource manager.

10. Under what circumstances are pay differentials justified?

## INCIDENT 12-1

### Compensation Administration at Reynolds Plastic Products

The Reynolds Plastic Products Corporation was recently purchased by a much larger organization, International Plastics Ltd. The human resources director of International Plastics is concerned that the wage and salary policies are irrational and in some cases actually violate the law. To evaluate the compensation system of the Reynolds Plastic subsidiary, a recent human resources management graduate, Thea Silverstein, was assigned to make an investigation. The key points of her report are summarized below.

a. The wage range for hourly employees is from $5.70 per hour to $13.96.

b. The amount of overtime paid by Reynolds is very modest; overtime is paid for all hours over 180 per month.

c. The wage rates for different workers vary widely even on the same job; those employees who are heads of households receive approximately 18% more than those workers who are not heads of households. Most of the heads of households are men.

d. On highly technical jobs, the firm pays a rate that is 20% above the prevailing wage rate for these jobs. All other jobs are paid an average of 15% below the prevailing rate.

e. Turnover averages a modest 12%. However, in technical jobs turnover is less than 2%; in nontechnical jobs turnover is nearly 20%. Absenteeism follows the same pattern.

1. What laws are probably being violated?

2. Develop a step-by-step plan of actions you would take and the order in which you would undertake them if you were made human resources director of the Reynolds subsidiary.

## INCIDENT 12-2

### Incentives at Karma Records

Joe Karma owned and operated Karma Records since its founding in 1979. Joe was often heard to say, "I believe in paying people for what they do, not for how many hours they work." This management philosophy was expressed through a variety of incentive plans that Joe designed himself. Although he was firmly committed to the use of incentives, he hired a management consulting team to make recommendations about his compensation programs.

To help the consultants, Joe wrote down the major features of each incentive program. His notes were as follows:

a. Executives do not own any stock, but they each get $1000 for each dollar the stock price goes up from the previous year.

b. Every time sales go up 10%, all the hourly employees get a day off with pay or can work one day at double-time rates.

c. Production workers get paid $.18 for each record they press and $.03 for each record they package.

d. Sales personnel get a $50 savings bond each time a new record store or department store starts stocking Karma Records.

1. What problems do you see with the incentives for (a) executives, (b) hourly workers, (c) production workers, (d) salespeople?

2. If you were a member of the consulting team, what incentives would you recommend for each group?

## SUGGESTED READINGS

Abella, Rosalie, *Equality in Employment: A Royal Commission Report,* Volumes I and II, Ottawa: Supply and Services, 1984.

Abella, Rosalie, ''Equality at Work and at Home,'' *Policy Options,* December 1985.

Bakker, J., ''Pay Equity in Ontario—More than a Defensive Victory,'' *Canadian Dimension,* March 1987.

Conway, Heather E. ''Equal Pay for Work of Equal Value Legislation in Canada: An Analysis,'' *Studies in Social Policy,* Ottawa (275 Slater Street, K1P 5H9), November 1987.

Gunderson, M., ''Discrimination, Equal Pay and Equal Opportunities in the Labour Market,'' in *Work and Pay: The Canadian Labour Market,* Research Studies of the Royal Commission on the Economic Union and Development Prospects for Canada, Volume 17, Toronto: University of Toronto Press for the Royal Commission, 1985.

Henderson, Richard I., *Compensation Management,* 5th ed., Englewood Cliffs, New Jersey: Prentice-Hall, 1989.

Milkovich, G.T., and J.M. Newman, *Compensation,* 2nd ed., Plano, Texas: Business Publications, 1987.

Nightingale, D.V., *The Profit Sharing Handbook,* Don Mills: Profit Sharing Council of Canada, 1983.

## REFERENCES

1. Milton L. Rock, *Handbook of Wage and Salary Administration,* New York: McGraw-Hill Book Company, 1972, p. xiii.

2. Bert L. Metzger, *Profit Sharing: A Natural for Today's Changing Work Force/Economy,* Evanston, Illinois: Profit Sharing Research Foundation, 1982, p. 7.

3. Edward E. Lawler III, *Pay and Organizational Effectiveness: A Psychological View,* New York: McGraw-Hill Book Company, 1971, p. 71.

4. Ibid., p. 244.

5. David W. Belcher, ''Pay Equity or Pay Fairness,'' *Compensation Review,* Second Quarter 1979, pp. 31-37. See also Elaine Wegener, ''Does Competitive Pay Discriminate?'' *The Personnel Administrator,* May 1980, pp. 38-43, 66.

6. Thomas M. Hestwood, ''Ensuring the Effectiveness of Compensation Programs,'' *Compensation Review,* First Quarter 1979, p. 14. See also Robert J. Greene, ''Thoughts on Compensation Management in the '80s and '90s,'' *The Personnel Administrator,* May 1980, pp. 27-28.

7. Allan N. Nash and Stephen J. Carroll, Jr., *The Management of Compensation,* Monterey, Calif.: Brooks/Cole Publishing Company, 1975, pp. 109-111; and Richard I. Henderson, *Compensation Management,* Reston, Va.: Reston Publishing Company, 1976, pp. 158-159.

8. Nash and Carroll, op. cit., p. 132.

9. Eugene J. Benge, ''Using Factor Methods to Measure Jobs,'' in Milton L. Rock (ed.), op. cit., pp. 242-256.

10. Nash and Carroll, op. cit., p. 128.

11. Edward Perlin, Irwin Bobby Kaplan, and John M. Curcia, ''Clearing Up Fuzziness in Salary Survey Analysis,'' *Compensation Review,* Second Quarter 1979, pp. 12-25.

12. The least squares method is explained in most introductory statistics books.
13. William A. Evans, ''Pay for Performance: Fact or Fable,'' *Personnel Journal*, September 1970, p. 731.
14. Douglas L. Fleuter, ''A Different Approach to Merit Increases,'' *Personnel Journal*, April 1979, pp. 225-226, 262. See also James T. Brinks, ''Is There Merit in Merit Increases?'' *The Personnel Administrator*, May 1980, pp. 59-64
15. Stephen H. Appelbaum and John B. Millard, ''Engineering a Compensation Program to Fit the Individual, Not the Job,'' *Personnel Journal*, March 1976, pp. 121-134.
16. Michael N. Wolfe and Charles W. Candland, ''The Impact of the Minimum Wage on Compression,'' *The Personnel Administrator*, May 1979, pp. 22-28, 40. See also Allen Flamion, ''The Dollars and Sense of Motivation,'' *Personnel Journal*, January 1980, pp. 51-52, 61.
17. Robert F. Johnston, ''Equal Pay for Work of Equal Value,'' *The Canadian Personnel & Industrial Relations Journal*, 18(2)(March 1981): 59-65.
18. Theresa Chruscinski, ''Equal Pay Front Pushes Forward,'' *Financial Post*, April 8, 1981.
19. Sherri Aikenhead, ''Women's Battle to Close the Wage Gap,'' *Maclean's*, Vol. 99, No. 43, October 27, 1986, p. 58-59.
20. W. Block and M. Walker, ''On Employment Equity,'' The Fraser Institute, Vancouver, 1985.
21. M. Gunderson, ''The Female-Male Earnings Gap in Ontario: A Summary,'' Ontario Ministry of Labour, Toronto, February, 1982.
22. C.C. Hoffmann and K.P. Hoffmann, ''Does Comparable Worth Obscure the Real Issues?'' *Personnel Journal*, Vol. 66, No. 1, January 1987, pp. 82-95. See also ''The Family in America,'' in *Public Opinion*, American Enterprise Insti-

tute, Washington, D.C., January 1986, pp. 25-32, and B. Berger, ''At Odds with America's Reality,'' in *Society*, Rutger's State University, July/August 1985, pp. 77-78.
23. ''Equal Pay for Male and Female Employees Who Are Performing Work of Equal Value,'' interpretation guide for section 11 of the Canadian Human Rights Act, Canadian Human Rights Commission, Ottawa, undated.
24. Ibid.
25. Hermann F. Schwind, ''Equal Pay for Work of Equal Value,'' *Commercial News*, a publication of the Halifax Board of Trade, July 1981, pp. 28-31.
26. Lester Thurow, ''Productivity Pay,'' *Newsweek*, May 3, 1982, p. 69.
27. Pearl Merey, ''Executive Compensation must Promote Long-Term Commitment,'' *Personnel Administrator*, May 1983, pp. 37-38, 40, 42. See also Carl J. Loomis, ''The Madness of Executive Compensation,'' *Fortune*, July 12, 1982, pp. 42-46.
28. Andrew Weiner, ''In the Family Way,'' *Canadian Business*, November 1980, pp. 113-124.
29. Personal communication.
30. ''Employees Share Ownership at Canada's Public Corporations,'' The Toronto Stock Exchange, 1987.
31. Robert J. Schulhop, ''Five Years with the Scanlon Plan,'' *Personnel Administrator*, June 1979, pp. 55-60, 62, 92. See also John Hoerr, ''Why Labor and Management Are Both Buying Profit Sharing,'' *Business Week*, January 10, 1983, p. 84; and Richard I. Henderson, ''Designing a Reward System for Today's Employee,'' *Business*, July-August 1982, pp. 2-12.
32. Allan M. Maslow and Gene Swimmer, *Wage Controls in Canada 1975-78: A Study of Public Decision Making*, Toronto: The Institute for Research on Public Policy, 1982.

# CHAPTER *13* ○ ○ ○ ○ ○ ○

## *EMPLOYEE BENEFITS AND SERVICES AND INCOME SECURITY*

*In many respects Canada's position in the area of fringe benefits is unique, striking a balance between the situation prevailing in the U.S. and that in Europe.*

BILL MEGALLI[1]

○ ○ ○ ○ ○ ○ ○ ○ ○ ○ ○ ○ ○ ○ ○ ○ ○ ○ ○ ○ ○ ○ ○ ○ ○ ○ ○

### *CHAPTER OBJECTIVES*

After studying this chapter, you should be able to:
1. **Describe** the objectives of indirect compensation.
2. **Identify** policies that minimize benefit costs.
3. **Explain** the key issues in designing pension plans.
4. **Identify** the administrative problems of employee benefits and services.
5. **Explain** how benefits and services can be better administered.
6. **Cite** benefits and services that are likely to become more common in the future.
7. **Explain** how government furthers employee security.
8. **Describe** the major Canadian laws relating to employee security.
9. **Identify** the implications of employee security programs.

○ ○ ○ ○ ○ ○ ○ ○ ○ ○ ○ ○ ○ ○ ○ ○ ○ ○ ○ ○ ○ ○ ○ ○ ○ ○ ○ ○ ○

*T*here are two types of benefits and services: those that an employer voluntarily gives and those that are legally required. We will focus first on the voluntary types.

## VOLUNTARY BENEFITS

To many people, compensation means pay. Anything else an employer might provide is often considered so minor that it is called a "fringe benefit." But since World War II, benefits and services have become a major part of employee compensation. No longer are benefits and services on the "fringe" of employee compensation.

> "Did you receive another job offer?" Carla asked her brother.
>
> "Yes. I received a letter yesterday from a bank in Vancouver. That's my problem; I don't know which to accept," Ed responded. "The pay, working conditions, and job duties are almost identical. The people I met at both banks seem equally pleasant."
>
> "What about fringe benefits?" Carla asked.
>
> "What about them? They are only the extras. They don't make much difference," Ed answered.
>
> "They don't make much difference? Are you kidding?" Carla questioned. "Some companies spend half as much on fringe benefits as they do on wages."
>
> "Now who is kidding? They're just fringes," Ed asserted.
>
> "I'm not kidding. Let me give you an example. Suppose one bank pays all your supplementary health and life insurance and the other pays half. At a cost of $1000 a year, you would be $600 better off with the bank that pays all of your benefits," Carla said confidently.
>
> Ed interrupted, "You mean $500."
>
> "Don't forget taxes," Carla added. "To pay your half of the $1000 you will have to come up with $500, true. But to have $500, you would probably have to earn $600 before taxes. And that is $50 a month."
>
> "Maybe I should find out more about their fringe benefits before I decide," Ed pondered.

When employees like Ed ignore benefits and services, they exclude from consideration all other forms of compensation except pay. Admittedly, pay is a major concern to employees. But since the typical organization spends a considerable share of its labour costs on benefits and services, ignorance like Ed's raises questions about the role of pay and benefits. Simply put, what is the difference between pay and benefits?

Pay is called *direct compensation* because it is based on critical job factors or performance. Benefits and services are *indirect compensation* because they are usually extended as a condition of employment and are not directly related to performance. They include insurance, security, time off, and scheduling benefits, in addition to educational, financial, and social services.

To explain the broad scope of benefits and services, this chapter discusses the objectives in indirect compensation. We follow this with an examination of the administration of voluntary benefit programs. The chapter concludes with a description of legally required benefits.

## THE ROLE OF INDIRECT COMPENSATION

Employee benefits and services seek to satisfy several objectives. These include societal, organizational, and employee objectives.

### Societal Objectives

Industrial societies have changed from rural nations of *independent* farmers and small businesses to urban nations of *interdependent* wage earners. This interdependence was illustrated forcefully by the mass unemployment of the Great Depression of the 1930s. Since that time, industrial societies have sought group solutions to societal problems.

To solve social problems and provide security for interdependent wage earners, governments rely on the support of employers. Through favourable tax treatment,

FIGURE 13-1    Benefits and Other Nonwage and Salary Cost Comparisons for Canadian Companies from 1954 to 1986

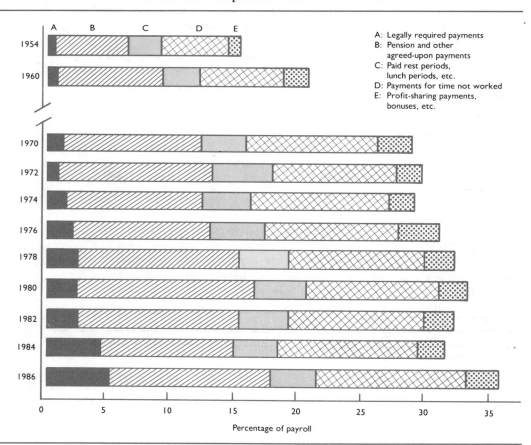

A: Legally required payments
B: Pension and other agreed-upon payments
C: Paid rest periods, lunch periods, etc.
D: Payments for time not worked
E: Profit-sharing payments, bonuses, etc.

Percentage of payroll

Source: Thorne Stevenson & Kellogg, "Employee Benefits in Canada," *Annual Surveys from 1954-1986.* Used with permission.

employees can receive most benefits tax-free, while employers can deduct the cost of benefits as a regular business expense. The result has been a rapid growth in indirect compensation since World War II.

Today, benefits and services give many employees financial security against illness, disability, and retirement. In fact, the growth of fringe benefits since World War II means that the average employer spends more than one-third of its payroll costs on benefits and services. No longer are benefits those "little extras" or "fringes." These outlays are a major and growing cost of doing business. As seen in Figure 13-1, the importance of such outlays has grown dramatically during the last twenty years. If this trend continues, benefits and services could amount to over one-half of most firms' payroll costs in the 1990s.

## Organizational Objectives

From these large outlays for fringe benefits, what do employers gain? Companies must offer some fringe benefits if they are to be able to recruit successfully in the labour market. If a company did not offer retirement plans and paid vacations, recruits and present employees would work for competitors who would offer these "fringes." Similarly, many employees will stay with a company because they do not want to give up benefits, so employee turnover is lowered by benefits. For example, employees may stay to save pension credits or their rights to the extended vacations that typically come with greater seniority.

Vacations, along with holidays and rest breaks, help employees reduce fatigue and may enhance productivity during the hours the employees do work. Similarly, retirement, health care, and disability benefits may allow workers to be more productive by freeing them from concern about medical and retirement costs. Likewise, if these benefits were not available to employees, they might elect to form a union and collectively bargain with the employer. (Although collective action is legal, many nonunion employers prefer to remain nonunion.) Therefore, it is accurate to state that indirect compensation may:

- Reduce fatigue
- Discourage labour unrest
- Satisfy employee objectives

- Aid recruitment
- Reduce turnover
- Minimize overtime costs

## Employee Objectives

Employees usually seek employer-provided benefits and services because of lower costs and availability. For example, company insurance benefits usually are less expensive because the employer may pay some or all of the costs. Even when the workers must pay the entire premium, rates are often lower because group plans save the insurer the administrative and selling costs of many individual policies. With group plans, the insurer also can reduce the *adverse selection* of insuring just those who need the insurance. Actuaries — the specialists who compute insurance rates — can pass these savings on to policyholders in the form of lower premiums.

Lower income taxes are another employee objective. For example, an employee in a 20% tax bracket has to earn $1000 to buy an $800 policy. But for $1000, the employer can buy the same insurance policy and give the worker a $200 raise. After taxes, the employee can keep $160 and the policy, while the employer is no worse off. And in many cases, the "buying power" of the company can allow it to negotiate a lower cost for the insurance policy. So the policy might cost only $600 instead of $800. Added to the $200 raise, the employer's outlays are only $800. By paying the employee to buy his or her own policy, the cost would have been $1000.

When the employer pays for a benefit, the employee achieves the benefit of partially being protected from inflation. For example, a two-week paid vacation is not reduced in value by inflation. The employee still gets two weeks off with pay. Or if a completely employer-paid insurance premium rises from $800 to $900, the worker is protected (although pay raises may be smaller since the employer has less money available for pay).

For some employees, the primary objective may be to obtain benefits and services —especially supplementary health and life insurance. Without employer-provided insurance, these policies may not be obtainable if the employee has a pre-existing medical condition.

The objectives of society, organizations, and employees have encouraged rapid growth of benefits and services. This growth has affected all areas of fringe benefits and services, including insurance, security, time-off, and scheduling benefits.

## INSURANCE BENEFITS

Insurance benefits spread the financial risks encountered by employees and their families. These risks are shared by pooling funds in the form of insurance premiums. Then, when an insured risk occurs, the covered employees or their families are compensated.

### Life Insurance

Life insurance was the first form of insurance offered to workers by employers. As a result, "group life insurance has become a practically universal element in corporate employee benefit programs."[2] In a recent survey that covered 171 large and small companies in Canada, 98.8% of the companies reported that they provide a group life insurance program for all of their employees.[3]

In the majority of firms, the amount of life insurance is a multiple of the employee's salary. For example, if the multiple is 2, a $20,000-a-year worker has $40,000 coverage. A few firms provide a flat amount for all workers. Employer-provided life insurance is typically not extended to the worker's family members. Most human resource managers and benefits experts reason that life insurance is to protect the family from loss of the worker's income. However, since group life insurance is considerably cheaper than most private policies, supplemental life insurance may be available; these policies allow employees to increase their coverage or include dependants. But employees must pay for this coverage.

### Health-Related Insurance

In Canada all citizens are covered by provincial health care programs that pay for basic hospital care and offer comprehensive coverage for medically required services of physicians, surgeons, and other qualified health professionals. For this reason, employers in Canada offer only supplementary health insurance plans. This is in contrast to the U.S., where health insurance is the most common form of coverage.[4]

## Supplementary Health Insurance Plans

The purpose of supplementary health insurance plans is to provide coverage for health care costs that are not included in provincial health care plans, such as private or semi-private rooms. Some supplementary plans provide for the payment of any amount in excess of the maximum coverage for a particular benefit as stipulated by the provincial plans. Other plans specify either some maximum overall coverage or some maximum coverage for specified services. Most employers bear the total cost of supplemental health plans; approximately one-third pay between 50% and 100%.[5]

## Dental Insurance

Dental insurance plans are one of the fastest-growing additions to the total benefit package.[6] According to the latest survey, 86% of the employers who responded offered dental plans.[7] Such plans, most of which are custom-designed, are usually provided at three levels: (1) simple fillings, x-rays, and extractions; (2) major restorative work such as bridgework, dentures, and crowns; (3) orthodontic work. Provincial dental plans cover emergency dental services required as a result of accidents. In addition, many provinces provide a limited dental care program for children.

## Salary Continuation Plans

If an employee misses a few days because of illness, it is usually not crucial from a financial point of view, since most employers grant paid sick leave for a limited time. It becomes more of a problem when an employee becomes disabled for a longer period of time or even permanently. Canadian companies offer short-term disability and long-term disability plans.

## Short-Term Disability Plans

Short-term disability plans comprise a variety of arrangements that provide sick or injured employees, temporarily incapable of working, with some form of income. The most common arrangement is the formal paid-sick-leave plan, financed and administered by the employer. Such a plan usually involves crediting or allocating a certain number of days to an employee, to be used as sick leave for nonoccupational accidents or illnesses. Sick-leave credits may be cumulative or noncumulative. A plan is cumulative if insured credits earned during one year may be transferred to the following year; it is noncumulative when the employee's entitlement is reviewed on a yearly basis or after each illness. In one survey all of the participating 171 companies offered paid-sick-leave plans.[8]

Another arrangement is the sickness indemnity insurance plan. This is an insured income protection plan provided through an insurance company or outside agency. The employer pays either all or part of the premiums. The typical plan will cover benefits only over a specified time interval and has a waiting period for illness that is waived in cases of accident. Benefits paid are usually expressed as a percentage of weekly

values by the on-going forces of inflation. However, the extent of protection is capped and is a function of the rate of inflation.

## Developing a Retirement Plan

When a human resource department decides to develop a retirement plan, several critical questions must be answered. One is: Who will pay it? In a *noncontributory plan,* the employer pays the entire amount. *Contributory plans* require both the employee and the employer to contribute.

Another question is: When will the pension rights vest? *Vesting* gives the workers the right to pension benefits even if they leave the company. Pension rights usually vest after several years of service. If an employee leaves before pension benefits are vested, the worker has no rights except to regain his or her contributions to the plan. Some pensions have *portability clauses.* They allow accumulated pension rights to be transferred to another employer.

A third question is: How will the firm meet its financial obligations? Some companies pay pensions out of current income when employees retire. This is called an *unfunded plan. Funded plans* require the employer to accumulate monies in advance so that the employer's contribution plus interest will cover the pension obligation.

Another important question is: Will the plan be *trusted* or *insured?* The trusted plan calls for all monies to be deposited into a trust fund, usually with a trust company. The company manages and protects the funds. It does not guarantee that the employer's pension liabilities will be met. These guarantees are provided by provincial or federal legislation covering pensions. With an insured plan, pension monies are used to buy employee annuities from the insurer. Each annuity represents an insurance company's pledge to pay the worker a given amount per month upon retirement.

Two significant problems have developed in the administration of pension plans. First, some employers go out of business, leaving the pension plan unfunded or only partially funded. Second, some companies minimize their pension costs by having very long vesting periods. Thus an employee who quits or is fired often has no pension rights. Since both of these problems may impose hardships on employees and on the nation's welfare burden, Parliament has passed the *Pension Benefits Standards Act.*

## Pension Benefits Standards Act

This act regulates pension plans in industries under the jurisdiction of the Government of Canada, such as banks, railways, shipping companies, and radio and other communication companies. In addition, seven provinces (Alberta, Saskatchewan, Manitoba, Ontario, Quebec, Nova Scotia, and Newfoundland) have enacted their own pension benefits acts which in content are similar to the federal act. Pension plans in the remaining provinces, to qualify for tax deductions, must conform to certain standards set forth in the federal legislation. The Pension Benefits Standards Act requires that pension funds be held in trust for members, and that the funds not be held under the complete custody and control of either the employer or the employees. To accomplish this, the funding of a private pension plan must be carried out by one or more of the following means:

· an insurance contract with a company authorized to conduct a life insurance business in Canada;

- a trust in Canada whose trustees are either a trust company or a group of individuals, at least three of whom live in Canada and one of whom must be independent of the employer and employees;
- a corporate pension society;
- an arrangement administered by the Government of Canada or a provincial government.

### Early Retirement

As retirement plans mature, companies tend to liberalize them. Increasingly, this has meant early retirement provisions, which allow workers to retire before age sixty-five. Benefits are normally reduced for early retirement, because statistically the employee draws benefits longer and the employer has less time to fund its share of the pension. Some pensions — those used by the military, for example — pay the retiree an amount based on years of service, regardless of age.

### Retirement Counselling

As part of the retirement program, some employers conduct pre-retirement and post-retirement counselling. The primary purpose of *pre-retirement counselling* is to encourage the employee to plan for retirement. The sooner counselling occurs, the more able the worker is to prepare emotionally and financially. These sessions are also used to explain the nature of the employee's retirement program and indicate the likely adjustments a retiree may face.

Post-retirement counselling is designed to ease the transition from worker to retiree. The retiree is made aware of community and company programs for retired people. Retired employees of Ontario Hydro, for example, can join an organization of other retired Hydro employees. This type of association provides social contacts, community projects, and recreational opportunities.

## PAID TIME-OFF BENEFITS

Time periods during which the employee is not working but is getting paid are the result of time-off benefits. Although time-off benefits may seem minor, according to one survey they were the costliest major category, comprising 11.2% of gross annual payroll.[14] (See Figure 13-1.)

### On-the-Job Breaks

Some of the most common forms of time-off benefits are those found on the job. Examples include rest breaks, meal breaks, and wash-up time. Through a break in the physical and mental effort of a job, productivity may be increased. The major problem for human resource and line managers is the tendency of employees to stretch these time-off periods.

When one human resource manager was confronted by a supervisor with the problem of stretched breaks, she suggested a simple solution. Each employee was assigned a specific break time — from 9:15-9:30 A.M., or 9:30 to 9:45 A.M., for example — but could not leave for break until the preceding employee returned.

Since each clerk was anxious to go on break, the peer group policed the length of breaks and the stretched breaks ended.

## Paid Sick Leave

Absences from work are unavoidable. Today, most companies pay workers when they are absent for medical reasons by granting a limited number of days of sick leave per year. Unfortunately, this is one of the most abused benefits; many workers take the attitude that these are simply extra days off. If the human resource policies prohibit employees from crediting unused sick leave to next year's account, absences increase near the end of the year. To minimize abuses, some companies require medical verifications of illness or pay employees for unused sick leave.

A few firms avoid the abuse question by granting "personal leave days." This approach allows an employee to skip work for any reason and get paid, up to a specified number of days per year. *Sick leave banks* allow employees to "borrow" extra days above the specified number when they use up their individual allocation. Then when they earn additional days, the days are repaid to the sick leave bank.

## Holidays and Vacations

About 75% of office and non-office employees and 85% of management and professional employees received eleven or more paid holidays in 1986, according to a survey by the Pay Research Bureau.[15] Like sick leave, however, this benefit is subject to abuse. Employees sometimes try to stretch the holiday by missing the work day before or after the holiday. Policies that require attendance the day before and after a holiday as a condition of holiday pay lessen this problem. The number of paid holidays for various categories of employees is shown in Figure 13-2.

FIGURE 13-2   Number of Paid Holidays

| NUMBER OF HOLIDAYS | % EMPLOYEES COVERED MANAGERIAL/ PROFESSIONAL | OFFICE | NON-OFFICE |
|---|---|---|---|
| Fewer than 10 days | 4.0 | 7.7 | 6.5 |
| 10–12 days | 69.0 | 72.6 | 78.5 |
| 13–15 days | 26.3 | 18.5 | 14.1 |
| 16–23 days | 0.7 | 1.2 | 0.9 |

Source: Adapted from *The Work Life Report,* Vol. 5, No. 3, 1987, p. 16.

Vacations are usually based on the employee's length of service, but federal and provincial laws specify a two-(in Saskatchewan three-) week minimum vacation entitlement. In some regions this increases to three weeks (in Saskatchewan four) after five, six, or ten years of service.

Policies for vacations vary widely. Some companies allow employees to use vacation days a few at a time. Other companies insist that the worker take the vacation all at once. A few employers actually close down during designated periods and require vacations to be taken during this period. Still other companies negate the reason for vacations completely by allowing employees to work and receive vacation pay as a bonus.

## Leaves of Absence

Leaves of absence are often granted for pregnancy, extended illness, accidents, summer military camps, jury duty, funeral services, and other reasons specified in a company's human resource policies. Extended leaves are normally without pay. Shorter absences —especially for jury duty or funerals of close relatives—are often with pay.

## WORK SCHEDULING BENEFITS

The length of the typical workweek has declined significantly since the early days of the Industrial Revolution, as illustrated by Figure 13-3. A norm of a five-day, forty-hour workweek remained relatively unchanged from the 1930s to the early 1970s. During the 1970s, however, several new approaches to scheduling work gained popularity: the shorter workweek, flextime, and job sharing.[16]

FIGURE 13-3  A Typical Work Schedule 100 Years Ago

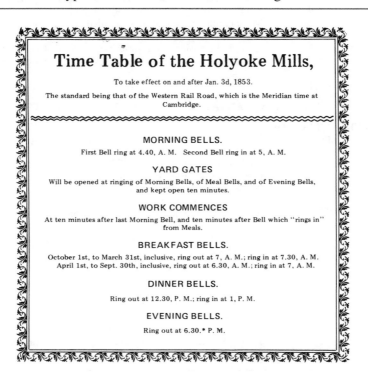

Source: *Labor's Long, Hard Road*, Air Line Employees Association, International, p. 4. Used by permission.

## Shorter Workweeks

A shorter workweek compresses forty hours of work into fewer than five full days. Some plans even shorten the workweek to fewer than forty hours. The most popular version has been forty hours of work compressed into four days. Figure 13-4 summarizes

FIGURE 13-4   Perceived Advantages and Disadvantages of the Shorter Workweek

### PERCEIVED ADVANTAGES OF THE SHORTER WORKWEEK

| RANK ORDER | PERCENTAGE OF RESPONSES | POTENTIALLY ADVANTAGEOUS FACTORS |
|---|---|---|
| 1 | 18.8 | Less total time would be lost due to startup, washup, breaks, and cleanup. |
| 2 | 15.8 | Absenteeism and turnover rates will be lower. |
| 3 | 13.2 | Efficiency would increase through better utilization of our equipment. |
| 4 | 12.9 | Employee morale and loyalty will be higher. |
| 5 | 8.1 | It would be good public relations and create a progressive image. |
| 6 | 7.9 | It will stimulate employee motivation and higher productivity. |
| 7 | 7.2 | More employees could be scheduled at peak workload days or times. |
| 8 | 6.2 | It would be easier to recruit a large supply of good workers. |
| 9 | 5.7 | It would provide an opportunity to implement other important changes. |
| 10 | 4.1 | It would fulfill the firm's social responsibility to our employees. |

### PERCEIVED DISADVANTAGES OF THE SHORTER WORKWEEK

| RANK ORDER | PERCENTAGE OF RESPONSES | POTENTIALLY DISADVANTAGEOUS FACTORS |
|---|---|---|
| 1 | 22.1 | Customers or suppliers would be inconvenienced. |
| 2 | 20.3 | It would create too many scheduling and communications problems. |
| 3 | 12.9 | Productivity would be lower once the novelty wore off. |
| 4 | 12.1 | All hours over eight per day would probably have to be paid as overtime. |
| 5 | 9.7 | The long hours would be boring, monotonous, and tiresome for employees. |
| 6 | 7.7 | Too many employees would be fatigued from moonlighting on second jobs. |
| 7 | 7.2 | If it fails, returning to the five-day workweek will be difficult. |
| 8 | 4.0 | Absenteeism and/or turnover would be greater under a shorter workweek. |
| 9 | 3.1 | Employees would dislike and resist the idea. |
| 10 | 0.9 | We might get bad publicity because as yet the program is not widely accepted. |

Source: John W. Newstrom and William B. Werther, Jr., "Managerial Perceptions of the Shorter Workweek," *Arizona Business*, February 1973, pp. 10, 11. Used by permission.

the major advantages and disadvantages commonly associated with shorter workweeks. The rankings of these factors are based on a U.S. survey of 223 firms.

The idea for a shorter workweek developed in 1973 in western Canada when the Oil, Chemical and Atomic Worker's International Union bargained for and was granted reduced working hours for 10,000 petrochemical and petroleum industry workers. Soon afterwards it suggested to management that workers be allowed to complete their thirty-seven and one-third hours in four days, giving them a free Friday. After a trial period, this feature became permanent. Although some companies are reluctant to change their schedules, employees generally seem to enjoy the greater opportunity for leisure activities. A survey in Ontario covered 10,600 employees in 175 companies where the short workweek had been implemented. The majority of employees reported improved employee morale, greater continuity in the work process, higher productivity, and lower absenteeism.[17]

## Flextime

*Flextime* abolishes rigid starting and ending times for the workday. Instead, employees are allowed to report to work at any time during a range of hours. For example, starting time may be from 7 A.M. to 9 A.M., with all employees expected to work the core hours of 9 A.M. to 3 P.M. The workday usually remains unchanged at eight hours. Therefore, the end of the workday is variable also.

The outcome of a flextime program, however, is contingent upon the nature of the firm's operations. For example, the major disadvantage of flextime is the difficulty in meeting minimum staffing needs early and late in the day. Assembly-line and customer service operations find this problem to be especially significant. But in many operations users have reported noteworthy successes.[18]

## Job Sharing

A third approach to employee scheduling that gained popularity during the 1970s is job sharing. *Job sharing* involves one or more employees doing the same job but working different hours, days, or even weeks. Most commonly, two people handle the duties of one full-time job.

> Karen and Bob Rosen both taught English at Queen Elizabeth High School. After Karen had her first child one summer, Karen, Bob, and their principal agreed to a job-sharing arrangement. Bob taught three classes of English literature and composition in the morning. He then drove home, gave Karen the car, and she returned to school and taught three English classes in the afternoon. The school benefitted because teachers normally had five classes and a planning period. With job sharing, the school received six classes of English instruction. Also, Bob and Karen were able to share in raising their child with neither of them completely giving up a career.

The major advantage claimed for job sharing is increased productivity from workers who are not fatigued. Problems arise from the increased paperwork and administrative burden associated with two employees' doing the job of one. Another problem is that of fringe benefits. Human resource specialists are forced to decide whether job sharers should be given benefits equal with other employees or benefits that are scaled down in proportion to the employee's hours.[19]

## EMPLOYEE SERVICES

Some companies go beyond pay and traditional benefits. They also provide educational, financial, and social services for their employees.

### Educational Assistance

Tuition refund programs are among the more common employer services. These programs partially or completely reimburse employees for furthering their education. They may be limited only to courses that are related to the employee's job, or the employer may reimburse workers for any educational expenditure. In the future, more companies may follow the lead of Kimberly-Clark Corporation in the U.S.:

> Kimberly-Clark created an educational savings account for employees and their dependants. The company gives employees credits for each year of service. Then when an employee or dependant wants to go to college, he or she can be reimbursed partially from the educational savings account established by the company.

### Financial Services

Probably the oldest service is employee discount plans. These programs — common among retail stores and consumer goods manufacturers — allow workers to buy products from the company at a discount.

Credit unions are another well-established employee service. The interest collected by the credit union on loans and investments is distributed to members in the form of dividends. The dividends (interest payments) are allocated in proportion to the amount employees have in their share (savings) account. The lower interest rate on loans, the higher interest on deposits, and payroll deductions for savings or loan repayment are the major employee advantages.

Stock purchase programs are another financial service. These plans enable employees to buy company stock — usually through payroll deductions. In some stock purchase programs, employee outlays may be matched by company contributions.

Profit sharing, increasingly popular in the United States, has also attracted the attention of the Canadian business community. The number of registered profit sharing plans in the U.S. increased from 186,000 in 1975 to well over 350,000 in 1982; the number in Canada grew from approximately 2000 registered plans in the middle 1950s to more than 32,000 by 1982. Since a recent study found that more than 50% of all profit-sharing plans are cash plans that do not require registration, the number of profit-sharing plans in Canada is probably well beyond 60,000.[20] Three types of plans exist in Canada:

**1.** *Current distribution* plans, which distribute a share of a company's profits to all employees in direct cash payments or company stock.

**2.** *Deferred payout* plans of two kinds: (a) employee profit-sharing plans (EPSP) and (b) deferred profit-sharing plans (DPSP), as defined in Sections 144 and 147 of the Income Tax Act. Both plans allow for deferred tax payments until the profits are actually paid out.

**3.** *Combination* plans, wherein plans 1 and 2 may be combined.

## Social Services

A wide range of social services is provided by employers. At one extreme are simple interest groups such as bowling leagues and softball teams. At the other extreme are comprehensive *employee assistance programs* designed to assist employees with personal problems.

> A large bank had a high turnover rate among its entry-level workers. After study, it appeared that many new workers had transportation, housing, child-care, and other problems. These difficulties were sometimes insurmountable for employees, and they would quit. To combat this situation, the bank created its "Contact" program. Each employee was informed of the program and given the telephone number to call whenever a work- or non-work-related problem occurred. Then when employees had child-care or transportation difficulties, they would call the Contact number. The contact staff provided individual counselling or a referral service by informing employees of groups in the community that could help them. The program was not limited to just new employees, however. To help build better employee relations, the Contact staff tried to assist with all types of employee problems. This involved the staff in resolving employee quarrels, advising managers of employee complaints, and even helping workers solve family disputes.

Although employee assistance programs like the one at this bank are rare, human resource managers realize that employee problems affect company performance. Employer services that can lessen these problems offer potential dividends in employee performance, loyalty, and turnover.

One employer service with a growing record of success is alcohol and drug rehabilitation. For example, human resource experts formerly recommended the discharge of alcoholic workers. During the last ten years, however, an increasing number of human resource departments have implemented *alcohol and drug rehabilitation programs*. This service has saved many otherwise good employees in companies such as Canadian National Railways and General Motors of Canada, Ltd. When rehabilitation has been effected, the company usually gains a hardworking, loyal employee.

> Canadian National Railways (CNR) spends $300,000 to run an employee assistance program (EAP), 85% of which is devoted to employees having alcohol-related or drug-related problems. CNR has twelve trained counsellors who deal with 400 problem drinkers annually. The company estimates that 80% of the 3000 workers referred to its EAP were rehabilitated, saving the company approximately $5 million.[21]

*Relocation programs* are the support in dollars or services a company provides to its transferred or new employees. At a minimum, this benefit includes payment for moving expenses. Some employees receive fully paid house-hunting trips with their spouse to the new location before the move, subsidized home mortgages, placement assistance for working spouses, and even family counselling to reduce the stress of the move. A transferred employee also may be able to sell his or her home to the employer for the appraised value in order to avoid having to sell it on the market.[22]

Additional employee assistance activities are discussed in Chapter 17 in connection with counselling.

## ADMINISTRATION OF VOLUNTARY BENEFIT AND SERVICE PROGRAMS

A serious shortcoming of human resource management has been poor administration of indirect compensation. Even in otherwise well-managed human resource departments, benefits and services have grown in a haphazard manner. Those costly supplements were introduced in response to social trends, union demands, employee pressures, and management wishes, and so human resource departments seldom established objectives, systematic plans, and standards to determine the appropriateness of benefits and services. This patchwork of benefits and services has caused several problems.

### Problems in Administration

The central problem in supplementary compensation is a lack of employee participation. Once a fringe benefit program is designed by the human resource department and the labour union (if there is one), employees have little discretion. For example, pension and maternity benefits usually are granted to all workers equally. Younger employees see pensions as distant and largely irrelevant; older workers find maternity benefits are not needed. This uniformity fails to recognize individual differences and wishes. Admittedly, uniformity leads to administrative and actuarial economies; but when employees receive benefits they neither want nor need, these economies are questionable.

Since employees have little choice in their individual benefit package, most workers are unaware of all of the benefits to which they are entitled.

> Two researchers designed a study to learn how knowledgeable selected workers were about their benefits. In two different plants—one with a union and one without — they asked employees to list all the benefits that they could recall. The average could not recall 15% of the employee-provided benefits.[23]

Ignorance and the inability to influence the mix of benefits often lead to pressure from employees for more benefits to meet their needs. For example, older workers may request improved retirement plans, while younger workers seek improved insurance coverage of dependants. Often the result is a proliferation of benefits and increased employer costs. These costs, which represented 15.1% of an employee's gross annual payroll in 1953, have escalated to 36.3% in 1986, an increase of 140%.[24] Still, employee ignorance and confusion can lead to complaints and dissatisfaction about their fringe benefit package.

## Traditional Remedies

The traditional remedy to benefit problems has been to increase employee awareness, usually through publicizing employee benefits. This publicity starts with orientation sessions that explain the benefit programs and provide employee handbooks. Company newspapers, special mailings, employee meetings, bulletin-board announcements, and responses to employee questions are also used to further publicize the organization's benefit package.

> William M. Mercer Ltd., a large consulting firm specializing in compensation and benefit issues, with branches in twelve cities in Canada, offers seminars to recipients of benefits and training courses to compensation officers. Interested employees of a client may ask for an individual assessment and for recommendations on more effective coverage.

Publicizing the benefits and services attacks only the symptoms of the problem: lack of employee interest. Moreover, this reactive approach further adds to the costs of administration through increased "advertising" expenses.

## A Proactive Solution: Cafeteria Benefits

*Cafeteria benefit programs,* or variable fringe benefit programs, allow employees to select benefits and services that match their individual needs. Workers are provided a benefit and services account with a specified number of dollars in the account. Through deductions from this account, employees shop for specific benefits from among those offered by the employer. The types and prices of benefits are provided to each employee in the form of a computer printout. This cost sheet also describes each benefit. Then, as illustrated in Figure 13-5, employees select their package of benefits and services for the coming year.

> Figure 13-5 indicates how two different workers might spend the $3500 the company grants each worker. Workers A and B select two different sets of benefits because their personal situations differ dramatically. Worker A is a young parent who is supporting a family and her husband. If they were to have another child or if they had some other health-related expense, it might seriously affect their plans, so they have elected to be well insured for pregnancy and supplemental health costs. Worker B can more easily afford unexpected medical expenses, so he bought less supplemental health insurance and allocated fewer dollars for weekly income benefits. Instead, he put a large portion of his benefit monies into the company pension plan.

Although this approach creates additional administrative costs and an obligation for the human resource department to advise employees, there are several advantages. The main

FIGURE 13-5   Hypothetical Benefit Selection of Two Different Workers

| WORKER A | | WORKER B |
|---|---|---|
| Age 27, female, married with one child. Husband in graduate school. | | Age 56, male, married with two grown and married children. Wife does not work. |
| | Supplemental health insurance: | |
| $245 | Maternity | 0 |
| 935 | $100 deductible | 0 |
| 0 | Prescription drug coverage | $625 |
| | Life insurance: | |
| 100 | $20,000 for worker | 100 |
| 150 | $10,000 for spouse | 0 |
| 600 | Vacations | 900 |
| 300 | Holidays | 300 |
| 200 | Pension plan | 1270 |
| 0 | Jury duty pay | 0 |
| 100 | Disability insurance | 100 |
| 870 | Weekly income benefit | 205 |
| $3500 | Total | $3500 |

advantage is employee participation. Through participation, employees come to understand exactly what benefits the employer is offering. And employees can better match their benefits with their needs.[25]

## LEGALLY REQUIRED BENEFITS

Legally required benefits and services are imposed upon organizations by the government. As a result, employers must comply with the law and its procedures. Most of these benefits and services are designed to help employees. In general, government seeks to ensure minimum levels of financial security for the nation's work force. Figure 13-6 shows that the objective of providing financial security is to ease the monetary burdens of retirement, death, long-term disability, and unemployment. The loss of income from these causes is cushioned by the security provisions. The financial problems of *involuntary unemployment* are lessened by unemployment compensation. And job-related inju-

FIGURE 13-6   Sources of Financial Protection for Workers

| PROTECTION FOR WORKERS | SOURCES OF PROTECTION | LEGISLATING GOVERNMENT |
|---|---|---|
| | FINANCIAL SECURITY | |
| Fair remuneration | Minimum wage acts | Federal and provincial |
| Retirement | Canada Pension Plan | Federal (except in Quebec) |
| Involuntary unemployment | Unemployment Insurance | Federal |
| Industrial accidents | Workers' compensation acts | Federal and provincial |
| Medical care | Health insurance plans | Provincial |
| Child sustenance | Family Allowances | Federal |

ries and death are compensated under workers' compensation laws. None of these programs fully reimburses the affected workers; nevertheless, each worker does get a financial base to which additional protection can be added.

Legally required benefits and services are important to the human resource department for two reasons. First, top management holds the human resource department responsible for meeting these legal obligations. If the department is to meet this responsibility, it must ensure that the firm is in compliance with the law. Second, if the obligations are improperly handled, the result can be severe fines and more taxes. None of these outcomes contributes to the organization's objectives.

## FINANCIAL SECURITY

A large majority of Canadians are financially dependent on their monthly paycheques. Only a small percentage of the population is self-employed; most others work for another person or organization. To protect the well-being of society, governmental regulations on fair remuneration, retirement plans, and disability compensation are imperative. The major legal provisions on the above matters will be discussed below. It should be emphasized that in Canada (unlike in the U.S. or in some other western countries), many of these regulations are provincially administered. To suit the specific work environments, many of these statutes and provisions vary from province to province in Canada.

### Minimum Wages

All the provinces have minimum wage legislation that applies to most classes of workers, other than farm labourers and domestic servants. The legislation provides for a board to set minimum wage rates, and these rates are imposed by means of minimum wage orders that are periodically issued.[26] Wide discretion is given to all provincial boards for determination of the classes of employees for which minimum wages are to be established. The general minimum wage rates at the provincial and federal levels are given in Figure 13-7. The rates shown are typical for persons eighteen years of age and over. For employees under eighteen the rates are somewhat lower.

**FIGURE 13-7  Minimum Hourly Wage Rates (1988 Status)**

| | |
|---|---|
| **Federal** (all employees 17 years of age and over) | $4.00 |
| **Alberta** (all employees 18 years of age and over) | $4.50 |
| **British Columbia** (all employees 18 years of age and over) | $4.50 |
| **Manitoba** (all employees 18 years of age and over) | $4.70 |
| **New Brunswick** (no special rates with respect to age) | $4.00 |
| **Newfoundland** (all employees 16 years of age and over) | $4.25 |
| **Northwest Territories** (all employees 17 years of age and over) | $5.39 |
| **Nova Scotia** (all employees 18 years of age and over) | $4.50 |
| **Ontario** (all employees 18 years of age and over) | $4.75 |
| **Prince Edward Island** (all employees 18 years of age and over) | $4.27 |
| **Quebec** (all employees 18 years of age and over) | $4.75 |
| **Saskatchewan** (all employees 18 years of age and over) | $4.50 |
| **Yukon Territory** (all employees 17 years of age and over) | $5.00 |

Source: Ministry of Labour (Research and Planning Division), Halifax, Nova Scotia.

The federal government passed the Minimum Wages Act in 1935, pursuant to one of the three conventions adopted by the International Labour Organization. However, under the British North America Act, minimum wage legislation comes under provincial jurisdiction. The federal Minimum Wages Act currently applies to all government agencies, Crown corporations, and some selected industries as mentioned in Chapter 3.

### Contracts With the Government

The Fair Wages and Hours of Labour Act applies to contracts made with the Government of Canada for all types of work. It is mandatory on the part of contractors dealing with the Government of Canada to pay fair wages and establish an eight-hour work day during all such work.[27]

### Staff Records

The Canada Labour Code requires every employer in those industries falling under federal jurisdiction to furnish information relating to wages of employees, their hours of work, general holidays, annual vacation, and conditions of employment whenever the Ministry of Labour demands it. Similar provisions exist in the provincial legislation. Accurate records are also to be kept on maternity leave, severance pay, etc., relating to all employees. This is to ensure that all provisions of the legislation relating to minimum wages, maximum weekly hours, overtime payments, etc., are strictly adhered to by each employer.

### Criticisms of Minimum Wage Regulation

It has been pointed out by some that minimum wage regulations increase the cost of production in Canada. This may eventually work against the workers rather than for them.

> In recent years, minimum wages across Canada have risen more than the average increase in manufacturing wages. And some economists are suggesting . . . [that] . . . it could lead to an intolerable increase [in unemployment] and cause the major burdens to fall precisely on the workers it was designed to help.[28]

Increases in minimum wages are usually accompanied by increases in unemployment figures of low-skilled and young persons in the work force. It is also pointed out by some that continual increases in minimum wage rates may actually contribute to the inflationary trends in the economy.[29] There is, however, no conclusive evidence on the matter one way or the other at this time. Figure 13-8 shows the average hourly wages paid in different Canadian industries for the years 1980, 1981, and 1988. As can be seen, there has been a steadily increasing trend in all industries. When all manufacturing industries are taken together, the average wages have gone up by approximately 56% in eight years.

### The Canada Pension Plan and the Quebec Pension Plan (CPP and QPP)

The Canada Pension Plan (Quebec Pension Plan in the province of Quebec), which came into effect on January 1, 1966, is a mandatory plan for all self-employed persons and

FIGURE 13-8   Average Hourly Wage, by Industry, 1980-1988

| MANUFACTURING | 1980 | 1981 | 1988 |
|---|---|---|---|
| Food and Beverages | $7.65 | $8.62 | $12.08 |
| Rubber Products | 8.22 | 9.37 | 12.94 |
| Leather Products | 5.35 | 5.97 | 8.09 |
| Textile Products | 6.44 | 7.07 | 10.26 |
| Clothing | 5.31 | 5.68 | 7.37 |
| Wood Products | 8.86 | 9.63 | 12.58 |
| Furniture, Fixtures | 6.37 | 6.99 | 9.06 |
| Paper and Products | 9.77 | 11.25 | 16.16 |
| Printing, Publishing | 8.98 | 9.97 | 13.95 |
| Primary Metals | 9.56 | 10.93 | 16.11 |
| Metal Fabricating | 8.52 | 9.58 | 12.65 |
| Machinery | 8.83 | 9.92 | 12.87 |
| Transportation Equipment | 9.33 | 10.39 | 14.84 |
| Electrical Products | 7.35 | 8.17 | 11.97 |
| Non-metallic Mineral Products | 8.92 | 10.05 | 13.35 |
| Petroleum and Coal Products | 11.12 | 12.53 | 16.60 |
| Chemicals and Chemical Products | 8.50 | 9.54 | 13.66 |
| All Manufacturing | 8.19 | 9.97 | 12.75 |
| Other Industries: | | | |
| Mining and Milling | 10.80 | 13.30 | 17.23 |
| Construction: | | | |
| Building | 12.47 | 14.07 | 14.84 |
| Engineering | 11.41 | 13.04 | 16.12 |
| Urban Transport | 9.44 | 10.44 | 15.32 |
| Highway, Bridge Maintenance | 7.79 | 8.69 | 13.18 |
| Laundries, Cleaners, and Pressers | 4.76 | 5.24 | 7.30 |
| Restaurants, Caterers, and Taverns | 4.50 | 4.89 | 8.38 |

Source: Statistics Canada, Labour Division, June 1988.

employees in Canada. Both plans are contributory, i.e., both the employer and the employee pay part of the costs. The plans are portable in Canada, i.e., pension rights are not affected by changes of job or residence. The plans are also tied to cost-of-living changes.

CPP and QPP pay retirement pensions, disability pensions, and pensions for surviving spouses. They also pay lump-sum death benefits to eligible applicants, benefits to children of disabled contributors, and orphans' benefits where applicable. Before 1987, the tax-deductible contributions to both plans were 3.6% of the total employee earnings, shared equally by employer and employee, up to a yearly maximum pensionable earning (YMPE) that is approximately the average industrial wage. Self-employed persons have to pay the full contribution. In 1987 the contribution from both parties increased to a total of 3.8% and will increase by 0.2% annually until 1991. The requirement for receiving a pension in Canada is being sixty-five years old (or sixty if not working) and having made contributions for at least one year. The retirement pension is approximately 25% of the employee's average pensionable earnings. Recent changes include the flexibility to draw CPP pension between age sixty and seventy with appropriate adjustments, and the possible splitting of the CPP pension following separation of legal or common-law spouses.

Since CPP and QPP provide retirees with only 25% of their average pensionable earnings as pension benefits, supplementary payments are available from the federal government through Old Age Security (OAS) and Guaranteed Income Supplements (GIS). OAS is a monthly benefit paid to all persons sixty-five years of age and over; it is not necessary to be retired to be eligible for OAS. GIS was set up mainly for those who retired prior to the enactment of the CPP and were therefore ineligible for CPP. It is a basic supplement to other over-sixty-five income. GIS and OAS are tied to the cost of living and will increase with the consumer price index. These additional benefits are designed to provide retirees with a guaranteed minimum income. To increase their pension benefits further, employees have to turn to private pension plans.

A comparative picture of Canada Pension Plan's revenues and disbursements is shown in Figure 13-9. As can be seen, the revenues of the CPP have risen by about 650% between 1970 and 1985, while the disbursements have increased by a whopping 5969%. This raises major concerns about the liquidity of the CPP in the next few decades when the number of pensioners in Canada is expected to rise dramatically.

FIGURE 13-9   Canada Pension Plan Revenues and Disbursements*

|  | 1970 | 1980 | 1985 |
|---|---|---|---|
| Revenues |  |  |  |
| Contributions | 812.9 | 2689.3 | 4495.1 |
| Interest on investments | 202.7 | 1427.3 | 3009.3 |
| Interest on operating balances | 4.0 | 91.4 | 152.3 |
| Total Revenues | 1020.1 | 4208.1 | 7656.7 |

|  | 1970 | 1980 | 1986 |
|---|---|---|---|
| Expenditure |  |  |  |
| Retirement benefits | 34.3 | 1218.2 | 3572.9 |
| Disability benefits | 1.8 | 225.6 | 681.4 |
| Child's benefits | 0.4 | 29.6 | 71.4 |
| Survivor's benefits | 21.8 | 313.1 | 832.1 |
| Orphans | 10.4 | 76.8 | 116.8 |
| Death | 9.2 | 48.7 | 118.2 |
| Total benefits paid | 77.9 | 1912.1 | 5392.9 |

Source: Ministry of National Health and Welfare: *Historical Studies in Canada Pension Plan*, December 1986, p. 9. Reproduced with the permission of the Minister of Supply and Services Canada.
*Figures in $ million

## Evaluation

Whether the government or private industry should plan and administer pensions is a question that has been debated for some time. It has been pointed out by some that compulsory national pension plans add to the costs of production, thus making Canadian goods uncompetitive in the international markets.[30] However, any welfare society has to take care of its old, disadvantaged, and poor. It should also be noted that CPP is much greater in scope than an old-age pension plan and provides for other contingencies not usually covered by common pension plans. On these dimensions CPP and QPP have indeed played a crucial role in the past.[31]

## Unemployment Insurance (UI)

In 1940 Canada started a program to help alleviate people's monetary problems during the transition from one job to another. The Unemployment Insurance Act of 1971 significantly changed and added to the program. Since 1971 there have been several modifications to eligibility criteria and payment schedules. Currently, approximately 12 million Canadians are covered by the UI scheme. In 1986, there were about 1.2 million beneficiaries under the plan. Statistics Canada's statistical review for February 1987 gives the following figures related to the UI scheme. All figures are approximate.

FIGURE 13-10   Unemployment Insurance Benefits

|  | Millions |
|---|---|
| Total benefits paid | $10,226.9 |
| Regular benefits | 8,975.3 |
| Sickness benefits | 220.7 |
| Maternity benefits | 432.5 |
| Retirement benefits | 22.4 |
| Fisherman's benefits | 179.8 |

Source: Statistics Canada, *Canadian Statistical Review February 1987*, Catalogue No. 11-003-E, Vol. 62, No.2, March 1987, p. 54.

Most salaried and hourly workers who are employed for at least fifteen hours a week are covered by UI. The self-employed are not eligible for benefits under the present regulations.

Jobs covered by UI are called *insurable employment.* All persons holding insurable employment are required to pay premiums to the Unemployment Insurance Commission (UIC). UIC premiums are deducted automatically from an employee's pay. All the premiums, along with the employers' contributions, are deposited together in the *unemployment insurance account,* out of which the final payments are made to persons who are temporarily out of their jobs.

Under the present regulations there are two kinds of payments: *regular* and *special.* To receive regular benefits the applicant should have had interruption of earnings for at least seven days. Further, the applicant must have worked in insurable employment for a certain number of weeks in the past fifty-two weeks. The number of weeks an applicant needs to have worked varies from ten to fourteen, depending on the unemployment rate in the economic region, and hence this period is called the *variable entrance requirement.* Special benefits are paid if the person is sick, injured, pregnant, or in quarantine. There is also a special one-time payment when a person reaches the age of sixty-five. To get special benefits a person needs to have worked at least twenty weeks immediately prior to the claim date.

## Benefits and Premiums

In 1980 the maximum weekly payment was $120, and total unemployment benefits paid to claimants exceeded $4.3 billion. The maximum weekly payments increased in 1987 to $318, and the total benefits paid out to claimants exceeded $12 billion, making UI the most expensive social program in Canada. The benefit rate is 60% of the average weekly insurable earnings of an employee. In 1987 the premium for employees was $2.35 and for employers $3.29 per $100 of weekly insurable earnings (maximum weekly contributions: employee $12.46 and employer $17.44). Benefits are payable for up to fifty weeks.

### Evaluation

A large part of the increase in UI payments in the past has been attributed to the ''loose'' manner in which the system is administered.

> Charlie Brown is upset. He's been trying—without success—for the past six months to hire two steady waiters or waitresses for his Toronto beer hall. ''The system has me beat,'' Brown says. ''I guess it's only natural that people would rather draw pogy (unemployment insurance) than work, but I don't feel very good about the present situation.
>
> ''About 50% of my customers are on unemployment, and they would probably take their business elsewhere if you used my name,'' he explains.
>
> So while Brown is having difficulty getting staff — he'll even settle for untrained workers—he benefits from the unemployment payments his customers get.
>
> Still, he's unhappy about what he calls the ''unemployment rip-off'' and believes changes should be made to make it more difficult for people to collect.
>
> ''The government thinks it is dealing with naive people,'' Brown says. ''This is not the case. These guys [his customers] should be awarded Ph.D.'s for their knowledge of the unemployment insurance system. They understand exactly how long they have to work before they can collect, how long they can collect and how much job hunting effort they have to exert to fool the government official handling their cases . . . ''[32]

Like Brown, many others believe that UI rules should be tightened. Some suggestions have been made to extend the minimum work period before a person can collect UI payments and to reduce the benefits as well as the benefit period (currently a maximum of fifty weeks). It is also contended by some that UI takes away all incentive to work. In a survey by the *Financial Times of Canada*, evidence of widespread abuse of the UIC system was found.[33] The MacDonald Commission in 1985 and the Forget Commission in 1986 investigated the present system and made suggestions for significant changes regarding financing and eligibility, but so far the government has not acted on these recommendations, which were strongly opposed by unions.[34] It is interesting to note that research indicates that increased benefits result in longer job search durations and, as a consequence, in higher unemployment levels.[35]

## Workers' Compensation Acts

All ten provinces, the Northwest Territories, and the Yukon have some act or other (usually called ''Workers' Compensation Act'' *or* ''Ordinance'') which entitles workers to compensation in the event of personal injury by accident during their regular work. The administration of the act is done provincially and all the provincial acts are of the ''collective liability'' type: that is, compensation is payable by employers collectively.

The industries covered by the act are classified into groups according to their special hazards, and all employers in each group are collectively liable for payment of compensation to all workers employed in that group. The annual contribution rate (a percentage of payroll) is determined on the basis of an employer's total annual payroll figures. However, an employer can also be charged a higher rate of contributions if there are many workers' compensation claims.

*Benefits*

Various types of benefits are available under the workers' compensation legislation: protection against accidents as a result of accident prevention activities of the Workers' Compensation Board or employer's association, first aid and all necessary medical aid, including hospitalization, cash benefits during the period of disablement (typically 75% of wages subject to an annual wage ceiling—see Figure 13-11), rehabilitation (physical and vocational), and a pension available for life for any resulting permanent disability. When disablement is slight, a lump-sum payment is made.[36] In the case of a fatal accident, cash benefits are provided for the spouse and dependent children of the deceased employee.

 The right of an employee to compensation is not affected by the employer's neglect or refusal to furnish information or to pay its assessment, or by its insolvency.[37] Also, the employee's right to compensation may not be assigned without Board approval and it cannot be waived or attached. All claims for compensation are received and adjudicated by the Workers' Compensation Board, whose decision is final (except in the four Atlantic provinces, where appeals are allowed).

FIGURE 13-11   Maximal Earnings Covered Under Provincial Workers' Compensation Acts

| PROVINCE | EARNINGS | ENACTED |
|----------|----------|---------|
| Alberta | $40,000 | 1982 |
| British Columbia | 41,300 | 1988 |
| Manitoba | 33,000 | 1988 |
| New Brunswick | 32,900 | 1988 |
| Newfoundland | 45,500 | 1983 |
| Nova Scotia | 28,000 | 1986 |
| Ontario | 35,000 | 1988 |
| Prince Edward Island | 22,000 | 1988 |
| Quebec | 36,500 | 1988 |
| Saskatchewan | 48,000 | 1985 |
| Northwest Territories | 38,800 | 1987 |
| Yukon Territories | 36,000 | 1988 |

Source: *Canadian Labour Law Report,* CCH Canadian Ltd., 1988.

*Employer's Liability*

All the provincial acts and those of the Yukon Territory are of the "collective liability" type: that is, compensation is payable by employers collectively. However, an individual liability act is still in force in the Northwest Territories. In addition to the collective liability laws, there are laws of individual liability that provide for payment of compensation by particular employers. For all types of employment in the shipping industry, for example, the Merchant Seamen Compensation Act assigns responsibility to individual employers. Similarly, while most industries in Ontario and Quebec are under the collective liability system, certain large corporations are individually liable to pay compensation. Part II of the acts in British Columbia, Manitoba, New Brunswick, Nova Scotia, Ontario, and Prince Edward Island specify industries wherein individual employer liability exists. Finally, compensation for federal government employees is covered under a separate enactment, the Government Employees Compensation Act.

There is a trend in most provinces to remove health and safety provisions from the Workers' Compensation Board and place them under a separate industrial safety or occupational health and safety division. British Columbia, Prince Edward Island, and the Yukon, however, continue to place occupational health and safety under the compensation board. In almost all cases the occupational health and safety jurisdiction of the board comes under the heading "accident prevention." In Nova Scotia, Newfoundland, and the Northwest Territories, concurrent powers are shared between the board and the occupational health and safety authorities.

## Health Insurance Plans

Canada's health and medical insurance is provided by provincial governments with assistance from the federal government. In April 1972 the scope of the Medical Care Act of 1966 was widened to include all of Canada. Since then, a major part of the cost of medical care has been paid for by taxes collected at the federal level.

In addition to the provincial health insurance, group life and disability insurance is widely provided as an employee benefit in Canada. Health insurance takes care of cost of hospitalization (room and board and hospital service charges), surgery, and other major medical goods and services. Some firms still offer major medical insurance for their employees whenever they travel outside the province or country. Increasingly, many organizations have also been providing dental insurance to their employees. In many cases, the cost of health and dental premiums is shared between the employer and the employee.

## Family Allowances

In 1944, through an act of Parliament, the family allowance scheme was inaugurated in Canada. Under this act, all mothers of Canadian children under sixteen years of age were to be given monthly payments for their children's sustenance and education. Under the original act, school attendance for children was required, although this was dropped in 1974. Currently, the average monthly payments are about $32 per child (compared to $5 in 1944), although variations across provinces exist. The family allowance payments are now taxable, except when the child is in a special institution or foster home.

## Implications for Human Resource Management

The implications of financial security plans for human resource departments are several. First, human resource managers should make sure that the firm adheres to all provisions relating to minimum wages and pension deductions. For example, the Canada Labour

Code requires every employer to furnish, from time to time, information relating to the employees' wages, hours of work, general holidays, annual vacations, and conditions of employment. As well, the Canada Labour Standards regulations require that the employee's social insurance number, sex, and occupational classification be recorded and kept ready for inspection. Accurate records of maternity leave, overtime, and termination should also be maintained.

Second, to avoid duplication, human resource managers need to consider CPP and other health benefits available to employees when designing their firm's own benefit and service plans. In many provinces, some of the items included in private group insurance plans are already covered under the workers' compensation and health insurance plans.

Often, workers are only vaguely aware of these compensation laws and even less aware of their rights. Consider the comments one employee made to a human resource specialist:

> It really came as a shock to learn that the province would pay me only 75% of my wage while I was unable to work. On top of that the province paid nothing for the first seven days I was out. I guess I am lucky that the disability wasn't permanent or my weekly benefit would have been even lower.

As this example illustrates, employees are sometimes unaware that workers' compensation pays only a fraction of the regular paycheque. For example, every province pays disabled claimants only part of their regular pay to discourage self-inflicted accidents or malingering. Another common provincial rule provides for waiting periods to lessen claims for trivial accidents. Payments are eventually reduced — or even discontinued — to encourage the permanently disabled to seek rehabilitation.

The inadequacy of workers' compensation coverage has two related implications for human resource departments. First, workers need to be informed by the human resource department of the limited financial security provided by these laws. Second, gaps in the employee's financial security need to be closed with supplemental disability and death insurance. By responding to these needs, human resource departments can show a genuine concern for employee welfare.

Human resource specialists also need to be concerned about reducing accidents in order to lower the cost of workers' compensation. These costs are directly related to the claims made against the company by employees. The more that must be paid to these employees, the greater the cost. Yet even aside from cost considerations, many managers feel a moral obligation to provide a safe working environment.

> George Fitzgerald, the new human resource manager in a machine shop, was appalled when he learned that in the past two years one employee was totally blinded and another lost an eye while operating a grinding machine. Mr. Fitzgerald posted a sign that said, "Any employee who runs the grinding machine without safety goggles will be fired!" After fifteen years (and several new signs) not one eye injury (or safety-related discharge) has occurred in the shop. A by-product of Mr. Fitzgerald's concern was that his workers' compensation premiums declined by 42%.

Unfortunately, too few human resource departments achieve such a dramatic success. As a result, government interest in the physical security of workers has increased and safety laws have been enacted (see following chapter).

As mentioned already, unemployment insurance payments have been increasing rapidly in the past few years. There are several things that human resource managers can do to improve the situation. First, they can institute human resource planning, which minimizes overhiring and subsequent layoffs. With such planning, shortages and surpluses of personnel are anticipated. Then retraining or attrition can lead to proper staffing levels without layoffs. Second, they can educate other decision makers — particularly production planners and schedulers. Production specialists may not realize that ''hire, then lay off'' policies increase payroll costs, which in turn raise production costs and selling prices. Third, human resource departments can review all discharges to make sure that they are justified. Unjustified dismissals by supervisors can be reversed or changed into intracompany transfers in order to prevent the higher payroll taxes that can result from dismissals or layoffs.[38]

A fourth approach is to challenge all unjustified claims for unemployment compensation made against employers. Those claims that are successfully challenged may reduce the costs in the future.

> Kevin Hirtsman was fired for stealing from the company, since the employee manual stated that stealing was grounds for immediate dismissal. When his claim for unemployment insurance was sent to the company for its comments, the human resource manager wrote back that Kevin was terminated for cause. Kevin's claim for unemployment compensation was denied.

## EMERGING SERVICES AND TRENDS

Several studies have attempted to predict the types of benefits that will be in demand over the next ten years.[39] The more popular options for employees seem to be:

1. Increased medical coverage, with dental plans and optometrist services being the favourites; also greater assumption of costs of medical coverage by employers.
2. More and longer vacations, coupled with reduced length of service requirements; more holidays.
3. Increased pension coverage, with greater contributions by employers.
4. Cost-of-living adjustments of pension plans.
5. Improved portability of pension rights and earlier vesting.
6. Sabbatical leaves for managers, and paid educational leave for rank-and-file employees.

The recessionary economy of the early 1980s does not hold promise that these popular wants will in fact be offered. However, current trends indicate that indirect compensation will form a greater proportion of total compensation offered. Perhaps the employer share of contributions to the various current benefit plans will rise without any new types of benefits being added. Employees may also be able to make choices among benefits, and it may well become easier for employees to enrol in benefits plans through liberalized eligibility requirements.

Given the trends outlined, it will be critical for top management in general and the human resource manager in particular to adopt a total compensation approach when decisions have to be made relating to pay. Organizations cannot afford to treat employee benefits and services independent of direct compensation, especially since they are growing at twice the pace of wages and salaries. For all practical purposes it can be said that benefits have lost much of their importance as an attraction for new employees since most organizations offer relatively similar benefit packages. Employees see benefits more and more as rights, not as privileges.

This change in employees' attitudes can be used by management in a positive way. If benefits are perceived as a normal part of a compensation package they will arouse an employee's interest only if they fulfil a need, i.e., have a perceived value. It is then management's responsibility to maximize this perceived value. This is not a difficult objective, given that certain preconditions are met. One is a willingness on the side of management to listen to its employees and to allow them to have input into the development of a benefits and services program. Secondly, a greater familiarity with trends in the area of benefits is required on the side of management. It probably is not enough to leave the human resource or compensation manager with the responsibility to monitor trends and to make recommendations, usually limited to collective bargaining demands by unions. Employee benefits and services programs have to be part of the overall organizational policy and strategy decisions that influence long-range planning.

Finally, management has to take into account the changes in the labour force that will take place over the next ten to twenty years. The average age of the labour force will increase, which will result in greater emphasis on pensions as part of the benefit package. More women will be working, and more will do it longer, i.e., will make their job a career. What impact will this have on benefits and services (paid maternity leave, day care centres, nurseries, etc.)? Part-time work will become more common, with still unforeseeable consequences, since traditionally part-timers received few or no benefits.

There can be little doubt that the issue of employee benefits and services will require more attention and occupy more of management's time than before. It would be time well spent.

## *Appendix* —

Listed on page 435 are the more common benefits and services, not all of which were mentioned in this chapter.

## *SUMMARY*

Employee benefits and services are the fastest-growing component of compensation. Employers have sought to expand them to discourage labour unrest, respond to employee pressures, and remain competitive in the labour market. Employees have desired to obtain benefits and services through their employer because of the low costs, tax advantages, and inflation protection they provide.

Benefits are classified into four major types: insurance, security, time-off, and scheduling benefits. Services include educational, financial, and social programs. This diversity contributes to several serious administrative problems. The most significant problem is the orientation of managers and human resource specialists towards cost savings. In pursuit of administrative and actuarial economies, most companies and unions do not allow individualized benefit packages in indirect compensation programs.

To further societal objectives, the Canadian government has instituted compulsory programs that provide citizens with certain benefits and services.

Financial security is achieved partially through such benefits as the Canada Pension Plan, unemployment insurance, and workers' compensation. The Canada Pension Plan provides income at retirement or upon disability. It also provides the family members of a deceased worker with a death benefit and a survivor's annuity, under certain conditions.

Unemployment insurance pays the worker a modest income to reduce the hardships of losing a job. These payments go to employees who are involuntarily separated from their jobs. Payments last until the worker finds suitable employment or until the worker receives the maximum number of payments permitted by the government.

Workers' compensation pays employees who are injured in the course of their employment. The payments are made to prevent the employee from having to sue to be compensated for injuries. If an employee dies, benefits are paid to the employee's survivors.

## TERMS FOR REVIEW

| | |
|---|---|
| Long-term disability insurance | Job sharing |
| Severance pay | Cafeteria benefit programs |
| Guaranteed annual wage (GAW) | Minimum wages |
| Supplemental unemployment benefits (SUB) | Canada Pension Plan (CPP) |
| Vesting | Unemployment Insurance |
| Contributory plans | Regular and special unemployment benefits |
| Portability clauses | Workers' compensation |
| Pension Benefits Standard Act | Health insurance |
| Shorter workweek | Family Allowances |
| Flextime | |

## REVIEW AND DISCUSSION QUESTIONS

1. What factors have contributed to the rapid growth of fringe benefits since World War II?

2. Suppose you are requested to explain why employees are better off receiving pay and benefits rather than just getting larger paycheques that include the monetary value of benefits. What arguments will you use?

3. Briefly describe the benefits that an organization might give employees to provide them with greater financial security.

4. Why was the Pension Benefits Standards Act needed? What are its major provisions?

5. For each of the following groups of employees, what types of problems are likely to occur if a company goes from a five-day, forty-hour week to a four-day, forty-hour week: (a) working mothers, (b) labourers, (c) assembly-line workers?

6. What are the common problems you would expect to find with the benefits and services program of a large company?

7. If you were asked to increase employee awareness of fringe benefits, what actions would you take without changing the way the company provides benefits? If you could change the entire benefits program, what other methods would you use to increase employee awareness?

8. Why has government been interested in providing financial security to workers through laws? What areas do you think are likely to receive government attention in the future, to ensure employee financial security?

9. Some people believe that unemployment insurance has over a period of time worked against workers rather than for them. What is your opinion of unemployment insurance? Why?

10. Suppose a friend of yours contracted lead poisoning on the job. What sources of income could this person rely on while recovering during the next two months? What if it took two years for your friend to recover? Are other sources of income available?

11. Besides retirement income, what other benefits are provided through the Canada Pension Plan?

12. What changes should be made to the unemployment insurance system to eliminate its present weaknesses?

## INCIDENT 13-1

### Soap Producers and Distributors Ltd.

Soap Producers and Distributors Ltd. faced a severe employee turnover problem. The company's annual turnover rate was nearly 40% among technical and white-collar workers. Among hourly paid employees, the rate was nearly 75%.

Wage and salary surveys repeatedly showed that the company's pay levels were 10 to 12% above comparable jobs in the labour market. The fringe benefit program was not as impressive, but management thought it was competitive. Employees received supplementary health and life insurance, paid vacations and holidays, and a Christmas bonus of $200. Although some employees complained about the company's benefits, complaints varied widely and no one benefit or lack of benefit seemed to be the key issue.

To make Soap Producers and Distributors' problems worse, they operated in a tight labour market, which meant jobs sometimes took weeks to fill. To hire specialized workers almost always meant recruiting them from other cities and paying their moving expenses.

1. What additions do you think should be made to the company's fringe benefit program?
2. What problem in the incident might be solved by a cafeteria approach?
3. To overcome the company's recruitment problems, what other changes do you suggest?

## INCIDENT 13-2

## International Sea Products' Pension Plan

In 1962 International Sea Products Ltd. established a private, noncontributory pension plan for all workers who had twenty years of service with the company. After the twenty years, workers were eligible for a pension beginning at the age of sixty-five. The pension plan was funded by putting 2 1/2% of each year's payroll into a trust fund administered by the company's vice president of finance. Although employees were told that there was an employer-paid pension fund, little explanation of the plan was offered. Whenever questioned, the president of the company would only state: "This company takes care of loyal employees."

1. What changes should be made in this company's pension plan to comply with the Pension Benefits Standards Act?
2. What other changes would you recommend to increase the effectiveness of the pension plan in improving employee morale?

## CASE STUDY

### ST. VINCENT COLLEGE

St. Vincent College of Applied Arts and Technology is situated in a small city near Toronto. It has a student population of approximately 5000 and is well known for the quality of its vocational program. Over the last three years its ability to attract faculty and administrative personnel has been seriously affected by budget cuts implemented by the Ontario government. Turnover has increased significantly and finding replacements has become more and more difficult. Although its salaries are now modest in comparison to those offered at other colleges and universities, its benefit program, implemented by the Board of Governors, seems to be elaborate and quite generous. It includes the following: (F = for faculty, A = for administrative personnel, FA = for both).

1. Contributions to the Canada Pension Plan (FA)
2. Workers' compensation (A)
3. Paid vacation — two weeks after one year of service, three weeks after two years, four weeks after five, and five weeks after ten. (Faculty has four weeks' paid vacation to be taken during the summer break.) (FA)
4. Paid holidays — eleven (FA)

5. Two twenty-minute coffee breaks daily (A)

6. Fully paid insurance plan, including (FA)

    a) life insurance — $50,000

    b) accidental death and dismemberment — $20,000

    c) sickness and accident insurance — $300/week

    d) extended disability — $1000/month

7. Free courses in the college program (FA)

8. A 50% tuition reduction for dependants for courses taken at the college (FA)

When asked, a surprisingly large number of employees, including faculty members, knew very little about the program, although brochures were given to every new employee and were readily available from the human resource department. Others, who had some knowledge about details of the program—usually quite sketchy—complained about its inadequacies. As one female employee put it:

Our benefit program does not fit our needs. We like to have medical insurance which goes beyond the minimum coverage provided by the provincial health care program, e.g., supplementary hospitalization coverage, dental insurance. Also group auto insurance, day-care centres, and good private pension plan. When the Board of Governors implemented their benefit program, they did not consult with us. What do they know what we need? They should have asked us.

A faculty member agreed with this statement and added:

Why don't we have a modern cafeteria benefit program? Then everybody could choose and select the benefits they want. The approach taken by the Board of Governors smacks of paternalism.

It should be added that neither the administrative personnel nor the faculty are unionized.

1. Comment on the implementation and administration of the benefit program.

2. How can it be used to aid in recruiting?

3. What can be done to increase its attractiveness?

4. What do you think of the suggestion to offer a cafeteria benefit plan? Discuss.

5. How would you approach the Board of Governors to suggest changes in the program?

## SUGGESTED READINGS

"Benefits Legislation in Canada," William M. Mercer Ltd., 1988.

Chilvers, G.A., "1988—The Year in Review," *Benefits Letter,* Peat Marwick, Vol. 15, No. 1, March 1989.

LaFleur, E.K., and W.B. Newsom, "Opportunities for Child Care," *Personnel Administrator,* June 1988, pp. 146-154

MacLeod, K., "Somewhere to Turn," *Office Management and Automation,* September 1988, pp. 46-48.

Mahoney, Kathleen, "Day Care and Equality in Canada," *Manitoba Law Journal,* Vol. 14, No. 3, 1985. pp. 305-334.

Schwind, Hermann F., "Employee Benefits and Services," in K.M. Srinivas, *Human Resource Management,* Toronto: McGraw-Hill Ryerson Ltd., 1984, pp. 400-424.

Sheffield, Lin, "Gilding the Golden Years," *Atlantic Business,* July/August 1988, pp. 23-29.

## REFERENCES

1. Bill Megalli, "The Fringe Benefit Debate," *Labour Gazette,* July 1978, p. 313

2. Mitchell Meyer and Harland Fox, *Profile of Employee Benefits,* New York: The Conference Board, Inc., 1974, p. 22.

3. Pay Research Bureau, *Benefits and Working Conditions,* Vol. 1, Ottawa: Public Service Staff Relations Board, January 1, 1980.

4. *Employee Benefits* 1975, Washington: Chamber of Commerce of the United States, 1976, p. 17. See also John J. Miller, "Trends and Practices in Employee Benefits," *The Personnel Administrator,* May 1980, pp. 48-51, 57.

5. Pay Research Bureau, op. cit.

6. Robert English, "Smiles All Round," *The Financial Post,* December 22, 1979, p. 55. See also Brent King, "Dental Plan Trend Something to Smile About," *The Financial Post,* May 9, 1981, p. 42.

7. *Employee Benefit Cost in Canada,* 1986, Toronto: Thorne Stevenson & Kellogg, p. 13.

8. Pay Research Bureau, op. cit., p. 76.

9. Ibid., p. 114

10. Dave Stack, "Legal Services: An Evolving Union Benefit," *The American Federationist,* January 1975, p. 18. See also Pay Research Bureau, op. cit., p. 68.

11. *Employee Benefit Cost in Canada,* p. 20

12. Pay Research Bureau, op. cit., p. 123.

13. L.W.C.S. Barnes, "One More Pension Milestone: The CAW-Chrysler Contract," *The Work Life Report,* Vol. 5, No. 5, 1987, p. 6.

14. *Employee Benefit Cost in Canada, p. 22.*

15. Survey results quoted in "Paid Holiday Provisions," *The Work Life Report, Vol. 5, No. 3, 1987, p. 16.*

16. John W. Newstrom and Jon L. Pierce, "Alternative Work Schedules: The State of the Art," *The Personnel Administrator,* October 1979, pp. 19-23.

17. Gordon Robertson and Peter Ferlejowski, "Effects of the Shorter Work Week on Ontario Firms," Ontario Ministry of Labour, 1975.

18. Geoff FitzGibbon, "Flexible Working Hours: The Canadian Experience," *The Canadian Personnel & Industrial Relations Journal,* January 1980, pp. 28-33.

19. R.W. Growly, "Worksharing and Layoffs," *Relations Industrielles,* 34 (1972) (2): 329-334. See also Dorothy Dearborn, "Pioneer Worksharing Fact," *The Financial Post,* December 3, 1977, p. 9.

20. H.F. Schwind, S. Pendse, and A. Mukhopadhyay, "Characteristics of Profit-Sharing Plans in Canada," *Journal of Small Business and Entrepreneurship,* Spring 1987, pp. 32-37.

21. Peter Silverman, "United Effort to Beat Alcoholism," *The Financial Post,* May 23, 1981, p. 25

22. Craig C. Pinder, "Comparative Reactions of Managers and Their Spouses to Corporate Transfer Policy Provisions," *Relations Industrielles,* 1978, Vol. 37, pp. 654-665. See also Craig C. Pinder and H. Das, "Hidden Costs and Benefits of Employee Transfers," *Human Resource Planning,* Vol. 2.3, 1979, pp. 135-145.

23. William H. Holley, Jr. and Earl Ingram II, "Communicating Fringe Benefits," *Personnel Administrator,* March-April 1973, pp. 21-22. See also Robert Krogman, "What Employees Need to Know about Benefit Plans," *The Personnel Administrator,* May 1980, pp. 45-47.

24. *Employee Benefit Cost in Canada,* p. 10.

25. William B. Werther, Jr., "A New Direction in Rethinking Employee Benefits," *MSU Business Topics,* Winter 1974, pp. 36-37. See also "Labour Letter," *Wall Street Journal,* Western ed., January 30, 1979, p. 1.

26. *Canadian Labour Law Reports,* Toronto: CCH Canadian Limited, 1988, p. 771.

27. Ibid.

28. *The Labour Gazette,* March 1976, pp. 155-156.

29. Clayton Sinclair, "Minimum Wage Increase 25% in Two Years," The *Financial Times of Canada,* January 10, 1977, p. 3.

30. Donald Coxe, "Pensions: Up to Government or Business?" *The Canadian Business Review,* Spring 1973, pp. 36-40.

31. See, for example, Roy LaBerge, "Canadian Retirement Policies," *The Labour Gazette,* June 1976, pp. 316-319; Donald Neelands, "Twin Threats to Pension Funds" *The Canadian Business Review,* Summer 1974, pp. 43-45.

32. *The Financial Post,* November 16, 1974, p. 4.

33. *The Financial Times of Canada,* February 3, 1975, p. 11.

34. Royal Commission on the Economic Union and Development Prospects for Canada (MacDonald Commission), Minister of Supply and Services Canada, 1985, Vol. II; Commission of Inquiry into Unemployment Insurance (Forget Commission), Minister of Supply and Services Canada, 1986.

35. Ibid.

36. *The Financial Times of Canada,* February 3, 1975, p. 11.

37. Canada Department of Labour, *Workmen's Compensation in Canada,* Ottawa: Information Canada, 1971.

38. Kathleen Classen-Ut Soff, "Unemployment Insurance: What Does It Really Do?" *Business Horizons,* February 1979, pp. 53-56.

39. Several studies have to be mentioned here. The most extensive is by T.J. Gordon and R.E. LeBleu, "Employee Benefits: 1970-1985," *Harvard Business Review,* January-February 1970, pp. 93-107. See also Gregor Caldwell, "Future Trends in Employee Benefits in Canada," *The Canadian Business Review,* Summer 1974, pp. 22-23; D.L. Salisbury, "Benefit Trends in the 80s," *Personnel Journal,* February 1982, pp. 104-108; Robert Schiele, "Spicing Up an Old Recipe," *The Financial Post,* February 2, 1987, pp. 33-40.

## APPENDIX

### Potential Benefits and Services

accidental death, dismemberment insurance
anniversary awards
annual reports to employees
athletic teams
attendance bonus
automobile lease plan
beauty parlours
bereavement leave
birthdays off
bonuses
business and professional memberships
cafeteria and canteen services
call-back and call-in pay
Christmas bonus
Christmas party
clean-up time
club membership
commissions
company medical assistance
company newspaper
company-provided automobile
company-provided housing
company-provided or subsidized travel
company stores
credit union
dances
day care centres
deferred bonus
deferred compensation plan
deferred profit sharing
dental and eye care insurance
dietetic advice
discount on company products
education costs
educational activities (time off)
executive dining room
family allowances
financial counselling
free chequing account
free or subsidized lunches
group automobile insurance
group homeowners' insurance

group life insurance
health maintenance organization fees
holidays (extra)
home health care
home financing
income tax service
interest-free loans
jury duty time
layoff pay (SUB)
legal, estate planning, and other professional assistance
library and reading room facilities
loans of company equipment
long-term disability benefits
low-interest company loans
lunch-period entertainment and music at work
magazine subscription payments
nursery
nursing home care
paid attendance at business, professional, and other outside meetings
paid sick leave
parking facilities
parties and picnics
payment of optical expenses
personal counselling
personal credit cards
personal expense accounts
political activities (time off)
purchasing service
private pension plan
profit sharing
quality bonus
recreational facilities
religious holidays
relocation expense plan
resort facilities
rest periods
retirement gratuity
room and board allowances
sabbatical leaves
safety awards
salary continuation

savings plan
scholarship for dependants
service bonus
severance pay
shorter or flexible work week
social service sabbaticals
stock appreciation rights
stock bonus plan
stock options plan
stock purchase plan
suggestion awards
supplementary hospital-surgical medical insurance

survivors' benefits
time spent on collective bargaining
time spent on grievances
training programs
vacations
vacation pay
voting time
waste-elimination bonus
weekly indemnity insurance
witness time
year-end bonus

# CHAPTER *14* ○○○○○○

## OCCUPATIONAL HEALTH AND SAFETY

*The existence of laws and regulations is not enough on its own. The regulations tend to become minimum standards whereby companies meet legal requirements. What is required on the part of business management is a comprehensive accident prevention and health program that is ongoing. Such a program not only involves tangible elements such as physical conditions but also has intangible elements such as the attitudes of employees and employers toward the problem.*

ROBERT SEXTY[1]

○ ○ ○ ○ ○ ○ ○ ○ ○ ○ ○ ○ ○ ○ ○ ○ ○ ○ ○ ○ ○ ○ ○ ○ ○ ○ ○ ○ ○ ○

### CHAPTER OBJECTIVES

After studying this chapter, you should be able to:
1. **Describe** the major Canadian laws relating to occupational health and safety.
2. **Assess** the traditional thinking with regard to occupational health and safety issues.
3. **Explain** the new thinking with regard to employee rights relating to occupational health and safety issues.
4. **Summarize** the safety and health responsibilities of employers and employees.

○ ○ ○ ○ ○ ○ ○ ○ ○ ○ ○ ○ ○ ○ ○ ○ ○ ○ ○ ○ ○ ○ ○ ○ ○ ○ ○ ○ ○ ○

*A*t the turn of the century, the thinking and attitudes of employers and employees towards accident prevention were quite different from today. Comments made during this period by employers illustrate this:

• ''I don't have money for frills like safety.''

437

- "Some people are just accident prone and no matter what you do, they'll hurt themselves some way."
- "... 90% of all accidents are caused by just plain carelessness."
- "We are not in business for safety."
- "There's no place for sissies in dangerous work."[2]

During this period, even the courts used a legal expression, "assumption of risk," meaning that the worker accepted all the customary risks associated with the occupation he or she accepted. Workers were also instructed to protect themselves from special hazards such as heat extremes or molten and sharp metal. It is interesting to note that the attitudes of employees paralleled those of the employers. Scars and stumps on fingers and hands were often proudly referred to as badges of honour. The thought that safety was a matter of "luck" was frequently reflected in such statements as, "I never thought he'd get it; he was always one of the lucky ones" or "When your number's up, there's not much you can do."[3]

Existing records of one steel company show that 1600 of its 2200 employees lost time from work because of injury during a four-year period in the early 1900s. Statistically speaking, 75% of this plant's entire work force lost time from work because of accidents on the job.[4]

The early approach to safety in the workplace used the "careless worker" model. It assumed that most of the accidents were due to a worker's failure to be careful or to protect himself. Even if training was provided to make workers more aware of the dangers in the workplace, it still assumed that it was mainly the worker's fault if an accident happened. A new approach, the shared responsibility model, assumes that the best method to reduce accident rates relies on the cooperation of the two main partners: the employer and the employees (often represented by a union).[5] Recent studies show that accident rates are reduced if:

- Management is committed to safety in the workplace
- Employees are informed about accident prevention
- Consultation between employer and employees takes place on a regular basis (e.g., creation of a Health and Safety Committee)
- There is a trusting relationship between employer and staff
- Employees have actual input into the decision-making process[6]

Over the last ten years, along with the increased concern about the environment, there has been a growing emphasis on health and safety in the workplace. Strong union pressure, together with an increased public interest in greater corporate responsibility, has resulted in better and more comprehensive federal and provincial legislation and health and safety measures.

In the last chapter, one of the topics was workers' compensation, which has as its aim the compensation of an employee for injuries suffered on the job. These programs have a serious defect: They are after-the-fact efforts. They attempt to compensate employees for accidents and illnesses that have already occurred. Many early supporters of these laws had hoped that costs would force employees to become more safety-conscious. Yet even with greater efforts by employers, accidents continue to grow along with economic activity. In addition, toxins and unhealthy work environments continue to create new health hazards.

An edger operator was struck by a kickback from a piece of lumber that was being processed. The edger in question was not equipped with an anti-kickback device for reasons of original design features. There were no violations of the Industrial Safety Act and Regulations. The company was directed to look into the possibility of having the manufacturer of the equipment incorporate some mechanical means of preventing a kickback from the edger.[7]

An explosion occurred in the hold of a car ferry that was in a shipyard for hull maintenance. Propane was being used to dry out areas in a hold that was being prepared for painting. An employee was blown out of the hold, suffered multiple injuries, and died in hospital some days later. The use of monitoring equipment and proper ventilation procedures was ordered to be carried out when propane is used for drying purposes. The employer was also directed to instruct his employees in the safe use of propane.[8]

Similar accidents occur every day. Labour Canada estimates that for every 100 employees, approximately five disabling injuries occur each year. Figure 14-1 shows some statistics of workplace fatalities in Canada. As may be noted, the number of fatal injuries has been decreasing overall; however, many problems still exist in occupational health and safety administration. Nor are accidents a phenomenon unique to the manufacturing sector:

FIGURE 14-1   Fatalities in Canada

| SECTOR | NUMBER OF FATAL INJURIES | | | | |
| --- | --- | --- | --- | --- | --- |
| | 1967 | 1970 | 1976 | 1981 | 1985 |
| Agriculture | 30 | 16 | 16 | 6 | 20 |
| Forestry | 106 | 94 | 58 | 67 | 65 |
| Fishing | 33 | 25 | 26 | 21 | 26 |
| Mining | 183 | 157 | 143 | 132 | 116 |
| Manufacturing | 187 | 183 | 161 | 117 | 115 |
| Construction | 223 | 195 | 167 | 149 | 122 |
| Transport | 237 | 187 | 197 | 183 | 122 |
| Trade | 64 | 62 | 52 | 62 | 71 |
| Finance | 5 | 4 | 7 | 7 | 4 |
| Services | 55 | 57 | 52 | 71 | 42 |
| Public Administration | 35 | 81 | 47 | 41 | 46 |
| Other (unspecified) | — | — | — | 15 | 19 |
| Total | 1,158 | 1,061 | 926 | 871 | 768 |

Source: The 1967, 1970, and 1976 figures are from *The Labour Gazette*, December, 1977, p. 557; the 1981 figures are from Labour Canada: *Canadian Employment Injuries and Occupational Illnesses*, 1982; the 1985 figures are from the *Canada Year Book*, 1988 issue.

> Kate McDonald has been working in a dentist's office in Winnipeg for the last several years. About four years ago she found that she had continual spells of headaches, nausea, fainting, and overall lethargy. When repeated use of pain killers and symptomatic treatments did not improve the situation, she went to a specialist. Her illness was diagnosed as prolonged mercury poisoning.

By and large, work accidents are caused by a complex combination of unsafe employee behaviour and unsafe working conditions.[9] Some of the key dimensions of the problem are shown in Figure 14-2. Unless solutions are found to all these issues, no significant reduction in industrial accidents may be achieved.

FIGURE 14-2   Reasons for the Complexity of the Safety Problem

- The effects of some industrial diseases do not show up for years.
- Industrial health problems may extend to families (as when contaminants are brought home on clothing or in vehicles) and to consumers who use the final products.
- Employers may not adequately monitor or disclose health hazards.
- Employers often "clean up" the situation just before the inspector arrives; problem identification hence becomes difficult.
- The medical profession is generally ignorant about, or not interested in, occupational health.
- Personal habits of employees, e.g., smoking, add to the problem.
- Strict safety guidelines may force an employer out of business because of increased costs.
- In collective bargaining, unions give higher priority to wages than to safety conditions.
- Workers often ignore safety regulations.

Source: Adapted from Robert W. Sexty, *Issues in Canadian Business*, Scarborough, Ontario: Prentice-Hall of Canada, 1983, p. 117.

## FEDERAL AND PROVINCIAL SAFETY REGULATIONS

Part IV of the Canada Labour Code (Safety of Employees) incorporates the provisions of the Canada Safety Code of 1968 (revised 1985). It details the elements of an industrial safety program and provides for regulations to deal with various types of occupational safety problems. All provinces and the territories have similar legislation. The key element of these laws is the *Joint Occupational Health and Safety Committee*, which is usually required in every workplace with twenty or more employees. Only the federal law and those of Saskatchewan and Ontario require committees to be formed unless specifically exempted. These committees have a broad range of responsibilities, such as those described here for the committee under federal jurisdiction:

- To deal with health and safety complaints by employees
- To identify hazards and to regularly monitor workplaces for hazards
- To monitor records of injuries and illnesses
- To participate in investigations of health and safety-related injuries
- To develop, establish, and promote health and safety programs and procedures

- To obtain information from the employer and government agencies concerning existing or potential hazards in the workplace[10]

Other relevant federal laws are the Hazardous Products Act (1969, revised 1985), the Transportation of Dangerous Goods Act (1981), and the Canadian Centre for Occupational Health and Safety Act (1978).

The Hazardous Products Act, which already had a broad industrial application, was amended in 1985. Its primary objective was the protection of consumers by regulating the sales of dangerous products. It is now an important part of *Workplace Hazardous Material Information System* (WHMIS), which became law during a transitional period from October 1, 1988, to October 1, 1989. It requires that suppliers label all hazardous products and provide a Material Safety Data Sheet (MSDS) on each one (see Figure 14-3 for class and division hazard symbols). All provinces will adopt similar provisions in their jurisdictions.

The Hazardous Products Act also requires that an employer provide training to enable employees to recognize the WHMIS hazard symbols and understand the information in the MSDS. In addition to the symbol on it, the MSDS must briefly describe the nature of the hazard that might result from misuse of the product, e.g., ''Toxic Material—eye and skin irritant.'' The training will allow employees to take the necessary precautions to protect themselves.

Ernest Meilleur, a construction worker in Ontario, was sprayed with a chemical called Uni-Crete XL, produced by Uni-Crete Canada under licence from Diamond Shamrock. As a result of the accident, he lost his eyesight. Although he was found to be 75% responsible for his injury because he did not wear safety goggles, Uni-Crete Canada was found 20% responsible and Diamond Shamrock 5%, because of inadequate labelling of the product.[11]

The Transportation of Dangerous Goods Act makes Transport Canada, a federal government agency, responsible for handling and transporting dangerous material by federally regulated shipping and transportation companies. It requires that such goods are identified, that a carrier is informed of them and that they are classified according to a coding system.

In the Canadian Centre for Occupational Health and Safety Act, the Parliament of Canada established a public corporation with the following objectives:

a) to promote health and safety in the workplace in Canada and the physical and mental health of working people in Canada;
b) to facilitate
   (i)  consultation and cooperation among federal, provincial, and territorial jurisdictions, and
   (ii) participation by labour and management in the establishment and maintenance of high standards of occupational health and safety appropriate to the Canadian situation;
c) to assist in the development and maintenance of policies and programs aimed at the reduction of elimination of occupational hazards; and

FIGURE 14-3   WHMIS Class and Division Hazard Symbols

| Class and Division Designation | Symbols |
| --- | --- |
| Class A – Compressed Gas |  |
| Class B – Flammable and Combustible Material<br><br>1. Flammable Gas<br>2. Flammable Liquid<br>3. Combustible Liquid<br>4. Flammable Solid<br>5. Flammable Aerosol<br>6. Reactive Flammable Material |  |
| Class C – Oxidizing Material |  |
| Class D – Poisonous and Infectious Material<br><br>1. Materials Causing Immediate and Serious Toxic Effect |  |
| 2. Material Causing Other Toxic Effects |  |
| 3. Biohazardous Infectious Material | |
| Class E – Corrosive Material |  |
| Class F – Dangerously Reactive Material | |

Source: Hazardous Products Act, June 1987, Parliament of Canada

d) to serve as a national centre for statistics and other information relating to occupational health and safety.[12]

The centre is supervised by a board of governors made up of representatives of the federal government (4), labour (11), and employers (11). More than 500 organizations are now connected electronically with the centre and have access to information relating to health and safety generally and to hazardous material specifically.[13]

The administration of safety programs comes mainly under provincial jurisdiction. Each province has legislated specific programs for the various industries and occupations within it. Examples from Nova Scotia are the Occupational Health and Safety Act, the Industrial Safety Act, the Construction Safety Act, the Steam Boiler and Pressure Vessel Act, the Elevators and Lifts Act, the Engine Operators Act, and the Amusement Devices Safety Act.

The responsibility for enforcing these laws was divided between several agencies: the Occupational Safety Division of the Department of Labour, the Occupational Health Division of the Department of Health, the Mine Safety Division of the Department of Mines and Energy, and the Accident Prevention Division of the Workers' Compensation Board. This situation was similar in most provinces. Over the last five years, however, there has been a strong tendency to streamline the fragmented responsibilities by combining the different agencies into one and — as was hoped — more efficient and effective body, the Occupational Health and Safety Division under the umbrella of the Ministry of Labour. Almost all provinces have now consolidated their health and safety laws in a similar way. Two, British Columbia and Prince Edward Island, left it under the jurisdiction of their Workers' Compensation Boards, while Alberta and Quebec delegated the enforcement to the Alberta Worker's Health, Safety, and Compensation Ministry and the Quebec Department of Social Development, respectively.

## Safety Enforcement

All industrial units are inspected at least once a year to confirm their safe operation. Depending on the unit's accident record and its size, the safety inspectors may visit more or less frequently. For the purposes of such inspection a safety officer may at any reasonable time enter any property or place used in connection with the operation of any business or undertaking. To carry out their duties effectively, the safety inspectors are given a wide range of powers. Section 91(2) of the Canada Labour Code, Part IV, details these powers:

A safety officer may, in the performance of his duties,
(a) inspect and examine all books and records relating in any way to conditions of work that affect the safety or health of any person employed upon or in connection with the operation of any federal work, undertaking or business;
(b) take extracts from or make copies of any entry in the books and records mentioned in paragraph (a);
(c) require an employer to make or furnish full and correct statements, either orally or in writing in such form as may be required, respecting the conditions of work affecting the safety or health of all or any of his employees, and the materials and equipment used by them in their employment;

(d) require any person employed upon or in connection with the operation of any federal work, undertaking or business to make full disclosure, production and delivery to him of all records or documents or copies thereof, or other information, orally or in writing, that he has in his possession or under his control and that in any way relate to the conditions of work affecting his safety or health, or that of his fellow workers, in his or their employment; and

(e) take or remove for purposes of analysis samples of materials and substances used or handled by employees, subject to the employer or his representative being notified of any samples or substances taken or removed for such purpose.[14]

Provincial laws provide similar powers to the safety officers under their jurisdiction.

The occupational health regulations in each province set standards relating to gases, vapours, mists, fumes, smoke, dust, and other chemical substances or physical agents associated with industrial activities. The ''Threshold Limit Values'' for chemical substances and physical agents are established and periodically revised. Figure 14-4 shows some adopted threshold limit values for a normal forty-hour workweek. It should be noted that these are used only as general guides in the control of health hazards.

FIGURE 14-4  Threshold Limit Values for Some Common Substances

| | $mg/m^3$* |
|---|---|
| Carbon monoxide | 55 |
| Coal dust | 4 |
| Chlorine | 3 |
| Graphite | 5 |
| Mica | 6 |
| Mercury | 0.05 |
| Lead | 0.15 |
| Ozone | 0.20 |
| Phosphorus | 0.10 |
| Silicone (tetrahydride) | 0.70 |
| *approximate milligrams of substance per cubic metre of air | |

Source: American Conference of Governmental Industrial Hygienists, *Threshold Limit Values for Chemical Substances in Workroom Air,* Cincinnati, Ohio: 1977, pp. 12-54.

## Implications for Human Resource Management

The Canada Labour Code requires that an employer:

(1) operating or carrying on . . . business shall do so in a manner that will not endanger the safety or health of any person employed thereupon or in connection therewith;

(2) shall adopt and carry out reasonable procedures and techniques designed or intended to prevent or reduce the risk of employment injury in the operation.[15]

Likewise, the act imposes a duty on employees to take all reasonable and necessary precautions to ensure their own safety and the safety of their fellow employees, and at all appropriate times to use such devices and wear such articles of clothing as are intended for employees' protection. This means that the human resource managers should (1) obtain organization-wide compliance, (2) maintain adequate records, (3) seek consistent enforcement of all rules and procedures, and (4) honour workers' rights to safety at the workplace.

Organization-wide compliance requires a detailed safety program. To be effective, the program should have several characteristics. Top management support is crucial to the human resource department's plans. Without such backing, other managers often fail to make the necessary commitment of time and resources. With this support, the human resource department needs to conduct a self-inspection so that health and accident hazards can be eliminated and unsafe practices corrected. Then training should include safety awareness programs for employees and supervisors, whose support is essential. Firm enforcement of safety rules by the supervisor quickly establishes a safety-conscious work environment. Supervisory commitment also requires that rewards (such as pay increases and promotions) depend on a good safety record. Finally, the human resource department must communicate directly with employees about safety. Not only do communications elevate safety awareness, but they reinforce supervisory actions. Some companies develop safety-slogan contests or offer rewards to employees to increase safety awareness.

The human resource manager should also ensure consistent enforcement of all safety and health rules. If human resource policies let one worker violate safety rules, others may follow. If an accident results, it is the employer that is fined by the government. By being firm — even if this means discharge of a valued employee — management quickly convinces employees that safety is important.

The law also permits employees to refuse to work when working conditions are perceived to be unsafe. In such instances, the employee should report the circumstances of the matter to his or her boss or to the boss's supervisor and to the safety committee in the firm. If a supervisor or representative of the safety committee advises the employee to continue to work and the employee refuses, he or she may lose pay for the time off if it is later determined that there was no danger.

## EMPLOYEE STRESS

Alain Simone had been a successful supervisor for Western Appliances for fifteen years. Then Central Electric took over the company—and his career changed drastically. As part of the restructuring after the acquisition, Alain was put in charge of purchasing, supervising one secretary and two clerks instead of twenty-five repairmen. He had taken over from a person who had chosen early retirement under the new management. He found a backlog of unprocessed purchase orders, piles of completed but unfiled orders, and a filing system in disarray. He worked hard and pushed his staff to the limits, but things seemed to get worse. Through the grapevine he heard that his position might be eliminated.

The pressure took its toll. Simone started drinking, lost weight, and suffered a nervous breakdown; then his wife left him. He went to a therapist and eventually filed a workers' compensation claim, blaming his condition on Central Electric. After several months of litigation Central Electric settled for $20,000, but refused to comment on the case.[16]

The term "stress management" is now part of the regular vocabulary of managers and even employees. The actual experience or the perceived threat of a corporate take-over, merger, downsizing, or plant closing, all of which could throw hundreds or even thousands of employees out of jobs, can lead to a variety of symptoms of stress that can harm employees' job performance. As shown in Figure 14-5, these symptoms involve both mental health and physical health. Persons who are stressed may become nervous and develop chronic worry. They are easily provoked to anger and are unable to relax. They may even develop stress-related physical ailments, such as stomach upsets. These conditions also occur from causes other than stress, but they are the common symptoms of stress.

FIGURE 14-5   Typical Symptoms of Stress

| | |
|---|---|
| • Nervousness and tension | • Excessive use of alcohol and/or tobacco |
| • Chronic worry | • Sleep problems |
| • Digestive problems | • Uncooperative attitudes |
| • High blood pressure | • Feelings of inability to cope |
| • Inability to relax | • Anger and aggression |

Whether stress will increase into something more serious depends on the severity and duration of the stress situation and the individual's ability to cope. What seems to be most important is whether the person feels helpless and out of control. Severe stress can lead to depression, and this can be fatal: Depressed individuals make up 60% of all suicides.[17]

## Causes of Stress

The basic theory of stress, often called a *person-environment fit,* states that "when the resources and demands of the work environment do not fit the needs and abilities of the worker, the worker will develop symptoms of strain."[18] These eventually can lead to problems with job performance, physical health, and mental health. Conditions that tend to cause stress are called *stressors.* Although major distress can occur from only one stressor, usually stressors combine to affect an employee in a variety of ways until distress develops.

> Bill felt that he was doing well, but then he failed to get a promotion that he had sought. At about the same time, two of his key employees quit, and he had difficulty replacing them. Then his son got into trouble in high school, and the transmission failed on an automobile that he had planned to trade for a new one the next week. So many different problems were hitting Bill that he began to show signs of stress. He became easily upset, less considerate of employees, and less successful in meeting his deadlines.

## Job Causes of Stress

Almost any job condition may cause stress, depending upon an employee's reaction to it.

For example, one employee will accept a new work procedure, while another employee rejects it. There are, however, a number of job conditions that frequently cause stress for employees.[19] Major ones are shown in Figure 14-6.

FIGURE 14-6 Typical Causes of Stress on the Job

- Work overload
- Time pressures
- Poor quality of supervision
- Insecure political climate
- Insufficient performance feedback
- Inadequate authority to match responsibilities
- Role ambiguity
- Frustration
- Interpersonal and intergroup conflict
- Differences between company and employee values
- Change of any type

It has been estimated that stress-related disabilities cost Canadian business annually more than $15 billion in lowered productivity, absenteeism, disability payments, and replacement payments.[20]

Work overload and time deadlines put employees under pressure and lead to stress. Often some of these pressures arise from supervision, and so a poor quality of supervision can cause stress. For example, the following stressful conditions are mostly created by supervision: an insecure political climate, lack of performance feedback, and inadequate authority to match one's responsibilities. Managers especially report that these conditions cause them to feel job stress.[21]

Another cause of stress is *role ambiguity*.[22] In situations of this type, superiors and coworkers have different expectations of an employee's responsibilities in a job, and so the employee does not know what to do and cannot meet all expectations. In addition, the job is often poorly defined, and so the employee has no official model on which to depend.

*Frustration* is a result of a motivation being blocked to prevent one from reaching a desired goal, and it is a major cause of stress.[23] If you are trying to finish a report before quitting time, you are likely to become frustrated by repeated interferences that prevent you from reaching your goal. You may become irritable, develop an uneasy feeling in your stomach, or have some other reaction. These reactions to frustration are known as *defence mechanisms*, because you are trying to defend yourself from the psychological effects of the blocked goal.

Both interpersonal and intergroup conflicts may cause stress. As people with different backgrounds, points of view, needs, and personalities interact there occur disagreements and other conflicts which may cause stress.

A further cause of stress is important differences between company values and employee values. In a sense, these differences "tear the employee apart" with mental stress as an effort is made to meet the requirements of both values.[24] For example, a salaried employee may value home life and regular quitting time. But that worker's manager may expect salaried employees to work overtime to meet department objectives. The company values employee loyalty, but the employee's loyalty may be family-centred.

A general and widely recognised cause of stress is change of any type, because it requires adaptation by employees. It tends to be especially stressful when it is major, unusual, or frequent.

> A sales representative named Dorothy Wang developed job stress as a result of certain management changes. During the last twelve months she had had three different sales managers, each with a different leadership style. As soon as Dorothy had adjusted to the style of one manager, she was forced to learn how to live with another. She felt insecure and under constant pressure. She longed for the day when she would have only one sales manager for two or three years and a measure of stability would return to her world.

A final source of stress on workers that is not listed in Figure 14-6, but which is increasingly becoming important, is sexual harassment on the job. Sexual harassment is typically aimed at women by males who are in positions of power. It can range from unwanted comments or suggestions to attempted physical contact or actual rape, and includes subtle acts like sexual jokes or requests for dates.[25] No matter how subtle it is, sexual harassment is real and often extremely stressful.

## Off-the-Job Causes of Stress

Causes of stress off the job are the full range of problems that can occur to people, but certain causes are fairly common. As shown in Figure 14-7, managers report that their primary cause of stress off the job are financial worries, problems with children, physical problems, marital problems, and change in residence. The problem most reported was financial worries, with 38% of top managers and 52% of middle managers reporting this problem.

Other studies have reported that the most stressful personal problems are the death of a spouse or other close family member, divorce, marital separation, and major injury or illness.[26] At these times the human resource department needs to be especially helpful with its policies, counselling, and other programs.

FIGURE 14-7   The Top Five Off-the-Job Causes of Managerial Stress

- Financial worries
- Problems with children
- Physical problems
- Marital problems
- Change in residence

Source: Adopted from Ari Kiev and Vera Kohn, *Executive Stress*, New York: AMACOM, 1979, p.35

## Burnout

Burnout is a condition of mental, emotional, and sometimes physical exhaustion that results from substantial and prolonged stress. It can occur for any type of employee—

whether one is a manager, professional, clerk, or factory worker. Even human resource managers may experience it.[27] Burned-out employees tend to feel used up, worn out, and "at the end of their rope."

People with burnout tend to have a variety of symptoms, such as depression and low self-image.[28] They may become withdrawn and detached from interpersonal contacts and day-to-day activities. They tend to be irritable and blame others for their difficulties, and they may develop health problems, such as sleep disorders and excessive use of alcohol. They eventually can become so emotionally exhausted that they go through the motions of work but accomplish very little. As one employee described a burned-out associate, "His body is here today, but his mind stayed home."

With regard to burnout, the human resource department's role is a proactive one to help employees prevent burnout before it occurs. For example, the human resource department can train supervisors to recognize stress and rearrange work assignments to reduce it. Jobs may be redesigned, staff conflicts resolved, counselling provided, and temporary leaves arranged. Many other approaches to stress reduction are discussed throughout this book. The popular statement that "prevention is better than curing" definitely applies to burnout, because it has high human and economic costs. Weeks or months of rest, reassignment, and/or treatment may be required before recovery occurs. Some emotional or health damage can be permanent.

> One large paper and forest products firm was faced with problems of employee absenteeism, a large number of accidents, and poor employee morale. After trying other methods that did not yield any great success, the company decided to make a counselling program available to all its employees. Most counselling problems related to the job, alcohol and drug abuse, marital relations, family problems, and personal finances. One year after the counselling program was started, there was a 43% reduction in absences and a 70% reduction in the number of accidents.

## Stress and Job Performance

Stress can be either helpful or harmful to job performance, depending upon the amount of it. Figure 14-8 presents a *stress-performance model* that shows the relationship between stress and job performance. When there is no stress, job challenges are absent and performance tends to be low. As stress increases, performance tends to increase, because stress helps a person call up resources to meet job requirements. It is a healthy stimulus to encourage employees to respond to challenges. Eventually it reaches a plateau that represents approximately a person's top day-to-day performance capability. At this point additional stress tends to produce no more improvement.

Finally, if stress becomes too great, performance begins to decline, because stress interferes with it. An employee loses the ability to cope, becomes unable to make decisions, and is erratic in behaviour. If stress increases to a breaking point, performance becomes zero, because the employee has a breakdown, becomes too ill to work, is fired, quits, or refuses to come to work to face the stress.

## Stress Thresholds

People have different tolerances of stressful situations. The level of stressors that one

FIGURE 14-8   A Stress-Performance Model

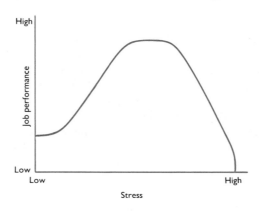

can tolerate before feelings of stress occur is one's *stress threshold*. Some persons are easily upset by the slightest change or emergency. Others are calm, cool, and collected, partly because they have confidence in their ability to cope. They feel very little stress unless a stressor is major or prolonged.

> Mabel Kelly worked at the driver's licence desk in a provincial government office. She faced a variety of problems, complaints, angry citizens, and red tape during the day, but it did not seem to trouble her. On the other hand, Malcolm Morgan, her associate at an adjoining desk, had difficulty with the complaints, anger, and abuse that he received. He began taking longer breaks and then extra breaks. He seemed nervous. Finally, he asked for a transfer to another office.

The two employees had different stress thresholds.

### Type A and Type B Persons

Reactions to stressful situations are often related to Type A and Type B persons.[29] *Type A persons* are those who are aggressive and competitive, set high standards, and put themselves under constant time pressure. They even make excessive demands on themselves in recreational sports and leisure activities. They often fail to realize that many of the pressures they feel are of their own making, rather than in their environment. Because of the constant stress that they feel, they are more prone to physical ailments related to stress, such as heart attacks. A group of Canadian researchers has suggested that company environment, job conditions, and individual characteristics all combine to generate Type A behaviour (see Figure 14-9).

*Type B persons* are more relaxed and easygoing. They accept situations and work within them, rather than fighting them competitively. They are especially relaxed regarding time pressures, and so they are less prone to problems associated with stress.

Figure 14-10 shows a model of occupational stress that takes into account organizational stress factors, individual reactions, and coping strategies.[30]

FIGURE 14-9   The Pathways of Type A Behaviour

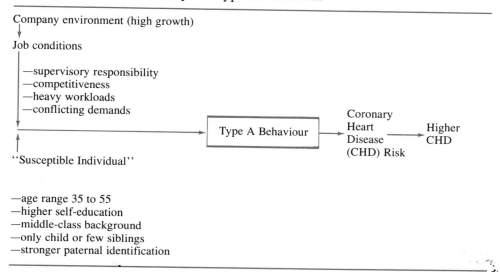

Company environment (high growth)

Job conditions

—supervisory responsibility
—competitiveness
—heavy workloads
—conflicting demands

Type A Behaviour

Coronary
Heart
Disease
(CHD) Risk

Higher
CHD

"Susceptible Individual"

—age range 35 to 55
—higher self-education
—middle-class background
—only child or few siblings
—stronger paternal identification

Source: John H. Howard, Peter A. Rechnitzer and David A. Cunningham, "Childhood Antecedents of Type A Behaviour," *ASAC (Organizational Behaviour Division) Meeting Proceedings*, Vol. 2, Part 5, 1981, p. 62.

Two University of Washington psychiatrists, Drs. Thomas Holmes and Richard Rahe, developed a stress factor measure that shows—on a 100-point scale—what degree of stress different factors generate (see Figure 14-11). For example, the death of a spouse rates highest with 100 points, followed by divorce, jail term, death of a close family member, personal injury or illness, and being fired. Even positive events may be responsible for stress. Marriage, receiving praise for an outstanding achievement, or even a vacation can raise blood pressure, anxiety, and irritation.[31]

## Stress Management

Until recently organizational stress has been considered to be a private matter. This attitude has changed significantly over the last years. Newspapers, magazines, and scholarly journals regularly discuss the topic and report on the latest developments in the field of stress management. There are several solutions to the problem. Curative solutions try to correct the outcome of stress, while preventive solutions attempt to change the cause of stress.

### Curative Measures

It has become quite popular to offer employees the opportunity to relax through aerobic exercises, yoga, meditation, and sensitivity training, among others. Some companies offer professional counselling services that assist in diagnosing the causes of stress and discuss ways to cope with it.[32]

### Preventive Measures

Management should look at the structure of the organization and the design of jobs. Dofasco, the largest steel producer in Canada, Supreme Aluminum of Canada, producer

FIGURE 14-10   Organizational-Occupational Stress

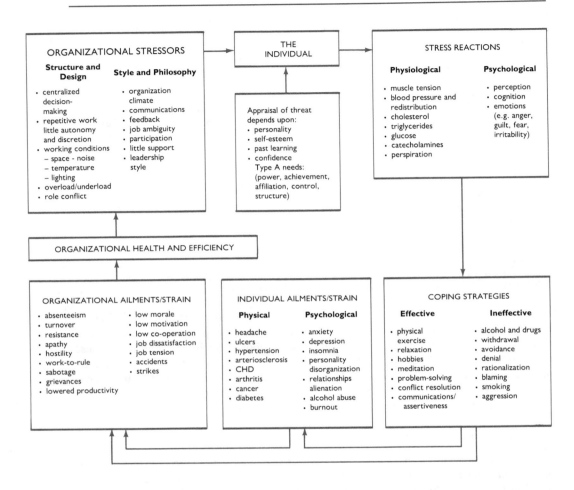

of aluminum products, and Britex Ltd., a Maritimes textile company, to name a few, have initiated programs that provide workers with more diversified tasks, greater control over decisions that affect their work, and a chance for wider participation in the overall production process.[33]

Some persons recover from stressful situations easily. For example, some recover away from the job daily and return to work the next day refreshed. Others can recover over a weekend. Although stress builds up during the week, they return to work the next week ready to absorb more stress. Other persons allow stress to build up, and it is these persons who are of special concern to the human resource department.

FIGURE 14-11   Stress Scale

| LIFE EVENT | MEAN VALUE |
|---|---|
| 1. Death of spouse | 100 |
| 2. Divorce | 73 |
| 3. Marital separation | 65 |
| 4. Jail term | 63 |
| 5. Death of close family member | 63 |
| 6. Personal injury or illness | 53 |
| 7. Marriage | 50 |
| 8. Fired at work | 47 |
| 9. Marital reconciliation | 45 |
| 10. Retirement | 45 |
| 11. Change in health of family member | 44 |
| 12. Pregnancy | 40 |
| 13. Sexual difficulties | 39 |
| 14. Gain of new family member | 39 |
| 15. Business readjustment | 39 |
| 16. Change in financial state | 38 |
| 17. Death of close friend | 37 |
| 18. Change to different line of work | 36 |
| 19. Change in number of arguments with spouse | 35 |
| 20. Mortgage over $10,000 | 31 |
| 21. Foreclosure of mortgage or loan | 30 |
| 22. Change in responsibilities at work | 29 |
| 23. Son or daughter leaving home | 29 |
| 24. Trouble with in-laws | 29 |
| 25. Outstanding personal achievement | 28 |
| 26. Wife begins or stops work | 26 |
| 27. Begin or end school | 26 |
| 28. Change in living conditions | 25 |
| 29. Revision of personal habits | 24 |
| 30. Trouble with boss | 23 |
| 31. Change in work hours or conditions | 20 |
| 32. Change in residence | 20 |
| 33. Change in schools | 20 |
| 34. Change in recreation | 19 |
| 35. Change in church activities | 19 |
| 36. Change in social activities | 18 |
| 37. Mortgage or loan less than $10,000 | 17 |
| 38. Change in sleeping habits | 16 |
| 39. Change in number of family get-togethers | 15 |
| 40. Change in eating habits | 13 |
| 41. Vacation | 13 |
| 42. Christmas | 12 |
| 43. Minor violations of the law | 11 |

Source: T.H. Holmes and R.H. Rahe, ''The Social Readjustment Rating Scale,'' *Journal of Psychosomatic Research*, Vol. 11, 1967, pp. 213-18. © Pergamon Press, Inc.

Figure 14-12 shows the stress responses of three employees to the same job. Employee A showed moderate stress in the beginning but adapted rapidly. Employee B showed higher stress. There was some recovery over weekends, but stress built up again during the week. In the case of employee C the stress was cumulative, becoming higher and higher. Each employee responded individually to stress.

FIGURE 14-12   Stress Responses of Three Employees to the Same Job

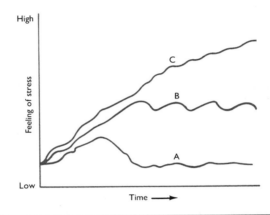

## Human Resource Actions to Reduce Stress

A desirable way to respond to stress is to try to remove or reduce its causes. For example, one option is to escape the stress, and the human resource department can help by arranging a transfer to another job, a different supervisor, and different work associates. Training and career counselling can be provided to qualify an employee for a new job.

Another way to reduce stress is to redesign jobs so that employees have more decision choices and authority to match their responsibility.[34] Job design can also reduce work overload, time pressures, and role ambiguity. Communication can be improved to give more performance feedback, and participation can be expanded.[35]

The human resource department also helps employees improve their ability to cope with stress. Better communication improves an employee's understanding of stressful situations, and training courses can be provided on the subject of coping with stress.[36] But counselling services may be the most effective way to help employees deal with stress (to be discussed in Chapter 16).

Figure 14-13 shows some of the specific actions that the human resource department should take to reduce employee stress and burnout.

Managers and supervisors should be trained in stress management since they tend to have a considerable impact on the work environment and the working atmosphere or climate in an organization. Important skills and characteristics that will assist in creating

## FIGURE 14-13   Actions to Reduce Stress and Burnout

- Develop a basic stress management policy for company approval.
- Communicate the policy to all employees in a sensitive, caring way. Then continue communication so that employees are always aware of the programs that are available to help them.
- Train managers to be sensitive to the early symptoms of stress so that they can take corrective action before it becomes severe. For example, an employee with signs of distress may be given less demanding work, encouraged to take a vacation, or referred to a counsellor.
- Train employees to recognize and cope with stress.
- Improve communication and participation throughout the organization so that employees understand what is affecting them and feel that they have a useful role in dealing with it.
- Monitor company activities to discover any conditions that unnecessarily lead to stress.
- Improve job and organization design to avoid stressful jobs.
- Provide counselling and other employee assistance programs to help employees in stressful situations.

## FIGURE 14-14   Health and Safety Aspects of Alcohol and Drug Use[38]

There is a high correlation between heavy use of alcohol or drugs and health and safety problems in the workplace, according to Bruce Cunningham, a consultant for the Addiction Research Foundation of Ontario.

Speaking at a conference on Drug Testing in the Workplace, organized by the Canadian Centre for Occupational Health and Safety, Mr. Cunningham noted that there is evidence of such a relationship from working with people who are undergoing treatment for a dependency problem. "People in treatment centres, whether they're referred from the workplace or seek help on their own, frequently report poor work performance, behaviour that proved a cost to the organization, and a higher frequency of accidents than would normally be expected."

There is evidence of such a relationship too in looking at persons referred to employee assistance programs. Their performance, he said, improves tremendously in the year after treatment.

More striking evidence of a relationship between alcohol and drug use and workplace accidents comes from surveys conducted by the Addiction Research Foundation which correlated what people said about the amount of alcohol or drugs they used and the extent to which their work activity was curtailed by injuries (on or off the job) during the past year. As shown in the accompanying tables, "once we get beyond the people who don't drink at all, we have an almost linear relationship. As reported frequency of usage went up, people having to curtail their work activity also went up." (Mr. Cunningham noted that among the non-drinkers, for whom the injury rate was higher than for those consuming less than 2 drinks a day, there may have been some people who used to drink heavily).

"We're convinced," said Cunningham, "that there is some risk to health and safety in the workplace from the consumption of alcohol and other drugs." They may not cause many accidents by themselves, but they are probably a factor in some.

There are various ways of intervening, he said. Education of the workforce about the health and safety risks associated with the use of alcohol and drugs can be a powerful weapon. "In a study of 100 people who were arrested for marijuana use, the ones who said they intended to stop cited health concerns based on information they had received as the reason for stopping." Many other interventions also have been found to be effective, including training supervisors to recognize some of the patterns that indicate a person is moving in the direction of becoming a safety risk, employee assistance programs, union counselling programs, and alerting security staff. "In some situations, urine tests may be relevant for certain jobs."

FIGURE 14-14 (continued)   Health and Safety Aspects of Alcohol and Drug Use[38]

### RELATIONSHIP BETWEEN ALCOHOL USE AND LOST TIME INJURIES IN 1987

| Alcohol use | Employees surveyed | Number with lost time injuries | % of total |
|---|---|---|---|
| Average daily alcohol consumption | | | |
| 0 drinks | 404 | 12 | 3.0 |
| >2 drinks | 739 | 13 | 1.8 |
| 2-3 drinks | 52 | 3 | 5.8 |
| 3-4 drinks | 31 | 2 | 6.5 |
| <4 drinks | 35 | 4 | 11.4 |

### RELATIONSHIP BETWEEN DRUG USE AND LOST TIME INJURIES IN 1987

| Drug use | Employees surveyed | Number with Lost time injuries | % of total |
|---|---|---|---|
| Never used drugs | 1,163 | 29 | 2.4 |
| Rarely used drugs | 116 | 6 | 5.2 |
| Occasionally/Often used drugs | 84 | 6 | 7.1 |

Source: Addiction Research Foundation *The Worklife Report*, Vol. 6, No. 2, 1988, p. 4.

a better organizational climate include interpersonal communication, democratic leadership style, willingness to delegate responsibilities and to accept input from employees into the management decision-making process.[37]

## AIDS

A modern book on human resource management would be incomplete if no reference were made to our most recent menace, the Acquired Immune Deficiency Syndrome or, as it is also known, the Human Immunodeficiency Virus (HIV), because of its potentially immense impact on the human resource function. How serious is the situation? Halfdan Mahler, the director-general of the World Health Organization, estimates the number of people with AIDS may total 500,000 to 3 million by 1993. It is estimated that 50 to 100 million people worldwide could develop AIDS in the next two decades.[39]

In Canada it is estimated that approximately 50,000 persons are infected with the AIDS virus, compared to 1.5 million in the U.S. It is expected that the majority of these will become active AIDS cases in the next ten years. Life expectancy once the disease develops is about two years.[40]

Cost estimates in Canada are not available, but a study by U.S. insurance companies has shown that 275 death benefit claims from AIDS victims had a price tag of $292 million. The medical costs of treating AIDS in 1987 in the U.S. is estimated to have been more than $2 billion and will increase to $4.5 billion in 1991.[41]

## AIDS and Human Resource Management

> Ron Lentz was hired January 4, 1988, by the Toronto Western Hospital as a nurse and fired on January 23. He complained to the Ontario Human Rights Commission that he was discriminated against because he had AIDS. The commission agreed and negotiated with the hospital a settlement that included reinstatement, about $14,000 in back pay, $1,400 in benefits, $5,000 in legal fees, restoration to seniority, and a clean employment record. Richard Shekter, Mr. Lentz's lawyer, said the case will send a clear message to employers across the country that there is no reason to refuse to hire a person with AIDS.[42]

This case points to problems that human resource managers have to face if one of their employees develops AIDS, or if an applicant happens to mention that he or she has an AIDS infection. It would be a breach of human rights laws to discriminate against that person. But what if colleagues refuse to work with him or her? What if the employee would have contact with customers? It is just a matter of time until many human resource managers encounter such a case. To be prepared for it, each employer should establish a policy and an action plan before the first AIDS case appears among employees or their dependants.

One of the problems human resource managers have to deal with is the general ignorance about the disease, despite the many articles in newspapers and magazines. There are still questions asked such as "Can I get AIDS from germs in the air? From a toilet seat? From infected water in a swimming pool? From insect bites?" Pregnant women are also concerned about whether their babies can catch the disease. It was found that a comprehensive education program for co-workers can halt the hysteria that often results when a colleague is diagnosed with AIDS.[43]

In May 1988 the Canadian Human Rights Commission agreed that being HIV infection-free may be a bona fide occupational requirement when an individual in a medical facility performs invasive procedures "which result in exposure to blood or blood products and the risk is real after all reasonable precautions have been taken."[44]

An information sheet on AIDS is reprinted in the Appendix.

## SUMMARY

Occupational health and safety has become an important aspect in organizations and will have an even higher priority for human resource managers in the future. The federal and provincial governments have created a variety of laws that require the attention of human resource professionals. Most occupational health and safety acts now require the establishment of safety committees in companies with twenty or more employees.

The Workplace Hazardous Material Information System (WHMIS) is a new law that requires suppliers to provide detailed information on any danger their material may pose, but it also asks the user to make sure that the information is available and that employees are trained to understand it.

Accident prevention is a major concern, but human resource managers should not forget to look at the psychological aspect of the work environment. Stress-related losses

— absenteeism, turnover, low productivity, accidents — cost Canada billions of dollars. Preventive programs — employee assistance programs, professional counselling, time management, fitness programs — can go a long way to reduce stress-related costs.

Acquired Immunity Deficiency Syndrome (AIDS) is a problem that currently is not a serious one for human resource managers, but there can be little doubt that it will be a significant one in five to ten years. In the meantime, some organizations will experience individual AIDS cases that, given present experiences, can lead to severe friction among work groups and irrational actions from some frightened employees. Human resource managers should be prepared for this by appropriate training and communication programs.

## TERMS FOR REVIEW

| | |
|---|---|
| Assumption of risk | Workplace Hazardous Material |
| Careless worker model | Information Systems (WHMIS) |
| Safety Committee | Stress management |
| Hazardous Products Act | Acquired Immune Deficiency Syndrome (AIDS) |

## REVIEW AND DISCUSSION QUESTIONS

1.  Explain the legal term "assumption of risk."
2.  What factors affect occupational accidents?
3.  Which organizational circumstances result in lower accidents?
4.  What responsibilities do Joint Occupational Health and Safety Committees have?
5.  Explain the requirements of the Workplace Hazardous Material Information System (WHMIS).
6.  What are the causes of organizational stress?
7.  Explain the symptoms of organizational stress and what the organization and the individual can do about them.
8.  What can be done to prepare an organization for an AIDS case?

## INCIDENT 14-1

### Safety at Canada Chemicals Limited

Canada Chemicals Limited is a large wholesaler of industrial chemicals in Ontario. It handles swimming pool supplies, industrial solvents, fertilizers, and special lubricants. The sales and clerical operations caused few safety worries, but the warehouse facilities caused Sam Peterson sleepless nights. Sam's title was manager of safety and security. He had worked in the human resources department since his job was created in 1981.

His biggest problem was the warehouse manager, Garfield McKenney. Gar simply did not appreciate safety. Nearly every action Sam took to improve safety resulted in objections from Gar, especially if it meant warehouse workers were to be slowed or delayed in their jobs. Most of the workers liked Sam, but they paid more attention to Gar. The only time employees wore their safety goggles, shoes, and acid-resistant gloves was when Sam was around. They knew Gar did not care and would not discipline good workers for safety violations unless company property was damaged.

One day a case of sulphuric-acid was dropped, badly burning a new employee. The employee recovered after four weeks and two plastic surgery operations. Immediately after the accident, Sam requested a meeting with Gar, the human resources manager, and the general manager.

1. If you were the general manager, what would you do to gain greater cooperation on safety from (a) Gar and (b) the workers under him?
2. Should Sam be given authority to discipline those who violate safety rules?

## INCIDENT 14-2

### Night Work in a Hospital

Ann LeBlanc is a laboratory technician in one of the city hospitals in Halifax. As a technician she has to work two day and three night shifts every week. She has been working at the hospital for the last eight years.

"This job is beginning to get to me," says Ann. "Night work is getting really harder and harder. I don't sleep or eat well on the three days when I have to work at night. I feel groggy most of the time."

Ann is one of four employees in the laboratory, three of whom have to work at night on a rotating basis. "All three of us have the same kinds of problems," Ann adds. "We all feel that our mental balance is lost at times. Sleep during the daytime does not help at all. It doesn't have the same depth as sleep at night. We also don't get a chance to spend time with our family most of the week. I would have quit a long time ago, but with the kids going to school we need the money.

"We are so sleepy at night that on several occasions we have been close to making serious mistakes. One day I mistook water for glycerine. . . . And Jackie almost fell down the stairs one day."

1. Can night work be called a health hazard? Why?
2. What can be done to eliminate the problems of night work?

## CASE STUDY

### A STRESSFUL CONDITION

#### Background

In late March, the joint Occupational Health and Safety Committee established pursuant to Section 24 of *The Occupational Health and Safety Act (1977)* at the Prince Albert Pulp Company Ltd. agreed to submit an unresolved problem pertaining to a complaint of stress by four recovery boiler operators to the Occupational Health and Safety Branch of the Saskatchewan Department of Labour.

## The Problem

In December 1977, a new recovery boiler came into operation at the pulp mill. The new boiler is only half the capacity of the old boiler and according to management is fitted with every conceivable self-regulatory and safety device. The main control panel is fitted into the old boiler control room, on the opposite wall, but the evaporator panels for the new boiler are on a lower floor.

In mid-March, the recovery boiler operators complained that they were feeling the effects of stress due to the extra responsibility of looking after two boilers whereas they had previously looked after only one. They felt that the stress is having an effect on their health, and that this in turn creates a danger to other workers anywhere in the vicinity of either boiler. The four boiler operators believe that the explosion hazards of black liquor recovery boilers are greater than ordinary steam or power boilers, and they were not getting sufficient support from supervision.

## Jurisdiction

The above unresolved Occupational Health and Safety Committee problem was appropriate for resolution by the Occupational Health and Safety Branch, Saskatchewan Department of Labour. Section 2, sub-section (k) of *The Occupational Health and Safety Act (1977)* defines "occupational health" as follows.

   (i)   the promotion and maintenance of the highest degree of physical, mental and social well-being of workers;

  (ii)  the prevention among workers of ill health caused by their working conditions;

 (iii)  the protection of workers in their employment from factors adverse to their health; and

 (iv)  the placing and maintenance of workers in occupational environments which are adapted to their individual physiological and psychological conditions.

Increased stress or distress not only can produce disease but also can increase the potential for accidents to the individual and fellow-workers.

Further, *The Boiler and Pressure Vessel Act (1977)* is also applicable to the above matter. Section 7, sub-section (d) states that the boiler and pressure vessel inspector may

give instructions orally or in writing to the owner, chief engineer, shift engineer or other persons responsible for or in immediate charge of a boiler, pressure vessel or plant on any matter pertaining to the construction fabrication, installation, operation, care, maintenance or repair thereof and require that those instructions shall be carried out within a specified time;

further, Section 37 states that

where exceptional circumstances exist, rendering strict compliance with the regulations impracticable, the chief inspector may, subject to such conditions as he may prescribe, grant special exemptions in individual cases if satisfied that such exemptions are not inconsistent with safe practice.

## Approach

In order to make a judgement two aspects of the problem require investigation.

(A) First, an assessment of the stressor—that is an assessment of the new working conditions resulting from the additional boiler. This evaluation should also address itself to the following questions:

1.  What change in *responsibility* occurs as a result of the additional boiler?

2.  What additional interactions between the new conditions and other features of work emerge?

3.  Are there any increases in hazards to workers, other workers and property, etc., as a result of the additional boiler?

In other words, *do increased responsibilities result in increased dangers?* The investigation of the above was appropriately assigned to the Boiler and Pressure Vessel Unit within the Occupational Health and Safety Branch, Saskatchewan Department of Labour.

(B) At the same time, the chief Occupational Medical Officer was asked to investigate the matter regarding stress or distress of the boiler operators as a result of the changed working conditions, or additional recovery boiler. The Chief Occupational Medical Officer's report would contain a medical evaluation of the operators as to the psychological and biological effects due to the "increased" stressors in their work environment.

## Summary of Investigation

**(A) Medical Assessment of Stress.** On March 29, 1978, Dr. L.E. Euinton visited the pulp mill and interviewed separately and privately the four recovery boiler operators. They all worked for Prince Albert Pulp Company Ltd., for ten years and have been recovery boiler operators for five to six years. For approximately one year, they have been working a 12-hour shift. More specifically, four days on day shift, three and a half days off, four days on night shift and four and a half days off, etc. The employees support this arrangement and maintain that their wives do so as well.

Afterwards, Dr. Euinton interviewed the boiler operators' supervisors. One supervisor stated that the responsibility of attending black liquor recovery boilers is not substantially greater than any other boilers, and that it is well within the compass of one operator to attend both boilers. He acknowledges that there have been recovery boiler explosions in the past with tragic results, but usually because someone has ignored signs that something was going wrong. His operators are experienced, are kept fully informed of the advisory com-

mittee's meetings, and are fully authorized to close down boilers or otherwise to act to avert serious mishaps, with no pressure to do otherwise for production motives.

The conclusion of Dr. Euinton's report is as follows:

There is no doubt whatsoever in my mind that these recovery boiler operators are feeling under considerable stress, and that they are worried about the dangers to other men that their stress may cause. What I think most difficult is to allocate the causes of the stress, since I think it comes from a combination of extra responsibility and twelve hour shifts. One of the operators, for instance, lives on a farm of three acres and although he says that he does not substantially "moonlight" he has a wife and a young family and he does have to travel forty-five miles to work. Under winter conditions, surely this in itself adds substantially to the strain of twelve-hour shifts. The other three operators all live in their own homes in Prince Albert, which is about fourteen miles away, also with wives and families.

**(B) Report of the Boiler and Pressure Vessel Inspectors.** On April 3, 1978, both Mr. Jim Crook and Mr. N. Uhrich, Inspection Engineers within the Boiler and Pressure Vessels Unit, inspected the boilers with a view of assessing the degree of responsibility in attending the black liquor recovery boiler, and whether this is substantially greater by having two boilers to look after instead of one.

The most significant and relevant findings in this report are as follows:

We find that there appears to be a stress situation. The cause could be through lack of communication, lack of training, working a twelve-hour shift, personality clashes between personnel or being over-committed on days off.

We feel that a realignment of job responsibilities should take place to provide for one man per shift to act as relief panel operator. This relief panel operator would be competent at operating the recovery panels. . . .

If, in the future, the turbine control panel is moved up to the control room, a further realignment of responsibilities could take place; however, there should be no reduction of manpower at that time.

### Director's Observations

As a result of the above two reports, I met with both the Chief Occupational Medical Officer and the Chief Boiler Inspector to discuss an appropriate resolution to the matter. All agreed that the boiler operators are genuinely feeling under stress, with a great deal of concern for safety. Further, we were quite convinced that the situation would worsen if the recovery boiler operators were to continue to look after two boilers on a twelve-hour shift.

Because of the degree of stress combined with responsibility, we concluded that the situation is intolerable.

Further, we could not understand why the workers at the Prince Albert Pulp Company Ltd., including the boiler operators, support a twelve-hour shift, apparently with no account for the responsibility of the work and the fact that most are married men with families, and some with travelling to do under seasonally hard conditions.

### Remedies

In order that the boiler operators properly cope with the additional recovery boiler while working a 12-hour shift, the following remedies are to be implemented forthwith:

1. That there be a realignment of job responsibilities so as to provide for one man per shift to act as relief panel operator.

2. The relief panel operators ought to be competent at operating the recovery panels and should assume greater responsibility for training the spoutmen.

3. The relief operator may be assigned other duties during upsets in the system, when required, so as to assist in the levelling out condition. This reassignment is not to contradict the prime or major purpose of this determination, which is to make an assistant available to the operator of the recovery boilers, but rather to allow for flexibility during critical periods. Consequently, such reassignments would be infrequent and for short periods of time.

4. If in the future the turbine control panel is moved up to the control room, a further realignment of responsibilities could take place, however there should be no reduction of manpower at that time.

5. Greater efforts must be made for proper training of the spoutman who is essential in the operation of the recovery boiler because he manually controls the liquor bed and the air flow over the bed.

6. Finally, consideration to the present communications system should be reviewed by higher management. This review should also take into consideration lack of support to the boiler operators by existing supervision.

We believe that the implementation of the above will greatly contribute to the reduction of stress for the boiler operators, and to a more competent and smoother operation of the mill, making for a safer and healthier work environment.

ROBERT SASS, Director, Occupational Health & Safety Division.

April 20, 1978

---

1. How is occupational health defined in Saskatchewan? How is it defined in your province?

2. Identify the stressors affecting the boiler operators.

3. How could the problem have been resolved in-house, without going to the Department of Labour's Occupational Health and Safety Division?

Reproduced with permission from Occupational Health and Safety Division, Department of Labour, Saskatchewan. The report was prepared by Director Robert Sass.

○ ○ ○ ○ ○ ○ ○ ○ ○ ○ ○ ○ ○ ○ ○ ○ ○ ○ ○ ○ ○ ○ ○ ○ ○ ○ ○ ○ ○ ○ ○ ○ ○ ○ ○ ○ ○ ○

# *REFERENCES*

1. R.W. Sexty, "Working Conditions," *Issues in Canadian Business*, Scarborough: Prentice-Hall of Canada, 1983, pp. 115-119.

2. F.E. Bird, Jr., *Management Guide to Loss Control*, Institute Press, Atlanta, 1974.

3. Ibid.

4. Ibid.

5. R.D. Clarke, "Worker Participation in Health and Safety in Canada," *International Labour Review*, March/April 1982, pp. 199-206; see also L. Gauthier, "Ontario's Occupational Health and Safety Act and the Internal Responsibility System: Is the Act Working?" *Canadian Community Law Journal*, Vol. 7, 1984, pp. 174-183; K.E. Swinton, "Enforcement of Occupational Health and Safety Legislation: The Role of the Internal Responsibility System," in *Studies in Labour Law*, K.P. Swan and K.E. Swinton (eds.), Toronto: Butterworths, 1983.

6. G.K. Bryce and P. Manga, "The Effectiveness of Health and Safety Committees," *Relations Industrielles*, Vol. 40, No. 3, 1983, pp. 257-283. See also R. Sass, "Alternative Policies in the Administration of Occupational Health and Safety Programs," *Economic and Industrial Democracy*, Vol. 8, 1987, pp. 243-257.

7. Nova Scotia Department of Labour, *Annual Report*, March 31, 1980, Halifax, N.S.: Queen's Printer, p. 28.

8. Ibid.

9. Sexty, op.cit. See also Keith Mason, *Accident Patterns by Time of Day of Week of Injury Occurrence*, Vancouver, B.C.: Workers' Compensation Board, September 1975; "Workers' Fall Blamed on Faulty Scaffolding," *The Calgary Herald*, March 3, 1981; Jean Surry, "Investigation, Tighter Standards Sought," Canadian Occupational Health and Safety News, April 14, 1980, p. 1; Robert Morgan, "Tracing Causes of Industrial Illness," *Canada Labour*, Vol. 23, No.1, March 1978, p. 19; Linda McQuaig, "Occupational Death," *Maclean's*, May 19, 1980, p. 45; Ray Sentes, *Hazards in the Work Place; Responses and Recommendations of Alberta's Unionized Workers*, Edmonton: Alberta Federation of Labour, 1981; "Utility Admits to Misleading Public," *The Calgary Herald*, July 22, 1980.

10. Labour Canada, "A Guide to the Revised Canada Labour Code" Part IV, Minister of Supply and Services Canada, Ottawa, 1985, p. 7.

11. *At the Centre*, the newsletter of the Canadian Centre for Occupational Health and Safety, July 1985, p. 13.

12. Canadian Centre for Occupational Health and Safety, *Report of the Council*, April 1, 1987, Hamilton.

13. Ibid.

14. Canada Labour Code, Part IV, revised in 1985.

15. Ibid.

16. Actual case, but names have been disguised.

17. "The Crippling Ills That Stress Can Trigger," *Business Week*, April 18, 1988, pp. 77-78.

18. *Coping with Job Stress*, ISR Newsletter (Institute for Social Research, University of Michigan), Winter 1982, p. 4, referring to work by John R.P. French, Jr., and others at the institute.

19. J.A. Lischeron, "Occupational Health: Psychological Aspects," in K. Srinivas, *Human Resource Management: Contemporary Perspectives in Canada*, McGraw-Hill Ryerson Ltd., 1984, pp. 425-455.

20. Canadian Institute of Stress, Toronto, 1988, personal communication. See also "Stress: The Test Americans are Failing," *Business Week*, April 18, 1988, pp. 74-76.

21. Lischeron, op.cit.

22. J. Howard, "To Reduce Stress Get Yourself A Senior Manager's Job," *The Canadian Personnel and Industrial Relations Journal*, Vol. 23, No. 1, January 1976, pp. 27-31; see also A. Kiev and V. Kohn, *Executive Stress*, N.Y.: AMACOM, 1979, pp. 20-23.

22. Gene Deszca, Ronald Burke and Victor N. MacDonald, "Organizational Correlates of Role Stress of Administrators In the Public Sector," *ASAC (Organizational Behaviour Division) Meeting Proceedings*, Vol. 3, Part 5, 1982, pp. 100-109; Lyons, R., "Role Clarity, Need for Clarity, Satisfaction, Tension and Withdrawal," *Organizational Behaviour and Human Performance*, 1971, 6, pp. 99-110. See also V.V. Baba and M.J. Harris, "Strain and Absence: A Study of White-Collar Workers in Quebec," Working Paper #83-010, Montreal: Concordia University, Faculty of Commerce, 1983.

23. Ari Kiev and Vera Kohn, 1979, op.cit. See also Muhammad Jamal, "Hours of Work, Use of Leisure Time, Physical and Psychological Health Problems, and Work Performance: A Study in Work and Leisure," *ASAC (Organizational Behaviour Division) Meeting Proceedings*, Vol. 1, Part 4, 1980, pp. 38-47; James S. Manuso, "Executive Stress Management," *The Personnel Administrator*, November 1979, pp. 23-26, and the model of frustration reported in Paul E. Spector, "Organizational Frustration: A Model and Review of Literature,"*Personnel Psychology*, Winter 1978, pp. 815-829.

24. Kurt R. Student, "Personnel's Newest Challenge: Helping to Cope with Stress," *The Personnel Administrator*, Novem-

ber 1978, pp. 20-24. See also John Howard, 1976, op.cit.; Gene Deszca, Ronald Burke and Victor N. MacDonald, 1982, op.cit.

25. Farida Shaikh, "Sexual Harassment: The Social Disease and How to Fight It," C.U.P.E.: *The Facts,* Vol. 2, March 1980, p. 107. See also "Harassment Exaggerated, Say Men," *The Calgary Herald,* February 18, 1981.

26. T.H. Holmes and R.H. Rahe, "The Social Readjustment Rating Scale," *Journal of Psychosomatic Research,* November 1968, pp. 213-218.

27. A.R. Cahoon and J.I.A.Rowney, "The Three Phases Model of Burnout: A Comparison by Sex and Level of Management Responsibilities," paper presented at the ASAC (Organizational Behaviour Division) meeting, University of Guelph, Ontario, May 29, 1984; Oliver L. Niehouse, "Burnout: A Real Threat to Human Resource Managers," *Personnel,* September/October 1981, pp. 25-32. For books on burnout, see Robert L. Veninga and James P. Spradley, *The Work Stress Connection: How to Cope with Job Burnout,* Boston: Little, Brown, 1981; and Herbert J. Freudenberger, with Geraldine Richelson, *Burn-Out; The High Cost of High Achievement,* New York: Anchor Press/Doubleday, 1980.

28. For discussion see Harry Levinson, "When Executives Burn Out," *Harvard Business Review,* May-June 1981, pp. 73-81; Susan E. Jackson and Randall S. Schuler, "Preventing Employee Burnout," *Personnel,* March-April 1983, pp. 58-68; and Morley D. Glicken and Katherine Janka, "Executives under Fire: The Burnout Syndrome," *California Management Review,* Spring 1982, pp. 67-72.

29. John H. Howard et al., "Childhood Antecedents of Type A Behaviour" *Proceedings of the Administrative Sciences Association of Canada,* May 23-24, 1981, Halifax: Dalhousie University, 1981. See also Meyer Friedman and Ray H. Rosenman, *Type A Behavior and Your Heart,* New York: Alfred A. Knopf, Inc. 1974, and Karl Albrecht, *Stress and the Manager: Making It Work for You,* Englewood Cliffs, N.J.: Prentice-Hall, Inc. 1979; John M. Ivancevich, Michael T. Matheson and Cynthia Preston "Occupational Stress, Type A Behaviour and Physical Well Being," *Academy of Management Journal,* June 1982, pp. 373-391.

30. Licheron, op. cit.

31. T.H. Holmes and R.H. Rahe, "The Social Readjustment Rating Scale," *Journal of Psychosomatic Research,* Vol. 11, 1967, pp. 213-218.

32. R.J. Shepard, M. Cox, and P. Corey, "Fitness Program Participation: Its Effect on Worker Performances," *Journal of Occupational Medicine,* Vol. 23, 1981, pp. 359-363; see also M. Cox, R.J. Shepard, and P. Corey, "Influence of an Employee Fitness Program upon Fitness, Productivity, and Absenteeism," *Ergonomics,* Vol. 24, 1981, pp. 795-806.

33. J. Dougall, R. Brookbank, H.F. Schwind, D. Clarimont, S. MacDonald, and R. Gardener, "Working Better, Feeling Better," report on a two-year QWL program for Maritime companies, The Institute of Public Affairs, 1986, Dalhousie

University; see also D.V. Nightingale, *Workplace Democracy: An Enquiry in Employee Participation in Canadian Work Organization,* University of Toronto Press, 1982; D.D. Umstot, C.H. Bell, and T.R. Mitchell, "The Effects of Job Enrichment and Task Goals on Satisfaction and Productivity: Implications for Job Design," *Journal of Applied Psychology,* Vol. 61, 1976, pp. 379-394.

34. Robert A. Karasek, Jr. "Job Demands, Job Decisions Latitude, and Mental Strain: Implications for Job Redesign," *Administrative Science Quarterly,* June 1979, pp. 285-308. General strategies for handling stress are summarized in John E. Newman and Terry A. Beehr, "Personal and Organization Strategies for Handling Job Stress: A Review of Research and Opinion," *Personnel Psychology,* Spring 1979, pp. 1-43. See also Muhammad Jamal, 1980, op.cit.

35. "Redesigning the Workplace," *The Financial Times of Canada,* November 14-20, 1977, p. 11. See also John M. Ivancevich, "An Analysis of Participation in Decision Making among Project Engineers," *Academy of Management Journal,* June 1979, pp. 253-269. See also Saroj Parasuraman and Joseph A. Alutto, "An Examination of Organizational Antecedents of Stressors at Work," *Academy of Management Journal,* March 1981, pp. 48-67; and James B. Shaw and John H. Riskind, "Predicting Job Stress Using Data from the Position Analysis Questionnaire," *Journal of Applied Psychology,*May 1983, pp. 253-261.

36. Charles R. Stoner and Fred L. Fry, "Developing a Corporate Policy for Managing Stress," *Personnel,* May-June 1983, pp. 66-76. The article also has two excellent lists of corrective policies and action programs for reducing stress. See also Morley D. Glicken, "A Counselling Approach to Burnout,"*Personnel Journal,* March 1983, pp. 222-228.

37. Lischeron, op.cit.

38. "Health and Safety Aspects of Alcohol and Drug Use," *The Worklife Report,* 1988, Vol. 6, No. 2, p. 4.

39. "AIDS," *The Bulletin,* William M. Mercer Meidinger Hansen, Inc., June 1988, No. 156.

40. Ibid.

41. Ibid.

42. J.J. Breckenridge, "Nurse with AIDS gets job back, but row over dismissal goes on," *Globe and Mail,* June 29, 1988, p. A10; see also letter to the Editor of the *Globe and Mail* by Raj Anand, Chief Human Rights Commissioner, Ontario Human Rights Commission, July 6, 1988, p. A6.

43. K. MacLeod, "Taking Fear and Loathing out of the Office," *Office Management and Automation,* April 1988, p. 30-32; see also M. Davids, "Panic Prevention," *Public Relations Journal,* March 1987, p. 18-43; S. Alaton, "The High Costs of AIDS," *Globe and Mail,* October 20, 1988, p. D1; G.E. Stevens, "Understanding AIDS," *Personnel Administrator,* August 1988, pp. 84-88.

44. "Acquired Immune Deficiency Syndrome (AIDS) in the Universities," *CAUT Bulletin* (Canadian Association of University Teachers), October 1988, p. 4.

## *APPENDIX*

### *Aids and the Workplace*

AIDS (Acquired Immune Deficiency Syndrome) is caused by a virus which is present in the blood, semen and other body fluids of an infected person.

The virus is spread when infected blood or semen enters into another person's bloodstream. That happens through:

· sexual contact with an infected person
· sharing contaminated needles or syringes

The virus can also pass from an infected mother to her unborn child in the womb.

Although very small traces of the virus have been found in tears and saliva, there have been no cases of anyone becoming infected from kissing or contact with saliva or tears.

The virus is **not** spread through non-sexual, everyday contact. Therefore there is little opportunity for infection in the workplace.

Not everyone infected with the AIDS virus has AIDS or will develop AIDS. Some people are exposed to the virus, carry it in their bloodstreams and have no symptoms. Some may develop mild symptoms which disappear; others develop more persistent symptoms. A number of people who have been infected with the AIDS virus will develop the serious, fatal disease known as AIDS.

**Can I get AIDS from a co-worker who has AIDS?**

There have been no cases of friends or coworkers being infected from nonsexual contact with persons with AIDS. Being in the same office, working on the same assembly line or using the same equipment as someone with AIDS, even for a long period of time, does not put you at any risk of becoming infected with the AIDS virus.

**Is there any risk in using cups, telephones, locker rooms or other facilities that are also used by a coworker who has AIDS or who has been infected with the AIDS virus?**

The AIDS virus has not been transmitted through air, water or food, or by touching the skin of a person with AIDS, or by touching any object handled, touched or breathed on by a person with AIDS. People can't get AIDS from public toilets, drinking fountains, telephones, public transportation or swimming pools.

Extensive studies of families of persons with AIDS have not found one case of the disease spread through sharing bathrooms, kitchenware or clothes.

**Can I get AIDS from eating in a restaurant where someone handling the food has AIDS?**

No cases of AIDS have been transmitted through food preparation or food handling. The AIDS virus is very fragile and survives for only a short time outside the human body. Even if the virus were present, it would be killed by the standard public health cleaning practices required of all restaurants or businesses handling food.

**Personal service workers (such as barbers and manicurists) have fairly close contact with customers. Are these workers at risk if the customer has AIDS or is infected with the AIDS virus?**

There has never been a case of a personal service worker becoming infected with the AIDS virus from nonsexual contact with a client or customer.

The risk of being exposed to the AIDS virus depends on the type of service performed. There is a potential risk *only* if the worker comes into contact with the client's blood *and* there is an opportunity for the virus to enter the worker's bloodstream.

Personal service workers such as hairdressers, barbers, beauticians, cosmetologists, manicurists and pedicurists may have close personal contact with clients, but they rarely come into contact with blood, and therefore have little risk of exposure.

Personal service workers who

- pierce ears
- give tattoos
- use acupuncture

may come into contact with blood and, therefore, could be at some slight risk.

To protect against *any* infection, all personal service workers should follow good hygiene practices. They should:

- wash their hands thoroughly
- cover any cuts or sores on their hands
- clean their equipment according to recommended procedures
- use disposable equipment where appropriate
- clean anything that has been contaminated with blood using rubbing alcohol or a bleach solution (1 part household, chlorine bleach — such as Javex — to 9 parts water).

These simple precautions will protect against hepatitis B and other blood-borne infections — including AIDS.

**If the personal service workers have AIDS or are infected with the AIDS virus, are their customers at risk?**

There has never been a case of someone becoming infected with the AIDS virus from nonsexual contact with a barber, hairdresser or other personal care worker. The good hygiene practices described for workers also protect customers.

**Are health care workers who are caring for persons with AIDS at risk?**

Health care workers and laboratory staff who handle body fluids such as blood, semen, feces and urine of AIDS patients run a slight risk of coming into contact with the AIDS virus. To protect themselves, they should follow the infection control practices and procedures recommended in their institutions so that the AIDS virus will not have the opportunity to enter their bloodstreams.

Studies have shown that, even in cases where health care workers have accidentally stuck themselves with needles contaminated with blood infected with the AIDS virus, the chance of becoming infected with the AIDS virus is very small — well over 100 times less than with hepatitis B.

More detailed information for health care workers is available through the Ministry of Health.

**Are patients at risk if the health care worker is infected with the AIDS virus?**

Infection control procedures in hospitals or clinics that protect health care workers also protect patients. In most hospital situations, there is little opportunity for a patient to be exposed to the blood of a health care worker and, therefore, there is very little risk.

During invasive procedures, such as surgery or kidney dialysis, precautions are already in place to prevent bloodborne infections such as hepatitis B, and they would also protect against AIDS.

**Are ambulance drivers, police officers, firefighters and other emergency workers at risk of AIDS virus infection?**

AIDS virus is not spread by touching, carrying or holding a person who is infected. Nonsexual contact is not risky.

However, ambulance or other emergency personnel will likely come into contact with blood and other body fluids in emergency situations. *Even if these fluids contain the AIDS virus, the risk of infection is very low.* There have been no cases of anyone becoming infected with the AIDS virus from providing emergency care for an infected person.

To protect against any infection, emergency workers should follow strict infection control practices in caring for emergency victims. They should:

· wash their hands thoroughly

· clean their equipment according to recommended procedures.

If they are likely to come into contact with blood or body fluids, they should:

· wear plastic, disposable gloves

· cover any cuts or sores on their hands

· clean any contaminated surfaces with a chlorine bleach solution.

These simple precautions will protect them from hepatitis B and other blood-borne infections — including AIDS.

Although very small quantities of the AIDS virus have been found in saliva, there have been no cases of AIDS virus infection transmitted through saliva. Emergency workers who *regularly* give mouth-to-mouth resuscitation or CPR to victims may protect themselves from a variety of diseases by using a specially designed mouthpiece. However, the risk of infection is so slight that no one should hesitate to give emergency mouth-to-mouth resuscitation without a mouthpiece.

**What should an employer's approach be to an employee who has AIDS?**

As long as the employee is able to perform the essential duties of his or her job, the employer's approach should be the same as with any other employee.

At certain stages in the illness, the employee may be too ill to work. When this happens, or when the workplace becomes dangerous to the employee's health, the approach to the person with AIDS should be the same as with any other employee who has a serious illness. Whenever possible, attempts should be made to adjust work requirements to accommodate the person's health.

The employer should be sensitive to the fact that ongoing employment for someone who has a life-threatening illness is important, and may help to prolong the employee's life.

**Can people be fired because they have AIDS or are infected with the AIDS virus?**

People who have AIDS or who are infected with the AIDS virus are not a health risk to coworkers so that there is no medical reason to dismiss them.

The Ontario Human Rights Code prohibits discrimination in employment based on a disabling condition. If a person were fired because he or she either:

- has AIDS,
- was infected with the AIDS virus, or
- was suspected of having AIDS,

that could be a violation of the employee's rights.

An employee who feels that his or her rights have been violated may file a complaint with the Ontario Human Rights Commission. In addition, the employee may be able to sue the employer for wrongful dismissal.

**Can an employee refuse to work with a coworker who has AIDS or who has been infected with the AIDS virus?**

The Occupational Health and Safety Act allows workers to refuse to do a job that threatens their health. However, there has not been a single incident reported of someone becoming infected with the AIDS virus through nonsexual contact with a coworker. Therefore, there is no medical reason to refuse to work with someone who is infected with the AIDS virus.

To prevent discrimination, a number of companies are developing internal policies on AIDS. Where policies exist, it may be a violation of the conditions of employment to refuse to work with someone who has AIDS or who is infected with the AIDS virus.

However, employers should be sensitive to coworkers' concerns and provide access to education to allay unreasonable fears.

**Can a health care worker refuse to provide care for a person with AIDS?**

If a health care worker who is a member of a regulated profession refuses to care for someone who has AIDS, it may be a violation of the profession's standards of conduct. The circumstances should be brought to the attention of the governing body of that profession.

A number of hospitals and institutions have developed guidelines or policies on treating AIDS patients. In those cases, refusing to care for someone who has AIDS could be a violation of the institution's conditions of employment. A worker who refused to care for an AIDS patient could be disciplined or dismissed.

Anyone who has been refused care also has the right to file a complaint with the Ontario Human Rights Commission.

**Can someone who provides a personal service refuse to serve someone who has AIDS or who is infected with the AIDS virus?**

There have been no cases of anyone becoming infected with the AIDS virus from providing a personal service (e.g., hairdressers, barbers, etc.) to someone who has AIDS or who is infected with the AIDS virus.

Anyone who is refused a personal service can lodge a complaint with the Ontario Human Rights Commission.

**Does an employer have the right to know if an employee has AIDS?**

Since AIDS cannot be transmitted by everyday contact in the workplace, there is no need for employers, coworkers, neighbours or anyone who does not have intimate sexual contact with a person with AIDS to know. The person with AIDS has a legal right to privacy and confidentiality.

An employer can only request medical information from an employee that is relevant to his or her job. An employer can only confirm this information with a physician with the employee's expressed consent.

**Should an employer request blood testing for employees?**

Available blood tests identify antibodies to the AIDS virus, which indicate that a person has been exposed to the virus.

Employers do not have the right to insist on mandatory blood testing.

Testing might be considered for health care workers who, through an injury in the workplace, have been exposed to infected blood or body fluids. In those cases, testing is for the benefit of the employee and should be voluntary — *not mandatory*.

In other work situations, there's no reason to test employees.

**What should employers do about AIDS?**

Employers should set an example for their employees and refrain from discrimination. They should also take action to prevent discrimination among employees in the workplace.

Employers should help employees become informed. General information about AIDS is available from the Ministry of Health, from your local public health unit, from the AIDS Committee of Toronto and from other local AIDS groups. Employers should distribute information that will help employees understand the AIDS virus and how it is transmitted. More knowledge will mean less fear, less discrimination and greater productivity.

**What should unions do about AIDS?**

Unions are a powerful force in communication and education and can help their members get accurate information about AIDS. They can also help prevent discrimination in the workplace. Union groups are forming committees to educate union leaders, staff and members about AIDS.

*Employers, employees and union groups who would like to know more about AIDS are encouraged to take advantage of the Ministry of Health AIDS Speakers Referral Service. Call the Ontario Public Education Panel on AIDS: in Toronto 965-2168, in the rest of Ontario 1-800-268-6066.*

If you have questions you would like to ask about AIDS, call the Ontario Ministry of Health AIDS hotline at 1-800-668-AIDS. In Toronto call 392-AIDS.

For more information, contact your doctor, your local STD (sexually-transmitted diseases) clinic, your public health unit (which is listed in the municipal section of the blue pages in your telephone directory), the AIDS Committee of Toronto or other AIDS organizations.

The following fact sheets are available from the Health Information Centre, 9th Floor, Hepburn Block, Queen's Park, Toronto, Ontario M7A 1S2:

Information About AIDS

Information for Parents and Teachers

Detecting AIDS

Women and AIDS

AIDS and the Workplace

The brochure AIDS: Let's Talk is available from the same address.

**The content of this fact sheet was prepared by the Ontario Public Education Panel on AIDS (OPEPA) with advice from the Provincial Advisory Committee on AIDS, the Ontario Human Rights Commission, the Ontario Federation of Labour and the Inter-Ministerial Working Group on AIDS.**

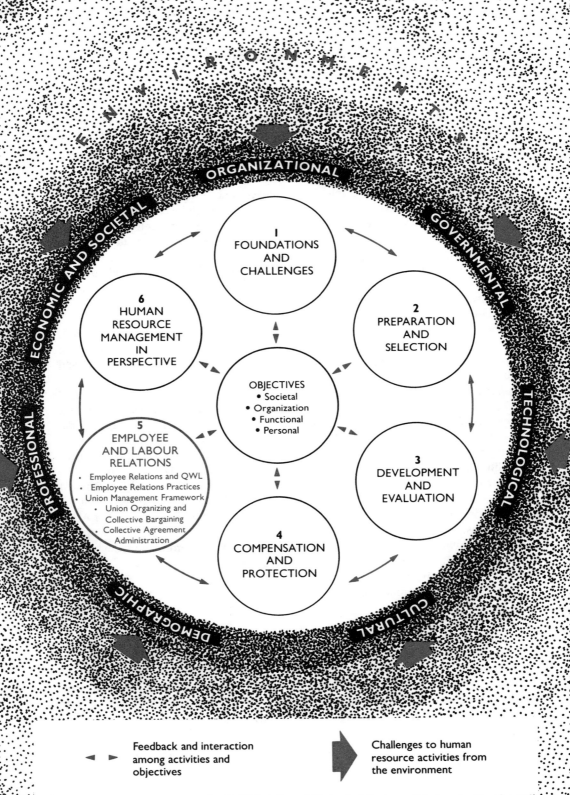

ENVIRONMENTS

ORGANIZATIONAL

GOVERNMENTAL

TECHNOLOGICAL

CULTURAL

DEMOGRAPHIC

PROFESSIONAL

ECONOMIC AND SOCIETAL

**1**
FOUNDATIONS AND CHALLENGES

**2**
PREPARATION AND SELECTION

**3**
DEVELOPMENT AND EVALUATION

**4**
COMPENSATION AND PROTECTION

**5**
EMPLOYEE AND LABOUR RELATIONS
- Employee Relations and QWL
- Employee Relations Practices
- Union Management Framework
  - Union Organizing and Collective Bargaining
- Collective Agreement Administration

**6**
HUMAN RESOURCE MANAGEMENT IN PERSPECTIVE

OBJECTIVES
- Societal
- Organization
- Functional
- Personal

Feedback and interaction among activities and objectives

Challenges to human resource activities from the environment

# PART 5 ○ ○ ○ ○ ○ ○

# *EMPLOYEE AND LABOUR RELATIONS*

*E*mployers and employees are concerned with the quality of the work environment. Quality of Work Life (QWL) programs have been implemented by many companies. Chapter 15 discusses the issues related to QWL programs.

Effective communication is a prerequisite for a good working climate. And, despite a good work environment, some employees experience personal problems that may affect their work performance. Furthermore, there are employees whose behaviour has disruptive consequences in the workplace. Chapter 16 describes how effective communication systems can be developed, discusses how employees can be counselled successfully, and elaborates on steps to be taken by management to control employee behaviour.

Chapters 17 to 19 explain the challenges management can expect when employees join unions. By understanding labour-management relations, managers can avoid serious errors that may have negative effects on their careers.

# CHAPTER *15* ○○○○○○

# *EMPLOYEE RELATIONS AND THE QUALITY OF WORK LIFE*

*The basic questions with regard to any work organization are:*
- *what are the critical requirements of the technology, and*
- *what are the characteristics of the human system?*

*The challenge lies in matching people and technology.*

DR. HANS VAN BEINUM
Executive Director, The Ontario Quality of Working Life Centre[1]

## *CHAPTER OBJECTIVES*

After studying this chapter, you should be able to:

1. **Explain** why human resource specialists are interested in the quality of work life.
2. **Identify** the efficiency and behaviourial considerations in job design.
3. **Discuss** the different techniques used to improve jobs and the quality of work life.
4. **Recognize** the nature of autonomous work groups in improving the quality of work life.
5. **Place** quality of work life in perspective with other human resource challenges.
6. **Explain** the concept of the quality circle.

*B*eyond the challenge of providing adequate financial rewards and benefits, human resource departments also seek to improve the quality of work life. Efforts to improve the *quality of work life* (QWL) make jobs more productive *and* satisfying. Although

many different techniques are used to improve the quality of work life, most involve
the participation of the workers who are affected.

> BOB WALTERS:   My job is very boring. All I do all day long is install the motors on
> electric typewriters. Every day it is the same task. I realize that someone
> must do it, but surely the job could be more fun.
>
> STAN BROWNE:   Well, several supervisors have talked with us in human resources
> about some of these assembly-line jobs. But the plant manager's big concern
> is maintaining productivity. Any changes we make must not mean fewer units
> per day. What do you suggest?
>
> BOB WALTERS:   I know high production is necessary to compete against foreign type-
> writers. But why can't several of us on the line be responsible for entire
> subassemblies instead of being responsible just for the parts we install?
>
> STAN BROWNE:   Well, what difference would that make?
>
> BOB WALTERS:   Probably not much difference. But when we got bored with one
> job we could swap jobs among us. Besides, when someone got behind, we
> could all pitch in.
>
> STAN BROWNE:   Maybe we should get together with the supervisor and the other
> workers and discuss this at lunch.

The quality of work life is affected by many factors: supervision, working conditions, pay, benefits, and the design of the job. But it is the nature of the job that most
intimately involves the worker. Even if management gave Bob Walters a pay raise, new
benefits, improved working conditions, and excellent supervision, his job would still be
boring. For most people a good work life means an interesting, challenging, and rewarding job. Admittedly, not all employee dissatisfactions can be solved by redesigning jobs.
Technology, production economies, and even tradition may block change. In Bob Walters's case, however, changing the job may be the best way to improve the quality of
his employment in the typewriter factory.

When jobs need to be redesigned, the changes are often handled by operating
managers without direct involvement of the human resource department. But other managers seek the assistance of the human resource department because it can help match
human needs with job needs. Either way, human resource specialists need to be knowledgeable about how to improve the quality of work life through job design.

Knowledge of job design is also important if human resource departments are to
respond proactively to the organizational, environmental, and behaviourial challenges
listed in Figure 15-1. Changes in any of these factors may affect the design of jobs and
the quality of work life. If the impact of these changes can be anticipated, human resource
departments are better able to respond. Consider how a knowledge of job design allowed
one human resource manager to be proactive:

> The development of a semiautomated steam box meant that Industrial Supply Serv-
> ice needed fewer employees to iron the uniforms the company rented. Instead of
> hand-ironing cotton uniforms, Industrial Supply changed to permanent press ones
> that only needed a four-minute trip through the steam box to remove wrinkles.

FIGURE 15-1 Environmental, Organizational, and Behavioural Factors that Influence Job Design and Quality of Work Life

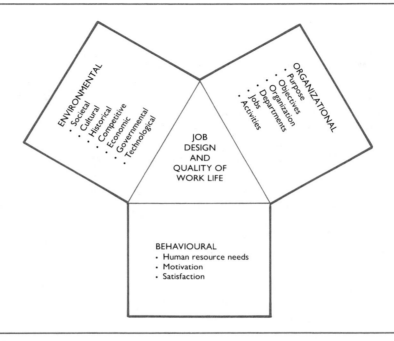

Since Helen Edgmon, the human resource manager, understood the work flow in the laundry room, she stopped hiring new workers when the steam box was ordered. She immediately began training the displaced ironers to fill other job openings.

Without an understanding of these jobs in the laundry room, Helen could not have undertaken such a proactive approach. She would have been forced to react by laying off workers. And layoffs do not contribute to societal, organizational, or employee objectives of stable employment.

Perhaps the most important need for understanding how job design affects quality of work life is the obvious point: *Jobs are the link between people and the organization.* Job openings are the reason organizations need human resources. If human resource departments are going to help the organization obtain and maintain a desired work force, people specialists must have a thorough understanding of job designs. The human resource management model from Chapter 1 is developed further in Figure 15-2 to indicate that quality of work life is an important challenge to human resource management. Every one of the major human resource activities in Figure 15-2 presupposes that human resource experts understand the organization's jobs. Without this knowledge, the human resource department cannot assist managers in redesigning jobs or performing other QWL activities.

FIGURE 15-2   A Model of the Human Resource Management System

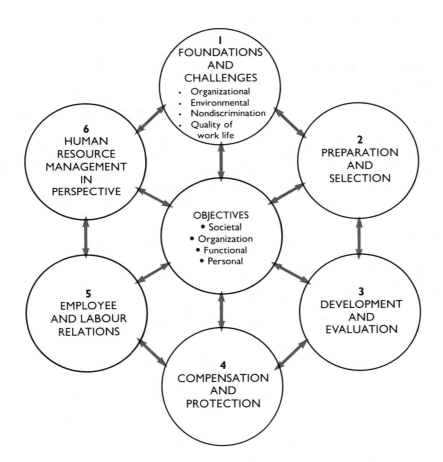

## *THE HUMAN RESOURCE DEPARTMENT'S ROLE*

The role of the human resource department in QWL efforts varies widely, although it is involved in almost every undertaking. In some organizations, top management has appointed an executive to ensure that QWL and productivity efforts occur throughout the organization.[2] In most cases, these executives have a small staff and must rely on the human resource department for help with employee training, feedback from attitude surveys, and other support.[3] In other organizations, the human resource department is responsible for initiating and directing the firm's QWL and productivity efforts.

Perhaps the most crucial role that the human resource department plays is winning the support of key managers. Management support—particularly top management support—appears to be a near universal prerequisite to successful QWL programs.[4] When full support from all levels of management does not exist, proactive human resource departments seek ways to document the success of individual QWL efforts.[5] By substantiating employee satisfaction and financial benefits, which range from lower absenteeism and turnover to higher productivity and fewer accidents, the human resource department can help convince doubting managers.[6] One telephone company, for example, achieved better sales from its phone installers, a reduction in lost inventory, fewer strikes, better employee attitudes, and improved productivity as a result of its QWL effort. Without the documentation of these favourable results, top management perhaps would not have given its on-going and strong support.

The remainder of this chapter takes a closer look at the key elements in job design, the trade-offs human resource specialists face between different design choices, and the tools of job design. Following this, there is a review of some specific approaches to QWL before concluding with a discussion of barriers that human resource departments are likely to encounter.

## ELEMENTS OF JOB DESIGN

To understand job design, Figure 15-3 provides a framework that identifies the goals of job design and the major demands it faces. The demands on job design are organizational, environmental, and behavioural. When they are carefully considered and correctly matched with a proper job design, the result is a productive and satisfying job. But when

**FIGURE 15-3**   The Job Design Input/Output Framework

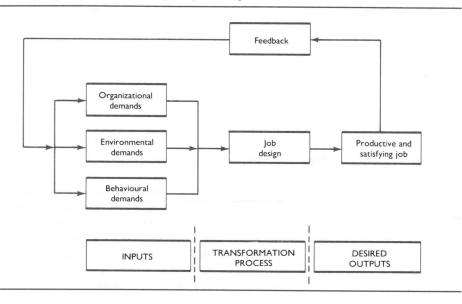

inputs or desired outputs are overlooked, problems result. For example, consider the following situation:

> Cal and Doris Shaeffer own the Shaeffer Car Rental Agency at Toronto's Pearson International Airport. Greg, a high school dropout, works weekends. Cal and Doris each give him parts of their job they dislike: fetching cars for customers, putting in gas, and posting the week's entries into the ledger. As a result, Greg's satisfaction and motivation are low.

Consider how Greg's job design compares with the model in Figure 15-3. The Shaeffers designed Greg's job to reflect their personal objectives, not organizational objectives. No apparent thought was given to Greg's needs. As a result, the job was not very satisfying to Greg. Nor did it make efficient use of his time; Greg faced long stretches with nothing to do, followed by periods of hectic activity each time a plane landed. Obviously, the quality of his work life was quite low under these circumstances.

Even if the Schaeffers had weighed the organization's objectives and Greg's needs, the job design may still have been ineffective. To create an effective job design requires an understanding of the factors listed in Figure 15-4. These organizational, environmental, and behaviourial elements of job design cannot be ignored if the demands placed on jobs are to be met. Had the Shaeffers considered the guidelines suggested by Figure 15-4, Greg's motivation and satisfaction might have been higher. Since these elements help ensure a high quality of work life, managers and human resource specialists should be familiar with them.

FIGURE 15-4   Elements of Job Design

| ORGANIZATIONAL ELEMENTS | ENVIRONMENTAL ELEMENTS | BEHAVIOURAL ELEMENTS |
|---|---|---|
| • Mechanistic approach<br>• Work flow<br>• Work practices | • Employee abilities and availability<br>• Social expectations | • Autonomy<br>• Variety<br>• Task identity<br>• Feedback |

## Organizational Elements of Job Design

Organizational elements of job design are concerned with efficiency. Efficiently designed jobs allow a highly motivated and capable worker to achieve maximum output. This concern for efficiency was formalized by management scientists around the turn of the century. They devoted much of their research to finding the best ways to design efficient jobs. Their success with stopwatches and motion pictures even gave rise to a new discipline, industrial engineering. They also contributed to the formal study of management as a separate discipline. From their efforts, we have learned that specialization is a key element in the design of jobs. When workers are limited to a few repetitive tasks, output is usually higher. The findings of these early researchers are still applicable today. They can be summarized under the heading of the mechanistic approach.

### Mechanistic Approach

The mechanistic approach seeks to identify every task in a job so that tasks can be arranged to minimize the time and effort of workers. Once task identification is complete, a limited number of tasks are grouped into a job. The result is *specialization*. Specialized jobs lead to short *job cycles*, the time to complete every task in the job. For example:

> An automotive assembly-line worker might pick up a headlight, plug it in, twist the adjustment screws, and pick up the next headlight within thirty seconds. Completing these tasks in thirty seconds means this worker's job cycle takes one-half a minute. The job cycle begins when the next headlight is picked up.

Headlight installation is a specialized job. It is so specialized that training takes only a few minutes. And the short job cycle means that the assembler gains much experience in a short time. Said another way, short job cycles require small investments in training and allow the worker to learn the job quickly. Training costs remain low because the worker needs to master only one job.

This mechanistic approach stresses efficiency in effort, time, labour, costs, training, and employee learning time. Today, this technique is still widely used in assembly operations. It is especially effective when dealing with poorly educated workers or workers who have little industrial experience. But the efficient design of jobs also considers such organizational elements as work flow and work practices.

### Work Flow

The flow of work in an organization is strongly influenced by the nature of the product or service. The product or service usually suggests the sequence of and balance between jobs if the work is to be done efficiently. For example, the frame of a car must be built before the fenders and doors can be added. Once the sequence of jobs is determined, the balance between jobs is established.

> Suppose it takes one person thirty seconds to install each headlight. Then in two minutes, an assembler can put on four headlights. If, however, it takes four minutes to install the necessary headlight receptacles, then the job designer must balance these two interrelated jobs by assigning two people to install the receptacles. Otherwise, a production bottleneck results. Since the work flow demands two receptacle installers for each headlight installer, one worker specializes in right-side receptacles and the other specializes in left-side receptacles.

### Work Practices

Work practices are set ways of performing work. These may arise from tradition or the collective wishes of employees. Either way, the human resource department's flexibility to design jobs is limited, especially when such practices are part of a union-management relationship. Failure to consider work practices can have undesired outcomes.

> In the United States, General Motors decided to increase productivity at its Lordstown, Ohio, plant by eliminating some jobs and adding new tasks to others. These design changes caused workers to stage a strike for several weeks because tradi-

tional practices at the plant had required a slower rate of production and less work by the employees. The additional demands on their jobs by management were seen as an attempt by the company to disregard past work practices.[7]

## Environmental Elements of Job Design

A second aspect of job design concerns environmental elements. As with most human resource activities, job designers cannot ignore the influence of the external environment. In designing jobs, human resource specialists and managers should consider the ability and availability of potential employees. At the same time, social expectations also have to be weighed.

### Employee Abilities and Availability

Efficiency considerations must be balanced against the abilities and availability of the people who are to do the work. When Henry Ford made use of the assembly line in the United States, for example, he was aware that most potential workers lacked any automobile-making experience. So jobs were designed to be simple and require little training. Thought must be given to who will actually do the work. An extreme example underlines this point.

Governments of less developed countries often think they can "buy" progress. To be "up to date," they seek the most advanced equipment they can find. Leaders of one country ordered a computerized oil refinery. This decision dictated a level of technology that exceeded the abilities of the country's available work force. As a result, these government leaders have hired Europeans to operate this refinery.

In less developed nations, the major risk is that jobs may be too complex. But in industrial nations with highly educated workers, jobs that are too simple can produce equally disturbing problems. For example, even when unemployment rates are high, many simple and overly specialized jobs are sometimes hard to fill, as long-standing newspaper want ads for dishwashers and cleaners attest.

### Social Expectations

The acceptability of a job's design is also influenced by the expectations of society.[8] Many uneducated immigrants to this country during the early days of the railway industry readily accepted highly specialized jobs that demanded long hours and hard physical labour. Often they had fled countries where jobs were unavailable; this made a job— any job—acceptable. Today, industrial workers are much better educated and have higher expectations about the quality of work life. Although work flow or work practices may suggest a particular job design, the job must meet the expectations of workers. Failure to consider these social expectations can create dissatisfaction, low motivation, hard-to-fill job openings, and a low quality of work life.

## Behavioural Elements of Job Design

Successful job designs consider behavioural elements if workers are to have a high quality of work life. Jobs cannot be designed by using only those elements that aid efficiency.

To do so overlooks the human needs of the people who are to perform the work. Instead, job designers draw heavily on behavioural research to provide a work environment that helps satisfy individual needs. Higher-level needs are of particular importance. One pair of researchers provided a useful framework when they suggested:

> People with a strong desire to satisfy higher order needs perform their best when placed on jobs that were high on certain dimensions. These were:
>
> - Autonomy — responsibility for work
> - Variety — use of different skills and abilities
> - Task identity — doing the whole piece of work
> - Feedback — information on performance[9]

### Autonomy

*Autonomy* is having responsibility for what one does. It is the freedom to control one's response to the environment. Jobs that give workers the authority to make decisions provide added responsibilities that tend to increase their sense of recognition and self-esteem. The absence of autonomy, on the other hand, can cause employee apathy or poor performance.[10]

> A common problem in many production operations is that employees develop an "I don't care" attitude because they believe they have no control over their jobs. On the bottling line of a small brewery, teams of workers were allowed to speed up or slow down the rate of the bottling line as long as they met daily production goals. Although the total output per shift did not change, there were fewer cases of capping machines jamming or breaking down for other reasons. When asked about this unexpected development, the supervisor concluded, "Employees pride themselves on meeting the shift quota. So they are more careful to check for defective bottle caps before they load the machine."

### Variety

A lack of variety may cause boredom. Boredom in turn leads to fatigue, and fatigue causes errors. By injecting variety into jobs, human resource specialists can reduce fatigue-caused errors. Being able to control the speed of the bottling line in the brewery example added variety to the pace of work and probably reduced both boredom and fatigue.

One research study found that diversity of work was partially responsible for effective performance.[11] And another study found that autonomy and variety were major contributors to employee satisfaction.[12]

### Task Identity

One problem with some jobs is that they lack any *task identity*. Workers cannot point to some complete piece of work when a job lacks task identity. They have little sense of responsibility and may lack pride in the results. After completing their job, they may have little sense of accomplishment. When tasks are grouped so that employees feel they are making an identifiable contribution, job satisfaction may be increased significantly.[13]

> The Crosswell and Black chartered accounting firm had two bookkeepers assigned to billing the firm's clients. One bookkeeper prepared and mailed the monthly bills, and the other one received incoming payments and credited them to each client's account. When problems arose, a partner in the firm had to check with both bookkeepers to find the cause of the problem. Since neither of them was completely responsible for individual accounts, neither took great interest in preventing errors. Mr. Crosswell decided to split the accounts equally between the bookkeepers and let each one prepare, mail, and post bills for the clients assigned to them. Besides making fewer errors, both bookkeepers expressed satisfaction with the arrangement and greater interest in the special needs of "their" clients.

### Feedback

When jobs do not give the worker any feedback on how well the job is being done, there is little guidance or motivation to perform better. By letting employees know how they are doing relative to the daily production quota in the brewery example, workers received feedback that allowed them to adjust their efforts. In the accounting firm example, each bookkeeper received feedback on client errors and was able to implement changes in billing or posting procedures to avoid future problems. In both examples, feedback led to improved motivation.[14]

## BEHAVIOURAL AND EFFICIENCY TRADE-OFFS

Behavioural elements of job design tell human resource specialists to add more autonomy, variety, task identity, or feedback. But efficiency elements point to greater specialization, less variety, minimal autonomy, and other contradictory elements. Thus to make jobs more efficient may cause them to be less satisfying. Conversely, satisfying jobs may prove to be inefficient. What should human resource specialists do?

There is no simple solution. Instead, human resource experts often make tradeoffs between efficiency and behavioural elements. Figure 15-5 depicts the most significant trade-offs faced by job designers in the human resource department.

### Graph A: Productivity Versus Specialization

The assumption that additional specialization means increased output is true only up to some point. As jobs are made more specialized, productivity climbs until behavioural elements such as boredom offset the advantages of further specialization. In Figure 15-5A, additional specialization beyond point *b* causes productivity to drop. In fact, jobs that are between *b* and *c* can have their productivity *increased* by reducing the degree of specialization.

### Graph B: Satisfaction Versus Specialization

Another interesting relationship exists between satisfaction and specialization. Here satisfaction first goes up with specialization and then additional specialization causes satisfaction to drop quickly. Jobs without any specialization take so long to learn that frustration and feedback are helped by some specialization. When specialization is carried past point *b* in Figure 15-5B, satisfaction drops because of a lack of autonomy,

FIGURE 15-5    Efficiency Versus Behavioural Trade-Offs in Job Design

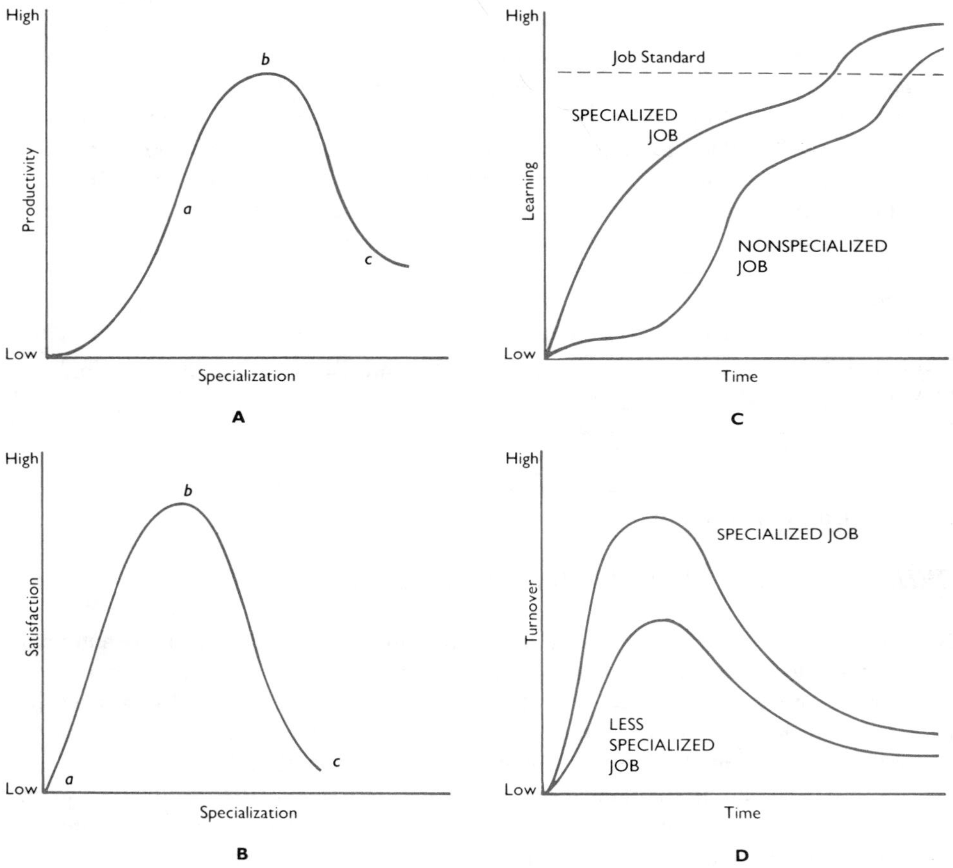

variety, and task identification. Notice that even while satisfaction is falling in graph B, productivity may still increase in graph A, from *a* to *b*. Productivity continues to go up only if the advantages of specialization outweigh the disadvantages of dissatisfaction.

## Graph C: Learning Versus Specialization

When a job is highly specialized, there is less to learn than in a nonspecialized job. Therefore, it takes less time to learn a specialized job. Graphically, this means that the rate of learning more quickly reaches an acceptable standard (shown as a dashed line). In the short run, the nonspecialized job takes longer to learn.

## Graph D: Turnover Versus Specialization

Although overspecialized jobs are quicker to learn, the lower levels of satisfaction generally associated with them can lead to higher turnover rates. When turnover rates are high, redesigning the job with more attention to behavioural elements may reduce this "quit rate."

## JOB REDESIGN TECHNIQUES

The central question often facing job designers is whether a particular job should have more or less specialization. As can be seen in graph A in Figure 15-5, the answer depends on whether the job is near point *a*, *b*, or *c*. Jobs near point *a* may need more specialization to increase their output. Those jobs near point *c* require less specialization to become more effective. Analysis and experimentation are the only sure ways to determine where a particular job is located on graph A.

### Underspecialization

When human resource specialists believe jobs are not specialized enough, they engage in *work simplification*. That is, the job is simplified. The tasks of one job may be split into two. Unneeded tasks are identified and eliminated. What is left are jobs that contain fewer tasks.

> When the Allyndale Weekly Newspaper operated with its old press, Guy Parsons could catch the newspapers as they came off the press, stack them and wrap them. But when a new high-speed press was added, he could not keep up with the output. So the circulation manager simplified Guy's job by making him responsible for stacking the newspapers. Two part-time high school students took turns catching and wrapping the papers.

The risk of work simplification is that jobs may be so specialized that boredom causes errors or resignations. This problem is more common in advanced industrial countries that have a highly educated work force. In less developed countries, highly specialized factory jobs may be acceptable and even appealing because they provide jobs for workers with limited skills.

### Overspecialization

As the labour force in advanced industrial societies becomes more educated and affluent, routine jobs that are very specialized, such as assembly-line positions, hold less and less appeal for many people. These jobs seldom offer opportunities for accomplishment, recognition, psychological growth, or other sources of satisfaction.

To increase the quality of work life for those who hold such jobs, human resource departments can use a variety of methods to improve jobs through redesign. The most widely practised techniques include job rotation, job enlargement, and job enrichment. Taken together, these techniques are usually referred to as quality of work life programs. When jobs are believed to be overly specialized, human resource specialists often recommend one of these approaches.

### Job Rotation

*Job rotation* is rotation of employees from job to job. Rotation breaks the monotony of highly specialized work by calling on different skills and abilities. The organization benefits because workers become competent in several jobs rather than only one. Knowing a variety of jobs also helps the worker's self-image and personal growth, and makes him or her more valuable to the organization.

Human resource experts should caution those who want to use job rotation. It does not improve the jobs themselves; the relationships between tasks, activities, and objectives remain unchanged. It may even postpone the use of more effective techniques while adding to training costs. Implementation should occur only after other techniques have been considered.

### Job Enlargement

*Job enlargement* means the expansion of the number of related tasks in a job, i.e., adding similar duties to provide greater variety. Enlargement reduces monotony by expanding the job cycle and drawing on a wider range of employee skills. According to one summary of job design research:

> IBM reported job enlargement led to higher wages and more inspection equipment, but improved quality and worker satisfaction offset these costs. The Maytag Company claimed that production quality was improved, labour costs declined, most workers preferred enlarged jobs, overall efficiency increased, and management had more flexibility in scheduling production.[15]

### Job Enrichment

*Job enrichment* means the addition of new sources of needed satisfaction to jobs. This increases worker responsibility, autonomy, and control. Adding these elements to jobs is sometimes called *vertical loading. Horizontal loading* occurs when the job is expanded by simply adding related tasks, as with job enlargement. Job enrichment sees jobs as consisting of three elements: plan, do, control.[16] Job enlargement (or horizontal loading) adds more things to *do*. Enrichment (or vertical loading) attempts to add more responsibility for *planning* and *control*. These additions to the job, coupled with rethinking the job itself, often lead to increased motivation and other improvements.

> In a pilot project with one unit of the Data Capture section of Statistics Canada, job enrichment and other changes resulted in increased employee satisfaction, lower absentee rates, increases in the quality of work done, and improved relationships between the union and management.
>
> One employee recalled that prior to the changes, "we were watched every second. We weren't able to talk. We had no responsibility or variety in our work. We'd just go to the basket and take the job that was on top." The changes implemented included more variety and more worker responsibility, both for completing the work and for attendance, hiring, training, appraisals, and discipline. Aside from the success indicators already mentioned, when the rest of the section was asked whether they were interested in being involved in similar changes for their units, 171 of the remaining 177 employees were in favour.[17]

Job enrichment, however, is not a cure-all; if it were, this book could end here.

Job enrichment techniques are merely tools, and they are not applied universally. When the diagnosis indicates jobs are unrewarding and unchallenging and limit the motivation and satisfaction of employees, human resource departments *may* find job enrichment to be the most appropriate strategy. Even then, however, job enrichment faces problems.

One author has listed twenty-two arguments against job enrichment.[18] The most compelling points are the existence of union resistance, the cost of design and implementation, and the scarcity of research on long-term effects. Another criticism of job enrichment is that it does not go far enough. To enrich the job and ignore other variables that contribute to the quality of work life may simply increase dissatisfaction with the unimproved aspects of the job environment. There is a need to go beyond job enrichment in some work situations.[19] Last but not least, the cultural values and social expectations surrounding the organization have to be carefully considered before any job redesign attempts are made.[20]

## QWL ON THE NATIONAL SCENE

In 1976, in the speech from the throne, the federal government's support for QWL was announced. The responsibility for the QWL program was assigned to the Employment Relations and Conditions of Work branch of Labour Canada. The activities of this organization over the past few years have been quite diverse. Rather than getting directly involved in QWL activities, it has opted for a policy of supporting and promoting QWL concepts and activities. This has been pursued by its being represented at and sponsoring conferences and workshops, publishing QWL information (including *Quality of Working Life: The Canadian Scene)*, and providing some financial and technical assistance for QWL training and research projects. This branch of Labour Canada has also endeavoured to develop a network of qualified QWL individuals across the country.

At the provincial level, most activities are less institutionalized. However, in 1978 Ontario established a QWL centre in its Department of Labour. The centre's activities include consultation, information services, research and field activities, and educational programs. McGill University has a QWL centre and there is a QWL forum in British Columbia. Yet these organizations represent only a small part of QWL activities in Canada. More and more public and private organizations are becoming involved in QWL.

The results of a typical industrial application of QWL are shown in Figure 15-6. The Alcan plant of Grande Baie, Quebec, an aluminum smelting facility with a staff of about 450, used QWL to improve morale in the workplace. After two years, management found that the working climate had changed significantly. They felt that there was more openness and employees showed more initiative and responsibility. In addition, turnover and absenteeism has decreased. Labour Canada compared the experience of this Canadian company with that of a U.S. company of similar size, the General Foods plant in Topeka, Kansas, which produces dog food. Managers from both companies report that besides the improvement in working climate there was also an increase in productivity and profitability. These two companies are compared in Figure 15-6 on several dimensions, which are contrasted with that of the traditional approach.[21]

FIGURE 15-6    Comparisons of QWL Approaches

| ALCAN, GRANDE BAIE | GENERAL FOODS, TOPEKA | TRADITIONAL |
|---|---|---|
| THE SOCIALIZATION AND RECRUITMENT SYSTEM | | |
| Team meetings held monthly | Team meetings held frequently | Team meetings non-existent |
| Team supervisor hires replacements | Team hires replacements via team committee | Management hires replacements |
| Team members perform a variety of functions | All team members have the opportunity to rotate jobs | Job rotation restricted |
| | Dismissals controlled by team committee | Dismissals controlled by management |
| | Team members learn a variety of jobs and skills | Job, skill enrichment limited to task |

| ALCAN, GRANDE BAIE | GENERAL FOODS, TOPEKA | TRADITIONAL |
|---|---|---|
| THE CONTROL AND REWARD SYSTEM | | |
| Discipline and control provided by first-level management with peer pressure | Discipline and control of team members provided internally by the team | Discipline and control of work force provided by management |
| Team problem solving negates the need for a formal grievance procedure | Team problem solving negates the need for a formal grievance procedure | Formal grievance procedure as set by company policy or union-management contract |
| Universal benefits plan to all employees | | Structured benefits plan based on a role |
| | Higher than average pay rate | Average or less than average pay rate |
| No probation period for new employees | No probation period for new employees | Probation period for new employees |
| | Attendance incentive | No attendance incentive |
| On full year net salary plus long-term disability plan | | Limited sick leave with benefits |
| Workers evaluated by supervisor | Workers evaluated by peers/ team members | Workers evaluated by supervisor or special department |

| ALCAN, GRANDE BAIE | GENERAL FOODS, TOPEKA | TRADITIONAL |
|---|---|---|
| THE VALUE SYSTEM | | |
| Managment expresses trust and confidence in ability of workers | Management is concerned about attitudes, interests, and goals of individuals | Management is concerned primarily with profit |

FIGURE 15-6 (continued) Comparisons of QWL Approaches

| ALCAN, GRANDE BAIE | THE VALUE SYSTEM GENERAL FOODS, TOPEKA | TRADITIONAL |
|---|---|---|
| Status symbols minimized (e.g., parking and common rooms are common areas) | Status symbols minimized (e.g., parking and lunch rooms are common areas) | Status symbols entrenched (e.g., preferred parking, executive only lunch rooms) |
| High worker morale, commitment, self-esteem, etc. | High worker morale, commitment, self-esteem, etc. | Morale, loyalty average or worse |

| ALCAN, GRANDE BAIE | SPECIFIC INDICATORS GENERAL FOODS, TOPEKA | TRADITIONAL |
|---|---|---|
| Absenteeism significantly lower than in traditional management plant | Absenteeism low (2%) | Absenteeism relatively high, 7 to 15% |
| High safety and housekeeping standards | Safety and housekeeping standards (a team responsibility) above industry norms | Safety and housekeeping standards (via specialized departments) average |
| Management-employee relations are cooperative; win-win | Employee relations, labour negotiations cooperative; win-win | Labour negotiations adversarial; win-lose |
| Lower than average employee turnover | Lower than average employee turnover | Average-to-high employee turnover |
| | Demeaning, repetitive, dirty work either shared or eliminated | Demeaning, repetitive work specified by job, not as part of shared function |

| ALCAN, GRANDE BAIE | PRODUCTIVITY, OUTPUT, AND PERFORMANCE GENERAL FOODS, TOPEKA | TRADITIONAL |
|---|---|---|
| Productivity superior to other plants, given innovative technology | Outperforms similar plants on any standard | Productivity average or worse |
| No work stoppages | Strikes nonexistent | Strikes common |
| Individuals are multiskilled | Teams are function-oriented | Individuals are task-oriented |
| | Workers highly motivated | Workers poorly motivated |
| | Quality control unsurpassed in industry | Quality control average and variable |
| | Overhead costs relatively low | Overhead costs relatively high |

Source: M. Chadwick and F. Clark, *Design of a New Plant at CSP Foods,* Labour Canada, cat. #1188-83E, pp. 8-11.

## QUALITY CIRCLES

A *quality circle* is a small group of employees with a common leader that meets regularly to identify and solve the work-related problems.[22] When quality circles started in Japan, they were called "quality control circles," because their primary focus was to improve the poor quality of products manufactured in Japan.

### Origins of Circles

Following World War II, the small island nation of Japan lacked virtually all types of resources except human ones. Japan found that to buy sufficient foodstuffs and raw materials it had to export. But in the 1950s and even the early 1960s, "Made in Japan" meant poor quality to many buyers. Government and business leaders realized that to import raw goods, add value, and export required the production of quality products that the world would buy. With the assistance of such United States experts as Drs. Demming and Juran, the concept of quality control circles was born in Japanese factories in the early 1960s. By the 1980s, most medium and large Japanese manufacturers had quality control circles in place among hourly employees. This effort began as a quality improvement program that has since become part of many Japanese managers' routine procedures and a key part of the QWL effort in many Japanese firms.

In the 1970s Lockheed Corporation and others adopted this approach to QWL and, with a few modifications, began using it in North America. The imported version is simply called "quality circles" or "employee participation groups," although many firms customize the name. For example, Tektronix, Inc. calls them "Tek Circles"; Control Data Corporation calls them "Involvement Teams"; and Union Carbide calls them "Pride Circles," which stands for *P*roductivity through *R*ecognition, *I*nvolvement, and *D*evelopment of *E*mployees.

### Unique Characteristics

Whatever they are called, quality circles (QC) are unique among the many QWL efforts being tried in North American firms. First, membership in the circle is voluntary for both the leader (usually the supervisor) and the members (usually hourly paid workers).[23] Typically, supervisors are given a brief explanation of the QC concept and asked if they want to start a circle. If they do, the supervisor's employees are given a briefing and volunteers are sought. Shortly thereafter training begins.

Second, the creation of quality circles is usually preceded by in-house training. Supervisors typically get two or three days of training. Most of the time is devoted to discussions of small-group dynamics, leadership skills, and indoctrination in the QWL and QC philosophies. About a day of the training is spent on different approaches to problem solving, such as those explained in Figure 15-7. Once the supervisor is trained, his or her employees are usually given one day of intensive training, primarily in the problem-solving techniques shown in Figure 15-7. Part of this training also explains the supervisor's role as the group's discussion leader and the concept of the quality circle.

Third, as is pointed out in the training, the group is permitted to select the problems

## FIGURE 15-7   Quality Circle Decision-Making Tools

**1. Brainstorming.** Brainstorming is a process by which members of the circle provide their ideas on a stated problem during a freewheeling group session. Some circles do request that members present their ideas in turn to ensure that each participates.

**2. Pareto Analysis.** Pareto analysis is a means of gathering data that is provided to employees by staff assistants or is collected by the workers themselves. Often this data describes types or causes of production problems. The data is then arranged in descending order of frequency, usually on a bar chart like the following. The bar chart helps workers to identify the most important causes of problems in order of priority.

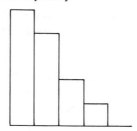

**3. Cause and Effect.** A cause-and-effect, or fishbone, diagram begins with a known effect, such as a defective part. From that effect, members of the circle use brainstorming and their knowledge of the production or service process to identify possible causes, in such standard areas as machines, people, methods, or materials.

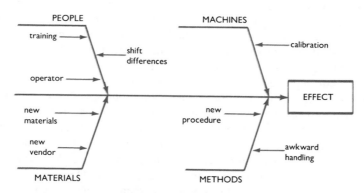

Each "bone," or branch, of the "fishbone" represents a possible cause of the effect under study. Once the group has identified all possible causes through brainstorming, members usually collect data on these causes to determine the source of the problem.

**4. Statistical Tools.** Workers also are taught a variety of statistical concepts to help them objectively determine causes of production problems. Common methods include random sampling, probability sampling, and the ability to compute arithmetical means and variances.

---

it wants to tackle. Management may suggest problems of concern to it, but the group decides which ones to select. Ideally, the selection process is made not by democratic vote but by consensus, in which everyone agrees on the problem to be solved first. (If management has pressing problems to be solved, they can be handled in the same way that problems were resolved before the introduction of quality circles.) The reason for relying on group consensus to select the problem is to allow employees to take on problems of concern and inconvenience to *them*.

> At Solar Turbines International (a Caterpillar Tractor Company subsidiary), employees were frustrated by the lack of power hand tools. They studied the lost production time caused by waiting for tools and showed management how to save more than $30,000 dollars a year by making a $2,200 investment in additional hand tools.

The employees at Solar Turbines did not select this problem to save management money; they did it because of the inconvenience that insufficient tools caused them. The fact that it saved more than a dozen times what it cost to fix is a typical by-product of successful quality circle efforts.

When employees select the problems they want to work on, they are likely to be more motivated to find a solution — and they are more likely to be motivated to remain in the circle and solve problems in the future.

## QC Process

After the training is completed, employees and their supervisor agree on a time and begin meeting, usually once a week for an hour. At the first meeting the supervisor often reviews the ground rules. Circles are intended to tackle problems in that group's area of responsibility. Company pay policies, union contracts, problems in remote departments, and personality issues are usually excluded from consideration. Instead, employees are asked to focus on how they can make their job easier. As a quality circle leader at Control Data Corporation once stated, "If we find ways to make the job easier, we cannot help but improve the QWL and productivity."

Following the discussion of ground rules, the group uses brainstorming to create a list of problems to be solved. Then through discussion, one is selected for further study and research. Data are collected about the problem and analyzed to see if there is a pattern from which causes and effects may be identified. If no pattern exists, the effect under study may be put into a "fishbone" diagram (Figure 15-7) so that additional brainstorming on other possible causes may be uncovered. These possible causes are ranked as to their likelihood by the group and then the most significant ones are researched.

Once a cause has been found for the problem, the group develops a solution. In its training, the group is taught to be able to justify the cost of the solution. For example, at Solar Turbines the workers believed that a $2200 dollar outlay by the company was justified because of the potential to save more than $30,000 in the first year.

At this point the group assembles its research, its proposed solution, and its justification for a presentation to management. This presentation explains to management the problem and the circle's recommended course of action. It also gives the circle members an opportunity for recognition by higher levels of management. Management, of course, reserves the right to accept or reject the recommendation, although more than 80% of a circle's ideas are typically accepted.[24]

Once an idea is presented, the burden falls to management to give the circle a timely authorization to implement the suggestion or an explanation as to why it is rejected. In the meantime, the circle begins the process over again and starts on another problem. This cycle repeats itself until the group solves all the problems it wishes to handle or until the members of the circle decide to disband. Circles usually disband when supervisors act autocratically rather than participatively or when upper levels of management repeatedly and arbitrarily reject circles' recommendations.

## Facilitators and Circle Coordination

Most organizations with multiple circles find that a coordinator or *facilitator* is needed. This person may be a line manager or a human resource specialist. Facilitators need good interpersonal skills — particularly the ability to communicate and train. The first facilitator usually receives five days of specialized training through the International Association of Quality Circles or the American Productivity Centre. These training programs concentrate on teaching the facilitator about quality circles and how to administer a QC effort. Training in teaching and consulting skills is typical too. Likewise, the facilitator also receives considerable training in group dynamics and the ability to coach supervisors. The facilitator reports to the *steering committee*, which includes the top manager and his or her staff. Once circles are operating, the facilitator may serve as a consultant to those supervisors who need additional help with their circles. The facilitator also serves as a link among the circles and others in the company who may have specialized knowledge needed by the circle to solve its problems.

## Costs and Benefits of Quality Circles

Quality circles have few costs to the organization. The primary expenditures are related to training. Included here are the costs of developing the training materials and the training of facilitators, supervisors, and employees. Perhaps the major cost of training is the wages and salaries paid to the trainees while they are being trained. Interestingly, the time spent in the circle meetings is not considered a significant cost because most facilitators and supervisors find that circle members get as much work done in thirty-nine hours as they did in forty hours, before quality circles.

> Solar Turbines International kept detailed track of their start-up costs over the first eighteen months. They included the costs of training materials, facilitator salaries, and the wage costs for employees while they were in training and attending circle meetings. The total amount spent was $79,000. However, during the same time period, documented and fully audited first-year savings from circle suggestions amounted to $90,000. And most of the circle ideas continued to save the company money during the second and subsequent years. After the start-up period, the facilitator estimated in a conversation with one of the authors that the annual savings were $3 for each dollar Solar Turbines spent on its quality circle effort.[25]

The measurable dollar savings from quality circle efforts are probably not the major benefits, however. Companies like Solar, Tektronix, Westinghouse, and others report that circles mean enhanced QWL for employees. Communications between supervisors and employees improve because they develop a less autocratic relationship. Supervisors and employees also learn to think more like executives because they begin to solve problems systematically and to cost-justify their recommendations. Often higher-level managers can spot particularly articulate employees who show promise to be supervisors based on their efforts in the circle group. In fact, some plant managers view it as their primary employee and supervisory development program, aside from solving workplace problems. They see quality circles as an effective way to train supervisors and workers, because circles allow the application of newly learned skills. The result may be a growing cadre of managers and human resource specialists with exceptional ''people skills.''[26]

## Quality Circles in Canada

Since the early 1980s, QCs have been growing in popularity in Canada. According to the Quality Circle Institute of Red Bluff, California, they are now used by more than 300 Canadian companies, such as B.C. Telephone, General Motors of Canada Ltd., Ford Motor Company of Canada Ltd., Northern Telecom Ltd., McCains Food Ltd., and the Toronto-Dominion Bank.[27] The institute predicted that by 1990 close to 1500 companies in Canada would have adopted this management technique. After the Ford Motor Company of Canada implemented QC in its Windsor, Ontario, plant the operating performance rose and employees' attitudes and perceptions of the company improved. Similarly, Vickers Inc., a manufacturer of hydraulic and pneumatic products and systems that employs about 7000 employees, reported annual savings of $250,000 because of the use of QC.[28]

> In the Maritimes, Andre Rousseau, vice-president of production of Maritime Beverages Ltd., Moncton, says QC provides another form of motivation to employees, beyond wages and benefits. Maritime Beverages has 400 workers throughout the Maritimes and is currently spending $50,000 annually to run five QCs at its Dartmouth plant. Employee grievances there have dropped by 75%. ''It's amazing the amount of detailed information that workers on the plant floor have,'' he says.
>
> On many occasions the workers' knowledge has been called on to improve plant efficiency. QC members have progressed from housekeeping and safety projects to more technical ones, such as doing a $15,000 redesign of a production line layout and a $7,000 modification to the ventilation system.[29]

## TEAM-BUILDING VARIATIONS

Quality circles are a very specialized form of *team building*. Some companies have undertaken other approaches to creating cohesive teams among their supervisors and employees. Some of these team approaches are a slight variation on the quality circle approach. The major difference is that the teams may consist of people from different departments, so they are more like a task force. Also, teams may exist only to solve one problem and then disband. Boeing uses a single-focus task force called ''Tiger Teams.'' Generally these teams are assembled to solve some production-delaying problem that the supervisor and employees cannot overcome.

These various forms of team building share a common underlying philosophy: Groups of people are usually better at solving problems than is an individual. And even though the ''purpose'' of these teams is to solve problems, a by-product is improved quality of work life.[30]

## SOCIO-TECHNICAL SYSTEMS

Another approach to QWL efforts are socio-technical systems. *Socio-technical systems* are interventions into the work situation that restructure the work, work groups, and relationship between workers and the technologies they use to do their jobs. More than just enlarging or enriching a job, these approaches may result in more radical changes in the work environment, as an article in *Business Week* points out:

> At a Siemens plant in Karlsruhe, West Germany, workers assembling electronics products used to perform simple tasks over and over, spending less than one minute on each unit as it moved along a belt conveyor. Today many employees work in groups of three to seven at well designed ''work islands,'' where they can avoid boredom by rotating jobs, socializing, and working in cycles of up to twenty minutes rather than a few seconds.[31]

This rearrangement of the social and technical relationships on the job offers workers an opportunity for greater QWL. This ''humanization'' of the workplace seems to be most advanced in West Germany, where the government even funds 50% of selected work restructuring and retraining efforts of private industry.[32]

West Germany also has done considerable work in the area of ergonomics. *Ergonomics* is the study of the biotechnical relationships between the physical attributes of workers and the physical demands of the job, with the object of reducing physical and mental strain in order to increase productivity and QWL. Germans have made considerable strides in reducing the strain of lifting, bending, and reaching through their ergonomic approach to structuring jobs, arranging equipment, and lighting.

Through ergonomics and socio-technical approaches to work, West Germany appears to lead the world in modifying assembly lines and increasing the worker's job cycle to minimize boredom and dissatisfaction. Individual work stations are being used that allow workers to assemble significant subassemblies which may take ten minutes or more. Through buffer stocks of partially completed products, employees are increasingly freed from the tedium of the assembly line.

## CODETERMINATION

One of the first attempts at industrial democracy on a broad scale occurred in West Germany under the name codetermination. *Codetermination* allows workers' representatives to discuss and vote on key management decisions that affect the workers through formal sessions with company management. This form of industrial democracy has since spread through most of free Europe. As a result, decisions to close plants or lay off large numbers of workers meet with far more formal resistance in Europe than in North

America. On the plus side, however, European firms are forced to plan more carefully their human resource needs and seek export markets to offset national economic cycles. Since major Canadian corporations operate in Europe under codetermination, human resource management in multinational corporations is affected. For international human resource experts, codetermination is a consideration in the design of overseas jobs. In North America, the first step towards codetermination may have begun when Chrysler Corporation appointed the president of the United Automobile Workers to its board of directors in the early 1980s.

## AUTONOMOUS WORK GROUPS

A more common, albeit still rare, approach to employee involvement is autonomous work groups. *Autonomous work groups* are teams of workers without a formal, company-appointed supervisor who decide among themselves most matters traditionally handled by a supervisor. These groups of workers typically decide daily work assignments, the use of job rotation, new-employee orientation, training, and production schedules. Some groups even handle recruitment, selection, and discipline. Perhaps the two best known experiments with these approaches are the Gaines Pet Food plant in the United States and Volvo's Kalmar plant in Sweden. These experiments are summarized in Figure 15-8.

FIGURE 15-8   A Summary of Gaines's and Volvo's Experiences with Autonomous Work Groups

### GAINES PET FOOD

At the Gaines Pet Food plant, jobs were radically changed. No longer were workers assigned specific tasks in traditional jobs. Instead, teams of workers were held responsible for a group of tasks that previously constituted several separate jobs. For example, the work group was held responsible for packaging and storing the completed products, instead of each worker having a narrow job that included only a few tasks in the packaging and storing operations. Employees were assigned to a work group, not a job. They were free to participate in the group decision-making processes. Members developed work schedules, interviewed new employees, performed quality control checks, maintained machinery, and performed other diverse activities. The work-group enrichment led to reduced overhead, higher productivity, better product quality, and lower turnover and absenteeism.

### VOLVO'S KALMAR PLANT

Volvo, the Swedish automobile producer, sought to design a more humane car production environment. It built the Kalmar plant around the concept of work teams, rather than the traditional assembly line. Again, workers were assigned to teams, not jobs. Teams built subsystems of the car: doors, cooling systems, engines, and other key components. Buffer stocks of partially completed cars reduced the dependence of one group on another. The physical work environment was made as quiet as the latest technology permitted.

The results of this experiment with autonomous work groups are not clear. Volvo claims higher satisfaction levels among employees because of the design changes, but productivity has remained behind that of other plants for years.

Whether these experiments at Gaines and Volvo herald a radically new approach to the quality of work life is still uncertain. Such innovations do illustrate the need of some employers and employees for more innovative solutions to the trade-off between efficiency and behavioural considerations. More, not less, attention will have to be paid by human resource experts to changing the socio-technical relationship in order to meet changing expectations about jobs. Improving the quality of work life may mean completely redesigning factories and workplaces, as Volvo and Gaines have done, to satisfy environmental and behavioural needs while maintaining efficiency.

In the refund services branch of Air Canada's finance department in Winnipeg, where more than 50,000 refunds were processed monthly, an innovative program involving workers, union, and management resulted in major work changes. Rather than specializing in one task, clerks learned a variety of skills and were formed into work teams with greater autonomy in handling refunds for their region. These changes are in part credited with an increase in job satisfaction and morale and with a 30% increase in job performance.[33]

Steinberg Limited, a grocery store chain that employs more than 25,000 people, with branches in Quebec, Ontario, and New Brunswick, created autonomous and semiautonomous production groups in their frozen-foods distribution centre in Dorval. By involving the employees in the creation and development of a new work environment, significant job improvements materialized. Prior to the change the absentee rate was 15% and the production of the employees involved was similar to that of other employees. However, the quality of working life (QWL) process employed resulted in significant increases in morale, a three-and-a-half-year absence of complaints from the stores receiving distribution-centre deliveries, an absentee rate of 5% (other centres had a 12% rate), and a productivity rate of 35% higher than the old frozen-foods distribution centre.[34]

QWL is more likely to improve as workers demand jobs with more behavioural elements. These demands are likely to emerge from an increasingly educated work force that expects more challenge and autonomy in jobs and more participation in decisions traditionally reserved to management. In Europe codetermination is more than thirty years old and still growing in popularity. And in both Europe and North America, experiments by Gaines, Volvo and other employers indicate that such new arrangements are economically feasible.[35]

If the population of industrial countries continues to grow at the slow rates of the last two decades, the scarcity of new workers entering the labour force will allow workers to be more selective, assuming the recessionary trends of the more recent years are reversed. Then employers may be forced by economic necessity to redesign jobs to achieve a higher quality of work life.[36] Or, as has happened in Europe, government may decree programs to improve the quality of work life.[37] In any event, increased on-the-job autonomy and participation in decision making seem likely during the coming decades.

Human resource departments will play an even more important role in organizations as social expectations increase the pressure for more autonomy. Rotation, enlargement, enrichment, and redesigning of jobs will be priorities. The training of present workers will receive greater attention from human resource departments. To attract scarce employees, human resource departments may have to offer a wide variety of part-time and full-time work schedules from which employees can choose the hours and days they wish to work. Whether these changes mean that any one approach to employee involvement will become more common is uncertain. What seems virtually certain, however, is the growing trend of employees toward participation in decisions affecting them.

## BARRIERS TO QUALITY OF WORK LIFE

As with many human resource department programs, barriers to implementation can undermine the success of any quality of work life program. These barriers are commonly erected by employees, management, or unions. Each of these groups usually fear the effect of unknown change. Even when the process and probable results are explained, the incentives for change may be too few.

To overcome these barriers, the human resource department usually must explain the need for change and the hoped-for results, and give whatever assurance it can. Workers and unions are sometimes suspicious because they may feel that any program to management's advantage is not likely to benefit them. Management often resists the change because it doubts that the benefits of change justify the potential disruption of production or service.

Although there is no certain way to gain the support of every group, most successful attempts at implementing quality of work life require broad participation. Through the participation of key managers, union officials, and affected employees, human resource specialists are more likely to overcome the barriers to new programs.[38] For example, consider how British Columbia Forest Products Ltd., MacKenzie Sawmill Division, was able to implement a program.[39]

Faced with an annual turnover rate of 200%, the company and the unions involved at MacKenzie collaborated with a research team to investigate the labour turnover problems. After a three-month pilot study that was coordinated by a joint steering committee comprising management, union, and research representatives, it was decided to begin an extensive change program in one of the company's three sawmills, "C" mill.

The "C" mill manager hoped that increased worker participation would lead to improvements in safety, quality, cost control, and production, but he also expressed his conviction that "working in the sawmill should not be like a jail sentence that we endure in order to live . . . [it] should be something that we enjoy doing and get some satisfaction or feeling of accomplishment from."

To implement the program, it was necessary to obtain the cooperation and support of the various organizational and individual units involved. After the management, union, and research people involved had reached agreement on the project, an unprecedented general meeting of all the plant's employees was called by the plant manager, and the sawmill was shut down. The mill manager described the project and explained that its intent was to involve the work force in the diagnosis and solution of work problems in the mill. However, some workers wondered whether they even wanted to be involved in such a program, and initially they all felt some degree of bewilderment and suspicion, because this approach to solving problems was quite alien to the company's previous practices.

During the next few weeks, numerous meetings were held with the various shifts of workers and foremen within the departments. It was agreed that the program should start in the most crucial part of the mill, the log infeed area, where the tree logs were transformed into rough lumber.

For each shift, decision-making groups were formed (largely comprising workers), which identified problems, did research, and made decisions related to production and other work-related projects. It was decided that if these groups could not reach a consensus on how a problem should be solved, the decision would be postponed or delayed.

The types of decisions reached encompassed all areas of the production operation; they involved technological work procedures, organizational role, and structure changes. Six months after the initiated activities in the infeed area, the QWL project was extended to another part of the plant, the planer mill.

The results achieved by a more participative and involved form of decision-making were significant. Production rose from 350,000 units of lumber per day to more than 410,000. There were no recorded accidents during this same period. The absentee rate in "C" mill fell by more than 50% and turnover was reduced to less than 30%. In the planer mill production efficiency rose from 50 to 70%. Absenteeism dropped from two per shift to one person every two shifts. As is evident, these represent significant improvements in morale and job satisfaction.

## QUALITY OF WORK LIFE IN PERSPECTIVE

The quality of work life represents another layer of challenges to human resource management. Proactive human resource departments must find better ways to achieve QWL. Otherwise, the purpose of human resource management remains only partially fulfilled at best. But as important as the challenge of improving the quality of work life is, it represents only one in a long line of challenges facing human resource departments.

These other challenges must be met if human resource management is to contribute to the organization's success. Although the quality of work life is important, human resource experts cannot disregard the challenges of fulfilling the purpose, objectives, and activities assigned to the human resource department. Nor can the environmental and equal-employment challenges be overlooked in designing jobs for maximum efficiency. All these challenges must be met simultaneously. The rest of this book explains how proactive human resource departments meet these challenges through a blend of traditional and innovative activities to achieve a high-quality work life through productive and satisfying jobs.

## SUMMARY

Jobs are the link between organizations and their human resources. The combined accomplishment of all jobs allows the organization to meet its objectives. Similarly, jobs represent not only a source of income to workers but also a means of fulfilling their needs. However, for the organization and its employees to receive these mutual benefits, jobs must provide a high quality of work life.

To achieve a high quality of work life requires jobs that are well designed. Effective job design seeks a trade-off between efficiency and behavioural elements. Efficiency elements stress productivity; behavioural elements stress employee needs. The role of human resource specialists is to achieve a balance between these trade-offs. When jobs are underspecialized, job designers may simplify the job by reducing the number of tasks. If jobs are overspecialized, they must be expanded or enriched.

Quality of work life efforts are systematic attempts by organizations to give workers a greater opportunity to take part in decisions that affect the way they do their job and the contribution they make to their organization's overall effectiveness. They are not a substitute for good, sound human resource practices and policies. However, effective QWL efforts can supplement other human resource actions and provide improved employee motivation, satisfaction, and productivity. QWL is most commonly improved through employee involvement. Whether that involvement is in solving workplace problems or participating in the design of jobs, employees want to know that their contribution makes a difference.

Many approaches to QWL exist. Aside from job design, one of the most popular is an import from Japan, quality circles. A quality circle is a small group of employees from the same work area who meet regularly with their supervisor to identify and solve workplace problems. Quality circles afford workers a chance to make a meaningful contribution by participating in decisions that affect them. Other forms of team building are similar to quality circles, although different groupings or objectives might be sought. Socio-technical systems seek to change the human and technical relationship that exists in the workplace. Typically, employees are involved in making these changes. Codetermination involves giving workers a formal voice in management decisions. Although common in Europe, it is almost nonexistent in Canada. Autonomous work groups also are uncommon, but have been more widely found in Canada than has codetermination. These groups consist of employees who collectively assume the supervisor's role for deciding work schedules, job assignments, and other duties typically reserved for first-level supervisors.

Management support and a long-term perspective are essential to any successful QWL effort. Unless the barrier of management support is overcome, even short-term success is unlikely.

## TERMS FOR REVIEW

| | |
|---|---|
| Quality of work life (QWL) | Job enlargement |
| Specialization | Job enrichment |
| Job cycle | Quality circles (QC) |
| Autonomy | Brainstorming |
| Task identity | Pareto diagrams |
| Work simplification | Cause-and-effect diagrams |
| Job rotation | Facilitators |

Steering committee
Team building
Socio-technical systems

Ergonomics
Codetermination
Autonomous work groups

## REVIEW AND DISCUSSION QUESTIONS

1. What role do human resource specialists play in ensuring a high quality of work life?

2. What are the major challenges of job design?

3. In their attempts to use autonomous work groups, Volvo and Gaines Pet Food had different outcomes with regard to productivity. Since Swedish workers are highly educated and enjoy a standard of living at least equal to that of workers in Canada and the United States, what other differences might account for these different outcomes?

4. What problems would you expect to arise in an organization that had carefully designed its jobs for maximum efficiency without careful consideration of each employee's individual priority of needs?

5. What were the contributions of scientific management to the design of jobs? What are the advantages of highly specialized jobs?

6. Suppose you have been assigned to design the job of ticket clerk for Air Canada.

   (a) Would you recommend highly specialized job designs to minimize training or very broad jobs with all clerks cross-trained to handle multiple tasks? Why?

   (b) Would you change your answer if you knew that employees tend to quit the job of ticket clerk within the first six months? Why or why not?

7. Assume that you were told to evaluate a group of jobs in a boat-building business. After studying each job for a considerable amount of time, you identified the following activities associated with each job. What job redesign techniques would you recommend for these jobs, if any?

   (a) *Sailmaker.* Cuts and sews material with very little variety in the type of work from day to day. Job is highly skilled and takes years to learn.

   (b) *Sander.* Sands rough wood and fibreglass edges almost continuously. Little skill is required in this job.

   (c) *Sales representative.* Talks with customers, answers phone inquiries, suggests customized additions to special-order boats.

   (d) *Boat preparer.* Cleans up completed boats, waxes fittings, and generally makes the boat ready for customer delivery. Few skills are required for this job.

8. Suppose you are a plant or division manager and you want to create a high QWL environment. Why could you not simply order it done and expect a high QWL environment almost immediately?

9. Explain where quality circles started and what makes them unique compared to other QWL efforts. What is management's responsibility after a quality circle group makes its presentation to management?

## INCIDENT 15-1

### Job Design at Marketing Newsletters, Inc.

Marketing Newsletters, Inc. is a small Montreal company that produces several different types of newsletters. These are sold to companies and individual salespeople. Although each series of letters has a different market, they all provide readers with useful tips on how to be more effective at selling.

Pierre Martel, president of Marketing Newsletters, discovered he could sell these letters by carefully tailoring them to the concerns of different types of specialized salespeople. For example, one letter was directed at new-car salespeople. Another was directed at sellers of industrial supplies. Although the sales of each letter were modest, Pierre succeeded in developing a new newsletter market about every three months.

In Pierre's firm there were two developmental editors, two copy editors, and two marketing editors. The developmental editors sought out likely authors to write and develop newsletters. The copy editors were responsible for editing each newsletter before it was printed and mailed. The marketing editors were responsible for advertising and for building the circulation of each newsletter.

Whenever a newsletter did not meet its sales goal, the marketing editors blamed the copy editors for not producing a quality product. In turn, the copy editors would complain that they could only improve so much on the quality of the contributions, and they blamed the developmental editors for not finding better writers.

Suppose Pierre asked you to help him solve the problem of identifying responsibility for the success or failure of each newsletter.

1.  What suggestions would you make to Pierre about the way editors' jobs are designed?
2.  If each editor were made responsible for developing, editing, and selling selected newsletters, what advantages would result for the firm? For the editors?
3.  If each editor were completely responsible for several newsletters, what kinds of favourable trade-offs might be encountered in the newly designed jobs?

## INCIDENT 15-2

### Cooperation, QWL, and Space

Psychologists Joseph Brady and Henry Emurian at Johns Hopkins Hospital have been doing research to learn how to increase productivity and reduce friction on future space missions. Under research grants from NASA, they are "studying the psychological and physiological effects of prolonged confinement on two- and three-person 'microsocieties.' Their goal is to develop behavioural guidelines for the most productive individual and group performance, with the least social friction, on future space and underwater missions."*

*For a more detailed explanation of this study, see Berkeley Rice, "Space-Lab Encounters," Psychology Today, June 1983, pp. 50-58.

Their studies have revealed the not-too-surprising conclusion that rewards and incentives are better motivators than sanctions and controls, and that cooperation leads to greater individual performance and greater satisfaction within the group.

1. Assume for the sake of this incident that these findings are applicable to larger societies called organizations. What implications do you see in these studies for improving QWL in organizations?
2. If you were a supervisor with six employees working for you, how could these findings make your quality circle group become more effective? Suggest specific actions you would implement to improve the effectiveness of the quality circle based on this brief research summary.

## EXERCISE 15-1

### A Good Work Environment

Think of some work-related situation that you have found enjoyable. Think of the job and identify the features that made it more enjoyable than other jobs you have held. The job need not have been a formal, full-time job. It may simply have been some temporary job or even some chore you have had to perform. Make a list of those characteristics of the job that made it so enjoyable.

1. In reviewing your answers with others, do you find any similarities between your list and the lists of others who did different jobs?
2. Do these characteristics indicate what job features provide a good work situation?

○ ○ ○ ○ ○ ○ ○ ○ ○ ○ ○ ○ ○ ○ ○ ○ ○ ○ ○ ○ ○ ○ ○ ○ ○ ○ ○ ○ ○ ○ ○ ○ ○ ○ ○

## CASE STUDY

### THE ALTA GAS PLANT

Utilizing a socio-technical system design, Alta Gas Plant near Calgary composed production teams so as to minimize turnover, improve the quality of production, maximize flexibility by having workers trained on various tasks, and reduce shutdown times by regularizing plant maintenance.

Under this new design, operation of the plant during a shift is handled by a five-member production team consisting of a coordinator and four technicians. Each technician rotates throughout the various jobs and qualifies by

examination for increasing salary levels. The team is centred in the control room and laboratory, and when their assignments scatter them throughout the plant, they maintain contact with portable radios. As the senior member of the team, the coordinator is not a supervisor in the usual sense. He rotates assignments with other members but maintains an overview of the plant's operations and serves as a linking pin between the team and upper levels.

Team members not only operate the plant

# CHAPTER 16 ○○○○○○○

## EMPLOYEE RELATIONS PRACTICES

*... organizational psychologists have had to contend with the fact that happiness and productivity may not necessarily go together.*
BARRY M. STAW[1]

*Although managers are not expected to be able to solve all employee problems, they should concern themselves with correcting poor job performance by helping employees work through their own problems.*
VICKI PAWLIK AND BRIAN H. KLEINER[2]

○ ○ ○ ○ ○ ○ ○ ○ ○ ○ ○ ○ ○ ○ ○ ○ ○ ○ ○ ○ ○ ○ ○ ○ ○ ○ ○ ○ ○ ○

## CHAPTER OBJECTIVES

After studying this chapter, you should be able to:
1. **Discuss** the common forms of downward communication used by human resource departments.
2. **Explain** different approaches to improving upward communication.
3. **Define** employee counselling and the major types of counselling.
4. **Describe** differences between directive and nondirective counselling.
5. **Explain** how progressive discipline works.
6. **Discuss** differences between preventive and corrective discipline.

○ ○ ○ ○ ○ ○ ○ ○ ○ ○ ○ ○ ○ ○ ○ ○ ○ ○ ○ ○ ○ ○ ○ ○ ○ ○ ○ ○ ○ ○

*In* many ways, this entire book has been about employee relations. How well the human resource department handles resource planning, staffing, placement, development, evaluation, compensation, and quality of work life largely determines the state of employee relations. A mistake in any one of these areas can harm the employee-employer relationship. However, even when these activities are performed properly, solid employee relations demand careful attention to organizational communications, employee counselling, and discipline.

The IBM corporation is one of the world's premier organizations. It is the leading producer of computers and microelectronic devices. In fact, IBM has been so dominant in its field that it is known in the industry as "Snow White and the Seven Dwarfs," which is a reference to IBM's former dress rule of white shirts and its relationship to its competitors. Technology and market dominance aside, IBM also excels in the management of its human resources.

Long ago top management at IBM realized that the company's future success rested with the people who developed its technology and sold its products. One example of IBM's commitment to its workers is a 1940s policy against putting full-time permanent employees on layoff. That policy has remained in effect since then. Another example comes from its view of human resources as found in an IBM training program: "The success of the IBM company is related directly to the ability and skill of its employees. Improvement of this ability and skill is a major objective of the company and the responsibility for bringing it about is shared by each member of management. This steady self-employment of employees is as important to the IBM organization as would be a technological breakthrough or the creation of a new product."

The management at IBM recognizes that the treatment of human resources must be approached from a systems viewpoint. Human resource activities, such as appraisal or training, lose their effectiveness if they occur in isolation and are not related to other aspects of employee development. To tie the various employee development activities together and to facilitate motivation and satisfaction, IBM relies heavily on communication. Some of its approaches to employee communication include extensive career planning information and assistance, attitude surveys, suggestion systems, open-door policies, daily newspapers at some sites, and near-daily bulletins on educational opportunities and promotions.

Beyond these formal methods, human resource specialists and line managers informally communicate with employees. This "management by walking around" is known at IBM as "trolling for open doors." IBM has an open-door policy whereby employees are free to walk into any manager's office with their problems. However, IBM management realizes that most workers are reluctant to take a problem to their boss's boss. Therefore, human resource specialists and line managers leave their offices and go out among the employees to learn what problems exist. As one IBM executive explained, "The only open-door policy that works is one where the manager gets up from the desk and goes through the door to talk to employees."

IBM's employee relations practices go beyond its extensive communications efforts. "Open doors," for example, allow employees to address their problems to higher levels of management, even executives. This "open" approach to communications demands that managers have skills in counselling and disciplining employees. Counselling skills are needed to draw out employee concerns before they become full-blown problems, requiring assistance from others. And, when an employee performs improperly, effective disciplinary tools are necessary to resolve the problem while maintaining the employee's commitment to high levels of performance.

Employee relations is a complex blend of corporate culture, human resource practices, and individual perceptions. Virtually everything the human resource department does affects employee relations directly or indirectly. But many human resource activities are largely unnoticed by employees, including, for example, recruitment, selection, orientation, benefits administration, and other important human resource functions. Other activities affect employees only periodically, as the performance and salary review sessions take place. But employee communications, counselling, and discipline are day-to-day activities shared by supervisors and human resource specialists.

This dual responsibility for the day-to-day activities of employee relations reflects the growing complexity of organizations, laws, and union-management relations. Earlier in this century, supervisors were solely responsible for employee relations practices. Today, under a need for uniform and proper approach to employees, many companies give human resource specialists considerable responsibility for organizationwide employee relations. Of course, the supervisor remains responsible for the communications within the work group, especially for task-related requirements. Supervisors are also responsible for counselling and disciplining their employees. When serious problems are uncovered in counselling or a major disciplinary action is planned, human resource specialists are commonly involved to ensure fairness and uniformity of treatment.

The dual responsibility and day-to-day impact of employee communications, counselling, and discipline merit special attention from human resource specialists and those who supervise others. This chapter examines each of these employee relations tools, beginning with communications.

## EMPLOYEE COMMUNICATIONS

Information is the engine that drives organizations.[3] Information about the organization, its environment, its products and services, and its people is essential to management and workers. Without information, managers cannot make effective decisions about markets or resources, particularly human resources. Likewise, insufficient information may cause stress and dissatisfaction among workers. This universal need for information is met through an organization's communication system. *Communication systems* provide formal and informal methods to move information through an organization so that appropriate decisions can be made. This section discusses the human resource department's role in managing the human resource communication system. Our focus is on organizationwide communication efforts, rather than on the primarily one-to-one communications of employee counselling and discipline discussed later in the chapter.

All organizations have human resource communication systems. In small or unsophisticated firms, communications may be informal and subject to infrequent management intervention. In large multi-billion-dollar enterprises, specialists may serve as employee communications directors. Most organizations use a blend of formal, systematically designed communications efforts and informal *ad hoc* arrangements. For convenience, most of these approaches can be divided into downward communication systems, which exist to get information *to* employees, and upward communication systems, which exist to get information *from* employees.

### Downward Communication Systems

Human resource departments operate large communication systems to keep people informed. They try to facilitate an open, two-way flow of information, although most messages are of the top-down variety. *Downward communication* is information that begins at some point in the organization and proceeds down the organization hierarchy to inform or influence others. Top-down methods are necessary for decision makers to have their decisions carried out. These communications also help give employees knowledge about the organization and feedback on how their efforts are perceived. In fact, a nationwide survey revealed that 42% of the people thought that "more and better information from management about decisions that affect employees" would improve productivity.[4] Likewise, a survey of 48,000 employees by the Opinion Research Corporation concluded: "Downward communication, measured by employees' ratings of their companies on letting them know what is going on, is rated favourably by fewer than half of employees in all groups."[5]

Organizations use a variety of downward communications. The reason for this diversity is that multiple channels are more likely to overcome barriers and reach the intended receivers. Some common examples of downward communication approaches include house organs, information booklets, employee bulletins, television films, jobholder reports, and meetings.

## House Organs

Many organizations publish company magazines, newspapers, or bulletins for employees. These publications are also called *house organs*. Their purpose is to inform employees about current developments and to build long-run understanding about company activities and goals.[6] Large organizations are able to publish well-designed magazines and/or newspapers, while small organizations may have only a weekly human resource information bulletin. Employees are encouraged to take employee magazines and newspapers home so that family members also may develop a better understanding of the organization. Frequently there are articles about company bowling teams, discount theatre tickets, and hobbies of employees that are designed to appeal to family members as well as employees.

Saint Mary's University in Halifax publishes a monthly paper called *The Times*, where details of the activities of the university faculty, staff, and students, as well as regional and national educational trends are recorded. For instance, details of faculty research, publications, and community involvements, staff and student activities, and information about government announcements are listed in each issue, thus enabling every member of the university and its alumni to know what is going on in and around the university. This is supplemented by other student newspapers, general circulars, bulletin board announcements, etc., all aiming to increase organizational communication.

Editors of in-house magazines and newspapers occasionally make readership surveys to determine what parts of their publication are being read and what additional information readers desire. In this way they can improve content, readability, and other features for better communication. Samples of questions asked on readership survey are as follows:

- What sections do you read regularly? (A list with check-boxes follows.)
- What articles did you read in the July issue? (A list of the articles, with check-boxes, follows.)

- What article in the July issue did you like most?
- What additional subjects would you like information about?

## Information Booklets

Human resource departments often distribute information booklets on various subjects to their employees. A well-known booklet is the employee handbook given to new employees to inform them about regulations and benefits. Other booklets are distributed on specialized subjects relating to human resource work, such as suggestion programs, wage incentives, retirement, and fringe benefits. When benefits such as life and medical insurance are purchased through an insurance company, that firm usually supplies the booklets. The following are examples of information booklets distributed by human resource departments:

- *How to Read Your Future* (the retirement program)
- *You've Got Something There* (the suggestion program)
- *Steps to Security* (programs for employee security)
- *The Employee Supplemental Health Insurance Plan*

## Employee Bulletins

Human resource departments publish a number of bulletins that concern their day-to-day operations. Usually these are placed on employee bulletin boards and copies are sent to each manager. For example, job openings are announced so that all employees have an equal opportunity for them. Holidays are announced, along with the regulations that govern payment and absences before and after holidays. Announcements are made about awards, retirements, and similar events. As a service activity it is the human resource function's responsibility to keep employees informed about all events relevant to their employment.

## Pre-recorded Messages

Since the public is conditioned to watching television sets, some organizations tape their own television programs for later replay to employees. These programs are viewed on television screens in company lunchrooms and other locations. Large firms with branch operations especially use this approach to keep their branch employees informed about corporate developments or assist with training. Other firms prepare information films for the same kind of use. As was noted by one manager:

> The importance of video as a means of communication has been recognized by a number of organizations in Canada . . . on the employee communications side such networks are used for training, induction, orientation, explaining salary and benefit plans and so on. . . . [7]

Some organizations use recorded telephone messages to present the latest information. Employees can dial a certain number from any telephone, and a recorded message is played to them. In a typical program the message takes one minute, and a new one is prepared daily.

## Jobholder Reports and Meetings

A few organizations give *jobholder reports* to employees.[8] These are reports to employees about a firm's economic performance. The reasoning is that company economic information is just as important to employees as it is to shareholders, and so the firm should report this information. The report is presented in the same style as the annual report, except that the jobholder report shows how the annual economic results affect jobholders.

> Some organizations follow the jobholder reports with jobholder meetings that are organized and conducted in the same way as shareholder meetings. Top management attends the meetings, and all employees are invited. Management presents its reports, and employees are invited to question management and make proposals in the same way that owners do in stockholder meetings. These meetings improve communication and give jobholders a stronger feeling of belonging.

## Upward Communications Systems

Perhaps no area of communications is more in need of improvement in most organizations than upward communications. *Upward communications* consists of information initiated by people who seek to inform or influence those higher up in the organization's hierarchy. The cornerstone of all such messages is the employee and the supervisor.[9] When a free flow of information travels between an employee and the supervisor, informal day-to-day communications are often sufficient for most situations. When open communications do not exist, or exist only for a limited range of issues, other tactics are needed. For example, an employee may have a good, open relationship with the supervisor about job-related matters such as supplies, work performance, quality of outputs and the like. However, that same employee may not be able to discuss interpersonal issues such as peer relations, relations between the employee and his or her supervisor, or issues pertaining to the conditions and the leadership style of the supervisor. A discussion follows of several programs and processes that facilitate upward communication.

How do organizations create open, upward communications? No universal formula exists. Each organization's human resource department must take an approach that is contingent upon the situation. However, one common element in most organizations is a genuine concern for employee well-being combined with meaningful opportunities for ideas to flow up the organization's hierarchy. Some of the more common upward communication channels include the grapevine, in-house complaint procedures, rap sessions, suggestions systems, and attitude survey feedback.

## Living with the Grapevine

There are two types of communication systems in an organization: the formal system and the informal one. The latter is usually called the "grapevine." A formal communication system is the one established by the organization for the official conduct of its activities. Examples of formal communications are job instructions, surveys, reports, and bulletins. *Grapevine communication* is an informal system that arises spontaneously from the social interaction of people in the organization.[10] It is the people-to-people system that arises naturally from human desires to make friends and share ideas. When two employees chat at the water cooler about their trouble with a supervisor, that is a grapevine communication.

The human resource department has a major interest in the grapevine for several reasons:

- The grapevine affects motivation and job satisfaction.
- The grapevine reflects breakdowns in communication.
- The grapevine provides valuable feedback of staff information.
- Supervisors tend to have poor understanding of the grapevine, and training is a human resource activity to improve understanding.

## Grapevine Patterns

Management did not establish the grapevine and cannot control it. This means that the grapevine can fly across chains of command or between departments as quickly as a telephone call or a chance meeting in the hallway. It is impossible to control these freewheeling communications. Even if control were possible, it is not desirable, because grapevines help satisfy social needs. Whenever normal people are together, they are going to share their ideas. All that management can do is learn to live with the grapevine. Management perhaps can influence it, but control is impossible.

Figure 16-1 shows how a grapevine moves easily across chains of command in an organization. It also can bypass levels of authority and even move to and from the community as it runs its course. Employee J originated the communication, which was interesting gossip about the love affair of employee H. The grapevine network then developed as follows:

J told I at the same organizational level.
I told L, a subordinate.
L told his wife, who did not work for the organization.
The wife told a friend, E, who was two levels higher than her husband.
E told C, an associate.
C told K two levels lower.

It is evident that the people involved in this grapevine could ignore chains of command, because they were communicating on the basis of their interests and friendships, not the organization structure.

## Grapevine Feedback from Employees

The grapevine provides a large amount of useful off-the-record feedback from employees. There are many opportunities for feedback, because human resource specialists are in regular contact with employees as they discuss fringe benefits, counsel employees, and perform other functions. Employees feel somewhat free to talk with human resource specialists, because the occupation of human resource management is oriented towards human needs and resources. In addition, employees feel safe to express their feelings, because human resource specialists do not directly supervise employees in other departments. The result is a large amount of useful input, provided the human resource department is prepared to listen, understand, and interpret the information. Some of the types

FIGURE 16-1   A Grapevine Network Compared with a Chain of Command

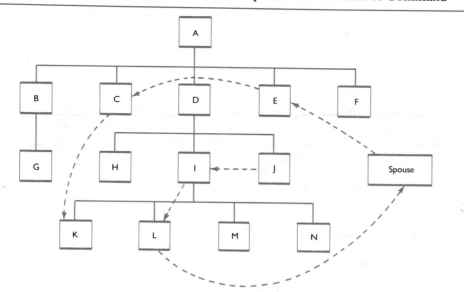

FIGURE 16-2   Types of Grapevine Feedback to the Human Resource Department

- Information about the problems and anxieties that employees have.
- Incorrect feedback that is evidence of breakdowns in communication.
- Insights into goals and motivations of employees.
- Identification of job problems that have high emotional content, because intense feelings encourage grapevine communication.
- Information about the quality of labour relations, including grievance settlements.
- Information about the quality of supervision. Complaints about supervision are often brought informally to the attention of human resource specialists with the hope that they will do something.
- Information about area of job dissatisfaction.
- Feedback about acceptance of new policies and procedures.

of grapevine feedback that come to the human resource department are shown in Figure 16-2.

If the human resource department shows that it is responsive and can handle off-the-record information in confidence without putting the communicator in jeopardy, then open communication is further encouraged. There are risks in this kind of communication, because supervisors may feel threatened by disclosures about their departments, but usually the benefits of more complete information are greater than the disadvantages.

A further point is that even when human resource specialists know that a grapevine input is incorrect, they should still listen, because the input may be helpful. Incorrect inputs tell management that there are communication breakdowns that need to be remedied. A useful guide to follow is: Always listen to the grapevine; it may be trying to tell you something.

## In-House Complaint Procedures

How does an employee solve a complaint if the supervisor is not receptive? In some organizations, the employee has no other option except to talk with the supervisor's superior. Although that may seem reasonable, most people in organizations are very reluctant to do that because they do not want to create negative feelings between themselves and their supervisor. To lessen the burden of "going over the boss's head" some organizations have installed in-house complaint procedures.

*In-house complaint procedures* are formal methods through which an employee can register a complaint. Normally these procedures are operated by the human resource department and require the employee to submit the complaint in writing. Then an employee relations specialist investigates the complaint and advises its author of the results. In some companies, the employee's name is known only by the employee relations investigator. However, if a supervisor is questioned about the issue, it is sometimes obvious who filed the complaint—so the person's anonymity is lost.

> IBM's program is called "Speak Up!" It is a confidential form designed as a pre-paid envelope. On the inside the employee completes a home address section and then writes up the complaint, opinion, or question. When the "Speak Up!" administrator receives the item, the name and address section are removed and the issue investigated. Once an answer is found, it is mailed to the employee's home address. No one but the "Speak Up!" administrator knows who submitted the form. If the employee does not provide a name and address, the issue and the response may be printed in the company newspaper. If the employee is not satisfied with the answer, an interview with an executive from corporate headquarters will be arranged, regardless of where the employee's job site is located.

Managers at IBM "troll for open doors" to avoid "Speak Ups!" that cause an executive to visit a disgruntled employee. If that employee is dissatisfied with some improper management action and talks with an executive about it, that manager's career with IBM may be affected adversely. What makes IBM's complaint procedure and open communications so effective is that IBM executives support the program with their actions; they are willing to get on an airplane and fly to a meeting with a dissatisfied employee. That level of commitment from top managers causes lower-level managers to pay close attention to employee communications. An *open-door policy* exists when employees are encouraged to come to their manager or even to higher management with any matter that concerns them. Probably the most effective open door is one that managers walk through to get out among their people. In this way they can learn more than they ever would sitting in their offices.

> The director of a large hospital reversed the usual "open door" by walking through all departments nearly every day. In this way he saw people he would not otherwise see, and he was able to observe operations directly. Over a period of time he developed personal contacts with many employees at different levels of the hospital. He discussed matters of interest with them and learned much more about his organization than if he had remained in his office. The result was low employee turn-

over and strong feelings of teamwork to accomplish the hospital's goals of quality medical care and personal concern for people.

## Rap Sessions

Closely related to in-house complaint procedures are rap sessions. *Rap sessions* are meetings between managers and groups of employees to discuss complaints, suggestions, opinions, or questions. These meetings may begin with some information sharing by management to tell the group about developments in the company. However, the primary purpose of these meetings is to encourage upward communications, often with several levels of employees and lower level management in attendance at the same time. When these meetings are face-to-face, informal discussions between a higher manager and rank-and-file workers, the process is called *deep-sensing* because it attempts to probe in some depth the issues that are on the minds of employees.[11] These meetings also are called *vertical staffing meetings,* because they put higher managers directly in touch with employees.[12] Attendance at rap sessions varies according to how the meetings are planned. In small facilities, it may be possible to get all the employees together annually or semiannually. In other large units different formats may be needed.

> One plant manager runs a "birthday club." All employees who have a birthday during the month meet with the manager and the human resource manager to have coffee and birthday cake. The occasion is used to discuss what changes these people think are needed.

Consider another example:

> One major bank's Open Meeting Program arranges meetings of about a dozen employees at a time. Meetings are held with different groups until at least one in five employees from each department attends. Employees are selected randomly and may decline to participate if they wish. A human resource specialist coordinates each meeting and develops the group report on a newsprint sheet in open discussions with the group. No employee names are used on the report, which becomes the basis of action plans with management. The program is repeated annually, and it has materially improved upward communication.

Two common problems often arise from these meetings. First, the top manager must be careful not to undermine other managers by countermanding orders without all the facts. Sometimes employees present a compelling case that does not contain all the facts. If the top manager reacts too quickly, a bad decision may result. Second, initial meetings tend to focus on employee complaints, such as pay, working conditions, fringe benefits, and the like. Many managers and human resource specialists become discouraged with the lack of constructive ideas and sometimes abandon these approaches too quickly. Human resource departments that have responded to employee complaints promptly and continued the rap sessions into a second year often find that complaints become constructive suggestions for improvement in operations policies and practices. Sometimes, constructive suggestions emerge in the early meetings, as the president of a major hotel chain discovered:

In an eight-month period, he held a dozen meetings with the hotel employees. Sometimes he heard serious problems that required immediate attention. More often he heard seemingly trivial complaints — but they concerned matters that can make day-to-day life miserable. "Every time I had one of these meetings, I realized that it's the little things that most often affect morale. . . . This is a way to make the employee feel like we care."

## Employee Letters and Question-Answer Programs

Some firms encourage employee letters, questions, and complaints, which are processed anonymously by a human resource specialist. The human resource specialist works with the appropriate manager to secure a reply that is prepared and signed by the manager. If a reply is of general interest, it may be published in the company newspaper or in a bulletin. All replies are routed back through the human resource specialist to the person who originally asked the question.

The R.S.V.P program of the Royal Bank of Canada encourages employee questions on special forms that are available throughout the bank. All letters are retyped in order to keep the employee's name confidential. A human resource specialist then discusses the retyped letter with those who can resolve the matter. The specialist has access to all management, including the president, and so full support for the program is assured. About 800 letters a year are received.

Instead of using letters, another company uses a telephone number that employees can call to leave their comments on a tape. The message is transcribed and processed by the vice president of industrial relations in a manner similar to that of the Royal Bank of Canada.

## Suggestion Systems

Suggestion systems are a formal method for generating, evaluating, and implementing employee ideas. If only one of these three elements — generating, evaluating, or implementing—is missing, the suggestion plan fails. All three are crucial to a successful suggestion system.

Figure 16-3 shows the key steps in successful suggestion systems. It begins with the employee's idea and a discussion with the supervisor. Once the suggestion form is completed, the supervisor reviews and signs the form, indicating awareness of the suggestion but not necessarily approval. The suggestion system office or committee receives the idea and acknowledges it to the employee through company mail. The idea is then evaluated and the decision is communicated to the employee. If it is a good idea, implementation follows with the employee receiving recognition and usually some award.[13] (Typically, awards are equal to 10% of the first year's savings.) The savings from the idea accrue to the organization.

Success is likely if management provides prompt and fair evaluations, supervisors are trained to encourage employee suggestions, and top management actively supports the program. Unfortunately, this source of upward communications is not very effective in many companies because evaluations often take months or supervisors see suggestions

FIGURE 16-3   Suggestion System Steps

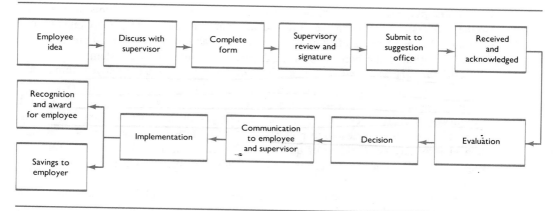

as more work for them with few personal benefits. As a result, many company suggestion plans exist on paper, but are not very effective.[14]

Although most suggestion systems pay employees a percentage of the first year savings, some companies pay a flat dollar amount in order to minimize the need for precision in evaluating the suggestion's exact dollar savings. This approach means that employees receive feedback about their suggestions much faster.

In a large, multinational electronics corporation, the supervisors' performances are evaluated in part by the effectiveness of the suggestion system among their employees. Obviously, this approach causes supervisors to encourage employee suggestions. Another organization gives $25 to the supervisors for each employee suggestion that has been found viable.

An airline company went a step further in encouraging employee feedback:

The company gave its supervisors the authority to make "quick look" awards. Supervisors were authorized to issue cheques for $10 immediately on receiving an idea that seemed useful. If the formal evaluation procedure rejected the idea, the employee could still keep the $10. This procedure facilitated quick feedback to the employees and encouraged them to generate good ideas.

Not all organizations have suggestion programs, because problems can develop unless they are administered carefully. Some employees feel that their award is not enough, and others resent the fact that their suggestion is not accepted. Other employees may object to a suggestion because it changes their jobs. They show their feelings by retaliation against the suggestor, who is discouraged from offering further ideas. In spite of the problems, suggestion programs offer an opportunity for management to explain job improvement needs to employees and for them to offer ideas to management. This exchange of ideas builds two-way communication, improves the organization's productivity, and can further the quality of work life for employees.[15]

### Attitude Survey Feedback

What do employees think about the organization? Do they have problems or concerns? Do they understand the human resource department's fringe benefit plan? Compensation program? Career planning efforts? Answers to these and many other questions can make a useful addition to the human resource department's information system.[16]

*Attitude surveys* are systematic methods of determining what employees think about their organization. These surveys may be conducted through face-to-face interviews, but usually are done through questionnaires that employees complete anonymously. An attitude survey typically seeks to learn what employees think about working conditions, supervision, and human resource policies. New programs or special concerns to management also may be a source of questions. The resulting information can be used to evaluate specific concerns, such as how individual managers are perceived by their employees.

Attitude surveys can be a frustrating experience for employees if they do not see any results. It is only natural that people would like to know what the survey questionnaire uncovered. Otherwise the survey has little meaning to them, especially if it is readministered in the future. Therefore, a summary of upward communication should be provided to employees for their reaction. When this feedback loop is closed, the overall process is called *attitude survey feedback*. However, feedback is not enough. Action is needed. Employees need to see that the survey results cause problems to be solved. Feedback of the results and action on the problem areas make attitude survey feedback a powerful communication tool. However, providing feedback in a constructive manner may require considerable assistance from the human resource department, especially for first-level supervisors who may have little experience in running meetings and listening to employee criticisms.

> Maple Leaf Automotive Products has for several years relied on employee surveys as a method of facilitating organizational communication. Supervisors in the company are given a workbook to analyze survey results. Trained internal facilitators help the supervisors to interpret the survey results. Then the facilitators conduct a role-playing exercise with the supervisors to prepare them for the questions that employees are likely to ask.
>
> After the role-playing, the supervisor meets with the employees and presents the results. Together, problems are identified and solutions sought. From this meeting a prioritized list of action items emerges with dates for their completion. The result of all these efforts is not only that employees know what others in the organization feel, but it also helps the organization to develop an action plan to resolve its immediate and potential problems.

Whether attitude survey feedback is appropriate for an organization depends on several factors. Is top management truly willing to take action based on the results of the survey feedback process? Are resources available to conduct the survey, train facilitators that might be needed, and follow-up on the prioritized action items? But the key question may be whether the organization and its leadership are ready for change. Dealing with change as a means of developing a more productive and satisfying organization is an ongoing concern of most proactive human resource departments.

## EMPLOYEE COUNSELLING

Communications often involve one person talking with another. The purpose may be to give an order, share information, or solve a problem. *Counselling* is the discussion of a problem with an employee, with the general objective of helping the worker cope with it. The purpose is to help employees either resolve or cope with the situation so that they can become more effective persons. The basic theory supporting counselling is that stress and personal problems are likely to affect both performance and an employee's general life adjustment; therefore, it is in the best interests of all those concerned (employer, employee, and community) to help the employee return to full effectiveness. Most counsellees are healthy people who are experiencing stress and need help to return to emotional wellness. Emotions are a normal part of life, but they can get out of control and cause workers to do things that are harmful to their own best interests and to those of the firm. Sometimes employees may leave the organization because of a trifling conflict that seems large to them, or they may undermine morale in their departments. Managers want their workers to maintain a reasonable emotional balance and channel their emotions along constructive lines so that everyone will work together effectively. Counselling is a useful tool to help accomplish this goal.

### Counselling Programs

Counselling programs usually are administered by the human resources department, which uses various combinations of in-house and external counselling services.[17] Large firms often employ their own counselling staff. Some are full-time counsellors while others may be part-time counsellors in the community who are available on the company premises for certain hours during the week. Other firms refer most problems to community agencies, even though there may be an in-house counsellor who coordinates the program. If the employer is located in a large city, expert community counselling services usually are available, so both large and small firms tend to use them. Community services are especially useful to smaller firms that would be unable to employ a full-time counsellor.

> One company has a slogan: "Employees are bright and well-trained enough to handle just about any problem — except their own." A program is available to employees and their families, and it covers both personal and work-related problems. It maintains a twenty-four-hour hot line and uses both company counsellors and community agencies. The service is strictly confidential.
>
> An average of 750 employees use the service each month. Many successes have been reported, although the program is unable to solve every employee problem. A study of alcoholic employees reported a remarkable 85% reduction in lost work hours, a 47% reduction in sick leave, and a 72% reduction in sickness and accident benefit payments. In a survey 93% of the employees reported that they believe that counselling is a worthwhile service.

### Chacteristics of Counselling

Counselling has a number of characteristics that make it a useful activity in the human resource department. As shown in Figure 16-4, counselling requires two people: a coun-

FIGURE 16-4 Counselling Types According to Amount of Direction Counsellors Provide Counsellees

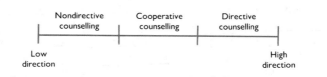

sellor and a counsellee. It is their exchange of ideas that creates a counselling relationship, and so counselling is an act of communication. Counselling can improve organizational performance because the employee becomes more cooperative, worries less about personal problems, or makes progress in other ways. Because it deals with people problems, counselling also helps organizations to be more human and considerate.

Counselling usually is performed by both professionally trained counsellors and nonprofessionals. For example, both human resource specialists in counselling and supervisors engage in counselling activities.

> A study of supervisors in seven companies reported that they spent an average of 2.5 hours a week discussing moderately serious personal problems with their employees. The most frequently discussed problems were work related, such as difficulties with associates, but more personal subjects, such as marital problems, were also discussed. The researchers' conclusion was that most supervisors "felt positively about being cast in the interpersonal helper role and considered that to be an important part of their job."[18]

Some firms, however, advise managers to avoid giving personal, nonjob advice to employees because the managers are not professionally qualified to do so. There is a chance that they will give inappropriate or wrong advice that aggravates an employee's problem.

## Counselling Functions

*Counselling functions* are the activities performed by counselling. Major counselling functions are as follows:

- *Advice.* Counsellors often give advice to counsellees in order to guide them towards desired courses of action.
- *Reassurance.* The counselling experience often provides employees with reassurance, which is confidence that they are following a suitable course of action and have the courage to try it.
- *Communication.* Counselling is a communication experience. It initiates upward communication to management, and also it gives the counsellor an opportunity to interpret management problems and give work insights to employees.
- *Release of emotional tension.* People tend to get emotional release from their tensions when they have an opportunity to discuss them with someone else.

- *Clarified thinking*. Serious discussion of problems with someone else helps a person to think more clearly about these problems.
- *Reorientation*. Reorientation involves a change in an employee's basic self through a change in goals and values. Deeper counselling of the type practised by psychologists and psychiatrists often helps employees reorient values. For example, it helps them recognize their own limitations.

## Types of Counselling

When we look upon counselling in terms of the amount of direction that a counsellor gives a counsellee, we see that it is on a continuum from full direction (directive counselling) to no direction (nondirective counselling), as shown in Figure 16-4. Between the two extremes is cooperative counselling. These three counselling types will be discussed in order to show how counsellors may vary their direction of a counsellee in a counselling situation.

### Directive Counselling

*Directive counselling* is the process of listening to an employee's emotional problems, deciding with the employee what should be done, and then telling and motivating the employee to do it. Directive counselling mostly accomplishes the counselling function of *advice*, but it may also reassure, communicate, give emotional release, and to a minor extent clarify thinking. Reorientation is seldom achieved in directive counselling.

Most everyone likes to give advice, counsellors included, and it is easy to do. But is it effective? Does the counsellor really understand the employee's problem? Does the counsellor have the knowledge and judgement to make a "right" decision? Even if the decision is right, will the employee follow it? The answer to these questions often is "no," and this is why advice may not be helpful in counselling. On other occasions an employee welcomes guidance because of a counsellor's broader knowledge and contacts in a situation.

### Nondirective Counselling

*Nondirective or client-centred counselling* is at the opposite end of the continuum. It is the process of skilfully listening and encouraging a counsellee to explain bothersome problems, understand them, and determine appropriate solutions. It focuses on the counsellee rather than on the counsellor as judge and advisor; hence it is "client-centred." Some variation on this type of counselling usually is practised by professional counsellors.

Professionals often accomplish four of the six counselling functions. Communication occurs both upward and downward through the counsellor. Emotional release takes place, even more effectively than with directive counselling, and clarified thinking tends to follow. The unique advantage of nondirective counselling is its ability to encourage the employee's reorientation. It emphasizes changing the person, instead of dealing only with the immediate problem in the usual manner of directive counselling. Here is the way nondirective counselling typically works.

Harold Pace comes to a counsellor, Janis Peterson, for assistance. Janis attempts to build a permissive relationship that encourages Harold to talk freely. At this point Janis defines the counselling relationship by explaining that she cannot tell Harold how to solve his problem, but that she may be able to help him understand his problem and deal satisfactorily with it.

Harold then explains his feelings, while Janis encourages their expression, shows interest in them, and accepts them without blame or praise. Eventually the negative feelings are drained away, giving Harold a chance to express tentatively a positive feeling or two, a step that marks the beginning of Harold's emotional growth. Janis encourages these positive feelings and accepts them without blame or praise, just as she did the negative feelings.

Harold at this point begins to get some insight into his problem and to develop alternative solutions to it. As he continues to grow, he is able to choose a course of positive action and see his way clear to try it. He then feels less need for help and recognizes that the counselling relationship should end.

### Participative Counselling

Nondirective counselling by employers is limited because it requires professional counsellors and is costly. Directive counselling often is not accepted by modern, independent employees. This means that the type of counselling used by many supervisors and human resource department employees is between the two extremes of directive and nondirective counselling. This middle ground is called participative (or cooperative) counselling because the counsellor and the counsellee participate in discussing a problem and developing a possible solution. *Particpative counselling* is a mutual counsellor-employee relationship that establishes a cooperative exchange of ideas to help solve an employee's problems. It is neither wholly counsellor-centred nor wholly counsellee-centred. Rather, the counsellor and counsellee use mutual discussion to apply their different knowledge, perspectives, and values to problems. Participative counselling integrates the ideas of both participants in the counselling relationship. It is, therefore, a balanced compromise that combines many advantages of both directive and nondirective counselling while throwing off most of their disadvantages. It also is best fitted to the skills of most company people who counsel employees.[19]

Participative counselling starts by using the listening techniques of nondirective counselling; but as the interview progresses, participative counsellors may play a more active role than a nondirective counsellor does. They may offer bits of information and insight. They may discuss the situation from their broader knowledge of the organization, thus giving an employee a different view of the problem. In general, participative counsellors apply the four counselling functions of reassurance, communication, emotional release, and clarified thinking.

### DISCIPLINE

Counselling does not always work. Sometimes the employee's behaviour is inappropriately disruptive or performance is unacceptable. Under these circumstances, discipline is needed. *Discipline* is management action to encourage compliance with organization standards. It is a type of training that seeks to correct and mould employee knowledge, attitudes, and behaviour so that the worker strives willingly for better cooperation and performance. There are two types of discipline: preventive and corrective.

## Preventive Discipline

*Preventive discipline* is action taken to encourage employees to follow standards and rules so that infractions are prevented. The basic objective is to encourage self-discipline among employees. In this way the employees maintain their own discipline, rather than having management impose it.

Management has the responsibility for building a climate of preventive discipline. In doing so, it makes its standards known and understood. If employees do not know what standards are expected, their conduct is likely to be erratic or misdirected. Employees will better support standards that they have helped create. They will also give more support to standards stated positively instead of negatively, such as ''Safety first!'' rather than ''Don't be careless!'' They usually want to know the reasons behind a standard so that it will make sense to them.

The human resource department has major responsibility for preventive discipline. For example, it develops programs to control absences and grievances. It communicates standards to employees and encourages employees to follow them. It also gives training programs to explain the reasons behind standards and to build a positive spirit of self-discipline. On other occasions, it develops employee participation in setting standards in order to build commitment to them. Effective discipline is a system relationship, and so the human resource department needs to be concerned with all parts of the system.[20]

## Corrective Discipline

*Corrective discipline* is an action that follows a rule infraction and seeks to discourage further infractions so that future acts are in compliance with standards. Typically the corrective action is a penalty of some type and is called a *disciplinary action*. Examples are a warning or suspension without pay.

The objectives of disciplinary action are as follows:

- To reform the offender
- To deter others from similar actions
- To maintain consistent, effective group standards

The objectives of disciplinary action are positive. They are educational and corrective, rather than a negative slapping back at employees who have done wrong. The goal is to improve the future rather than punish the past. A negative, punishing approach introduces too many undesirable side effects, such as emotional relations, apathy, absences, and fear of the supervisor.[21]

The corrective disciplinary interview often follows a ''sandwich model,'' which means that a corrective comment is sandwiched between two positive comments in order to make the corrective comment more acceptable. An example is: ''Your attendance is excellent, Roy (a positive comment), but your late return from coffee breaks disrupts our repair operations (negative). Otherwise, your work is among the best in our department (positive).'' The supervisor then focuses on ways in which the two of them can work together to correct the problem.

## Dismissal

The ultimate disciplinary action is *dismissal*, which is separation from the employer for cause. (Other terms used in this situation are fired, terminated, discharged, or separated.) Usually there is a carefully planned termination interview to ensure that the separation is as positive and constructive as possible.[22] It has been said that every employee dismissal is evidence of management and human resource department failure, but this view is not realistic. Neither managers nor employees are perfect, so some problems cannot be solved regardless of how hard people try. Sometimes dismissal is better for both the worker and the company. It gives the employee a chance to seek a new job where his or her abilities and temperament may be more appropriate. Many discharged employees move to another company and are successful, sometimes receiving promotions to top positions.

## Restrictions on Corrective Discipline

In general, discipline is substantially restricted by unions and government and the rules, laws, and regulations that have grown up around them. Corrective discipline is an especially sensitive subject with unions. They see it as an opportunity to protect employees from unreasonable management authority and to show employees that the union leadership cares for their interests. Employees also are sensitive about disciplinary issues, because these issues can be a threat to employee pay and jobs. If there is a hint of unfairness in a disciplinary action, it can lead to a prolonged, costly dispute and eventual arbitration.[23] Walkouts and strikes can occur, and new bargaining issues about discipline may develop for the next bargaining session. The human resource department's job is to reduce chances for conflict by working with supervisors and union representatives to assure that corrective discipline is fairly and uniformly applied, and that employees and unions will accept such discipline as appropriate.

Government is increasing its regulation of discipline, making it more difficult to justify. The historical employer right to terminate an employee at any time without cause (the *termination-at-will doctrine*) is increasingly becoming restricted.[24] For example, an employee cannot be disciplined or dismissed for union activities (as determined by law), conditions controlled by human rights legislation (such as race, sex, religion) or refusing to perform very hazardous or unsafe or unlawful activities. Other employment restrictions may also apply, depending on the circumstances and on the laws in the provinces concerned.

In all cases, *due process* for discipline may be required of the employer by courts of law, arbitrators, and labour unions. Due process means that established rules and procedures for disciplinary action are followed and that employees have an opportunity to respond to charges made against them.[25] It is the human resource department's responsibility to ensure that all parties in a disciplinary action follow the correct rules and procedures so that due process will be used.

If a disciplinary action is challenged, the human resource department also must have sufficient documentation to support the action; therefore, human resource policy usually requires proper documentation for all employer disciplinary actions.[26] Proper documentation should be specific, beginning with the date, time, and location of an incident. It also describes the nature of the undesirable performance or behaviour and how it relates to job and organizational performance. Specific rules and regulations that relate to the incident are identified. Documentation also states what the manager said to the employee and how the employee responded, including specific words and acts. If there were witnesses, they should be identified. All documentation needs to be recorded promptly, while the supervisor's memory is still fresh. It should be objective, based on observations and not impressions. Documentation need not be lengthy, but it should be complete, precise, and accurate. If a supervisor follows these practical documentation guidelines, then the employer is reasonably protected in case of challenges by employees, unions, regulatory bodies such as the Human Rights Commission, and lawsuits.

## The Hot-Stove Rule

A useful guide for corrective discipline is the hot-stove rule, as shown in Figure 16-5. The *hot-stove rule* states that disciplinary action should have the same characteristics as the penalty a person receives from touching a hot stove. These characteristics are that discipline should be with warning, immediate, consistent, and impersonal.

FIGURE 16-5   The Hot-Stove Rule for Discipline

Disciplinary action should be like the penalty from touching a hot stove:

- With warning
- Immediate
- Consistent
- Impersonal

*Warning* is essential. It requires communication of the rules to all employees. If an employee can show that management failed to give adequate notice of rules, management will have difficulty justifying the discipline before a union or arbitrator.

Dorothy Settler was given a one-day suspension for smoking in a restricted area. She was able to show that there was no "No Smoking" sign, and that she had had no other notice that smoking in the area was a fire hazard. The arbitrator revoked the penalty and ordered one day of back pay for Dorothy.

Discipline also should be *immediate*. When the discipline quickly follows an infraction, there is a connection between the two events in the employee's mind, and there is less probability for a future infraction.

*Consistent* discipline is required, because consistency is an important part of fairness. Lack of consistency causes employees to feel discriminated against. On the other hand, occasional exceptions can be justified.[27]

Walter Miller, who had worked eighteen years without a disciplinary infraction, came to work slightly intoxicated three weeks after the death of his wife. Different treatment for him was justified, compared with the penalty for Betina Rouse, who had only two years of seniority, had been warned twice about coming to work intoxicated, and then again came to work slightly intoxicated.

The hot-stove rule also requires *impersonal* discipline, just as a stove burns men and women, young and old, equally. The supervisor's like or dislike of an employee is not relevant to disciplinary action. Effective discipline condemns the employee's wrongful act, not the employee as a person. There is a difference between applying a penalty for a job not performed and calling an employee a lazy loafer. (Of course, managers should be personal and considerate enough of employee feelings to administer discipline in private.)

## Progressive Discipline

Most employers apply a policy of *progressive discipline*, which means that there are stronger penalties for repeated offences. The purpose of this is to give an employee an opportunity to take corrective action before more serious penalties are applied. Progressive discipline also gives management time to work with an employee to help correct infractions.

> When Margaret Stoner had two unauthorized absences, the human resource department provided counselling. It also arranged for her to join a ride pool that allowed her to leave home thirty minutes later than with public transportation. Eventually her unauthorized absences stopped.

A typical progressive discipline system is shown in Figure 16-6. The first infraction leads to a verbal reprimand by the supervisor. The next infraction leads to a written reprimand, with a record placed in the files. Further infractions build up to stronger discipline, leading finally to discharge. Usually the human resource department becomes involved at Step 3 or sooner, in order to assure that company policy is applied consistently in all departments.

FIGURE 16-6   **A Progressive Discipline System**

1. Verbal reprimand by supervisor
2. Written reprimand, with a record in file
3. One- to three-day suspension from work
4. Suspension for one week or longer
5. Discharge for cause

Some progressive systems allow minor offences to be removed from the record after one to three years, allowing each employee to return to Step 1. But specified serious offences, such as fighting or theft, are usually not dealt with by means of progressive discipline. An employee who commits these offences may be discharged on the first offence.

## A Counselling Approach to Discipline

Most organizations use counselling in connection with discipline, but a few firms have moved a step further and taken a counselling approach to the entire procedure. In this approach, an employee is counselled rather than progressively penalized for the first few breaches of organizational standards. Here is how the program works in one organization.[28]

> The philosophy is that violations are employee malfunctions that can be constructively corrected without penalty. The first violation results in a private discussion with the supervisor. The second violation brings further discussion with the supervisor with a focus on correcting causes of the behaviour. A third violation leads to counselling with the immediate supervisor and the shift supervisor to determine roots of the employee's malfunction. For example, does the employee dislike the job and want a transfer? Is the employee prepared to abide by the standard? The result of the discussion is given to the employee in a letter.
>
> A fourth infraction within a reasonable time, such as a year, results in final counselling with the superintendent. The offender is released from duty with pay for the remainder of the day to consider willingness to abide by standards. The offender is told that a further violation, regretfully, will result in termination, because it shows that the employee is unable or unwilling to work within the standards of the organization.

The counselling approach is fact-finding and guiding, instead of retaliatory. In this manner the employee's self-image and dignity are retained and the supervisor-employee relationship remains cooperative and constructive.

## *SUMMARY*

The human resource department's role in organizational communication is to create an open two-way flow of information. Part of the foundation of any organizational communication effort is the view held by management of employees. If that view is one that sincerely strives to provide an effective downward and upward flow of information, then the human resource department can help develop and maintain appropriate communication systems.

Downward communication approaches include house organs, information booklets, employee bulletins, television and films, and jobholder reports and meetings. Multiple channels are used to help ensure that each message reaches the intended receivers.

Perhaps the greatest difficulty in organizational communication is to provide an effective upward flow of information. In-house complaint procedures, rap sessions, suggestion systems, and attitude survey feedback are commonly used tools.

Counselling is the discussion of a problem with an employee to help the worker cope with the situation. It is performed by human resource department professionals as well as supervisors. In the typical firm most counselling for day-to-day problems is in the broad middle ground between directive and nondirective methods. Counselling programs include both job and personal problems, and there is extensive cooperation with community counselling agencies.

Discipline is management action to enforce organizational standards, and it is both preventive and corrective. The hot-stove rule is a useful general guide for corrective discipline. Most disciplinary action is progressive, with stronger penalties for repeated offences. Some disciplinary programs primarily emphasize a counselling approach.

## TERMS FOR REVIEW

| | |
|---|---|
| Open communication | Attitude survey feedback |
| Open-door policy | Counselling |
| Downward communication | Counselling functions |
| House organs | Directive counselling |
| Grapevine communication | Nondirective counselling |
| In-house complaint procedures | Participative counselling |
| Rap sessions | Preventive discipline |
| Deep-sensing meetings | Corrective discipline |
| Vertical staffing meetings | Hot-stove rule |
| Suggestion systems | Progressive discipline |

## REVIEW AND DISCUSSION QUESTIONS

1.  Discuss the "dual responsibility for communications" shared by the human resource department and supervisors.
2.  Discuss how grapevines work in an organization and the kinds of feedback management can get from them.
3.  Think of a situation in which you learned some new information from the grapevine and took action on the basis of that information. Discuss.
4.  List and discuss different programs that the human resource department manages in order to improve communications.
5.  Explain the three types of counselling and the ways in which they differ.
6.  Discuss differences between preventive and corrective discipline. What examples of either one were applied to you on the last job you had?
7.  Discuss different government restrictions on an employer's right to discipline or dismiss an employee "at will," and explain why each of these restrictions probably exists.
8.  Discuss what progressive discipline is and how it works. Is its basic approach realistic in work situations?

## INCIDENT 16-1

### The Machinist's Abusive Comments to the Supervisor

William Lee, a machine operator, worked as a machinist for Horace Gray, a supervisor. Horace told William to pick up some trash that had fallen from William's work area, and William replied, "I won't do the janitor's work."

Horace replied, "When you drop it, you pick it up." William became angry and abusive, calling Horace a number of uncomplimentary names in a loud voice and refusing to pick up the trash. All employees in the department heard William's comments.

The situation was as follows. Horace had been trying for two weeks to get his employees to pick up trash in order to have a cleaner workplace and prevent accidents. He talked with all employees in a weekly department meeting and to each employee individually at least once. He stated that he was following the instructions of the superintendent. Only William objected with the comment, "I'm not here to do the janitor's work. I'm a machinist."

William had been in the department for six months and with the company for three years. Horace had spoken to him twice about excessive horseplay, but otherwise his record was good. He was known to have a quick temper.

After William finished his abusive outburst, Horace told him to come to the office and suspended him for one day for insubordination and abusive language to a supervisor. The discipline was within company policy, and similar acts had been disciplined in other departments.

When William walked out of Horace's office, Horace called the human resource director, reported what he had done, and said that he was sending a copy of his action for William's file.

1.  As human resource director, what comments would you make?
2.  What follow-up actions should the human resource director take or recommend that Horace take? For example, do you recommend counselling for William? Would you reconsider disciplinary procedures and policies?

## INCIDENT 16-2

## A Counselling Program for Drug Abuse

Windsor Electronics, a growing electronics manufacturing firm, has increasingly faced problems with employees who abused alcohol and other drugs. Supervisors had previously been dealing with these employees in whatever ways seemed appropriate; however, both the supervisors and the human resource director now agreed that drug abuse problems were serious enough to require a company policy and a procedure to implement it. They also believed that the company needed a consistent, dependable policy to protect itself from possible human rights complaints of discrimination in counselling or treatment.

The human resource director asked his assistant, Carolyn Stevens, to prepare a policy and procedure for working with employees when drug abuse was suspected. Carolyn had been in the human resource department for three years following her graduation with a major in human resource management from a nearby university.

Form teams of three to five members and develop an appropriate drug abuse policy and procedure for Carolyn. Be sure to include specific steps covering who will work with drug abusers and what they should do. Then present your report to the entire classroom group and compare it with statements by other teams.

**528**    PART 5    EMPLOYEE AND LABOUR RELATIONS

∘ ∘ ∘ ∘ ∘ ∘ ∘ ∘ ∘ ∘ ∘ ∘ ∘ ∘ ∘ ∘ ∘ ∘ ∘ ∘ ∘ ∘ ∘ ∘ ∘ ∘ ∘ ∘ ∘ ∘ ∘ ∘ ∘ ∘ ∘ ∘ ∘ ∘

*CASE STUDY*

## JIM McNAB

Jim McNab is employed as an account officer with Central Canada Trust Company. He emigrated from Great Britain to Canada when the employment situation at home deteriorated during the early eighties. He joined Central Canada Trust shortly after his arrival.

Jim came from a large family, and since his father could not afford to pay for a college education Jim worked his way through college, holding evening jobs and working during the summer. He graduated with a Bachelor of Commerce degree. His grades were not impressive, but he would say, "I went through the school of hard knocks. I know the requirements for doing a good job, and good grades are not one of them!"

He was an active member of the Anglican Church and attended church services regularly. After two years in Canada, he joined the Progressive Conservative Party and was selected twice as a local representative at party conventions. He was married and had two children.

Central Canada Trust Company is one of the smaller trust companies in Central Canada and has its main branch in Ottawa. Its services are aimed mainly at middle income earners, mostly civil servants. It takes great pride in the quality of its services, the company slogan being "You Can Trust Us." Every employee had to undergo a thorough orientation program and was afterwards trained regularly.

One of the company policies required that employees who had direct contact with customers had to follow a dress code, which specified that male employees had to wear dark or grey suits, white shirts and ties, and a hat when on duty outside the office. Female employees were asked not to wear pants, and to avoid "deep-cut" blouses. Most employees followed the code and very few could recall

that anyone had been reprimanded for wearing something objectionable. As a matter of fact, it was generally felt that management had relaxed the code because nothing had been said for quite some time.

On a hot day during the summer, shortly after his birthday, Jim came to the office wearing a modern safari suit with a yellow shirt and a nice tie. The outfit had been the collective birthday present from his wife and children. He looked very fashionable and elegant in it and several of the employees commented on it.

Shortly after his arrival on that day his direct supervisor, Michelle Tremblay, called him in.

**Michelle:** Jim, I am not happy that I have to do this, but Rich Chan [the branch manager] was quite upset when he saw you coming in and he asked me to talk to you. As you know he has a Chinese upbringing and is very conservative. He asked me to remind you that our company's image is at stake when you don't wear a white shirt and a suitable tie.

**Jim:** Mich, you must be kidding. We aren't living in medieval times when companies could prescribe even private activities of employees. I know about the dress code, but it has never been enforced. Besides, this outfit looks very good on me, and some customers even commented positively about it.

**Michelle:** Well, that may be. We haven't had a case like this for some time, but Mr. Chan feels that you have gone too far. We have the policy and you were informed about it during the orientation program. You even confirmed in writing that you had read it.

**Jim:** Yes, I read it, but you can't call my dress outrageous or offensive. It is modern, looks good and is certainly more comfortable than a three-piece suit, especially in these temperatures.

**Michelle:** Personally I agree with you, but Mr. Chan is adamant. He really feels that the image of the company is at stake. You know that we compete against the banks and that we try to be perceived by our customers as solid and trustworthy. Mr. Chan thinks that the way our employees dress has an impact on this image. I have to give you an official warning, which becomes part of your file. I am sorry about this, but I have to do it.

**Jim:** Well, I am not happy about it either, but if that is what the company wants, so be it. It isn't that important to me.

Richard Chan had been born in Hong Kong, but had come to Canada with his parents when he was fifteen. His father had been an unskilled labourer and had died at an early age, leaving Richard as the main breadwinner for the family. He had worked his way up in Central Canada Trust from a teller to branch manager and was very proud of his accomplishment. He was considered a hard worker who expected a lot from his employees, but he was considered a fair supervisor.

Michelle Tremblay had been hired as a management trainee after she graduated with a degree in economics from the University of Ottawa. She was considered to be a good manager and was well liked as a supervisor.

Jim was not too concerned about the incident. His performance was good enough that he received the highest merit pay increases in his department. He was convinced that Mr. Chan would think twice before he would take any drastic action against a high performer.

Employees of the Central Canada Trust Company had been told that it would be good for the image of the company if employees were involved in community work. Management was even willing to compensate employees for certain expenses, e.g., taxi or bus fares, or the cost of a meal. Jim, for example, was a counsellor for the local Junior Achievers, a group of high school students who work on small business assignments under the guidance of experienced managers.

A few weeks after the incident in the office, he was invited by Junior Achievers to give a presentation on sound financial management. Since it was part of a promotional campaign for the Achievers, a local TV station showed some excerpts during the evening news.

For the presentation, Jim had dressed casually since he knew the students quite well and he saw his talk as part of his regular work as a Junior Achiever Counsellor. He was not aware that the TV station had planned to broadcast part of the presentation.

The next day Michelle Tremblay received a memo from Mr. Chan which stated:

> Michelle, I saw Mr. McNab yesterday evening on the TV news, giving a public presentation. He wore a sport shirt and no tie. Since this is the second time he disregarded the company's dress code and my explicit warning a few weeks ago, I ask you to arrange for his immediate termination. We cannot tolerate employees who violate official company policies and challenge my authority.

Michelle immediately went to see Mr. Chan and tried to change his mind, but to no avail. He was especially upset that Jim had appeared on TV and had been introduced as an employee of Central Canada Trust Company. He felt that since Jim had been warned about his inappropriate attire before, the second occasion was a deliberate snub.

1. Assume that you are the human resource manager. Discuss the issue from the company's point of view. (Are dress codes legal? How valid are claims that the company's image may be influenced by the attire of employees?)

2. Michelle has come to you for your advice. She would like to retain Jim since he is an excellent

employee. She also feels that such drastic action will have a negative effect on the morale of other employees. What actions would you want to take?

○ ○ ○ ○ ○ ○ ○ ○ ○ ○ ○ ○ ○ ○ ○ ○ ○ ○ ○ ○ ○ ○ ○ ○ ○ ○ ○ ○ ○ ○ ○ ○ ○ ○ ○ ○

## SUGGESTED READINGS

Corbett, W.J., "The Communication Tools Inherent in Corporate Culture," *Personnel Journal*, April 1986, pp. 71-72, 74.

"Employee Discipline: Firm but Fair," *Business Update*, September 1985, pp. 1-15.

Macintosh, J.C.C., "Reporting to Employees: Identifying the Areas of Interest to Employees," *Accounting and Finance*, Vol. 27, No. 2, November 1987, pp. 41-52.

Orth, C.D., H.E. Wilkinson and R.C. Benfari, "The Manager's Role as Coach and Mentor," *Organizational Dynamics*, Spring 1987, pp. 66-74.

Postain, H., P. Allan and S. Rosenberg, "New York City's Approach to Problem-Employee Counselling," *Personnel Journal*, April 1980, pp. 305-309, 321.

Veiga, J.F., "Face Your Problem Subordinates Now!" The Academy of Management *Executive*, Vol. 11, No. 2, 1988, pp. 145-152.

## REFERENCES

1. Barry M. Staw, "Organizational Psychology and the Pursuit of the Happy/Productive Worker," *California Management Review*, Summer, 1986, p. 41.
2. Vicki Pawlik and Brian H. Kleiner, "On-the-Job Employee Counselling: Focus on Performance," *Personnel Journal*, November 1986, p. 31
3. Everett M. Rogers and Rekha Agarwala-Rogers, *Communication in Organizations*, New York: Free Press, 1976, p. 26.
4. Amitai Etzioni, *Perspectives on Productivity: A Global View*, Philadelphia: Louis Harris, 1981, p. 45.
5. Walter Kiechel, III, "No Word From on High," *Fortune*, January 6, 1986, p. 125.
6. For example, see Roger M. D'Aprix, "The Believable House Organ," *Management Review*, February 1979, pp. 23-28. American Express Company publications for employees are summarized in "How Amex Employees Learn What's Happening," *Management Review*, February 1980, pp. 48-49.
7. Troyer, op.cit., p. 39. See also "TV that Competes with the Office Grapevine," *Business Week*, March 14, 1977, pp. 49-54.
8. "Spreading the Word about the Facts of Life in the Corporation," *Personnel*, May–June 1976, pp. 4-5.
9. Walter D. St. John, "Successful Communications between Supervisors and Employees," *Personnel Journal*, January 1983, p. 73.
10. See Keith Davis, *Human Behavior at Work: Organizational Behavior*, 6th ed., New York: McGraw-Hill Book Company, 1981, pp. 335-346.
11. "Deep Sensing: A Pipeline to Employee Morale," *Business Week*, January 29, 1979, pp. 124-128.
12. "Vertical Staffing Meetings Open Lines of Communication at Rocketdyne Plant," *World of Work Report*, April 1979, pp. 27-28. See also Adri A. Boudewyn, "The Open Meeting —A Confidential Forum for Employees," *Personnel Journal*, April 1977, pp. 192-194.

13. "Employee Recognition: A Key To Motivation," *Personnel Journal*, February 1981, pp. 103-106.
14. The *"Key Program,"* Chicago: National Association of Suggestions Systems, 1983.
15. Lee A. Graf, "Suggestion Program Failure: Causes and Remedies," *Personnel Journal*, June 1982, pp. 450-454.
16. William J. Rothwell, "Conducting an Employee Attitude Survey," *Personnel Journal*, September 1982, pp. 689-691.
17. Surveys of counselling practices are reported in Helen LaVan, Nicholas Mathys, and David Drehmer, "A Look at the Counselling Practices of Major U.S. Corporations," *The Personnel Administrator*, June 1983, pp. 76ff.; Hermine Zagat Levine, "Employee Counselling Services," *Personnel*, March–April 1981, pp. 4-11; and Robert C. Ford and Frank S. McLaughlin, "Employee Assistance Programs: A Descriptive Survey of ASPA Members," *The Personnel Administrator*, September 1981, pp. 29-35; Beverly L. Wolkind, "North American Congress on FAPs Comes Through," *EAP Digest*, September/October, 1986, pp. 44-48.
18. Elizabeth M. Kaplan and Emory L. Cowen, "Interpersonal Helping Behavior of Industrial Foremen," *Journal of Applied Psychology*, October 1981, pp. 633-638. See also Ronald J. Burke, "Mentors in Organizations" *ASAC (Organizational Behaviour Division) Meeting Proceedings*, Vol. 3, Part 5, 1982, 41-48.
19. A participative counselling program is discussed in Steven H. Appelbaum, "A Human Resources Counselling Model: The Alcoholic Employee," *The Personnel Administrator*, August 1982, pp. 35-44.
20. James A. Belohlav and Paul O. Popp, "Making Employee Discipline Work," *The Personnel Administrator*, March 1978, pp. 22-24. See also Ira G. Asherman, "The Corrective Discipline Process," *Personnel Journal*, July 1982, pp. 528-531; Frank E. Kumits, "No Fault: A New Strategy for Absenteeism Control," *Personnel Journal*, May 1981, pp. 387-390.

21. Henry P. Sims, Jr., "Tips and Troubles with Employee Reprimand," *The Personnel Administrator*, January 1979, pp. 57-61; and idem, "Further Thoughts on Punishment in Organizations," *Academy of Management Review*, January 1980, pp. 133-138.

22. Maria Leonard, "Challenges to the Termination-at-Will Doctrine," *Personnel Administrator*, February 1983, pp. 49-56; and Edward Mandt, "Employee Termination: Proceed with Care," *Management Review*, December 1980, pp. 25-28. For a general discussion of restrictions on the right to dismiss, see David W. Ewing, *Do It My Way or You're Fired!* New York: Wiley, 1983; Edward L. Harrison, "Legal Restrictions on the Employer's Authority to Discipline," *Personnel Journal*, February 1982, pp. 136-141; David W. Ewing, "Your Right to Fire," *Harvard Business Review*, March–April 1983, pp. 33-42. See also John Huberman, " 'Discipline without Punishment' Lives," *Harvard Business Review*, July–August 1975, pp. 6-8.

23. Laurence J. Stybel, Robin Cooper, and Maryanne Peabody, "Planning Executive Dismissals: How to Fire a Friend," *California Management Review*, Spring 1982, pp. 73-80; Stanley J. Schwartz, "How to Dehire: A Guide for the Manager," *Human Resource Management*, Winter 1980, pp. 22-25; and Robert Coulson, "The Fine Art of Informing an Employee: You're Fired!" *Management Review*, February 1982, p. 37; Jeffrey C. Pingpank and Thomas B. Mooney, "Wrongful Discharge: A New Danger for Employers," *Personnel Administrator*, March 1981, pp. 31-35.

24. See M. Leonard, op. cit.

25. David W. Ewing, "Due Process: Will Business Default?" *Harvard Business Review*, November–December 1982, pp. 114-122; and Bryan P. Heshizer and Harry Graham, "Discipline in the Nonunion Company: Protecting Employer and Employee Rights," *Personnel*, March–April 1982, pp. 71-78.

26. Ira G. Asherman and Sandra Lee Vance, "Documentation: A Tool for Effective Management," *Personnel Journal*, August 1981, pp. 641-643.

27. For differences between disciplinary policies for professional and nonprofessional employees see Irene Unterberger and S. Herbert Unterberger, "Disciplining Professional Employees," *Industrial Relations*, October 1978, pp. 353-359.

28. John Huberman, 1975, op. cit., Richard C. Grote, "Positive Discipline: Keeping Employees in Line Without Punishment," *Training*, October 1977, pp. 42-44; James A. Belohlav and Paul O. Popp. "Making Employee Discipline Work," *The Personnel Administrator*, March 1978, pp. 22-24.

# CHAPTER *17* ○○○○○○

# *THE UNION-MANAGEMENT FRAMEWORK*

*The principles which underlie the Canadian Industrial Relations system are reflected in Canada's heritage of fundamental Western values, in the liberal democratic system adopted in this country and in the modified capitalistic or mixed enterprise economy that has developed.*

TASK FORCE ON LABOUR RELATIONS[1]

○ ○ ○ ○ ○ ○ ○ ○ ○ ○ ○ ○ ○ ○ ○ ○ ○ ○ ○ ○ ○ ○ ○ ○ ○ ○ ○ ○ ○ ○ ○ ○ ○

## *CHAPTER OBJECTIVES*

After studying this chapter, you should be able to:
1. **Explain** the relationship between unions, employers and government.
2. **Describe** the nature and priorities of union objectives.
3. **Identify** illegal management and union activities.
4. **Distinguish** between various government agencies that enforce labour laws.
5. **Discuss** the major reasons that workers join unions.
6. **Describe** how unions affect the human resource management environment.

○ ○ ○ ○ ○ ○ ○ ○ ○ ○ ○ ○ ○ ○ ○ ○ ○ ○ ○ ○ ○ ○ ○ ○ ○ ○ ○ ○ ○ ○ ○ ○

*W*hen employees are dissatisfied, they may band together and form a *union*. This does not mean the end of an organization's success. Many successful companies have one or more unions among their employees. But the use of collective action puts new limits on the role of human resource management. Many times, operating managers find these new limitations hard to accept. Consider the views of one plant manager in the following dialogue:

"As plant manager, I don't think we need to worry about unions. Our company pays good wages and has a sound benefit program," argued Dave Weldon.

"Sure, our pay and benefits are fair. But a union could promise our employees even more. Besides, workers don't always join unions for higher pay or better benefits. They may want a union as a protest of company policies or simply because they feel unfairly treated," Stan commented.

"Well, if any supervisor is treating workers unfairly, they could tell me. I would take action quickly. Since management at this plant takes care of workers, I don't think workers should want to join a union. If they did, I would try to stop it before it got out of hand," Dave added with little thought.

"When your boss does something you don't like, do you complain to the company president?" Stan questioned. "Most workers are probably reluctant to complain to you about their supervisors. And workers have a legally protected right to join a union!"

The union-management framework consists of three principal actors: workers and their representatives (unions); managerial employees (management); and government representatives.[2] Each of these parties depends upon the others, as shown in Figure 17-1. For example, the union relies on management for jobs and on the government for protection of workers' rights. Government protection is why Dave Weldon legally cannot fire employees who want to start a union. Managers depend on the union to honour its obligations. Government needs both unions and management to provide productive organizations that meet society's needs.

Although each party depends on the other, the parties are not equals. Government

FIGURE 17-1   The Interdependence of Unions, Management, and Government

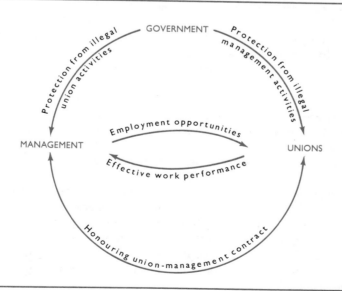

is the dominant force because it defines the roles of management and unions through laws. Within these laws, unions and management may use their respective powers to shape their relationship. For example, a powerful union may force management to make concessions in order to avoid a crippling strike. Likewise, when the union is weak, management can get concessions from the union because the threat of an effective strike is remote. The power of each side depends on the capacity of each to influence or threaten the other.

Durability is another characteristic of the labour-management framework. The process of collective bargaining between employers and unions has survived in its present form since the 1930s. Admittedly, the framework has undergone continuous refinements in law and practice. And unions, management, and the government have grown more sophisticated. But the three-way relationship has shown considerable stability, while remaining flexible enough to adjust to countless legal, social, and economic challenges.

This chapter explains the labour-management framework. It begins with a look at the goals, structure, and impact of unions on the work environment. Then the government's role is discussed. The chapter ends by examining the challenges that unions hold for human resource management.

## LABOUR UNIONS AND HUMAN RESOURCE MANAGEMENT

Labour unions do alter the work environment. Their presence changes the relationship between employees and the organization, especially the role of supervisors and the human resource department. As seen through the eyes of one veteran supervisor, the human resource department's response to unions is not always well received by lower levels of management:

> When I started working here in 1972, supervisors had it made. We handled our own discipline, hiring, and firing. We had clout around here. Then we got a union. Immediately, the human resource department grew and got involved in everything we did. We had training in how to deal with the union, training in the labour laws, training in what the contract meant, and training in all the new rules we had to follow.
>
> Even worse, the human resource department started to have a bigger part in hiring, firing, and discipline. At the same time, I had to deal with the union representative. Of course, my manager still expected me to meet my department's objectives and its budget. Supervising sure is less satisfying than it used to be before the union and the human resource department made all these changes.

As this supervisor's comments indicate, unions have a major effect on the work environment, but in many other ways the environment remains unchanged. Supervisors and managers retain their primary responsibility for employee performance. Profit objectives and budgetary goals are not usually shared with the union. Nor do unions reduce the need for effective human resource department procedures. In short, management must still manage; and the union does not assume the responsibilities of the human resource department.

To understand how and why unions influence human resource management, it is necessary to examine their goals and structure.

## Union Goals and Philosophy

Like other organizations, unions are social systems that pursue objectives. Their objectives are influenced internally by the wishes of their members, aspirations of their leaders, and the financial and membership strength of the union. And like other organizations, unions are open social systems that are affected by their external environment. The financial condition of the employer, the gains of rival unions, the inflation and unemployment rates, and government policies influence the union's objectives.

Yet among all these internal and external considerations, there does exist a common core of widely-agreed-upon objectives. According to one prominent labour leader, the mission for the labour movement is to protect workers, increase their pay, improve their working conditions, and help workers in general.[3] This approach has become known as *business unionism,* primarily because it recognizes that a union can survive only if it delivers a needed service to its members in a businesslike manner. But some unions have chosen to address broader social issues of politics and economics when such concern is in the best interest of their members. This second kind of union, engaged in what is called *social (or reform) unionism,* tries to influence the economic and social policies of government at all levels—municipal, provincial, and federal.[4] In practice, union leaders pursue the objectives of social unionism by speaking out for or against government programs. For example, many union leaders rejected federal government wage and price control in 1975 because it seriously impeded the collective bargaining process.[5]

Business and social unionism present unions with multiple, and sometimes conflicting, objectives. Figure 17-2 explains these trade-offs. For example, when the union bargains with management, it seeks high pay and good working conditions. But higher costs may cause the company to hire fewer workers or encourage management to use more automation. The social unionism trade-offs are less obvious.

FIGURE 17-2   Trade-Offs Faced by Unions Under Business and Social Unionism

| PHILOSOPHICAL APPROACHES | TRADE-OFFS BETWEEN UNION OBJECTIVES | | |
|---|---|---|---|
| Business Unionism | Maximize number of employed members. | OR | Maximize pay and benefits of members. |
| Social Unionism | Maximize welfare of members. | OR | Maximize welfare of working people. |

Examples of this would be the unions' support of industrial safety acts. These acts improve the safety and health of all working people. But the cost of compliance may lessen the ability of union employers to provide pay raises. Thus social unionism causes labour organizations to face the trade-off of maximizing the welfare of its members.[6]

Human resource management is influenced by both business and social unionism goals. The growth of benefits discussed in Chapter 13 has resulted partly from union pressure. Even nonunionized employers have added many benefits in order to remain competitive in the labour market or to forestall unionization among their employees. Social unionism goals affect human resource management through such union-supported actions as the Canada Pension Plan and others. Consider how one human resource department responded to the business and social goals of unions.

> Michelin Tire (Canada) Ltd. has two plants in Nova Scotia, employing more than 4000 workers. To prevent the employees from seeking unionization, management pays wages significantly above those of other unionized companies in the region. Since some unions were able to negotiate dental plans with their employers, the management of Michelin offered its employees free dental insurance coverage as an extra inducement not to unionize. So far, two attempts to unionize the company have failed.

## Union Structure and Functions

Some writers believe that employees lost direct contact with the owners as employers grew large, and so unions emerged to help workers influence workplace decisions.[7] Through unions, workers were able to exert control over "their jobs" and "their work environment."[8] Then when attempts were made by employers to cut wages, the employees relied on their unions to resist these actions.[9]

Early attempts to control the work environment were merely local efforts, because most employers were small local operations. As employers, particularly the railway companies, began to span municipal and then provincial boundaries, some labour organizations created national unions composed of locals all over the country; their locals either became affiliated with or were directly organized by strong U.S. unions, thus forming international unions. When social problems affected several national or international unions at once, they joined together and formed multiunion associations like the Canadian Labour Congress (CLC) or the American Federation of Labor and Congress of Industrial Organizations (AFL-CIO). In Canada there are several such associations, but the CLC is the most influential. A brief review of these four levels—the locals, the nationals, the internationals, and the multiunion association as represented by CLC and AFL-CIO—will illustrate the functions and structure of the unions that human resource departments encounter.[10]

### Quebec

The development of the labour movement in Quebec is relatively independent of its development in the rest of Canada. Perhaps the most active role in organizing workers in Quebec was played by the clergy of the Roman Catholic Church. In 1921, there were enough unions to form the first national confederation, the Canadian and Catholic Confederation of Labour (C.C.C.L.). Because of their religious nature, the unions in the C.C.C.L. strongly opposed the international unions, whom they perceived as antireligious and too materialistic. Only after World War II did the religious character of the C.C.C.L. change; the change became official by 1960, when the organization adopted its present name, the Confederation of National Trade Unions (CNTU). Although the CLC's Quebec arm, the Quebec Federation of Labour (QFL), with about 250,000 members, represents most of the province's unionized workers, the CNTU is the largest independent labour federation in Quebec, with about 93,000 members. A number of large unions have chosen not to affiliate with either the QFL or the CNTU, e.g., the 75,000 teachers organized in the Centrale de l'Enseignement du Québec, and 30,000 provincial civil servants, members of the Syndicat des Fonctionnaires Provinciaux du Québec.

### Local Unions

For human resource administrators, the *local unions* are the most important part of the union structure.[11] They provide the members, the revenue, and the power of the entire union movement. There are three types of local unions: craft, industrial, and mixed local. *Craft unions* are composed of workers who possess the same skills or trades; these include, for example, all the carpenters who work in the same geographical area. *Industrial unions* include the unskilled and semiskilled workers at a particular location. When an employer has several locations that are unionized, employees at each location are usually represented by a different local union. Members of the Canadian Auto Workers are an example. A *mixed local* combines both unskilled and skilled employees. This arrangement is common, for example, in the electric utility industry, where the International Brotherhood of Electrical Workers includes skilled, semiskilled, and unskilled workers.

Figure 17-3 shows the structure of a typical local. The *steward* is usually elected by the workers and helps them present their problems to management. If the steward of an industrial or mixed local cannot help the employee, the problem is given to the

**FIGURE 17-3   Structure of a Typical Local Union**

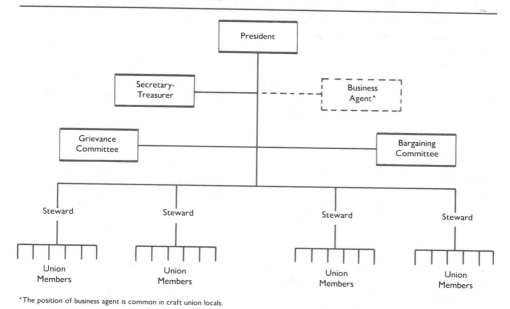

*The position of business agent is common in craft union locals.

*grievance committee,* which takes the issue to higher levels of management or to the human resource department.[12] In craft unions, the steward, who is also called the representative, usually takes the issue directly to the *business agent,* who is a full-time employee of the union.

This process of resolving employee problems, called the *grievance procedure,* limits human resource specialists and line managers because it challenges their decisions. If the challenge is successful, the result may serve as a precedent that limits future decisions.

> Christine Rae was a department manager in a large retail store. Whenever she needed someone to work overtime, she asked the first employee she saw. One employee, Ian George, filed a formal grievance, complaining that overtime was not granted fairly to all employees. Eventually the problem reached the regional human resource manager and the union president. They agreed that in the future overtime would be rotated among all departmental employees. The solution of this grievance set a precedent that other managers of union workers must follow in granting overtime.

An even more important limitation on supervisors and human resource specialists is the collective agreement. It normally specifies wages, hours, working conditions, and related issues such as grievance procedures, safety standards, probationary periods, and benefits. It is usually negotiated between the local union's *bargaining committee* and the human resource or industrial relations department.

## National Unions
Most local unions are part of a larger association called the *national union.* It exists to organize and help local unions. It also pursues social objectives of interest to its members.

Most national unions maintain a staff that assists the local unions with negotiations, grievance handling, and expert advice. Among the craft unions, the national tends to leave many key decisions to the locals. Mixed and industrial nationals are more likely to be involved with their locals. For example, a national union may require that locally bargained contracts receive its approval. Sometimes the national union may actually bargain an industry-wide contract, as the Canadian Auto Workers union does in the automobile industry.

## International Unions
An international union provides services similar to those of a national union, the major difference being that the international union operates in Canada *and* the U.S. and has headquarters in the U.S. Since international unions are usually stronger financially, they are in better condition to support locals in a prolonged strike.[13]

## Secession
Canadian members of international unions have often complained that they receive a disproportionate share of union benefits. The secession trend started in 1971 when Canadian members of the Communication Workers of America separated from the international union and founded the Communications Workers of Canada (CWC). The most

dramatic breakaway occurred in 1985 when the Canadian Auto Workers Union (CAW) held its founding convention in Toronto. Although it was expected that it would be difficult to work out a financial arrangement, the separation from the United Automobile Workers Union (UAW), the American parent, was amicable. Of the $600 million American strike fund, the Canadians received $36 million, approximately 5% (the 125,000 Canadian members represented close to 10% of the total union membership).[14] Today, CAW represents not only auto workers, but also salt miners, airline agents, baggage handlers, brewery workers, and even fishermen.[15]

## CLC

The CLC represents most of the unions in Canada, and has a total membership of more than two million.[16] It is primarily a service organization composed of seventy-seven national and international unions who finance the CLC through dues based on the size of their membership. Figure 17-4 illustrates the structure of the CLC and Figure 17-5 shows the membership of the sixteen largest unions in Canada.

One of the major objectives of the CLC is to influence legislation and promote programs that are relevant to the labour force. It achieves these objectives through lobbying, education, and research.

## AFL-CIO

The AFL-CIO is the U.S. counterpart of the CLC. The two organizations operate inde-

**FIGURE 17-4   Structure of the Canadian Labour Congress**

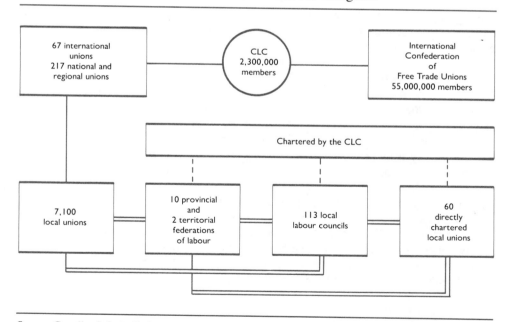

Source: Canadian Labour Congress, "The Structure of Labour in Canada," *Notes on Unions*, Ottawa: CLC, 1988, p. 2.

FIGURE 17-5    Membership of Canada's Sixteen Largest Unions, 1982-1987

| | CANADIAN MEMBERSHIP ('000) | | | |
| --- | --- | --- | --- | --- |
| | 1982 | 1985 | 1986 | 1987 |
| Canadian Union of Public Employees (CLC) | 274.7 | 296.0 | 304.3 | 330.0 |
| National Union of Provincial Government Employees (CLC) | 230.0 | 245.0 | 254.3 | 278.5 |
| Public Service Alliance (CLC) | 157.6 | 181.5 | 182.0 | 179.8 |
| United Steelworkers of America (CLC) | 197.0 | 148.0 | 160.0 | 160.0 |
| United Food and Commercial Workers (CLC) | 135.0 | 146.0 | 156.0 | 160.0 |
| Canadian Auto Workers (CLC) | 121.8 | 135.9 | 140.0 | 143.0 |
| International Brotherhood of Teamsters (Ind.) | 93.0 | 91.5 | 91.5 | 91.5 |
| Quebec Teaching Congress (CEQ) | 82.1 | 90.0 | 91.2 | 87.6 |
| Social Affairs Federation Inc. (CNTU) | 84.0 | 93.0 | 93.0 | 93.0 |
| United Brotherhood of Carpenters (AFL-CLO) | 89.0 | 73.0 | 68.0 | 66.0 |
| International Brotherhood of Electrical Workers (CFL) | 71.0 | 68.6 | 68.6 | 68.6 |
| Service Employees International Union (CLC) | 65.0 | 70.0 | 70.0 | 70.0 |
| International Association of Machinists (CLC) | 64.4 | 58.6 | 58.6 | 58.6 |
| Canadian Paperworkers Union (CLC) | 66.2 | 63.0 | 57.0 | 57.0 |
| Labourers' International Union (AFL-CIO) | 55.4 | 51.4 | 46.7 | 46.7 |
| International Woodworkers of America (CLC) | 63.0 | 51.2 | 48.0 | 48.0 |

Source: P. Kumar, "The Current Industrial Relations Scene in Canada," Industrial Relations Centre, Queen's University, 1987.

pendently, but since most international unions in the AFL-CIO are also members of the CLC, a certain degree of common interest exists. Most international unions are dues-paying members of both organizations.

### Union Membership

In recent years, the number of women members in Canadian unions has been increasing rapidly. In 1962, women made up only 16.4% of total union membership; the corresponding figure in the mid-1980s was about 36%. Between 1962 and 1984, women accounted for 54% of total membership growth in this country.[17] However, women are still a long way from being represented on the executive boards of unions in proportion to their numbers. Though comprising 36% of the total union membership, they accounted for only 18.1% of the executive board members.

Out of nearly 370 labour organizations in Canada, 114 were affiliated with the CLC, representing 57.6% of all union members in the mid-1980s. Approximately 35% of the current Canadian labour force is unionized. Public administration was the most highly unionized at 72.4%, followed by transportation, communication, and other utilities with 56.4%. Agriculture, finance, and trade sectors had the lowest rate of unionization with 1.1%, 6.7%, and 9.8% respectively.[18]

### Unions and Productivity

The number of worker days lost due to work stoppages decreased marginally in the last few years (see Figure 17-6). As may be seen from the figure, paper and allied industries

FIGURE 17-6  Number of Work Stoppages in Canada

| | TOTAL (000 WORKER DAYS) | FOOD AND BEVERAGES | WOOD | PAPER AND ALLIED INDUSTRIES | TRANS-PORTATION EQUIPMENT | TRANS-PORTATION |
|---|---|---|---|---|---|---|
| 1984 | 3871.6 | 438.1 | 166.7 | 551.3 | 537.8 | 550.1 |
| 1985 | 3180.7 | 314.0 | 76.0 | 95.2 | 373.2 | 478.8 |
| 1986* | 2903.6 | 166.4 | 99.2 | 1.6 | 90.0 | 564.8 |

*Figures for the months of January-March are actual; for other months, projected.

Source: Statistics Canada, *Canadian Statistical Review,* February, 1987, Catalogue # 11-003E, Vol. 62, No. 2, p. 55. Reproduced with permission of the Minister of Supply and Services Canada.

and transportation were the biggest losers during work stoppages in 1984; however, this picture changed for the better in 1986.

What are the effects of unions on profitability of organizations? A study in 1986 that considered rates of return on capital, sales, and assets of firms belonging to twenty Canadian industries over a ten-year period concluded that unions, overall, have a negative effect on productivity. Whether this occurs only through effects on wages and labour productivity or through other channels is not clear at present.[19]

Unions need not always play this negative role. Indeed there are many instances where powerful unions can work with management and be a catalyst in major organizational change and productivity improvement programs.

### Effects of Strikes

How expensive are strikes from the point of view of employers? Results of a survey conducted among 127 Canadian firms indicate a variety of costs associated with work stoppages (see Figure 17-7). Fixed overheads (item 9) and loss of sales (item 4) were viewed by most employers as the most important costs; the least important costs were advertising (item 13), customer penalties (item 12), additional insurance costs (item 10), and increased costs through sabotage (item 11).[20]

Do strikes help employees get better wage negotiations? Not necessarily, according to one Canadian study reported in 1986. Robert Lacroix of l'Université de Montréal analyzed 1915 wage settlements in the Canadian manufacturing industry during 1968-1981 and found that "on average . . . there will be no difference between wage settlements reached after a strike and other negotiated wage agreements." According to Lacroix, "A strike does not change existing bargaining powers, it only reveals them more accurately to the two bargaining parties." As such, it is unlikely that strikes can change the capacity of firms to pay more wages; indeed the probability of a negative effect of a strike on the firm's resources increases with the length of a strike.[21]

## GOVERNMENT AND HUMAN RESOURCE MANAGEMENT

Government shapes the union-management framework through laws and their interpretation. The federal government's role comes from its obligation to protect the welfare of society and from the authority found in Section 91 of the British North America Act, which states that the Canadian Parliament shall have the power to "make laws for the

FIGURE 17-7  Costs of Strikes

| COSTS OF WORK STOPPAGES | MEAN[a] | SD | PERCENT IMPORTANT[b] |
|---|---|---|---|
| **I.  Costs incurred before a work stoppage** | | | |
| 1.  Loss of sales due to order splitting by strike-sensitive customers | 1.7 | 1.41 | 31 |
| 2.  Time spent by legal counsel and company executives on contract negotiations | 2.2 | .94 | 33 |
| 3.  Cost of building inventories in anticipation of a strike | 1.7 | 1.32 | 28 |
| **II.  Costs incurred during a work stoppage** | | | |
| 4.  Loss of sales due to inability to fulfil orders | 2.7 | 1.48 | 66 |
| 5.  Loss of production in related manufacturing plants | 1.5 | 1.46 | 27 |
| 6.  Overtime costs for administrative or supervisory personnel | 1.4 | 1.08 | 12 |
| 7.  Costs for additional security arrangements | 1.6 | 1.02 | 15 |
| 8.  Time spent by legal counsel and company executives on negotiations | 2.3 | 1.02 | 40 |
| 9.  Fixed overhead for idle plant capacity | 2.8 | .99 | 66 |
| 10.  Costs of increasing insurance coverage for production facilities and other property | 0.8 | .96 | 5 |
| 11.  Damages caused by sabotage | 1.1 | 1.25 | 14 |
| 12.  Penalties paid to customers for delay in delivery or inability to meet other contract provisions | 0.9 | 1.14 | 11 |
| 13.  Advertising expenses to inform the public of your case | 0.6 | .72 | 2 |
| 14.  Costs incurred in the process of conciliation, mediation, or arbitration | 1.6 | .86 | 10 |
| **III.  Costs incurred after a work stoppage** | | | |
| 15.  Loss in production due to low productivity in the early post-strike period | 1.8 | 1.29 | 28 |
| 16.  Start-up costs | 2.1 | 1.02 | 36 |
| 17.  Overtime costs to rebuild inventories | 1.5 | 1.09 | 15 |
| 18.  Recruiting and training expenses for newly hired employees to replace those leaving the company for good | 1.1 | 1.04 | 8 |
| 19.  Loss of goodwill from present and potential customers | 1.7 | 1.31 | 27 |
| 20.  Bad publicity and reduced confidence from investors, creditors, and government agencies | 1.2 | 1.15 | 14 |
| **Savings from work stoppages** | | | |
| 1.  Savings on labour costs during the work stoppage | 1.8 | 1.13 | 27 |
| 2.  Savings on other variable or semi-variable costs during the work stoppage | 1.4 | 1.03 | 12 |
| 3.  Savings on labour costs after the work stoppage due to concessions made by the union | 0.9 | 1.14 | 13 |

[a]Based on a 5 point scale with 4 extremely important and 0 not incurred.
[b]Percentage of firms indicating the item was either extremely or very important (m = 127)

Source: T.Y.W. Tang and A. Ponak, "Employer Assessment of Strike Costs," *Relations Industrielles,* Vol. 41, No. 3, 1986, p. 560.

Peace, Order, and Good Government of Canada,'' in relation to those matters not assigned exclusively to the provinces. The latter part of this statement is quite significant for human resource practitioners, because the Canadian Parliament is restricted in its jurisdiction over labour relations matters to organizations involved in interprovincial trade and commerce, e.g. banks, airlines, railways, and federal government agencies. All other organizations fall under the jurisdiction of the provinces. It has been estimated that only about 10% of the Canadian labour force comes under federal jurisdiction, in contrast to about 90% in the United States.[22] Nevertheless, a number of federal laws are relevant to all employees in Canada. Those laws, and the appropriate provincial laws, will be discussed in the following sections.

## *Canada Labour Code*

The backbone of Canadian labour legislation has been—and still is, with modifications —the Industrial Disputes Investigation Act of 1907, now the Canada Labour Code, in effect since 1971. Two major components make this legislation unique as compared to similar laws in the United States and the United Kingdom: the creation of a tripartite Labour Relations Board and the delay of the right to strike or to lockout until conciliation efforts have failed. Otherwise, the law gives employees the right to organize without interference by employers. It also requires any party to organize without interference by employers. It also requires any party to a collective agreement to bargain in good faith.

To prevent employers from interfering with employee rights, the law prohibits specific *unfair labour practices* by management. These legal prohibitions are summarized in Figure 17-8. They require that management neither interfere with nor discriminate against employees who undertake collective action. These unfair labour practices also make firing these employees illegal and outlaw ''blacklisting'' and ''yellow dog'' contracts.

## FIGURE 17-8 Unfair Labour Practices by Management

The Canada Labour Code makes it an unfair labour practice for members of management to:
1. **Suspend**, transfer, lay off, or otherwise discriminate against employees who want to unionize.
2. **Impose** any condition in a contract of employment that restricts an employee's rights under the code.
3. **Suspend**, discharge, or impose any penalty on an employee for refusing to perform the duties of another employee who is participating in a legal strike.
4. **Deny** pension rights or accrued benefits to an employee because of involvement in a legal strike.
5. **Intimidate** or threaten an employee to compel that person to refrain from becoming or to cease to be a member, officer, or representative of a trade union.
6. **Bargain** collectively with a trade union if another trade union is the bargaining agent of that bargaining unit.

---

Before the Canada Labour Code was passed, a common human resource policy was to require new employees to sign a ''yellow dog'' contract. This employment contract meant that if an employee assisted a union in any way, that person could be fired. Those who agreed to these contracts were often called ''yellow dogs.''

And anyone who supported unions might be "blacklisted" by the previous employer's giving a negative reference.[23]

The Canada Labour Code also makes company-dominated unions illegal. In the past, some employers believed that if they could not prevent their employees from organizing, the next best thing would be to encourage a union they could dominate. Through threats, bribes, or infiltration, some companies tried to control union activities. For example:

Robin Hood Multi-Foods Inc. in Ontario arranged for an employee to infiltrate the Service Employees International Union, take part in its deliberations, and report back to general management about its activities. The Ontario Labour Relations Board issued a "cease and desist" order and required the company to post a notice in the plant explaining the board's order and making it clear that the company would not engage in any of a long, specified list of unfair labour practices.[24]

The law also prohibits employers from discriminating against anyone who brings charges against a company for violating the law. And to make the result of unionization meaningful, employers must bargain with the union in good faith over wages, hours, and working conditions.

Unfair labour practices by unions are also prohibited. Such practices are described in Figure 17-9.

FIGURE 17-9    Unfair Labour Practices by Unions

The Canada Labour Code makes it an unfair labour practice for a trade union to:
1. **Seek** to compel an employee to bargain collectively through it if the trade union is not the bargaining agent of a unit that includes that employee.
2. **Bargain** collectively with an employer if the trade union knows or ought to know that another trade union is the bargaining agent for the unit of employees.
3. **Participate** in or interfere with the foundation or administration of an employers' organization.
4. **Attempt**, at the workplace and during working hours, to persuade an employee to become a union member—except with the consent of the employer.
5. **Require** an employer to discharge an employee because he or she has been expelled or suspended by the trade union for reasons other than failure to pay membership dues.
6. **Expel** or suspend an employee from membership, or deny membership, by applying union membership rules in a discriminatory manner.
7. **Intimidate**, coerce, or penalize a person because he or she has filed a complaint or testified in any proceedings pursuant to the code.

To illustrate how few constraints unions faced before this law was passed, consider how one powerful union arranged for a large number of its unemployed members to picket a small trucking firm. The pickets so severely interfered with deliveries that the owner was forced to recognize the union against the wishes of his employees.

When negotiations on the first contract began, the union leader refused to meet with the company's lawyer. The owner was told to pick someone else to represent

> the firm. The owner, having no legal remedies and fearing more disruption, hired a new lawyer. Then the union presented the lawyer with a completed contract and said, ''Sign or we strike.'' There was no negotiation, and the company signed.

Although most unions do not abuse their power, isolated cases like this one contributed to legal restrictions on unions.

The law makes it illegal for unions to force employees into a union or to interfere with an employer's selection of its collective-bargaining representative. It also requires unions to bargain with management in good faith.

As has been mentioned before, federal legislation like the Canada Labour Code is relevant only to employees and employers under federal jurisdiction, whereas most employees and employers are governed by provincial legislation. Fortunately for the human resource practitioner, the content of provincial laws is similar to that of the federal law. Nevertheless, for specific legal problems the relevant jurisdiction and appropriate laws have to be determined.

Despite the fact that Canada has eleven independent jurisdictions affecting employee-employer relations, it is possible to distinguish some common characteristics, which are outlined in Figure 17-10.

FIGURE 17-10   Common Characteristics of Federal and Provincial Labour Legislation

---

1. All jurisdictions create labour relations boards to decide who has the right to participate in collective bargaining and what bargaining unit should be permitted to represent those who are organized.
2. All jurisdictions (except Saskatchewan) prohibit strikes during the life of an agreement.
3. All jurisdictions (except Saskatchewan and British Columbia) contain regulations that delay strike action until a conciliation effort has been made and has failed.
4. All jurisdictions require that a collective agreement be in force for at least one year.
5. All jurisdictions specify and prohibit certain ''unfair practices'' by management and unions.

---

## Labour Relations Boards

To enforce the Canada Labour Code at the federal level and related legislation in the provinces, the federal and all provincial governments have created their own Labour Relations Boards (LRB). These agencies investigate violations of the law and have the power to determine: (1) whether a person is an employee for the purposes of the law; (2) whether an employee is a member of a trade union; (3) whether an organization is an appropriate bargaining agent for bargaining purposes; (4) whether a collective agreement is in force; and (5) whether or not any given party is bound by it. The enforcement procedures of an LRB are summarized in Figure 17-11.

In comparison to traditional courts of law, LRBs are more flexible in their procedures for solving a conflict. They may rely on expert testimony instead of looking for precedents, suggest a compromise, or even impose a solution upon the parties. In all jurisdictions, the boards' decisions are final and binding and cannot be appealed except on procedural matters. On the other hand, the boards may revise, rescind, or override any of their decisions.

When charges have been filed against an employer, the human resource department

FIGURE 17-11   LRB Procedures for Redressing Unfair Labour Practices

1. The aggrieved individual or organization contacts the appropriate LRB office (federal or provincial) and explains the alleged violation.
2. If the case appears to have merit, the LRB informs the other party of the complaint and asks for a response.
3. The LRB gives the parties involved the opportunity to present evidence and to make representations. If the complaint cannot be solved informally, the LRB conducts an official hearing with the interested parties present and usually represented by legal counsel.
4. On the basis of the evidence, the board will either dismiss the case or, if one party is found guilty of a violation, issue a cease-and-desist order. In the event of noncompliance, this order is enforceable in a court of law.
5. It is up to the board to decide whether a verdict can be appealed or not. In any case, an appeal can be made in matters of jurisdiction, failure to pursue legitimate complaints, and procedural irregularities.

usually assists the company's lawyer in preparing the case. The department compiles performance appraisals, attendance records, and other documents that help the company prove its case. Sometimes the department's investigation reveals that the company is guilty. At this point, time and legal costs are saved by admitting guilt and accepting the LRB's proposed settlement.

Human resource departments also become involved when the LRB holds an employee election. This other function of the LRB comes into play when a union applies for certification as a bargaining unit. The election is held to determine if a majority of the employees want a union.

In cases where a substantial number of employees (usually between 50 and 60%, depending on jurisdiction) have signed union cards, the LRB may certify the unit without an election. However, if the number of signed union cards is less than the majority but over some figure between 35 and 45% (again depending on jurisdiction), an election is mandatory. A secret ballot is taken under the supervision of the LRB at the employees' place of business. If the union loses, another election among the same employees cannot be held for one year. If the union wins, then the human resource department must prepare to bargain with the union and reach a collective agreement.

*Conciliation and Mediation*

In their legislation, all jurisdictions provide for conciliation and mediation services. Actually (with the exception of Saskatchewan and British Columbia), no strike action is permitted before a conciliation effort has been made and has failed. The terms conciliation and mediation are often used interchangeably, but in Canada some jurisdictions give them different definitions. "Conciliation" usually implies a relatively passive role by the third party (conciliator) involved, the major purpose being to bring the parties together and keep them talking. "Mediation" connotes a more active involvement of the third party. A mediator may make suggestions and recommendations after having determined the positions of the parties. Often a mediator will meet separately with each bargaining team, especially when the negotiations take place in a hostile atmosphere. Effective mediation requires a high degree of sensitivity, patience, and expertise in the psychology of negotiation. An example will illustrate how a skillful mediator enabled deadlocked negotiations to get moving again.

I had a case where the union had asked for a 15% increase in a one-year contract. Their spokesman told me he would go to 10, but not now—not until the company indicated some movement. The company was holding at 5, but said to me they would go to 7, if the union would come down a little. Both of the parties convinced me that they would go no further, and a strike seemed certain.

In some cases, if I knew the parties well, I would tell them exactly what the other said. However, in this case I simply indicated to each bargaining team in separate meetings that there was some flexibility in the other's position, but I didn't know how much. Then I said to the union: "I'd like to see you get 10% or even 15, but I don't believe the company will go that high. In my opinion the most you can get is 7 or 8%. I may be mistaken, but if you hold to the 10% figure I think you'll have a strike."

Then I went to the company and said: "If you hold to the 5 or 7% figure I can almost assure you that you'll have a strike. Now the decision is yours, and it's not for me to tell you how to spend your money, but in my opinion the settlement will eventually be 10%, and I think 10% might do it now. You might have to go as high as 13. If you want me to explore 7%, I'll give it a try, because, as I've said, the union has indicated some flexibility. But I don't think 7% will get a settlement."[25]

Conciliators and mediators are appointed by the federal or provincial ministers of labour, at the request of either one or both of the parties involved or at the discretion of the ministers. A conciliator is requested to submit a report to the minister within a specified time period. If conciliation fails, strikes or lockouts can legally commence, usually two weeks after the submission of the conciliator's report. A mediator is not required to write a report on the legality of a strike or lockout and in fact has no influence in this matter.

### Arbitration

All jurisdictions, with the exception of Saskatchewan, require that collective agreements include a provision for final settlement by arbitration, without stoppage of work, of all differences concerning the interpretation or administration of a contract. This means that as long as a collective agreement is in force, any strike or lockout is illegal. An arbitrator is selected from a list furnished by the appropriate ministry of labour, and the choice must be approved by both parties. The arbitrator's decision is final and cannot be changed or revised, except in cases wherein corruption, fraud, or a breach of natural justice has been proven.

### Corporations and Labour Unions Returns Act

In the 1960s and early 1970s, Parliament created a number of royal commissions and study groups that investigated many aspects of organized labour and labour-management relations. The investigations were largely fact-finding exercises, conducted in hopes of providing information and recommendations that would be useful in the drafting of new legislation. Of considerable concern to the federal government and the public were reports of mismanagement of funds and corruption by officials of national and inter-national unions. Based upon the results of some investigations, Parliament in 1962 passed the Corporations and Labour Unions Returns Act, designed primarily to gather information on the activities and financial dealings of international unions and corporations. The act requires unions and corporations to submit annual reports containing statements of assets and liabilities, income and expenditures, and other more detailed information relating to financial matters. This information is published annually (in summary form to maintain anonymity) by Statistics Canada and is available to interested parties.[26]

## Public Sector Bargaining

### Unions at the Federal Level

The first Canadian union representing civil servants and other government employees was the Civil Service Federation of Canada (CSFC), founded in 1909. It had more than 80,000 members in 1958, when a group broke away and founded the Civil Service Association of Canada (CSAC). These two unions merged again in 1967 to form the Public Service Alliance of Canada (PSAC), now the third largest union in the Canadian Labour Congress with close to 180,000 members (1988). There are seventeen other unions representing federal employees. The best known, mainly for its militancy and strike activities, is the Canadian Union of Postal Workers (CUPW).

### Unions at the Provincial and Municipal Level

The National Union of Provincial Government Employees (NUPGE) was formed in 1976 as an umbrella organization for the unions in all provinces. It is the second largest union with approximately 292,000 members (1988). The largest union in the municipal field and at the same time the largest union in Canada is the Canadian Union of Public Employees (CUPE) with 342,000 members (1988).

### Public Sector Employers

It would be natural to assume that the employer of civil servants is either the government of Canada, the government of a province, or that of a municipality. However, a variety of employment relationships exist, differing among provinces and municipalities. At the federal level, it is the Treasury Board that deals with employees under federal jurisdiction, comprising approximately 10% of the Canadian labour force. At the provincial level authority may be vested in a provincial treasury board or its president (New Brunswick and Newfoundland), a management board (Ontario), in any person designated by the treasury board (Prince Edward Island), the Public Service Commission (Nova Scotia), or the government itself (Quebec). The laws of Alberta, Manitoba, and Saskatchewan do not mention any specific government body.

## LEGISLATION AND TRIBUNALS AT THE FEDERAL LEVEL

When Parliament passed the Public Service Staff Relations Act (PSSRA) in 1967, it essentially gave federal civil servants bargaining rights similar to those granted workers in the private sector: usually the right to bargain for wages, hours, and certain working conditions. More importantly, it also gave them the right to strike. This is in contrast to civil servants in the United States, who since 1962 have had the right to bargain collectively, but not to withhold their services. The PSSRA created the Public Service Staff Relations Board (PSSRB), a body equivalent to the Canada Labour Relations Board in the private sector. However, the PSSRB possesses a wider range of responsibilities than the CLRB. The reason for this lies mainly in the conflict-of-interest situation that arises with the federal government having to protect the public welfare on the one hand and being in the role of an employer on the other. Like the CLRB in the private sector, the PSSRB is responsible for certification of unions as bargaining agents for appropriate groups of employees. The methods of conflict resolution, however, are different. Before a bargaining agent can give notice that it wishes to bargain, a decision must be made whether a conciliation-strike procedure or a binding-arbitration procedure will be used should a deadlock occur. Once that decision is made and the PSSRB has been informed, the employer must accept it. The union has the right to choose different procedures for each subsequent collective agreement. If the strike route has been chosen, conciliation procedures must be followed before a strike can begin. The chairman of the PSSRB will appoint a conciliation officer at the request of either party. Once the officer has submitted his or her report, the chairman of the PSSRB will decide whether or not to appoint a conciliation board. If a board is not appointed, or if an appointed board is unsuccessful in settling the dispute, the union may initiate strike action. (See Figure 17-12 for a diagram of the collective bargaining process in the public sector.)

FIGURE 17-12   Collective Bargaining in the Public Sector

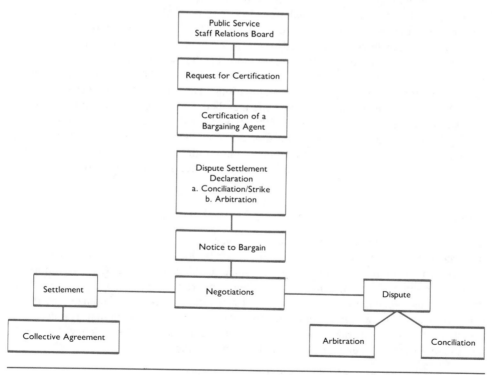

Source: Alton W.J. Craig, *The System of Industrial Relations in Canada*, Second Edition, Prentice-Hall Canada Inc., 1986, p. 258.

Another difference from the private sector is that the law allows the employer to designate certain employees as performing essential services, thus divesting them of the right to strike. The union, however, may challenge the list of "designated employees," in which case the PSSRB makes the final decision. This latter function gives the board a certain responsibility for the safety and security of the public, since in a strike of civil servants it must decide which services are essential.

### Provincial Legislation

A comparison of the federal and provincial legislation for public service labour relations reveals little uniformity of treatment across Canada. In Saskatchewan the public sector is treated the same as the private sector (meaning there is no special legislation), whereas in Alberta, Ontario, Nova Scotia, and Newfoundland, there are different legal frameworks for the public and private sectors, with severe restrictions on or even total prohibition of strikes. The remaining provinces are somewhere in between. It can be said, however, that the general trend is towards granting public sector employees the same rights as private employees.

## THE CHALLENGE TO HUMAN RESOURCE MANAGEMENT

Today, many human resource managers and union leaders perceive government intervention as a threat to the traditional freedoms they both have enjoyed. Their common concern rises out of the fear of more government laws that will control their affairs. And since existing laws are enforced by agencies with the power to "make laws" by their interpretation of existing ones, regulations are bound to grow.

Closer union and management cooperation to improve labour relations is a major way to slow the growth of government regulations. This does not mean that either party must abandon its constituents: rank-and-file members and stockholders. On the contrary, both sides must continue to perform. What is needed is a realization that cooperation, not legalistic advocacy, represents the shortest route away from additional government constraints. Otherwise, political expediency and public welfare will demand, for better or worse, further legislative action, new agency decisions, and more government constraints.[27]

### The Human Resource Department's Proactive Response

Unions cause changes in the behaviour of managers and in the operation of the human resource function. In nonunionized facilities, an implicit objective of human resource management is often to remain nonunion. Since the Canada Labour Code prohibits the use of coercion or discrimination, management must rely on a proactive approach. That is, it must use *effective* human resource practices that discourage unionization, if that is the company's policy. For example, this approach requires that human resource specialists (within the constraints of organizational effectiveness and efficiency, law, technology, and other challenges) carefully do the following:

- *Design* jobs that are personally satisfying to workers.
- *Develop* plans that maximize individual opportunities while minimizing the possibility of layoffs.

- *Select* workers who are qualified.
- *Establish* fair, meaningful, and objective standards of individual performance.
- *Train* workers and managers to enable them to achieve expected levels of performance.
- *Evaluate* and reward behaviour on the basis of actual performance.

In other words, human resource managers need to apply actively the ideas discussed in earlier chapters of this book! Failure to implement sound human resource policies and practices provides the motivation *and* justification for workers to form unions.

## Human Resource Management Implications

When unions are present, the human resource function is changed. Organizationally, the human resource department is expanded by the addition of a labour relations section. This section allows labour specialists to deal with such critical areas as negotiations and contract administration, while human resource professionals attend to their more traditional roles. In fact, human resource and labour relations may form two equal divisions within a broader department, typically called *industrial relations*.

Operationally, the human resource section seeks sound employee relations through effective policies. "Open door" policies and in-house complaint procedures are two examples. The labour relations section has a complementary role. It wants to minimize the restrictions on management by diligent negotiations and fair administration of the union contract. Or to use a sports analogy, human resource management serves as the offensive team and labour relations as the defensive team.[28]

Unions can cause greater centralization of employee record keeping and discipline to ensure uniformity. This change can mean that line managers lose some of their authority to the human resource department. They also find their jobs more difficult because of the new rules imposed by the contract. In other words, line managers may become dissatisfied because their authority diminishes while their responsibility increases. These added responsibilities are likely to be imposed at the request of human resource administrators, who now need more information from the line managers. To illustrate, the line manager may have to compile new reports on absenteeism, tardiness, productivity, and comments voluntarily made by workers about the union. Often these demands on supervisors create a fertile ground for friction between line managers and human resource staff members.

Besides the high costs for record keeping, additional staff, negotiations, and occasional strikes, management has less freedom to make unilateral changes. No longer can a manager decide what is desirable and then make a change. Instead, union-management agreements and the labour laws must also be considered.

A large manufacturing company was losing money on the company cafeteria in one of its plants. Although the company never expected to make money from this operation, it certainly wanted to break even. To correct the deficit, the company raised prices slightly without discussing this with the union. The union threatened to file an unfair labour practice charge unless management reduced the prices and agreed to negotiate the matter.

Although this incident is relatively minor, every year there are thousands of unfair labour practice cases. And even more significant than the time and costs of such legal actions are the inefficiencies caused when unilateral decisions must be reversed. The processes used to create a bilateral relationship will be discussed in the next chapter.

## SUMMARY

The labour-management framework consists of unions, governments, and management. Although each union is unique, unions share the common objectives of protecting and improving their members' wages, hours, and working conditions. To further these objectives, the union movement has created local, national, and international structures, plus federations at the provincial and federal levels. Moreover, most unions are loosely incorporated into the Canadian Labour Congress (CLC).

In Canada the federal government has jurisdiction in labour relations matters over only Crown-corporations, airlines, most railways, communication companies, and federal government agencies — or approximately 10% of the labour force. All other organizations fall under the jurisdiction of the provinces, who have enacted separate but similar legislation. Every jurisdiction has its own labour relations board which is responsible for the enforcement of the law in that jurisdiction.

Management's role is to integrate resources to meet society's needs within an environment substantially shaped by union and government constraints. Although unions may represent the employees, management remains ultimately responsible for obtaining organizational performance and effectively utilizing the human resources. Only through proper utilization of human resources can management fulfil its labour-management role.

## TERMS FOR REVIEW

| | |
|---|---|
| Business unionism | Canadian Labour Congress (CLC) |
| Social unionism | Canada Labour Code |
| American Federation of Labor and Congress | Labour Relations Board |
|   of Industrial Organization (AFL-CIO) | Unfair labour practices |
| Local unions | Conciliation and mediation |
| Craft unions | Corporations and Labour Unions Returns Act |
| Industrial unions | Public Service Staff Relations Act (PSSRA) |
| National unions | Public Service Staff Relations Board (PSSRB) |
| International unions | |

## REVIEW AND DISCUSSION QUESTIONS

1. In your own words, summarize the primary objectives of unions.
2. What distinguishes craft, industrial, and mixed unions from each other?
3. Suppose an employee in your department is an active member of the union but is performing improperly. After several sessions with the employee, performance is

still unacceptable. What type of support would you want to gather before you terminated that employee? What legal complications might result from your action?

4.  What roles does the Labour Relations Board serve in labour-management relations?

5.  Why are sound human resource policies necessary even when no union is present?

6.  If you work in the human resource department of a small company that is suddenly unionized, what changes would you expect to occur in the human resource department?

7.  What role do you think federal and provincial governments will play in future labour-management relations? What actions can unions and management take to reduce the probability of future government involvement?

## INCIDENT 17-1

### Union Pressures at Halby Ltd.

After the employees at Halby Ltd. won the Labour Relations Board election, they selected Tom York to be the local union president. Tom had no experience in the role of union president, but he was well liked by the other employees and was largely responsible for starting the local union.

About two weeks after the election, the human resource manager, the company lawyer, Tom, and the union's vice president began negotiating the contract. Among the union's demands, Tom listed the following:

- A 75-cent-an-hour raise to be given all employees in the union
- The removal of the company lawyer from negotiations, since the union had no lawyer and could not afford one
- The termination of Hal Sinkin and Francis Ellison because they had fought against the union's representation of the workers
- The discharge of all employees who do not join the union before the contract is signed
- Free supplementary medical insurance for all employees in the union

Although Tom had other demands, he said these were the ones that were most important.

1.  Do any of Tom's demands violate the labour law? Which ones?

2.  If Tom insisted on each of these demands, what legal action could the company take?

## INCIDENT 17-2

### A Routine Discharge at ITC

On October 2, 1988, Pete Ross was discharged from ITC. The supervisor requested that the human resource department discharge Pete because he was caught drinking in the employee's locker room. Drinking on company property was prohibited, as it had been since publication of the ITC Employees'Handbookin 1971.

All employees of ITC were given a copy, and whenever new employees joined, as had Pete in 1980, they too were given one. The handbook stated in part: "The consumption of alcoholic beverages on company premises is grounds for immediate termination . . . ."

The discharge appeared rather routine to the human resource manager and to the plant manager. Although drinking violations were uncommon, the plant manager believed clear-cut violations of company policy should be punished. Besides, he was frequently heard to say, "We must support our first-line managers."

Pete's fellow machinists did not see it as a "routine discharge." John Briggs, a fellow machinist, summed up the group's feelings: "Pete was a darn good machinist. He was seldom tardy, never absent, and always did a first-class job. If Pete did it, it was done right! That bugged George (the supervisor) because George would pressure Pete to get out the work and say, 'Don't worry about the quality; they only measure quantity.' But Pete wasn't slow. He'd turn out a quality product as fast as some people turned out junk. I don't think George liked Pete. I don't know if Pete took a belt before leaving the plant Wednesday evening, but I think George just wanted to can Pete."

The following Monday John Briggs spent his rest breaks and lunch hour talking with the other machinists, telling them that "if we don't want to end up like Pete, we'd better get a union." He even had cards from the International Association of Machinists Union. By Monday evening, Briggs had thirty-two signed cards. (There were thirty-nine machinists in the shop.)

On Tuesday morning John Briggs was called into the supervisor's office. The plant manager and the supervisor grilled him. They asked him if he had been distributing authorization cards, who had signed them, and how many he had obtained. Briggs simply replied by saying, "That is none of your business." The plant manager adjourned the meeting without saying a word.

On Thursday (payday at ITC), Briggs received a termination notice with his pay-cheque. The notice was effective immediately. The notice said termination was for low productivity and excessive absences during the previous twelve months.

1. What unfair labour practices may have occurred?
2. Should management offer reinstatement to Pete Ross or John Briggs?
3. Was Briggs correct when he answered, "That is none of your business," to the questions about the authorization cards?

○ ○ ○ ○ ○ ○ ○ ○ ○ ○ ○ ○ ○ ○ ○ ○ ○ ○ ○ ○ ○ ○ ○ ○ ○ ○ ○ ○ ○ ○ ○ ○ ○ ○ ○ ○ ○ ○ ○ ○ ○ ○ ○

## CASE STUDY

### UNIONIZATION OF SERVICE LABS INC.*

Service Labs started three years ago. The executive manager through aggressive recruitment efforts brought in a core of about six experienced technicians from another lab that had been in town for over twenty years. These skilled technicians gave up their secure unionized jobs at the old lab for the non-union- ized jobs in the new plant. Although the wages were a bit lower, the new plant offered a clean, new environment as well as equipment that was new (and therefore less prone to breakdowns). They perceived the manage- ment at the new plant to be liberal (i.e., no time clocks, etc.). They liked the small size of the plant and the fact that they had direct access to the big boss. There was also a prom- ise that once the new lab got established, the wage rates would go up. In the next eighteen months several other less experienced work- ers also moved from the old lab to the new lab.

Service Labs quickly gained a reputation for the quality of its service. Expansion began to occur in the second year and continued in the third year, at the time of events narrated below. The fact that this expansion was occur- ring in the downswing economy of 1982-83 said something about the strong market hold the company's services had acquired. Also early in the third year a general manager and a production manager were hired.

The third year was also the year when the plant was organized by a militant union. The number of employees at this time was slightly in excess of forty and operated in two shifts. They were predominantly female and over half on the younger side of age twenty-five. The following is one employee's account of why unionization occurred at Service Labs.

"It all started with this new one-day service business. They started an evening shift so they can provide one-day service, and hired a num- ber of new people off the street. The new workers were posted mostly to the night shift. Because of their inexperience, lots of prob- lems began to occur in the night shift. But the bosses were not in at this time. So it was the day shift that got yelled at. We naturally resented that. And then some of us were asked to work evening and split shifts, and that didn't go too well. Most of the girls here have families or are single. Either way their evenings

are precious. All these things started a rest- lessness and there was a lot of bitching around during coffee time.

"The promised increase in wages never came about. They kept saying that they were still a new lab just getting established and could not afford to bring up the wages to the level of older established labs. But the business was booming as we could see. They were buying all sorts of new machines.

"In the meanwhile, the wages at the old lab had gone up and up. So much so, some of us here were making two to two and a half dol- lars an hour less than comparable jobs at the old lab. Some people started saying, 'We need a union'. Finally around October-November the management said our wages would go up soon, that all jobs would be systematically classified into categories. While this helped keep the restlessness under control, it also got our hopes up, perhaps unreasonably up. In anticipation of these raises we worked our butt off during the November to December peak season.

"We expected our salaries to go up on the first of the year. By mid-February we had lost faith and many uncomplimentary things about management were on the lips of everyone, just like after they put in a time clock a few months earlier. The new managers also intro- duced all kinds of new controls. They checked waste bins to check out our wastage rates, and they brought in consultants with stop-watches. Whereas before we had only two working supervisors or lead-hands, now in addition, we had a production manager and a general man- ager between the supervisors and the execu- tive manager. If these two new managers had been older or had experience in our business, it wouldn't have been so bad. They were in their early twenties.

"Finally in early March we got the long- awaited pay raises. The day on which the new rate paycheques were given out was some- thing else. We normally get them before noon. But on that day they didn't come around even an hour after lunch. We were getting a bit apprehensive . . . that they would pull some number on us. So finally the general manager calls a meeting and goes on and on about the hard days the company was facing . . . that the times were getting rough and so on. At this point our executive manager storms into the meeting and starts swearing at people, that we were all a bunch of stupid idiots; that we don't learn fast and this and that and the new rates are going to cost the company a bundle and we have to pull our socks up . . . Having said his piece, he leaves the meeting and the general manager again goes on and on saying the same things he said before. About the new wage rates, he says, 'If you don't think you got a good rate, come and talk to us. But we might not be able to do anything about it.'

"Here everybody was waiting anxiously to find out what their new rates were and they get called names and yelled at. It made a lot of people angry, very very angry. There was no appreciation of what we had done for the company during the past peak season.

"So, when we finally got our paycheques in our hands, we found out what the new raises were. They were nowhere near what people were making in the other lab. Some people got fairly decent raises and some almost nothing. That is when some people again started talking union.

"We also didn't have any kind of sick leave. If you got sick for a week you just lost your pay. If you stayed sick longer, there was no guarantee your job would be held for you. We didn't have a dental plan or anything. Not even parking facilities. In the winter it gets to be really a pain if you have to find street parking.

"So all these things added up. When management started calling names and made us feel like beggars, that was the last straw! The delaying of the cheque distribution was like playing games. If it was a technical problem with the computer or something, why didn't they bother to explain? It was like they were

showing us who was boss . . . that our bread depended on them.

"I didn't want to have the union. When you have a union, there are lots of restrictions. There comes a rule for everything. And the union can't do anything about the everyday stuff anyway, the stuff that gets on your nerves! Where I worked before there was a union and it got us good rates but that's all it did. Then we had a four month strike, and that wiped it all out. We lost more than we gained. And about management harassment, the union couldn't do anything. That is the reason I quit there, because of management harassment, especially after the strike, and the kind of job they posted me to.

"It was too heavy a job for me. For my size and weight, I couldn't handle it. On top of it, my boss was an 'ugly' person. And you have to deal with him in the dark room. I was scared to. Not that he did anything, but he didn't think anything of touching a person. For me that is an ugly thing. The union didn't do anything. What is the point in having a union then?

"That is the reason why I wasn't particularly keen about a union. But when it came to signing union pledge cards, I didn't want to stand out as a sore thumb. I had good relationships with everybody. I didn't want to risk it. You spend most of your day with your co-workers and if they are not pleasant, your eight-hour day is most miserably spent. I would rather stay home than work where people are nasty and unpleasant.

"So when the union filed for certification and management found out about it, they were very upset, stunned I should say. They didn't expect this to happen. They right away laid off ten people . . . the same afternoon as a matter of fact. As if that wasn't enough, one day we find the production manager playing spy by sitting up behind the storage boxes listening to see who is for the union and who is not. Among the people laid off were also the ones who were most active in getting people to sign the union pledge cards. Management said there wasn't enough work. That was true only to a degree. If they had laid off just two or three people it wouldn't have been that bad. With that many laid off, the pressure was on the rest of us to do more.

"It was dumb! Of course the union went straight to the Labour Relations Board and complained about management's 'dirty tricks.' So the certification was granted just for that. Management had to take back all the people it laid off and had to give them their pay for the laid off period.

"So the plant got organized because management did some dumb things . . . the way they treated people . . . they should have known it was coming. They say one of the new managers had worked in a unionized plant. I believe he was actually responsible to get the union there and was the shop steward. He should have known better. So you see management got what it deserved. The prom-

ised wage raises take forever to come . . . they are too little and too late . . . then they yell and scream at us and call us names . . . suggest we go talk to them if we have gripes, but in the same breath they say they won't do anything about it. Some, who got only a five cent raise, did go and talk. Management said that is what they considered fair and that was that. They also said nothing could be done for another three or six months now because the computer system locks-in a given rate for a certain period. So why didn't they tell people what new rates they were going to get and give them a chance to appeal? I got a dollar increase, but that was still a dollar less than what my job got paid at this other lab. Then they shoved me to do two people's load by not replacing this girl who had quit. If they had back paid me it would have helped how I felt.

"So, that's how we got unionized."

1. Do you think the employee's feelings are generally shared by other workers in the lab? What factors would you say led to the unionization of Service Labs Inc.?

2. Did management engage in unfair labour practices?

3. If employees felt pressured to sign the union pledge card, is it unfair labour practice on the part of the union?

4. Identify, in order of priority, the issues that will be taken to the first collective bargaining negotiation by the union, and by the management.

*The company is given a fictitious name. The case was written by Prof. Jai Ram of Wascana Institute of Applied Arts and Sciences, Regina. Used with permission.

○ ○ ○ ○ ○ ○ ○ ○ ○ ○ ○ ○ ○ ○ ○ ○ ○ ○ ○ ○ ○ ○ ○ ○ ○ ○ ○ ○ ○ ○ ○ ○ ○ ○ ○ ○ ○ ○ ○ ○ ○ ○

## SUGGESTED READINGS

Anderson, John, Morley Gunderson and Allen Ponak, *Union-Management Relations in Canada*, 2nd ed., Toronto: Addison-Wesley Publishers, 1989.

Craig, Alton W.J., *The System of Industrial Relations in Canada*, 2nd. ed., Scarborough: Prentice-Hall Canada, 1986.

Kumar, Pradeep, Mary Lou Coates and David Arrowsmith, *The Current Industrial Relations Scene in Canada*, Industrial Relations Centre, Queen's University, Kingston, Ontario, 1988.

Jamieson, Stuart M., "Industrial Conflict in Canada, 1966-75," Discussion Paper No. 142, Centre for the Study of Inflation and Productivity, Economic Council of Canada, 1979.

Labour Canada, *Directory of Labour Organizations in Canada*, Ottawa: Supply and Services Canada, 1989.

Williams, Brian C., "Collective Bargaining in the Public Sector: A Re-examination," *Relations Industrielles/ Industrial Relations*, Vol. 28, No. 1, pp. 17-33.

# REFERENCES

1. *Canadian Industrial Relations*, the Report of Task Force on Labour Relations, Ottawa: Privy Council Office, December 1968, p.9.

2. Alton W. J. Craig, "A Model for the Analysis of Industrial Relation Systems," in Harish C. Jain (ed.), *Canadian Labour and Industrial Relations*, Toronto: McGraw-Hill Ryerson Limited, 1975.

3. Samuel Gompers, *Labour and the Common Welfare*, Freeport, N.Y.: Books for Libraries Press, 1919, p. 20.

4. An editorial in *Canadian Labour*, June 1968, p. 5.

5. Ed Finn, "Collective Bargaining under Wage Controls Seen as a Charade," *Toronto Star*, January 26, 1976.

6. J.W. Miller, Jr., "Power, Politics, and the Prospects for Collective Bargaining: An Employer's Viewpoint," in Stanley M. Jacks (ed.), *Issues in Labour Policy*, Cambridge, Mass.: MIT Press, 1971, pp. 3-10.

7. Frank Tannenbaum, *The Labour Movement, Its Conservative Functions and Consequences*, New York: Alfred A. Knopf, Inc., 1921.

8. Selig Perlman, *A Theory of the Labour Movement*, New York: The MacMillan Company, 1928.

9. Charles Lipton, *The Trade Union Movement in Canada 1827-1959*, Montreal: Canadian Social Publications Ltd., 1967, p. 4.

10. See Charles Lipton, op. cit.; John Crispo, *The Canadian Industrial Relations System*, Toronto: McGraw-Hill Ryerson Limited, 1978; Gerald E. Phillips, *The Practice of Labour Relations and Collective Bargaining in Canada*, Toronto: Butterworth and Co. (Canada) Ltd., 1977; and Stuart Jamieson, *Industrial Relations in Canada* 2nd ed., Toronto: Macmillan of Canada, 1973.

11. Leonard Sayles and George Strauss, *The Local Union*, New York: Harcourt, Brace & World, 1967.

12. Phillips, op. cit., pp. 143-145.

13. John Crispo, *International Unionism—A Study in Canadian-American Relations*, Toronto: McGraw-Hill of Canada Limited, 1967.

14. A.W.J. Craig, *The System of Industrial Relations in Canada*, Second Edition, Scarborough: Prentice-Hall Canada Inc., 1986, p. 104.

15. D. Jenish, C. White and C. Wood, "Union Fighting Unions," *Maclean's*, April 27, 1987, pp. 41-42.

16. Canadian Labour Congress, "The Structure of Labour in Canada," *Notes on Unions*, Ottawa: CLC, 1983, p. 2.

17. *Work Life Report*, Vol. 5, No. 3, 1987, p. 8.

18. *Work Life Report*, op. cit.

19. D.R. Maki and L.N. Meredith, "The Effects of Unions on Profitability," *Relations Industrielles*,, Vol. 41, No. 1. 1986, pp. 54-67.

20. R.Y.W. Tang and A. Ponak, "Employer Assessment of Strike Costs," *Relations Industrielles*, Vol. 41, No. 3, 1986, pp. 552-571.

21. R. Lacroix, "A Microeconometric Analysis of the Effects of Strikes on Wages," *Relations Industrielles*, Vol. 41, No. 1, 1986. pp. 111-127.

22. R.M. Lyon, M. Reiner, and E.R. Teple (eds.), *The Labour Relations Law of Canada*, Washington, D.C.: Bureau of National Affairs, 1977, p. 18.

23. Jack Williams, *The Story of Unions in Canada*, T.M. Dent & Sons (Canada) Ltd., 1975.

24. Wilfred List, "Food Processing Firm Used Employee as Spy, Board Certifies Union," *Globe & Mail*, July 30, 1981, p. 2.

25. D.A. Peach and D. Kuechle, *The Practice of Industrial Relations*, Second Edition, Toronto: McGraw-Hill Ryerson Ltd. 1985, p. 210.

26. *Annual Report of the Minister of Supply and Services Canada under the Corporations and Labour Unions Returns Act, Part II: Labour Union*, Ottawa: Minister of Supply and Services, published annually.

27. William B. Werther, Jr., "Government Control v. Corporate Ingenuity," *Labour Law Journal*, June 1975; pp. 360-367.

28. John R. Bangs, *Collective Bargaining*, New York: Alexander Hamilton Institute, Inc., 1964, pp. 29-34.

# C H A P T E R *18* ○ ○ ○ ○ ○ ○ ○

## *UNION ORGANIZING AND COLLECTIVE BARGAINING*

*Collective bargaining may be described as a joint endeavour on the part of workers to bring their combined pressure to bear on their employers in order to persuade them to better their wages, fringe benefits, and other conditions of employment.*

JOHN CRISPO[1]

○ ○ ○ ○ ○ ○ ○ ○ ○ ○ ○ ○ ○ ○ ○ ○ ○ ○ ○ ○ ○ ○ ○ ○ ○ ○ ○

## *CHAPTER OBJECTIVES*

After studying this chapter, you should be able to:
1. **Discuss** the major reasons that workers join unions.
2. **Identify** conditions that indicate unionization may occur.
3. **Describe** how human resource departments respond to unionization attempts.
4. **Explain** the key steps in negotiating a union contract.
5. **Define** the major topics of collective bargaining.

○ ○ ○ ○ ○ ○ ○ ○ ○ ○ ○ ○ ○ ○ ○ ○ ○ ○ ○ ○ ○ ○ ○ ○ ○ ○ ○

*U*nions do not just happen. They are usually caused by some management action or inaction that seems unfair to the workers. For example, consider how two people viewed the discharge of their coworker Pete Ross.

> JOHN BRIGGS: Our supervisor finally found an excuse to fire Pete. All Pete did was take a drink in the locker room after his work shift ended. He wasn't even on company time.
>
> KATE VANDER: I know, and it really scares me. I have a family to support. If the supervisor ever decided to fire me, my family would suffer a lot.

JOHN BRIGGS:   It frightens me too, especially since the human resource department approved the discharge without an investigation. Everybody in the shop knew the supervisor didn't like Pete's happy-go-lucky attitude.

KATE VANDER:   If the supervisor had liked Pete, the drinking in the locker room would have been overlooked. It is all a matter of favouritism around here. But what can we do?

JOHN BRIGGS:   Well, if we had a union, at least we might get a fair hearing. A union can stand up to management. I wonder if we can start a union?

Whether John and Kate can start a union depends on the support they can get from other workers. If others feel a need to join together, then a union can be organized successfully. Once it is created, the union and management may negotiate a contract that defines their roles. These two actions of organizing and bargaining create the union-management relationship.

Each relationship between a union and an employer is unique. To explain why, this chapter examines the causes of unions and the methods used to organize them. It also discusses the negotiation process and its goals.

## CAUSES OF UNIONS

The reasons for joining a union vary from person to person. Even workers in the same organization may have different reasons for joining a union because of their different perceptions. For example, consider the views of two bank tellers at a recently organized branch bank.

MARIA TOMAS:   I decided to join the union for many reasons. I'm not even certain which one was the main reason. One thing for sure, the branch manager now must prepare work schedules fairly. Before the union, we never had any say about them. The manager told us what hours we worked, and it was final. Now we can appeal to the union. Sure, I could have complained to the human resource department at head office. But then the manager might have become angry. That sure would reduce my chances for a merit raise or promotion. I supported the union, and I am proud of it.

PAUL ANGLIN:   I really don't know why so many people wanted a union at this branch. This is the best job I have ever had, and the boss is really nice. All the union means is dues, rules, and maybe even a strike. I simply can't afford to miss a paycheque over some strike. To me, we were better off without a union.

Although it is hard to believe, both tellers have the same boss, work in the same bank branch, receive the same pay, and have the same job. The big difference between Maria and Paul is their views of the bank and the union. Had someone at the bank realized Maria's dissatisfaction and reacted favourably, she might agree with Paul's feelings. But when employees like Maria think they are being treated unfairly and believe that the human resource department is unable to help, union membership may seem desirable.[2]

Since individual perceptions vary, there is no single force that motivates people to join unions. Instead, perceptions are shaped by a variety of reasons. Some of the more important ones are shown in Figure 18-1, according to the types of unions that may result. A further discussion of the figure explains why some people join unions and others do not.

FIGURE 18-1   Workers' Major Reasons for Joining or Not Joining Unions

| TYPE OF ORGANIZATION (AND WORKERS) | MAJOR REASONS FOR JOINING | MAJOR REASONS FOR NOT JOINING |
|---|---|---|
| **Craft Unions** (Blue-collar workers) | • Learn a trade<br>• Find employment through union<br>• Receive union benefits<br>• Acquire collective power | • Dislike unions<br>• Possess steady employment<br>• Receive fair treatment |
| **Industrial Unions** (Blue- and white-collar workers) | • Seek change in management practices<br>• Dislike supervision<br>• Receive peer pressure<br>• Required by union shop<br>• Want benefits promised during organizing drive | • Want a management position<br>• Afraid of strikes<br>• Dislike dues<br>• Dislike unions<br>• Receive fair treatment |
| **Professional Associations** (White-collar workers) | • Seek professional contacts<br>• Dislike supervisory practices<br>• Resolve professional issues<br>• Want better pay | • Reject as unprofessional<br>• Unions not needed for self-employed<br>• Want a management position<br>• Receive fair treatment |

## Craft Unions

As described in Chapter 17, craft unions exist to organize workers who have similar skills, such as carpenters or plumbers. People join these unions for practical reasons. They hope to learn a useful skill through the union's apprenticeship program, which offers them both a job and training.

Workers who already have a trade often use craft unions to find jobs. In the construction industry (where many skilled tradespeople are employed), craft workers are hired on a per-project basis. When the project is over, the contractor lays them off. Then workers typically ask the union for a referral to another contractor who has requested their skills. Thus membership in a craft union makes it easier to find a job.

Craft unions also offer other services. The union may provide supplemental health insurance, life insurance, pension plans, and other benefits to members. Besides the employment service and benefits, the union's collective bargaining power can mean favourable wages and working conditions.

Some skilled workers do not join craft unions, however. Aside from those who dislike unions, most nonmembers have acceptable management, human resource policies, employment security, and fringe benefits.

## Industrial Unions

If the workers of a single employer decide to organize without regard to individual skill, the result is an industrial union. Workers usually form these unions when human resource policies or supervisors cause mistreatment.

Human resource management policies guide managers in their treatment of employees. Policies that affect discipline, layoffs, compensation, job design, and communications are especially important. When these policies are ignored or do not address employee needs, a union may be formed by workers to make changes.

Possibly even more important than policies are first-level supervisors. These people serve as the link between employees and management. If supervisors do not provide fair treatment, employees may look to unions for protection.

> As manager of CGKS TV and Radio Station Ltd., Lily Konna had to cut expenses since sales of advertisements had declined 10%. She ordered a freeze on all hiring, a stop to the annual cost-of-living raise, and a 10% layoff. Kevin DeFleur, the human resource manager, suggested a policy of keeping 90% of the workers that had been with the company the longest.
>
> Lily responded, "Are you kidding? Those are the highest-paid workers and not necessarily the best ones. Besides, layoffs allow supervisors to get rid of their deadwood. Let the supervisors decide whom to keep."
>
> "You're going to open us up to charges of favouritism," Kevin argued.
>
> "I doubt it." Lily added, "My order stands!"
>
> Four months later, the Communications Workers of Canada organized a union among the remaining workers. The union's organizing slogan was "End favouritism, join the CWC."

Once a union exists, members may pressure their peers to join. This *peer pressure* is most effective on new workers, who are often uncertain of their roles and want to "feel like I belong." This pressure also can cause other employees (who might otherwise be indifferent) to join a union.

Labour leaders and management may also agree to a *union shop*. Under this agreement, all workers are obligated to join the union to keep their jobs. If they fail to join, management must fire those workers. Union shops are allowed in all provinces.[3]

Reasons for nonmembership are equally diverse. Workers who want to become managers may believe union membership damages their chances for promotion. Other employees view unions as "just another boss" that leads to extra costs, such as union dues or lost wages from strikes. Likewise, past experiences or isolated stories of union wrongdoing may cause some people to form a negative opinion of collective action.[4] Or, more simply, policies and supervisory treatment may be fair, so that employees lack motivation to join a union.

## Professional Associations

Most professionals do not join unions. Instead, they belong to *professional associations* that are designed to further their knowledge and improve the image of the profession. But when professionals are also employees, their association may become more like a union.[5]

Some professional groups — provincial education associations and provincial nurses' associations, for example—have evolved into unions. This change usually results from poor treatment by management. These "unions" emerge when supervisory practices, human resource policies, or professional issues are unacceptable. For example, a few years ago the Nova Scotia Registered Nurses Association complained bitterly about poor management and unpleasant working conditions in Nova Scotia hospitals. A short time later the first union for nurses was certified.

There are several reasons why professionals do not join unions. Those who are self-employed would receive few benefits from such membership. Even those who work for an employer have little to gain if their treatment is professionally favourable. And many professionals view unions as degrading and inappropriate.

## UNION ORGANIZING

It is worth remembering that a union begins only when workers create it.[6] Though this is a simple observation, it is a key to understanding the process of unionization. While unions use professional organizers, the outcome of the organizing drive depends primarily upon the employees. As George Meany, the first president of the AFL-CIO in the U.S., once commented:

> Despite the well-worn trade union phrase, an organizer does not organize a plant. Now, as in the beginning, the workers must organize themselves. The organizer can serve only as an educator; what he organizes is the thinking of the workers.[7]

*Union organizers* educate the workers by explaining how the union can reduce mistreatment. These professionals only assist workers; they do not cause workers to join a union. Organizers are less successful when confronted by a proactive human resource department because there is little that a union can offer. Even the most experienced organizers find it difficult to organize a truly well-managed and growing company. IBM provides an appropriate example:

> In more than thirty-five years, IBM claims the company has never laid off a worker for economic reasons. Instead, it retrains workers unneeded in one job and assigns them to another. Since 1970 it has retrained and physically relocated 5000 employees as part of the most extensive corporate education program in the U.S.
>
> Not surprisingly, IBM has never been the target of a major union organizing drive in the U.S. . . . "I don't know what a union at IBM would do," says one salesman, incredulously, when asked if he would join a union.[8]

### Signs of Organizing Activity

Human resource departments can estimate the chances of union organizing by looking for the proper signs. One set of signs is found in the work environment. Figure 18-2 lists specific questions that can alert a human resource department to union activity. The higher the number of "yes" answers to the questions in the figure, the more likely it is that union activity will occur. The external factors shown in the figure are largely

FIGURE 18-2   Environmental Factors that May Lead to Unionization

---

### EXTERNAL FACTORS

- Have there been recent changes in the labour laws that affect your industry that might cause interest in your firm by union organizers?
- Has there been a sudden increase in unionization activity in your community or industry?
- Is your company planning a major increase in its work force that might stimulate union interest in organizing the firm before it becomes larger and more expensive to organize?

### INTERNAL FACTORS

- Has your organization failed to resolve systematically the union complaints made during previous, unsuccessful organizing attempts?
- Are employee turnover and absenteeism rates worse than the norms for your industry or community?
- Has the company failed to conduct job satisfaction surveys? Or, if they have been conducted, do they reveal a trend towards dissatisfaction?
- Are pay and fringe benefits below average for the industry, community, or unionized firms?
- Is the company's procedure for resolving employee complaints largely not used by workers?

---

FIGURE 18-3   Employee Behaviour that Suggests Unionization Activity

---

- Do some employees seem to be suddenly popular?
- Are workers making unusual inquiries about fringe benefits, wage levels, raises, promotions, grievance procedures, or other employee-related matters?
- Do criticisms of management decisions and policies seem more vocal?
- Have employee directories been disappearing at a high rate?
- Are employees asking about management's reaction to unions?
- Are questions being asked about company rules on solicitation?
- Have employees discussed past or future group meetings?
- Are there strangers in the cafeteria or parking lots?
- Do employees exclude supervisors from their conversations?
- Are cards or handbills being distributed?

---

outside the human resource department's control. But external developments can cause the department to pay greater attention to the internal factors over which it has influence.

> When the federal government and some provinces changed the labour laws to allow employees of organizations run by federal or provincial governments to participate in the collective bargaining process, many human resource managers under their jurisdiction realized that union organizing would become more likely. Rather than wait for a union drive to begin, some human resource managers began an assessment of the internal factors over which they had control. This prompt, proactive action gave them a wide range of options for improving the work environment. Their counterparts who did not respond to this external sign had less flexibility once union activity had started.

Another set of signs comes from changes in employee behaviour that suggest a union drive may be underway. Figure 18-3 indicates the type of behaviour to which supervisors and human resource specialists should be alert. Again, a high number of "yes" answers may mean unionization is occurring. It is important to remember that these are only indications, not proof.

> One manager who observed some suspicious activities notified the human resource department. A few days later she was embarrassed "pleasantly" when the employees presented her with a gift certificate and a card as a Christmas present. What this manager saw was a group of employees passing around a card and collecting contributions for a gift. She thought they were signing up to join a union.

## Limits on Management's Response

Once a union drive begins, management's choice of responses becomes limited in several important ways. First, Labour Relations Boards (LRB) protect workers' rights from management reprisals. For example, the discipline of union supporters can result in legal violations, unless the employer can prove the wrongdoer received the same punishment as other employees normally receive.[9] Even an *increase* in wages or fringe benefits during an organizing drive may be considered a violation because the employer is trying to "buy" employee support.

> When the Union of Bank Employees tried to organize branches of the Canadian Imperial Bank of Commerce, bank management granted pay increases to all employees except where the union had already been certified or where certification was pending. Management contended that any salary adjustment for unionized employees was a matter of future negotiations. The Canadian Labour Relations Board declared this action to be unfair labour practice and ordered the bank to compensate employees who had not received an increase.[10]

Another limit results when a *union organizing committee* is present.[11] This committee consists of those workers who are leading the union drive. Their responsibility is to convince other employees to join the union. To do this, they use handbills, speeches, conversations, and even home visits. The committee's goal is to get workers to sign *authorization cards*, which evidence the employees' interest in the union. Once a certain percentage of the employees sign cards, the committee can ask an LRB to conduct a representative election or grant certification of the union. During this process, the organizing committee may raise questions about management actions that affect employees, even if management's actions are fair.

> After the Blue Water Swimming Pool Company fired Reed Creaseman for stealing, the organizing committee mailed a letter to each employee's home. The letter never questioned Reed's guilt or innocence. Instead, the union raised questions about the swimming pool company's discipline procedures. One paragraph of the letter read as follows:
> "Have you ever taken home a pen or pencil from work? If you have, you might be fired like Reed Creaseman. He took home some company tools and the main-

tenance yard guard stopped him. Will a guard stop you with company property? Will you get fair treatment, or will you end up like Reed? Fired! Before you are next, sign an authorization card. Join the union for your own protection.''

A third limit during unionization is the actions of management. Human resource administrators should stress to every manager, from supervisor to chief executive officer, the following two cautions:

- Will management actions be ruled as unfair labour practices?
- Will management actions provide fuel for the organization drive?

When an unfair labour practice is committed by any member of management, it can lead to expensive, time-consuming lawsuits. What is equally damaging, the organizing committee can point to violations as further justification for a union. Even when management actions are legal, union leaders may claim credit for new policies favourable to employees.

The human resource manager and president of a small insurance company were surprised by what happened after they gave a 10% raise during a union organizing campaign. The day after the pay raise was announced, the union circulated handbills that read as follows:

"Beware! Management is trying to trick you. They gave you a 10% raise to con you into voting against the union next week. What will happen if the union loses? Will it take another drive to get a raise? Isn't it odd that with the union here, management suddenly cares about your pay? Don't be tricked! Vote for the Teamsters Union! Show management that you are smarter than they think. . . . ''

Even worse than the union's counterattack was the LRB's charging the employer with an unfair labour practice. The union then promptly circulated another handbill titled "LRB Catches Company Breaking Labour Laws." The union won the election thirty-seven to fourteen.

## Management's Campaign

Most employers mount a careful campaign to counteract a union drive. Normally, the human resource department is responsible for fending off the union, although outside consultants and labour lawyers often help.

The campaign usually begins by getting needed information. The most important information is top management's attitude towards unionization.[12] Although management officials usually oppose unions, the human resource department must determine what response, if any, top management wants to make. Assuming management wants to keep the company nonunion, the human resource department collects data about the (proposed or campaigning) union. Human resource specialists learn about the union's dues, strike record, if any, salaries of officers, and any other relevant facts that might cause workers to reject the union.

Armed with this detailed information, the human resource department arranges for speeches to workers about the need to stay nonunion. Speeches are usually supplemented with group meetings, handbills, letters to employees, and articles in the company newspaper.

To coordinate these activities, an *information clearing office* may be established in the human resource department. This office provides information to supervisors about the need to stay nonunion and answers their questions. Sometimes telephone "hot lines" are installed so that supervisors and employees can get quick answers to questions raised during the organizing drive. The human resource department uses the clearing office to remind employees of the company's good points while refuting the union's claims. Ideally, the employer's case is presented in a factual, honest, and straightforward manner. However, the human resource department's success is determined only partially by its campaign. More important is the treatment employees have received before the organizing drive began.

## COLLECTIVE BARGAINING

When a union wins an election, the LRB requires both the union and management to bargain in good faith. The failure of either party to do so can lead to unfair practice charges. Clearly, it is important for management to bargain in good faith. Should it needlessly postpone negotiations, refuse to meet with the union, fail to discuss relevant issues, or undertake any other action that represents a failure to bargain in good faith, the results can be costly. Besides the cost of legal expenses, the workers are free to strike. If the strike is caused by management's refusal to bargain or other illegal activities, the strikers can get their jobs back *plus* the wages they would have earned.

> The editor of a now-defunct newspaper found out the hard way what "bargaining in good faith" means. He had decided to automate by installing computerized typesetting machines. When he told the president of the local typographical union, the president said, "Let's talk about it."
>
> "No! I've made up my mind and my decision is final. I own this newspaper, and I'll do with it what I want," the editor concluded.
>
> "Well, I guess we are at an impasse. I'm going to call a strike. We'll end the strike after we settle this automation nonsense," added the union president.
>
> The union charged the newspaper with refusal to bargain. Thirty months later a court of appeals upheld the LRB and ordered the owner to pay thirty months' back wages, with interest, to every striker. The total bill was $374,000.00.

The process of collective bargaining has three overlapping phases. Preparation for negotiations is the first and most critical stage. The success of the second stage, face-to-face negotiations, largely depends on how well each side has prepared. The third phase involves the follow-up activities of contract administration. To conduct these new duties, a labour relations department may be added to the human resource function.

### Preparations for Negotiations

The purpose of negotiations is to achieve a *collective agreement*. The agreement specifies the rights and responsibilities of management and the union.

Detailed preparations are required if the agreement is to achieve a balance of rights and responsibilities.[13] Figure 18-4 shows the major stages of collective bargaining. As can be seen, several steps are required before actual negotiations begin.

FIGURE 18-4   The Stages of Collective Bargaining

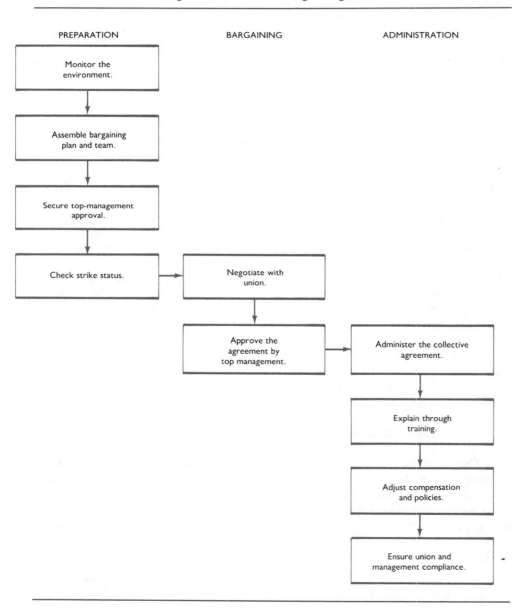

## Monitor the Environment

Collective bargaining does not occur in a vacuum. Labour relations specialists need to monitor the environment to find clues about likely union concerns. These clues can be found in several ways. First, the labour department must be sensitive to the inflation rate and the gains made by other unions. Since union leaders are elected, they seldom accept wage increases that are less than those of rival unions. Otherwise, they may be voted out of office. Acceptable increases usually exceed the inflation rate by a few percentage points, unless the employer cannot afford the usual pattern. For example, the United Auto Workers allowed Chrysler Corporation in Canada and the U.S. to give a smaller wage increase in 1979, because of its weaker financial position in comparison with General Motors and Ford.

A second class of clues can be found among union promises made during the organizing drive or among unmet demands from previous negotiations.

> During an organizing drive at an electronics company in the Maritimes the union promised to make day-care facilities for children of employees the key issue for the first negotiations. The majority of the employees were women who several times before had put forward similar requests to management, to no avail. The union won the election by a 155-to-28 margin, although the year before it had failed to get a majority.
>
> During the following negotiations, management again refused to consider day-care facilities, but relented when 95% of the employees voted for strike action. A day-care centre was organized on a trial and cost-sharing basis. When the agreement expired and was renegotiated the following year, the union demanded that the company accept the full cost of the centre. Since management had just secured a lucrative supply contract and could not afford a strike, it agreed to the demand.

A third source of bargaining issues is *management rights*. Those rights are the freedoms that supervisors and managers need to do their jobs effectively.[14] They often include the right to reassign employees to different jobs, to make hiring decisions, and to decide other matters important to management. If these rights are not protected in the contract, the union may hinder management's effectiveness. For example, supervisors may want all job descriptions to include the phrase ''and other duties assigned by management.'' This clause prevents workers from refusing to work because it is not in their job description. The clause also gives supervisors greater freedom in assigning employees. Labour relations specialists in the human resource department discover which rights are important on the basis of discussions and surveys among supervisors and managers.[15]

## Assemble a Bargaining Plan

After monitoring union demands and management rights, this information is compiled into a *bargaining book*. The ''book,'' or more commonly a computer tape, contains estimates of likely union demands and management's counterproposals. It represents the employer's plans for the upcoming negotiations.

### Secure Top-Management Approval

Top management should approve the overall bargaining plans and goals since it is responsible for the organization's success. These goals serve as controls that enable top management to gauge the bargaining team's effectiveness. Knowledge of the controls also may help the bargaining team because it knows the limits on its authority to bargain with the union.

### Check Strike Status

Most contracts are negotiated without a strike. But labour specialists usually plan for a possible strike to strengthen their bargaining position. Their preparations depend upon the likelihood of a strike. If employees strongly support union demands, a strike is more likely and plans are more thorough.

The goal of labour specialists is to reduce the damage from a strike if it occurs. Their efforts include special arrangements with important buyers and suppliers. If operations are to be stopped during a strike, close-down and start-up plans are made. When top management seeks to continue production or service, work schedules for managers and nonstriking employees are developed. These preparations signal to union leaders that the employer is ready for a strike. This signal may cause union leaders to rethink their demands and agree to a negotiated settlement without a strike.

## Bargaining

After preparations, the second phase of collective bargaining is face-to-face negotiations with the union. Discussions usually start sixty to ninety days before the end of the present contract. If the negotiations are for the first time, they begin after the union is recognized by the employer or wins an LRB election.

### Negotiate with the Union

Negotiations cover wages, hours, and working conditions. These three areas are interpreted broadly. *Wages* mean all forms of compensation such as pay, insurance plans, retirement programs, and other benefits and services. *Hours* include the length of the workday, breaks, holidays, vacations — in fact, any component of the work schedule. *Working conditions* involve safety, supervisory treatment, and other elements of the work environment.[16]

Once face-to-face bargaining begins, it is important to follow the techniques listed in Figure 18-5. Otherwise confusion may develop that can cause needless delays or even a strike.[17]

General Electric in the U.S. used to follow an approach called Boulwarism.[18] Instead of following the suggestions in the figure, GE simply presented the union with its final offer at the beginning of negotiations. This approach created confusion because the unions did not know that GE's first offer was also its last. Politically, the union leaders did not dare accept this offer. If they did, members might question the need for leaders who merely accepted the company's first offer. As a result, bitter strikes occurred between GE and its unions. Eventually, the U.S. National Labor Relations Board ruled this approach to be illegal because GE was not really bargaining. It only made an offer on a take-it-or-leave-it basis.

FIGURE 18-5   Guidelines for Negotiations

---

### THE "DOs" OF NEGOTIATIONS

1. Do seek more (or offer less) than you plan to receive (or give).
2. Do negotiate in private, not through the media.
3. Do let both sides win; otherwise the other side may retaliate.
4. Do start with easy issues.
5. Do remember that negotiations are seldom over when the agreement has been signed; eventually, it will be renegotiated.
6. Do resolve deadlocks by stressing past progress, another point, or counterproposals.
7. Do enlist the support of the federal or provincial conciliator if a strike seems likely.

---

### THE "DON'Ts" OF NEGOTIATIONS

1. Do not make your best offer first; that is so uncommon that the other side will expect more.
2. Do not seek unwanted changes; you may get them.
3. Do not say "no" absolutely, unless your organization will back you up absolutely.
4. Do not violate a confidence.
5. Do not settle too quickly; union members may think a quick settlement is not a good one.
6. Do not let the other side bypass your team and go directly to top management.
7. Do not let top management actually participate in face-to-face negotiations; they are often inexperienced and poorly informed.

---

Successful bargaining usually begins with easy issues to build a pattern of give-and-take. This give-and-take occurs in private, since off-the-record comments may be embarrassing to either side when repeated out of context. This way management does not have to worry about what stockholders may think of its bargaining comments, and union leaders can focus on bargaining without guarding against member reactions.

When deadlocks do occur, several tactics can keep negotiations moving towards a peaceful settlement. By settling easy issues first, bargainers can often point to this progress and say, "We've come too far to give up on this impasse. Surely, we can find a solution." This sense of past progress may increase the resolve of both sides to find a compromise.

Compromises may be achieved by offering counterproposals that take into account the objections of the other party. Sometimes progress is made by simply dropping the issue temporarily and moving on to other items. Further progress on other issues may lead to compromises regarding earlier impasses. If no progress results, bargainers may request the assistance of federal or provincial mediators or conciliators, as discussed in Chapter 17.

The suggestions in Figure 18-5 also imply common bargaining strategies. For example, most management teams will exclude top executives. They are kept out of negotiations because top managers are often not experienced in collective bargaining. But their exclusion also gives management bargainers a good reason to ask for a temporary adjournment when the union produces demands that require a careful review. Rather than refusing the union's suggestion, management bargainers may ask for a recess to confer with top management.

Experienced management bargainers also realize that the union must "win" some concessions. If the employer is powerful enough to force an unacceptable contract on the union, union leaders may seek revenge by refusing to cooperate with management once the collective agreement goes into effect. They may encourage slowdowns and other uncooperative actions. Or when the agreement is renegotiated, the union may be strong enough to cause a long strike. Besides, an unfavourable agreement may not be ratified by union members. If it is rejected, many union constitutions require the parties to resume collective bargaining.[19]

### Approve the Proposed Agreement

The negotiation stage of collective bargaining is completed when the agreement has been approved. Often final approval for the employer rests with top management, although the bargaining team may have the authority to commit the company.

Negotiations are not complete until the union also approves the proposed agreement. Union bargainers usually submit the proposal to the membership for ratification. If a majority of the members vote for the proposal, it replaces the prior agreements. When members reject it, union and management bargainers reopen negotiations and seek a new compromise. Administration of the agreement begins when both sides sign it.

## Administration of the Collective Agreement

Once the agreement is accepted by union members and top management, the human resource department normally explains it by means of training programs and also adjusts pay, fringe benefits, and policies to conform with it. At this point, the agreement needs to be administered to ensure union and management compliance with its provisions. Chapter 19 explains this third stage of collective bargaining more fully.

## SUMMARY

A union-management relationship occurs when workers perceive the need for a union. Their perceptions depend upon many factors. However, treatment by management is the single most important factor in most cases.

Union organizing usually begins with a small group of dissatisfied workers. Cases of an outside organizer's suddenly appearing and gaining widespread employee support seldom occur. Even when this happens, this is because of basic dissatisfactions among the work force.

The organizing process finds workers (with or without a professional organizer) trying to convince others to join the union. Management's response is limited severely by laws and employee reactions. The employer's primary defence is sound policies implemented by competent supervisors *before unionization begins*.

If workers form a union, the federal or provincial Labour Relations Boards require management and the union to bargain in good faith. The success of the human resource department at the bargaining table is affected by its actions before negotiations begin. Labour relations specialists must monitor changes in the collective bargaining environment and assemble a detailed bargaining plan. Then after top management approval and strike preparations, bargainers begin to negotiate. Negotiations with the union result in an agreement that must be approved by union members and top management. Once negotiated, the agreement is administered by the union and management.

## TERMS FOR REVIEW

Union shop
Professional associations
Union organizers
Union organizing committee
Authorization cards

Information clearing office
Collective agreement
Management rights
Bargaining book
Boulwarism

## REVIEW AND DISCUSSION QUESTIONS

1.  What conditions must be met before a labour-management relationship comes into existence?

2.  In your own words, summarize the reasons why workers join (a) craft unions, (b) industrial unions, and (c) professional associations.

3.  ''Unions do not happen, they are caused — by management.'' Do you agree or disagree with that statement? Why?

4.  The major role of human resource departments occurs before union organizing begins. In what ways does the human resource department influence employee decisions to unionize?

5.  In preparing to negotiate an agreement with a union, what types of information would you gather before arriving at the bargaining table?

6.  If you were asked to explain why various types of people are on the employer's bargaining team, what reasons would you give for (a) the company lawyer, (b) the director of industrial relations, (c) a wage and salary specialist, (d) a benefit specialist, and (e) the assistant plant manager?

7.  If you had to advise the manager of a small chain of bakeries how to prepare for a possible strike, what would you suggest?

8.  Suppose you decided to make the union the best offer you could to begin negotiations. What problems might you expect?

## INCIDENT 18-1

### Decorative Mail Boxes Ltd.

During the past three years, Decorative Mail Boxes Ltd. had received contracts from Sears and Eaton's to supply large quantities of decorative mailboxes. This rapid expansion left Amy and Chuck Minor with little time to create a human resource department. Their wage and salary clerk did a good job of keeping wages in line with local pay scales and benefit programs. But little was done about the workers' complaints of poor supervisory practices.

One day, several employees stormed into Chuck's office and threatened to get a union unless he fired two supervisors. Not wanting a union, Chuck transferred the two supervisors. About a month later, the same group of employees said they wanted to change the company's policy on vacations and holidays. Chuck refused to discuss these policies with the group, but said that he was willing to talk with each person individually. From these discussions, Chuck learned that:

- Employees were tired of ten-hour days and work on Saturday, even though they received overtime pay for hours over forty in a week.
- Employees were fed up with having orders yelled at them by supervisors.
- Employees felt that the shop area should be cleaned more regularly.

Although other problems were mentioned, these issues seemed to be the main ones. So Chuck began to solve each problem as time permitted.

1.   By using a reactive approach to employee complaints, what impression is Chuck leaving with employees?
2.   If a union drive began at Decorative Mail Boxes and Chuck suddenly solved all the problems that employees had mentioned, how do you think the union organizing committee would react?
3.   If you were hired as human resource manager, what would be your first action?

## INCIDENT 18-2

### Nicholson and Sons Ltd.

Nicholson and Sons Ltd., a large fish-product manufacturer in Atlantic Canada, experienced a serious drop in fresh fish supplies when the local fishermen preferred to sell their catches to Russian fishing ships that paid higher prices. Management of Nicholson and Sons Ltd. asked the government to regulate the amount of fish local fishermen could sell to foreigners. The Minister of Fisheries and Ocean Resources promised to study the issue.

In the meantime the collective agreement with the Seafood Workers' Union was close to expiration. The president and the human resource manager of the company met to discuss their bargaining plans. According to the information available to the human resource manager, the union would probably ask for 15% wage increases, two more holidays, and a dental plan.

The president was shocked. It was obvious that the company could not afford to meet the union demands, at least not until the situation had improved. And if it did not improve, the company would either have to reduce its volume of business considerably or shut down completely.

The three managers then decided to ask the union to forgo any pay or benefit increases during the term of the next agreement. To make this idea more acceptable, the human resource manager was told to offer the union a one-year agreement instead of the traditional two-year one. The president said: "Tell the union bargaining committee we'll make it up to them if business improves. For us to give any more to the workers would aggravate our losses and may mean more layoffs. I'm sure they don't want that to happen. Also tell them that if they want to strike, it would be fine with us; we probably could reduce our losses if we shut down the plant until we secure more supplies."

1. What action would you take before negotiations begin if you were the human resource manager?
2. Suppose that the situation improves after the collective agreement has been signed. What action do you think the union may take under these circumstances?

○ ○ ○ ○ ○ ○ ○ ○ ○ ○ ○ ○ ○ ○ ○ ○ ○ ○ ○ ○ ○ ○ ○ ○ ○ ○ ○ ○ ○ ○ ○ ○ ○ ○ ○ ○ ○ ○ ○ ○ ○ ○

## *CASE STUDY*

## BRIDGETOWN MANUFACTURING vs. CBCFW*

Bridgetown Manufacturing Company is a medium size manufacturer of home and office furniture, which employs 250 employees, many of whom have been with the company over fifteen years. The employees are represented by the Canadian Brotherhood of Cabinet and Furniture Workers, Local 555. The contract provides for a union shop.

The relationship between the company and the union has been cordial and most of the contracts were negotiated without any third-party assistance.

During the 1975 contract which expired in June 1978, some cracks began to appear in the relationship which hitherto existed between the company and its employees. The rank and file were unhappy about the impact of inflation on their wages and their inadequate fringe benefits package. The union had fought for a COLA clause in the last agreement, but management was adamant in its refusal to discuss this demand. The 1975 settlement was ratified by only 60% of the membership after a bitter and acrimonious ratification meeting.

In an attempt to improve its profit position, the company recently subcontracted work to a private contractor which would normally have been done by the workers in the plant. This reduced the overtime available to the workers and caused a great deal of resentment and frustration.

Three months before the contract was to expire, the company dismissed a shop steward for drinking on company premises during his lunch period. Another employee, with ten years' service, was suspended one week without pay for excessive tardiness and absenteeism.

In the union elections conducted in January 1978, a young, aggressive and militant executive was elected on the platform of "increased democratic control over production," a better pension plan, and greater job security. Jim Trimble, a member of the Marxist-Leninist Party and leader of the militant faction, was elected president of Local 555.

### Negotiations: Week 1

Negotiations in past years were based on "a cooperative bargaining" concept. Two months prior to negotiations both sides submitted to each other proposals for changes in the existing contract and their initial bargaining positions. Because relationships between the union and the company had deteriorated, this practice was not followed in 1978, and the union waited for the first formal negotiation session to submit its demands.

They included the usual demand for changes in vague and ambiguous wording in the hundred paragraphs of the old agreement. Since some recent arbitration decisions supported management's position, some amendments were requested to the relevant clauses to nullify management's advantage. The union also presented an impressive list of new demands, some of them obviously "fillers" to be traded away later in the negotiation sessions.

The company's negotiation team accepted the new demands without comment and agreed to meet within a week. This would give them time to study the demands and prepare counterproposals.

It was agreed that the next session would start with a revision of the contractual language of the existing contract, and then proceed with the new demands. There was an air of cautious optimism at the bargaining table and each party left the initial session with renewed confidence that a settlement would not be difficult. They agreed in advance that they would try to conclude negotiations within four weeks. The union set a strike deadline four weeks from the commencement of negotiations.

Representing the union were:

1. Jim Trimble — newly elected president of Local 555, Chairman;
2. Peter Tull — representative of the Canadian Cabinet and Furniture Workers Union;
3. Rick Kennedy — Secretary Treasurer, Local 555;
4. Peter Hermann, Don Lindsay, Lloyd Campbell — shop stewards;
5. Arthur Black — representing the membership at large.

Representing the management were:

1. Lance Gibbs — General Manager, Chairman;
2. Andy Jacobs — Director of Human Resources and Industrial Relations;
3. Dale Andrews — Production Manager.

## Week 2 (Monday)

There were very few disagreements over the revision of the contractual language in the existing contract and the management team was anxious to begin discussing the list of forty-two union demands. It was confident that the union was serious about twelve of them, and that the others were mere bargaining tools to gain concessions later in the negotiations.

Its strategy, therefore, was to determine which of these demands had "top priority" status and to focus the negotiations on them. The quicker this was done, the easier it would be to reach an early settlement.

Peter Tull, the union's national representative, was not interested, however, in discussing specific demands, but preferred to review in great detail job titles, job descriptions and classifications, which had already been discussed and revised by the Joint Management-Union Evaluation Committee. A recent evaluation resulted in eight job classes being upgraded and four job classes being downgraded.

The next two days were spent on this exercise much to the annoyance of the management team. Management perceived the analyzing and questioning of the judgment of the Joint Committee as an obvious "go slow" tactic on the part of the union.

## Week 2 (Wednesday)

Lance Gibbs, chairman of the management's negotiation team, attempted to counter the union's delaying tactics at the start of the meeting.

**Mr. Gibbs:** Let's get on with the job at hand. Your strategy is clear. You are trying to stall, and force us into a strike to squeeze the last dollar out of us, but it won't work. The decisions of the Joint Evaluation Committee are not topics for negotiations.

**Mr. Trimble:** We have a responsibility to our membership to look after their welfare to the best of our ability. We feel that it is the duty of the negotiation team to review the deliberations of the Committee.

**Mr. Gibbs:** You have that right, but not at the negotiating table. When you are ready to enter into serious negotiations let us know.

(Mr. Gibbs and his team stormed out of the room, muttering that the union was not bargaining in "good faith.")

Later, an agreement was finally reached on this contentious issue, and the decision of the Joint Committee, by agreement, was considered as binding on both parties.

Mr. Gibbs was convinced that the union's strategy was to extend negotiations to the strike deadline, and to coerce management into accepting their demands under the threat of strike action. "Crisis bargaining" was clearly their game plan. He, therefore, reported his suspicions to John Chapman, plant manager, and advised him to make the necessary preparations for a strike. Extra overtime was scheduled and instructions were sent to their suppliers of raw materials to "hold off" on deliveries. The services of a security guard were also secured.

### Week 3 (Monday)

No serious negotiations took place since the management team abruptly left the last session. Attempts to resume serious bargaining were rebuffed by the union. Mr. Gibbs was prepared to begin serious negotiations:

**Mr. Gibbs:**  Are you ready to tell us what exact wage increases you are demanding?

**Mr. Trimble:**  For the past three years our workers have been receiving wages much less than the average for this region, and the high cost of living is making it difficult to feed our families and meet our mortgage payments. The company is making substantial profits, and we are expecting a substantial increase.

**Mr. Gibbs:**  What I want to hear from you is an exact amount. What is a substantial increase?

**Mr. Trimble:**  First we want to hear what the company is prepared to offer.

**Mr. Gibbs:**  O.K., can we have a half-hour coffee break?

The parties returned to their respective hotel suites to plan strategy. Each side wanted the other to take the initiative and put an exact wage increase on the table. The company representatives did not want to take the initiative since they wanted to start well below the union's initial demand. The union team was in no hurry to state a precise wage demand with the hope that, as the deadline approached, management would be forced to offer a higher wage increase.

After the recess, Mr. Gibbs revealed the company's offer to make the union tip its hand.

**Mr. Gibbs:**  I will give you the total package amount by which the company is willing to increase its overall labour costs. You can break up the amount any way your membership wishes for all your economic demands. You can allocate the total dollar package between wages and fringe benefits. The company cannot afford any more and remain in business. If you press for more, we might have to consider shifting some production to our nonunionized Quebec plant.

**Mr. Trimble:**  How are we to determine how this total amount should be broken down? We have no way of determining the cost of each of our demands, such as the cost of O.H.I.P., shift premiums, etc., to the company. We will, however, discuss your offer over the weekend and meet with you again next Monday.

During the weekend there was considerable activity on both sides. The company was busy preparing for a strike and managers were told to prepare for a three or four week work stoppage. On the union side, the word went out to the membership to refuse overtime. Union officers and stewards began to condition the membership for strike activity. "We have been shafted long enough" became somewhat of a slogan. Strike signs were hastily prepared and picket captains were being instructed as to their conduct and responsibilities on the picket lines. Letters went out to the District Labour Council enlisting moral and monetary support from the locals of the Council.

### Week 4 (Monday)

This was the final week of negotiations, and Friday at midnight was the strike deadline set earlier by the union. The company persisted in negotiating a package deal while the union preferred to negotiate on an item-by-item basis.

The company offered a package totalling $200,000 to cover a three-year contract. The union promptly turned down this offer and countered with its proposal.

**Mr. Trimble:**   We have decided to negotiate for a one-year contract.

**Mr. Gibbs:**   Forget it.

**Mr. Trimble:**   Then we shall not give you any proposals at all.

**Mr. Gibbs:**   Sure you can — just adjust them to a three-year contract.

At this point in the negotiations Mr. Trimble gave the company the union's demands based on a one-year contract.

The list consisted of ten major demands including a 25-cent an hour general wage increase — the first time that a precise wage increase was put on the table. In addition, there were some non-economic items — e.g., plant-wide, instead of departmental, seniority governing layoffs, a sub-contracting clause, and a job security clause.

The company's negotiating team left the room to discuss the union's demands. On returning, Mr. Gibbs said that he was willing to negotiate a one-year contract, but that the cost of the union's demands were far beyond what the company was capable of paying.

**Mr. Gibbs:**   Do you want to drive us into bankruptcy? The most we can afford — and I am being generous — is a 10 cent general wage increase. I am very upset over the conduct of these negotiations. In the past we had a good working relationship and negotiations were conducted with very little rancour. We compromised, made concessions, and signed contracts that were fair and realistic. I am very dissatisfied with the slow pace of negotiations, and I am not going to be "sucked in."

**Mr. Trimble:**   The union will adjust its demands if you allow our accountants to inspect your financial statements. Our membership helped to make your company a success over the years, and we are entitled to a fair share of its wealth.

Mr. Gibbs did not reply to the union's request to examine the company's financial statements, but reiterated "that if the union persisted in making unreasonable demands, and if the company could not be assured of labour stability in the plant, management would postpone plans for further expansion. It would seriously consider moving the plant to their other location. Ten cents increase per hour is all the company could afford."

### Week 4 (Wednesday)

The union resumed negotiations with some significant changes in its demands. It would accept a two-year agreement calling for 15 cents an hour in each year of the agreement, four weeks vacation after ten years of service instead of eight as set out in demands, and twelve paid holidays instead of fourteen.

**Mr. Gibbs:**   I thought as much. You come to the negotiations with a large shopping list and you expect me to raise my offer a couple of cents each time you drop a demand.

It was decided to postpone negotiations on the wage issue and discuss some of the non-economic demands. The session lasted until midnight, and agreement was reached on most of the clauses. The parties agreed to take another look at "job security" the following morning.

### Week 4 (Thursday)

With the strike deadline only twenty-four hours away, the pressure was on. Both sides wanted to avert a strike, but each side was waiting for the other side to make concessions. The union picket leaders had met to plan the final strike strategy, but the membership was having second thoughts although by an overwhelming majority it had given the negotiation team a strike mandate earlier. Most of them could not survive a strike of more than two weeks, and the union's strike fund would last for only about three weeks.

Little was achieved in the first hour of negotiations, since both sides merely traded insults. After lunch, however, the company submitted its final offer — 12 cents an hour general wage increase for each year of a three-year contract together with an improved life and health benefits package.

The union assessed its position. It would agree to a three-year contract as proposed by management with the addition of COLA and sub-contracting clauses. The company's representatives agreed to discuss the union's latest position with senior management and meet the following day. The union negotiators reminded Mr. Gibbs that the strike deadline was only hours away.

Week 4 (Friday)
(Contract expires midnight)

The management team disagreed as to what should be done about the union's latest proposal.

**Mr. Jacobs (Human Resource Director):** Our relations with the union have not been very stable lately, and I think that a compromise now would be a great help in improving relationships. Further, I think we should consult more with the union committee before bringing about changes in the plant — anything to restore our workers' morale and confidence in the company. I do not think that they can afford to strike, but we should offer them a few more cents, or at least try to negotiate a COLA clause.

**Mr. Andrews (Production Manager):** With the new executive in charge and the present mood of the workers, a strike is a distinct possibility, if only for a couple of weeks. We have a backlog of production orders and I am afraid that we could lose some of our customers if there is a strike. Let's "sweeten the pot." We can find ways of increasing production and we can still be competitive with a moderate increase in prices.

**Mr. Gibbs (General Manager):** The union is bluffing. They are in no position to withstand a lengthy strike. If they do strike, they will be begging us to take them back when their credit has dried up. They are behind in their mortgage payments, and their wives are beginning to get on their backs. We should show the new executive who runs the plant. If we stand up to the union, its influence with the membership would be somewhat weakened. We should "hang tough."

The management team, unable to reach an agreement, decided to let Jack Anderson, the company president, review the situation and resolve the impasse. The president, after a thorough analysis of the situation, agreed with Mr. Gibbs, and directed the management team to reject the union's proposal.

Mr. Gibbs met with Mr. Trimble at 10:00 P.M. and informed him that the company was not prepared to accept the union's latest proposal. The company, however, would now pay 70% of O.H.I.P., and 100% of the premiums for the employees' group insurance package. The company's right to subcontract was not negotiable. It would not consider a COLA clause.

Mr. Trimble hastily convened a meeting of the union executive. They decided to submit the company's latest offer to the membership with a recommendation that it be rejected.

1. What does the case tell you about how union-management bargaining takes place?
2. Identify the negotiation strategies employed by each of the parties.
3. Were these strategies effective? Explain.
4. What alternatives do you advocate in place of such collective bargaining?

5.  What impact will this round of negotiations have upon the next round and upon labour-management relations in the interim?

*Excerpted from a case written by Mr. E.L. Roach, Department of Management Studies, Algonquin College, Ottawa, and reproduced here with his permission. This case was prepared for educational purposes, and is entirely fictional.

○ ○ ○ ○ ○ ○ ○ ○ ○ ○ ○ ○ ○ ○ ○ ○ ○ ○ ○ ○ ○ ○ ○ ○ ○ ○ ○ ○ ○ ○ ○ ○ ○ ○ ○ ○ ○ ○ ○ ○ ○ ○ ○

## SUGGESTED READING

Adams, G.W., *Canadian Labour Law*, Toronto: Canada Law Book Inc., 1985.

Arthurs, H.D., D.D. Carter and H.J. Glasbeek, *Labour Law and Industrial Relations in Canada*, 2nd ed., Toronto: Butterworths, 1984.

Bemmels, B., E.G. Fisher and B. Nyland, ''Canadian-American Jurisprudence on 'Good Faith' Bargaining,'' *Relations Industrielles/Industrial Relations*, Vol. 41, No. 3, 1986, pp. 596-621.

Herman, E.E., *Determination of the Appropriate Bargaining Unit by Labour Relations Boards in Canada*, Ottawa: Canada Department of Labour, 1966.

Kochan, T., et al., ''Determinants of Intraorganizational Conflict in Collective Bargaining in the Public Sector,'' *Administrative Science Quarterly*, March 1975, pp. 10-22.

Pantich, L., and D. Swartz, ''Towards Permanent Exceptionalism: Coercion and Consent in Canadian Industrial Relations,'' *Labour/Le Travail*, Spring 1984, pp. 133-157.

## REFERENCES

1.  John Crispo, *The Canadian Industrial Relations System*, Toronto: McGraw-Hill Ryerson Limited, 1978, pp. 378-383.

2.  Randall Brett, ''No Need for a Union Today,'' *The Personnel Administrator,* March 1979, pp. 23-24. See also James H. Hopkins and Robert D. Binderup, ''Employee Relations and the Union Organizing Campaigns,'' *The Personnel Administrator,* March 1980, pp. 57-61.

3.  International Labor Law Committee, Section of Labor Relations Law, American Bar Association, *The Labor Relations Law of Canada*, Washington, D.C.: Bureau of National Affairs, Inc., 1977, p. 97.

4.  Joseph W.R. Lawson, II, *How to Meet the Challenge of the Union Organizer*, Chicago: The Dartnell Corporation, 1972, pp. 7-24.

5.  Hermann F. Schwind and Vance F. Mitchell, ''Attitudes of Canadian Middle Managers toward Unionization,'' *Proceedings of the Administrative Science Association of Canada*, microfiche, Edmonton, 1975.

6.  George Meany, ''Organizing: A Continuing Effort,'' *The American Federationist*, July 1976, p. 1.

7.  Ibid.

8.  ''How IBM Avoids Layoffs through Retraining,'' *Business Week*, November 10, 1975, pp. 110,112.

9.  International Labor Law Committee, p. 156.

10.  Canada Labour Relations Board, ''Union of Bank Employees and Canadian Imperial Bank of Commerce,'' *Reasons for Decisions*, No. 202, *di 35*, November 30, 1979, pp. 105-112.

11.  Edward S. Haines and Alan Kistler, ''The Techniques of Organizing,'' *The American Federationist*, July 1967, pp. 30-32. See also James F. Rand, ''Preventative-Maintenance Techniques for Staying Union-Free,'' *Personnel Journal*, June 1980, pp. 497-499.

12.  Lawson, op. cit., pp. 25-45.

13.  Gerard I. Nierenberg, *The Art of Negotiating*, New York: Cornerstone Library Publications, 1968, pp. 47-61.

14.  Crispo, op. cit., pp. 378-383.

15.  George E. Constantino, Jr., ''Defining Line and Staff Roles in Collective Bargaining,'' *Personnel Journal*, October 1979, pp. 689-691, 717.

16.  David A. Peach and David Kuechle, *The Practice of Industrial Relations*, Toronto: McGraw-Hill Ryerson Limited, 1975, pp. 94-117.

17.  George E. Constantino, Jr., ''The Negotiator in Collective Bargaining,'' *Personnel Journal*, August 1975, pp. 445-447.

18.  See Herbert R. Northrup, *Boulwarism*, Ann Arbor: Bureau of Industrial Relations, Graduate School of Business, The University of Michigan, 1964. For an excellent discussion of negotiation see Richard E. Walton and Robert B. McKersie, *A Behavioral Theory of Labor Negotiations*, New York: McGraw-Hill Book Company, 1965, pp. 13-46. See also Nierenberg, op. cit., pp. 7-12.

19.  Crispo, op. cit., pp. 244-245.

# CHAPTER *19* ○○○○○○

## *COLLECTIVE AGREEMENT ADMINISTRATION*

*The most important aspect of industrial relations involves day-to-day administration of the collective bargaining agreement.*

DAVID A. PEACH AND DAVID KUECHLE[1]

○ ○ ○ ○ ○ ○ ○ ○ ○ ○ ○ ○ ○ ○ ○ ○ ○ ○ ○ ○ ○ ○ ○ ○ ○ ○ ○ ○ ○ ○ ○

## *CHAPTER OBJECTIVES*

After studying this chapter, you should be able to:
1. **Explain** how a collective agreement limits human resource management.
2. **Describe** the major provisions of a collective agreement.
3. **Discuss** common techniques to resolve disputes.
4. **Identify** the human resource department's role in handling grievances and in arbitration.
5. **Suggest** ways to build union-management cooperation.

○ ○ ○ ○ ○ ○ ○ ○ ○ ○ ○ ○ ○ ○ ○ ○ ○ ○ ○ ○ ○ ○ ○ ○ ○ ○ ○ ○ ○ ○ ○

*T*he outcome of organizing and negotiating is the *collective agreement*, or contract. This agreement limits management's flexibility. For example, labour contracts often specify how work assignments, promotions, wages, benefits, and other employee matters are to be handled. In other words, the agreement is an important challenge to managers and human resource specialists.

Fran Harper manages the sporting goods department of a large department store. After the store and the Retail, Wholesale and Department Store Union negotiated their first contract, Fran received a copy. Since she was busy with the new work schedule, the contract was set aside. Shortly after the schedule was posted on the bulletin board, one of Fran's best salesmen, Jake Renna, complained that the schedule was wrong.

Jake said, "I'm the most senior salesman; I should be able to pick the schedule I want."

"You know we don't do things that way around here," Fran firmly responded.

"You're wrong!" Jake shouted. "You haven't heard the end of this."

Fran said, "What do you mean?"

"The new collective agreement says that senior employees in each department get first choice of schedules," Jake added. "I want off on Mondays, or I'll file a complaint with the union."

"But I need you to help with inventory on Mondays," Fran argued.

"I don't care. The collective agreement says I get first choice," Jake angrily replied.

Even under the most restrictive contracts, managers, like Fran, must still manage. Decisions are made; orders are given. When a manager violates the agreement, employees like Jake may demand their rights. If their rights are denied, these employees may call on the union to help them.

The ideal is for the union and management to act cooperatively. Through cooperation, management can become more effective and can better meet the union's demands. But the extent of cooperation is shaped by the day-to-day administration of the contract. If properly administered, the contract is the basis for a cooperative relationship. Otherwise, violations lead to employee complaints that may reduce the organization's effectiveness.

This chapter describes the scope of contract administration and the resolution of complaints. It concludes with a discussion of union-management cooperation.

## THE SCOPE OF CONTRACT ADMINISTRATION

Once ratified by union members and approved by management, the contract must be carried out. As Figure 19-1 shows, the agreement affects many areas of human resource management. As a result, its administration often limits human resource practices in a number of ways. These limitations come from the contract's terms, past practices, and resolution of disputes.

### Contract Provisons

Every labour agreement contains specific terms and provisions. The most common ones are listed in Figure 19-2. These clauses are important because they define the rights and obligations of the employer and the union. Since nearly every provision affects the management of human resources, these clauses merit the attention of human resource specialists.

Whether the collective agreement contains all the provisions found in Figure 19-2 depends on the parties. For example, the employer is never required by law to grant a union security clause. Management bargainers may agree to a *union shop* or *checkoff* provision when it leads to a lessening of other demands. Often these security clauses are given in return for a provision that protects important management rights.

FIGURE 19-1    Sources of Contract Limitations on Human Resource
Management

| SOURCE OF CONSTRAINTS | MEANS OF ACHIEVEMENT | MAJOR AREAS AFFECTED |
|---|---|---|
| Contract Provisions | Negotiations | Human resource practices and policies; costs; discipline; management, union, and employee rights; promotions; layoffs, work assignments; overtime; pay; benefits |
| Past Practices | Management and union actions while administering the contract | Human resource practices and policies; costs; discipline; management, union, and employee rights |
| Dispute Resolution | Decisions made while resolving disputes between union and management | Human resource practices and policies; costs; discipline; management, union, and employee rights |

FIGURE 19-2    Common Provisions in Union-Management Agreements

• **Union recognition.** Normally near the beginning of a contract, this clause states management's acceptance of the union as the sole representative of designated employees.

• **Union security.** To ensure that the union maintains members as new employees are hired and present employees quit, a union security clause is commonly demanded by the union. Forms of union security include:

　**a. Union shop.** All new workers must join the union shortly after being hired.

　**b. Agency shop.** All new workers must pay to the union an amount equal to dues.

　**c. Checkoff.** Upon authorization, management agrees to deduct the union dues from each union member's paycheque and transfer the monies to the union.

• **Wage rates.** The amount of wages to be paid to workers (or classes of workers) is specified in the wage clause.

• **Cost of living.** Increasingly, unions are demanding and receiving automatic wage increases for workers when price levels go up. For example, a common approach is for wages to go up by one cent an hour for each 0.3 or 0.4% increase in the consumer price index.

• **Insurance benefits.** This section specifies which insurance benefits the employer provides and how much the employer contributes towards these benefits. Frequently included benefits are life and supplemental hospitalization insurance and dental plans.

• **Pension benefits.** The amount of retirement income, years of service required, penalties for early retirement, employer and employee contributions, and vesting provisions are described in this section if a pension plan exists.

• **Income maintenance.** To provide workers with economic security, some contracts give guarantees of minimum income or minimum work. Other income maintenance provisions include severance pay and supplements to unemployment insurance.

• **Time-off benefits.** Vacations, holidays, rest breaks, wash-up periods, and leave-of-absence provisions typically are specified in this clause.

• **Seniority clause.** Unions seek contract terms that cause human resource decisions to be made on the basis of seniority. Often senior workers are given preferential treatment in job assignments, promotions, layoffs, vacation scheduling, overtime, and shift preferences.

• **Management rights.** Management must retain certain rights to do an effective job. These may include the ability to require overtime work, decide on promotions into management, design jobs, and select employees. This clause reserves to management the right to make decisions that management thinks are necessary for the organization's success.

FIGURE 19-2 (continued)   Provisions in Union-Management Agreements

- **Discipline**. Prohibited employee actions, penalties, and disciplinary procedures are either stated in the contract or included in the agreement by reference to those documents that contain the information.
- **Dispute resolution.** Disagreements between the union and management are resolved through procedures specified in the contract.
- **Duration of agreement.** Union and management agree on a time period during which the collective agreement is in force.

With the exception of clauses on management rights, most clauses in the agreement limit human resource actions. Some of these limitations are minor and similar to the self-imposed policies of well-managed organizations. For example, even without a union, most employers provide competitive wages, benefits, and working conditions. The collective agreement merely formalizes these obligations. But other contract terms may change the policies used before the contract was negotiated. Seniority and discipline clauses are two constraints that are commonly added.

*Seniority*

Unions typically prefer to have employee-related decisions determined by the length of the worker's employment, called *seniority.* Seniority assures that promotions, overtime, and other employee concerns are handled without favouritism. But as the following example illustrates, seniority may limit management's flexibility in making staff decisions.[2]

Three weeks before the retirement of the senior clerk in the parts department, the manager of the Anderson Buick dealership sought a replacement. The collective agreement stated that "all job openings must be posted on the employee bulletin board for one week. Interested employees must submit their bids during the one-week open period. After the open period, the most senior, qualified employee will be selected from among those who submitted job bids." Accordingly, this was done.

Two workers applied. One, Jacob Marls, had been with the car agency for almost three years. His performance as a junior clerk was efficient and courteous. In fact, many parts customers asked for Jacob by name. John Abbott also submitted a bid. He had been with the dealership for three years and two months. John was dependable, but sometimes he was moody in dealing with customers. The general manager wanted to reward Jacob's good performance. But the contract required that the promotion go to John since he was qualified and had the most seniority.

Seniority also is used to decide overtime and layoff rights. As with promotions, merit cannot always be rewarded. For example, suppose that a supervisor needs three subordinates to finish a job. Since seniority must be honoured, the supervisor cannot select the best employees. Likewise, when a company plans a layoff, the most recently hired workers are the first to go. Those who are left probably get higher wages if there is a premium for longevity. Thus the higher-paid employees are retained, even though the layoff was probably needed to reduce costs. And these layoffs may undermine the company's affirmative-action plan, since employees hired through the program may have low seniority.

## Discipline

Unions often challenge any discipline of a union member. Therefore, discipline must abide by the contract and be backed with evidence. The need for proof requires management to document employee discipline, which means more (not necessarily productive) paperwork. Even when discipline is done correctly, the union may argue that special circumstances should be considered.

> One Monday, Georgia Green was late for work. She explained to her supervisor that her son was sick and so child-care arrangements delayed her. Sally, Georgia's supervisor, said, "Okay, but get here on time from now on. You know how strict my boss is." The following three days Georgia was late. The contract stated, "Any employee late four days in one month is subject to a two-day layoff without pay." On Thursday morning, Sally told Georgia to go home, citing the contract clause.
>
> Georgia told the union what had happened. The union complained that Georgia's sick child should be grounds for an exception. The human resource manager disagreed. When the union representative asked to see Georgia's file, it was discovered that Sally did not give Georgia a written warning after the second tardiness. Again, the contract was specific: "No worker can be given a layoff for tardiness or absenteeism unless a written notice is given after the second occurrence." The company had to pay Georgia for the two days she was off because the contract's procedure was not followed.

## Past Practices

The actions of managers and union officials sometimes change the meaning of the agreement. Consider again the incident involving Georgia Green. Suppose the supervisor had failed to discipline Georgia. Or suppose that human resource management had been sympathetic to Georgia's problem and decided against approving the layoff. The result might have been to set a precedent.

A *precedent* is a new standard that arises from the past practices of either party. Once a precedent results from unequal enforcement of disciplinary rules, the new standard may affect similar cases in the future. Then any other tardy employee with child-care problems might demand special treatment too. In time, it may become difficult for management to control tardiness because precedents have created exceptions to the rules. If the human resource manager felt that an exception in Georgia's case was appropriate, the union and the company can sign a letter stating that this exception is not a binding precedent. Then other employees cannot rely on Georgia's case to win exceptions from the rule.

The fear of past practices usually causes two changes in human resources procedures. First, employee-related decisions are often centralized in the human resource department. Supervisors are stripped of their authority to make decisions on layoffs, discipline, and other employee matters. Instead, supervisors are required to make recommendations to the human resources department to ensure uniformity and prevent precedents.

The other change is to increase the training of supervisors in the administration of the contract. The training is needed to ensure that supervisors administer the remaining portions of the contract uniformly. For example, if each supervisor applies a different standard to tardiness, some employees may be disciplined while others with more lenient supervisors may escape discipline. In time, the union might argue that unequal treatment makes it unfair to discipline those who are late. The enforcement of the contract terms by supervisors then can lead to damaging precedents. Through centralization and training, human resource departments create a more uniform enforcement of the contract to avoid such damaging precedents.

In addition to contract provisions and past practices, a third constraint is dispute resolution, which is discussed in the following section.

## THE RESOLUTION OF DISPUTES

Constraints on management during contract administration also come from the resolution of disputes with the union. Since in Canada the use of strikes as a weapon is limited — strikes are illegal when a collective agreement is in force — disputes have to be settled through *grievances*. A grievance is defined as a complaint by an employee or employer that alleges that some aspect of a collective agreement has been violated. Almost every collective agreement in Canada contains some type of formalized procedure for resolving disputes. All jurisdictions (with the exception of Saskatchewan) require that a grievance which cannot be solved between the parties be submitted to an arbitrator or arbitration board whose decision will be final and binding.

### Grievance Procedures

Either management or the union may file a grievance when the contract is violated. But since most decisions are made by management, there are few opportunities for the union to break the agreement and cause a grievance to be initiated by management. More commonly, unions file grievances because of an alleged violation by management.

The *grievance procedure* consists of an ordered series of steps. Figure 19-3 describes the steps through which an employee's grievance typically passes. An example further explains how grievances arise and are settled.

> Hanson Environment Services had an opening for the job of service representative. The job required making house calls to repair home air conditioners and heaters sold by the company. Only two employees applied for the job. The contract with the International Brotherhood of Electrical Workers stated: "Promotions are made on the basis of seniority, provided ability is equal." Mr. Hanson, the owner, selected the second most senior employee for the promotion.
>
> When Rick West found out he did not get the job even though he had more seniority, he talked with his supervisor. The supervisor said, "It is Mr. Hanson's decision. But you didn't get the job because you use profanity. We can't have you swearing in some customer's home. We would lose too much business."
>
> Together, Rick and the union representative wrote up a formal grievance and submitted it to the supervisor. Although the supervisor had two days to review the complaint before making a written decision, he handed it back to Rick immediately

FIGURE 19-3   Typical Steps in a Union-Management Grievance Procedure

- **Preliminary discussion**. The aggrieved employee discusses the complaint with the immediate supervisor with or without a union representative.
- **Step 1.** The complaint is put in writing and formally presented by the shop steward to the first-level supervisor. Normally, the supervisor must respond in writing within a contractually specified time period, usually two to five days.
- **Step 2.** The chief steward takes the complaint to the department superintendent. A written response is required, usually within a week.
- **Step 3.** The complaint is submitted to the plant manager/chief administrative officer by the union plan or grievance committee. Again, a written response is typically required.
- **Step 4.** If Step 3 does not solve the dispute, arrangements are made for an arbitrator or an arbitration board to settle the matter.

> with "Denied" written across it. Then the union submitted the complaint to the shop manager, which was the next step in the procedure. The result was the same. Finally, the grievance was taken to Mr. Hanson. He explained his fear of losing business over Rick's profanity and denied the grievance.
>
> Finally, the union requested that the issue be submitted to arbitration and that a single arbitrator be chosen. Management agreed to that. The arbitrator ruled that management had no evidence that Mr. West ever used profanity in the presence of customers, and that the mere assumption he would do so was not sufficient grounds for denying his promotion.

The number of steps in the grievance procedure and the staff involved at each step will vary from organization to organization. The purpose of a multistep grievance procedure is to allow higher-level managers and union representatives to look at the issue from different angles and to assess the consequences of alternative further actions. This approach will increase the chance that the dispute gets resolved without submission to arbitration.

### Types and Causes of Grievances

Even though the human resource department may not handle grievances in their early stages, it plays an important role. Each supervisor sees only a small number of complaints. But the human resource department has an organization-wide view from which it can identify the types and causes of grievances. With this information, human resource management can create programs to improve grievance handling.[3]

Grievances can be classified into three types: legitimate, imagined, and political. *Legitimate grievances* occur when there is reasonable cause to think there has been a contract violation. Even in a cooperative environment, contract clauses may have different meanings to different people. In the Hanson Environment Services example, the union thought the contract meant that promotions were decided on the basis of seniority if workers were technically qualified. Mr. Hanson, the owner, used a different perspective. He thought that "qualified" included both technical and personality variables. Misunderstanding of the agreement caused a legitimate grievance.

*Imagined grievances* occur when employees believe that the agreement has been violated even though management is exercising its contract rights reasonably. Again, misunderstanding is the primary cause of these grievances. A cooperative union can help settle such complaints quickly by explaining management's rights. Otherwise, when a manager says the complaint is without merit, the worker may feel that management is trying to save face for a bad decision.

*Political grievances* are the most difficult to solve. They occur when a complaint is pursued to further someone's political aspirations. For example, a union representative may be reluctant to tell union members that their grievances are without merit. To do so may mean a loss of political support in the next union election. Instead, the union leader may process a worthless grievance. Likewise, management also files political grievances.[4]

> Jake Renna filed a grievance against his manager, who had failed to abide by the contract. Jake's grievance demanded that he get first choice of work schedules since he was the most senior employee in the sporting goods department. The store manager wanted to show his support for the department manager, Fran Harper, and so he denied Jake's grievance without even reviewing the contract. The corporate human resource department agreed that Jake was right and directed that he get first selection of work schedules. The human resource manager also sent a memo to the store manager and Fran telling them that their refusal to follow the contract may lead to other grievances and employee dissatisfaction.

### Handling Grievances

Once a grievance has been submitted, management should seek to resolve it fairly and quickly. Failure to do so can be seen as a disregard for employee needs. In time, morale, motivation, performance, and company loyalty may be damaged.[5]

In adjusting grievances, several precautions should be followed.[6] Most importantly, grievances should be settled on their merits. Political considerations by either party weaken the grievance system. Complaints need to be carefully investigated and decided on the facts, not emotional whim. Otherwise, damaging precedents may result. Second, the cause to each grievance should be recorded. Many grievances coming from one or two departments may indicate personality conflicts or a poor understanding of the contract. Third, employees should be encouraged to use the grievance procedure. Problems cannot be solved unless management and union officials know what they are. But before employees can use the grievance process, it must be explained through meetings, employee handbooks, or bulletin-board notices. Lastly, whatever the final solution, it needs to be explained to those affected. Even though union leaders usually do this, management should not fail to explain *its* reasoning to the worker.[7]

### Arbitration

*Arbitration* is the submission of a dispute to a neutral third party. The arbitrator acts in the role of a judge and hears both sides to the dispute. Based on the facts, the arbitrator renders a binding decision.

In Canada, federal and provincial legislation (except in Saskatchewan) requires that every collective agreement contain a provision for final settlement, by arbitration or otherwise, without work stoppage, of all differences concerning its interpretation, application, administration, or alleged violations. Although the law permits the use of means other than arbitration for settlement, unions and management so far have not found a viable alternative.[8]

Arbitration holds two potential problems for human resource administrators: costs and unacceptable solutions. Although the employer and the union usually share expenses, a case may cost from several hundred to several thousand dollars.

Another potential problem occurs when an arbitrator renders a decision that is against management's best interest. Since the ruling is binding, it may alter drastically management's rights. Suppose, for example, that management lays off several hundred workers, and the union convinces an arbitrator that management did not follow the contract's layoff procedure. The arbitrator may rule that all workers get their jobs back with back pay. Or if an arbitrator accepts the union's argument of extenuating circumstances in a disciplinary case, those extenuating circumstances may be cited in future cases. For example, consider what happened in a chain of convenience markets:

> The Quick Foods Market had a policy that stealing from the company was grounds for immediate discharge. Sam Sample, a new employee, took a sandwich from the cooler and consumed it without paying. He was fired when caught by the store manager. The union argued that Sam should get a second chance since he was a new employee. The arbitrator upheld management. But he added that discharge for such a minor theft might be too harsh a penalty if Sam had not been a probationary employee.

This ruling implies that the judgement may have been different had a senior employee been caught stealing. The union may then use this argument to argue that discharge is an inappropriate penalty. There is a possibility that a different arbitrator may agree.

It is important for human resource specialists to seek a solution with the union before arbitration. In this manner they avoid additional costs, delays, and the possibility of an unsatisfactory decision. When arbitration is unavoidable, human resource specialists should follow the guidelines in Figure 19-4. These suggestions offer the best chance of winning a favorable decision. If these guidelines reveal serious flaws with the employer's case, a compromise solution with the union before arbitration is usually advisable.

## Form of Arbitration

In Canada most arbitration cases are decided by an arbitration board, in contrast to the U.S., where the majority of cases are handled by individual arbitrators.[9] The interested parties each appoint one of the three-member body. These two members, in turn, select a neutral chairman. The advantage of using a board lies in the fact that representatives of the parties are directly involved in the decision-making process. The disadvantage is that boards usually take more time to make their decisions, not to mention the higher costs involved when there are three arbitrators instead of one.[10]

FIGURE 19-4   Preparation Guidelines for Arbitration Hearings

**1.** Study the original grievance and review its history through every step of the grievance machinery.

**2.** Determine the arbitrator's role. It might be found, for instance, that while the original grievance contains many elements, the arbitrator is restricted by the contract to resolving only certain aspects.

**3.** Review the collective bargaining agreement from beginning to end. Often, other clauses may be related to the grievance.

**4.** Assemble all documents and papers you will need at the hearing. Where feasible, make copies for the arbitrator and the other party. If some of the documents you need are in the possession of the other party, ask in advance that they be brought to the arbitration.

**5.** Make plans in advance if you think it will be necessary for the arbitrator to visit the plant or job site for on-the-spot investigation. The arbitrator should be accompanied by representatives of **both** parties.

**6.** Interview all witnesses. Make certain that they understand the whole case and the importance of their own testimony within it.

**7.** Make a written summary of what each witness will say. This serves as a useful checklist at the hearing to make certain nothing is overlooked.

**8.** Study the case from the other side's point of view. Be prepared to answer the opposing evidence and arguments.

**9.** Discuss your outline of the case with others in your organization. A fresh viewpoint will often disclose weak spots or previously overlooked details.

**10.** Read as many articles and published awards as you can on the general subject matter in dispute. While awards by other arbitrators for other parties have no binding precedent value, they may help clarify the thinking of parties and arbitrators alike.

Source: *Labour Arbitration Procedures and Techniques,* New York: American Arbitration Association, 1972, pp. 15-16. Used with permission.

## *UNION-MANAGEMENT COOPERATION*

Although dispute resolution techniques stop most complaints from erupting into a strike, they are after-the-fact measures. Even the "winner" of a favourable arbitration decision loses the time and money it took to argue the case. Through cooperation, both parties can replace reactive measures with proactive approaches. Proactive efforts benefit the union and the company by saving time and expenses. These savings can mean higher profits for the employer and better contracts for the union.

As human resource manager for the East Coast Logging Company Ltd., Joe VonKampen spent about 40% of his time on some phase of dispute resolution. Although the Teamsters represented only 125 of the employees, there were usually 275 to 300 grievances a year. About 10% of these cases went to arbitration. These costs seriously affected the company's profitability, which forced the union to accept the lowest wage rates in the area. To change the situation, which was uncovered by research into the company's grievance records, the town's mayor offered to help.

The mayor devised a training program that involved the union leader's and the human resource manager's taking turns reading the contract to an audience of supervisors and union representatives. After each paragraph, the human resource manager and the union president both summarized what the paragraph meant. The mayor did not let them go on to the next paragraph until both agreed on the meaning of the previous one. After several sessions, the entire contract was reviewed. Lower-ranking union and management officials learned what the contract meant and that they were expected to cooperate with each other. The following year, fourteen grievances were filed and only one went to arbitration. The company's profitability improved dramatically, and the local union obtained its largest wage increase in the next negotiations.

## Union-Management Attitudes

Severe conflicts between a company and union often can be traced to the attitudes each holds about the other.[11] In the East Coast Logging example, supervisors felt that the union was intruding on their rights. When supervisors denied workers their rights, the union had to fight back with grievances. Sometimes members of a union get so upset that they conduct a *wildcat strike*. These strikes are spontaneous acts that take place in violation of the contract, regardless of the objections raised by union leaders. Even after such a strike is over, the underlying problems still have to be settled.

If the attitudes between the parties remain hostile, the organization suffers poor performance. Serious disruptions can affect even the very survival of the organization and the union.[12] Sometimes extreme disruptions may require the two parties to cooperate in preventing bankruptcy and mass layoffs.

## Building Cooperation

Proactive human resource departments cannot wait for disaster before they attempt to build cooperation with the union. They realize that cooperation is not automatic and must be initiated by human resource specialists. However, there are several obstacles to cooperation.

### Obstacles to Cooperation

Human resource specialists often seek union cooperation to improve the organization's effectiveness. But effectiveness is usually far less important to union leaders. Quite naturally, these officials are more concerned about the welfare of their members and winning reelection to union office. So when cooperation fails to be attractive politically, union leaders have little incentive to cooperate. In fact, if leaders do cooperate, they may be accused by workers of forgetting the union's interests. These accusations can mean defeat by political opponents within the union. Thus cooperation may not be in the leader's best interest.

For many years, negotiations in the U.S. steel industry were marked by strikes and threats of strikes. The result was lower profitability and even a loss of markets to foreign producers. In turn, many members of the United Steel Workers union were put on layoff. Both the union and the steel companies were being damaged.

The unions and major steel producers reached a cooperative arrangement called the *Experimental Negotiations Agreement*. This agreement called for concessions from the producers and no nationwide strikes by the union against the steel industry. This cooperative move was intended to benefit both the union and employers. But some members saw it as a loss of rights, particularly the right to strike. In the union's national elections, a splinter group was able to make a serious challenge to the established leadership by attacking this cooperative agreement.

Besides political obstacles, union leaders may mistrust the human resources department. For example, bitter remarks during the organizing drive may convince union officials that human resource specialists are antiunion. Within this climate, cooperative gestures may be seen as tricks against the union. If cooperative proposals threaten the members or leaders, mistrust increases and cooperation usually fails.

## Cooperative Methods

Once human resource specialists realize the political concerns and suspicions of union leaders, several cooperative methods can be tried. These techniques are summarized in Figure 19-5 and are explained in the following paragraphs.

FIGURE 19-5   Methods of Building Union-Management Cooperation

---

Managers and human resource specialists can build cooperation between the employer and the union through:
- **Prior consultation** with union leaders to defuse problems before they become formal grievances.
- **Sincere concern** for employee problems and welfare even when management is not obligated to do so by the collective agreement.
- **Training programs** that objectively communicate the intent of union and management bargainers and reduce biases and misunderstandings.
- **Joint study committees** that allow management and union officials to find solutions to common problems.
- **Third parties** who can provide guidance and programs that bring union leaders and managers closer together to pursue common objectives.

---

One of the most basic actions is *prior consultation* with the union. Not every management decision must be approved by the union. But actions that affect the union or its leaders may cause a grievance unless explained before the action is taken. Consider once more the Hanson Environment Service example given earlier in this chapter. Suppose human resource management had explained to the union leaders that the use of profanity by the most senior worker could mean a loss of valuable business and jobs for union members; perhaps the union leader would have accepted the promotion of the junior worker. At least politically, the union president would be less likely to challenge the promotion decision of Mr. Hanson. Some managers even call on union leaders to talk with problem employees before management takes action that might lead to a grievance. For example, Mr. Hanson could have asked the union leader to talk to Rick West about his profanity.

Human resource specialists can also build cooperation through a *sincere concern* for employees. This concern may be shown through the prompt settlement of grievances, regardless of who wins. Or management can bargain sincerely with the union to reduce the need for a strike. Even when a strike occurs, management can express its concern for workers. For example, during the 1970 strike at General Motors in the U.S. and Canada, GM continued to pay the strikers' insurance premiums to prevent a lapse in their insurance coverage.

*Training programs* are another way to build cooperation. After a new contract is signed, the human resource department usually trains just managers. The union does the same for its leaders. The result is that both sides continue their biases and misunderstandings. If human resource management sponsors training for both the union and management, a common understanding of the contract is more likely to be brought about. The training can be as simple as taking turns paraphrasing the contract, as done in the East Coast Logging Company example. Or outside neutrals can be hired to do the training. Either way, supervisors and union officials end the training with a common understanding of the contract and a new basis for cooperation.

When a complex problem confronts the union and employer, *joint study committees* are sometimes formed.[13] For example, the three largest automobile companies have agreed to create separate committees with the United Auto Workers union to study healthcare costs. If the idea is successful, costs will grow more slowly and there will be more money available for other benefits.[14]

A final method of building cooperation is through *third parties,* such as consultants or government agencies, who may act as catalysts to cooperation. In Canada, this is the most common approach, since parties to a collective agreement are required by law to ask for conciliation before any strike or lockout action can be taken.

There is no single best approach to building cooperation. Since each relationship is unique, the methods used will depend upon the situation. But if human resource administrators can build more cooperative relations with their unions, the employer gains higher productivity. In turn, there are more resources against which the union and its members can make demands. Improving union-management relations, therefore, is a potentially significant role that can be played by human resource departments in unionized organizations.

## SUMMARY

Contract administration begins after union organizing and contract negotiations. In administering the agreement, human resource specialists face several challenges. First, contract clauses place limits on management. Second, day-to-day administration of the contract can lead to precedents. Third, limitations often result from the dispute resolution procedures: grievance handling and arbitration help interpret the contract, sometimes in ways that limit management.

Yet managers still must manage in spite of these constraints. Only through increased cooperation between the company and the union can these limitations be lessened. Responsibility for improving the relationship must be assumed by the human resource department, if political barriers and mistrust are to be overcome. Through prior consultation, concern for employees, training programs, or joint committees, human resource specialists can lay the foundations of a cooperative union-management relationship.

## TERMS FOR REVIEW

Collective agreement          Political grievances
Seniority                     Arbitration
Precedent                     Wildcat strikes
Grievance procedure           Cooperative methods

## REVIEW AND DISCUSSION QUESTIONS

1.  In your own words, explain why most grievances are usually filed by unions.
2.  What are the major sources of constraints on human resource management during the administration of a collective agreement?
3.  During one union organization drive, a plant manager told employees: "A union means less flexibility in dealing with your individual problems. With a union present, the company must follow the collective agreement." Explain how this loss of freedom might be to the employees' disadvantage.
4.  Suppose one of your unionized employees wanted to leave work early to see her child play in the minor hockey league. Further, suppose she offered to work through her lunch hour so no loss of work or production would occur. If you agreed to her suggestions, what problems might result?
5.  Since grievance procedures are found in most contracts, both managers and unions must want them. Explain why both managers and unions want grievance procedures.
6.  Suppose several supervisors said they had hoped to create enough problems for the union to cause it to go away. What advice would you give them?
7.  What are the disadvantages of using arbitration as a last step in the grievance procedure?
8.  Suppose your union and company had very hostile relations. What steps would you recommend to the human resource manager?

## INCIDENT 19-1

### The Reindeer Lake Paper Mill

The Reindeer Lake Paper Mill in Saskatchewan has been plagued with numerous problems since it began operations in 1980. In 1983, the Canadian Paperworkers Union was successful in organizing the workers and negotiating a three-year collective agreement. After two years of operation under the agreement, human resource problems were growing worse. In 1985, there were several illegal walkouts by small groups of workers to protest unresolved grievances. Management decided not to prosecute the employees although the wildcat strikes disrupted production.

Now, the human resource director expects a strike at the expiration of the collective agreement, because of low wages and unpleasant working conditions. The workers are claiming that inflation has exceeded the wage increases granted in the

1987 agreement. In addition, although working conditions meet federal and provincial health and safety regulations, the workers complain that heat, smell, and humidity in the plant make working very uncomfortable, especially during the summer months.

1. This incident suggests several changes that should be made in the next collective agreement, given the company's past experiences. What changes do you think the human resource department should recommend?

2. What actions could the human resource department undertake immediately to reduce the problems that exist between workers and the company?

3. If management decided to implement the changes you suggest, what actions should be taken to win the support of union leaders?

## INCIDENT 19-2

### In-Flight Food Services Company

The In-Flight Food Services Company provides prepared meals for several airlines at a major airport in the East. Food handlers cook and package meals to be reheated in airplane galleys for service to passengers while in flight. Most of the 535 food handlers belong to the Independent Food Handlers Union, which has represented these employees for over five years.

Each year, the industrial relations department has noticed that the number of grievances filed by members of the union increases by about 15%. The time spent by union representatives, employees, and supervisors was affecting productivity in the company's cafeteria. The general manager was concerned that the company's costs and low productivity could lead to a loss of several key contracts with major airlines.

The industrial relations department studied all the grievances during the past year and provided the following analysis.

| | |
|---|---|
| Total grievances filed | 803 |
| Number settled at: | |
|   First-level supervision | 104 |
|   Second-level supervision | 483 |
|   General manager level | 205 |
|   Arbitration | 11 |

Although some grievances involved more than one issue, most of them were single-issue matters. When the industrial relations department classified the grievances, the following results were reported:

| | |
|---|---|
| Grievance issues: | |
|   Tardiness or absence control | 349 |
|   Overtime disputes | 265 |
|   Other discipline or discharge | 77 |
|   Incorrect job schedules | 75 |
|   Multiple-issue disputes | 37 |

1. Assuming the industrial relations director asked you to design a training program to reduce the high number of grievances, who do you think should attend the training sessions?

2. What topics would you cover in the training?

3. If you felt that many of the grievances resulted from poor wording in the contract, what could you do to make changes before the expiration of the contract?

○ ○ ○ ○ ○ ○ ○ ○ ○ ○ ○ ○ ○ ○ ○ ○ ○ ○ ○ ○ ○ ○ ○ ○ ○ ○ ○ ○ ○ ○ ○ ○ ○ ○ ○ ○ ○ ○ ○ ○ ○ ○

## CASE STUDY

### LADBROKE VALVE CO., INC.*

The Ladbroke Valve Company manufactured two lines of gauges and instruments. One of these lines was sold to industrial users such as refineries and chemical works, the other to the food industry. Its office employees were members of the Instrument and Gauge Artisans Union (IGAU), Local 22. Although they were generally assigned to work either in the Industrial or Food divisions, they were all members of the same local and there was one seniority schedule covering all unionized office employees.

John Jeremy was an estimator who worked on the Food line of products. He had been employed with Ladbroke for twenty-five years and had been one of the first employees to become a member of the IGAU when it organized the office staff in 1963. He was a former president of the local and had served in other local offices for most of the last ten years.

In early 1983, sales of the Food line of products declined sharply and, as a result, there were only about twenty hours a week of estimating to be done. The company assigned additional estimating and scheduling duties on the Industrial product line to Mr. Jeremy. This resulted in a more junior employee, Mr. Wilson, being placed on temporary layoff. However, after about one month, the sales supervisor in the Industrial division complained that Mr. Jeremy was unable to cope with

working on both the Food and Industrial products. He was returned to the job of estimating the Food products only and Mr. Wilson was recalled.

Mr. Jeremy was clearly underemployed in this job. The office manager, Frank Webster, decided to place Mr. Jeremy on a shortened work week; he would work (and be paid for) only twenty hours per week although he would continue to receive full company benefits, including vacation entitlement, as if he were working full time. This would continue until sales picked up in the Food division and Mr. Jeremy could return to full-time estimating. In Mr. Webster's view, the company could do this since the Management's Rights clause of the collective agreement stated:

The Union further recognizes the undisputed right of the Company to operate and manage its business in all respects in accordance with its responsibilities and commitments. The products to be manufactured, the schedule of production, the methods, processes, and means of manufacturing and office methods are exclusively the responsibility of the Company.

When advised that this would happen, Mr. Jeremy and his union representative spoke with Mr. Webster. They pointed out that, according to Article 9 of the collective agreement, Mr. Jeremy had the right to displace (or "bump") a more junior employee who was

*This is based on a real situation. All names have been disguised.

doing a job that Jeremy was qualified for. There were several jobs in the production scheduling office that Jeremy was qualified for and that were filled by employees with much less seniority. Article 9 of the agreement said:

> In the event of a reduction in the work-force, employees will be laid off in inverse order of seniority provided there are available other employees able and willing to do the work of the employees to be laid off.

Mr. Webster spoke with the supervisor of the production scheduling office before responding to this request. The supervisor was opposed to allowing Mr. Jeremy to ''bump'' one of the production scheduling clerks. He pointed out that the four production scheduling clerks had full workloads and that the department was running very smoothly. Mr. Webster also realized that if Mr. Jeremy was allowed to displace one of those employees, he would not have time to do the twenty hours per week estimating on the Food line of products. Jeremy was the only qualified person who could do that estimating.

At a meeting that afternoon with Mr. Jeremy, the union representative, and the industrial relations manager, Mr. Webster denied Mr. Jeremy's request. He also pointed out that no reduction in work force was taking place. Mr. Jeremy was not being laid off; he was only being placed temporarily on a short work week. There were still the same number of employees in the office. Therefore, the question of layoff and the ''bumping'' of less senior employees did not arise. Neither Mr. Jeremy nor his union representative were prepared to accept this decision and they indicated that a formal grievance would be filed.

1. What rights does Mr. Jeremy have to insist on ''bumping'' a more junior employee in the production office?

2. Do you think that the union will actually file a grievance? If the company denies the grievance, will they take this case to arbitration? What will be the outcome?

3. What alternatives does Mr. Webster have in this situation? What should he do now?

○ ○ ○ ○ ○ ○ ○ ○ ○ ○ ○ ○ ○ ○ ○ ○ ○ ○ ○ ○ ○ ○ ○ ○ ○ ○ ○ ○ ○ ○ ○ ○ ○ ○ ○ ○ ○ ○ ○ ○ ○ ○ ○

## SUGGESTED READINGS

''Avoiding the Arbitrator: Some New Alternatives to the Grievance Procedure,'' *Proceedings, 30th annual meeting Washington, D.C.: National Academy of Arbitrators*, 1977.

Brown, D.J.M. and D.M. Beatty, *Canadian Labour Arbitration*, 2nd ed., Aurora, Ontario: Canada Law Book Ltd., 1984.

Dalton, D.R. and W.D. Todor, ''Antecedents of Grievance Filing Behavior: Attitude/Behavior Consistency and the Union Steward,'' *Academy of Management Journal*, Vol. 25, No. 1, 1982, pp. 158-160.

Harris, D. *Wrongful Dismissal*, Toronto: Richard DeBoo Publishers, 1984.

Palmer, E.E., *Collective Agreement Arbitration in Canada*, 2nd ed., Toronto: Butterworths, 1983.

Trudeau, G., ''Employee Rights vs. Management Rights: Some Reflections Regarding Dismissals,'' in S.L. Dolan and R.S. Schuler (eds.) *Canadian Readings in Personnel and Human Resource Management*, Toronto: West Publishing Co., 1987, pp. 367-3.

# *REFERENCES*

1. David A. Peach and David Kuechle, *The Practice of Industrial Relations,* Toronto: McGraw-Hill Ryerson Limited, 1975, p. 181.

2. Gerald E. Phillips, *Labour Relations and Collective Bargaining in Canada,* Toronto: Butterworth and Co. (Canada) Ltd., 1977. 160-161.

3. William B. Werther, Jr., "Reducing Grievances through Effective Contract Administration," *Labor Law Journal,* April 1974, pp. 211-216.

4. Ross Stagner and Hjalmar Rosen, *Psychology of Union-Management Relations,* Belmont, Calif.: Wadsworth Publishing Company, Inc., 1965, pp. 110-111.

5. Jeffrey Gandz, "Grievance Initiation and Resolution: A Test of the Behavioural Theory," *Relations Industrielles,* 34 (1979) (4): 790.

6. Thomas F. Gideon and Richard B. Peterson, "A Comparison of Alternate Grievance Procedures," *Employee Relations Law Journal,* Autumn 1979, pp. 222-223. See also "The Antiunion Grievance Ploy," *Business Week,* February 12, 1979, pp. 117, 120.

7. James C. McBrearty, *Handling Grievances: A Positive Approach for Management and Labor Representatives,* Tucson: Division of Economics and Business Research, University of Arizona, 1972, pp. 3-6. See also George W. Bohlander, "Fair Representation: Not Just a Union Problem," *The Personnel Administrator,* March 1980, pp. 36-40, 82.

8. Peach and Kuechle, op. cit., p. 284.

9. Ibid., p. 243.

10. Ibid., p. 244.

11. Joseph Tomkiewicz and Otto Brenner, "Union Attitudes and the 'Manager of the Future,'" *The Personnel Administrator,* October 1979, pp. 67-70, 72.

12. Richard E. Walton and Robert B. McKersie, *A Behavioral Theory of Labor Negotiations,* New York: McGraw-Hill Book Company, 1965, pp. 184-221.

13. Edger Weinberg, "Labor-Management Cooperation: A Report on Recent Initiatives," *Monthly Labor Review,* April 1976, p. 13.

14. "A Joint Look at Cutting Health Care Costs," *Business Week,* November 17, 1975, p. 49.

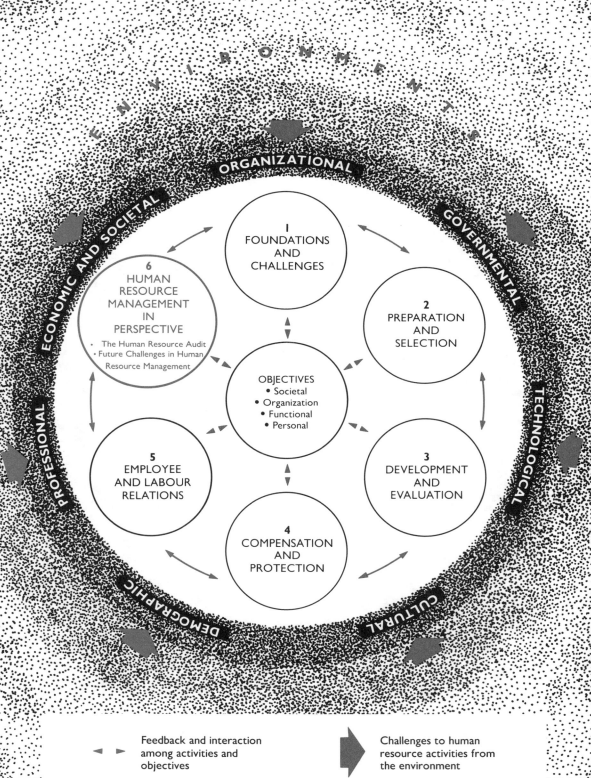

ENVIRONMENTS

ORGANIZATIONAL

GOVERNMENTAL

TECHNOLOGICAL

CULTURAL

DEMOGRAPHIC

PROFESSIONAL

ECONOMIC AND SOCIETAL

**1**
FOUNDATIONS
AND
CHALLENGES

**2**
PREPARATION
AND
SELECTION

**3**
DEVELOPMENT
AND
EVALUATION

**4**
COMPENSATION
AND
PROTECTION

**5**
EMPLOYEE
AND LABOUR
RELATIONS

**6**
HUMAN
RESOURCE
MANAGEMENT
IN
PERSPECTIVE
• The Human Resource Audit
• Future Challenges in Human
  Resource Management

OBJECTIVES
• Societal
• Organization
• Functional
• Personal

Feedback and interaction
among activities and
objectives

Challenges to human
resource activities from
the environment

PART *6* ○ ○ ○ ○ ○ ○

# *HUMAN RESOURCE MANAGEMENT IN PERSPECTIVE*

*A* human resource department must not become content with its performance. It must proactively search for new ways to help the firm and its people. One way is through an audit of its activities. The research findings from an audit point to opportunities for improvement. Another way to help the firm and its people is to anticipate future challenges. As a manager or human resource professional, audits give you feedback on how you perform, and so they may change the way you manage in the future.

# C H A P T E R *20* ○○○○○○○

# *HUMAN RESOURCE AUDIT*

> *. . . managers are focusing on improved human resources management as a means of restoring the competitive position of their companies in an increasingly challenging global marketplace.*
>
> RAYMOND E. MILES AND CHARLES C. SNOW[1]

○ ○ ○ ○ ○ ○ ○ ○ ○ ○ ○ ○ ○ ○ ○ ○ ○ ○ ○ ○ ○ ○ ○ ○ ○ ○ ○ ○ ○ ○ ○
## *CHAPTER OBJECTIVES*
After studying this chapter, you should be able to:
1. **Identify** the benefits of a human resource audit.
2. **Describe** the most common approaches to audits.
3. **Explain** the research tools used in a human resource audit.
4. **Recommend** the components of a successful human resource audit report.
○ ○ ○ ○ ○ ○ ○ ○ ○ ○ ○ ○ ○ ○ ○ ○ ○ ○ ○ ○ ○ ○ ○ ○ ○ ○ ○ ○ ○ ○ ○

*A* human resource department cannot assume that everything it does is correct. Errors happen. Policies become outdated. By evaluating itself, the department finds problems before they become serious. Audits of past practices also reveal outdated assumptions that can be changed to help the department better meet future challenges. Research into those practices and procedures may uncover better ways for the department to contribute to the societal, organizational, functional, and personal objectives discussed in Chapter 1. If the evaluation is done properly, it can also build support between the human resource department and operating managers. For example, consider the following conversation between a manager and a member of the human resource department.

"As manager of the underwriting department, I know we make mistakes. Most errors are caught and corrected before any damage is done. But sometimes outside auditors catch our mistakes for us, so I am glad that you are auditing the human resource department's procedures. I was beginning to wonder if your department thought it was above outside review," commented Linda Desmarais.

"We realize that there is room for improvement. In fact, the reason we are doing this review is to check our methods and learn how we can better serve managers like yourself," Fred Nolin reacted.

"What do you hope to discover?" Linda asked.

"First, we want to see if our present procedures are being followed. We need uniformity in our selection, career planning, compensation, and other activities. If there is a lack of consistency, we want to find out why. Maybe people do not understand our procedures. Or maybe our methods are not practical and should be changed. Second, we are checking to ensure compliance with employee relations laws such as human rights, safety, and others. This audit is not a 'witch hunt.' We are simply trying to improve our performance," Fred concluded.

A human resource *audit* evaluates the human resource activities used in an organization.[2] The audit may include one division or an entire company. It gives feedback about the human resource function to operating managers and human resource specialists. It also provides feedback about how well managers are meeting their human resource duties. In short, the audit is an overall quality control check on human resource activities in a division or company.

As the opening dialogue indicates, several benefits result from a human resource audit. Figure 20-1 lists the major ones. An audit reminds managers like Linda of the department's contribution.[3] It also creates a more professional image of the department among managers and human resource specialists. And the audit helps clarify the department's role and leads to greater uniformity. Perhaps most importantly, it uncovers problems and ensures compliance with a variety of laws. These benefits explain the increasing interest in human resource audit by major Canadian firms in recent years.

## FIGURE 20-1  Benefits of Human Resource Management Audit

- **Identifies** the contributions of the human resource department to the organization.
- **Improves** the professional image of the human resource department.
- **Encourages** greater responsibility and professionalism among members of the human resource department.
- **Clarifies** the human resource department's duties and responsibilities.
- **Stimulates** uniformity of human resource policies and practices.
- **Finds** critical human resource problems.
- **Ensures** timely compliance with legal requirements.
- **Reduces** human resource costs through more effective human resource department procedures.
- **Creates** increased acceptance of needed changes in the human resource department.
- **Includes** a thorough review of the department's information system.

Human resource research grows more important with each passing year for several reasons. First, human resource work carries with it many legal implications for the employer. Failure to comply with equal employment or safety laws, for example, subjects the organization to lawsuits. Second, people costs are significant. Pay and benefits often are a major operating expense for most employers. Improper compensation plans can be costly, even fatal, to the company's survival. Third, the department's activities help shape an organization's productivity and its employees' quality of work life. And, the growing complexity of human resources work makes research necessary.

As discussed in Chapter 1, human resource activities are simply more important to competitive survival. More and more executives expect the department to make significant, even strategic, contributions and to be professionally managed.[4] For example, in a research study involving interviews with seventy-one chief executive officers (CEO) of U.S. companies, it was found that the human resource function (especially activities aimed at productivity improvement, succession planning, and cultural change) was critical to business success.

For modern human resource departments to make a strategic contribution and better meet their organizations' needs, they face a fundamental challenge to balance societal, organizational, functional, and human resource objectives. It must be done in a way that respects the importance and dignity of human beings, called the human resource approach in Chapter 1. At the same time, specialists must not lose sight of the systems approach, which *subordinates* the departmental subsystem to the larger system of the organization. The organization's success, not the department's, is what really matters.

Achieving departmental objectives also depends on providing service to managers and employees through a proactive approach. The department does not usurp each manager's human resource responsibilities. Instead, a professional management approach assumes a dual responsibility between the worker's immediate supervisor and the human resource department, with the department playing a major and proactive role. However, with all other systems, human resource management also needs to be evaluated to ensure that it meets organizational, departmental, and individual objectives. This chapter examines the scope, approaches, and tools used to conduct human resource audits. Although the audit is usually done by human resource experts, their findings affect both the human resource function and operating managers.

## THE SCOPE OF HUMAN RESOURCE AUDITS

The scope of an audit extends beyond just the human resource department's actions. The department does not operate in isolation. Its success depends on how well it performs *and* how well its programs are carried out by others in the organization. For example, consider how supervisors at Ontario Electronics and Electrical Manufacturers reduced the effectiveness of the performance appraisal process.

> To appraise performance, Ontario Electronics and Electrical Manufacturers used a critical-incident procedure, which means supervisors had to record both positive and negative incidents as they occurred. To become a section supervisor, an employee needed three years of good or superior performance evaluations. However, in practice, supervisors stressed employee mistakes when they recorded incidents; as a result, few employees received the three years of good ratings needed to qualify for a promotion. Many of them blamed the human resource department's appraisal process for their lack of promotions.

An audit uncovered this misuse of the program and led to additional training for supervisors in the use of the critical-incident method. If the audit had not uncovered this problem, employee dissatisfaction might have grown worse.

As the example of Ontario Electronics and Electrical Manufacturers illustrates, people problems are seldom confined to just the human resource department. Thus these audits must be broad in scope to be effective. They should evaluate the human resource department's function, the use of personnel procedures by managers, and the impact of these activities on employee goals and satisfaction.

In recent years, however, this "inward looking perspective" has become insufficient. Human resource professionals find that the scope of the audit must transcend even the concerns of the department and operating managers. Although not all human resource audits review corporate strategy and its fit with the external environment, these broader concerns merit mention.

## Audit of the Corporate Strategy

Human resource professionals do not set corporate strategy, but as discussed in Chapter 1, they strongly determine its success.[5] Corporate strategy is concerned with how the organization is going to gain a competitive advantage. Based upon such things as an assessment of the firm's environment, weaknesses, opportunities, and strengths, senior management devises ways of gaining an advantage. Whether the company stresses superior marketing (McCain Foods), service (IBM), innovation (Northern Telecom), low-cost operations (Canadian Tire), or some other approach, human resource management is affected.[6] Understanding the strategy has strong implications for human resource planning, staffing, compensation, employee relations, and other human resource activities.

Although the department may lack both the expertise and resources to audit the corporate strategy and its fit with the external environment, the strategy/environmental fit cannot be ignored. Human resource professionals must audit their function, managerial compliance, and employee acceptance of human resource policies and practices against the firm's strategic plans. For example, high turnover in entry-level jobs may keep wages near the bottom of the rate range, lowering labour costs. Thus, employee turnover in a large accounting firm may be a low-cost way to keep the firm's overall labour costs competitive. An audit, however, might reveal considerable dissatisfaction among recent accounting graduates about the number of billable hours required of them each week. Knowledge of the firm's strategy (to hire excess entry-level accountants) affects the value of audit information (about employee satisfaction, for example).

Human resource auditors can learn more about the firm's strategy through interviews with key executives, reviews of long-range business plans, and systematic environmental scans designed to uncover changing trends.[7]

## Audit of the Human Resource Function

Audits should logically begin with a review of the human resource department's work.[8] Figure 20-2 lists the major areas they cover. As shown in the figure, an audit should focus on the human resource management information system, staffing and development,

FIGURE 20-2   Major Areas Covered in a Human Resource Audit

### HUMAN RESOURCE MANAGEMENT INFORMATION SYSTEM

| | |
|---|---|
| **Human rights legislation** | **Human resource plans** |
| • Information on compliance | • Supply and demand estimates |
| | • Skills inventories |
| | • Replacement charts and summaries |
| **Job analysis information** | **Compensation administration** |
| • Job standards | • Wage and salary levels |
| • Job descriptions | • Fringe benefit package |
| • Job specifications | • Employer-provided services |

### STAFFING AND DEVELOPMENT

| | |
|---|---|
| **Recruiting** | **Selection** |
| • Source of recruits | • Selection ratios |
| • Availability of recruits | • Selection procedures |
| • Employment applications | • Human rights legislation compliance |
| **Training and orientation** | **Career development** |
| • Orientation program | • Internal placement success |
| • Training objectives and procedures | • Career planning program |
| • Learning rate | • Human resource development effort |

### ORGANIZATION CONTROL AND EVALUATION

| | |
|---|---|
| **Performance appraisals** | **Labour-management relations** |
| • Standards and measures of performance | • Legal compliance |
| • Performance appraisal techniques | • Management rights |
| • Evaluation interviews | • Dispute resolution problems |
| **Human resource controls** | **Human resource audits** |
| • Employee communications | • Human resource function |
| • Discipline procedures | • Operating managers |
| • Change and development procedures | • Employee feedback on human resource department |

and organizational control and evaluation. These three areas of audit supplement one another and integrate with one another. As such, no single area should be overemphasized in the audit.

An audit touches on virtually every topic discussed in this book. A review of only a few aspects of the human resource management system may ignore topics that affect the department's effectiveness. For each item in the figure, the audit team of human resources specialists should:

- *Identify* who is responsible for each activity.
- *Determine* the objectives sought by each activity.
- *Review* the policies and procedures used to achieve these objectives.
- *Sample* the records in the human resource information system to learn if policies and procedures are being followed correctly.

- *Prepare* a report commending proper objectives, policies, and procedures.
- *Develop* a plan of action to correct errors in objectives, policies, and procedures.
- *Follow up* on the plan of action to see if it has solved the problems found through the audit.[9]

Admittedly, an audit of every human resource activity is time consuming. As a result, very large organizations have full-time audit teams similar to those who conduct financial audits. These teams are especially useful when the human resource department is decentralized into regional or field offices. Through the use of audits, the organization can maintain consistency in its practices even though there are several human resources offices in different locations. And the mere existence of an audit team encourages compliance and self-audits between visits by the audit team.

> Cliff Robertson, a regional human resource manager, realized that his chances for promotion to the corporate headquarters in Toronto depended on how well his region's human resource offices performed. The company's human resource audit team reviewed his region's performance every June. So in preparation for the audit, Cliff had each human resource office in the central region conduct a self-audit in April. Then in early May the human resource administrators from the three branches met in Winnipeg to review the results of the audit, and during May errors uncovered through the audit were corrected, if possible. Thus when the corporate audit team completed its own review in June, they always gave Cliff's region high marks for compliance with company policies and with laws.

## *Audit of Managerial Compliance*

An audit also reviews how well managers comply with human resource policies and procedures. If managers ignore these policies or violate employee relations laws, the audit should uncover these errors so that corrective action can be taken. Compliance with laws is especially important for when human rights, safety, compensation, or labour laws are violated, the government holds the company responsible.

> The manager of a fast-food restaurant hired two high school students to do janitorial work on a part-time basis. The two boys were glad to earn $3 an hour. But one boy's father complained to the government that the restaurant was paying below minimum wage. Not only was the parent company found guilty of violating the minimum wage laws, but the complaint triggered an investigation of the pay and overtime practices of the firm's other restaurants. Had this company used an internal human resource audit, the error could have been corrected before formal government action was taken.

Besides assuring compliance, the audit can improve the human resource department's image and contribution to the company. Operating managers may gain a higher respect for the department when an audit team seeks their views. If the comments of managers are acted upon, the department will be seen as more responsive to their needs. And since it is a service department, these actions may improve its contribution to organizational objectives. For example, consider what one audit team learned when it talked with managers of local claims offices:

> After several interviews with claims office managers, the audit team discovered a pattern to their comments. Most managers believed that although the human resource department filled job vacancies quickly, it did not train recruits before assigning them to a claims office. Day-to-day pressures in the claims office caused training to be superficial and led to many errors by new adjusters. The managers felt that the training should be done at the regional office by the human resource department.
>
> After reading the team's report, the regional human resource manager was pleased to learn that the selection process was satisfactory, and to solve the problem of field training, she created a one-week training program for claims adjusters with her next budget increase.

### Audit of Employee Satisfaction

Effective human resource departments meet both company objectives and employee needs. When employee needs are not met, turnover, absenteeism, and union activity are more likely. To learn how well employee needs are met, the audit team gathers data from workers. The team collects information about wages, benefits, supervisory practices, career planning assistance, and the feedback employees receive about their performance.

> The audit team of an automobile parts distributor received one common complaint from employees: they felt isolated because they worked in retail stores or warehouses located all over Canada. They had little sense of belonging to the large company of which they were a part. To bolster sagging morale and to help employees feel that they were members of a fast-growing and dynamic company, the human resource department started a biweekly "Employee Newsletter." The two-page letter was stuffed in every pay envelope each payday. It gave tips on new developments at headquarters and different field locations. In this way, the department used the audit to make the firm more responsive to its employees' needs.

In more progressive organizations such as IBM Canada, employee attitude surveys are done regularly. This enables the organization to solve problems before they evolve into larger and more complex issues.

### RESEARCH APPROACHES TO AUDITS

Human resource activities are evaluated through research.[10] Several research approaches are used because the scope of audits includes the human resource function, operating managers, and employees. Sometimes the "research" is little more than an informal investigation or fact-finding effort. At other times, the approach may be advanced and rely on sophisticated research designs and statistics.[11] Whether informal or rigorous, this research seeks to improve the human resource activities of the organization. These applications-oriented efforts are called *applied research*. The most common forms of applied human resource research are summarized in Figure 20-3 and are explained in the following paragraphs.[12]

FIGURE 20-3   Research Approaches of Human Resource Audits

---

· **Comparative approach.** The human resource audit team compares its firm (or division) with another firm (or division) to uncover areas of poor performance. This approach commonly is used to compare the results of specific human resource activities or programs. It helps to detect areas of needed improvement.

· **Outside authority approach.** The audit team relies on the expertise of a consultant or published research findings as a standard against which human resource activities or programs are evaluated. The consultant or research findings may help diagnose the cause of problems.

· **Statistical approach.** From existing records, the audit team generates statistical standards against which activities and programs are evaluated. With these mathematical standards, the team may uncover errors while they are still minor.

· **Compliance approach.** By sampling elements of the human resource information system, the audit team looks for deviations from laws and company policies or procedures. Through their fact-finding efforts, the team can determine whether there is compliance with company policies and legal regulations.

· **MBO approach.** When a management-by-objectives (MBO) approach is applied to the human resource area, the audit team can compare actual results with stated objectives. Areas of poor performance can be detected and reported.

---

Perhaps the simplest form of research is the *comparative approach*. It uses another division or company as a model. The audit team then compares their results or procedures with those of the other organization. The comparative approach is often used to compare absence, turnover, and salary data. This approach also makes sense when a new procedure is being tried for the first time. For example, if a company installs an alcoholic rehabilitation program, it may copy a similar program at another firm or division. Then the results of the two programs are compared.

Alternatively, the human resource department may rely on an *outside authority approach*. Standards set by a consultant or from published research findings serve as benchmarks for the audit team. For example, the consultant or industry-wide research may indicate that the human resource budget is usually about three-quarters of 1% of gross sales. This figure then serves as a rough guidepost when evaluating the human resource department's overall budget. At present, external comparison is one of the most popular approaches to evaluating human resource activities and services.

A third approach is to develop statistical measures of performance based on the company's existing information system. For example, research into the company's records reveals its absenteeism and turnover rates. These data indicate how well human resource activities and operating managers control these problem areas. This *statistical approach* is usually supplemented with comparisons against external information, which may be gathered from other firms. This information is often expressed as ratios that are easy to compute and use. For example, an employer that averages two hundred employees during the month and has twelve quit finds that its turnover rate is 6%.[13]

$$\frac{\text{Number of separations (12)}}{\text{Average number of employees (200)}} \times 100 = 6\%$$

Likewise, if eight employees miss work on a particular day, the absenteeism rate is 4%.

$$\frac{\text{Number of employees absent (8)}}{\text{Total number scheduled to work (200)}} \times 100 = 4\%$$

The *compliance approach* is another human resource audit strategy. This method reviews past practices to determine if those actions followed company policies and procedures. Often the audit team reviews a sample of employment, compensation, discipline, and employee appraisal forms. The purpose of the review is to ensure that field office and operating managers comply with internal rules and legal regulations.

> An internal audit of the selection process used at Bio-Genetics Ltd. revealed that the employment manager followed the correct procedures. But the audit team noticed that many applications had comments written in the margins. These comments were added by operating managers who also interviewed applicants. Most of their notes referred to personal data that were not asked on the form, such as sex, age, marital status, ages of dependants, and race. Managers did this to help them remember individual candidates. But if some applicant was not hired, these comments could lead to charges of discrimination on the basis of age, sex or race.

A final approach is for human resource specialists and operating managers to set objectives in their area of responsibility. This *MBO* (management-by-objectives) *approach* creates specific objectives against which performance can be measured.[14] Then the audit team researches actual performance and compares it with the previously set objectives. For example, operating managers may set a goal of resolving a higher percentage of grievances before they reach arbitration. Then the audit evaluates the trends in this area. This is also a popular approach to evaluating the human resource department's function.

No one of these audit approaches can be applied to all parts of human resource management. More commonly, audit teams use several of these strategies, depending on the specific human resource activities under evaluation. Then, as Figure 20-4 suggests, the audit team selects specific research tools to collect audit information. This information serves as feedback on human resource activities. Unfavourable feedback leads to corrective action that improves the contribution of human resource activities.

## TOOLS OF HUMAN RESOURCE RESEARCH

Regardless of the audit team's approach, it must collect data about the organization's human resource activities. In practice, this is a very difficult task. Part of the reason lies in the fact that it is very difficult to define its effectiveness. Many of the indices available are subjective in nature and organization-dependent. Further, human resource management effectiveness at the organizational level may be quite different from the effectiveness and efficiency of the human resource department itself. Typically, a number

FIGURE 20-4    An Overview of the Human Resource Management Audit
Process

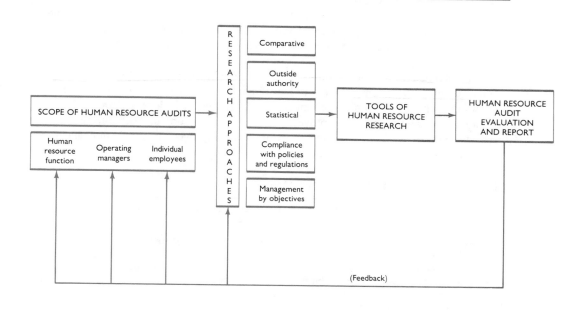

of tools may be needed to gauge human resource management effectiveness even approximately. Each research tool provides partial insights into the firm's human resource
activities. If these tools are used skillfully, the team can weave these insights into a clear
picture of the organization's human resource activities. These tools include:

· Interviews
· Questionnaires and surveys
· Record analysis

· External information
· Human resource experiments

*Interviews*

Interviews with employees and managers are one source of information about human
resource activities. Their comments help the audit team find areas that need improvement. Criticisms by employees may pinpoint those actions that the department should
take to meet their needs. Likewise, suggestions by managers may reveal ways to provide
them with better service. When their criticisms are valid, changes should be made. But
when it is the human resource department who is right, it may have to educate others
in the firm by explaining the procedures being questioned.

Bob Gordon served as a member of the audit team at Canadian Furniture Company.
He interviewed various managers, who complained that the frequent transfer of

managerial staff was a problem. Bob understood their concerns. He explained that the unique type of furniture the company dealt with led to too many fluctuations in market demand for the company's products. Unless senior managers were frequently transferred to faraway branches, the sales of these branches could not be pulled up. Although many managers still disliked the situation, the audit interview helped them understand the need for the frequent transfers of managers.

Another useful source of information is the exit interview.[15] *Exit interviews* are conducted with departing employees to learn their views of the organization. Figure 20-5 shows the typical questions asked during the interview. It is done separately from the human resource audit, and the employees' comments are recorded. Then during the audit these answers are reviewed to find the causes of employee dissatisfaction and other human resource management problems.

FIGURE 20-5   An Exit Interview Form

**SASKATOON KITCHEN APPLIANCES LTD.**
**Exit Interview Form**

Employee's name _____   Date hired _____
Interviewed by _____   Interviewed on _____
Supervisor's name _____   Department _____

1. Were your job duties and responsibilities what you expected? _____
   If not, why? _____
2. What is your frank and honest opinion of:
   **a.** Your job? _____
   **b.** Your working conditions? _____
   **c.** Your orientation to your job? _____
   **d.** Your training provided by the company? _____
   **e.** Your pay? _____
   **f.** Your company-provided benefits and services? _____
   **g.** Your treatment by your manager? _____
3. What is your major reason for leaving the company? _____
4. What could we have done to keep you from leaving? _____
5. What could be done to make Saskatoon Kitchen Appliances a better place to work? _____
   _____

## Questionnaires and Surveys

Many human resource departments supplement interviews with questionnaires and surveys. These tools are used because interviews are time consuming, costly, and usually limited to only a few people. Through surveys of employees, a more accurate picture of employee treatment can be developed. Also, questionnaires may lead to more candid answers than face-to-face interviews.

One common questionnaire is an *attitude survey*. These multipage paper-and-pencil tests are used to learn how employees view their manager, their job, and the human resource department. Sometimes several hundred questions are asked. These questions seek answers to the critical issues listed in Figure 20-6. Then the answers are grouped into areas of analysis to find out where employee attitudes are high and where low. Further analysis may identify problems with specific supervisors, jobs, or benefits.

FIGURE 20-6   Critical Concerns to Be Answered by Attitude Surveys

### EMPLOYEE ATTITUDES ABOUT SUPERVISORS

- Are some supervisors' employees exceptionally satisfied or dissatisfied?
- Do specific supervisors need training in supervisory and human relations skills?
- Have attitudes improved since the last survey?

### EMPLOYEE ATTITUDES ABOUT THEIR JOBS

- What are common elements of jobs that cause negative attitudes? Positive attitudes?
- Can jobs that cause poor attitudes be redesigned to improve satisfaction?
- Can jobs that cause poor attitudes be given alternative work schedules (such as shorter workweeks or flextime)?

### PERCEIVED EFFECTIVENESS OF THE PERSONNEL DEPARTMENT

- Do employees think they work for a good or bad employer?
- Do employees think they have a career or merely a job?
- Do employees feel they have some place to turn in order to solve their problems, besides to their immediate superior?
- Do employees feel informed about company developments?
- Do employees know what is expected of them in their jobs?
- Are employees satisfied by the amount and type of feedback they get about their performance?
- Are employees satisfied with their pay? Benefits?

After an attitude survey, the manager of a small steel mill found that the detailers in the design department were dissatisfied. Their dissatisfaction stemmed from their jobs, supervision, and medical insurance.

Detailers are typically responsible for executing detailed drawings. However, at the mill some detailers specialized in doing the drawings, while others labelled the blueprints. Also, they worked under a supervisor who rigidly enforced company rules and was very autocratic. Finally, they were upset at the human resource department because it usually took nearly two months for them to be reimbursed for claims against the supplementary dental insurance plan.

The mill manager, the human resource manager, and the design department supervisor met to discuss the attitude problem among the detailers. They agreed to redesign the jobs so that each detailer was responsible for all phases of a drawing. The human resource and mill managers convinced the supervisor to implement flexible working hours and move these workers from hourly pay to salary. The supervisor also agreed to enroll in the company's sixteen-week human relations training program. Since dissatisfaction with dental expenses reimbursement existed throughout the company, the human resource manager arranged for all employees to send their claims directly to the insurance company. The next survey revealed that this problem no longer existed.

As the example shows, attitude surveys give valuable feedback. Operating managers can learn where changes in jobs or supervision are needed. The human resource department learns how its efforts are viewed by employees. And when surveys are conducted periodically, the audit team can identify trends. Perhaps more importantly, changes made after an attitude survey show employees management's commitment to their welfare.

## Record Analysis

Not all problems are revealed through employee attitudes. Sometimes problems can be found only by studying records. These reviews are done to ensure compliance with company procedures and laws. The records normally reviewed by an audit team are listed in Figure 20-7 and discussed in the following paragraphs.

**FIGURE 20-7**   Records Commonly Reviewed as Part of Human Resource Audit

---

### SAFETY AND HEALTH RECORDS

- Determine differences before and after human resource programs aimed at lowering turnover or absenteeism.

### GRIEVANCE RECORDS

- Are there patterns to grievances arising from specific contract clauses or supervisors?
- Are there sections of the agreement that are unclear to union or management officials?

### COMPENSATION STUDIES

- Are wages externally and internally equitable?
- Are fringe benefits understood by employees?
- Does the fringe benefit package compare favourably with those of local firms and national competitors?

### HUMAN RIGHTS PLANS

- Is the firm in compliance with all human rights laws?
- Should there be an affirmative-action plan to address those areas where the firm is not in compliance?
- Has the firm made acceptable progress toward meeting its human rights goals?

### PROGRAM AND POLICY STUDIES

- Does each human resource program meet its stated goals?
- Are human resource policies and procedures being followed by the human resource department and line managers?

### SCRAP RATES

- Determine if training, bonuses, or other human resource programs have reduced scrap rates.

### TURNOVER/ABSENTEEISM

- Are there patterns or discernible causes? By age? Sex?
- How do these records compare with those of other employers?
- Determine differences before and after human resource programs aimed at lowering turnover or absenteeism.

FIGURE 20-7 (continued)    Records Commonly Reviewed in Human Resource Audit

---

### PRETEST/POSTTEST SCORES

- Determine if orientation or training programs improve test scores or job performance.
- How well do test scores relate to job performance?

---

### INTERNAL PLACEMENT RECORDS

- What percentage of jobs are filled internally?
- How well do internally promoted candidates perform?
- Do replacement charts/summaries indicate sufficient promotable talent?

---

### SELECTION RECORDS

- Is the performance of recruits better according to the source from which they were recruited?
- Are recruitment and selection costs comparable with those of other firms?

---

### EMPLOYEE FILES

- Are employee files in order and properly completed?
- Do records contain accurate, up-to-date information that is useful for making employee decisions?
- Is this employee making reasonable career progress?
- Is this employee a source of discipline or interpersonal problem?

---

### SPECIAL PROGRAMMING REPORTS

- Are special programs achieving the desired results?

---

## Safety and Health Audits

An analysis of safety and health records may reveal violations of provisions of the Canadian Labour Code and other provincial safety and health regulations. Under the record-keeping requirements of the Canada Labour Code, Part IV, accurate records of all matters coming under the jurisdiction of the Safety and Health Committee should be kept by every organization. A human resource audit can help to document the firm's compliance with safety and health requirements in each province.

## Grievance Audits

The audit team may also be able to uncover a pattern in employee grievances. Patterns may emerge by jobs, supervisors, union representatives, age groups, or contract provisions. If patterns are detected, human resource specialists seek out the underlying causes and take corrective action to reduce the causes of these complaints. Interviews with supervisors and union officials may reveal the underlying causes of grievances. And if union officials participate in finding patterns of grievances, they may support management's suggested changes.

A grievance audit at the Kelowna Logging Company indicated that supervisors and managers were spending too much of their time dealing with grievances. In fact, the lost production time by workers and costs of arbitration were seriously reducing the company's profitability. Low profitability meant that the union had to accept the smallest wage increases in the area.

The audit team asked the two top union officials to help review the causes of grievances. The union leaders thought the problem was a poor understanding of the contract by both supervisors and union representatives. The audit team's analysis fit the union leaders' comments. As a result, the company asked the town's part-time mayor to help train both sides. The training led to a noticeable drop in grievances.

### Compensation Audits

Audit teams carefully review the human resource department's compensation practices.[16] Primarily, they study the level of wages, benefits, and services that are provided. If jobs have been priced properly through job evaluations and salary surveys, pay levels will be fair. Benefits and services are also studied, to learn if they are competitive with those of other employers and in compliance with government regulations.

### Human Rights Compliance Audits

Although several large companies employ one or more persons to monitor the company's compliance with Canadian human rights legislation, the audit team serves as a further check on compliance. The team usually concentrates its attention on hiring, placement, and compensation of all minority groups; if discriminating practices exist, it informs management of the need for corrective action.

### Program and Policy Audits

Besides safety, grievance, compensation, and human rights corrective action programs, audits evaluate many other human resource programs and policies. The purpose of these audits is to determine whether other programs and policies are doing what was intended.

Two years after Seafood Canners Ltd. adopted a "promotion from within" policy, most supervisors were still recruited from outside the firm. Few workers applied for supervisory openings, even though these jobs were posted throughout the plant and employees were encouraged to apply. The audit team learned that during peak seasons, production workers earned more money than supervisors because of over-time pay and the incentive system. Many employees viewed supervisory jobs as entailing more responsibility and less pay. To remedy the problem, supervisors were given a percentage of their department's production bonus. A year later, 90% of the supervisory openings were being filled internally.

As the Seafood Canners example illustrates, policies ("promote from within") may conflict with other programs (the incentive system). And legal requirements (over-time pay) may conflict with the department's goals. Virtually every human resource policy and program affects at least one other. Thus a thorough audit needs to include all the major human resource policies and programs and how they relate to each other.

Figure 20-7 also identifies other typical records reviewed by audit teams. These records are evaluated to find areas of poor performance and conflicts between policies, programs, and employee relations laws. The use of these records in an audit is wide-ranging, as suggested by the questions raised in the figure.

## External Information

Another tool of the audit team is external information.[17] Research that is limited to just the organization's internal attitudes and records may uncover unfavourable trends. But outside comparisons also give the audit team a perspective against which their firm's activities can be judged. Some needed information is available readily, while other data may be difficult to find.

Most of the external information is available from the publications of Statistics Canada and Labour Canada. These agencies regularly publish information about future employment opportunities, employee turnover rates, work-force projections, area wage and salary surveys, severity and frequency rates of accidents, and other data that can serve as benchmarks for comparing internal information. Statistics Canada, Labour Canada, Employment and Immigration Canada, and provincial labour and manpower offices provide information that can also be used for comparative purposes. Work-force demographics—age, sex, education, and national-ethnic composition—are commonly available from provincial agencies.

Industry associations and boards of trade usually make available to members specialized data related to the industry. Of most use to audit teams are statistics on industry norms — such as turnover rates, absenteeism rates, standard wage rates, growth rates, standardized job descriptions, accident rates, fringe benefit costs, and sample union-management agreements.

Professional associations often provide similar information to members of the profession. Studies conducted by the association may include salary and benefit surveys, demographic profiles, and other data that can serve as standards against which the human resource department's efforts are measured.

Consultants and university research bureaus may be able to provide other needed information through research.

## Human Resource Experiments

A final tool available to human resource departments and audit teams is research experiments. The ideal research design is a *field experiment* that allows the human resource department to compare an experimental and a control group under realistic conditions. For example, the human resource department may implement a safety training program for half of the department supervisors. This half is the experimental group. The control group is the supervisors who are not given training. Then the subsequent safety records of both groups are compared several months after the training is completed. If the experimental group has significantly lower accident rates, this is evidence that the safety training program was effective.

Experimentation does have some drawbacks. Many managers are reluctant to experiment with only some workers because of morale problems and potential dissatisfaction among those who were not selected. Those involved may feel manipulated.

And the experiment may be confounded by changes in the work environment or simply by the two groups' talking with each other about the experiment.

These problems are lessened by using a research design that involves two organizations, as did one school board:

> The human resource department of a rural school district gave all the elementary school teachers of one school a special two-day training program. The teachers at another school thirty kilometres away did not receive the training. At the end of the year, the school board's audit team compared the teacher evaluations and pupil scores on province-wide tests to assess the success of the development program.

This design reduced the likelihood of the experimental and control groups' discussing the training. It also prevented the problem of principals' having half of their faculty in each group. Of course, the difficulty with this design is that it assumes that the two organizations, their teachers, and their students were comparable before the experiment began.

## AUDIT REPORT

Research approaches and tools are used to develop a picture of the organization's human resource activities. For this information to be useful, it is compiled into an audit report. The *audit report* is a comprehensive description of human resource activities, which includes both commendations for effective practices and recommendations for improving practices that are ineffective. A recognition of both good and bad practices is more balanced and encourages acceptance of the report.

Often an audit report is in three parts. One part is for operating managers, another for managers of specific human resource functions, and the third for the human resource manager.

### Report for Operating Managers

The audit report for operating managers summarizes their human resource objectives and responsibilities. Their goals may seek to reduce absenteeism or turnover, further employee development, improve union relations, or achieve other objectives. Specific duties of line managers also may be included. These duties may involve interviewing applicants, training employees, evaluating performance, motivating workers, and satisfying employee needs.

The report also identifies human resource problems. Violations of human resource policies and employee relations laws are highlighted. Poor management practices are revealed in the report along with recommendations where appropriate. For example, consider an excerpt of a report received by the manager of a bottling plant.

> **Employee turnover.** Overall, the turnover rates in the Sydney Bottling Plant compare favourably with turnover rates in the community and the industry. Plant management appears to be sensitive to the needs of long-service employees.
>
> Turnover among recently hired employees tends to be very high. Attitude surveys

and exit interviews reveal two problems. First, new employees sometimes quit because their job duties were not what they had expected. Second, among those new employees who stay, many report feelings of isolation and not being part of the "team." If applicants were given realistic job previews by showing them the actual duties and working conditions, fewer of them would resign during the ninety-day probationary period. It is also recommended that each supervisor start a departmental orientation program. This program should introduce new hires to the people, facilities, and policies of their department. Then new employees should be assigned to a senior worker to create a "buddy system" that will help them become part of the work team and the informal organization.

## Report to Human Resource Specialists

Those specialists who handle employment, training, compensation, and other human resource activities also need feedback. The audit report they receive isolates specific areas of good and poor performance. For example, one audit team observed that many jobs did not have qualified replacements. This information was given to the manager of training and development along with the recommendation for more programs to develop promising supervisors and managers.

The report may also provide these specialists with other feedback, such as attitudes of operating managers about the specialists' efforts. Sometimes comparative data are included to show what other companies are doing and to provide standards of comparison.

## Report to Human Resource Manager

The human resource manager's report contains all the information given to line managers and specialists within the human resource department. In addition, the human resource manager gets feedback about:

· Attitudes of operating managers and employees about the human resource department's benefits and services.
· A review of the department's objectives and its organization to achieve them.
· Human resource problems and their implications.
· Recommendations for needed changes, which may be stated in the priority seen by the audit team.

With the information contained in the audit report, the human resource manager can take a broad view of the human resource function. Instead of solving problems in a random manner, the manager now can focus on those areas that have the greatest potential for improving the department's contribution to the firm.[18] Emerging trends can be studied and corrective action taken while the problems are still minor. Prompt response to the problems of operating managers may earn added support among them. Even morale and motivation within the human resource department may be increased — for example, through timely congratulations to those who have performed well. The organization could ensure that actual management actions are seen to result from these audits. Otherwise audits may serve only to raise the employees' expectations and in fact make matters worse than before.

Perhaps most importantly, the audit serves as a map for future efforts and a reference point for future audits. With knowledge of the department's present performance, the manager can make long-range plans to upgrade crucial activities. These plans identify new goals for the department. And these goals serve as standards — standards that future audit teams will use to evaluate the firm's human resource management activities.

## SUMMARY

A human resource audit evaluates the human resource activities used in an organization. Its purpose is to ensure that operating managers and human resource specialists are following human resource policies and maintaining an effective work force.

The scope of the audit involves human resource specialists, operating managers, employees, and the external environment. Inputs are sought from all four sources because each has a unique perspective. And to be truly effective, human resource activities cannot meet just the wishes of experts in the field. They also must meet the needs of employees and operating managers and the challenges from the environment.

The audit team uses a variety of research approaches and tools to evaluate human resource activities. Along with internal comparisons, audit teams need to compare their firm's efforts against those of other companies or against standards developed by external authorities and internal statistics. Or their approach may evaluate compliance with laws or with objectives set by management.

Data are gathered through interviews, questionnaire surveys, internal records, external sources, or experimentation. Through these tools, the audit team is able to compile an audit report. The audit report gives feedback to top management, operating managers, human resource specialists, and the human resource manager. Armed with this information, the human resource manager then can develop plans to ensure that human resource activitites better contribute to the organization. If human resource management is to be responsible, it needs to review its past performance through audits and research. At the same time, it needs a future orientation to anticipate upcoming challenges. Finally, a proactive view encourages human resource management to contribute to both people and company goals.

## TERMS FOR REVIEW

| | |
|---|---|
| Human resource audit | Exit interviews |
| Audit team | Attitude survey |
| Applied research | Field experiment |
| Research approaches | Audit report |
| MBO approach | |

## REVIEW AND DISCUSSION QUESTIONS

1.  In your own words, what are the benefits of a human resource audit to an organization?

2.  Why does a human resource audit go beyond just the actions of human resource specialists?

3.  If you were asked to conduct a human resource audit on the compensation function (or any other function within the human resource department), what steps would you follow?

4.  If you had to conduct an audit of employee job satisfaction, what tools would you use?

5.  What research approach do you think should be followed for each of the following areas of concern to the human resource audit team: (a) evaluation of a new company-sponsored drug rehabilitation program, (b) an analysis of employee tardiness patterns, (c) the appropriateness of present recruiting costs?

6.  Why are exit interviews an effective source of insight into employee problems in the organization?

7.  How would you design a field experiment to evaluate the advantages of two different employee compensation programs?

8.  What types of information should be put in an audit report for (a) the employment manager, (b) the assistant plant manager, and (c) the human resource director?

9.  In the last two decades, many cultural values have changed—some rather drastically. Briefly describe how human resource management might be affected by (a) a trend toward smaller families, (b) increased participation of women in the work force, (c) increased acceptability by society of divorce.

10. Explain why a human resource department should be proactive in its approach.

## INCIDENT 20-1

### Maritime Coal Industries Limited

Maritime Coal Industries ran two underground coal mines and a coke oven for converting coal into industrial coke. The locations were about sixty kilometers distant from one another, and so each operation had a branch human resource office. The branch offices did their own hiring, administration of employee benefits, safety programs, and labour relations with the local union. After reading an article about the merit of a human resource management audit, the human resource director at Maritime, Gabe Robertson, discussed the need for an audit with the three branch human resource officers. Their individual reactions are summarized below:

**Tony Masone:** We don't need an audit. It will take weeks to conduct, and it won't change a thing. Each of us branch human resource managers does the best job we know how. Besides, most of our actions are audited daily by the union. If we make a mistake in employee treatment, pay, benefits, safety, or most of the traditional audit areas, the union lets us know promptly. When you have a union, an audit is not needed.

**Joyce McDonald:** I disagree with Tony. The union would complain if we made an error against their members. But if our error were detrimental to the best interests of Maritime, I doubt the union would say anything. Besides, in the matter of recruiting, selection, orientation, and training, the union has little say or interest. An audit might even reveal areas where each branch might improve. I for one welcome an audit and a chance to see how my office compares with the other two.

**Sylvie Gagnon:** Joyce makes a good case for an audit, but if we were having problems in training, selection, or the other areas she mentions, we'd know it. We have gotten along for years without an audit; I see no need to put in a lot of overtime and disrupt everything else just to compile a report that will tell us what we already know.

1.  Assuming you agree with Joyce, what other arguments would you add to justify the overtime and disruption that worry Sylvie?

2.  Even though the union contract specifies many areas in detail, briefly describe the possible benefits from an audit of Maritime's (a) compensation program, (b) safety program, (c) grievance process, and (d) labour relations training for supervisors.

3.  Do you think Tony and Sylvie would have a different attitude if they and Joyce were assigned to the audit team? Why?

## INCIDENT 20-2

### Employee Attitudes at Anko Ltd.

Anko Ltd. rents sports equipment. Its main business is renting out ski equipment and snowmobiles. During the winter, the number of employees ranges between fifty and sixty at five locations in various winter resort areas. Al Anko, the owner, hired a management consultant to evaluate employee satisfaction and attitudes. After interviewing nearly twenty employees and supervisors, the consultant developed an attitude survey that was mailed to all employees. From the interviews and attitude surveys, the consultant made the following observations:

• Nearly two-thirds of the employees felt little loyalty to the firm because they considered their jobs temporary.

• Many employees applied to work at Anko because they were interested in skiing.

• Although the firm gave few benefits, many employees commented about the reduced rental rates on equipment as an important "extra" of their jobs.

• Every supervisor mentioned that the most important selection criterion was whether an applicant knows how to fit and adjust ski bindings.

• Over half of the employees worked split shifts from 7 to 10 A.M. and from 4 to 7 P.M., which were the hours most skis were rented and returned. Some employees liked those hours because they could ski during the day. However, employees who lived in the resort area all year long generally disliked the hours.

• Employee turnover was very low. But many employees indicated that they would quit if they could find a better-paying job.

> • Several employees who had worked for Anko in previous years thought it was unfair that they received the same hourly wage as new employees.

1.  If you were the consultant, what recommendations would you make to the owner about (a) the use of split shifts, (b) the types of people recruited, and (c) the treatment of employees who have worked for Anko more than one season?
2.  Should Anko treat employees who permanently live in the resort areas differently from those who move there just for the ski season? If so, what differences in treatment would you recommend?

○ ○ ○ ○ ○ ○ ○ ○ ○ ○ ○ ○ ○ ○ ○ ○ ○ ○ ○ ○ ○ ○ ○ ○ ○ ○ ○ ○ ○ ○ ○ ○ ○ ○ ○ ○

## CASE STUDY

### PACIFIC MINES LIMITED: BRIAN BOYDELL'S LETTER

As he left the office for the day, Brian Boydell felt pleased with himself. Everything seemed to be going well at last. The eight plant operators were back from Holland and Texas and were now writing training manuals. He felt proud of the way the operators were developing as a team. "I've done my best to be open and above board with them," he thought. "It's been hard work but I think we finally have the relationship we need to make the team concept work."

#### Plant Background

As Brian recalled the past year, he remembered how apprehensive and excited he'd been when he accepted his new post in the fall. Pat Irving, project manager, had asked him to join a group of people who were devising a training program for the operators of Pacific Mines Ltd.'s new plant in Carseland. He knew then that he would be the management person working with the developing operations. Pacific Mines, specializing in ammonia-urea fertilizer production, was opening the new $135-million-dollar plant forty kilometres east of Calgary in September of next year. It was to be highly automated, with a total operating group of eight workers on each of the five shifts, and twenty maintenance people on a day shift. Its capacity would be 430 000 tonnes of ammonia or 475 000 tonnes of urea per year. Initially, the consulting engineers would be responsible for the start-up of the operations, but the operating teams would take over the running of the plant after the plant had been checked out.

The new plant would use a well-known process to produce ammonia and urea. Natural gas fuelstock and nitrogen would be converted into ammonia in a high temperature, high pressure continuous flow process. Ammonia would then be combined with carbon dioxide to produce urea.

The competitive advantages of the new plant would result from the scale of the operation and the efficiency of production. The latter would depend primarily on fine-tuning a complex set of interdependent processes and upon the elimination of "downtime" — the period of time when the plant computer was not functioning. Estimates of the cost of downtime were based on the cost of lost production. Contribution per tonne of ammonia was estimated at $150 per tonne. Refining the process would allow for an increase in production tonnage. There was generally no product differentiation and, consequently, the price for ammonia and urea was set as a commodity.

The eight operators would be expected to play an important role in diagnosing problems in the plant and eliminating downtime. In theory, the computer was supposed to run the plant. However, if something did go wrong, it would be up to the operators to take action — from manually adjusting valves and the production flows to shutting down the plant if the automatic controls failed. Plans had been made to have the operators periodically take over control of the plant from the computer in order to sharpen their skills. In a similar plant in Holland, virtually all problems were handled by the computer and operators did not get the chance to control the plant under normal conditions.

### Team Concept

The new plant was to be run on the basis of "team concept." There were to be no supervisors. Elected, unpaid team representatives would be responsible for voicing concerns, jobs would rotate on a periodic basis, salaries would be based on knowledge and training, not

---

EXHIBIT I

The Carseland Plant: Training and Operating Staff

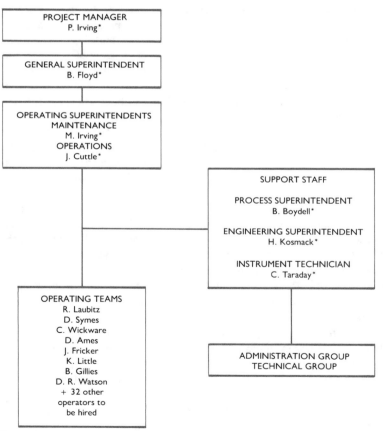

*Members of the core team

on job position, and there would be training provided in team building.

Pat Irving had really sold Brian on the concepts, saying that the traditional styles of management were passé in the eighties. Pat was fond of reiterating four questions he'd picked up from some management course at an Eastern business school:

1. What are we trying to do?

---

EXHIBIT 2

Extracts from Employee Relations Document

GENERAL

*Objective*

The basic objective of the employee relations system is to ensure safe, highly efficient and uninterrupted operations with an integrated approach to the management of human resources. The system must respond to the needs, interests and aspirations of people.

*Management Philosophy*

The following statement of management philosophy represents the type of environment and relationships for which we are striving:

> Company competitors differ from each other in the degree of creativity and initiative shown by their employees. Each person has an obligation to use all his or her capacities and those of his or her colleagues in contributing to the growth and betterment of the company's operations at Carseland.

Management has an obligation to provide an environment in which each person has freedom to develop and to use all his or her capacities.

*Management Style*

All levels of management will be expected to partake on a team basis and to support an integrated approach within and among teams, while encouraging personal initiative and responsibility.

A high value will be placed on obtaining sound creative decisions through understanding and agreement by team members. Decision making will take place by those who are close to the source of the problem and have the appropriate know-how. Ideas, opinions and attitudes of people will be sought out in the continuing process of improving operating and administrative techniques. When conflict arises, every effort will be made to deal with it in an open manner, and to identify and resolve its underlying causes. Emphasis will be placed on developing talent and potential and encouraging, by example, a high degree of effort and participation. Openness, courtesy and respect will be expected in all interpersonal relationships.

HUMAN RESOURCE POLICIES AND PROGRAMS

*Organization*

The organization will be designed is such a way as to establish a relationship among jobs which promotes flexible, integrated work teams. This goal will be achieved in the Carseland organization by means of the following:

(1) The number of authority levels will be kept at a minimum.
(2) All employees will be encouraged to develop their job-related skills.
(3) Versatility of operating and maintenance people is considered essential and will be encouraged by such innovations as block training, job rotation, and cross-trades training.

2. What is my part in it?

3. What is keeping me from doing better?

4. What am I doing about it?

Brian agreed that these questions seemed to keep everyone on track and he agreed with Pat that leaders in an organization should be "first among equals." The new "servant leadership" approach to management, as Pat described it, meant that while those with ability should lead, leadership should become service to others. Under such a system, traditional hierarchies would be eliminated.

The new plant was to be organized without supervisors and Brian sincerely felt that the team was making progress towards self-management. The team concept could only be beneficial to the employees, he mused. Pat had expressed the opinion that the employees had a claim on the business, along with the share-holders, the customers, and the community. If any group was short-changed, it would act to increase its share of return. The team concept was an attempt to give the employees a fair share of the pie.

So far, Brian had been pleased at how well the team building was going. He knew that the training team or "core" team (see Exhibit 1) hadn't met with the operators as often as he would have liked, but everyone was very busy working on the technical side of the new plant. Except for the last few weeks, he'd had frequent contact with the operators. It would be good when Bruce Floyd and the rest of the core team were together in one location. Bruce had been a central figure in the project for several years and frequently was away on technical matters. It would be the end of August before he moved to Calgary.

The first team-building session held in Banff

---

EXHIBIT 3

Training Schedule for Operators

| April 1 | Hire first eight operators | |
|---------|----------------------------|---|
| April | Introduction to the company<br>Training techniques<br>Team building (Banff Springs Hotel)<br>Ammonia familiarization | 1 week<br>1 week<br>1 week<br>1 week |
| May | Urea familiarization<br>Specialty training—ammonia or urea<br>(4 operators for each specialty) | 1 week<br><br>3 weeks |
| June | Visits to Geleen, Holland and Borger, Texas | 3-4 weeks |
| July | Return home<br>Writing of training and operating manuals begins | |
| August<br>September | Writing of training and operating manuals | 6-8 weeks |
| September<br>October | Begin training other operators | 8 weeks |

last May had produced the EmployeeRelations Document (see Exhibit 2 for excerpts). It had been developed by both the members of the operating team and the core team and expanded on Pat's ideas. "How many drafts did we work through?" Brian asked himself. "Was it four or five? We really put a lot of effort into that document. Thank heavens, head office in Vancouver approved it." And the organization development people had put on a good program. Normally, he didn't trust those guys. They were too "touchy-feely" for him. The operators had liked the opportunity to work on the issues. During the week they had focused on Pat Irving's four questions as well as engaging in team building exercises. Brian had been worried when only a few of the core team could attend but that did not seem to matter now. The after-hours socializing that week seemed to strengthen the group and make everything more fun (see Exhibit 3 for the training schedule for operators).

One thing did bother Brian slightly. It was four months since they had hired the first eight operators and gone through the team building session and it would be difficult to start again. "The cost alone is scary," thought Brian. "I wish we had some guarantee that things would work out. The training is my responsibility, so the $1.5-million-dollar program had better pay off. Not using the team concept would have saved us a lot of money and meant that we could have started training later" (see Exhibit 4 for breakdown of the training costs developed in July of the previous year).

Brian also thought that the operator's trips to Holland and Texas had been a little unnerving. Four operators had travelled overseas for three weeks and four had visited the U.S. for four weeks to observe plants similar to the new Carseland operation. "I wonder how much they got out of the three weeks there?" Brian reflected. "Three weeks is a long time away from home and we had hoped they wouldn't party so much. It was surprising that

Jim Cuttle and Mike Irving, who also went, hadn't ensured that they work harder. The group doing the instructing didn't seem to help much either." Several of the operators had mentioned that the trip to the States could have been shortened since there was nothing to do at night in Borger, where the Texas plant was located. However, the Texas group had indicated they had learned a lot about ammonia production on the trip.

Brian congratulated himself and the core team on getting the operators involved—they seemed to be caught up in working out the technical details of the new plant. Brian had been pleased when Bill Gillies had asked Craig Tarady, the instrumentation expert, to bring in the computer person from head office to talk to the operators. And the operators had liked being a part of the recent recruiting process to hire eighteen more operators. They had provided a major source of information since thirty-six of the forty-two applicants were personally known to them. In fact, many operators with steam certification in Alberta knew each other because there were so few in the province. Four of the eight operators hired had come from the same company and knew each other well (see Exhibit 5 for a brief description of the operators).

Brian also believed that the operator's role in decision making was expanding. Doug Ames, one of the eight, had suggested moving everyone from the team room where they had been working to the empty offices upstairs. (The group was sharing the building with the Calgary operators until the Carseland buildings were ready in December.) The team room led to a lot of group cooperation but it was crowded and those operators who were trying to write their manuals were easily disturbed by the others. Brian wondered if too much group interaction was dangerous. He knew that the operators had developed the habit of going drinking together on occasion and was concerned that the group might become socially rather than work oriented.

EXHIBIT 4

Pat Irving's Memo on January 28
The Carseland Plant: Training Costs

January 28

Memorandum

To: Vice President, Pacific Region, Vancouver
From: Manager, Operations
Subject: Appropriation of Pre-Production Expenses

This is a request for funds to carry on with pre-production training.

The amount requested is $1.5 million as outlined in my memo of July 24, attached. We are negotiating with the Alberta Department of Manpower and Labour to share this cost. We, therefore, request that $1.5 million be appropriated and $1.0 million be authorized at this time.

A budget is being prepared and monthly control statements will be issued.


P.W. Irving:mb
Enc.

c.c. B. Floyd
    B. Boydell
    J. Homes
    P.W. Irving

Pat Irving's Memo of July 24
The Carseland Plant: Training Costs

July 24

Memorandum

Subject: Training Costs

It is important that those people who will be operating the new plant receive adequate training. Any operating errors will be extremely costly. The cost of this training should be carried as a separate cost centre to allow proper control.

The operators now involved—Irwing, Floyd, Kilborn, Bydell, Hind and Mintsberg—are not taken into account here. The cost of pre-production training at the plant is also not included in this estimate.

The estimated breakdown is:

For 24 months:

| | |
|---|---:|
| 1 Supervisor @ $2 400/month | $ 60 000 |
| Expenses and travel $ 1 500/month | 36 000 |
| | $ 96 000 |

EXHIBIT 4 continued

Pat Irving's Memo of July 24

For 21 months:

| | | |
|---|---|---|
| 6 shift supervisors @ $28 000/year | $300 000 | |
| 3 maintenance supervisors @ $26 000/year | $136 000 | |
| 1 assistant supervisor @ $26 000/year | $ 45 000 | |
| | $481 000 | |
| Expenses @ 52% | 249 000 | $ 730 000 |
| Total staff | | $ 826 000 |
| Air fares | | 25 000 |
| | | $ 851 000 |

Purchase of 2 Carmody trainers (simulators) has been included in the capital estimates.

| | | |
|---|---|---|
| Programming of trainers | $ 10 000 | |
| Labour of Murray Williams (trainer 4 months @ $2 000/month) | 8 000 | |
| Training films, tapes, etc. | 10 000 | |
| Total training equipment | | $ 28 000 |
| 4 junior engineers 6 months @ $25 000/year | $200 000 | |
| 20 operators 6 months @ $20 000/year | $200 000 | |
| Steaming engineer training | $ 30 000 | |
| Total operator training | | $ 430 000 |
| Total | | $1 359 000 |
| Unaccounted and contingency | | 141 000 |
| | | $1 500 000 |

P.W. Irving:ft

cc: F.A. Moore, Vancouver
B. Floyd, Head Office

## Brian Boydell's Plans

Brian was aware that he would have to get to work on the new salary schedules. The "pay for knowledge" concept was a good idea but it created difficulty in establishing rates, as there were no comparable jobs. Usually compensation was tied to a particular job. Esti-mates were made of the job's difficulty, its skill and education requirements, and the working conditions involved. A salary would be determined accordingly. Under the "pay for knowledge" plan, an operator was paid for the amount of training and knowledge he or she had, regardless of the job performed. Thus a

EXHIBIT 5

Operator Profiles


Doug Ames
>    Married, two children
>    Third Class Certificate
>    District manager of distillery sales for two years
>    Operator and shift supervisor of Calgary ammonia plant for seven years
>    Plant operator for eleven years
>    Hobbies: hockey, golf, curling, fastball
>    Member of Fraternal Order of Eagles


Keith Little
>    Married, two children
>    Second Class Certificate: St. John's First Aid Certificate
>    Plant operator for five years
>    Previous supervisory experience
>    Hobbies: ball, golf, curling, swimming


Joe Fricker
>    Married, one child
>    Second Class Certificate, SAIT Power Engineering Diploma; one year university
>    Operator of two different thermal power electrical generating stations for four years
>    Hobbies: curling, badminton, mechanics


Dave Symes
>    Married, two children
>    Second Class Certificate; one year university
>    Operator of ammonia plant for four years, including gas and steam plants (Calgary)
>    Worked as salesman for Western Canada Steel (summer job)
>    Machine operator on railroad tie gang and signal helper for three summers
>    Hobbies: tropical fish, astronomy, oil painting, cave exploring
>    Member of Moose Lodge


Rob Laubitz
>    Married, two children
>    Third Class Certificate; Part A, Second Class; NAIT Gas Technology Diploma; St. John's First Aid
>    Certificate
>    Operator in steam, and process of sulphur recovery and gas processing plant at Okotoks for three
>    years
>    Engineering technologist with oil company for three years
>    Hobbies: woodworking


Chris Wickware
>    Married, two children
>    Operator for eight years
>    Millwright at Edmonton Steel Mill for five years

EXHIBIT 5 continued

       Hobbies: hunting, fishing
       Member of Royal Canadian Legion, Fraternal Order of Eagles
       Union steward for several years

Don R. Watson
       Married, three children
       Third Class Certificate; two years university engineering
       Operator and relief shift supervisor in Calgary ammonia plant for ten years
       Operator of fertilizer plants in Calgary for five years
       Hobbies: skiing, snowshoeing, motorcycling: Member of YMCA
       Union president in previous job

Bill Gillies
       Married, two children
       Second Class Certificate
       Operator and relief shift supervisor in Calgary ammonia plant for ten years
       Operator in Fort Saskatchewan ammonia plant for three years
       Hobbies: hunting, football, carpentry, mechanics
       Member of Western Coop Social Club, and Canton Meadows Community Association

---

low skill job would provide a high salary for a trained individual. This plan increased flexibility, as people could be switched quite easily from one job to another. At the same time, it allowed the operators to earn more money through their own efforts.

"It looks as if we will have to pay more money if we want to hire good people in September," Brian mused, "especially if we hope to get eighteen more. Who knows what the pay will be when we hire the final fourteen in December. Wages really seem to be getting out of hand. I'll be glad when the October 1 raise comes through. It will make my job of hiring easier. Setting the pay schedule for these operators took from last December until April before we got approval from head office. I wonder if the reorganization announced last week will speed up the process? Ron Holmes, the new VP, has a reputation of being a hard-nosed but fair and extremely competent manager. He must be, to be where he is at forty-four. I hope he knows what we're trying to do but I'll bet he doesn't, considering his background at General Coal Co., with its strong union. I guess I'll find out when I meet with him next week on the suggestion that we review salaries three times rather than twice a year."

As Brian left the building, he noticed a car coming towards him. It was one of the operators. Brian was surprised to see him, as most of the operators had been on a writing course at the Southern Alberta Institute of Technology (SAIT). The writing course was designed to help the operators develop the skills needed to write the training and operating manuals and was held at the other end of town. Pat and Brian believed that by having the operators write their own manuals, the final product would be intelligible to other operators and would encourage everyone to be more committed to the project.

When the car pulled up the operator handed Brian two envelopes saying, "I've been delegated to hand these to you." One envelope was addressed to him and the other to Pat Irving. As he read the letter (see Exhibit 6 for a copy of the letter), Brian's feeling of dismay turned to anger: "How could they do this to me? They aren't following the team concept at all! What are they trying to pull off anyway?"

---

EXHIBIT 6

Brian Boydell's Letter

July 21

Dear Mr. Irving:

During the latter part of June and early July, in response to our earlier request, Brian Boydell indicated the possibility of a July pay raise. However, this morning, Brian indicated that a raise in July would be impossible.

We, of the operator trainer team, respectfully submit this letter of discontent regarding the negative feedback to our request.

The reasons for the raise are as follows:

(1) All of us took wage cuts to come to the company.
(2) The cost of living has escalated substantially.
(3) We are receiving lower wages than competition staff for similar jobs.
(4) We have a desire to maintain a strong and loyal team.

We also note that a 37.3 hour work week has been adopted by numerous companies. We believe that Pacific Mines should not be among the exceptions.

We feel confident that you will give this letter your every consideration.

Sincerely,


The Operating Team

| | |
|---|---|
| Doug Ames | Dave Symes |
| Chris Wickware | Keith Little |
| Don R. Watson | Rob Laubitz |
| Joe Fricker | Bill Gillies |

c.c. Mr. Brian Boydell

---

1. In your opinion, was the change to a new approach handled properly by management of the Pacific Mines Limited?
2. Was Brian correct when he said: "They aren't following the team concept at all!" when he received the letter from the team of operators?
3. If you had to conduct a human resource audit, what factors would you take into account?
4. What is your overall assessment of the human resource management at Pacific Mines Limited?

Case prepared by T. Cawsey, R. Hodgson and E. Watson. The University of Western Ontario.

## SUGGESTED READINGS

Anderson, J.S., "Mission Statements Bond Corporate Culture," *Personnel Journal*, Vol. 66, No. 10, October 1987, pp. 120-122.

Long, J., and J.H. Ormsby, "Stamp Out Absenteeism," *Personnel Journal*, Vol. 66, No. 11, November 1987, pp. 94-96.

Tsui, Anne S., "Personnel Department Effectiveness: A Tri-partite Approach," *International Relations,* Spring 1984, pp. 184-197.

LaPointe, Joel R., "Human Resource Performance Indexes," *Personnel Journal*, July 1983, pp. 545-600.

Schmidt, Frank L., John E. Hunter and Kenneth Pearlman, "Assessing the Economic Impact of Personnel Programs on Workforce Productivity," *Personnel Psychology*, Vol. 35, No. 2, 1982, pp. 333-347.

Landy, Frank J., James L. Farr and Rick R. Jacobs, "Utility Concepts in Performance Measurement," *Organizational Behavior and Human Performance*, Vol. 30, No. 1, 1982, pp. 15-30.

## REFERENCES

1. Raymond E. Miles and Charles C. Snow, "Designing Strategic Human Resources Systems," *Organizational Dynamics,* Summer, 1984, p. 36.

2. Terry Hercus and Diane Oades, "A Diagnostic Instrument to Evaluate Personnel Practices," *The Canadian Personnel & Industrial Relations Journal,* September 1980, pp. 24-32.

3. Ibid.; Eugene Schmuckler, "The Personnel Audit: Management's Forgotten Tool," *Personnel Journal,* November 1973, pp. 977-980; Walter R. Mahler, "Auditing Pair," in Dale Yoder and Herbert G. Heneman, Jr. (eds.), *Planning and Auditing Pair,* Washington: Bureau of National Affairs, Inc., 1976, pp. 2-92; Paul Schiebar, "Personnel Practices Review: A Personnel Audit Activity," *Personnel,* March-April, 1974, pp. 211-217; Anne S. Tsui, "Personnel Department Effectiveness: A Tri-Partite Approach," *Industrial Relations,* Spring, 1984, pp. 184-197; Joel R. LaPointe, "Human Resource Performance Indexes," *Personnel Journal,* July 1983, pp. 545-600; Michael Gordon, "Three Ways to Effectively Evaluate Personnel Programs," *Personnel Journal,* July 1972, pp. 498-504; J. Fitz-Enz, "Quantifying the Human Resources Function," *Personnel,* March-April 1980, pp. 41-52.

4. Miles and Snow, op. cit., pp. 36-52; Karen A. Golden and Uasudevan Ramanujam, "Between a Dream and a Nightmare: On the Integration of Human Resource Management and Strategic Business Planning Process," *Human Resource Management,* Winter 1985, pp. 429-452; see also John Hoerr, "Human Resource Managers Aren't Corporate Nobodies Anymore," *Business Week,* December 2, 1985, pp. 58-59.

5. "Becoming a Business Partner First," *Personnel Administrator,* December 1986, pp. 61-65, 118.

6. Thomas J. Peters and Robert H. Waterman, Jr., *In Search of Excellence: Lessons from America's Best-Run Companies,* New York: Harper & Row, 1982.

7. John A. Hooper, Ralph F. Catalanello, and Patrick L. Murray, "Showing Up the Weakest Link," *Personnel Administrator,* April 1987, p. 53.

8. Hercus and Oades, loc. cit.; Mahler, loc. cit.; George E. Biles and Randall S. Schuler, *Audit Handbook of Human Resource Practices: Auditing the Effectiveness of the Human Resource Function,* Alexandria, Va.: The American Society for Personnel Administration, 1986; Robert L. Mathis and Gary Cameron, "Auditing Personnel Practices in Smaller-Sized Organizations: A Realistic Approach," *The Personnel Administrator,* April 1981, pp. 45-50.

9. Dean F. Berry, *The Politics of Personnel Research,* Ann Arbor: Bureau of Industrial Relations, Graduate School of Business Administration, University of Michigan, 1967, pp. 89-103.

10. Fred Crandall, "Personnel Research for Problem-Solving," *The Personnel Administrator,* September 1978, pp. 13-16. See also Victoria Kaminski, "There's a Better Way to Conduct Attitude Surveys," *The Personnel Administrator,* July 1983, pp. 62-63; Dow Scott, Diana Deadrick, and Stephen Taylor, "The Evolution of Personnel Research," *Personnel Journal,* August 1983, pp. 624-629; Barry A. Macy and Phillip H. Mirris, "A Methodology for Assessing the Quality of Work Life and Organizational Effectiveness in Behavioral and Economic Terms," *Administrative Science Quarterly,* June 1976, pp. 212-226.

11. Fred Luthans and Terry L. Maris, "Evaluating Personnel Programs through the Reversal Technique," *Personnel Journal,* October 1979, pp. 692-697.

12. George Odiorne, "Evaluating the Personnel Program," in Joseph Famularo (ed.), *Handbook of Modern Personnel Administration,* New York: McGraw-Hill Book Company, 1972, Ch. 8. See also Walter R. Mahler, op. cit.; Vytenis P. Kuraitis, "The Personnel Audit," *Personnel Administrator,* November 1981, pp. 29-34.

13. Thomas F. Cawsey and William C. Wedley, "Labour Turnover Costs: Measurement and Control," *Personnel Journal,* February 1979, pp. 90-95, 121; Joseph Lowman and Tom Snediker, "Pinpointing Avoidable Turnover with 'Cohort Analysis'," *Personnel Journal,* April 1980, pp. 310-315.

14. Odiorne, loc. cit.

15. Wanda R. Embrey, R. Wayne Mondy, and Robert M. Noe, "Exit Interview: A Tool for Personnel Management," *The Personnel Administrator,* May 1979, pp. 43-48; Donald A. Drost, Fabius P. O'Brien, and Steve Marsh, "Exit Inter-

views: Master the Possibilities,'' *Personnel Administrator,* February 1987, pp. 104-110.

16. Carl H. Driessnack, ''Financial Impact of Effective Human Resource Management,'' *The Personnel Administrator,* January 1976, pp. 22-26. See also Frank L. Schmidt, John E. Hunter, and Kenneth Pearlman, ''Assessing the Economic Impact of Personnel Programs on Workforce Productivity,'' *Personnel Psychology,* Vol. 35, No. 2, 1982, pp. 333-347; John W. Boudrean, ''Economic Considerations in Estimating the Utility of Human Resource Productivity Improvement Programs,'' *Personnel Psychology,* Vol. 36, No. 4, 1986, pp. 551-576; John E. Hunter, Frank L. Schmidt, R.C. McKenzie and T.W. Muldrow, ''Impact of Valid Selection Procedures on Workforce Productivity,'' *Journal of Applied Psychology,* Vol. 64, 1979, pp. 609-626.

17. Richard W. Beatty, ''Research Needs of PAIR Professions

in the Near Future,'' *The Personnel Administrator,* September 1978, pp. 17-20. See also Jac Fitz-Enz, ''Measuring Human Resource Effectiveness,'' *The Personnel Administrator,* July 1980, pp. 33-36.

18. Dennis C. King and Walter G. Beevor, ''Long-Range Thinking,'' *Personnel Journal,* October 1978, pp. 542-545; William C. Byham, *The Uses of Personnel Research,* American Management Association Research Study 91, New York: American Management Association, 1968; Henry Dahl, ''Measuring the Human ROI,'' *Management Review,* January 1979, pp. 44-50; Henry Dahl and K.S. Morgan, *Return on Investment in Human Resources,* (Upjohn Company Report) 1982; Wayne F. Cascio, ''Responding to the Demand for Accountability: A Critical Analysis of Three Utility Models,'' *Organizational Behavior and Human Performance,* Vol. 25, No. 1, 1980, pp. 32-45.

# CHAPTER 21 ○○○○○○

# *FUTURE CHALLENGES*

*Tomorrow's crises are already taking shape, but they can be minimized
— and possibly avoided — if human resource executives take the time
to observe the evolutionary path of today's work related issues.*

ERIC G. FLAMHOLTZ, YVONNE RANDLE, AND SONJA SACKMANN[1]

○ ○ ○ ○ ○ ○ ○ ○ ○ ○ ○ ○ ○ ○ ○ ○ ○ ○ ○ ○ ○ ○ ○ ○ ○ ○ ○ ○

## *CHAPTER OBJECTIVES*

After studying this chapter, you should be able to:
1. **Explain** the major challenges facing human resource practices in the future.
2. **Identify** the emerging forces in society that will challenge human resource management.
3. **Describe** how third parties cause changes in human resource management.
4. **List** major workplace innovations that are likely to occur by the year 2000.
5. **Explain** why careers in human resource management affect most managers.

○ ○ ○ ○ ○ ○ ○ ○ ○ ○ ○ ○ ○ ○ ○ ○ ○ ○ ○ ○ ○ ○ ○ ○ ○ ○ ○ ○

As one view of the future, consider the lunchtime conversation between a human resource manager, a new trainee, and a management consultant:

TRAINEE: Both of you have worked in the human resource field for a long time. You must have some opinions about its future.

MANAGER: Well, I don't have a crystal ball, but some of the trends of the 1970s and 1980s are likely to continue. I expect, and hope, most women will continue to enter the work force. We are going to need high participation rates of women to offset the low birthrates of the 1960s.

As traditional values about family and work continue to change, those of us in human resources are going to have to be more innovative. We are going to have to find new ways to meet employee and company needs. Undoubtedly, we will see more moves towards professionalism. Unfortunately, I fear we will also see more government intervention during the next couple of decades.

CONSULTANT:  Even if government involvement should lessen, special-interest groups and unions will pressure for change. But the big change that must come in human resource management is convincing top managers to use a human resource approach.

TRAINEE:   What do you mean?

CONSULTANT:   Few operating managers are convinced that sound human resource policies, practices, and programs directly benefit the company.

MANAGER:   I think many believe it, but we sometimes fail to demonstrate the dollars-and-cents payoff of our human resource programs. Too often we promise more than we can deliver. So when a line manager faces a choice between investing in people or equipment, the equipment decision is sometimes more certain.

CONSULTANT:   Or worse, we suggest programs that benefit the employee with little regard for the impact on profitability. Don't misunderstand me. Someone in the organization must consider employees' needs, but those needs must be balanced by the organization's objectives.

TRAINEE:   But through human resource management audits and research, aren't ineffective programs uncovered?

MANAGER:   Sure, audits and research weed out mistakes and poor programs. But mistakes will be fewer from top management's view point if we consider the impact on both employees and the bottom line.

Human resource management must seek a balance between company objectives and employee needs. To be responsible, the human resource department cannot just audit itself, as discussed in the last chapter. Audits are necessary, but they are backward-looking. They uncover only the results of past decisions. Although past performance should be evaluated, human resource departments also should look to the future in order to be more proactive.[2]

A proactive approach requires human resource managers and their staff to develop a *future orientation*. They must constantly scan their professional and social environment for clues about the future. New developments may mean new challenges. For example, high divorce rates may lead to more employer-provided child-care facilities and flexible work schedules so that working parents can fulfill their parental duties.

Without a future orientation, the human resource department becomes reactive, not proactive. And reactive approaches allow minor problems to become major ones. The area of planning provides an appropriate example.

Several top managers of West Coast Paper Products, Ltd. seldom took more than a one-week vacation. They felt that no one else was qualified to take their place for longer than a week. When one mill manager quit, the replacement problem became a crisis for several weeks until a new manager was found. Even then, the mill had problems for months until the new manager had learned the company's policies.

Had the human resource office used human resource planning, replacement could have been developed ahead of time. Even without human resource planning, a future-oriented human resource manager would have questioned the lack of replacements.

But a proactive approach is insufficient by itself. A systems orientation also is needed. Human resource specialists must view company objectives and employee needs as part of the total system. When managers fail to keep this perspective in mind, they may misuse human resources to achieve company objectives. Likewise, if human resource specialists forget this relationship, they may pursue employee needs to the exclusion of company objectives.[3] The appropriate focus is a proactive, human resource approach to human resource management within a systems framework. As explained in Chapter 1:

- *Proactive approach* means having a future orientation in order to anticipate challenges before they arise. Therefore, human resource management needs to be sensitive to emerging trends.
- *Human resource approach* means that employees should be treated with importance and dignity. Since the standards of fair treatment and dignity change through time, human resource management should be sensitive to future developments.
- *Systems approach* means that human resources management takes place within a larger context, the organization and its environment. Human resource management can be evaluated only with respect to its contribution to the organization. And since organizations are open systems, human resource management needs to relate to the external environment.

By applying these three approaches, human resource departments are better able to meet the future challenges discussed in this chapter.[4] These challenges arise from the department's day-to-day practices and from the external challenges it faces.

## CHALLENGES TO HUMAN RESOURCE MANAGEMENT PRACTICES

Although human resource management practices have matured rapidly in recent years, improvements still are needed to meet future challenges.[5] Many challenges are unique to individual employers. But demands for an expanded contribution, modern information systems, and professionalism are likely to touch all human resource departments.

## CONTRIBUTION TO OBJECTIVES

Human resource departments need to increase their contribution to organizational objectives. But this expanded contribution requires the support of line managers, particularly top management. And many operating managers question the department's contribution to the firm's objectives. Too often, top managers see human resource experts as worrying

FIGURE 21-1    Traditional Concerns of Operating and Human Resource
Managers

| OPERATING MANAGERS AND ORGANIZATIONAL OBJECTIVES | HUMAN RESOURCES MANAGERS AND HUMAN RESOURCE NEEDS |
|---|---|
| • Control cost.<br>• Improve efficiency.<br>• Improve performance.<br>• Increase profitability.<br>• Help the organization grow.<br>• Comply with legal requirements.<br>• Improve earnings per share. | • Improve employee satisfaction.<br>• Lower employee turnover.<br>• Meet employee needs.<br>• Raise employee morale.<br>• Provide job security.<br>• Comply with legal requirements.<br>• Improve reputation as an employer. |

about records, employee rights, and laws — instead of costs, performance, and profitability. This difference between operating and human resource managers is shown in Figure 21-1. Line managers often view people's needs as important only to the extent that profitability is affected.

Perhaps the biggest challenge facing human resource managers is convincing line managers that human resource practices do contribute to overall performance.[6] That is, human resource specialists need to evaluate their efforts against the company objectives in Figure 21-1. To gain management support, human resource experts need to emphasize cost, performance, and profitability.

This challenge requires more than just a change in the human resource manager's vocabulary. Human resource specialists must realize that company performance sometimes assumes priority over employee needs.[7] Ideally, human resource practices can benefit employees *and* the organization. But the ideal is not always attainable, as the following dialogue illustrates:

> ANN:  As human resource manager, I cannot support the layoff of 3200 workers. Consider what that means to all those families. This close to Christmas, we are going to look like Scrooge reborn. Besides, imagine the impact on the Hamilton area. We should cancel the layoff altogether, or at least put it off until after the Christmas holidays.
>
> BOB:  Put it off? Are you kidding? Every week we wait, it costs nearly $1 million in added wages. This division isn't so profitable that we can afford to absorb costs like that for seven weeks. I am sorry for those who are put on layoff. I truly am. But your suggestion might cause headquarters to close the entire division. Consider the impact of 8000 people being unemployed. What would that do to the local economy? As plant manager, I need to take the broad perspective.

This conflict between Ann, the human resource manager, and Bob, the plant manager, can be explained by viewing Figure 21-2. Ann's concern is for the employees. Bob's focus is the organization's survival. Since Ann's efforts were directed at employee needs only, they were not supported by the plant manager. In fact, Ann's comments

FIGURE 21-2   Area of Overlap Between Organizational Objectives and
Employee Needs

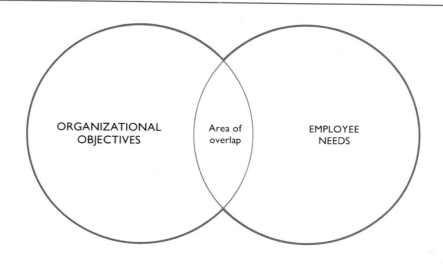

ORGANIZATIONAL
OBJECTIVES

Area of
overlap

EMPLOYEE
NEEDS

probably convinced the plant manager that Ann is a humane person, but not unduly
concerned with bottom-line performance.[8]

If human resource managers are to contribute meaningfully, they must show how
organizational objectives are furthered by meeting employee needs. For example, the
human resource manager might get the layoff postponed if she stressed profits and costs.
Suppose Ann had said:

> The division cannot afford this layoff if it is only for a few weeks. It will raise our
> unemployment tax for the next three years; it will renew employee interest in
> unions; and it will cost nearly a half-million dollars in layoff and recall expenses. Our
> best employees — particularly engineers — will be recruited by competitors. Besides,
> wages won't fall for two weeks since most employees will use their vacation time.
> Our studies in the human resource department show that if the layoff lasts for more
> than three weeks, savings will exceed the direct costs. When employee morale,
> community reactions, and the loss of key employees are considered, I would rec-
> ommend against the layoff if it is to be less than five weeks. I recommend we consider
> a reduced workweek for a period of time. We should be able to get employee
> support for it during this season.

## Human Resource Information Systems

To contribute to the organization, human resource specialists need a modern human
resource *information system,* which is the total of all human resource data and plans.
The department is a staff function that exists in part to advise management. Its role
cannot be more effective than the information it makes available to line managers.

To provide useful advice, large human resource departments have computerized much of their information base.[9] Smaller departments are also able to reap the advantages of a computerized information system by installing personal computers. A variety of software covering practically all aspects of the human resource function is currently available in Canada. The human resource departments of today have the technology to provide answers to almost all queries from operating managers on human resource matters. Historically, before the advent of computers, records were often organized for ease of use by specialists, rather than managers. The emergence of computers and their easy access have meant that data storage can be done in such a way as to accommodate the needs of *both* functionaries. The modern information system can also help the human resource manager to prove his or her department's contribution to the organization.

> As director of human resource research at United Chemical, Ltd. Christine Krigsman was assigned to improve the morale and productivity of one of its manufacturing plants. After extensive surveys, she made changes in job designs and started a training program. In time, productivity increased by 25% and absenteeism dropped from 5 to 3%, and much of it appeared to be the result of the improvements. Without a good information system, Krigsman would have been unable to demonstrate the human resource department's contribution to the company's profitability.

Human resource information systems (HRIS) are, thus, an inventory of all positions, skills, human resource needs, goals, and costs in a given organization. However, HRIS is more than a simple aggregation mechanism; it should enable an organization's management to plan, direct, reward, control, and motivate its human resources. More specifically, a good HRIS system should enable the manager to:

- Track basic attributes of all its employees (such as age, sex, education level, length of service, etc.) to eliminate any form of discrimination and to aid affirmative action.
- Track skill levels of employees to aid succession planning.
- Counsel their subordinates regarding training needs, career progress possibilities, and reward prospects.
- Build alternative scenarios about skill shortages and surpluses, employee turnover patterns, productivity levels of employees, career paths for its managers, etc.
- Forecast future demand for and supply of various types of employees.
- Forecast probable future composition of society's workforce and the firm's own labour force to enable proactive planning.
- Forecast the effects of changes in job descriptions, specifications and standards on a firm's training, compensation, evaluation and counselling processes and the overall organizational structure.
- Evaluate the costs and benefits associated with alternative human resource decisions.

In order to achieve these objectives, many large Canadian firms today maintain a variety of information on their employees. This includes personal data, details of employment (e.g., date of hire, retirement date, benefit plans enrolled in, etc.), employment history data (e.g., all previous jobs held outside the organization, duties carried out within the firm), and details of education and on the job training. With the advent of personal computers and the emergence of a number of cheap software programs relevant for using for HRIS, even smaller organizations in this country are beginning to reap the benefits of a full-fledged HRIS.

## Professionalism

Another challenge is professionalism. As mentioned in Chapter 2, human resource activities are too important to be carried out by the untrained. To ensure competency within the field, many provincial human resource associations have created certification programs. The Personnel Association of Ontario (PAO), for example, which presently has more than 4000 members, offers a certification program that requires the completion of eight courses related to the human resources field. These credits, plus a minimum of three years of managerial experience as a human resources manager or professional, are the preconditions for full membership in the association.[10] Although certification does not elevate the human resource field to the professional standing of medicine or law, it is an important first step.

Professionalism may lead to more widely accepted standards within the human resource management field. As standards in employment, development, and other activities become widespread, more firms are likely to upgrade their human resource practices accordingly.

Professionalism also created a need to stay informed about advances in the field.[11] This need causes self-renewal through reading, seminars, and work with professional associations of human resource experts. These renewal efforts can also produce a greater awareness of external challenges. It should be mentioned that almost all associations in Canada offer a variety of seminars, lectures, or complete courses on human resource related topics to improve the management skills of current human resource officers and managers.

## EXTERNAL CHALLENGES TO HUMAN RESOURCE MANAGEMENT

Changes in society also affect human resource management. Many of those changes will challenge human resource management during the 1990s and beyond. They arise from changes in demographics, values, pressures from third parties, and other sources. These challenges are likely to stimulate many innovations in human resource management over the next decade. Some of the more important challenges are listed in Figure 21-3 and are discussed further in the following paragraphs.

## Demographic Changes

The work force of the future has already been born. Only the number of people who will seek jobs is unknown. This rate of participation in the labour force determines the size and composition of the work force. Although these rates are unknown, Statistics Canada does make projections of the work force available based on low and high estimates. One projection appears in Figure 21-4. An examination of that figure indicates that, in general, the number of workers between fifteen and nineteen years old was expected to decline during the 1980s. Likewise, between 1983 and 1989, the availability

FIGURE 21-3   Selected Challenges Facing Human Resource Management in the 1990s

---

• **Demographic changes**. The birthrate decline that started in the 1950s means the average age in the work force will rise. Employee productivity may go up as workers gain experience. But those same people are likely to seek more job security and improved pensions.

• **Changing values**. Cultural and work values change through time. These changes affect the attitudes of people towards work, retirement, loyalty, attendance, tardiness, and work effort. In turn, these changes shape the demands placed on human resource management. Providing employee motivation and satisfaction during periods of changing values is a significant challenge.

• **Third-party interests**. Government, unions, and special-interest groups make demands on organizations and human resource activities. As a result, these activities must take place within many constraints. However, as the needs of society grow, the interests of third parties may grow closer to those of organizations.

• **Innovation**. Coping with the many challenges facing human resource managers and specialists will require continued innovation in order to meet both employee needs and company goals.

• **Canada Pension costs**. As the work force grows older, the burden on the government pension system will grow. Government may need employers to shoulder more of the burden with private pension plans.

• **Portable pensions**. Workers are mobile. Since people change jobs, even careers, during their life, human resource departments may see a greater need to make pensions portable. Portable pensions will allow employees who go to another employer to take their accrued pension benefits with them to ensure a comfortable retirement.

• **Retirement programs**. As larger numbers of workers approach retirement in coming years, they may seek improved pensions and other retirement-related services. Pre-retirement counselling will grow in popularity, and more firms will be expected to provide post-retirement benefits to meet the social and insurance needs of the employees.

• **Immigration**. The number of immigrants to Canada has generally been decreasing in the past few years. However, international upheavals may result in large numbers of immigrants arriving in a relatively short period of time. Because of their different social and cultural backgrounds, the effective integration of such employees into the work force will be a challenge for human resource specialists.

• **Free trade**. The removal of all tariffs between the U.S. and Canada could open up markets for virtually all Canadian organizations while also making them vulnerable to foreign competition.

• **Technological changes**. Remarkable changes in electronic technology are likely to mean radical changes in the types of jobs and skill levels needed by organizations in the 1990s. Training, development, and career planning activities are areas of tremendous growth potential within the human resource field as employers try to adjust the work force to technological change.

• **Privacy legislation**. With the growth of computerized information systems, companies maintain ever-growing data banks on employees. The need to ensure privacy of employees against abuse of this information may cause greater attention to be paid to the privacy of employee records.

FIGURE 21-3 (continued)   Selected Challenges Facing Human Resource
Management in the 1990s

• **Women workers**. The higher participation rates of women in the work force will create
demands for greater equality in pay or career advancement opportunities. The limited number of
women in top management means many women will be unable to find the mentors that are more
available to men. Human resource departments may be expected to respond with more extensive
career planning assistance.

• **Dual-career families**. With the increased participation of women in the work force, human
resource departments will become involved more with helping spouses find suitable employment
as a condition of employment transfers.

• **Employee reward**. Inflation has caused many firms to put less emphasis on merit increases
and more emphasis on "across-the-board" raises to adjust wages for inflation. Inflation and
strong demand for skilled workers have caused "wage compression" where the gap between the
pay of new and senior workers has narrowed. As a result, wage and salary differentials offer
small rewards for experience and loyalty. If these trends continue, employee rewards may focus
more and more on noncash compensation.

• **Quebec**. In 1988, Quebec used the "notwithstanding clause" in the Charter of Rights to
override a Supreme Court decision giving equal status to the use of the English language in the
province. This has sparked a new controversy and brought new concerns to the province's
linguistic minorities. The subsequent events may have serious implications for inter-provincial
migration patterns and supply of human resources to firms operating in Quebec.

• **Meech Lake Agreement**. The unwillingness of Manitoba and New Brunswick to sign the
Meech Lake Agreement (until a satisfactory solution to the minority language rights in Quebec is
found) has brought in fresh political uncertainties in this country. Depending on the final shape of
Canada's Charter of Rights, human resource practices (especially in the area of employee
discrimination) may have to undergo major changes.

FIGURE 21-4   Projected Rate of Change in Population Levels (in %)

| Age | LOW-GROWTH PROJECTION | | | HIGH-GROWTH PROJECTION | | |
|---|---|---|---|---|---|---|
| | 1983 to 1989 | 1989 to 1995 | 1995 to 2001 | 1983 to 1989 | 1989 to 1995 | 1995 to 2001 |
| 15 years and over | 5.30 | 4.15 | 3.74 | 7.80 | 7.07 | 7.52 |
| 15 to 19 years | − 14.89 | − 0.31 | 4.66 | − 11.40 | 7.20 | 15.37 |
| 20 to 24 years | − 16.02 | − 12.18 | 2.65 | − 13.47 | − 8.13 | 11.26 |
| 25 to 34 years | 9.11 | − 8.29 | − 15.52 | 12.41 | − 5.53 | − 11.22 |
| 35 to 44 years | 19.63 | 11.48 | 4.70 | 23.61 | 15.81 | 7.18 |
| 45 to 54 years | 8.41 | 25.25 | 16.94 | 9.81 | 27.74 | 21.12 |
| 55 to 64 years | 3.13 | 0.43 | 14.35 | 3.77 | 1.29 | 15.86 |
| 65 and over | 16.13 | 11.84 | 6.58 | 18.07 | 12.74 | 7.35 |
| Total Population | 4.40 | 2.91 | 1.46 | 8.48 | 7.12 | 5.54 |

Source: Developed from data provided in Statistics Canada, *Population Projections for Canada and the Provinces 1976-2001*, Catalogue 91-520, Ottawa: Industry, Trade and Commerce, 1979.

of twenty to twenty-four-year-olds was also expected to drop. These trends were good news for government officials and sociologists who had anticipated high unemployment rates among these groups. But for human resource administrators who work for restaurant chains, retail outlets, and other large employers of young workers, recruiting and retention programs may become more important than ever.

A more recent, and somewhat different projection by Statistics Canada, is given in Figure 21-5. As may be seen, these projections again indicate a declining young labour force, while the number of older (65 and over) workers is expected to more than double in the next fifty years or so.

FIGURE 21-5   Population Projection in Canada

| YEAR | FORECAST PERCENTAGE DISTRIBUTION OF POPULATION IN CANADA (ASSUMPTION: FERTILITY RATE = 1.5) | | | AVERAGE AGE OF POPULATION (YEARS) |
|---|---|---|---|---|
| | Age Group 0-14 | 15-64 | 65 + | |
| 1991 | 20.51 | 68.10 | 11.40 | 35.46 |
| 1996 | 18.99 | 68.87 | 12.14 | 36.84 |
| 2001 | 17.20 | 70.16 | 12.63 | 38.24 |
| 2011 | 15.15 | 70.53 | 14.33 | 40.82 |
| 2021 | 14.30 | 66.65 | 19.06 | 43.16 |
| 2051 | 12.99 | 61.18 | 25.83 | 46.22 |

Source: Statistics Canada, *Current Demographic Analysis: Fertility in Canada—from Baby Boom to Baby Bust.* Catalogue 91-524 E, November 1984, p. 151.

## Changing Values

Changing cultural and work values confront human resource experts with future challenges.[12] To return to Figure 21-4, some of these changes are already evident in the demographic trends. For example, as a result of a declining birth rate that began about twenty-five years ago, the work force is becoming proportionately older and older. The 1983-to-1989 projections for fifteen-to-nineteen and twenty-to-twenty-four age categories vividly showed this decline. As a result, the overall values of the work force may well change as the proportion of older employees increases. Likewise, although it is not shown in Figure 21-4, the percentage growth of women over fifteen in the labour force is higher than for men over fifteen. These projections show an increase in the participation rate of women in the work force. This trend, coupled with growing demands for women's rights, will continue to challenge human resource specialists to find meaningful employment opportunities for women.

Many human resource professionals believe that mandatory retirement at any age will be abolished nationwide in the 1990s. Here, the challenge for human resource management is to honour the rights of senior workers while providing promotional opportunities for younger workers (whose promotion rate may be slowed by older employees who elect to work rather than retire).[13]

Some experts suggest that work may become a less important aspect of people's lives in the future. Jobs may not be as central to the lives of some people. Extended periods of education, flexible lifestyles, changes in traditional male-female roles, and improved welfare benefits may cause a decline in work-force participation rates. Some knowledgeable researchers even suggest that rapidly growing technology may lead to shorter work-weeks and job sharing, as the benefits of electronics and automation spread through society. In this environment, human resource departments may find it exceedingly difficult to attract and retain workers with anything less than an ideal work environment. As a result, consider one possible scenario:

> In the 1990s, we may see life patterns undergo major revisions. The traditional education-work-retirement pattern that became popular with the Industrial Revolution may become less common. Although all three elements are likely to be present, their sequence may be more jumbled. For example, education may be followed by work for a few years. Then "retirement" might be elected for five years followed by education and work. These elements — education, work, and retirement — may be interchanged throughout one's life without a formal or permanent retirement.[14]

If values and the workforce change as radically as suggested by this scenario, human resource planning, career counselling, and human resource development will all have to be rethought carefully.

## Third-Party Interests

As discussed throughout the book, government, unions, and special-interest groups are concerned with the employment relationship. And since jobs are likely to remain the primary way most people earn their livelihood, third parties will continue to be an important force in shaping the practice of human resource management.

Although pressures from these third parties add complexity to human resource management, greater cooperation in the future may be possible.[15] As more people realize that the well-being of society is tied to the health of its organizations, especially its business firms, pressures may mount for increased government-business cooperation. Regulations may become fewer, or at least grow more slowly. Those rules that remain are more likely to be designed with both employer *and* employee interests in mind.

Unions, too, show signs of becoming more cooperative.[16] As other nations become more effective competitors in world markets, union leaders increasingly recognize the benefits of greater cooperation with the employer. Of course, their goals are likely to remain focused on employee welfare; but when competition threatens firms or entire industries, their interests and the employers' may be closer.[17]

Although demands from special-interest groups will undoubtedly grow during coming decades, human resource departments have an established record of meeting the needs of such groups and the objectives of the employer. Even with this record of success, human resource specialists must remain sensitive to demands for equality and improved community relations.

## *Other Challenges to Human Resource Management*

Changes in society and business practices mean that there will be many other challenges facing human resource management in the future. Figure 21-3 mentions those that are likely to stimulate innovation in human resource management. Each of these challenges holds unseen implications. And as this list grows in coming years, the role of human resource management will grow and become more dynamic.

One of the most critical challenges facing Canada today is preparing for a free trade framework with the U.S. With the election of a Conservative majority in November 1988, the free trade deal with the U.S. was implemented in January 1989. Although the exact consequences of free trade for the country in general and Canadian organizations in particular are currently hard to predict, free trade in general is bound to make the marketplace much more competitive than ever before.[18] This means that many Canadian organizations will have an opportunity to compete in much larger North American (rather than Canadian) markets. In turn, this could help them reap the economies of large-scale production and distribution. However, it could also lead to the arrival of many U.S. products on the Canadian market, which could, in turn, put pressure on Canadian manufacturers to keep their production and operating costs low. Human resource activities such as job analysis, job design, training, productivity improvement programs, etc., are likely to be more important than ever before. Canadian labour costs are high by international (and U.S.) standards and may have to be tightly controlled if we are to maintain our competitiveness in the 1990s. Compensation and benefits planning in the future may have to be very carefully undertaken, while negotiations with unions may become even more difficult. Employers may be caught between rising worker expectations on the one hand and the cost squeeze (imposed by increased competitiveness) on the other. Given the new conditions, workplace innovations increasing the efficiency and productivity of workers may indeed be the greatest challenge of all. Human resource managers and specialists will have to be creative, dedicated, and hardworking. They will have to find new ways to meet the demands of employees that contribute to their organization's success. Many of these innovations involve the job and the job setting.[19]

## WORKPLACE INNOVATIONS IN THE FUTURE

Future challenges to human resource management will require workplace innovations. Some of these will develop in response to increased professionalism and more advanced human resource information systems. Others will be intended to meet the challenges of changing demographics, values, and external pressures.

Although it is impossible to list all the innovations that are likely to occur by the end of the century, several trends appear likely to affect human resource management. Among these trends are improved employee participation, security, assistance, and work schedules.

## *Employee Participation*

Throughout western Europe—especially in Scandinavia—employees are gaining rights to participate in the decisions that affect them. As described in Chapter 4, these rights may include participation in decisions through their involvement in autonomous work groups. In these groups, employees are often responsible for the day-to-day decisions that produce goods or services. Although the motivation behind these programs appears to be the improvement of the quality of work life, North American versions may seek to improve productivity.

Also in Europe, codetermination laws require employee representation on supervisory boards and in other top-management decision-making groups. These employee (usually union) representatives have the right to vote on key management decisions that affect employees. Although most North American union leaders claim no interest in codetermination, its continued use in Europe may create interest among workers, unions, and politicians on this side of the ocean. For example, in the U.S. Chrysler Corporation installed the president of the United Automobile Workers union on the board of directors to win collective bargaining concessions.

## Employee Security

The desire to participate in management decisions may come from a desire for greater employment security. Generally speaking, workers in western Europe and Japan have higher levels of employment security than their Canadian or American counterparts. In those overseas countries, employers give high priority to maintaining stable employment even during recessions. Besides extensive unionization, government pressure, and different economies, the higher level of security may result from greater employee participation in decision making.

North American workers may seek greater employment security and rights, especially if international events or technology lead to major changes in the nature of industry. The pressure for security likely will come through traditional avenues such as unions or legislation or both. Some experts believe it will take the form of an employee "bill of rights," which will grant workers increased civil liberties on their jobs. It may include guarantees of free speech, job security, and outside review of disciplinary actions.[20] If these changes do evolve, the role of human resource management will grow, and employee satisfaction and motivation may move to even higher levels throughout industry.

## Employee Assistance

A clear trend since World War II has been growing employer assistance to employees. During the 1990s, more employers are likely to provide help through *employee assistance programs* that follow the pioneering work done by Control Data Corporation and others.

> Control Data's efforts to help employees solve their problems have been formalized into an employee assistance program. Its purpose is to provide employees with a broad range of counselling and other professional services. It includes career guidance services, drug and alcoholic rehabilitation programs, outplacement assistance, and referral to community groups that can provide help with housing, food, medical, marital, and other employee problem areas.

When employee assistance programs are combined with the more common insurance and time-off benefits, workers find the employer as a source of solutions to personal, financial, and family problems. Although lifetime employment security, company housing, vacation resorts, and employer-operated schools are not as common as in Japan, the trend toward "womb-to-tomb" care seems well advanced in most developed countries and is likely to expand.

A continuation of this trend may appear in the form of flexible compensation programs. Under these plans, employees are allowed to select the mix of fringe benefits they want from among those the employer provides. This cafeteria approach recognizes human differences. It also allows employees to maximize their satisfaction from the employer's fringe benefits. Although these programs present administrative, actuarial, and tax problems to employers, they may be a logical continuation of ever-expanding benefit programs.[21]

## Child Care

Day care for employees' children has emerged as a major employee benefit since the late 1980s. Indeed, given the record numbers of women who have entered the labour force in recent years, day care may be an absolute necessity in future years.

> More than a hundred hospitals and municipalities in this country have set aside space for day care centres for employees' children. Most of these centres are run as independent, non-profit ventures. Several large hospitals in this country (such as the Riverdale Hospital in Toronto) have found that the presence of a good day-care system increases an organization's ability to recruit employees and increases morale.[22]

In the years to come, the importance of child care as an employee benefit is bound to increase. An Ontario Hydro survey found that over 70% of female employees viewed day care as a social right and wanted to include it as a bargaining issue during negotiations.[23] With the demand for day-care services increasing, the employers of the future may have to begin cost-effective, on-site facilities for this purpose.

## High-Tech Operations

During the last half of the 1980s, computer-based technology quickly penetrated practically all the key spheres of operations in this country. Although much of the new technology introduced in the past involved personal computers, word processors, and office applications, a number of organizations have also implemented process automation and applied robots in the workplace. The introduction of the new technology has been most prevalent in Western Canada—British Columbia being a leader—and least prevalent in Atlantic Canada (81% of B.C. firms surveyed had employed some form of new technology while only about 67% of those in Atlantic Canada had done so).[24] The adoption of new technology was also more common among U.S.-owned firms (94%) and foreign-owned firms (88%) than Canadian-owned enterprises (72%). The rate of introduction of technology was also found to be a function of the industry sector.

What impact will high-tech operations have on work and non-work? How will it affect the overall quality of life of Canadians? Precise predictions are hard to make. By and large, it would seem that high-technology operations may:[25]

- Raise the overall quality of the work life by transferring mundane, boring, repetitive jobs to machines.
- Result in loss of jobs as many of the current jobs will become obsolete.
- Increase the predictability and hence safety of the workplace.
- Increase the complexity of maintenance functions (as robots are more complex to maintain than traditional machines).
- Permit the establishment of smaller, yet economically viable, plants.
- Necessitate considerable retraining of workers.
- Permit cost-benefit analysis to be carried out to a much greater extent than ever before.
- Change the structure and hierarchical ordering in organizations probably resulting in a flatter organization structure.
- Raise new issues of invasion into the individual's privacy and safety of centrally stored information bases.

As may be concluded, the switch-over to high technology will affect practically all human resource functions, the ones that will be most affected being job design, human resource planning, selection, training, appraisal, and union relations.

## Employee Work Schedules

The trend towards flexible work schedules began in earnest during the 1970s. During that decade a variety of different schedules gained increased use. Many of these innovations were not new but were given exposure to large numbers of people for the first time.

The common element of these schedules is that they avoid the traditional eight-hour day, five-day workweek with fixed starting and ending times for fifty weeks a year.[26] One variation is called the *compressed workweek*. It shortens the workweek to less than five days; four days at ten hours each is a common type of compressed workweek schedule. *Flextime* may involve five days a week, but it gives the employee some control over when the workday start and ends. *Flexyear* is a newer variation that allows employees to work only part of the year, which is helpful in seasonal businesses.

The most common variation and perhaps the oldest is part-time employment. It merits mention because of its growing popularity and flexibility. Some employers are allowing two part-time workers to team up to handle a full-time job. Often called *job sharing*, this practice may grow as employees seek different lifestyles. In Scandinavia, job sharing is popular among new parents because it allows them to share job and parental responsibilities more fully. In the United States, part-time employment appears to be used as a recruiting tool to better utilize plant and equipment or to meet peak demands in retailing.

A Honeywell plant in the Boston area adopted a "mothers' shift" as a means of recruiting additional workers. These shifts coincide with school hours, so that working mothers can attend to parental duties by arriving at work after the children have gone to school and getting home when school ends each day. During the summer, these employees are replaced by college students.

DuPont wanted to make greater use of a chemical plant near the University of Georgia, so it created a weekend shift staffed largely by college students.

## AN OVERVIEW OF HUMAN RESOURCE MANAGEMENT

As mentioned earlier, future challenges require that human resource activities be considered as a system of connected activities, each of which may be affected by the others and the external environment. The numbered circles in Figure 21-5 represent the different parts of this book, which are summarized in the following paragraphs.

For human resource specialists to be successful, they must balance the human, societal, personnel, and organizational objectives that form the core of every human resource department. At the same time, human resource specialists need to be aware of the challenges they face. These challenges come from the environment and the design of jobs. Within these challenges, human resource experts must collect human resource information. Information about jobs is a key input for human resource plans. These plans then serve as the basis for external and internal staffing activities.

External staffing is based on the recruitment needs estimated in the human resource plan. Applicants are recruited; selection begins. The selection process screens out those who are unqualified and selects those who possess the potential to perform. Orientation and training then translate potential into ability.

Internal staffing prepares present employees to assume future duties. In a growing number of companies, the internal staffing process begins with career planning. Employees also are urged to pursue development activities that further both their careers and the organization's staffing needs. Along the way, the human resource department must contend with change and organization development. To verify the internal staffing process and previous human resource activities, employees are evaluated with performance appraisals.

But human resource activities do not end with staffing. Once a staff is assembled, it must be motivated and satisfied. A major aspect of motivation and satisfaction is compensation. Wages and salaries must be paid in exchange for employee performance. Today that exchange includes numerous fringe benefits and employee services.

Human resource specialists also need to maintain communications with employees. It is through communications that management controls its human resources. When that control fails, counselling or discipline may be necessary.

If employees are not satisfied with the treatment they receive from the organization, they may form a labour organization. Unions mean new limits on human resource management. The collective bargaining relationship limits the roles of management and employees through a collective agreement and its administration.

Responsible human resource management also requires an audit of the department's policies, practices, and programs. Only through research can the department uncover areas in need of improvement. However, responsible human resource management means

FIGURE 21-6   An Overview of Human Resource Management

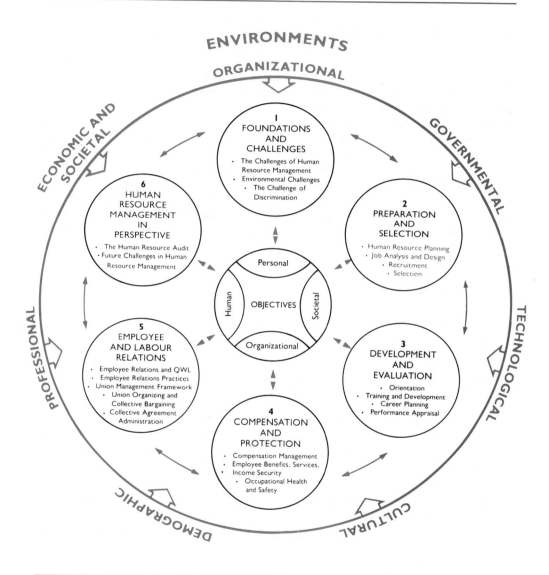

more than just evaluating past actions. It requires a future orientation if people are to be managed proactively within a systems framework.

Without a future orientation, the most creative inventions of our time — organizations — will fail. But with a proactive outlook, our organizations will benefit from the contributions of human resource management and human resources.

## SUMMARY

If human resource management is to be responsible, its practitioners need to review their past performance through audits and research. At the same time, they need a future orientation that causes them to anticipate upcoming challenges.

A proactive view encourages human resource management to contribute to both people and company goals. But to be proactive requires modern information systems and increased professionalism. Otherwise, the human resource department will not be able to meet the challenges of changing demographics, values, and third-party pressures. These evolving challenges will cause human resource managers to find new approaches. Some possible new approaches are suggested by overseas employers, particularly Europe and Japan. Likely developments include more employee participation, security, assistance, free trade with the U.S. and work schedule flexibility.

With all the challenges facing human resource management, its role is sure to grow in scope and importance. The key to this growth is unlocking the contribution that people make to organizations. It is through this contribution that organizations prosper. And it is through our life-giving and life-sustaining organizations that we prosper as individuals and as a society.

## TERMS FOR REVIEW

Employee assistance programs          Flexyear
Compressed workweek                   Job sharing

## REVIEW AND DISCUSSION QUESTIONS

1.  How do human resource specialists prepare for the future?
2.  In some firms the human resource manager is not considered a key part of the top-management team. In other firms human resource managers are considered important executives. In your own words, what may be the cause of this different perception?
3.  How do you think the growing professionalism of the human resource management field will affect the preparation and performance of human resource specialists?
4.  Several times in this book, demographics have been mentioned as an area of concern to human resource managers. Why should human resource managers be concerned with population demographics?
5.  In the last two decades, many cultural values have changed, some rather drastically. Briefly describe how human resource management might be affected by these values: (a) a trend towards smaller families, (b) increased participation of women in the work force, (c) increased acceptability to society of divorce.
6.  ''With the average employer paying over 30% of payroll costs for employee fringe benefits and with the long list of fringe benefits now available to workers, it is

unlikely that fringe benefits will experience much change during the 1990s.'' Do you agree or disagree? Discuss.

7.   What are some of the reasons that employers might adopt more flexible work schedules? Discuss which type of work schedule you would prefer.

## *INCIDENT 21-1*

### *Future Scenarios Ltd.*

Future Scenarios Ltd. is a West Coast ''think tank'' that accepts contracts from business and government to research possible trends in the future. One recent contract required a broad estimate of the future of work. A summary of their report appears below:

Excluding the possibility of a global energy crisis, ecological disaster, or war, we at Future Scenarios hold a realistically optimistic view of the world of work. Slow but continually increasing productivity during the 1990s will lead to a much improved work environment. The design of jobs will reflect the needs of workers more fully. Unpleasant jobs will be the focus of major innovations in automation, which will all but eliminate the monotonous assembly-line jobs of the industrial era. Some menial tasks will be left in the service area; restaurant, retail, and clerical jobs will absorb the bulk of young, inexperienced, or undereducated workers.

Employees will be able to set their own hours of work in most establishments. Those people still working an average workweek will be employed thirty-two hours a week. Most people will work more hours per week, but they will work less than the normal forty-four-week workyear. About one-third of the work force will work part-time, which means less than twenty-five hours per week.

Fringe benefits will amount to nearly 65% of most employers' payroll costs, and employees will be able to select the mix of fringe benefits they want. Moreover, benefit costs will be rising quickly because of the growing demand by workers for more time off with pay.

Participation rates by men and women will be essentially equal, when adjusted for maternity and paternity leave. Pay differentials between males and females and between white and minority workers will be narrowed considerably. Statistical differences will be explained primarily by educational differences and by the greater concentration of women in teaching, nursing, and clerical positions.

Growing numbers of workers will be working into their seventies and eighties. This trend will be encouraged by extended leaves at partial pay during one's working lifetime. These leaves will be financed by a deduction from employee retirement accounts. The greater participation of people over seventy years old in the work force will greatly reduce the pressure on the Canada/Quebec Pension Plans and employer pension plans.

Although unions still will carry on their traditional roles of collective bargaining and representing employees to members of management, they will begin to copy the union patterns now found in Europe. Union leaders will sit on company boards of directors and will become much more cooperative with management. Union leaders will spearhead company productivity improvement programs and will often be given the position of chairperson of the employer's productivity committee.

1. Assuming this seemingly unlikely scenario occurs, what implications does it hold for the future of human resource management?
2. Do you think these predicted developments will increase or decrease the importance of the human resource function in most organizations? Why?
3. What other changes do you think might occur?

## SUGGESTED READINGS

Halcrow, A., "Operation Phoenix: The Business of Human Resources," *Personnel Journal*, Vol. 66, No. 9, September 1987, pp. 92-101.

London, Manuel, *Change Agents: New Roles and Innovation Strategies for Human Resource Professionals*, San Francisco, Calif.: Jossey Bass, 1988.

Magnus, M., "Personnel Policies in Partnership with Profit," *Personnel Journal*, Vol. 66, No. 9, 1987, pp. 102-109.

Manzini, A.O., and J.D. Gridley, *Integrating Human Resources and Planning*, New York: ANACOM, 1966.

Miles, R. and H.R. Rosenberg, "The Human Resources Approach to Management: Second Generation Issues," *Organizational Dynamics*, Winter 1982, pp. 26-41.

## REFERENCES

1. Eric G. Flamholtz, Yvonne Randle, and Sonja Sackmann, "Personnel Management: The Tone of Tomorrow," *Personnel Journal*, Vol. 66, No. 2, July 1987, p. 43.

2. For a discussion of the issues of the next decade, see R. Gordon Cassidy and E. H. Neave, "Management Issues in the 1980s," *Proceedings of the Atlantic School of Business Conference*, Sydney, N.S.: College of Cape Breton, 1980. See also Flamholtz, Randle, and Sackman, 197, op. cit.; Fred K. Foulkes, "The Expanding Role of the Personnel Function," *Harvard Business Review*, March-April 1975, p. 84.

3. Walter R. Nord and Douglas E. Durand, "What's Wrong with the Human Resource Approach to Management?" *Organizational Dynamics*, Winter 1978, pp. 13-25.

4. For a discussion of some of the emerging trends, see "Labour movement unsure about its public image," *The Globe and Mail*, November, 5, 1979, p. B5; "Rights to strike gets heat from business," *The Financial Post*, August 15, 1981, p. 3; "Workers in Management," *Alberta Report*, June 13, 1980, p. 21; Donald V. Nightingale, *Workplace Democracy: An Inquiry into Employee Participation in Canadian Work Organizations*, Toronto: University of Toronto Press, 1982; "Manpower — A High Technology Problem," *Canada Commerce*, special supplement, 1982, pp. 20-21; James Bagnell, "Urgent Priority to Job Training,"

*The Financial Post*, January 16, 1982, p. 3; *Work for Tomorrow: Employment Opportunities for the '80s*, Report of the Parliamentary Task Force on Employment Opportunities for the '80s, Ottawa: Speaker of the House of Commons, Cat. No. XC2-321/4-OIE, 1981; Marilyn Goneau, "Discrimination is still Part of the Work Place," *The Financial Post*, November 21, 1981, p. 27; Solomon Barking, "Troubled Worker Militancy," *Relations Industrielles*, Vol. 38, no. 4, 1983, pp. 713-727; Robert L. Perry, "Pointing the Way Ahead," in a special Report on Careers and the Job Market, *The Financial Post*, September 26, 1981; "Industrial Relations 1986: Coping with Change," *Canadian Business Review*, Summer 1986, pp. 26-31.

5. George S. Odiorne, "Personnel Management for the '80s," *The Personnel Administrator*, August 1977, pp. 20-24. See also James C. Toedtman, "A Decade of Rapid Change: The Outlook for Human Resources Management in the '80s." *Personnel Journal*, January 1980, pp. 29-35; Peter C. Newman, "New Masters of the Bottom Line," *Maclean's*, vol. 99, no. 37, Sept. 15, 1985; Pierre Lortie, "The World's not Changing: It Already Has," *Commercial News*, April 1987, pp. 7-9.

6. Carl H. Driessnack, "The Financial Impact of Effective Human Resource Management," *The Personnel Administrator*, January 1976, pp. 22-26.

7.  Nord and Durand, op. cit., p. 15.

8.  Erwin S. Stanton, "Last Change for Personnel to Come of Age," *The Personnel Administrator,* November 1975, pp. 14-16, 49. See also "Reflections on the Profession and ASPA," *The Personnel Administrator,* June 1980, pp. 51-54; and Fred R. Edney, "The Greening of the Profession," *The Personnel Administrator,* July 1980, pp. 27-30, 42; also see, Clay Carr, "Personnel World: Injecting Quality into Personnel Management," *Personnel Journal,* September 1987.

9.  Sidney H. Simon, "Personnel's Role in Developing an Information System," *Personnel Journal,* November 1978, pp. 622-625, 640. See also Michael N. Wolfe, "Computerization—It Can Bring Sophistication into Personnel," *Personnel Journal,* June 1978, pp. 325-326, 336; A.J. Walker, "The 10 Most Common Mistakes in Developing Computer Based Personnel Systems," *The Personnel Administrator,* July 1980, pp. 39-42; "Technological Change Presents Dilemmas to Labour Movements," *The Globe and Mail,* April 14, 1986, p. B10; "Computers Blamed for Making Jobs Dead Ends," *The Globe and Mail,* November 17, 1986, p. C11.

10.  Dan A. Ondrack, "P/IR Professional Certification in Ontario: The PAO Model," paper presented at a symposium on professional education in P/IR, Canadian Industrial Relations Association, Dalhousie University, Halifax, N.S. 1981.

11.  "The New Personnel Professional," *Personnel Journal,* January 1979, pp. 17-19; also see "Will Canadian Workers Accept Japanese Ways?" *The Globe and Mail,* September 6, 1986, p. D1.

12.  Daniel Yankelovich, "The New Psychological Contracts at Work," *Psychology Today,* May 1978, pp. 46,47,49,50. See also Patricia A. Renwick and Edward E. Lawler, "What You Really Want from Your Job," *Psychology Today,* May 1978, pp. 53-58,60,62,65,118; Rae Corelli, "A Turning Away from Politics," *Maclean's,* vol. 100, no. 1, January 5, 1987; "A Volatile National Mood," *Maclean's,* vol. 100, no. 1, January 5, 1987, pp. 26-39.

13.  James W. Walker and Harriet Lazer, *The End of Mandatory Retirement,* New York: John Wiley & Sons, Inc., 1979.

14.  *The Changing Nature of Work, Trends Analysis Report 17,* Washington: American Council of Life Insurance, 1978. See also "The Great Male Cop-Out from the Work Ethic," *Business Week,* November 14, 1977, pp. 156,161,164,166.

15.  William B. Werther, Jr., "Government Control vs. Corporate Ingenuity," *Labour Law Journal,* June 1975, pp. 36-37.

16.  George S. McIssac, "What's Coming in Labor Relations," *Harvard Business Review,* September-October 1977, pp. 22-23, 26, 30, 34, 35, 190.

17.  Gus Tyler, "Labor in the 1980s — A New Challenge," *The AFL-CIO American Federationist,* November 1979, pp. 3-7. See also, Robert Ferchet, "Science Is Key to Future Wellbeing," *The Financial Post,* August 23, 1986, p. 8.

18.  John Crispo (ed.), *Free Trade: The Real Story,* Toronto: Gage Educational Publishing, 1988. See also Joseph R.D'cruz and James D. Fleck, "The 1986 Score Card on Canada's Competitiveness: Mixed but Encouraging," *Business Quarterly,* Summer 1986, pp. 78-87.

19.  Lawrence A. Wrangler, "The Intensification of the Personnel Role," *Personnel Journal,* February 1979, pp. 111-119. See also "Technological Change Presents Dilemmas to Labour Movement" *The Globe and Mail,* April 17, 1986, p. B1.

20.  D. Quinn Mills, "Human Resources in the 1980's," *Harvard Business Review,* July-August 1979, pp. 158-159. See also "The New Personnel Professional," op. cit., p. 49.

21.  William B. Werther, Jr., "Flexible Compensation Evaluated," *California Management Review,* Fall 1976, pp. 40-46. See also Economic Council of Canada, *Workplace Futures: Notes on Emerging Technologies,* Ottawa: Supply and Services Canada, 1986. (Catalogue No. EC22-132/1986E).

22.  Bureau of Municipal Research, *Work Related Day-Care — Helping to Close the Gap.* (Toronto: BMR), 1981, p. 30. See also Jay Paul, "How to Boost Productivity — Put a Nanny on Your Payroll," *Canadian Business,* March 1986, pp. 122-123; "Day Care Becoming Management Issue," *Financial Post,* October 18, 1986, p. 43; George Milkovich and Luis Cromez, "Day Care and Selected Employee Work Behaviours" *Academy of Management Journal* March 1976, p. 111-15.

23.  See Bureau of Municipal Research op. cit., 1981. See also Oscar Ornato and Carol Buckham, "Day Care: Still Waiting Its Turn as a Standard Benefit," *Management Review,* May 1983, pp. 57-62. Jacquelyn McCroskey, "Work and Families: What Is the Employer's Responsibility?" *Personnel Journal,* January 1982, pp. 30-38; Kathleen Mahoney, "Day Care and Equality in Canada," *Manitoba Law Journal,* 1985, vol. 14, no.3 pp. 305-334.

24.  Gordon Betcherman and Kathryn McMullen, *Working with Technology: A Survey of Automation in Canada,* Report prepared for the Economic Council of Canada (Ottawa: Ministry of Supply and Services Canada), 1986, Catalogue No. EC22-133/1986E.

25.  See *In the Chips: Opportunities, People, Partnerships,* Report of the Labour Canada Task Force on Microelectronics and Employment, Ottawa: Ministry of Supply and Services Canada, 1982, Catalogue No. L35-1982/IE. See also Carol A. Beatty, *Promoting Productivity with CAD,* Kingston, Ontario: School of Business, Queen's University, September 1986, Working Paper Series no. MC 96-05; "Factory of the Future," *The Economist,* May 30, 1987; Richard Brandt and Otis Port, "How Automation Could Save the Day," *Business Week,* March 3, 1986, pp. 72-74; Edward M. Knod, Jr., Jerry L. Wall, John P. Daniels, Hugh M. Shane, and Theodore A. Wernimont, "Robotics: Challenges for the Human Resources Manager," *Business Horizons,* March-April 1984, pp. 38-46.

26.  Joann S. Lublin, "Firms and Job Seekers Discover More Benefits of Part-Time Positions," *Wall Street Journal,* Western ed., October 4, 1978, pp. 1, 27. See also William B. Werther, Jr., "Beyond Job Enrichment to Employment Enrichment," *Personnel Journal,* August 1975, pp. 438-4442; and William B. Werther, Jr., "Part-Timers: Overlooked and Undervalued," *Business Horizons,* February 1975, pp. 13-29. "Part Time Workers Fastest Growing Element of the Canadian Workforce," *The Evening Telegram,* December 1, 1986, p. 25. "Employers Split over Benefits for Part Timers," *The Globe and Mail,* July 25, 1986, pp. A1-A2.

# G L O S S A R Y OOOOOO

**Absentees.** Employees who were scheduled to be at work but are not present.

**Accident and sickness policies.** Policies that pay the insured a specific amount during short periods when the employee is unable to work because of an accident or sickness.

**Accreditation/certification.** The process by which the standards and credentials for members of a profession are established. Accreditation may be based on, among other things, written or oral tests, letters of recommendation from established professional members, or experience.

**Achievement tests.** Tests of an individual's performance, often of a work sample, but also paper-and-pencil test (see also *paper-and-pencil test*).

**Active listening.** Requires the listener to stop talking, to remove distractions, be patient, and to emphathize with the talker.

**Adverse selection.** This occurs when a disproportionately high percentage of those who are likely to file claims against their insurance are granted insurance coverage.

**Advisory authority.** (See *Staff authority*.)

**Affirmative-action programs.** Detailed plans developed by employers to undo the result of past employment discrimination or to ensure equal employment opportunity in the future.

**Agency shop.** A provision in a collective-bargaining agreement that requires that all employees in the bargaining unit who do not join the union pay, as a condition of employment, a fixed amount monthly, usually the equivalent of union dues, to help defray the union's expenses in acting as bargaining agent. Under some arrangements, the payments are allocated to the union's welfare fund or to a recognized charity.

**American Federation of Labor and Congress of Industrial Organizations (AFL-CIO).** An American federation of many national unions in the U.S. and Canada. It exists to provide a unified focal point for the labour movement, assist national unions, and influence government policies that affect members and working people.

**American Society for Personnel Administration (ASPA).** The major association of professional human resource specialists and administrators in the U.S.

**Applied research.** A study of practical problems, the solution of which will lead to improved performance.

**Aptitude Requirements (APT).** One of the job attributes used in the *Canadian Classification and Dictionary of Occupations* to define a job. The aptitude factors measured are intelligence, verbal ability, numerical ability, spatial ability, form perception ability, clerical perception ability, eye-hand-foot coordination, and colour discrimination.

**Aptitude test.** A measure of an individual's potential to perform.

**Arbitration.** The resolution of a dispute by a neutral third party.

**Arbitration board.** A panel consisting of a neutral chairman and a member representing each of the parties to an arbitration. When the members of the board are unable to agree, the chairman's decision normally governs.

**Arbitration clause.** A provision in a collective agreement stipulating that disputes arising during the term of the contract be settled by arbitration. All jurisdictions in Canada except Saskatchewan have legislated for the insertion of an arbitration clause in all collective agreements.

**Assessment centres.** A standardized form of employee appraisal that relies on several types of evaluation and several raters.

**Attitude surveys.** Systematic methods of determining what employees think about their organization through the use of a broad survey of employee attitudes, usually done through a questionnaire. Attitude survey feedback results when the information collected is reported back to the participants who initially provided the information. This process then is usually followed by action planning to identify and resolve specific areas of employee concern.

**Attrition.** The loss of employees due to their leaving the organization.

**Audit report.** A comprehensive description of human resource activities, which includes both commendation for effective practices and recommendations for improving practices that are ineffective.

**Audit team.** Those people who are responsible for evaluating the performance of the human resource department.

**Authorization cards.** Forms that prospective union members sign to indicate their wish to have an election that determines whether the workers want to be represented by a labour organization in their dealings with management.

**Autonomous work groups.** Any of a variety of arrangements that allow employees to decide democratically how they will meet their group's work objectives.

**Autonomy.** Independence; in a job context, having control over one's work.


**Bargaining book.** A compilation of the negotiation team's plans for collective bargaining with labour or management.

**Barriers to change.** Factors that interfere with employee acceptance and implementation of change.

**Barriers to communication.** Factors that interfere with the receiver's understanding of a communication.

**Behaviour modification.** A psychological theory that behaviour depends on its consequences.

**Behavioural modelling.** Relies on the imitation or emulation of a desired behaviour. A repetition of behaviour modelling helps develop appropriate responses in specified situations.

**Behaviourally anchored rating scales (BARS).** Evaluation tools that rate employees along a rating scale by means of specific behaviour examples on the scale.

**Benchmark jobs.** Well-established jobs specifically chosen to serve as a guide to compare the value of other jobs on compensable factors. (See *Job evaluation*.)

**Benefit plan.** One of various types of schemes established by employers to provide some degree of financial protection for employees against accident, illness, old age, and death.

**Bereavement pay.** Pay to a worker, usually for a limited period, for time lost because of the death and funeral of a member of the immediate family.

**Blind ads.** Want ads that do not identify the employer.

**Body language.** A form of nonverbal communication that communicates by body movements during face-to-face communication.

**Bona fide occupational qualification (BFOQ).** A justified business reason for discriminating against a member of a protected class.

**Boulwarism.** A negotiation strategy developed and used by the General Electric Company in the U.S. The strategy caused the company to make its "best" offer to the union at the beginning of negotiations. Then the company remained firm in not increasing its offer unless the union could find where management had erred in its calculations used to arrive at the ''best'' offer. This strategy has been ruled an unfair labour practice by U.S. courts.

**Brainstorming.** A process by which participants provide their ideas on a stated problem during a freewheeling group session.

**''Buddy system.''** The ''buddy-system'' of orientation exists when an experienced employee is asked to show a new worker around the job site, conduct introductions, and answer the newcomer's questions.

**Burnout.** A condition of mental, emotional, and sometimes physical exhaustion that results in substantial and prolonged stress.

**Business agent.** Generally, a full-time, paid employee or official of a local union whose duties include day-to-day dealing with employers and workers.

**Business unionism.** The practice of unions that seek to improve the wages, hours, and working conditions of their members in a businesslike manner. (See *Social unionism.*)

**Buy-back.** A method of convincing an employee who attempts to resign to stay in the employ of the organization; normally, it involves an offer of an increased wage or salary.


**Cafeteria benefit programs.** Programs that allow employees to select the mix of fringe benefits and services that answer their individual needs.

**Canada Employment and Immigration Commission (CEIC).** A federal agency responsible for administering employment and immigration programs.

**Canada Employment Centres (CECs).** Centres administered by the Canada Employment and Immigration Commission (CEIC) that match jobseekers with employers who have job openings, and provide counselling and testing services.

**Canada Labour Code.** Federal law regulating labour relations under federal jurisdiction.

**Canada Labour Relations Board.** A federal board whose responsibilities include the determination of appropriate bargaining units, certification and decertification of unions, and decisions on unfair labour practices.

**Canada Manpower Training Program.** A federal program that supports institutional (classroom) and industrial (on-the-job) training.

**Canada Occupational Forecasting Program (COFOR).** One of the publications of Canada Employment and Immigration providing long-term forecasts on the demand for various types of labour in Canada.

**Canada Pension Plan (CPP).** A mandatory, contributory, and portable pension plan applicable to all self-employed persons and employees in Canada, except those working for the federal government. It pays retirement pensions, disability pensions, pensions for surviving spouses, lump-sum death benefits, and benefits to children of disabled contributors.

**Canadian Classification and Dictionary of Occupations (CCDO).** A publication of Canada Employment and Immigration in 1971, periodically updated, providing detailed job definitions for all jobs in government and industry.

**Canadian Human Rights Act.** A federal law, enacted in 1977, prohibiting discrimination on the basis of race, national or ethnic origin, colour, religion, age, sex, marital status, conviction for an offence for which a pardon was issued, and physical handicap. It applies to all federal government agencies and Crown corporations and to businesses and industries under federal jurisdiction.

**Canadian Human Rights Commission (CHRC).** A federal body, consisting of a Chief

Commissioner, a Deputy Chief Commissioner, and from three to six other members; all members are appointed by the Governor in Council. The commission supervises the implementation and adjudication of the Canadian Human Rights Act.

**Canadian Labour Congress.** A central labour congress formed in 1956 by the merger of the Trades and Labour Congress of Canada and the Canadian Congress of Labour.

**Career.** All the jobs that are held during one's working life.

**Career counselling.** A process that assists employees to find appropriate career goals and paths.

**Career development.** Those personal improvements one undertakes to achieve a personal career plan.

**Career goals.** The future positions one strives to reach as part of a career. The goals serve as benchmarks along one's career path.

**Career path.** The sequential pattern of jobs that forms one's career.

**Career planning.** The process by which one selects career goals and paths to those goals.

**Career plateau.** This occurs when an employee is in a position that he or she does well enough not to be demoted or fired, but not so well that the person is likely to be promoted.

**Cash plan.** Type of profit sharing offering cash instead of deferred payments.

**Change agents.** People who have the role of stimulating and coordinating changes in a group.

**Change objective of the human resource department.** The change objective of the human resource department is to manage change in ways that increase its benefits and reduce its costs.

**Charter of Rights and Freedoms.** Federal law enacted in 1982, guaranteeing individuals equal rights before the law.

**Check-off.** A procedure whereby the employer, by agreement with the union, deducts union membership dues and assessments from the pay of all employees in the bargaining unit and turns these monies over to the union.

**Closed shop.** A form of union security that requires the employer to hire only union members and retain only union members.

**Codetermination.** A form of industrial democracy, first popularized in West Germany, giving workers the right to have their representatives vote on management decisions.

**Cognitive dissonance.** Cognitive dissonance results from a gap between what one expects and what one experiences.

**Cognitive models of motivation.** These models depend on the thinking or feeling (that is, cognition) within each individual.

**Coinsurance clause.** A provision in an insurance policy that requires the insured and the insurer to share the costs of a claim on some basis.

**Collective agreement.** A legal document negotiated between the union and the employer. It states the terms and conditions of employment.

**Collective bargaining.** The procedure by which the representatives of employers and unions negotiate the terms and conditions of their employment. The term also applies beyond the negotiating process to encompass the actual interpretation and administration of the agreement, including the day-to-day activities of the employer and union.

**Collective liability.** In the Workmen's Compensation Act, the collective responsibility of all employers to pay compensation to workers for any work-related injury. The industries covered by the act are classified according to how hazardous they are, and employers in each group are collectively liable for payment of compensation to workers employed in that group.

**Communication.** The transfer of information and understanding from one person to another.

**Communication overload.** A condition that exists when employees receive more communication inputs than they can process or than they need.

**Communication process.** The method by which a sender reaches a receiver; it requires that an idea be developed, encoded, transmitted, received, decoded, and used.

**Communication system.** Provides formal and informal methods to move information throughout an organization so that appropriate decisions are made.

**Comparable work.** (See *Equal pay for work of equal value.*)

**Comparable worth.** U.S. terminology for *Equal pay for work of equal value.*)

**Compa ratio.** Measure of average salary for a given pay grade relative to the midpoint of that grade. A CP of above 1 indicates that more employees are paid in the upper range of that grade (less desirable); a CP of below 1 indicates that more employees are paid in the lower range (more desirable).

**Compensation.** Whatever employees receive in exchange for their work.

**Concentration in employment.** A condition that exists when a department or employer has a higher proportion of members of a protected class than is found in the employer's labour market. (See *Underutilization.*)

**Concilation.** The process whereby a third party, usually a government official or a person appointed by the government, attempts to bring together the parties in an industrial dispute for reconciling their differences. The conciliator has no power to enforce a settlement.

**Concilation board.** A board, usually legally required and consisting of a chairperson and a member representing each of the parties to the dispute, formed to effect a settlement in a negotiation dispute.

**Concurrent validation.** Relationship between a predicator (test) score and a job criterion (job performance) score, whereby predicator and criterion scores are measured concurrently.

**Confederation of National Trade Unions (CNTU).** Quebec-based central labour body.

**Conservative syndrome.** A tendency to be guided by tradition, to accept the decision-making functions of elites, and to put a strong emphasis on the maintenance of order and predictability in society.

**Constructs.** Substitutes for actual performance; for example, a score of a test is a construct for actual learning.

**Consumer Price Index (CPI).** A monthly index prepared by Statistics Canada, to measure the percentage change through time in the cost of purchasing a fixed basket of consumer goods and services representing the purchases by families and individuals living in urban centres with populations of 30,000 or over.

**Content theories of motivation.** Describe the needs or desires within us that initiate behaviour.

**Content validity.** Estimate of how well test items reflect elements of the job domain.

**Contract labour.** People who are hired (and often trained) by an independent agency that supplies companies with needed human resources for a fee.

**Contributory benefit plans.** Fringe benefits that require the employer to contribute to the cost of the benefit. (See *Noncontributory benefit plans.*)

**Cooperative counselling.** A mutual counsellor-employee relationship that establishes a cooperative exchange of ideas to help solve an employee's problems. (See *Directive counselling* and *Nondirective counselling.*)

**Corrective discipline.** Action that follows a rule infraction and seeks to discourage further infractions so that future actions are in compliance with standards. (See *Preventive discipline.*)

**Correlation coefficient.** Measure of the degree of relationship between two variables (e.g., test scores and job performance scores).

**Cost-of-living adjustment (COLA).** An increase or decrease in wages or salaries in accordance with changes in the cost of living as measured by a designated index, such as the Consumer Price Index.

**Council of Canadian Personnel Associations (CCPA).** A Canadian federation of provincial human resource associations.

**Counselling.** Discussion of a problem with an employee, with the general objective of helping the employee cope with it better.

**Counselling functions.** The activities performed by counselling, which include advice, reassurance, communication, release of emotional tension, clarified thinking, and reorientation.

**Craft union.** A labour organization that limits membership to workers having a particular craft or skill or working at closely related trades.

**Criterion** (plural: criteria). A standard or norm to assess performance.

**Critical incident method.** An employee evaluation method requiring the rater to record statements that describe extremely good or bad behaviour related to performance.

**Cut-off scores.** Test scores below which nobody will be hired.


**Decertification.** Loss of a union's privilege to represent a bargaining unit.

**Decision-making authority.** (See *Line authority.*)

**Deductible clause.** A provision in an insurance policy that requires the insured to pay a specified amount of a claim before the insurance company is obligated to pay. Usually the insured must pay the first $50 or $100.

**Delegation.** The process of getting others to share a manager's work; it requires the manager to assign duties, grant authority, and create a sense of responsibility.

**Delphi technique.** The soliciting of predictions about specified future developments from a panel of experts. Their collective estimates are then reported back to the panel so that members may adjust their opinions. This process is repeated until general agreement on the future trends emerges.

**Demographics.** The study of population characteristics.

**Demotions.** Demotions occur when an employee is moved from one job to another that is lower in pay, responsibility, and organizational level.

**Dental insurance plan.** A group benefit plan whereby the employer pays in whole or in part the individual premium for dental insurance coverage of its employees.

**Development.** A process of preparing an employee for future job responsibilities. (Compare with *Training.*)

**Differential validity.** The applicability of tests or other selection criteria to different subgroups (such as women or minorities).

**Directive counselling.** The process of listening to an employee's emotional problems, deciding with the employee what should be done, and then telling and motivating the employee to do it. (See *Nondirective counselling* and *Cooperative counselling.*)

**Discipline.** Management action to encourage compliance with the organization's standards.

**Discrimination.** The systematic exclusion of particular persons from consideration for a job, or the payment of different wages to such persons, because of their age, sex, race, or some other characteristic not relevant to job ability or performance.

**Dismissal.** The ultimate disciplinary action; it separates the employee from the employer for a cause.

**Downward communication.** Information that begins at some point in the organization and feeds down the organization hierarchy to inform or influence others in the organization.

**Dual responsibility for human resource management.** Since both line and staff managers are responsible for employees, production, and quality of work life, a dual responsibility for human resource management exists.

**Due process.** It means that established rules and procedures for disciplinary action are followed and that employees have an opportunity to respond to the charges made against them.

**Early retirement.** When a worker retires from an employer before the "normal" retirement age.

**Empirical validity.** Validity achieved through studies that relate test scores to a job-related criterion, usually performance.

**Employee assistance programs (EAPS).** Comprehensive company programs that seek to help employees overcome their personal and work-related problems.

**Employee handbook.** A handbook explaining key benefits, policies, and general information about the employer.

**Employment Equity Act.** Federal law, enacted in 1987, to remove employment barriers and to promote equality for women, aboriginal peoples, persons with disabilities, and visible minorities.

**Employment freeze.** Occurs when the organization curtails future hiring.

**Employment function.** That aspect of human resources work that is responsible for recruiting, selecting, and hiring new workers. It is usually found in the employment section of large human resource departments.

**Employment involvement (EI).** Consists of a variety of systematic methods that enable employees to participate in the decisions that affect them in relation to the organization.

**Employment references.** Evaluations of an employee's past work performance, provided by past employers.

**Employment tests.** Devices that assess the probable match between applicants and job requirements.

**Environmental conditions (EC).** One of the job attributes described in the *Canadian Classification and Dictionary of Occupations*, consisting of the significant physical surroundings of a worker, such as noise, mechanical hazards, and fumes and dust.

**Equal employment opportunity.** The principle whereby employment is based on the qualifications of the applicant rather than upon sex, race, or other factors not related to ability or performance.

**Equal pay for equal work.** The principle or policy of equal rates of pay for all employees in an establishment performing the same kind and amount of work, regardless of sex, race, or other characteristics of individual workers not related to ability or performance.

**Equal pay for work of equal value.** The principle of equal pay for men and women in jobs with comparable content; criteria used: skill, effort, responsibility, and working conditions; part of the Human Rights Act.

**Equifinality.** The attribute of paths that lead to a common objective.

**Equity theory.** Equity theory suggests that people are motivated to close the gap between their efforts and the perceived amount and appropriateness of the rewards they receive.

**Ergonomics.** The study of biotechnical relationships between the physical attributes of workers and the physical demands of the job with the object of reducing physical and mental strain in order to increase productivity and quality of work life.

**Error of central tendency.** An error in rating employees that consists in evaluating employees as neither good nor poor performers even when some employees perform exceptionally well or poorly.

**Esteem needs.** The needs people have for recognition from others and for a personal sense of self-worth.

**Evaluation interviews.** Performance review sessions that give employees feedback about their past performance or future potential.

**Existence-Relatedness-Growth (ERG) Theory.** Alderfer's Existence-Relatedness-Growth Theory suggests that lower-order needs can be grouped under the heading of Existence; Relatedness needs encompass interpersonal relationships and include acceptance, belonging and security that come from approval of those in the organization. Growth needs include challenging an individual's capabilities that cause personal growth on the job.

**Exit interviews.** Conversations with departing employees to learn their opinion of the employer, managers, policies, and other aspects of employment with the company. These interviews also seek to learn why the employee is leaving.

**Expectancy.** The strength of a person's belief that an act will lead to a particular outcome.

**Expectancy theory.** Expectancy theory states that motivation is the result of the outcome one seeks and one's estimate that action will lead to the desired outcome.

**Experiential learning.** Learning by experiencing in the training environment the kinds of problems one faces on the job.

**Exposure.** Becoming known by those who decide on promotions, transfers, and other career opportunities.

**Extrapolation.** Extending past rates of change into the future.

**Face validity.** Subjective assessment (appearance) of how well a test will predict job success by examining the test items.

**Facilitator.** Someone who assists quality circles and the quality circle leader to identify and solve workplace problems.

**Factor comparison method.** A form of job evaluation that allocates a part of each job's wage to the key factors of the job. The result is a relative evaluation of the organization's jobs.

**Family Allowances.** A scheme introduced in 1944 by which all Canadian mothers of children under sixteen years of age are to be given monthly payments for their sustenance and education.

**Feedback.** Information that helps evaluate the success or failure of an action or system.

**Field experiment.** Research that allows the researchers to study employees under realistic conditions to learn how experimental and control subjects react to new programs or other changes.

**Field review method.** A method of preparing an employee performance evaluation, whereby skilled representatives of the human resource department go into the field and gather information about employee performance.

**Final-offer arbitration.** Choice of an arbitrator between the final offer of either management or union.

**Flextime.** A scheduling innovation that abolishes rigid starting and ending times for each day's work. Instead, employees are allowed to begin and end the workday at their discretion, usually within a range of hours.

**Flexyear.** An employee scheduling concept that allows employees to be off of the job part of the year. Employees usually work a normal work year in less than the twelve months.

**Forced-choice method.** A method of employee performance evaluation that requires the rater to choose the most descriptive statement in each of several pairs of statements about the employee being rated.

**Ford Occupational Imbalance Listing (FOIL).** A quarterly publication by CEIC that projects the short-term imbalances based on supply-and-demand information.

**Forecasts.** Forecasts predict the organization's future needs.

**Functional authority.** Authority that allows staff experts to make decisions and take actions normally reserved for line managers.

**Funded retirement plans.** A retirement plan in which the employer has set aside sufficient monies to meet the future payout requirements of the retirement plan.

**General Educational Development (GED).** One of the job attributes used in the *Canadian Classification and Dictionary of Occupations* to define a job; it reflects the approximate direction of schooling and/or qualification needed for effective performance on the job in question.

**General Industrial Training Program.** A federal program supported by CEIC that reimburses employers for the direct cost of industrial training and a portion of the trainee wages.

**Good-faith bargaining.** The requirement that two parties meet and confer at reasonable times with the sincere intention of reaching agreement on new contract terms.

**Grapevine communication.** An informal communications system that arises spontaneously from the social interaction of people in the organization.

**Grievance.** Any complaint or expressed dissatisfaction by an employee or by a union concerning the job, pay, or any other aspect of the employment relationship.

**Grievance procedure.** Usually, a formal plan set up in the collective agreement to resolve grievances, involving discussions at progressively higher levels of authority in the company and the union, culminating, if necessary, in arbitration.

**Guaranteed annual wage plans.** Agreements wherein an employer assures employees that they will receive a minimum annual income regardless of layoffs or a lack of work. The guaranteed amount is usually a fraction of the employee's normal full-time earnings.

**Halo effect.** A bias that occurs when an evaluation allows some information to disproportionately affect the final evaluation.

**Handicapped workers.** Workers whose earning capacity is impaired by age, physical or mental deficiency, or injury.

**Harassment.** Harassment occurs when another member of an organization treats an employee in a disparate manner because of that person's sex, race, religion, age, or other protective classification.

**Health insurance plans.** Health and medical insurance provided by provincial governments with assistance from a federal government. In April 1972, the scope of the Medical Care Act of 1966 was extended to all of Canada. Since that date, the cost of medical care has been paid for by taxes.

**Hierarchy of needs.** Since all needs cannot be expressed at once, they have some priority in the way in which they find expression. The ordering or priority of these needs forms a hierarchy beginning with physical and security needs and continuing with social, esteem, and self-fulfillment needs.

**Higher-order needs.** Higher-order needs include the need of social acceptance, esteem, and self-fulfillment.

**Hiring hall.** An office, usually run by the union, or jointly by employers and union, for referring workers to jobs or for the actual hiring operation. Common in construction and related trades.

**Hot-stove rule.** The principle that disciplinary action should have the same characteristics as the penalty a person receives from touching a hot stove—that is, the discipline should be with warning, immediate, consistent, and impersonal.

**House organ.** Any regularly published organizational magazine, newspaper, or bulletin directed to employees.

**Human resource audits.** An extensive survey of each employee's skills and abilities.

**Human resource forecasts.** Predictions of the organization's future demand for employees.

**Human resource management.** The function primarily concerned with utilization and development of the human resources in a particular company or organization. It involves the planning of human resource needs, staffing, training, and compensation.

**Human resource planning.** Organizational planning based on systematic forecasts of an organization's future supply and demand of employees.

**Human resources.** The people who are ready, willing, and able to contribute to organizational goals.

**Human rights legislation.** Federal and provincial laws against discrimination. (See *Canadian Human Rights Act*.)

**Imminent danger.** An unsafe or unhealthy work condition that is likely to lead to death or serious injury if it is allowed to continue.

**Incentive systems.** Incentive systems link compensation and performance by paying employees for actual results, not seniority or hours worked.

**Indexation.** A method of estimating future employment needs by matching employment growth with some index, such as sales growth.

**Industrial democracy.** The policy of giving employees a larger voice in work-related decisions that affect them.

**Industrial relations.** A broad term that includes relations between unions and management, between management and the government, between unions and the government, and between employers and employees—the latter often being referred to as human resource relations.

**Industrial union.** A union that represents all or most of the production, maintenance, and related workers, both skilled and unskilled, in an industry or company. It may also include office, sales, and technical employees of the same companies.

**In-house complaint procedures.** Organizationally developed methods for employees to register their complaints about the various aspects of the organization.

**Initiation fee.** A payment to the union required of a worker when he or she joins, usually as set forth in the union's constitution.

**Injunction.** A court order restraining one or more persons, corporations, or unions from performing some act that the court believes would result in irreparable injury to property or other rights.

**Insurable employment.** Jobs covered by unemployment insurance.

**Interest Factors (INT).** One of the job attributes used in the *Canadian Classification and Dictionary of Occupations* (CCDO) to define a job. Five pairs of interest factors are provided in the CCDO; positive concern for one factor of a pair usually implies rejection of the other factor (e.g., routine vs. creative work).

**International union.** A union that charters locals in the United States and Canada.

**Job analysis.** Systematic study of a job to discover its specifications, its mental, physical, and skill requirements, its relation to other jobs in the plant, etc., usually for wage-setting or job-simplification purposes.

**Job analysis schedules.** Checklists or questionnaires that seek to collect information about jobs in a uniform manner. (Also called *Job Analysis Questionnaire*.)

**Job banks.** Job banks are maintained in employment offices. They are used to match job applicants with openings.

**Job classification.** The arrangement of tasks in an establishment or industry into a limited series of jobs or occupations, rated in terms of skill, responsibility, experience, training, and similar considerations, usually for wage-setting purposes.

**Job code.** A job code uses numbers, letters, or both to provide a quick summary of the job and its content.

**Job cycle.** The time it takes a worker to complete every task in his or her job before repeating the cycle.

**Job description.** A recognized list of functions and tasks included in a particular occupation or job.

**Job enlargement.** Adding more tasks to a job in order to increase the job cycle.

**Job enrichment.** Adding more responsibilities, autonomy, and control to a job.

**Job evaluation.** The process of assessing job content and ranking jobs according to a consistent set of job characteristics and worker traits, such as skill, responsibility, experience, etc. Commonly used for setting relative rates of pay.

**Job families.** Groups of different jobs that require similar skills.

**Job grading.** A form of job evaluation that assigns jobs to predetermined job classifications according to their relative worth to the organization. This technique also is called the job classification method.

**Jobholder reports.** Reports to employees about a firm's economic performance.

**Job instruction training.** Training received directly on the job and used to train workers in how to do their job.

**Job performance standards.** The work performance expected from an employee on a particular job.

**Job posting.** Involves informing employees about unfilled job openings and the qualifications for those jobs.

**Job progression ladder.** A particular career path where some jobs have prerequisites.

**Job ranking.** One form of job evaluation whereby jobs are ranked subjectively according to their overall worth to the organization.

**Job rotation.** A process of moving employees from one job to another in order to allow employees more variety in their jobs and to learn new skills.

**Job satisfaction.** The favourableness or unfavourableness with which employees view their work.

**Job sharing.** A plan whereby available work is spread among all of the workers in the group in order to prevent, or reduce the extent of, a layoff when production requirements result in a substantial decline in available work.

**Job specifications.** A written statement that explains what a job demands of employees who do it and the human skills and factors that are required.

**Joint study committees.** Committees which incude representatives of management and the unions who meet away from the bargaining table to study some topic of mutual interest in hopes of finding a solution that is mutually satisfactory.

**Jurisdiction, union.** The authority of a union to represent certain groups of workers within specific occupations, industries, or geographic areas.

**Key jobs.** Jobs that are common in the organization and its labour market.

**Key subordinates.** Those employees who are crucial to a manager's success in a particular job.

**Laboratory training.** A form of group training primarily used to enhance interpersonal skills.

**Labour agreement.** A legal document, also called a labour contract, that is negotiated between the union and employer. It states the terms and conditions of employment.

**Labour market.** The area in which the employer recruits.

**Labour market analysis.** The study of the employer's labour market to evaluate the present or future availability of workers.

**Labour relations board.** A board set up in the federal and all provincial jurisdictions to administer labour relations legislation. Its powers and duties generally include the determination of appropriate bargaining units, the certification and the decertification of trade unions, decisions as to unfair labour practices, and failure to bargain in good faith.

**Labour standards.** Standards concerning employment and working conditions found acceptable by labour and management through collective bargaining and by the legislator through labour laws and legislation.

**Labour standards legislation.** Legislation designed primarily to provide protection to unorganized workers but which increasingly affects the operation of negotiated collective agreements. The legislation sets the minimum standards permissible in the areas of statutory school-leaving age, minimum age for employment, minimum wages, equal pay for equal work, hours of work, weekly rest-day, annual vacations, general holidays, termination of employment, maternity protection, and severance pay.

**Labour union.** Any organization in which workers participate as members and that exists for the purpose of dealing with employers concerning grievances, wages, hours, and conditions of employment.

**Law of effect.** The principle that people learn to repeat behaviours that have favourable consequences and to avoid behaviours that have unfavourable consequences.

**Layoff.** A temporary or indefinite dismissal of one or more employees because of lack of work.

**Learning curve.** A visual representation of the rate at which one learns given material through time.

**Learning curve for change.** A chartered representation of the period of adjustment and adaptation to change required by an organization.

**Learning principles.** Guidelines to the ways in which people learn most effectively.

**Leave of absence.** A grant to an employee of time off from his or her job, generally without loss of job or seniority.

**Legally required benefits.** Employee benefits programs to which employers must contribute, or insurance that they must purchase for employees, by law.

**Leniency bias.** A tendency to rate employees higher than their performance justifies.

**Leveraging.** Resigning in order to further one's career with another employer.

**Liability, joint.** Responsibility on the part of both union and employer for unfair labour practices.

**Lie detector.** Misnomer for polygraph. Does not detect lies, but measures body reactions, e.g., heart beat. (See *Polygraph*.)

**Life insurance plan.** Group term insurance coverage for employees, paid for in whole or in part by the employer.

**Life plan.** A person's hopes, dreams, personal ambitions, and career goals.

**Line authority.** Authority allowing managers to direct others and to make decisions about the organization's operations.

**Listening.** A receiver's positive effort to receive an understanding of a message transmitted by sound.

**Local.** The basic unit of union organization, formed in a particular plant or locality. Members participate directly in the affairs of their local, including the election of officers, financial and other business matters, and relations between their organization and employers, and pay dues to the local.

**Lockout.** A temporary withholding of work or denial of employment to a group of workers by an employer during a labour dispute in order to compel a settlement at or close to the employer's terms.

**Long-term disability plan.** A benefit plan that provides the employee with an income, usually a percentage of normal take-home pay, in the case of long-term illness or injury.

**Maintenance factors.** Those elements of the work setting that lead to employee dissatisfaction when they are not provided adequately. These factors also are called dissatisfiers or hygiene factors.

**"Make-whole" remedies.** Measures taken when an individual is mistreated in violation of employment laws, whereby the wrongdoer is usually required to make up losses to the employee that were suffered because of the wrongdoing.

**Management by objectives (MBO).** Requires an employee and superior to jointly establish performance goals for the future. Employees are subsequently evaluated on how well they have obtained these agreed-upon objectives.

**Management inventories.** Management inventories summarize the skills and abilities of management personnel. (See *Skills inventories*, which are used for nonmanagement employees.)

**Management rights.** As used in union-management relationships, this term encompasses those aspects of the employer's operations that do not require discussion with or concurrence of the union, or rights reserved to management that are not subject to collective bargaining. These rights may be expressly noted as such in a collective agreement. Such prerogatives generally include matters of hiring, production, scheduling, price-fixing, the maintenance of order and efficiency, and the processes of manufacturing and sales.

**Maternity benefit.** Medical benefits, and partial compensation for loss of income for maternity, as provided under health and disability insurance systems or under private benefit plans.

**Maternity leave.** The period of time off work generally granted persons who are pregnant. Many jurisdictions have legislation setting minimum standards for maternity leave.

**Maturity curves.** A statistical device used to calculate compensation for workers based on their seniority and performance. Normally, such compensation plans are limited to professional and technical workers.

**Maximum hours.** The number of hours that can be worked at straight-time rates under federal and provincial laws.

**Mediation.** The process whereby disputing parties seek to reconcile their differences through a third party who actively seeks to assist by making suggestions, providing background information, and noting avenues open to the parties for settlement.

**Mediator.** A person who undertakes mediation of a dispute.

**Medical and health benefits plans.** Public and private insurance plans to protect the individual from the costs resulting from illness.

**Medical and health benefits provisions.** Provisions made by an employer, contractually or otherwise, to pay entirely or in part the cost to the employee of public or private medical and health benefits.

**Mentor.** Someone who offers informed career guidance and support on a regular basis.

**Merit-based promotion.** Promotion of superior performance in the present job.

**Merit raises.** Pay increases given to individual workers according to an evaluation of their performance.

**Metropolitan Order Processing System (MOPS).** A computerized system that automatically conveys information about job vacancies to all Canada Employment Centres within a large metropolitan area.

**Minimum wage.** The rate of pay established by statute or minimum wage order as the lowest wage that may be paid for any category of work or workers. All provinces in Canada have legislation establishing minimum wages for most classes of workers. In 1935, the federal government passed the Minimum Wages Act, which applies to all governmental agencies.

**Modified union shop.** A union security provision that specifies that only new employees are required to join the union. It may or may not stipulate that present union members maintain such membership.

**Motivation.** A person's drive to take action because that person wants to do so.

**Motivational factors.** Those elements of the work environment that motivate people to perform and be satisfied.

**National Job Bank (NJB).** A national system for conveying information about vacancies in any region of the country to all other regions; it is administered by Canada Employment and Immigration and operates through Canada Employment Centres.

**National union.** A union that charters locals in Canada only.

**Needs assessment.** A diagnosis that presents problems and future challenges that can be met through training or development.

**Net benefit.** A surplus of benefits after all costs are included.

**No-lockout clause.** Statutory provision prohibiting lockouts during the term of a collective agreement.

**Nominal group techniques (NGT).** A group method of drawing out ideas from people on a specified topic. It requires participants to list their ideas and then share those ideas in round-robin fashion with the group and a facilitator. Once all ideas of the group are vented, duplicate ideas are eliminated and clarification follows. Following clarification, members of the group vote on what they believe to be the best or most important items they uncovered through the NGT process.

**Noncontributory benefit plans.** Fringe benefits that are paid entirely by the employer. (See *Contributory benefit plans*.)

**Nondirective (or client-centred) counselling.** The process of skillfully listening to and encouraging an employee to explain bothersome problems, understand them, and determine appropriate solutions. (See *Directive counselling* and *Cooperative counselling*.)

**Nonverbal communication.** Actions that communicate, as opposed to words.

**Objectives.** Benchmarks against which actions are evaluated.

**Obsolescence.** A condition that results when an employee no longer possesses the knowledge or abilities to perform successfully.

**Open communication.** A condition that exists when people feel free to communicate all relevant messages.

**Open-door policy.** A policy of encouraging employees to come to their manager or even to higher management with any matter that concerns them.

**Open system.** (See *System.*)

**Organization character.** The product of all the organization's features, such as its people, objectives, technology, size, age, unions, policies, successes, and failures.

**Organizational climate.** The favourableness or unfavourableness of the environment for people in the organization.

**Organizational development (OD).** An intervention strategy that uses group processes to focus on the whole organization in order to bring about planned change.

**Organizational development process.** A complex and difficult process that consists of seven steps. These steps begin with initial diagnosis, data collection, data feedback and confrontation, action planning and problem solving, team building, and conclude with inter-group development and evaluation and follow-up.

**Organizing committee.** A group of workers who guide the efforts needed to organize their fellow workers into a labour organization.

**Orientation programs.** Programs that familiarize primarily new employees with their roles, the organization, its policies, and other employees.

**Outplacement.** The action of an organization in assisting its present employees to find jobs with other employers.

**Overtime.** Hours worked in excess of the standard workweek or work day established either by law, by the collective agreement, or by company policy.

**Paper-and-pencil test.** Measures of job-related knowledge rather than work samples of the job itself.

**Pareto analysis.** A means of collating data about the types or causes of production problems by arranging the data in descending order of frequency.

**Participation rates.** The percentage of working age men and women who are in the work force.

**Participative counselling.** This type of counselling seeks to find a balance between directive and nondirective counselling techniques with the counsellor and the counsellee participating in the discussion and solution of the problem. (See *Cooperative counselling.*)

**Part IV of the Canada Labour Code.** A section dealing with safety of employees and incorporating many of the provisions of the Canadian Safety Code of 1968.

**Part-time layoffs.** When an employer lays off workers without pay for a part of each week, such as each Friday.

**Paternalism.** The attitude of an organization whose management assumes that it alone is the best judge of employee needs and that it need not seek and act upon inputs about their needs.

**Patterns and practices.** When discrimination is found to exist against a large number of individuals who are in a protected class, a *pattern and practice* of discrimination exists.

**Pension plan.** Any plan whose primary purpose is to provide specific and determinable benefits to employees over a period of years following retirement. The term private pension plan is often used to distinguish voluntary plans from the social insurance system. If the employee shares in the cost, the plan is *contributory.*

**Pension plan, registered.** An employee's superannuation or pension fund or plan registered for purposes of the Income Tax Act.

**Performance appraisal.** The process by which organizations evaluate employee job performance.

**Performance measures.** The ratings used to evaluate employee performance.

**Performance standards.** The benchmarks against which performance is measured.

**Personal barriers.** Communication interferences that arise from human emotions, values, and limitations.

**Personal failure.** Nonachievement of one's most important goals in life. Research studies indicate that contradictory life demands, disconfirmation of one's expectancies and beliefs about the environment, a sense of external control, and feelings of loneliness are associated with a person's feelings of personal failure.

**Personal leave days.** Normal work days that an employee is entitled to be off. (In some firms personal leave days are used instead of sick days.)

**Personnel audit.** A systematic review of the personnel activities used in an organization.

**Peter Principle.** The Peter Principle states that in a hierarchy, people tend to rise to their level of incompetence.

**Physical Activities (PA).** In the *Canadian Classification and Dictionary of Occupations*, the physical requirements of the job and the physical capacities or traits a worker must have to meet those requirements (e.g., seeing, lifting).

**Picketing.** Patrolling by union members at or near an employer's place of business in order to publicize the existence of a labour dispute or union's desire to represent the employees, to attempt to persuade workers to join the work stoppage, to discourage customers from patronizing a business, etc.

**Piecework.** A type of incentive system that compensates workers for each unit of output.

**Placement.** The assignment of the employee to a new or a different job.

**Point system.** A form of job evaluation that assesses the relative importance of the job's key factors in order to arrive at the relative worth of jobs.

**Polygraph.** Machine that measures body reactions to stress, e.g., heart beat, galvanic skin response (sweating), and changes in breathing. Often called lie detector.

**Portability clauses.** Allow accumulated pension rights to be transferred to another employer when an employee changes employers.

**Portable pensions.** Pension plans with a feature allowing employees to move from one employer to another without losing their accrued pension credits.

**Position analysis questionnaire (PAQ).** A standardized, preprinted form that collects specific information about jobs.

**Precedent.** A new standard that arises from the past practices of either the company or the union.

**Preferential quota system.** This situation exists when a proportion of the job openings, promotions, or other employment opportunities are reserved for members of a protected class who have been previously discriminated against.

**Prevailing wage rate.** The wage rates most commonly paid for a given job in a geographical area. The prevailing wage rate is determined by a wage and salary survey.

**Preventive discipline.** Action taken prior to any infraction, to encourage employees to follow the standards and rules so that infractions are prevented. (See *Corrective discipline*.)

**Price index.** A statistical device used to show relative price changes over time. Prevailing prices in a selected base year are assigned a value of 100; in subsequent years, the prices of the components of the overall index are weighted by their relative importance in the base year in order to determine the current price level, which is then divided by the base year price to yield the index.

**Private placement agencies.** For-profit organizations that help job seekers find employment.

**Proactive management.** A type of management wherein decision makers anticipate problems and take affirmative steps to minimize those problems rather than waiting until after a problem occurs before taking action.

**Probationary period.** The initial period of employment during which a worker is on trial and may be discharged with or without cause.

**Problem-solving interviews.** Interviews that rely on questions limited to hypothetical situations or problems. The applicant is evaluated on how well the problems are solved.

**Production bonuses.** A type of incentive system that provides employees with additional compensation when they surpass stated production goals.

**Productivity.** The ratio of a firm's output (goods and services) divided by its input (people, capital, materials, energy).

**Professional associations.** Groups of workers who voluntarily join together to further their profession and their professional development. When these associations undertake to negotiate for their members, they are also labour organizations.

**Profit sharing.** A system whereby an employer pays compensation or benefits to employees in addition to their regular wage based upon the profits of the company. This is usually done on an annual basis.

**Programmed instruction.** Systematic and stepwise presentation of teaching material broken down into steps (frames) where each step must be successfully completed before going on to the next. Immediate feedback allows users to assess their comprehension of the material and to place themselves.

**Progressive discipline.** A type of discipline whereby there are stronger penalties for repeated offences.

**Promotion.** When an employee is moved from one job to another that is higher in pay, responsibility, and/or organization level.

**Protected groups.** Classes of people who are protected from employment discrimination under one or more laws.

**Provincial federation.** An organization formed by a labour congress at the provincial level that consists of the congress affiliates in the province. It functions similarly to the congress in the appropriate provincial area except that it does not charter local unions. Funds are obtained through a per capita tax on affiliates.

**Psychic costs.** The stresses, strains, and anxieties that affect a person's inner self during periods of change.

**Pygmalion effect.** The Pygmalion effect occurs when people live up to the highest expectations others hold of them.

**Qualified handicapped.** Those handicapped individuals who can perform jobs with reasonable employer accommodation.

**Quality circles.** A small group of employees with a common leader who meet together regularly to identify and solve work-related problems.

**Quality of work life (QWL).** A generic term emphasizing the humanization of work. The elements relevant to a worker's quality of work life involve the task, the physical work environment, the social environment within the workplace, the administrative system of the enterprise, and the relationship between life on and off the job.

**Quality of work life efforts.** Systematic attempts by an organization to give workers a greater opportunity to affect their jobs and their contributions to the organization's overall effectiveness.

**Quebec Pension Plan (QPP).** A mandatory, contributory, and portable pension plan applicable to all self-employed persons and employees in the province of Quebec except those working for the federal government. This plan is identical to the Canada Pension Plan in most of its provisions.

**Quitting.** Voluntary resignation from employment, initiated by the employee.

**Raiding.** The efforts of a union to bring into its organization individuals who are already members of another union.

**Rand formula.** A union security plan developed by Judge Rand, in an arbitration decision handed down in 1946, that requires the employer to deduct union dues from the pay of all employees, union and non-union, and remit the amounts to the union.

**Rank and file, the.** Union members, collectively, who have no special status as either officers or shop stewards in the plant.

**Rap sessions.** Meetings between managers and groups of employees to discuss complaints, suggestions, opinions, or questions.

**Rate range.** A pay range for each job class.

**Ratification.** Formal approval of a newly negotiated agreement by vote of the union members affected.

**Rating scale.** A scale that requires the rater to provide a subjective evaluation of an individual's performance along a scale from low to high.

**Rational validity.** A characteristic of tests that include reasonable samples of the skills needed to perform successfully or that are based on an obvious relationship between performance and other characteristics assumed to be necessary for successful job performance.

**Reactive management.** A type of management wherein decision makers respond to problems rather than anticipate them.

**Realistic Job Preview (RJP).** Allows the employee to understand a job and the job setting where the hiring decision is made. It involves showing the candidate the type of work, equipment, and working conditions involved in the job before the hiring decision is finalized.

**Recall.** The procedure followed by an employer for the return of individuals who have been laid off.

**Recency effect.** A rater bias that occurs when the rater allows recent employee performance to sway unduly the overall evaluation of the employee's performance.

**Recognition clause.** A mandatory clause in Canadian collective labour agreements that provides that the trade union is recognized as the exclusive agent of the employees in the bargaining unit.

**Recruitment.** The process of finding and attracting capable applicants to apply for employment.

**Recruitment channels.** Different sources of prospective applicants for a job.

**Red-circle rate.** A rate of pay higher than the contractual, or formerly established, rate for a job. The special rate is usually attached to the incumbent worker, not to the job as such.

**Refreezing.** Requires integrating what has been learned into actual practice.

**Registered pension plan.** (See *Pension plan, registered.*)

**Regulations.** Legally enforceable rules developed by governmental agencies to ensure compliance with laws that the agency administers.

**Reinforcement schedules.** The different ways that behaviour reinforcement can be given, in terms of frequency, type of stimulus, etc.

**Relation to Data, People and Things (DPT).** One of the job attributes used in the *Canadian Classification and Dictionary of Occupations* to define a job. DPT code numbers indicate the functional relationships of the worker in relation to data (e.g., analyzing, synthesizing), people (e.g., negotiating, supervising), and things (e.g., handling, tending).

**Reliability.** A quality of a selection device (usually a test) such that it yields consistent results each time an individual takes it.

**Relocation program.** A company-sponsored fringe benefit that assists employees who must move in connection with their job.

**Repetition.** Facilitates learning through repeated review of the material to be learned.

**Replacement charts.** Visual representations of who will replace whom in the organization when a job opening occurs. (See *Replacement summary*.)

**Replacement summary.** A list of likely replacements and their relative strengths and weaknesses for each job. (See *Replacement charts*.)

**Resistance to change.** Employee opposition to change.

**Résumé.** A brief listing of an applicant's work experience, education, personal data, and other information relevant to employment qualifications.

**Reverse discrimination.** This situation occurs when an employer seeks to hire or promote a member of a protected class over an equally (or better) qualified candidate who is not a member of such a protected class.

**Reward-performance model.** This model combines the strengths of other motivational approaches. It argues that behaviour that is properly reinforced enhances an individual's self-image and, therefore, the individual's self-expectations. These self-expectations lead to greater effort, which is met with rewards and continues to reinforce that behaviour.

**Role ambiguity.** Uncertainty of what is expected of one in a given job.

**Role playing.** A training technique that requires trainees to assume different identities in order to learn how others feel under different circumstances.

**Sandwich model.** The human relations principle that corrective comments should be sandwiched between two positive comments in order to make corrective comments more acceptable.

**Scanlon Plan.** An incentive plan developed by Joseph Scanlon, which has as its general objective the reduction of labour costs though increased efficiency and the sharing of resultant savings among workers.

**Search firms.** Private for-profit organizations that exist to help employers locate hard-to-find applicants.

**Selection interview.** A step in the selection process where the applicant and the employer's representative have a face-to-face opportunity to explore their mutual interests in the employment relationship.

**Selection process.** A series of specific steps used by an employer to decide which recruits should be hired.

**Selection ratio.** The ratio of the number of applicants hired to the total number of applicants.

**Self-actualization.** (See *Self-fulfilment needs*.)

**Self-fulfilment needs.** The needs people have that make them feel they are becoming all they are capable of becoming. This need is also called self-actualization.

**Semantic barriers.** Limitations that arise from the words with which we communicate.

**Seniority.** A certain type of employee status relative to other employees, used for determining order of promotion, layoffs, vacation, etc. *Straight seniority* is seniority acquired solely through length of service. *Qualified seniority* depends on other factors besides length of service, such as ability.

**Seniority-based promotion.** When the most senior employee is promoted into a new position.

**Settlement.** The agreement reached between labour and management.

**Severance pay.** Payment to a worker upon permanent separation from the company, usually for causes beyond the worker's control.

**Shelf-sitters.** This is a slang term for upwardly immobile manages who block promotion channels.

**Shift differentials.** A premium rate paid to workers on other than the regular day shift. Payment may be a fixed cents-per-hour above or a percentage over the regular day-shift rate.

**Shop steward.** A local union's representative in a plant or department usually elected by union members to carry out union duties, adjust grievances, collect dues, and solicit new members. Usually a fellow employee.

**Shorter workweeks.** Employee scheduling variations that allow full-time employees to complete their week's work in less than the traditional five days. One variation is forty hours' work in four days.

**Sick leave.** Time off work allowed to an employee because of illness, accident, or some other incapacity. A paid sick leave plan provides for full or partial pay for such absence.

**Skills inventories.** Summaries of each employee's skills and abilities. (Skills inventories usually refer to nonmanagement workers. See *Management inventories*.)

**Social insurance.** Insurance devised by governments to give wage earners and their dependants a minimum of income during periods when, through conditions largely beyond control, the workers' earnings are impaired or cut off.

**Socialization.** The process by which people adapt to an organization.

**Social unionism.** A characteristic of unions that seek to further their members' interests by influencing the social, economic, and legal policies of governments at all levels — city, district, province, and nation. (See *Business unionism*.)

**Socio-technical systems.** Interventions into the work situation that restructure the work, work groups, and the relationship between workers and the technology they use to do their jobs.

**Specialization.** Specialization occurs when a very limited number of tasks is grouped into one job.

**Specific Vocational Preparation (SVP).** In the *Canadian Classification and Dictionary of Occupations*, the additional special training (apart from general education) needed by a job holder to perform the job effectively. SVP ratings are shown in terms of a range; for example, 8 means: over 4 years up to and including 10 years.

**Sponsor.** A person in an organization who can create career development opportunities for others.

**Staff authority.** Authority to advise, but not to direct, others.

**Staffing table.** A list of anticipated employment openings for each type of job.

**Statistics Canada.** A federal agency responsible for providing a broad range of statistical information.

**Steering committee.** Part of a quality circle or other employee involvement effort. It usually includes the top manager of the work site (such as a plant manager) and his or her direct staff.

**Steward.** A union official elected by workers (or appointed by local union leaders) to help covered employees to present their problems to management.

**Stock options.** A fringe benefit that gives the holder the right to purchase the company's stock at a predetermined price.

**Strategic plan.** An identification of a firm's long-range objectives and its proposals for achieving those objectives.

**Stress.** A condition of strain that affects one's emotions, thought processes, and physical conditions.

**Stress interviews.** Job interviews that rely on a series of harsh, rapid-fire questions intended to upset the applicant and learn how the applicant handles stress.

**Stressors.** Conditions that tend to cause stress.

**Stress-performance model.** This model shows the relationship between stress and job performance.

**Stress threshold.** The level of stressors that one can tolerate before feelings of stress occur.

**Strictness bias.** A tendency to rate employees lower than their performance justifies.

**Strike.** A temporary stoppage of work by a group of employees to express a grievance, enforce a demand for changes in the conditions of employment, obtain recognition, or resolve a dispute with management.

**Strike benefits.** Union payments made to members who are on strike.

**Structured interviews.** Interviews wherein a predetermined checklist of questions usually asked of all applicants is used.

**Suggestion programs.** Specific procedures designed to encourage employees to recommend work improvements.

**Suitable employment.** For the purposes of unemployment compensation laws, employment in a position to which a person is suited by training, education, or experience. Those receiving compensation are not required to accept any available job, but only a suitable one in his sense.

**Supplementary unemployment benefits (SUB).** Private plans providing compensation for wage loss to laid-off workers, usually in addition to benefits provided under a government unemployment insurance programs. SUB plans are employer-financed.

**Suspension.** A form of disciplinary action that consists in removing a worker from his or her job for a stipulated time with the consequent loss of pay.

**System.** Two or more parts (or subsystems) working together as an organized whole with identifiable boundaries. An *open system* is one that is affected by the environment.

**Task identity.** The feeling of responsibility and pride that results from doing an entire piece of work rather than only a small part of it.

**Task significance.** Means knowing that the work one does is important to others in the organization or outsiders.

**Time studies.** Measurements of how long a job takes to be performed.

**Training.** Teaching employees how to perform their present jobs. (Compare with *Development*.)

**Transfer.** When an employee is moved from one job to another that is relatively equal in pay, responsibility, and organizational level.

**Transference.** Applicability of training to actual job situations, as evaluated by how readily the trainee can transfer the learning to his or her job.

**Tripartite board.** A board whose membership is composed of three elements: one or more members selected by management, an equal number of members selected by the union, and one or more neutral members, whose selection may be achieved by agreement of the partisan members or by other means.

**Turnover.** The rate of loss of employees by the organization. It represents those employees who depart the organization for a variety of reasons.

**Two-way communication.** The exchange of messages between a sender and a receiver such that a regular flow of communication is maintained.

**Type A persons.** Persons who are aggressive and competitive, set high standards, and put themselves under constant time pressure.

**Type B persons.** Persons who accept situations and work within them rather than fighting them competitively or putting themselves under constant time pressure.

**Underemployment.** Employment which does not fully utilize a worker's potential, whether in terms of skill or time or both.

**Underutilization.** The condition that exists when a department or entire employer has a smaller proportion of members of a protected class than are found in the employer's labour market. (See *Concentration*.)

**Unemployment benefits.** Payments to those who have lost their jobs, are willing and able to accept new employment, and are actively looking for work.

**Unemployment insurance.** A program started in 1940 to help alleviate the monetary problems of workers in Canada during the transition from one job to another. The Unemployment Insurance Act of 1971 has made some significant changes and additions to the program.

**Unfair labour practices.** Those employer or union practices that are classed as ''unfair'' by labour relations acts.

**Unfreezing.** Refers to casting aside old ideas or practices so that new ones can be learned.

**Union-management agreement.** (See *Collective agreement*.)

**Union organizers.** Persons who assist employees in forming a local union.

**Union rights.** Those freedoms of action that individual union members or organizations claim as theirs by constitutional right, statute, or practices recognized over a period of time. These may include the right of assembly, the freedom to form a union, the freedom to strike, etc.

**Union security.** A provision in a collective agreement designed to protect the status of the union by establishing a union shop, a closed shop, an agency shop, or a maintenance-of-membership arrangement.

**Union shop.** A union security provision in which the employer may hire anyone he wants, but all workers must join the union within a specified period.

**Unstructured interview.** An interview using few if any planned questions, to enable the interview to pursue, in depth, the applicant's responses.

**Upward-communication.** Communication that begins at some point in the organization and proceeds up the organization hierarchy to inform or influence others in the organization.

**Valence.** The strength of a person's preference for one outcome in relation to others.

**Validity.** An attribute of a selection device (usually a test) that exists when it is related significantly to job performance or some other relevant criterion.

**Variable entrance requirement.** The number of weeks an applicant for unemployment insurance needs to work before he or she becomes eligible for payments. The requirement varies with the unemployment rate in the economic region.

**Variety.** An attribute of jobs wherein the worker has the opportunity to use different skills and abilities.

**Vertical mosaic.** Canadian society, with reference to its multiracial, multiethnic, and multicultural nature.

**Vertical staff meetings.** When managers meet with two or more levels of subordinates to learn of their concern.

**Vestibule training.** Training that occurs off the job on equipment or method that are highly similar to those used on the job. This technique is used to minimize the disruption to operations caused by training activities.

**Vesting.** A provision in employer-provided retirement plans that gives workers rights to a pension after a specified number of years of service. Once a pension has been vested, the employee is entitled to a pension payout even if he or she quits before retirement.

**Wage and salary surveys.** Studies made of wages and salaries paid by other organizations within the employer's labour market.

**Wage compression.** A narrowing of the difference between the top and lowest jobs in an organization or industry. This compression usually results from giving larger pay increases to the lower-paid jobs than to the higher-paid ones.

**Walk-ins.** Job seekers who arrive at the human resource department in search of a job without any prior referrals and not in response to a specific ad or request.

**Want ads.** Advertisements in a periodical that solicit applicants for a job; these ads describe the job and its benefits, identify the employer, and tell those who are interested how to apply.

**Weighted checklist.** Requires the rater to select statements or words to describe an employee's performance or characteristics. After those selections are made, different responses are given different values or weights in order that a quantified total score can be determined.

**Welfare secretary.** A forerunner of modern human resource specialists, who existed to help workers meet their personal needs and to minimize any tendency of workers to join unions.

**Wildcat strikes.** Spontaneous work stoppages that take place in violation of a labour contract and are officially against the wishes of union leaders.

**Work flow.** The sequence of jobs in an organization needed to produce the firm's goods or services.

**Work measurement techniques.** Methods for evaluating what a job's performance standards should be.

**Workers' compensation.** Compensation payable by employers collectively for injuries sustained by workers in the course of their employment. Each province has a workers' compensation act.

**Work practices.** The set ways of performing work in an organization.

**Work sampling.** The use of a variety of observations on a particular job to measure the length of time devoted to certain aspects of the job.

**Work sharing.** A plan whereby work available during slack periods is spread among all of the workers in the group by reducing each worker's daily or weekly hours in order to prevent or reduce a layoff.

**Work simplication.** The elimination of unnecessary tasks in a job, or the reduction of the number of tasks by combining them.

**Work stoppage.** Cessation of normal business operations due to a strike or lockout.

**Write-ins.** People who send in their written inquiry, often seeking a job application.

**Yellow Dog Contracts.** Contracts signed by employees when hired, promising not to join a union.

# Name Index

# Subject Index

## ACKNOWLEDGEMENTS

The writing of a text book requires the cooperation and support of many people. *Canadian Human Resource Management* is no exception. We are deeply indebted to the followng persons for reviewing and commenting on the second edition and the third edition manuscript: Doreen Bell of Humber College, W.F. Chadwick of University of Regina, Armin Gabauer of N.A.I.T., Margo McMahan of University of Regina, Lloyd Steier of University of Alberta, and Andrew Templar of University of Windsor. Jennifer Mix, Sponsoring Editor at McGraw-Hill Ryerson, deserves a special thanks as she played the impossible task of meeting tight publication deadlines, preserving high quality in all aspects of production, and maintaining good relations with the text's authors! Not forgotten should be the encouragement and assistance provided by Kathleen Price, Production Editor, and Wendy Thomas, Editor in charge of this third edition. We are also thankful to the instructors who took the time to respond to our extensive questionnaire. Their responses assisted us in our revision plans for the third edition. Finally, we are deeply indebted to the many students, instructors, researchers, and practitioners who have used and commented on our last edition. Ultimately, it is the users of a book who can tell us about what we did right in the past and what we should do in the future. We hope the readers will find this third edition even more useful in teaching and learning about human resource management.

WILLIAM B. WERTHER, JR.
KEITH DAVIS
HERMANN F. SCHWIND
HARI DAS

January, 1990